FATWA
ON
TERRORISM
AND
SUICIDE BOMBINGS

FATWA
ON
TERRORISM
AND
SUICIDE BOMBINGS

Shaykh-ul-Islam
Dr Muhammad Tahir-ul-Qadri

Foreword by
Prof John L. Esposito

Introduction by
Dr Joel S. Hayward

First Published December 2010

Published by Minhaj-ul-Quran International (UK)
292–296 Romford Road
Forest Gate
London, E7 9HD
United Kingdom

www.minhaj.org | www.minhajuk.org
www.fatwaonterrorism.com

Copy editor: Abdul Aziz Suraqah

ISBN–13: 978–0–95518–889–3
ISBN–10: 0–9551888–9–X

Library of Congress Control Number: 2010939059

Printed by MPG Biddles Book Printers, Norfolk UK

بِسْمِ اللَّهِ الرَّحْمَٰنِ الرَّحِيمِ

In the name of God, Most Compassionate, Ever-Merciful

Saying of God ﷻ

﴿مَنْ قَتَلَ نَفْسًا بِغَيْرِ نَفْسٍ أَوْ فَسَادٍ فِى ٱلْأَرْضِ فَكَأَنَّمَا قَتَلَ ٱلنَّاسَ جَمِيعًا﴾

Whoever kills a person [unjustly], *except as a punishment for murder or* [as a prescribed punishment for spreading] *disorder in the land, it is as if he killed all of humanity*. [Qurʾān 5:32]

Saying of the Prophet ﷺ

عَنْ أَبِي بَكْرَةَ رضي الله عنه عَنِ النَّبِيِّ ﷺ أَنَّهُ قَالَ: «إِنَّ دِمَاءَكُمْ وَأَمْوَالَكُمْ وَأَعْرَاضَكُمْ عَلَيْكُمْ حَرَامٌ، كَحُرْمَةِ يَوْمِكُمْ هَذَا، فِي شَهْرِكُمْ هَذَا، فِي بَلَدِكُمْ هَذَا، إِلَى يَوْمِ تَلْقَوْنَ رَبَّكُمْ».

Abū Bakra رضي الله عنه reported that the Prophet ﷺ said, ‘Indeed, your blood and your property and your honour are inviolable, like the inviolability of this day of yours and this month of yours and this land of yours until the day you meet your Lord’. [al-Bukhārī and Muslim]

Shaykh-ul-Islam Dr Muhammad Tahir-ul-Qadri

Shaykh-ul-Islam Dr Muhammad Tahir-ul-Qadri is a scholar and intellectual leader of extraordinary proportions. He is a living model of profound classical knowledge, intellectual enlightenment, practical wisdom, pure spirituality, love, harmony and humanism. He is well known for his ardent endeavours to strengthen bonds amongst people by bringing them together through tolerance, dialogue, integration and education. He successfully bridges the past with his image of the future and finds convincing solutions for contemporary problems. Dr Qadri has been teaching Hadith, Qur᾽ānic exegesis, jurisprudence, theology, Sufism, Prophetic biography, Islamic philosophy and many other rational and traditional sciences to thousands of people, including scholars, students, intellectuals and academics in the east and the west.

Dr Qadri was born in 1951 in the city of Jhang, Pakistan, hailing from a family of Islamic scholars and teachers. His formal religious education was initiated in Medina at the age of 12 in Madrasa al-ᶜUlūm al-Sharᶜiyya, a traditional school situated in the blessed house of the Companion of the Prophet Muhammad ﷺ, Abū Ayyūb al-Anṣārī ؓ. He completed the traditional studies of classical and Arabic sciences under the tutelage of his father and other eminent scholars of his time. He continued to travel around the Islamic world in pursuit of sacred knowledge, and studied under many famous scholars of Mecca, Medina, Syria, Baghdad, Lebanon, the Maghreb, India and Pakistan, and received around five hundred authorities and chains of transmission from them in Hadith and classical Islamic and spiritual sciences.

Amongst those is an unprecedented, unique, highly blessed and honoured chain of authority which connects him, through four teachers, to ᶜAbd al-Razzāq, the son of Sayyidunā Shaykh ᶜAbd al-Qādir al-Jīlānī al-Ḥasanī al-Ḥusaynī (of Baghdad), al-Shaykh al-Akbar Muḥyī al-Dīn Ibn al-ʿArabī (author of *al-Futūḥāt al-Makkiyya*) (Damascus) and Imam Ibn Ḥajar al-ʿAsqalānī, the great Hadith authority of Egypt. Through another chain he is linked to Imam Yūsuf al-Nabahānī directly via only one teacher. His chains of transmission are published in two of his *thabat*s (detailed list): *al-Jawāhir al-bāhira fī al-asānīd al-ṭāhira* and *al-Subul al-wahabiyya fī al-asānīd al-dhahabiyya*.

In the academic sphere, Dr Qadri received a First Class Honours Degree from the University of the Punjab in 1970. After earning his MA in Islamic studies with distinction in 1972 and achieving his LLB in 1974, Dr Qadri began to practise law in the district courts of Jhang. He moved to Lahore in 1978 and joined the University of the Punjab as a lecturer in law and completed his doctorate in Islamic Law. He was later appointed as a professor of Islamic Law and was head of the department of Islamic legislation.

Dr Qadri was also a jurist advisor to the Federal Shariah Court and Appellate Shariah Bench of the Supreme Court of Pakistan and advisor on the development of Islamic Curricula to the Federal Ministry of Education. Within a short span of time, Dr Qadri has emerged as one of the Pakistan's leading Islamic jurists and scholars and one of the world's most renowned and leading authorities on Islam. A prolific author, researcher and orator, Dr Qadri has written around one thousand books, out of which four hundred have been published, and has delivered over six thousand lectures (in Urdu, English and Arabic) on a wide range of subjects.

Dr Qadri is also the founder and head of Minhaj-ul-Quran International (MQI), an organisation with branches and centres in more than ninety countries around the globe; he is the chairman of the Board of Governors of Minhaj University Lahore, which is chartered by Government of Pakistan; he is founder of Minhaj Education Society, which has established more than 572 schools and colleges in Pakistan; and he is the chairman of the Minhaj Welfare Foundation, an organization involved in humanitarian and social welfare activities globally.

Transliteration Key

ا/آ/ى	ā	ظ	ẓ
ب	b	ع	ʿ
ت	t	غ	gh
ث	th	ف	f
ج	j	ق	q
ح	ḥ	ك	k
خ	kh	ل	l
د	d	م	m
ذ	dh	ن	n
ر	r	ه	h
ز	z	و	w/ū
س	s	ي	y/ī
ش	sh	ة	a
ص	ṣ	ء	ʾ
ض	ḍ	أ	a
ط	ṭ	إ	i

Formulaic Arabic Expressions

ﷺ (*Ṣalla-llāhu ʿalayhi wa ālihī wa sallam*) an invocation of God's blessings and peace upon the Prophet Muhammad and his family: 'God's blessings and peace be upon him and his family'

ﷺ (*ʿAlayhis-salām*) an invocation of God's blessings and peace upon a Prophet or an angel: 'May peace be upon him'

ﷺ (*ʿAlayhimus-salām*) an invocation of God's blessings and peace upon three or more Prophets: 'May peace be upon them'

ﷺ (*Raḍiya-llāhu ʿanhu*) an invocation of God's pleasure with a male Companion of the Prophet: 'May God be pleased with him'

ﷺ (*Raḍiya-llāhu ʿanhā*) an invocation of God's pleasure with a female Companion of the Prophet: 'May God be pleased with her'

ﷺ (*Raḍiya-llāhu ʿanhumā*) an invocation of God's pleasure with two Companions of the Prophet: 'May God be pleased with both of them'

ﷺ (*Raḍiya-llāhu ʿanhum*) an invocation of God's pleasure with more than two Companions of the Prophet: 'May God be pleased with them'

Contents

Foreword

From the Iranian revolution to the 9/11 and 7/7 attacks, and continued acts of global terrorism by militants in the name of Islam, questions have been raised and charges made regarding the relationship of Islam to religious extremism, violence, suicide bombing and terrorism. A common question often raised is: Why haven't more Muslims, especially Muslim religious leaders, spoken out and aggressively condemned the attacks of 9/11 and subsequent acts of terrorism? In fact, Muslims have.

The relationship of Islam to extremism and terrorism, at home and abroad, remains critical in the twenty-first century. The primary causes of global terrorism, most often political and economic grievances, are sometimes obscured by extremists' use of religious language and symbolism. In recent decades, religion has proven a potent force, used not only by Muslims but by Jewish, Christian, Hindu and Buddhist terrorists to recruit, legitimate their actions and mobilize popular support. In the Muslim context, the Gallup World Poll, the largest and most systematic poll of Muslims in some 35 Muslim countries, from North Africa to Southeast Asia, representing the voices of a billion Muslims, has demonstrated that the majority of respondents who were asked in an open-ended question to explain their views of 9/11, those who condemned terrorism cited religious as well as humanitarian reasons. For example, 20 per cent of Kuwaitis who called the attacks 'completely unjustified' explained this by saying that terrorism was against the teachings of Islam. By contrast, not a single respondent who condoned the attacks used the Qur'ān or Islam as justification. Instead, they relied on political rationalizations, for example, calling the United States an imperialist power or accusing it of wanting to control the world. The Gallup World Poll found that the vast majority of respondents (93 per cent) belong to the mainstream, who believe the 9/11 attacks were unjustified though many in this group, like many non-Muslims, hold critical views of US foreign policy. Seven per cent, though not necessarily engaged in violence, themselves condoned the 9/11 attacks. Contrary to the popular notion, in the Gallup World Poll those who belong to the politically radicalized group proved to be no more religious than the mainstream. Large majorities of all groups report that religion is an important part of their daily lives, and there is no significant difference in mosque attendance.

At the same time, from almost immediately after the attacks against the World Trade Center and the Pentagon, major Muslim religious leaders did speak out publically and continue to do so but, more often than not, the media has rarely covered this story, preferring to emphasize statements and threats from a dangerous and deadly minority of terrorists and preachers of hate. Yet a problem still remains. While the majority of Muslim leaders have condemned terrorism and suicide bombing in the name of Islam, some have regarded attacks against civilians and suicide bombing in Israel-Palestine as legitimate. Timothy Winter, for example, dismisses those who hold this view, such as Bin Laden and his right-hand man, Ayman al-Zawahiri, as unqualified, un-Islamic vigilantes who violate basic Islamic teachings.

> Their proclamations ignore 14 centuries of Muslim scholarship. . . . [They use] lists of anti-American grievances and of Koranic quotations referring to early Muslim wars against Arab idolators. . . . All this amounts to an odd and extreme violation of the normal methods of Islamic scholarship. . . . An insurrectionist who kills non-combatants is guilty of baghy, 'armed transgression', a capital offence in Islamic law. A jihad can be proclaimed only by a properly constituted state; anything else is pure vigilantism.

Internationally prominent and influential religious scholar and leader, Yusuf Qaradawi and others issued fatwas condemning the 9/11 attacks. Qaradawi on September 12, 2001 issued a fatwa, declaring:

> Islam, the religion of tolerance, holds the human soul in high esteem, and considers the attack against innocent human beings a grave sin; this is backed by the Qur'anic verse which reads: 'Whoever kills a human being for other than manslaughter or corruption in the earth, it shall be as if he has killed all mankind, and who so ever saves the life of one, it shall be as if he had saved the life of all mankind'. [Qurʾān 5:32] . . . I categorically go against a committed Muslim's embarking on such attacks.

But he and others have also regarded suicide bombing against Israelis in Israel-Palestine and American troops in Iraq as legitimate. And so the 'war of fatwas' has not only occurred between a majority of mainstream muftis and the fatwas issued by terrorists and their supporters but also existed between conflicting positions taken by muftis to whom many mainstream Muslims look for guidance.

Suicide attacks that target innocent civilians or non-combatants have spark sharp debate among prominent religious authorities in the Muslim world. Sheikh Ahmad Yassin, the late religious leader and founder of Hamas in Palestine, and Akram Sabri, the Grand Mufti of Jerusalem, along with many other Arab and Palestinian religious leaders, have argued that suicide bombing is necessary and justified to counter Israel's illegal occupation and overwhelming military power. Likewise, although Yusuf Qaradawi had condemned acts of terrorism and suicide bombings, in 1995, he was also one of the first religious scholars to issue a fatwa justifying such attacks in Israel, based on the premise Israelis were not civilians but combatants in a war of occupation waged against the Palestinians.

In sharp contrast, Abdul Aziz Al-Shaykh, Grand Mufti of Saudi Arabia, condemned all suicide bombing without exception as un-Islamic and forbidden by Islam. Shortly after 9/11, on September 15, 2001, he stated:

> Enmity and hatred do not justify aggression or injustice. . . . Firstly: the recent developments in the United States

> including hijacking planes, terrorizing innocent people and shedding blood, constitute a form of injustice that cannot be tolerated by Islam, which views them as gross crimes and sinful acts. Secondly: any Muslim who is aware of the teachings of his religion and adheres to the directives of the Holy Qur'an and the sunnah [the teachings of the Prophet Muhammad] will never involve himself in such acts, because they will invoke the anger of God Almighty and lead to harm and corruption on earth. Thirdly: it is the duty of the Muslim ulema [religious scholars] to make facts clear in this respect, and to clarify that Islam never accepts such acts. Fourthly: the media, which try to defame Islam and Muslims in order to rally against them the feelings of various nations, should immediately stop this unacceptable and unjustifiable practice, since all reasonable and just people know that such biased accusations have nothing to do with Islam.

Two important initiatives of Muslim religious leaders to globally to address and delegitimate religious extremism and global terrorism are the Amman Message [2004–05] and 'A Common Word Between Us and You' [2007]. In the Amman Message religious leaders issued a statement on the nature of true Islam, declaring 'what Islam is and what it is not, and what actions represent it and what actions do not', emphasizing Islam's core values of compassion, mutual respect, acceptance and freedom of religion. The Amman Message intended to reject extremism as a deviation from Islamic beliefs and affirmed Islam's message of tolerance and humanity as a common ground among different faiths and peoples. They addressed the critical questions: (1) Who is a Muslim? (2) Is it permissible to declare someone an apostate [*takfīr*]? (3) Who has the right to issue fatwas? The opinions of these scholars then became the basis in July 2005 of a major international Islamic conference of two hundred Muslim scholars from over fifty countries. Based on fatwas provided by three of the most senior Sunni and Shia religious authorities, among them Sheikh Muhammad Sayyid Tantawi of al-Azhar University,

Iraq's Grand Ayatollah Ali al-Sistani, and Yusuf Qaradawi, scholars addressed intra-Muslim conflict and violence and tried to delegitimate extremists who issue fatwas to justify their agendas.

Participants issued a final declaration that emphasized the underlying unity and validity of the three major branches of Islam [Sunni, Shia and Ibadi], forbade declarations of excommunication or apostasy [*takfīr*] between Muslims and delineated the conditions for a valid fatwa. Over five hundred leading Muslim scholars worldwide unanimously endorsed the Amman Message. Thus for the first time in history a large number of diverse religious leaders and representatives of global Islam joined together to issue an authoritative statement.

In a second major document in October 2007, 138 prominent Muslim leaders [muftis, academics, intellectuals, government ministers and authors] from across the world sent another open letter, 'A Common Word Between Us and You', to the heads of the world's major Christian churches. This initiative emphasized the importance of Muslims and Christians, who make up over half of the world's population, working together for global peace on the basis of their shared 'Common Word', the very foundational principles of both faiths: love of the One God, and love of the neighbour.

The response to 'A Common Word' from Christian leaders and scholars was immediate and global. The archbishop of Canterbury, Pope Benedict XVI, Orthodox Patriarch Alexei II of Russia, the presiding bishop of the Lutheran World Federation, and many others acknowledged its importance, as did many individuals and groups who posted their comments and criticisms on the official website of 'A Common Word'. The number of Muslim leaders and scholars who signed the initiative increased from the original 138 to over 300 with more than 460 Islamic organizations and associations also endorsing it.

It is within this context that Dr Muhammad Tahir-ul-Qadri's *Fatwa on Terrorism and Suicide Bombings* has been welcomed as an important document. Tahir ul-Qadri's distinctive and voluminous fatwa is an exhaustive study of what the Qur'ān and

Islamic sources have to say about the use of violence, terrorism and suicide bombing and is a categorical and unequivocal rejection of all acts of illegitimate violence, terrorism and every act of suicide bombing against all human beings, whether Muslim or non-Muslim. At the same time, he also distances himself from all, whether fellow prominent religious leaders or Muslim youth who have the potential to be radicalized, who would seek to justify and excuse suicide bombing and terrorism for any reason. As he noted in an interview with Christiane Amanpour, 'Terrorism and violence cannot be considered to be permissible in Islam on the basis of any excuse. . . . Any good intention or any mistake of foreign policy of any country or any pretext cannot legalize the act of terrorism'.

This important fatwa is a major contribution to Islamic discourse and teaching and to inter-religious understanding in the 21st century, offering a thought-provoking message and lesson for all who seek global peace and justice.

Prof John L. Esposito
Georgetown University, Washington DC

Introduction

When terrorists hijacked four commercial airliners on 11 September 2001 and succeeded in crashing three of them into civilian-filled buildings which symbolically projected American economic and military power, they conducted the worst act of violence on American soil since the Japanese attack on Pearl Harbor on 7 December 1941. With a death toll six times greater than history's worst terrorist attack, the dreadful events of 9/11 were so ingenious in their planning, audacious in their method and indiscriminate in their victims that it was clear to strategists everywhere that someone would have to pay for the evil and effrontery. The United States and several key allies responded swiftly by invading Afghanistan in pursuit of the perpetrators to punish the Taliban regime that seemed to be aiding them. Intended as a short and intense campaign, the military operation quickly swept the regime from power and ushered in what the Coalition called a new beginning for Afghanistan; with human rights, the rule of law and equitable and representative governance. For reasons still questioned and debated, the Coalition felt compelled in 2003 to invade Iraq in order to replace the government led by Saddam Hussein with a government sharing the values of that sought in Afghanistan. The invasion of Iraq degenerated surprisingly quick into a costly and bloody counter-insurgency campaign. A resurgent Taliban resistance movement in Afghanistan soon came to resemble, and then outperform, the Iraqi insurgency.

The so-called 'War on Terror' has done little so far to enhance regional security, let alone restore a sense of peace to the world. Regardless of the injustice of the grievance that prompted the Coalition's military response, the invasion of Afghanistan and especially of Iraq proved highly controversial and divisive. Despite the fact that the 9/11 terrorists were themselves Muslims, the invasion of two Islamic lands seemed so unnecessary and disproportionate to the world's 1.6 billion Muslims (and a vast number of non-Muslims) that the Coalition inadvertently drove a deep wedge between its member nations and virtually the entire Muslim world. Not only did these campaigns seem to most Muslims to be unwarranted and excessive, but they also seemed to be aimed at making all Muslims pay for the misdeeds of a few. Rather than inhibit terrorism, some commentators argue that the campaigns have inflamed tensions to such a heightened state that terrorism has increased, not decreased, as a consequence.

As a scholar of war and strategy I have often felt concerned throughout the last decade by the spiralling cycle of violence, punishment, increased violence, increased punishment and so on. With the benefit of hindsight I suspect most of the Western politicians and military leaders who sent their forces into Afghanistan and Iraq now wish they had adopted different strategies, or at least carried out the same strategies in different ways. Even without the benefit of hindsight it should have been clear in 2001 and 2003 that the pattern of military history would continue. From the beginning of recorded history every military occupation had given rise to a counter-occupation, usually characterised by asymmetric guerrilla warfare. Another lesson from history is that asymmetric insurgencies are routinely difficult, unpopular and lengthy affairs for the occupying states. We see this today.

We also see new trends in the types and occurrence rates of terrorist attacks that now plague the world and make governments and populations highly jittery. Although suicide bombing existed before 9/11, it did not become frequent and common amongst Muslim terrorists until afterwards. It has now become alarmingly popular amongst aggrieved young men and women in communities troubled by occupation or perceptions of unjust governance. This has of course deeply troubled many non-Muslims who worry that there may be something inherently violent within the faith of Islam itself.

I have watched gentle, inclusive, tolerant and peaceful Muslims condemn terrorist attacks and suicide bombings. Their religion, they say, is not inherently warlike or violent. It rests upon a code of human interaction that stresses equality, harmony and the value of human dignity. I have felt tremendously proud at the condemnations of evil made by so many good Muslims. Yet I have also been acutely aware that, with terrorist attacks continuing unabated, their condemnations have not convinced all non-Muslims that Islam is a religion of peace, or persuaded those Muslims drawn to terrorism that they must not commit acts of evil, regardless of any perceived justification. Throughout this troubled decade of war and tension, I have watched numerous imams, shaykhs and clerics condemn terrorism as un-Islamic. I have felt relieved and comforted by their efforts to demonstrate that, according to the Qur'ān and the Sunna, acts of lethal violence committed outside of organised warfare between states (and directed by legitimate leaders) are unjust and therefore un-Islamic. I have also felt frustrated that so many of the scholars who have condemned terrorism and suicide bombings have lacked sufficient international credibility and eminence to prove influential throughout the world. Moreover, some scholars have strangely equivocated on issues. That is, they have developed confusing and occasionally inconsistent arguments relating to the motivations of the perpetrators that could, by not closing the door completely, unintentionally allow would-be terrorists to slip through the gap into sinful action.

In March 2010 I breathed a huge sigh of relief when I read that an internationally renowned Islamic scholar, recognised throughout the world as an authority on the Qur'ān and the Sunna, had issued a prodigiously researched fatwa which demonstrated from scrupulously reliable sources that terrorism and suicide bombings are so wickedly unjust and un-Islamic that their evil cannot be justified by recourse to discussions of intention. Regardless of intention, the evil act remains an evil act. I was struck by the fact that the scholar behind this fatwa, unlike any previously issued, is unquestionably a scholar of unimpeachable reputation whose almost four decades of meticulous research have produced scores of influential books.

His Eminence Shaykh-ul-Islam Dr Muhammad Tahir-ul-Qadri has emerged in recent decades as one of the world's foremost authorities on Islamic jurisprudence. In addition to many humanitarian activities, he founded and still heads Minhaj-ul-Quran, a broad-based international organisation with branches and centres in ninety countries which has a remarkably positive vision: to promote the well-being of all humans through religious moderation, accessible education, and dialogue based on mutual respect and cooperation instead of competition between the world's great faith communities. Make no mistake: Minhaj-ul-Quran promotes Islam globally. It merely aspires to do so in the manner of Islam's Beloved Prophet: through impeccable teachings that stress peace, patience, respect and tolerance.

The Shaykh's scholarship is remarkable. The fatwa rests upon a granite-solid foundation of research and references from the Qur'ān, reliable Hadith of established provenance, opinions of the Beloved Prophet's Companions and the classical texts of Islamic scholarship that are widely accepted by all main schools of thought. I have pored over not only the exhaustive text of the fatwa, but also over its hundreds of footnotes. Carefully selected for their reliability and clarity, the citations are employed by the Shaykh with obvious and commendable scholarly concern for precision and accuracy and after all issues of truth, objectivity and bias have been carefully weighed on the scales of his mind. In selecting sources, building his case brick-by-brick and expressing his argument powerfully and clearly, he has demonstrated profoundly good judgment.

The power of Dr Tahir-ul-Qadri's argument stems from its completeness and comprehensiveness as well as from the fact that, for the first time in a fatwa, an internationally renowned scholar has left no stone unturned in his determination to demonstrate that there can be no possible justification for deliberate violence in the name of Islam outside of the context of organised warfare. This is itself only permissible when undertaken according to strict criteria based only on self-defence and adherence to justice. Dr Tahir-ul-Qadri categorically demonstrates with dependable scholarship that regardless of any claimed motives, however righteous they may seem, evil acts will remain evil. Indeed, the Shaykh demonstrates that suicide bombings and other forms of terrorism are so unjust and wicked that they place the perpetrators outside of Islam. That is, these acts are the acts of unbelievers, not martyrs, and they will expose those who do them to the gravest likelihood of eternal punishment after death.

As a strategic thinker who studies and teaches on war, ethics and justice, I have worried for a decade about the unnecessary misunderstandings that seem to divide the world's communities and I have felt gnawing frustration that so few actions have eased tensions or reduced suspicions and hatreds. I genuinely believe that Shaykh-ul-Islam Dr Muhammad Tahir-ul-Qadri's marvellous fatwa should be read by everyone. It is the most important single work yet to appear that has any chance of explaining to the Islamic community what most Muslims intuitively believe but sometimes cannot adequately convey: the precise reasons why terrorism can never be condoned and must always be condemned. Dr Tahir-ul-Qadri's fatwa is also the most likely of all publications in recent years to convince any non-Muslim readers or observers that Islam advocates peace, love and harmony and decries all unjust violence. Most importantly, if we are able to get this fabulous fatwa into the hands of any misguided Muslims, it just might, God willing, prevent them from committing un-Islamic acts of barbarity in the name of a great religion of peace.

Dr Joel S. Hayward
Dean of the Royal Air Force College, Cranwell
Head of Air Power Studies, King's College London

Preface

THE HORRENDOUS ONSLAUGHT OF TERRORISM THAT HAS CONTINUED unabated in recent years has brought the Muslim *Umma* (nation) in general, and Pakistan in particular, into disrepute. The overwhelming majority of Muslims oppose and condemn terrorism in unequivocal terms and are unwilling to accept it as even remotely related to Islam. However, a negligible—albeit highly visible and vocal—minority amongst them seems to openly approve of terrorism, and instead of opposing and condemning it, resorts to misleading and fallacious reasoning.

It may be conceded that the local, national and international factors underpinning global terrorism include the injustices inflicted against Muslims in certain areas, the apparent double standards displayed by the major state powers and their open-ended and the long-term military engagements in a number of countries under the pretext of combating terror. That said, the terrorists' recourse to violence and indiscriminate murder has become a routine affair, taking the form of suicide bombings against peaceful people, as well as bomb blasts directed towards mosques, shrines, educational institutions, bazaars, governmental buildings, trade centres, markets, security installations and other public places: heinous, inhuman and barbarous acts in their very essence.

The perpetrators of these crimes justify their actions in the name of jihad, and thus they distort, twist and confuse the sacred Islamic concept of jihad. This situation is causing some Muslims—amongst the youth in particular—to fall prey to doubts and reservations, resulting in confusion about the concept of jihad, because those who perpetrate these atrocities are self-professed Muslims. They and their cohorts practise Islamic rituals, perform acts of worship and display the outward forms of religiosity encapsulated in the Shariah (Islamic Sacred Law). This has put not only the common Muslims into a dilemma, but also a significant number of religious scholars and intellectuals. They are perturbed and curious to know the real Islamic stance on the methods these individuals and groups have adopted to wreak their havoc.

Furthermore, international media consistently over-reports incidents of terrorism and extremism around the Muslim world, and is reluctant to highlight the positive and constructive aspects of Islam, its peaceful teachings and philanthropic philosophy and orientation. Moreover, they do not report the condemnation and opposition prevalent within Muslim communities towards extremists, militants and terrorists. Lumping both Islam and terrorism together has led only to negative consequences. The Western mind conjures up images of terrorism and extremism at the merest mention of the word Islam. This in turn leaves Western-bred and educated Muslim youth in a most difficult position. In fact, the present generation of young Muslims all over the Islamic world is falling victim to intellectual confusion and deterioration in the practical fields and in the domain of beliefs and religious tenets.

This precarious situation has led to damage on two levels: damage to Islam and the Muslims and damage to the Western world. The damage to Islam and the Muslim world is that many Muslim youth, unaware of the normative teachings of Islam, and under the influence of the media, erroneously believe that terrorism and extremism emanate from religious teachings and the attitudes of religious people. This misplaced thinking has alienated many of the youth from the religion, and has even led some of them to atheism or rejection of religion altogether. On the other hand, the danger threatening the Western world is from the governmental policies and subsequent stereotyping of Muslims, which provoke a negative response amongst some of the Muslim youth, who regard these as attacks against Islam and an organised conspiracy from certain influential circles in the Western world.

As a reaction, some youth are gradually becoming extreme and militant in their outlooks. Some of them are eschewing moderation and expressing hatred and desire for revenge, and ultimately becoming terrorists, or at the very least, adopting the terrorist worldview or being groomed for their nefarious designs. Thus, such policies are instrumental in producing potential terrorist recruits and supporters, with no end in sight. Consequently, both the Muslim *Umma*, as well as humanity, are heading towards catastrophe.

Moreover, these circumstances are heightening tensions, and creating an atmosphere of mistrust between the Islamic and Western worlds. The upsurge in terrorism is paving the way for greater foreign interference in and pressure on the Muslim nation-states. This widening gulf is not only pushing humanity towards interfaith antagonism at the global level but also reducing the possibilities of peace, tolerance and mutual coexistence amongst the different societies in this rapidly shrinking and globalized world.

Under these dire circumstances, I thought it necessary to explain to the Western and Islamic worlds the proper Islamic stance on terrorism: in the light of the Qurʾān, the prophetic traditions (hadith) and classical books of jurisprudence and theology. The underlying purpose is to present this point of view to significant institutions of learning, important think tanks and influential opinion-making organisations around the world, so that both the Muslims and non-Muslims who entertain doubts and reservations about Islam are able to understand Islam's stance on terrorism more clearly.

The first part of this book explains the meaning of Islam and discusses its three categories: Islam (peace), *Īmān* (faith) and *Iḥsān* (spiritual excellence). These three words, literally and figuratively, represent peace, safety, mercy, tolerance, forbearance, love, kindness, benevolence and respect for humanity. Using Qurʾānic verses and prophetic traditions, it demonstrates that the killing of Muslims and the practice of terrorism against common people are not only unlawful and forbidden in Islam, but also represent a rejection of faith (*kufr*). Referencing the expositions and opinions of jurists and experts of Qurʾānic exegesis and hadith, it has established that virtually all of the learned Islamic authorities have held the same unanimous opinion about terrorism throughout the entire 1400-year history of Islam. The concluding part of this book takes an account of the proper means of effecting a change in society and the correct way to redress wrongs, as well as the Muslim's responsibilities when he or she resides in a non-Muslim country.

Perhaps the most important aspect of this book is that it explains the ideology and mindset that pits one Muslim against another and leads to bloodshed in society. This mindset not only regards it permissible to kill schoolgirls and women in markets, but also considers these heinous acts a means of earning rewards and spiritual benefits in the Hereafter. What power or conviction rouses someone to kill people gathered in a mosque and causes him to believe that he will earn Paradise through wanton carnage? Why does a terrorist decide to end his own life—one of the greatest blessings of God—with his own hands through suicide bombing? How does he come to believe that by killing people through suicide bombing he will become a martyr and enter Paradise? These are the questions that spring to the mind of every person possessing common sense. In answering these questions, I have relied on historical facts which the Prophet ﷺ (may God bless him and grant him peace) himself foretold. The book offers a comprehensive analysis of the signs, beliefs and ideologies of the Kharijites—an extremist group that appeared in the Muslim community over one thousand years ago—and establishes that the terrorists of today are their modern offshoots.

An oft-repeated contention these days is that since foreign powers are aggressing against Muslim countries, including Pakistan, the so-called jihadi groups have thwarted them by launching the offensive and inflicting upon them devastating blows, and that, therefore, their actions—though incorrect—should not be reviled and condemned because their intention is to defend Islam. This is a flawed argument and a morally reprehensible position. I have addressed this contention, and explained that, in the light of the Qur'ān and hadith, evil cannot become good under any circumstance, nor can oppression transform itself into virtue due to a good intention.

Some Important Questions

The heartbreaking and ghastly scenes of terrorism will no doubt disturb the minds of all decent and common folk around the world, and will prompt some perplexing questions that demand satisfactory answers.

Question One

Is it lawful for a group or organization to use force to promote and implement its own doctrine and beliefs in the name of reforming others, presuming itself to be on the right path? Does Islam in any way allow the killing of people because of doctrinal differences, and does it permit the usurpation of their wealth and properties and the destruction of mosques, religious sites and shrines?

Answer

Islam is a religion of peace and safety and champions love and harmony in society. According to Islamic teachings, a Muslim is one from whose hands the lives and properties of all Muslims and non-Muslims remain safe. The sanctity of human life and its protection occupies a fundamental place in Islamic law. Taking anyone's life is an act that is forbidden and unlawful, and in some cases amounts to disbelief. These days, the terrorists who, in a futile attempt to impose their own ideas and beliefs, ruthlessly and indiscriminately, kill people in mosques, marketplaces, governmental offices and other public places, are in fact committing a clear act of disbelief. They are warned of a humiliating torment in this world and in the Hereafter.

Terrorism in its very essence symbolizes disbelief and is a rejection of what Islam stands for. When the forbidden element of suicide is added to it, its severity and gravity becomes even greater. Scores of Qur'ānic verses and prophetic traditions prove that terrorism is unlawful in Islam and that it is an act of disbelief. This has been the opinion of many Islamic scholars through the 1400 years of Islamic history, including the eminent Imams of Qur'ānic exegesis and hadith and the authorities on logic and jurisprudence.

Islam has kept the door of negotiation and discussion open to convince others by reasoning, instead of taking up arms to denounce the viewpoints of others and to enforce one's own opinion. Only the victims of ignorance, jealousy and malice take recourse to attacks against public. Islam declares them as rebels who will abide in Hell.

Question Two

What are the rights of the non-Muslim citizens of a Muslim state?

Answer

Islam not only guarantees the protection of the life, honour and property of Muslim citizens of an Islamic state, but also guarantees the equal protection of the life, honour and property of non-Muslim citizens, as well as those with whom it has entered into a peace treaty. The rights of non-Muslim citizens in an Islamic state are just as sacrosanct as those of Muslim citizens. There is no difference between them as human beings. That is why Islamic law metes out equal treatment to both parties in the matters of blood money and legal retribution (*qiṣāṣ*). Non-Muslims have complete personal and religious freedom in a Muslim society and their properties and places of worship also enjoy complete protection.

In addition to the non-Muslim citizens, even the ambassadors of non-Muslim countries and others working on diplomatic assignments have been guaranteed complete protection. Likewise, the protection of the lives and properties of non-Muslim traders is the responsibility of the Islamic state. Islam forbids the use of violence against peaceful and non-combatant citizens. Those who attack peaceful non-Muslim citizens, kidnap them for ransom and torture them mentally or physically, or keep them under unlawful custody are in fact committing major violations of Islamic teachings.

Question Three

Does Islam offer clear commands regarding the sanctity of human life? Is it lawful to kidnap and assassinate foreign delegates and peaceful non-Muslim citizens in order to avenge injustices and disrupt the non-Muslim global powers?

ANSWER

The importance Islam lays on the sanctity and dignity of human life can be gauged from the fact that it forbids indiscriminate killing even when Muslim armies are engaged in war against enemy troops. The killing of children, women, elderly people, religious leaders and traders is strictly prohibited. Similarly, those who surrender their arms, confine themselves to their homes and seek shelter cannot be killed. The general public must not be targeted, and likewise, places of worship, buildings, crops and even trees must not be destroyed.

On the one hand, there is a clear set of Islamic laws based on extreme discretion, and on the other hand, there are people who invoke the name of Islam to justify the indiscriminate and wanton killing of men, women and children everywhere. It is a pity that such barbaric people claim that their activities are jihad. In no way is it permissible to hold foreign delegates under unlawful custody and murder them and other peaceful non-Muslim citizens in retaliation for the interference, injustice and aggression of their countries. The one who commits these acts has no relation to Islam or the Prophet Muhammad ﷺ.

QUESTION FOUR

Is armed struggle permissible against Muslim rulers in order to remove their governments because of their un-Islamic policies, or to bring them to the right path or to force them to give up their impious activities? Is rebellion against the constitutional government and its authority Islamically mandated? What should be the legitimate way to change the rulers or make them mend their ways?

ANSWER

Islam is not merely a religion; it is a complete *dīn*, or code of life. It provides a complete set of principles for every aspect of life, and has also made arrangements for the protection of society as a whole. The rights and duties of state institutions have been clearly detailed. All citizens of a Muslim state are duty-bound to abide by its laws, rules and regulations. One of these principles is that a Muslim state and society should be a paragon of peace and coexistence. For this reason, Islam strictly prohibits taking up arms against it, challenging its authority and declaring war against it. Islamic law considers such actions as rebellion. God forbid if such conditions are created, then it is the primary responsibility of the Islamic state to take urgent measures to decisively eliminate rebellion and terrorism so that no individual or group can dare destroy the harmony of society, ruin peace and shed blood. Islam holds the peace and tranquillity of society in general, and of the Muslim state in particular, so dear that it does not allow people to raise the banner of revolt in the name of confronting injustice, oppression and other vices committed by the ruling elite. The banner of rebellion against a Muslim state cannot be raised unless the rulers commit explicit, declared and unequivocal disbelief, and use force to prevent the performance of religious rituals, like prayer.

The evidence for the prohibition of armed rebellion is explicitly outlined in the Qur'ān, the prophetic traditions and the expositions of the classical jurists. If reference is made to the noble Companions of the Prophet ﷺ, their successors, as well as Imam Abū Ḥanīfa, Imam Mālik, Imam al-Shāfiʿī, Imam Aḥmad b. Ḥanbal and other leading jurists, consensus would approve to exist that it is totally forbidden to rebel against the Muslim state—and there is no difference of opinion between any schools of thought on this matter. Any armed rebellion that challenges the authority of the state is nothing but a civil war, a blatant act of terrorism and a clear act of strife. Under no circumstances can it be called jihad. As for the struggle to reform an impious Muslim ruler or state, that is not at all prohibited.

The prohibition of rebellion and armed struggle does not imply that an evil should not be called an evil and that no effort should be made to stop its spread or that the religious obligation to enjoin the good and forbid the evil should be abandoned. The act of upholding the truth and rejecting falsehood is mandatory for all Muslims, and seeking to reform society and fight off evil forces is a religious obligation. The adoption of all constitutional, legal, political and democratic ways to reform the rulers and the system of governance and prevent them from the violation of human rights is not only lawful but a binding duty upon Muslims. Indeed, it is from the obligations of faith to strive at the individual and collective levels—through the appropriate means—for the establishment of truth, abolishment of terror and oppression and restoration of justice.

QUESTION FIVE

The sect of the Kharijites has left behind an indelible mark in the history of terrorism. The question arises: Who were the Kharijites? How are they judged in Islamic Revealed Law? Are the present-day terrorists a continuation of the Kharijites of old?

ANSWER

The Kharijites were rebels and apostates from Islam. Their initial appearance was during the lifetime of the Prophet Muhammad ﷺ, and their intellectual growth and emergence took place during the caliphates of ʿUthmān b. ʿAffān and ʿAlī b. Abī Ṭālib ؓ. The Kharijites were so punctual and regular in the performance of religious rituals and acts of worship that they would appear more pious than the Companions of the Prophet ﷺ; however, according to the clear statement of the Prophet ﷺ, they were absolutely out of the fold of Islam.

The Kharijites regarded the killing of Muslims as lawful, rejected the Companions for their disagreement with them, and, with the slogan of '*there is no rule but for God*', considered it lawful to wage armed struggle against ʿAlī ؓ. The Kharijites were in fact the first terrorist group to challenge the authority of the Muslim state and raise the banner of armed struggle against it. The hadith texts clearly establish that the elements of the Kharijites will continue to emerge and reappear in every age.

The term Kharijite is not restricted to the group that took up arms against the Rightly Guided Caliphs, but it encompasses—from then until the Day of Judgement—every group and individual who possesses their attributes and beliefs and who commits terrorism in the name of jihad. Despite being compulsive and obsessive in their performance of the outward religious rituals, the Kharijites are considered out of the fold of Islam for their mistaken and erroneous beliefs.

A Muslim state cannot be allowed to give them any concession in the name of dialogue, or stop military actions against them until they are eliminated—and this is according to the explicit instructions of the Prophet ﷺ. The only time they can be spared is when they willingly lay down their arms, repent of their actions and vow to honour the authority of the Muslim state.

Question Six

What are the measures that a government should take to end terrorist activities and armed strife?

Answer

The government and the law enforcement agencies should, at the outset, remove all factors and stimuli that contribute to making the common man a victim of doubts regarding the impermissibility of terrorism as a method of change. The ringleaders and supporters of terrorism are able to snare impressionable youth and lead them to militancy due to these doubts and misgivings. They are easily able to groom them for terrorist activities by exploiting their emotions and sensibilities. The policies, events and circumstances the terrorist elements use as fuel for their evil agenda must be remedied and set right as a priority. This will certainly help eradicate the root causes of the spread of this plague. Similarly, as long as the world powers continually fail to attend to the real hardships of people and take note of their complaints, and until they abandon their deceptive policies, the restoration of real peace will remain a distant dream.

Question Seven

Can the atrocities of terrorism be justified and deemed permissible if they are done with the intention of promoting Islam and securing the rights of the Muslims?

Answer

Even today the Kharijites invoke Islam and raise slogans to establish the divine order, but all of their actions and steps constitute a clear violation of Islamic teachings. When the supporters of the Kharijites do not have a legal argument to defend their actions, they draw people's attention to the vices and corruption of the ruling elite and the oppression committed by foreign forces. By way of this moral equivocation, they attempt to justify unlawful murder. They are content in the belief that, although the terrorists are doing wrong, their intention is good and beyond reproach. This is a major intellectual *faux pas*, and many people, both educated and uneducated, suffer from this doubt. An evil act remains evil in all its forms; whether it is interpreted as injustice, this principle remains the same. Therefore, no forbidden action can ever become a virtuous and lawful deed due to the goodness of intention.

Killing the common people, engaging in oppression and behaving with cruelty and violence cannot become pardonable offenses due to the presence of a good intention or pious conviction. There is no place for deviation from this fundamental principle. Thus, this argument of the terrorists and their well-wishers is invalid as per the Islamic Sacred Law. Therefore, I begin my arguments with the clarification of the same issue: that an evil deed cannot transform into a pious deed due to a good intention from where it supposedly arises.

Good Intentions do not Change Vices into Virtues

If a good intention gives rise to bloodshed and massacre, the question arises whether such tyranny and barbarism can be declared lawful on its basis. Some people think that, although suicide bombings are evil and the destruction of educational, training, industrial, commercial and welfare centres is a heinous crime, still the suicide bombers are doing these acts with good intentions and pious motives, and are therefore justified. They are justified—so the logic goes—as retaliation for foreign aggression against Muslims. They are carrying out a jihad, it is argued, and so they cannot be given any blame.

This brief discussion analyses this thought in the light of the Qurʾān and Sunna. The Qurʾān rejected the idol worship that was carried out with the intention of attaining nearness to God and called it disbelief. The Qur'ān says,

﴿أَلَا لِلَّهِ ٱلدِّينُ ٱلْخَالِصُ وَٱلَّذِينَ ٱتَّخَذُواْ مِن دُونِهِۦٓ أَوْلِيَآءَ مَا نَعْبُدُهُمْ إِلَّا لِيُقَرِّبُونَآ إِلَى ٱللَّهِ زُلْفَىٰٓ إِنَّ ٱللَّهَ يَحْكُمُ بَيْنَهُمْ فِى مَا هُمْ فِيهِ يَخْتَلِفُونَ إِنَّ ٱللَّهَ لَا يَهْدِى مَنْ هُوَ كَٰذِبٌ كَفَّارٌ﴾

'Listen, sincere devotion is only God's due. But those who take others as protectors besides God [say], *"We only worship them in order that they may bring us nearer to God". Truly God will judge between them in that wherein they differ. But God guides not such as are liars and ingrates'.*[1]

When the idolaters of Mecca were asked why they worshipped idols, they said the idols would bring them closer to God. Their intention to attain closeness to God was good, but their idol-worship was blasphemy and disbelief. Idolatry, therefore, cannot be justified because of good intentions.

Furthermore, the terrorists' claim that they are fighting injustice is rejected because they are shedding blood and spreading fear, and are not engaging in constructive work or reformation. God says,

﴿وَمِنَ ٱلنَّاسِ مَن يُعْجِبُكَ قَوْلُهُۥ فِى ٱلْحَيَوٰةِ ٱلدُّنْيَا وَيُشْهِدُ ٱللَّهَ عَلَىٰ مَا فِى قَلْبِهِۦ وَهُوَ أَلَدُّ ٱلْخِصَامِ. وَإِذَا تَوَلَّىٰ سَعَىٰ فِى ٱلْأَرْضِ لِيُفْسِدَ فِيهَا وَيُهْلِكَ ٱلْحَرْثَ وَٱلنَّسْلَ وَٱللَّهُ لَا يُحِبُّ ٱلْفَسَادَ. وَإِذَا قِيلَ لَهُ ٱتَّقِ ٱللَّهَ أَخَذَتْهُ ٱلْعِزَّةُ بِٱلْإِثْمِ فَحَسْبُهُۥ جَهَنَّمُ وَلَبِئْسَ ٱلْمِهَادُ﴾

'And amongst people there is he whose conversation seems pleasing to you in the life of the world, and he calls God to bear witness to that which is in his heart, but in truth he is the most quarrelsome of opponents. And when he turns away, he runs about in the land to cause corruption and destroy crops and life, and God does not like corruption. And when it is said to him, "Fear God",

---

1 Qur'ān 39:3.

his arrogance leads him to more sins. Hell is, therefore, sufficient for him. And that is indeed an evil abode'.[1]

These verses explain that many people will speak with seemingly pleasant words and employ superficial arguments. They will swear on their good intentions, and declare God witness to their noble objectives and pious aims. Despite their assertions and claims, however, God declared them miscreants and wrongdoers who will face the torment of Hell. Their swearing on their intentions has been refuted because they are committing wanton acts of violence, strife and terrorism. Their crimes, therefore, cannot be forgiven due to their 'good' intentions and noble designs that they declare on oath. This is a basic principle drawn from the Qur᾽ān and the Shariah. Another Qur᾽ānic verse explains the same point:

﴿وَإِذَا قِيلَ لَهُمْ لَا تُفْسِدُوا۟ فِى ٱلْأَرْضِ قَالُوٓا۟ إِنَّمَا نَحْنُ مُصْلِحُونَ. أَلَآ إِنَّهُمْ هُمُ ٱلْمُفْسِدُونَ وَلَٰكِن لَّا يَشْعُرُونَ﴾

'And when it is said to them, "Do not spread corruption in the land", they say, "We are only reformers!" Truly, it is they who spread corruption but they perceive it not'.[2]

Here again, the corrupt and criminal mentality of terrorists is described. This verse explains that the offenders never regard their activity as disruption, violence and strife; rather, they may call it jihad and reconstruction and reformation. They presume that the criminal activities they engage in are for the greater good of society. Today's tragedy is that terrorists, murderers and rioters try to prove—claiming to uphold the banner of Islam and national interests—that their criminal, rebellious, brutal and blasphemous activities are justified reactions to foreign aggression.

They should know that, just as a good intention can never justify an unlawful act, and just as pious motives can never transform blasphemy into righteousness, similarly, the intention to perform jihad can never justify unlawful violence or make terrorism lawful. The intention to protect Islam, defend it against

---

[1] Ibid., 2:204–206.

[2] Ibid., 2:11–12.

foreign aggression and avenge the wrongs and excesses inflicted upon the Muslim *Umma* is one thing, but the brutal mass murder of peaceful citizens, the destruction of property and the ruthless target killings are altogether different. The former can never prove the latter lawful; the two have no relation to one another. Terrorism, carnage and mass destruction can neither be justified in the name of enforcing Islamic commands, nor can they be exceptions to the rule or pardonable.

An in-depth study of the Qur'ān and hadith literature clearly establishes that Islam makes the realisation of lawful objectives conditional upon lawful means only, and decrees that the attainment of noble aims can only be through noble methods. A sacred goal can never be achieved by following an evil and criminal path. Constructing a mosque, for example, is a pious act, but it cannot be funded by robbing a bank or through ill-gotten means. The objectives of mercy cannot be achieved through cruelty and oppression, and the designs of a religious person cannot be materialised by adopting shameful methods. Fair is fair and foul is foul; it is Satan who says, 'Fair is foul and foul is fair'. This illustrates the majesty and purity of Islam, which has purified and reformed both the destination and its path and has made both objective and method pure and upright.

Those who base their argument on the famous hadith, 'Actions are judged according to intentions', in order to justify their brutal ways and cursed means, make false and heretic claims. They cannot set a wrong thing right. This hadith speaks only about those actions that are proven pious, permissible and lawful. Their acceptability has been based on the soundness of intention; if the intention is pure, they will be accepted, and if not, they will be rejected. If the intention is corrupt, or if it does not exist, the actions will not be considered acts of worship, despite their apparent righteous value. But the actions that are from the start forbidden, unjust, unlawful and blasphemous cannot be made permissible or lawful by good intentions.

This is such a crucial Islamic principle that not one of the Companions, pious predecessors, Imams and authorities of hadith and Qur'ānic exegesis has opposed it to date. Some scholars have also interpreted the hadith, 'Actions are judged according to intentions', saying that actions take shape according to their intentions. So a terrorist's actions speak of his intentions: his killings and destructive activities prove his foul intentions and condemnable ideas and beliefs. His heinous actions cannot stem from pious intentions and beliefs. The bloodshed he causes only proves his internal cruelty and lack of mercy. It is, therefore, evident that whatever false implications and foul justifications these rebels, criminals and brutes may put forth to prove their atrocities as acts of jihad, they have nothing to do with the teachings of Islam whatsoever.

The Qur'ān has vividly described them as:

﴿ٱلَّذِينَ ضَلَّ سَعْيُهُمْ فِى ٱلْحَيَوٰةِ ٱلدُّنْيَا وَهُمْ يَحْسَبُونَ أَنَّهُمْ يُحْسِنُونَ صُنْعًا﴾

> *'Those whose entire struggle is wasted in the life of this world, but they presume they are doing good'.*[1]

I also regard it my fundamental duty to inform the respected readers that I am writing this book solely for the sake of Islam's dignity and in service to humanity. This book has not been written to condone or approve of the unpopular and unwise policies of global powers, nor does it seek to justify the wrong policies and actions of any government, including that of Pakistan. I neither seek the pleasure of any government, nor the tribute or appreciation from any international power or organisation. As always, I have taken the initiative to perform this task as a part of my religious obligation. The objective is to wash off the stain of terrorism from Islam, to familiarise the Muslims with the real teachings of the Qur'ān and Sunna (the Prophet's way) and to attempt to prevent human suffering from the flames of terrorism.

May God bless this endeavour with His benevolent acceptance through the means of His Beloved Messenger, Muhammad, may God bless him and grant him peace!

Muhammad Tahir-ul-Qadri

---

[1] Ibid., 18:104.

Chapter 1

The Meaning of Islam

1.1 Islam as Peace and Security

Islam is a religion of peace and security, and it urges others to pursue the path of peace and protection. The most significant proof of this is that God has named it as Islam.[1] The word Islam is derived from the Arabic word *salama* or *salima*. It means peace, security, safety and protection. As for its literal meaning, Islam denotes absolute peace. As a religion, it is peace incarnate. It encourages humankind to be moderate, peaceful, kind, balanced, tolerant, patient and forbearing.

If we look for the definition of a Muslim or *muʾmin* [believer] mentioned in the Qurʾān and hadith, it will become evident that, in the sight of God and His Messenger ﷺ, a Muslim is someone who embodies peace and security, and a *muʾmin* is the one who is endowed with love, affection, peace, tranquillity, tolerance and coexistence, and upholds the cause of human dignity. Everyone is protected and safe from him at all levels, individually and collectively.

1.2 The Three Levels of Islam

The Messenger of God ﷺ described three levels of religion: *Islām*, *Īmān* and *Iḥsān*. These are the levels of the religion applicable to actions, beliefs and inner spiritual states. All Islamic teachings revolve around these three levels, as proven by an agreed upon hadith.[2]

It is reported that ʿUmar b. al-Khaṭṭāb ؓ said:

بَيْنَمَا نَحْنُ عِنْدَ رَسُوْلِ اللهِ ﷺ ذَاتَ يَوْمٍ إِذْ طَلَعَ عَلَيْنَا رَجُلٌ شَدِيْدُ بَيَاضِ الثِّيَابِ،
شَدِيْدُ سَوَادِ الشَّعْرِ، لَا يُرَى عَلَيْهِ أَثَرُ السَّفَرِ، وَلَا يَعْرِفُهُ مِنَّا أَحَدٌ، حَتَّى جَلَسَ إِلَى

[1] God says: '*Truly, Islam is the only* dīn [religion] *in God's sight*' [Qurʾān 3:19]; '*And I have chosen for you Islam as a* dīn' [Qurʾān 5:3]; and '*He* [God] *has named you Muslims in the previous* [Books] *as well as in this* [Qurʾān]' [Qurʾān 22:78].

[2] A hadith that is 'agreed upon' is a rigorously authentic narration reported

النَّبِيِّ ﷺ، فَأَسْنَدَ رُكْبَتَيْهِ إِلَى رُكْبَتَيْهِ، وَوَضَعَ كَفَّيْهِ عَلَى فَخِذَيْهِ، وَقَالَ: يَا مُحَمَّدُ! أَخْبِرْنِي عَنِ الإِسْلَامِ، فَقَالَ رَسُوْلُ اللهِ ﷺ: الإِسْلَامُ أَنْ تَشْهَدَ أَنْ لَا إِلَهَ إِلاَّ اللهُ، وَأَنَّ مُحَمَّدًا رَسُوْلُ اللهِ وَتُقِيمَ الصَّلَاةَ، وَتُؤْتِيَ الزَّكَاةَ، وَتَصُوْمَ رَمَضَانَ، وَتَحُجَّ الْبَيْتَ إِنِ اسْتَطَعْتَ إِلَيْهِ سَبِيْلًا. قَالَ: صَدَقْتَ. قَالَ: فَعَجِبْنَا لَهُ يَسْأَلُهُ وَيُصَدِّقُهُ! قَالَ: فَأَخْبِرْنِي عَنِ الإِيْمَانِ. قَالَ: أَنْ تُؤْمِنَ بِاللهِ، وَمَلَائِكَتِهِ، وَكُتُبِهِ، وَرُسُلِهِ، وَالْيَوْمِ الآخِرِ، وَتُؤْمِنَ بِالْقَدَرِ خَيْرِهِ وَشَرِّهِ. قَالَ: صَدَقْتَ. قَالَ: فَأَخْبِرْنِي عَنِ الإِحْسَانِ. قَالَ: أَنْ تَعْبُدَ اللهَ كَأَنَّكَ تَرَاهُ، فَإِنْ لَمْ تَكُنْ تَرَاهُ فَإِنَّهُ يَرَاكَ. قَالَ: فَأَخْبِرْنِي عَنِ السَّاعَةِ. قَالَ: مَا الْمَسْئُوْلُ عَنْهَا بِأَعْلَمَ مِنَ السَّائِلِ. قَالَ: فَأَخْبِرْنِي عَنْ أَمَارَتِهَا. قَالَ: أَنْ تَلِدَ الأَمَةُ رَبَّتَهَا، وَأَنْ تَرَى الْحُفَاةَ الْعُرَاةَ الْعَالَةَ رِعَاءَ الشَّاءِ يَتَطَاوَلُونَ فِي الْبُنْيَانِ. ثُمَّ انْطَلَقَ، فَلَبِثْتُ مَلِيًّا، ثُمَّ قَالَ: يَا عُمَرُ، أَتَدْرِي مَنِ السَّائِلُ؟ قُلْتُ: اللهُ وَرَسُوْلُهُ أَعْلَمُ. قَالَ: فَإِنَّهُ جِبْرِيْلُ أَتَاكُمْ يُعَلِّمُكُمْ دِيْنَكُمْ.

'One day as we were sitting with the Messenger of God ﷺ, there appeared before us a man whose clothes were exceedingly white and whose hair was exceedingly black. No signs of travel were seen upon him and none of us knew him. He walked up and sat down by the Prophet ﷺ. Resting his knees against his and placing the palms of his hands on his thighs, he said, "O Muhammad! Tell me about Islam". The Messenger ﷺ said, "Islam is to bear witness that there is no god but God, and that Muhammad is the Messenger of God, and to perform the prayers, to give the alms, to fast in Ramaḍān and to make the pilgrimage to the House [the Kaʿba in Mecca] if you are able". The man said, "You have spoken truthfully". We were amazed at him for asking the Prophet ﷺ a question and then saying that he had spoken truthfully. Then he said, "Then tell me about *Īmān*". The Messenger ﷺ said, "*Īmān* is to believe in God, His Angels, His Books, His

by the two most famous scholars of hadith traditions: Imam Muhammad b. Ismāʿīl al-Bukhārī, and Imam Muslim b. al-Ḥajjāj al-Nīshābūrī. ED.

Messengers, and the Last Day and to believe in Divine destiny, both its good and evil". He said, "You have spoken truthfully". Then he said, "Tell me about *Iḥsān*". The Messenger ﷺ said, "It is to worship God as though you see Him, and if you don't see Him, know that He sees you". He said, "So tell me about the Final Hour". The Messenger ﷺ said, "The one asked about it knows no better than the one asking". He said, "So tell me about its signs". The Messenger ﷺ said, "That the slave-girl will give birth to her mistress and that you will see the barefooted, naked and destitute herdsmen competing in the construction of tall buildings". Then the man left and I stayed for a time. The Prophet ﷺ then said, "O ʿUmar! Do you know who the questioner was?" I said, "God and His Messenger know best". He ﷺ said, "It was Gabriel, who came to you to teach you your religion".'[1]

Replying to Angel Gabriel's question about Islam, the Prophet ﷺ described the basic practices of Islam; when asked about *Īmān*, he described the basic tenets of belief in the *dīn*; and when asked about *Iḥsān*, he described the inner states of the heart and the spiritual experiences pertaining to the *dīn*, which bring about the purification of the inner self, spiritual elevation and stability and strength in character and personality.

The details of these three levels of the *dīn* have been elucidated in a number of hadith reports. Similarly, God Most High revealed

---

[1] Narrated by al-Bukhārī in *al-Ṣaḥīḥ: Kitāb al-Īmān* [The Book of Faith], chapter: 'On Gabriel's Asking the Prophet ﷺ about *Īmān*, Islam, *Iḥsān* and Knowledge of the Final Hour', 1:27 §50; Muslim in *Kitāb al-Īmān* [The Book of Faith], chapter: 'The Explanation of *Īmān*, Islam and *Iḥsān*', 1:36 §8–9; al-Tirmidhī in *al-Sunan: Kitāb al-Īmān* [The Book of Faith], chapter: 'What Has Come to Us Regarding Jibrīl's Description of Faith and Islam to the Prophet ﷺ', 5:6 §2601; Abū Dāwūd in *al-Sunan: Kitāb al-Sunna* [The Book of the Sunna], chapter: 'On the Divine Decree', 4:222 §4695; al-Nasāʾī in *al-Sunan: Kitāb al-Īmān wa sharāʾiʿuhu* [The Book of Faith and its Revealed Laws], chapter: 'The Description of Islam', 8:97 §4990; and Ibn Mājah in the introduction to *al-Sunan*, section: 'Concerning Faith', 1:24 §63.

details about these levels on different occasions in the Qurʾān. As for the first level, God says:

﴿ٱلْيَوْمَ أَكْمَلْتُ لَكُمْ دِينَكُمْ وَأَتْمَمْتُ عَلَيْكُمْ نِعْمَتِي وَرَضِيتُ لَكُمُ ٱلْإِسْلَٰمَ دِينًا﴾

‘*Today I have perfected your* dīn *for you, and have completed My Blessing upon you, and have chosen for you Islam as a* dīn’.[1]

Regarding the second level, God says:

﴿قَالَتِ ٱلْأَعْرَابُ ءَامَنَّا قُل لَّمْ تُؤْمِنُوا۟ وَلَٰكِن قُولُوٓا۟ أَسْلَمْنَا وَلَمَّا يَدْخُلِ ٱلْإِيمَٰنُ فِى قُلُوبِكُمْ وَإِن تُطِيعُوا۟ ٱللَّهَ وَرَسُولَهُۥ لَا يَلِتْكُم مِّنْ أَعْمَٰلِكُمْ شَيْـًٔا إِنَّ ٱللَّهَ غَفُورٌ رَّحِيمٌ﴾

‘*The Bedouins say, “We have believed”. Say, “You have not believed. Rather say, ‘We have accepted Islam’, for true belief has not yet entered your hearts”.*’[2]

And regarding the third level, God says:

﴿وَمَنْ أَحْسَنُ دِينًا مِّمَّنْ أَسْلَمَ وَجْهَهُۥ لِلَّهِ وَهُوَ مُحْسِنٌ وَٱتَّبَعَ مِلَّةَ إِبْرَٰهِيمَ حَنِيفًا وَٱتَّخَذَ ٱللَّهُ إِبْرَٰهِيمَ خَلِيلًا﴾

‘*And with regard to* dīn, *who can be better than he who submits his whole being entirely to God while he also observes spiritual excellence?*’[3]

Elsewhere in the Qurʾān, God Most High mentions these three levels together. He says:

﴿لَيْسَ عَلَى ٱلَّذِينَ ءَامَنُوا۟ وَعَمِلُوا۟ ٱلصَّٰلِحَٰتِ جُنَاحٌ فِيمَا طَعِمُوٓا۟ إِذَا مَا ٱتَّقَوا۟ وَّءَامَنُوا۟ وَعَمِلُوا۟ ٱلصَّٰلِحَٰتِ ثُمَّ ٱتَّقَوا۟ وَّءَامَنُوا۟ ثُمَّ ٱتَّقَوا۟ وَّأَحْسَنُوا۟ وَٱللَّهُ يُحِبُّ ٱلْمُحْسِنِينَ﴾

‘*There is no sin on those who believe* [have *Īmān*] *and do righteous deeds with regard to what they have eaten* [of the unlawful things before the prohibitions came],

[1] Qurʾān 5:3.

[2] Ibid., 49:14.

[3] Ibid., 4:125.

> *so long as they observed piety and possessed firm faith and practised pious deeds consistently, and later,* [after the revelation of the prohibitions] *they desisted from* [unlawful things] *and believed* [with certainty regarding their unlawfulness], *became people of piety and* [finally] *rose to the station of those of spiritual excellence* [*Iḥsān*]. *And God loves those who observe spiritual excellence*'.[1]

If we consider the general meaning of the word Islam, we see that it refers to the *dīn* as a whole; however, if we reflect on a particular meaning of the word, we see that it denotes the basic—although significant—practices known as the 'pillars of Islam'. It is these pillars that shape the Muslim's individual and collective life into a practical mould. In the same way, the teachings of the religion that pertain to actions and commands fall under Islam. However, the teachings that pertain to beliefs and doctrine fall under *Īmān*. They describe the theological aspect of human life. Consequently, the teachings of Islam bless us with lofty inner feelings of connection to God, and the spiritual states of heart converge on the third level of *dīn*, *Iḥsān*. These teachings purify Muslims morally and spiritually. The *muʾmin*'s heart and inner self is developed and elevated, which is the main objective of Islam and *Īmān*.

Let us now discuss these three levels, one by one, and explain their literal and lexical meanings. This will, in turn, demonstrate that these three levels imply peace, security and protection.

1.3 On the Literal Meaning of the Word Islam

The word *Islam* is derived from the root words *salima, yaslamu, salāman* and *salāmatan*, as well as other variations. God says:

﴿يَـٰٓأَيُّهَا ٱلَّذِينَ ءَامَنُوا۟ ٱدْخُلُوا۟ فِى ٱلسِّلْمِ كَآفَّةً﴾

'*O believers! Enter Islam* (Ar. *silm*) *perfectly and wholly*'.[2]

---

[1] Ibid., 5:93.

[2] Ibid., 2:208.

The famous philologist, Abū ʿAmr al-Shaybanī, interpreted the word *silm* as Islam.

The Prophet ﷺ said,

اَلْمُسْلِمُ مَنْ سَلِمَ الْمُسْلِمُونَ مِنْ لِسَانِهِ وَيَدِهِ.

> 'The Muslim is he from whose tongue and hand the Muslims are safe'.[1]

Embracing Islam, therefore, means to enter the door of peace and protection, until people become safe from his harm and evil. According to Abū Manṣūr Muhammad al-Azharī, Abū Isḥāq al-Zujāj narrated from Muhammad b. Yazīd in *Tahdhīb al-lugha* who interpreted the Qurʾānic verse,

﴿فَقُلْ سَلَٰمٌ عَلَيْكُمْ كَتَبَ رَبُّكُمْ عَلَىٰ نَفْسِهِ ٱلرَّحْمَةَ﴾

> '*Say, "Peace be upon you!" Your Lord has made Mercy incumbent upon Himself*'.[2]

In Arabic, the word *salām* has four meanings. Firstly, *salām* is the verbal noun of *salima* (to be free of blemish). Secondly, it is the plural form of *salāma* (safety and security). Thirdly, it is one of the beautiful names of Almighty God (al-Salām, the Flawless). And fourthly, it is a tree which is shady and evergreen.

According to al-Zujāj, *salām* comes from *sallama*, which denotes supplication for man to remain safe and secure from hardships and troubles. It implies deliverance from miseries and disasters.[3]

---

[1] Narrated by al-Bukhārī in *al-Ṣaḥīḥ: Kitāb al-Īmān* [The Book of Faith], chapter: 'The Muslim is He from Whose Tongue and Hand the Muslims Are Safe', 1:13 §10; Muslim in *al-Ṣaḥīḥ: Kitāb al-Īmān* [The Book of Faith], chapter: 'Explaining the Ranks of Virtue within Islam and which of its Affairs are Most Virtuous', 1:65 §41; al-Tirmidhī in *al-Sunan*: *Kitāb al-Īmān* [The Book of Faith], chapter: 'What Has Come to Us Concerning the Fact That the Muslim is He from Whose Tongue and Hand the Muslims Are Safe', 5:17 §2627; Aḥmad b. Ḥanbal in *al-Musnad*, 3:440 §15673; and Ibn Ḥibbān in *al-Ṣaḥīḥ*, 1:406 §180.

[2] Qurʾān 6:54.

[3] Muhammad Al-Azharī, *Tahdhīb al-lugha*, 4:292.

Paradise has also been named the Abode of Peace (*Dār al-Salām*) because it will be free from death and extinction. No one dwelling in it will be in danger or exposed to any malady. It will be a home exclusively permeated with calmness and tranquillity, pleasure and protection, peace and security. No fear, grief, pain or remorse will touch any of its inhabitants. God says,

﴿لَهُمْ دَارُ السَّلَامِ عِندَ رَبِّهِمْ﴾

> '*For them is the home of peace and security with their Lord*'.[1]

God also says,

﴿وَٱللَّهُ يَدْعُوٓا۟ إِلَىٰ دَارِ ٱلسَّلَٰمِ﴾

> '*And God calls towards the Abode of Peace*'.[2]

Dār al-Salām means the abode of *salāma* (safety and protection), because true safety will be available only in Paradise. It is blessed with permanence that will not face extinction. It provides honour that will not see any humiliation and its health has no decay. According to Imam al-Aṣfahānī, *salām* and *salāma* denote freedom from all known and hidden troubles. God says,

﴿إِلَّا مَنْ أَتَى ٱللَّهَ بِقَلْبٍ سَلِيمٍ﴾

> '*But he alone* [will enter Paradise] *who appears before God with a sound* [*salīm*] *heart* [protected from evils]'.[3]

The sound heart is a heart free of tyranny and violence. Security, therefore, is related to the inner self. When God says regarding the heifer in the story of the Children of Israel,

﴿مُسَلَّمَةٌ لَّا شِيَةَ فِيهَا﴾

> '*Sound without any blemish*',[4]

---

1 Qur'ān 6:127.

2 Ibid., 10:25.

3 Ibid., 26:89.

4 Ibid., 2:71.

the soundness implied is physical and external. In other verses, peace, security and protection have been mentioned:

﴿وَلَٰكِنَّ ٱللَّهَ سَلَّمَ﴾

'*But God saved* [*sallam*]';[1]

﴿ٱدْخُلُوهَا بِسَلَٰمٍ ءَامِنِينَ﴾

'*Enter them with peace* [*bi salām*] *and security*';[2]

﴿ٱهْبِطْ بِسَلَٰمٍ مِّنَّا﴾

'*Get down* [from the Ark] *with peace* [*bi salām*] *and blessings from Us*';[3]

﴿يَهْدِى بِهِ ٱللَّهُ مَنِ ٱتَّبَعَ رِضْوَٰنَهُۥ سُبُلَ ٱلسَّلَٰمِ﴾

'*By this God guides those who seek His pleasure to the paths of peace* [*subul al-salām*]';[4]

﴿وَإِذَا خَاطَبَهُمُ ٱلْجَٰهِلُونَ قَالُوا۟ سَلَٰمًا﴾

'*When the ignorant people say to them something* [with bad words] *they reply back with mild words and gentleness* [*salāman*]';[5]

﴿سَلَٰمٌ قَوْلًا مِّن رَّبٍّ رَّحِيمٍ﴾

'"*Peace* [be upon you]*!" This greeting will be conveyed* [to them] *from the Ever-Merciful Lord*';[6]

﴿سَلَٰمٌ عَلَيْكُم بِمَا صَبَرْتُمْ﴾

'*Peace be upon you as a reward for your patience*'.[7]

---

1 Ibid., 8:43.

2 Ibid., 15:46.

3 Ibid., 11:48.

4 Ibid., 5:16.

5 Ibid., 25:63.

6 Ibid., 36:58.

7 Ibid., 13:24.

These verses provide the proof for the first lexical meaning of Islam. They also illustrate that every noun or verb derived from Islam, and every derivative or word conjugated from it, essentially denotes peace, protection, security and safety.

God Most High has also mentioned al-Salām as one of His beautiful names, for He is flawless and free of any shortcoming. Due to its being one of God's beautiful names, this word reflects all the shades of peace, beauty, betterment and goodness. It totally negates all forms of mischief and strife as well. For this reason, the salutation of peace is a distinctive greeting between Muslims, which identifies them as such. Whenever two Muslims meet, they invoke peace on each other, wish security and safety and deliver the message of calmness and tranquillity. They also wish each other protection from every evil, mischief, violence and strife. The ritual prayer performed by Muslims is completed by turning the face right and left, invoking peace on all the Muslims.

Furthermore, a green tree is another meaning of the word Islam. The two famous Arabic lexicons, *Lisān al-ʿArab* and *Tahdhīb al-lugha*, quote the saying of Imam Abū Ḥanīfa:

اَلسَّلَامُ هُوَ شَجَرٌ عَظِيْمٌ وَهُوَ أَبَدًا أَخْضَرُ.

'*Al-Salām* is a magnificent evergreen tree'.[1]

The Imams of the Arabic lexicons maintain that calling an evergreen tree *al-salām* is based on the linguistic meaning of the word. It is a tree safe from decay and the vicissitudes of autumn, so it is called *al-salām*. According to Ibn Barrī, this tree is called *salm* and *salām* is its plural form. It is so named because it is evergreen and shady. This implies that everything providing shade, benefit, peace and security will be conceived as *silm, salm* and *salām*. Moreover, a ladder is called *sullam* in Arabic. According to al-Zujāj,

السُّلَّمُ سُمِّيَ سُلَّمًا لِأَنَّهُ يُسَلِّمُكَ إِلَى حَيْثُ تُرِيْدُ.

'A ladder is called *sullam*, because it takes one safe and

[1] Ibn Manẓūr al-Afrīqī, *Lisān al-ʿArab,* 12:297.

sound wherever one wants to climb'.[1]

All other methods of climbing without a ladder or staircase, like jumping, would end up in some fall, injury or even loss of life. However, by taking a ladder to climb, one becomes safe and protected from threats and dangers. As it provides safety and protection, a ladder is called *sullam* in Arabic. There is a mention of a ladder in the Qur'ān as well:

﴿أَوْ سُلَّماً فِي السَّمَآءِ﴾

'[They should seek] *some ladder* [climbing up] *to heaven*'.[2]

According to Ibn Manẓūr, the author of *Lisān al-ʿArab*,

اَلسُّلَّمُ هُوَ الدَّلْوُ الْعَظِيْمَةُ.

'*Al-Sullam* means a large bucket'.[3]

A bucket is a means of fetching water from a well, and before the advent of machines, people would draw water from wells by means of buckets. But why is a bucket called *al-sullam*? It is because people quench their thirst by drawing water with its help. The needy fetch water and take it home to store for use. In the old days, people used it for water required for ablution and bathing. Due to its usefulness and life-giving utility, it has been given the name *al-sullam*. Water is the fountainhead of life, irrigation, coolness, calm, pleasantness, vegetation and greenery. The means of fetching it, therefore, is called *al-sullam* because it is a means of peace and survival.

The lexical and literal meanings of the word Islam illustrate that it inherently means peace, security, protection, safety and safeguard. In other words, Islam implies safety from violence and killing and also means protection and security. There is no room in Islam for strife, mass murder, destruction, anarchy and chaos. That is why all its aspects negate extremism and terrorism.

---

1 Ibid., 12:299.

2 Qur'ān 6:35.

3 Ibn Manẓūr al-Afrīqī, *Lisān al-ʿArab,* 12:201.

Consequently, it guarantees prosperity, betterment, positive progress, peace, security, protection and development. Therefore, a person exhibiting conduct contrary to the basic meaning of the word Islam has no link at all with *dīn*.

In addition to the Qur'ānic verses, there are prophetic traditions that emphasize the lexical meaning of Islam. ʿAbd Allāh b. ʿAmr b. al-ʿĀṣ reported that the Messenger of God ﷺ said,

اَلْمُسْلِمُ مَنْ سَلِمَ الْمُسْلِمُونَ مِنْ لِّسَانِهِ وَيَدِهِ.

> 'The Muslim is he from whose tongue and hand the Muslims are safe'.[1]

Abū Mūsā al-Ashʿarī also said, 'I asked the Prophet ﷺ, "What kind of [person's] Islam is best?" He said,

مَنْ سَلِمَ الْمُسْلِمُونَ مِنْ لِّسَانِهِ وَيَدِهِ.

> "The one from whose tongue and hand the Muslims are safe!".'[2]

Through the reply of the Prophet ﷺ in this hadith, he has removed the objection of some people, who question, 'Whose Islam should we accept and whose Islam should we reject?' He ﷺ

---

[1] Narrated by al-Bukhārī in *al-Ṣaḥīḥ: Kitāb al-Īmān* [The Book of Faith], chapter: 'The Muslim is He from Whose Tongue and Hand the Muslims Are Safe', 1:13 §10; Muslim in *al-Ṣaḥīḥ: Kitāb al-Īmān* [The Book of Faith], chapter: 'Explaining the Ranks of Virtue within Islam and which of its Affairs are Most Virtuous', 1:65 §41; al-Tirmidhī in *al-Sunan*: *Kitāb al-Īmān* [The Book of Faith], chapter: 'What Has Come to Us Concerning the Fact That the Muslim is He from Whose Tongue and Hand the Muslims Are Safe', 5:17 §2627; Aḥmad b. Ḥanbal in *al-Musnad*, 3:440 §15673; and Ibn Ḥibbān in *al-Ṣaḥīḥ*, 1:406 §180.

[2] Narrated by al-Bukhārī in *al-Ṣaḥīḥ: Kitāb al-Īmān* [The Book of Faith], chapter: 'The Muslim is He from Whose Tongue and Hand the Muslims Are Safe', 1:13 §10; Muslim in *al-Ṣaḥīḥ: Kitāb al-Īmān* [The Book of Faith], chapter: 'Explaining the Ranks of Virtue within Islam and which of its Affairs are Most Virtuous', 1:65 §41; Aḥmad b. Ḥanbal in *al-Musnad*, 3:372 §15037, 2:112 §16027; Ibn Ḥibbān in *al-Ṣaḥīḥ*, 11:579 §5176; Ibn Abī Shayba in *al-Muṣannaf*, 8:320 §26497; al-Ḥākim in *al-Mustadrak*, 1:55 §26; and ʿAbd al-Razzāq in *al-Muṣannaf*, 11:127 §20107.

provided a crystal clear vision of Islam and said that the best Islam is of those from whose hands and tongues all humans are safe. They uphold the banner of peaceful coexistence, love, tolerance, moderation, forbearance and interfaith harmony. Conversely, if someone becomes an extremist and adopts hatred, prejudice, disunity, chaos and coercion, and kills peaceful citizens as a means to preach and enforce *dīn*, his claim to be a Muslim cannot be accepted—even if he appears outwardly as a devout worshipper—because the basic criterion given by the Prophet ﷺ to judge true Islam is peace and security.

ʿAbd Allāh b. ʿUmar ؓ said, 'A man asked the Messenger of God ﷺ, "What kind of Islam is best?" The Prophet ﷺ replied,

تُطْعِمُ الطَّعَامَ، وَتَقْرَأُ السَّلَامَ عَلَى مَنْ عَرَفْتَ وَمَنْ لَمْ تَعْرِفْ.

> "That you serve food and give the salutation of peace to the one whom you know and the one whom you do not know".'[1]

According to Jābir ؓ the Messenger of God ﷺ said,

أَكْمَلُ الْمُؤْمِنِيْنَ مَنْ سَلِمَ الْمُسْلِمُونَ مِنْ لِّسَانِهِ وَيَدِهِ.

> 'The most complete of the believers is he from whose tongue and hand the Muslims are safe'.[2]

According to Ibn ʿUmar ؓ the Messenger of God ﷺ said,

اَلْمُسْلِمُ أَخُو الْمُسْلِمِ. لَا يَظْلِمُهُ وَلَا يُسْلِمُهُ، مَنْ كَانَ فِي حَاجَةِ أَخِيْهِ كَانَ اللهُ فِي حَاجَتِهِ، وَمَنْ فَرَّجَ عَنْ مُسْلِمٍ كُرْبَةً فَرَّجَ اللهُ عَنْهُ كُرْبَةً مِنْ كُرُبَاتِ يَوْمِ الْقِيَامَةِ، وَمَنْ سَتَرَ مُسْلِمًا سَتَرَهُ اللهُ يَوْمَ الْقِيَامَةِ.

---

[1] Narrated by al-Bukhārī in *al-Ṣaḥīḥ: Kitāb al-Īmān* [The Book of Faith], chapter: 'Serving Food is a Part of Islam', 1:13 §12, and in chapter: 'Spreading Salutations of Peace is from Islam', 1:19 §28; Muslim in *al-Ṣaḥīḥ: Kitāb al-Īmān* [The Book of Faith], chapter: 'Explaining the Ranks of Virtue within Islam and which of its Affairs Entail Half of It', 1:65 §39.

[2] Narrated by al-Ḥākim in *al-Mustadrak*, 1:54 §23; and Ibn Ḥibbān in *al-Ṣaḥīḥ*, 1:426 §197.

'The Muslim is the brother of his fellow Muslim. He does not wrong him or leave him helpless. Whoever attends to his brother's need, God will attend to his need. If someone relieves a Muslim of a distress in the world, God will relieve him of one of the distresses of the Day of Resurrection. And if someone covers the fault of a Muslim, God will cover his faults on the Day of Resurrection'.[1]

According to Abū Hurayra ﵁ the Messenger of God ﷺ said,

اَلْمُسْلِمُ أَخُو الْمُسْلِمِ. لَا يَظْلِمُهُ، وَلَا يَخْذُلُهُ، وَلَا يَحْقِرُهُ، اَلتَّقْوَى هَاهُنَا (وَيُشِيرُ إِلَى صَدْرِهِ ثَلَاثَ مَرَّاتٍ). بِحَسْبِ امْرِئٍ مِنَ الشَّرِّ أَنْ يَحْقِرَ أَخَاهُ الْمُسْلِمَ. كُلُّ الْمُسْلِمِ عَلَى الْمُسْلِمِ حَرَامٌ، دَمُهُ، وَمَالُهُ، وَعِرْضُهُ.

'The Muslim is the brother of a fellow Muslim; he does not wrong him, abandon him or look down upon him. Piety [*taqwā*] is right here [and the Prophet ﷺ pointed to his blessed chest thrice]. It is evil enough for a Muslim to look down upon his brother Muslim. The Muslim's blood, property and honour are forbidden for the other Muslim'.[2]

---

[1] Narrated by al-Bukhārī in *al-Ṣaḥīḥ*: *Kitāb al-maẓālim* [The Book of Wrongdoings], chapter: *'The Muslim Does Not Wrong or Forsake a Fellow Muslim'*, 2:862 §2310; Muslim in *al-Ṣaḥīḥ*: *Kitāb al-birr wa al-ṣila wa al-ādāb* [The Book of Piety, Filial Duty and Good Manners], chapter: 'On the Prohibition of Oppression', 4:1996 §2580; al-Tirmidhī in *al-Sunan*: *Kitāb al-ḥudūd* [The Book of Prescribed Punishments], chapter: 'What Has Come to Us Concerning the Hiding of a Muslim's Faults', 4:34 §1426; and Abū Dāwūd in *al-Sunan*: *Kitāb al-adab* [The Book of Good Manners], chapter: 'On Brotherhood', 4:273 §4893.

[2] Narrated by Muslim in *al-Ṣaḥīḥ*: *Kitāb al-Birr wa al-ṣila wa al-ādāb* [The Book of Piety, Filial Duty and Good Manners], chapter: *The Prohibition of Wronging a Muslim or Deserting Him, Despising Him, His Goods, His Blood and His Wealth*, 4:1986 §2564; Aḥmad b. Ḥanbal in *al-Musnad*, 2:277 §7713; ʿAbd b. Ḥumayd in *al-Musnad*, 1:420 §1442; and al-Bayhaqī in *al-Sunan al-Kubrā*, 6:92 §11276, and in *Shuʿab al-Īmān*, 5:280 §6660.

According to ʿAbd Allāh b. Masʿūd ﵁ the Prophet ﷺ said,

سِبَابُ الْمُسْلِمِ فُسُوقٌ، وَقِتَالُهُ كُفْرٌ.

> 'Reviling a Muslim is immorality, and fighting him is disbelief'.[1]

According to this hadith, using foul words and abusive language against someone is corruption, and fighting and killing amounts to disbelief; how worse it would be to take up arms and kill civilians?

1.4 Islam Means Safety for All of Humanity

Abū Hurayra ﵁ reported that the Messenger of God ﷺ said,

اَلْمُسْلِمُ مَنْ سَلِمَ النَّاسُ مِنْ لِّسَانِهِ وَيَدِهِ.

> 'The Muslim is he from whose tongue and hand all people are safe'.[2]

Imam Aḥmad b. Ḥanbal narrated in his *Musnad* from ʿAbd Allāh b. ʿAmr b. al-ʿĀṣ ﵁ who reported that a man said, 'O Messenger of God! What [person's] Islam is best?' The Prophet ﷺ replied,

مَنْ سَلِمَ النَّاسُ مِنْ لِّسَانِهِ وَيَدِهِ.

---

[1] Narrated by al-Bukhārī in *al-Ṣaḥīḥ*: *Kitāb al-Īmān* [The Book of Faith], chapter: 'On the Muslim's Fear That His Deeds Might be in Vain, Without His Being Aware', 1:27 §48; Muslim in *al-Ṣaḥīḥ: Kitāb al-Īmān* [The Book of Faith], chapter: 'Explanation of the Prophet's Saying ﷺ, "Reviling A Muslim is Immorality and Fighting Him is Disbelief"', 1:81 §64; al-Tirmidhī in *al-Sunan: Kitāb al-Birr wa al-ṣila* [The Book of Piety and Filial Duty], chapter 52, 4:353 §1983; al-Nasāʾī in *al-Sunan: Kitāb taḥrīm al-dam* [The Book on the Prohibition of Bloodshed], chapter: 'On Fighting A Muslim', 7:121 §4105; and Ibn Mājah in the introduction to his *al-Sunan*, section: 'On Faith', 1:27 §69.

[2] Narrated by al-Nasāʾī in *al-Sunan*: *Kitāb al-Īmān wa sharāʾiʿuhu* [The Book of Faith and its Revealed Laws], chapter: 'The Quality of the True Believer', 8:104 §4995, and in his *al-Sunan al-kubrā*, 6:530 §11726; Ibn Mājah in *al-Sunan*: *Kitāb al-fitan* [The Book of Tribulations], chapter: 'The Sanctity of a Believer's Blood and Property', 2:1298 §3934; and Aḥmad b. Ḥanbal in *al-Musnad*, 2:379 §8918.

> 'The one from whose tongue and hand all people are safe'.[1]

Imam al-Ṭabarānī has also narrated from ʿAbd Allāh b. ʿAmr who said that a man asked the Prophet ﷺ, 'O Messenger of God! Whose Islam is best?' The Prophet ﷺ replied,

مَنْ سَلِمَ النَّاسُ مِنْ لِّسَانِهِ وَيَدِهِ.

> 'The one from whose tongue and hand all people are safe'.[2]

Using the word '*al-nās*' in some of these hadith reports, the Prophet ﷺ indicated that a Muslim or *muʾmin* is the one from whom everyone's life and property are safe and secure—without any discrimination based on faith and creed. Therefore, a person who does not consider human dignity worth any regard, and treads the path of violence, bloodshed and strife, cannot be a *muʾmin*, despite his devout worship and pious efforts. If someone keeps a beard and glorifies God day and night, offers prayers five times a day, keeps fasts, observes night vigil prayers, performs Hajj and visitation every year in addition to his preaching—yet despite all that, the lives and properties of others are unsafe and insecure from him, none of his deeds will save him from the torment of God. True prosperity depends on a heart protected from mischief and tyranny,[3] not solely on outward acts of worship. The Prophet ﷺ said,

إِنَّ اللهَ لَا يَنْظُرُ إِلَى صُوَرِكُمْ وَأَمْوَالِكُمْ، وَلَكِنْ يَّنْظُرُ إِلَى قُلُوبِكُمْ وَأَعْمَالِكُمْ.

> 'God does not observe your forms and your properties, but He does observe your hearts and your deeds'.[4]

---

[1] Narrated by Aḥmad b. Ḥanbal in *al-Musnad*, 2:187 §6753.

[2] Narrated by al-Ṭabarānī in *al-Muʿjam al-awsaṭ*, 3:287 §3170.

[3] Qurʾān 26:89.

[4] Narrated by Muslim in *al-Ṣaḥīḥ*: *Kitāb al-birr wa al-ṣila wa al-ādāb* [The Book of Piety, Filial Duty and Good Manners], chapter: 'The Prohibition of Wronging a Muslim, Deserting Him, Scorning Him, Shedding His Blood and Assaulting His Honour and Property', 4:1987 §2564; and Aḥmad b.

If the inner self does not undergo any change and remains brutal, one cannot deceive God by adorning oneself with the outward trappings of piety and goodness.

1.5 On the Literal Meaning of the Word *Īmān*

According to al-Liḥiyānī, the word *īmān* is derived from *amina, ya'manu, amnan* and *amanan*, *amānatan* and *amanatan*. This word also indicates peace and protection. Abū Manṣūr Muhammad al-Azharī quoted Abū Zayd in *Tahdhīb al-lugha*: 'So-and-so provided shelter [*āmana*] to the enemy, so the enemy felt safe [*amina*], and is thus protected [*mu'man*]'.[1]

This is *īmān*, or the providing of safety. When an enemy has been provided with protection, he will be called *mu'man* [passive participle], while the provider of shelter will be called *mu'min* [active participle]. Similarly, the Qur'ān has taken an oath by Mecca calling it '*the city of peace*'.[2] In it, the word *amīn* has been used to imply *ma'mūn* (the object of safety).

Peace is the opposite of fear. Al-Amīn is also one of the beautiful names of God, as reported by the exegete al-Mujāhid, while al-Mu'min is one of His beautiful names mentioned in the Qur'ān. Both, however, mean the same thing: the One Who provides shelter to His friends. The Qur'ān says,

﴿فَلْيَعْبُدُوا۟ رَبَّ هَـٰذَا ٱلْبَيْتِ. ٱلَّذِىٓ أَطْعَمَهُم مِّن جُوعٍ وَءَامَنَهُم مِّنْ خَوْفٍ﴾

> '*So they should worship the Lord of this Sacred House* [the Ka'ba], *Who has fed them in hunger and secured them from fear*'.[3]

Īmān and *amāna* are transitive as well as intransitive. *Mu'min*, therefore, has two meanings: the one who attains peace and the provider of peace. The sanctuary of Mecca has been mentioned in the Qur'ān:

Ḥanbal in *al-Musnad*, 2:258.

[1] Ibn Manẓūr al-Afrīqī, *Lisān al-'Arab,* 13:21.

[2] Qur'ān 95:3.

[3] Ibid., 106:3–4.

﴿أَوَلَمْ يَرَوْا۟ أَنَّا جَعَلْنَا حَرَمًا ءَامِنًا﴾

'*And have they not seen that We have made the Sanctuary* [of the Kaᶜba] *a safe haven?*'[1]

It also says about the Sacred House of God,

﴿وَإِذْ جَعَلْنَا ٱلْبَيْتَ مَثَابَةً لِّلنَّاسِ وَأَمْنًا﴾

'*And* [remember] *when We made this House* [the Kaᶜba] *a central place for mankind to turn to* [and assemble] *and a sanctuary for peace*'.[2]

Abū Isḥāq al-Zujāj ruled that the words *āmin, amin* and *amīn* all share the same meaning. The stars have been called *amana* in the prophetic traditions, implying that they are the security of the heavens. When they collide, the Day of Resurrection will begin and the universe will perish. The Prophet ﷺ said,

اَلنُّجُومُ أَمَنَةُ السَّمَاءِ، فَإِذَا ذَهَبَتِ النُّجُوْمُ أَتَى السَّمَاءَ مَا تُوعَدُ.

'The stars are the source of security for the heavens, and when they go the heavens will receive what has been promised it'.

Similarly, the Messenger of God ﷺ called himself the security of his Companions:

أَنَا أَمَنَةٌ لِأَصْحَابِي، فَإِذَا ذَهَبْتُ أَتَى أَصْحَابِي مَا يُوعَدُونَ.

'I am the source of security for my Companions. When I [physically] leave the world that which was promised them [disruptions, rebellions and hostilities] will come'.

That is exactly what happened and, consequently, the Rightly Guided Caliphs and thousands of other Companions were martyred. Then the Prophet ﷺ said,

أَصْحَابِي أَمَنَةٌ لِأُمَّتِي، فَإِذَا ذَهَبَتْ أَصْحَابِي أَتَى أُمَّتِي مَا يُوعَدُونَ.

---

[1] Ibid., 29:67.

[2] Ibid., 2:125.

> 'My Companions are a source of security for my *Umma*. When they leave my *Umma* will receive what was promised it'.[1]

That is how the word *amana* has been used to denote peace and protection. This word and all its derivatives relate to peace and protection. That is why if someone acts contrary to the way of peace and security and spreads terror, he has no link with *Īmān*.

This linguistic analysis of the meanings of Islam and *Īmān* fully reveals that both levels of *dīn* demand peace, protection and security in every matter. Whatever action is performed to destroy peace—under any slogan, and with whatever justification fabricated to prove it valid—cannot be in the fold of either Islam or *Īmān*; rather, it will be in conflict with them. That is why the Prophet ﷺ declared *Īmān* conditional upon peace, protection and security.

The beloved Messenger of God ﷺ blessed the *Umma* with countless exhortations and instructions drawn from the linguistic reality of *Īmān*, so that all Muslims become embodiments of love and affection, tolerance and forbearance, human dignity and mercy and clemency. If these instructions are applied, society entire will become a haven of peace and calmness, security and protection, ease and comfort.

Jābir ؓ reported that the Messenger of God ﷺ said,

أَكْمَلُ الْمُؤْمِنِيْنَ مَنْ سَلِمَ الْمُسْلِمُونَ مِنْ لِّسَانِهِ وَيَدِهِ.

> 'The most complete of the believers is he from whose tongue and whose hand the Muslims are safe'.[2]

Abū Mūsā al-Ashʿarī ؓ reported that the Messenger of God ﷺ said,

اَلْمُؤْمِنُ لِلْمُؤْمِنِ كَالْبُنْيَانِ. يَشُدُّ بَعْضُهُ بَعْضًا (وَشَبَّكَ بَيْنَ أَصَابِعِهِ).

---

[1] Narrated by Aḥmad b. Ḥanbal in *al-Musnad*, 4:398 §19584.

[2] Narrated by al-Ḥākim in *al-Mustadrak*, 1:54 §23 and Ibn Ḥibbān in *al-Ṣaḥīḥ*, 1:426 §197.

'The believer is to another believer like an edifice, each part of it strengthens the other', and he interlaced his fingers to illustrate this.[1]

Al-Nuʿmān b. al-Bashīr ﷺ reported that the Messenger of God ﷺ said,

مَثَلُ الْمُؤْمِنِيْنَ فِي تَوَادِّهِمْ وَتَرَاحُمِهِمْ وَتَعَاطُفِهِمْ مَثَلُ الْجَسَدِ. إِذَا اشْتَكَى مِنْهُ عُضْوٌ تَدَاعَى لَهُ سَائِرُ الْجَسَدِ بِالسَّهَرِ وَالْحُمَّى.

'In their mutual love, mercy and compassion, the true believers are like the physical body. If one of its organs is afflicted with pain, the rest of the body rallies to it with sleeplessness and fever'.[2]

According to Abū Hurayra ﷺ the Messenger of God ﷺ said,

أَكْمَلُ الْمُؤْمِنِيْنَ إِيْمَانًا أَحْسَنُهُمْ خُلُقًا، وَخِيَارُكُمْ خِيَارُكُمْ لِنِسَائِهِمْ.

'The most complete of the believers in faith is the finest of them in moral character, and the best of you are those

---

[1] Narrated by al-Bukharī in *al-Ṣaḥīḥ*: *Kitāb al-maẓālim* [The Book of Oppression], chapter: 'Assisting the Oppressed', 2:863 §2314; Muslim in *al-Ṣaḥīḥ*: *Kitāb al-birr wa al-ṣila wa al-ādāb* [The Book of Piety, Filial Duty and Good Manners], chapter: 'The Mutual Compassion of the Muslims, Their Mutual Affection and Their Mutual Support', 4:1999 §2585; al-Tirmidhī in *al-Sunan*: *Kitāb al-birr wa al-ṣila* [The Book of Piety and Filial Duty], chapter: 'What Has Been Reported Concerning the Muslim's Compassion for a fellow Muslim', 4:325 §1928; and al-Nasāʾī in *al-Sunan*: *Kitāb al-Zakāt* [The Book of Zakat], chapter: 'The Remuneration of the Treasurer When He Gives Charitable Donations with His Master's Permission', 5:79 §2560.

[2] Narrated by al-Bukhārī in *al-Ṣaḥīḥ*: *Kitāb al-adab* [The Book of Good Manners], chapter: 'Compassion for People and Their Livestock', 5:2238 §5665; Muslim in *al-Ṣaḥīḥ*: *Kitāb al-birr wa al-ṣila wa al-ādāb* [The Book of Piety, Filial Duty and Good Manners], chapter: 'The Mutual Compassion of the Muslims, Their Mutual Affection and Their Mutual Support', 4:1999 §2586; Aḥmad b. Ḥanbal in *al-Musnad*, 4:270; al-Bazzār in *al-Musnad*, 8:238 §3299; and al-Bayhaqī in *al-Sunan al-kubrā*, 3:353 §6223, and *Shuʿab al-Īmān*, 6:481 §8985.

who are the kindest towards your womenfolk'.[1]

ʿAbd Allāh ﷺ reported that the Messenger of God ﷺ said,

لَيْسَ الْمُؤْمِنُ بِالطَّعَّانِ وَلَا اللَّعَّانِ وَلَا الْفَاحِشِ وَلَا الْبَذِيءِ.

'The true believer is not a defamer or curser or one given to vulgarities and obscenities'.[2]

ʿAbd Allāh b. ʿUmar ﷺ said, 'I saw the Messenger of God ﷺ circumambulating around the Kaʿba and addressing it, saying,

مَا أَطْيَبَكِ وَأَطْيَبَ رِيحَكِ! مَا أَعْظَمَكِ وَأَعْظَمَ حُرْمَتَكِ! وَالَّذِي نَفْسُ مُحَمَّدٍ بِيَدِهِ، لَحُرْمَةُ الْمُؤْمِنِ أَعْظَمُ عِنْدَ اللهِ حُرْمَةً مِنْكِ مَالِهِ وَدَمِهِ، وَأَنْ نَظُنَّ بِهِ إِلَّا خَيْرًا.

"How excellent you are and how sweet your smell is! How grand you are and how grand your sacredness is! By the One in Whose Hand is Muhammad's soul, the inviolability of a believer's property and blood is greater in the sight of God than your sacredness. We must think only well of a believer".'[3]

Anas b. Mālik ﷺ reported that the Messenger of God ﷺ said,

ثَلَاثٌ مِنْ أَخْلَاقِ الْإِيْمَانِ: مَنْ إِذَا غَضِبَ لَمْ يُدْخِلْهُ غَضَبُهُ فِي بَاطِلٍ، وَمَنْ إِذَا رَضِيَ لَمْ يُخْرِجْهُ رِضَاهُ مِنْ حَقٍّ، وَمَنْ إِذَا قَدَرَ لَمْ يَتَعَاطَ مَا لَيْسَ لَهُ.

---

[1] Narrated by al-Tirmidhī in *al-Sunan*: *Kitāb al-raḍāʿa* [The Book of Suckling], chapter: 'What Has Come to Us About the Wife's Right upon Her Husband', 3:466 §1162; Aḥmad b. Ḥanbal in *al-Musnad*, 2:472 §10110; Ibn Ḥibbān in *al-Ṣaḥīḥ*, 2:227 §479; al-Ḥākim in *al-Mustadrak*, 1:43 §2; al-Dārimī in *al-Sunan*, 2:415 §2792; and Abū Yaʿlā in *al-Musnad*, 7:237 §4240.

[2] Narrated by al-Tirmidhī in *al-Sunan*: *Kitāb al-birr wa al-ṣila* [The Book of Piety and Filial Duty], chapter: 'What Has Come to Us About Cursing', 4:350 §1977; al-Bukhārī in *al-Adab al-mufrad*, p. 116 §312 and 332; Ibn Ḥibbān in *al-Ṣaḥīḥ*, 1:421 §192; and al-Ḥākim in *al-Mustadrak*, 1:57 §29.

[3] Narrated by Ibn Mājah in *al-Sunan: Kitāb al-fitan* [The Book of Tribulations], chapter: 'The Inviolability of a Believer's Blood and Property', 2:1297 §3932; al-Ṭabarānī in *Musnad al-Shāmiyyīn*, 2:396 §1568; and al-Mundhirī in *al-Targhīb wa al-tarhīb*, 3:201 §3679.

'There are three characteristics of faith: if someone is angry, his anger does not lead him to commit an evil act; if someone is pleased, his pleasure does not cause him to depart from the truth; and if someone is powerful, he does not engage in that which is not his right'.[1]

1.6 Īmān Means Safety for All of Humanity

Imam al-Nasāʾī and Aḥmad b. Ḥanbal reported from Abū Hurayra ﷺ that the Messenger of God ﷺ said,

اَلْمُؤْمِنُ مَنْ أَمِنَهُ النَّاسُ عَلَى دِمَائِهِمْ وَأَمْوَالِهِمْ.

'The true believer [*muʾmin*] is he whom people trust with regard to their blood and their properties'.[2]

Fuḍāla b. ʿUbayd ﷺ reported that the Messenger of God ﷺ said during his Farewell Pilgrimage,

اَلْمُؤْمِنُ مَنْ أَمِنَهُ النَّاسُ عَلَى أَنْفُسِهِمْ وَأَمْوَالِهِمْ.

'The true believer [*muʾmin*] is he whom people trust with regard to their lives and their properties'.[3]

Abu Hurayra ﷺ reported that the Messenger of God ﷺ said,

مَنْ كَانَ يُؤْمِنُ بِاللهِ وَالْيَوْمِ الْآخِرِ فَلَا يُؤْذِ جَارَهُ، وَمَنْ كَانَ يُؤْمِنُ بِاللهِ وَالْيَوْمِ الْآخِرِ فَلْيُكْرِمْ ضَيْفَهُ، وَمَنْ كَانَ يُؤْمِنُ بِاللهِ وَالْيَوْمِ الْآخِرِ فَلْيَقُلْ خَيْرًا أَوْ لِيَصْمُتْ.

'He who believes in God and the Last Day, let him

---

[1] Narrated by al-Ṭabarānī in *al-Muʿjam al-ṣaghīr*, 1:114 §164; al-Daylamī in *al-Firdaws bi maʾthūr al-khiṭāb*, 2:87 §2466; Ibn Rajab in *Jāmiʿ al-ʿulūm wa al-ḥikam*, 1:148; and al-Haythamī in *Majmaʿ al-zawāʾid*, 1:59.

[2] Narrated by al-Nasāʾī in *al-Sunan*: *Kitāb al-Īmān wa sharāʾiʿuhu* [The Book of Faith and its Revealed Laws], chapter: 'The Quality of the True Believer', 8:104 §4995; and Aḥmad b. Ḥanbal in *al-Musnad*, 2:379 §8918.

[3] Narrated by Ibn Mājah in *al-Sunan*: *Kitāb al-fitan* [The Book of Tribulations], chapter: 'The Sanctity of the Believer's Blood and Property', 2:1298 §3934; Aḥmad b. Ḥanbal in *al-Musnad*, 6:21 §24004; al-Ḥākim in *al-Mustadrak*, 1:54 §24; and al-Ṭabarānī in *al-Muʿjam al-awsaṭ*, 1:81 §232.

abstain from harming his neighbour; he who believes in God and the Last Day, let him honour his guest; and he who believes in God and the Last Day, let him say that which is good, or remain silent'.[1]

Abū Shurayḥ ﷺ reported that the Prophet ﷺ said,

وَاللهِ لَا يُؤْمِنُ، وَاللهِ لَا يُؤْمِنُ، وَاللهِ لَا يُؤْمِنُ.

'By God, he does not truly believe! By God, he does not truly believe! By God, he does not truly believe!'

Someone asked, 'Who, O Messenger of God?' He said:

الَّذِي لَا يَأْمَنُ جَارُهُ بَوَائِقَهُ.

'He whose neighbour is not safe from his hurtful behaviour'.[2]

This concept is also validated by the hadith,

لَا إِيْمَانَ لِمَنْ لَا أَمَانَةَ لَهُ.

---

[1] Narrated by al-Bukhārī in *al-Ṣaḥīḥ*: *Kitāb al-adab* [The Book of Good Manners], chapter: 'If Someone Believes in God and the Last Day, He Must Not Harm His Neighbour', 5:2240 §5672, and *Kitāb al-adab* [The Book of Good Manners], chapter: 'Honouring the Guest and Serving Him Personally', 5:2273 §5785, and *Kitāb al-riqāq* [The Book of Heart-softening Narrations], chapter: 'Safeguarding the Tongue', 5:2376 §6110; Muslim in *al-Ṣaḥīḥ*: *Kitāb al-Īmān* [The Book of Faith], chapter: 'Urging Piety for the Neighbour and the Guest, and the Necessity of Maintaining Silence Except when Having Something Good to Say', 1:6968 §§47–48; al-Tirmidhī in *al-Sunan*: *Kitāb al-adab* [The Book of Manners], chapter 50, 4:659 §2500; Abū Dāwūd in *al-Sunan*: *Kitāb al-Adab* [The Book of Good Manners], chapter: 'The Rightful Due to the Neighbour', 4:339 §5154; and Ibn Mājah in *al-Sunan*: *Kitāb al-adab* [The Book of Good Manners], chapter: 'The Right Due to the Neighbour', 2:1211 §3672.

[2] Narrated by al-Bukhārī in *al-Ṣaḥīḥ*: *Kitāb al-adab* [The Book of Good Manners], chapter: 'The Sin of Someone Whose Neighbour is Not Safe from His Mischief', 5:2240 §5670; Muslim in *al-Ṣaḥīḥ*: *Kitāb al-Īmān* [The Book of Faith], chapter: 'Explanation of the Prohibition of Harming the Neighbour', 1:68 §46; al-Ḥākim in *al-Mustadrak*, 1:53 §21; and al-Ṭabarānī in *al-Muʿjam al-kabīr*, 22:187 §487.

'He who is untrustworthy has no faith'.[1]

For that reason, when someone asked the Messenger of God ﷺ, 'Who is a believer?' he replied,

مَنِ ائْتَمَنَهُ النَّاسُ عَلَى أَمْوَالِهِمْ وَأَنْفُسِهِمْ.

'[The believer is he] whom people trust with their property and their persons'.[2]

This is the lowest level denoted by the word *Īmān*. The Prophet ﷺ made it a precondition for one to attain good character:

مَا آمَنَ بِي مَنْ بَاتَ شَبْعَانًا وَجَارُهُ جَائِعٌ.

'If someone spends the night satiated while his neighbour is hungry, he has not believed in me'.[3]

1.7 On the Literal Meaning of the Word *Iḥsān*

The word *Iḥsān* is the verbal noun of the trilateral verb *ḥasana/ḥasuna, yaḥsunu, ḥusnan*. It means beauty, balance, betterment, benevolence, piety and goodness. It is the opposite of ugliness and evil, sin and vice and bad deeds. The antonym of *Iḥsān* is *isāʾa*, which means the same thing as ugliness.

In *Tahdhīb al-lugha* Imam Abū Manṣūr Muhammad al-Azharī quoted the saying of al-Layth al-Shaybānī regarding the basic meaning of *Iḥsān*. Regarding the verse:

﴿وَقُولُوا۟ لِلنَّاسِ حُسْنًا﴾

[1] Narrated by Ibn Ḥibbān in *al-Ṣaḥīḥ*, 1:422 §194; Ibn Khuzayma in *al-Ṣaḥīḥ*, 4:51; al-Bayhaqī in *al-Sunan al-kubrā*, 4:97; Ibn Abī Shayba in *al-Muṣannaf*, 6:159; and al-Ṭabarānī in *al-Muʿjam al-kabīr*, 8:195.

[2] Narrated by Ibn Mājah in *al-Sunan: Kitāb al-fitan* [The Book of Tribulations], chapter: 'The Inviolability of a Believer's Blood and Property', 2:1298 §3934 and recorded by Ibn Manẓūr al-Afrīqī in *Lisān al-ʿArab*, 13:24.

[3] Narrated by al-Ṭabarānī in *al-Muʿjam al-kabīr*, 1:259 §751; and al-Ḥākim in *al-Mustadrak*, 2:15.

'*And speak with goodness* [*ḥusnan*] *to people*',[1]

Al-Layth said that it means to say good and pleasant words to others. Al-Zujāj also maintained that it is to talk to people in a nice manner and possess beauty, goodness and benevolence, because *ḥasīn* has been derived from *ḥasuna*, as *ʿaẓīm* is from *ʿaẓuma* and *karīm* is from *karuma*. Al-Mundhirī reported from Abū al-Haytham that the words *ḥusnan* and *ḥasanan* both imply a beautiful thing. It points to beauty in everything, whether in utterance or action, moral acts or general behaviour. The divine command is to be nice and refined not only in conversation but in general behaviour. One must interact with others cordially, piously, and with a sentiment of well-wishing, goodness and beauty.

This word has also been employed as a command for benevolent and beautiful behaviour with parents. God Most High says,

﴿وَوَصَّيْنَا ٱلْإِنسَـٰنَ بِوَالِدَيْهِ حُسْنًا﴾

'*And We have enjoined man to behave benevolently with his parents*'.[2]

The intention of this divine decree is to teach us that we should speak nicely to our parents, treat them with refined conduct and behave with them in every matter with beauty, kindness, good manners, love and affection, and that under no circumstances should we be harsh with them. This entire manner of behaviour and conduct is called *Iḥsān*. The Qurʾān has further made it easy:

﴿وَيَدْرَءُونَ بِٱلْحَسَنَةِ ٱلسَّيِّئَةَ﴾

'*And they repel evil by means of good*'.[3]

The *muʾmin* and *muḥsin* repel evil with good, and vice with virtue. They respond to what is painful with pleasant behaviour. Similarly, the Qurʾān has mentioned another divine principle:

---

[1] Qurʾān 2:83.

[2] Ibid., 29:8.

[3] Ibid., 13:22.

﴿إِنَّ ٱلْحَسَنَٰتِ يُذْهِبْنَ ٱلسَّيِّئَاتِ﴾

'*Surely, good actions remove the evil actions*'.[1]

Spiritually, the impact of pious deeds is so strong that they eliminate evil deeds, and the acts of *Iḥsān* defeat wrongs and render sins into nothingness. The Qur'ān has further explained,

﴿وَلَا تَسْتَوِى ٱلْحَسَنَةُ وَلَا ٱلسَّيِّئَةُ﴾

'*And good and evil cannot be equal*'.[2]

The message here is that a wrong action should not receive a wrong reaction. Muslims should respond to a vice with virtue. When they hear something bad, they should reply to it with something good and beautiful. A beautiful act or saying effaces the odious act or saying, and permeates the environment with love and cooperation. Evil leads to disunity and division, while good leads to unity and strength. Evil conduct and wrong-doing generate hatred, while good conduct and piety bring about goodness, benevolence, love and harmony. That is the truth of *Iḥsān*. That is why God has ordained the Muslims to beg for '*ḥasana*' in this world as well as in the Hereafter:

﴿رَبَّنَآ ءَاتِنَا فِى ٱلدُّنْيَا حَسَنَةً وَفِى ٱلْأَخِرَةِ حَسَنَةً وَقِنَا عَذَابَ ٱلنَّارِ﴾

'*O our Lord, grant us excellence* [*ḥasana*] *in this world, and excellence in the Hereafter, and save us from the torment of Hell*'.[3]

One must realize that in this verse, the word *ḥasana* does not only imply good deeds and acts of worship—because it is not possible to perform meritorious acts in the Hereafter—*ḥasana* means *Iḥsān* both here and Hereafter. In this Qur'ānic supplication, goodness, benevolence, beauty and conduct based on *Iḥsān* are requested. When we ask for '*ḥasana*' in this life, we beg for a peaceful life,

---

[1] Ibid., 11:114.

[2] Ibid., 41:34.

[3] Ibid., 2:201.

free of every evil, mischief, wrong-doing and strife. And when we beg for '*ḥasana*' in the Hereafter, we beg for *Iḥsān*, which is superior to justice alone.

The *ḥasana* in this world refers to goodness and betterment and protection from evil and pain, and *ḥasana* in the Hereafter signifies emancipation and deliverance from torment, hardships on the Last Day, reckoning and Hell. This meaning of *ḥasana* has been elaborated by Anas b. Mālik's saying, quoted by the Imams of Qur'ānic exegesis, including Ibn Kathīr. Similarly, Imam al-Ḥasan al-Baṣrī, Abū Wā'il, al-Suddī, Ibn Zayd, Qatāda, Muqātil, Sufyān al-Thawrī and Ibn Qutayba also maintain that *ḥasana* in this world connotes 'knowledge, bounty, worship, expansion of sustenance and security and protection from every evil, mischief and disruption'. The *ḥasana* in the Hereafter implies 'Paradise, forgiveness, and protection from torment and hardships'. In both cases, *ḥasana* means goodness, betterment, expansion, facility and protection. Deliverance is being implored from torment in both the worlds. This highlights the inherent meaning of goodness, and security that *Iḥsān* conveys.

Two modes of action have been described in the Qur'ān: justice and *Iḥsān*. God says,

﴿إِنَّ ٱللَّهَ يَأْمُرُ بِٱلْعَدْلِ وَٱلْإِحْسَٰنِ﴾

'*Indeed, God enjoins justice and benevolence* [towards everyone]'.[1]

According to Imam al-Rāghib al-Aṣfahānī, justice means that whatever is obligatory for man to give should be given, and whatever he has the right to take, he should take. *Iḥsān*, however, means to give more than is due and to take less than is one's right. This conduct emphasizes benevolence when giving to others and taking from others. *Iḥsān* is, therefore, a higher grade than justice. Justice is due compensation while *Iḥsān* is added excellence. God says,

﴿هَلْ جَزَآءُ ٱلْإِحْسَٰنِ إِلَّا ٱلْإِحْسَٰنُ﴾

[1] Ibid., 16:90.

'And is the reward of good anything but good?'[1]

That is what has been ordained. Someone who gives to others more than their due demonstrates *Iḥsān*, and God will reward him or her more than what is due. God says,

﴿لِّلَّذِينَ أَحْسَنُوا۟ ٱلْحُسْنَىٰ وَزِيَادَةٌ﴾

'For those who do pious works there is good recompense and more [added to it]'.[2]

The benevolent will be awarded Paradise and will also be awarded more than what is their due. The Qur'ānic exegetes have further elaborated the meaning of 'more' [*ziyāda*], and held that it implies the beholding of God's Countenance.

By revealing to us his beautiful name of al-Salām, God shows us the meaning of peace that is inherent in Islam, and by revealing to us His name al-Mu'min, He highlights the inherent sense of peace and protection found in the word *Īmān*. And how beautiful it is that God, after revealing the concept of *Iḥsān*, informed us that His names are all *ḥusnā* (beautiful)! He says,

﴿وَلِلَّهِ ٱلْأَسْمَآءُ ٱلْحُسْنَىٰ﴾

'And to God alone belong the most beautiful names [*al-asmā' al-ḥusnā*]'.[3]

The Qur'ān orders us to exemplify *Iḥsān* and benevolence and give others their rightful due. God says,

﴿وَأَدَآءٌ إِلَيْهِ بِإِحْسَـٰنٍ﴾

'And it should be paid in a graceful manner [*bi iḥsān*]'.[4]

God loves *Iḥsān* and blesses the people of *Iḥsān* with His companionship, saying,

---

[1] Ibid., 55:60.

[2] Ibid., 10:26.

[3] Ibid., 7:180.

[4] Ibid., 2:178.

﴿إِنَّ ٱللَّهَ لَمَعَ ٱلْمُحْسِنِينَ﴾

'*Certainly, God is with the people of* Iḥsān'.[1]

He declares His love for them, saying,

﴿إِنَّ ٱللَّهَ يُحِبُّ ٱلْمُحْسِنِينَ﴾

'*Certainly, God loves the people of* Iḥsān'.[2]

He pronounces His guarantee for the people of *Iḥsān* that they will have His exclusive protection and divine shelter, and He declares them free of all blame,

﴿مَا عَلَى ٱلْمُحْسِنِينَ مِن سَبِيلٍ﴾

'*The people of* Iḥsān *are not to be blamed*'.[3]

God also says,

﴿وَمَنْ أَحْسَنُ دِينًا مِّمَّنْ أَسْلَمَ وَجْهَهُۥ لِلَّهِ وَهُوَ مُحْسِنٌ﴾

'*And with regard to* dīn, *who is better than the one who submits his whole being entirely to God, while he also holds spiritual excellence?*'[4]

Certainly, those who conduct themselves benevolently are the people of excellence. According to the Qurʾān, it was said to the Prophet Joseph ﷺ,

﴿إِنَّا نَرَىٰكَ مِنَ ٱلْمُحْسِنِينَ﴾

'*Surely, we see you one of the spiritually excellent* [*muḥsinīn*]'.[5]

According to Abū Manṣūr al-Azharī and Ibn Manẓūr, a

---

[1] Ibid., 29:69.

[2] Ibid., 2:195.

[3] Ibid., 9:91.

[4] Ibid., 4:125.

[5] Ibid., 12:36.

beautiful green tree is called *al-ḥasan*, because it provides coolness and pleasant shade to people. Even the mere sight of it pleases hearts. Due to its trait of benevolence, it is named *al-ḥasan*. According to Abū Naṣr al-Fārābī al-Jawharī in *al-Ṣiḥāḥ*, the moon is also known as *al-ḥāsin* because its light shows the path to travellers, and the moonlit nights are a great source of soothing for those who are stricken with anxiety and concern. Moreover, the moon is a metaphor of light and light eliminates darkness. *Iḥsān* is, therefore, light, guidance, calm and comfort. This is why *Iḥsān* has been given the third and highest level in the religion. The zenith of Islam culminates in *Īmān* and the apex of *Īmān* is identified as *Iḥsān*. The hadith of Gabriel ﷺ verifies this hierarchy. Islam relates to verbal and physical obedience, while *Īmān* is its internal aspect, comprising the verification of the inner self and its commitment and conviction; and *Iḥsān* points to their spiritual fruition and inner states of divine love and beauty. *Iḥsān* bestows upon us authenticity and sincerity which ensure protection from disaster and extinction. It is for this reason that the Qur᾿ān regards *Iḥsān* as a way out of disaster. God says,

﴿وَأَنفِقُواْ فِى سَبِيلِ ٱللَّهِ وَلَا تُلْقُواْ بِأَيْدِيكُمْ إِلَى ٱلتَّهْلُكَةِ وَأَحْسِنُوٓاْ إِنَّ ٱللَّهَ يُحِبُّ ٱلْمُحْسِنِينَ﴾

‘*And spend in the cause of God and do not cast yourselves into destruction with your own hands—and adopt spiritual excellence* [*Iḥsān*]. *Verily, God loves the spiritually excellent* [*muḥsinīn*]’.[1]

Iḥsān is obligatory for everyone and in every matter, so much so that killing someone by torture, or even teasing an animal at the time of slaughter, are forbidden acts—as evidenced by the many prophetic traditions on this subject. Shaddād b. Aws ﷺ reported that the Messenger of God ﷺ said,

إِنَّ اللهَ كَتَبَ الْإِحْسَانَ عَلَى كُلِّ شَيْءٍ، فَإِذَا قَتَلْتُمْ فَأَحْسِنُوا الْقِتْلَةَ، وَإِذَا ذَبَحْتُمْ فَأَحْسِنُوا الذَّبْحَ، وَلْيُحِدَّ أَحَدُكُمْ شَفْرَتَهُ، فَلْيُرِحْ ذَبِيحَتَهُ.

[1] Ibid., 2:195.

> 'God has prescribed spiritual excellence in everything, so if you kill, do so with excellence, and if you sacrifice an animal, do so with excellence, and let one of you sharpen his blade, in order to set his sacrificial animal at rest [causing it the least discomfort]'.[1]

Abū Shurayḥ al-Khuzāʿī ﵁ reported that the Messenger of God ﷺ said,

> مَنْ كَانَ يُؤْمِنُ بِاللهِ وَالْيَوْمِ الْآخِرِ فَلْيُحْسِنْ إِلَى جَارِهِ.
>
> 'Whoever believes in God and the Last Day, let him behave with excellence towards his neighbour'.[2]

Abū Dharr ﵁ reported that the Messenger of God ﷺ said,

> اِتَّقِ اللهَ حَيْثُمَا كُنْتَ، وَأَتْبِعِ السَّيِّئَةَ الْحَسَنَةَ تَمْحُهَا، وَخَالِقِ النَّاسَ بِخُلُقٍ حَسَنٍ.
>
> 'Fear God wherever you may be, follow up a bad deed with a good deed and it will efface it, and deal with

---

[1] Narrated by Muslim in *al-Ṣaḥīḥ*: *Kitāb al-ṣayd wa al-dhabāʾiḥ wa mā yuʾkal min al-ḥayawān* [The Book of Hunting, Sacrificing Animals and What Animals May be Eaten], chapter: 'The Injunction to Perform the Slaughter and Cutting well, and to Sharpen the Cutting Blade', 3:1548 §1955; al-Tirmidhī in *al-Sunan: Kitāb al-diyāt* [The Book of Blood Money], chapter: 'What Has Come to Us About the Prohibition of Mutilation [*muthla*]', 4:23 §1409; Abū Dāwūd in *al-Sunan*: *Kitāb al-ḍaḥāyā* [The Book of Sacrificial Animals], chapter: 'The Prohibition of Keeping Animals Waiting, and the Injunction to Treat the Sacrificial Animals Gently', 3:100 §2815; al-Nasāʾī in *al-Sunan*: *Kitāb al-ḍaḥāyā* [The Book of Sacrificial Animals], chapter: 'The Injunction to Sharpen the Cutting Blade', 7:227 §4405; and Ibn Mājah in *al-Sunan: Kitāb al-ḍaḥāyā* [The Book of Sacrificial Animals], chapter: 'When You Slaughter, You Must Perform the Slaughter Well', 2:1058 §3170.

[2] Narrated by Muslim in *al-Ṣaḥīḥ*: *Kitāb al-Īmān* [The Book of Faith], chapter: 'The Encouragement to Honour the Neighbour and the Guest, and the Necessity of Maintaining Silence Except when Having Something Good to Say', 1:69 §48; Ibn Mājah in *al-Sunan*: *Kitāb al-adab* [The Book of Good Manners], chapter: 'The Right Due of the Neighbour', 2:1211 §3672; al-Dārimī in *al-Sunan*, 2:134; and al-Ṭabarānī in *al-Muʿjam al-kabīr*, 22:192 §501.

people with good character'.[1]

ʿAbd Allāh b. Masʿūd ﷺ reported, 'A man said, "O Messenger of God! When shall I become spiritually excellent?" The Prophet ﷺ replied,

إِذَا قَالَ جِيْرَانُكَ: أَنْتَ مُحْسِنٌ، فَأَنْتَ مُحْسِنٌ، وَإِذَا قَالُوا: إِنَّكَ مُسِيءٌ فَأَنْتَ مُسِيءٌ.

"If your neighbours say, 'You are spiritually excellent', you are spiritually excellent, and if they say, 'You are an evildoer', then you are an evildoer"!'[2]

Anas b. Mālik ﷺ reported that the Messenger of God ﷺ said,

إِذَا جَمَعَ اللهُ الْأَوَّلِيْنَ وَالْآخِرِيْنَ يُنَادِي مُنَادٍ فِي صَعِيْدٍ وَاحِدٍ مِنْ بُطْنَانِ الْعَرْشِ: أَيْنَ الْمُحْسِنُونَ؟ قَالُوا: نَحْنُ الْمُحْسِنُونَ. قَالَ: صَدَقْتُمْ. قُلْتُ لِنَبِيِّ: ﴿مَا عَلَى ٱلْمُحْسِنِينَ مِنْ سَبِيلٍ﴾ مَا عَلَيْكُمْ مِنْ سَبِيْلٍ، ادْخُلُوا الْجَنَّةَ بِرَحْمَتِي.

'When God assembles the first and the last, a herald will call out from a plain under the pedestals of the Heavenly Throne: "Where are the people of spiritual excellence [*muḥsinūn*]?" . . . A group of people will say, "We are the spiritually excellent!" God will say, "You have told the truth! I said to My Prophet: '*The people of* Iḥsān *are not to be blamed*'.[3] So there is no cause of reproach against you. Enter the Garden of Paradise with My Mercy"!'

---

[1] Narrated by al-Tirmidhī in *al-Sunan*: *Kitāb al-birr wa al-ṣila* [The Book of Piety and Filial Duty], chapter: 'What Has Come to Us About Social Interaction', 4:355 §1987; al-Dārimī in *al-Sunan*, 2:415 §2791; Aḥmad b. Ḥanbal in *al-Musnad*, 5:153 §21392; Ibn Abī Shayba in *al-Muṣannaf*, 5:211 §25324; al-Bazzār in *al-Musnad*, 9:416 §4022; and al-Ṭabarānī in *al-Muʿjam al-kabīr*, 20:144 §296. Abū ʿĪsā [al-Tirmidhī] said, 'This is a fine authentic tradition [*ḥasan ṣaḥīḥ*]'.

[2] Narrated by Ibn Mājah in *al-Sunan*: *Kitāb al-zuhd* [The Book of Renunciation], chapter: 'On Goodly Mention', 2:1411 §§4222–3; Ibn Ḥibbān in *al-Ṣaḥīḥ*, 2:284 §525; al-Ḥākim in *al-Mustadrak*, 1:534 §1399; and al-Bayhaqī in *Shuʿab al-Īmān*, 7:85 §1399. Al-Ḥākim said, 'This is a rigorously authentic [*ṣaḥīḥ*] tradition'.

[3] Qurʾān 9:91.

Anas ﷺ added, 'Then, the Messenger of God ﷺ smiled and said,

لَقَدْ نَجَّاهُمُ اللهُ مِنْ أَهْوَالِ بَوَائِقِ الْقِيَامَةِ.

"Indeed, God will deliver them from the miseries and calamities of the Resurrection!".'[1]

Jābir ﷺ reported that the Messenger of God ﷺ said,

إِنَّ مِنْ أَحَبِّكُمْ إِلَيَّ وَأَقْرَبِكُمْ مِنِّي مَجْلِسًا يَوْمَ الْقِيَامَةِ أَحَاسِنُكُمْ أَخْلَاقًا.

'Indeed, amongst the dearest of you to me, and those of you seated closest to me on the Day of Resurrection, are the finest of you in moral character'.[2]

ʿĀʾisha ﷺ reported that the Messenger of God ﷺ said,

إِنَّ الْمُؤْمِنَ لَيُدْرِكُ بِحُسْنِ خُلُقِهِ دَرَجَةَ الصَّائِمِ الْقَائِمِ.

'The believer will surely attain, by the excellence of his moral character, the degree of the one steadfast in prayers and fasting'.[3]

Ibn Masʿūd ﷺ reported that the Messenger of God ﷺ said,

حُرِّمَ عَلَى النَّارِ كُلُّ هَيِّنٍ، سَهْلٍ، قَرِيْبٍ مِنَ النَّاسِ.

'The Hellfire is forbidden for every mild-mannered and

---

[1] Narrated by Abū Nuʿaym in *Kitāb al-arbaʿīn*, p. 100 §51; and al-Munāwī in *Fayḍ al-Qadīr*, 1:420 §4.

[2] Narrated by al-Tirmidhī in *al-Sunan*: *Kitāb al-birr wa al-ṣila* [The Book of Piety and Filial Duty], chapter: 'What Has Come to Us Concerning the Nobility of Lofty Character', 4:370 §2018; Aḥmad b. Ḥanbal in *al-Musnad*, 2:185 and 217 §§6735, 7035; Ibn Ḥibbān in *al-Ṣaḥīḥ*, 2:235 §485; and al-Bayhaqī in *Shuʿab al-Īmān*, 6:234 §799. Abū ʿĪsā [al-Tirmidhī] said, 'This is a sound [*ḥasan*] tradition'.

[3] Narrated by Abū Dāwūd in *al-Sunan*: *Kitāb al-adab* [The Book of Good Manners], chapter: 'On Goodness of Character', 4:252 §4798; Aḥmad b. Ḥanbal in *al-Musnad*, 6:90 §24639; Ibn Ḥibbān in *al-Ṣaḥīḥ*, 2:228 §480; al-Ḥākim in *al-Mustadrak*, 1:128 §199; and al-Bayhaqī in *Shuʿab al-Īmān*, 6:236 §7997.

even-tempered person who is close to people'.[1]

ʿĀʾisha ﷺ reported that the Messenger of God ﷺ said,

يَا عَائِشَةُ! إِنَّ اللهَ رَفِيْقٌ؛ يُحِبُّ الرِّفْقَ فِي الْأَمْرِ كُلِّهِ.

'O ʿĀʾisha, God is Gentle and Kind and He loves gentleness in everything'.[2]

In another narration she reported that he ﷺ said,

يَا عَائِشَةُ! إِنَّ اللهَ رَفِيْقٌ وَيُحِبُّ الرِّفْقَ، وَيُعْطِي عَلَى الرِّفْقِ مَا لَا يُعْطِي عَلَى الْعُنْفِ.

'O ʿĀʾisha, God is Gentle and He loves gentleness. He bestows for the sake of gentleness what He does not bestow due to harshness'.[3]

Abū Hurayra ﷺ reported that the Messenger of God ﷺ said,

كَانَ تَاجِرٌ يُدَايِنُ النَّاسَ، فَإِذَا رَأَى مُعْسِرًا، قَالَ لِفِتْيَانِهِ: تَجَاوَزُوا عَنْهُ، لَعَلَّ اللهَ أَنْ يَتَجَاوَزَ عَنَّا، فَتَجَاوَزَ اللهُ عَنْهُ.

'There was a merchant who used to give people credit. When he saw someone in difficulty, he would say to his employees: "Make allowances for him, so that perhaps God will make allowances for us". So as a result, God

---

[1] Narrated by Aḥmad b. Ḥanbal in *al-Musnad*, 1:415 §3938; Ibn Ḥibbān in *al-Ṣaḥīḥ*, 2:215 §469; al-Ṭabarānī in *al-Muʿjam al-kabīr*, 10:231 §10562; Abū Yaʿlā in *al-Musnad*, 8:467 §5053; and al-Bayhaqī in *Shuʿab al-Īmān*, 7:353 §2697.

[2] Narrated by al-Bukhārī in *al-Ṣaḥīḥ*: *Kitāb istitāba al-murtaddīn wa al-muʿānidīn wa qitālihim* [The Book on Demanding the Repentance of the Apostates and Reprobates, and Fighting Them], chapter: 'What is to be Done When a Non-Muslim Citizen [or Anyone Else] Presents Himself', 6:2539 §6528; and Ibn Mājah in *al-Sunan: Kitāb al-adab* [The Book of Good Manners], chapter: 'On Kindness', 2:1216 §3688.

[3] Narrated by Muslim in *al-Ṣaḥīḥ*: *Kitāb al-birr wa al-ṣila wa al-ādāb* [The Book of Piety, Filial Duty and Good Manners], chapter: 'The Virtue of Gentleness', 4:2003 §2593; Abū Dāwūd in *al-Sunan*: *Kitāb al-adab* [The Book of Good Manners], chapter: 'On Gentleness', 4:254 §4807; and Aḥmad b. Ḥanbal in *al-Musnad*, 1:112 §902.

made allowances for him'.[1]

Abū Hurayra ﷺ also reported that the Messenger of God ﷺ said,

إِنَّ رَجُلًا لَمْ يَعْمَلْ خَيْرًا قَطُّ وَكَانَ يُدَايِنُ النَّاسَ. فَيَقُولُ لِرَسُولِهِ: خُذْ مَا تَيَسَّرَ وَاتْرُكْ مَا عَسُرَ، وَتَجَاوَزْ لَعَلَّ اللهَ تَعَالَى أَنْ يَّتَجَاوَزَ عَنَّا. فَلَمَّا هَلَكَ، قَالَ اللهُ لَهُ: هَلْ عَمِلْتَ خَيْرًا قَطُّ؟ قَالَ: لَا، إِلَّا أَنَّهُ كَانَ لِي غُلَامٌ، وَكُنْتُ أُدَايِنُ النَّاسَ، فَإِذَا بَعَثْتُهُ لِيَتَقَاضَى، قُلْتُ لَهُ: خُذْ مَا تَيَسَّرَ وَاتْرُكْ مَا عَسُرَ، وَتَجَاوَزْ لَعَلَّ اللهَ يَتَجَاوَزُ عَنَّا. قَالَ اللهُ تَعَالَى: قَدْ تَجَاوَزْتُ عَنْكَ.

'There was a man who was extremely lax in performing good deeds and he used to loan money to people. [When he would loan money out] he would say to his secretary, "Take [in repayment of a loan] that which is easy and leave that which is difficult and overlook it, for perhaps God Most High will overlook us [our faults]". When that man perished, God Most High said to him, "Did you ever do any good deeds?" The man replied, "No, but I did have a young servant and I used to loan money to people, so when I would send him to collect the money owed, I would say to him, 'Take that which is easy and leave that which is difficult and overlook it, for perhaps God Most High will overlook us'." God then said to him, "I have overlooked your faults".'[2]

[1] Narrated by al-Bukhārī in *al-Ṣaḥīḥ*: *Kitāb al-buyūʿ* [The Book of Sales], chapter: 'On Someone Giving a Person in Difficulties Time to Pay', 2:731 §1972; Muslim in *al-Ṣaḥīḥ*: *Kitāb al-musāqāt* [The Book of Sharecropping], chapter: 'The Virtue of Giving a Person in Difficulties Time to Pay', 3:1196 §1562.

[2] Narrated by al-Nasāʾī in *al-Sunan: Kitāb al-buyūʿ* [The Book of Sales], chapter: 'On Dealing with Others Well and Being Kind in Seeking Repayment of Loans', 7:381 §3696; Aḥmad b. Ḥanbal in *al-Musnad*, 2:361 §8715; Ibn Ḥibbān in *al-Ṣaḥīḥ*, 11:422 §5403; and al-Ḥākim in *al-Mustadrak*, 2:33 §2223.

1.8 Summary

This lexical research has demonstrated that the three levels of our *dīn*, Islam, *Īmān* and *Iḥsān*, are synonymous with peace and security, safety and protection, tolerance and forbearance, love and affection, benevolence and human dignity, and all their resultant pleasures. Islam is a perfect and complete code of life that ensures protection, mercy, clemency, patience, tolerance, balance, justice and moderation for all. A Muslim, therefore, is the one who embodies peace, sanctity and protection for the whole of humankind. A *mu'min* is the one who, at the same time, possesses the traits of human dignity, coexistence, tolerance, moderation and love and peace. And a *muḥsin* is the one who is a blend of the first two levels along with the spiritual and divine experiences that are useful for others. In sum, Islam, in its wider perspective, is a religion that ensures peace and security for everyone at all levels, individually and collectively.

Chapter 2

The Unlawfulness of Indiscriminately Killing Muslims

2.1 The Sanctity of a Believer is Greater Than the Kaʿba

There are some people who declare that the majority of the Muslims are disbelievers, polytheists and innovators on account of political, ideological or religious differences, and subsequently massacre them ruthlessly. They must know the sanctity and honour of a believer's life in the sight of God and His Messenger ﷺ. The Prophet ﷺ declared the honour and dignity of a believer greater than that of the Kaʿba, the Sacred House of God. Imam Ibn Mājah transmitted a hadith on this subject.

عَنْ عَبْدِ اللهِ بْنِ عُمَرَ رضي الله عنهما قَالَ: رَأَيْتُ رَسُولَ اللهِ ﷺ يَطُوفُ بِالْكَعْبَةِ، وَيَقُولُ: مَا أَطْيَبَكِ وَأَطْيَبَ رِيْحَكِ! مَا أَعْظَمَكِ وَأَعْظَمَ حُرْمَتَكِ! وَالَّذِي نَفْسُ مُحَمَّدٍ بِيَدِهِ، لَحُرْمَةُ الْمُؤْمِنِ أَعْظَمُ عِنْدَ اللهِ حُرْمَةً مِنْكِ، مَالِهِ، وَدَمِهِ، وَأَنْ نَظُنَّ بِهِ إِلَّا خَيْرًا.

ʿAbd Allāh b. ʿUmar رضي الله عنهما said, 'Once, I saw the Messenger of God ﷺ circumambulating the Kaʿba and he was addressing it: "How excellent you are and how sweet your smell is! How grand you are and how grand your sacredness is! By the One in Whose Hand is Muhammad's soul, the inviolability of a believer's property and blood is greater in the sight of God than your sacredness. We must think only well of a believer".'[1]

2.2 Merely Pointing a Weapon at a Believer is Prohibited

Killing people with explosives or other weapons is a grave sin, but even pointing a weapon towards a believer is forbidden, and

[1] Narrated by Ibn Mājah in *al-Sunan*: *Kitāb al-fitan* [The Book of Tribulations], chapter: 'The Inviolability of a Believer's Blood and Property', 2:1297 §3932; al-Ṭabarānī in *Musnad al-Shāmiyyīn*, 2:396 §1568; and al-Mundhirī in *al-Targhīb wa al-tarhīb*, 3:201 §3679.

the one who does it is cursed. Abū Hurayra ﷺ reported that the Messenger of God ﷺ said,

لَا يُشِيرُ أَحَدُكُمْ إِلَى أَخِيْهِ بِالسِّلَاحِ، فَإِنَّهُ لَا يَدْرِي أَحَدُكُمْ لَعَلَّ الشَّيْطَانَ يَنْزِعُ فِي يَدِهِ، فَيَقَعُ فِي حُفْرَةٍ مِنَ النَّارِ.

> 'None of you should point a weapon at his brother, for he does not know, for perhaps the devil may draw it out while it is in his hand, resulting in his falling into a pit of Hell'.[1]

Here, metaphorical language has been employed. Someone who wields a weapon might fire it at the spur of the moment and hit someone. This act has been linked to Satan so that people regard it as a satanic act and stay away from it. This has been elaborated in another hadith in which the Prophet ﷺ said,

مَنْ أَشَارَ إِلَى أَخِيْهِ بِحَدِيْدَةٍ، فَإِنَّ الْمَلَائِكَةَ تَلْعَنُهُ حَتَّى يَدَعَهُ، وَإِنْ كَانَ أَخَاهُ لِأَبِيْهِ وَأُمِّهِ.

> 'Whoever points a piece of iron [e.g., a gun] at his brother, the angels will curse him until he puts it down, even if he [the one at whom it is pointed] is his brother of the same father and mother'.[2]

The Prophet ﷺ not only forbade pointing a weapon at someone, but he also forbade displaying it. Jābir ﷺ said,

---

[1] Narrated by Muslim in *al-Ṣaḥīḥ*: *Kitāb al-birr wa al-ṣila wa al-ādāb* [The Book of Piety, Filial Duty and Good Manners], chapter: 'On the Prohibition of Pointing a Weapon at Someone Else', 4:2020 §2617; al-Ḥākim in *al-Mustadrak*, 3:587 §6176; and al-Bayhaqī in *al-Sunan al-kubrā*, 8:23 §2617.

[2] Narrated by Muslim in *al-Ṣaḥīḥ*: *Kitāb al-birr wa al-ṣila wa al-ādāb* [The Book of Piety, Filial Duty and Good Manners], chapter: 'On the Prohibition of Pointing a Weapon at Someone Else', 4:2020 §2616; al-Tirmidhī in *al-Sunan*: *Kitāb al-fitan* [The Book of Tribulations], chapter: 'What Has Come to Us Regarding the Muslim who Points a Weapon at His Brother', 4:463 §2162; al-Ḥākim in *al-Mustadrak*, 2:171 §2669; Ibn Ḥibbān in *al-Ṣaḥīḥ*, 13:272 §5944; and al-Bayhaqī in *al-Sunan al-kubrā,* 8:23 §15649.

نَهَى رَسُولُ اللهِ ﷺ أَنْ يُتَعَاطَى السَّيْفُ مَسْلُولًا.

'The Messenger of God ﷺ forbade that an unsheathed sword be handed to someone else'.[1]

While a drawn sword—or any other weapon for that matter—may cause injury, displaying it might provoke one to violence. What can be a greater proof of Islam's status as a religion of peace, security and advancement, for the word '*maslūl*' used in the aforementioned hadith essentially indicates that defence institutions charged with keeping arms must also adopt foolproof security measures to ensure that their weapons will not be misused!

If displaying weapons and pointing them at others are strictly prohibited—as proven in the above mentioned hadith—then how grave a sin and atrocity it is to challenge the authority of a Muslim state and destroy the lives and properties of civilians through bomb blasts and suicide attacks!

2.3 The Unlawfulness of Violence against Muslims

Islam not only outlaws the mass killing of Muslims but the whole of humanity, without any discrimination on the basis of caste, colour, race or religion. One can appreciate the value and inviolability of human life in Islam by realising that the act of killing a human being has been equated with slaughtering the entire human race. In connection with human dignity, God says in the Qur'ān,

﴿مَن قَتَلَ نَفْسًا بِغَيْرِ نَفْسٍ أَوْ فَسَادٍ فِى ٱلْأَرْضِ فَكَأَنَّمَا قَتَلَ ٱلنَّاسَ جَمِيعًا﴾

'*Whoever kills a person* [unjustly], *except as a punishment for murder or* [as a prescribed punishment for bloodshed, robbery and spreading] *disorder in the land, it is as if he*

---

[1] Narrated by al-Tirmidhī in *al-Sunan*: *Kitāb al-fitan* [The Book of Tribulation], chapter: 'What Has Come to Us Regarding the Prohibition of Handing Someone an Unsheathed Sword', 4:464 §2163; Abū Dāwūd in *al-Sunan*: *Kitāb al-jihād* [The Book of Martial Jihad], chapter: 'What Has Come to Us Regarding the Prohibition of Handing Someone an Unsheathed Sword', 3:31 §2588; al-Ḥākim in *al-Mustadrak*, 4:322 §7785; and Ibn Ḥibbān in *al-Ṣaḥīḥ*, 13:275 §5946.

killed all of humanity'.[1]

This verse highlights the sanctity of human life in general. The sanctity of a man or woman, the old or the young, the rich or the poor has not been specified. The point being that the Qur'ān has not only prohibited killing a man without any justification, but has also declared that it is akin to the murder of humanity entire. As for the law of retribution, which authorizes capital punishment for a murderer, it has been legislated for safeguarding the sanctity of human life.

2.4 The Unlawfulness of Killing Someone Who Accepts Islam in the midst of Fighting

Although the common notion expressed around the world is that all is fair in love and war, Islam does not agree. It has laid down rules and regulations for the battlefield, and the life and blessed practice of the Prophet of Islam ﷺ enjoin us to observe caution, care and fair play, even in the most critical and troubled moments of war. The Prophet ﷺ showed his strong displeasure over the killing of a man who declared his acceptance of the faith (which *was* perhaps under the fear of death) when he was under the sword and about to be slain. If that was his displeasure over someone killed in a state of battle, what about killing Muslims and people of knowledge only because their views differ with the extremist ideologies of the rebel terrorist groups?

Usāma b. Zayd b. Ḥāritha ؓ said,

بَعَثَنَا رَسُولُ اللهِ ﷺ إِلَى الْحُرَقَةِ مِنْ جُهَيْنَةَ، فَصَبَّحْنَا الْقَوْمَ، فَهَزَمْنَاهُمْ، وَلَحِقْتُ أَنَا وَرَجُلٌ مِنَ الْأَنْصَارِ رَجُلًا مِنْهُمْ، فَلَمَّا غَشِيْنَاهُ قَالَ: لَا إِلَهَ إِلَّا اللهُ. فَكَفَّ عَنْهُ الْأَنْصَارِيُّ، وَطَعَنْتُهُ بِرُمْحِي حَتَّى قَتَلْتُهُ. قَالَ: فَلَمَّا قَدِمْنَا، بَلَغَ ذَلِكَ النَّبِيَّ ﷺ فَقَالَ لِي: يَا أُسَامَةُ، أَقَتَلْتَهُ بَعْدَ مَا قَالَ لَا إِلَهَ إِلَّا اللهُ؟ قَالَ: قُلْتُ: يَا رَسُولَ اللهِ، إِنَّمَا كَانَ مُتَعَوِّذًا، قَالَ: فَقَالَ: أَقَتَلْتَهُ بَعْدَ مَا قَالَ لَا إِلَهَ إِلَّا اللهُ؟ قَالَ: فَمَا زَالَ يُكَرِّرُهَا عَلَيَّ حَتَّى تَمَنَّيْتُ أَنِّي لَمْ أَكُنْ أَسْلَمْتُ قَبْلَ ذَلِكَ الْيَوْمِ.

---

[1] Qur'ān 5:32.

> 'The Messenger of God ﷺ dispatched us to fight against Ḥuraqa, a branch of the Juhayna tribe, so we reached the tribesmen in the morning and defeated them. One of the *Anṣār* and I jointly caught up to a man of that tribe. When we overpowered him, he said, "There is no god but God". Upon hearing this, the *Anṣārī* held back from him, but I stabbed him with my spear until I killed him. When we came back, the news had already reached the Prophet ﷺ so he said to me, "O Usāma, did you kill him after he said, 'There is no god but God'?" I said, "O Messenger of God, he was merely seeking refuge. (He uttered the formula to save his life)!" He said again, "Did you kill him after he said, 'There is no god but God'?" He kept repeating that to me, until I wished that I had not embraced Islam before that day!'[1]

The version of Imam Muslim reads:

> فَدَعَاهُ فَسَأَلَهُ، فَقَالَ: لِمَ قَتَلْتَهُ؟ قَالَ: يَا رَسُولَ اللهِ، أَوْجَعَ فِي الْمُسْلِمِيْنَ، وَقَتَلَ فُلَانًا وَفُلَانًا، وَسَمَّى لَهُ نَفَرًا. وَأَنِّي حَمَلْتُ عَلَيْهِ، فَلَمَّا رَأَى السَّيْفَ، قَالَ: لَا إِلَهَ إِلاَّ اللهُ. قَالَ رَسُولُ اللهِ ﷺ: أَقَتَلْتَهُ؟ قَالَ: نَعَمْ. قَالَ: فَكَيْفَ تَصْنَعُ بِلَا إِلَهَ إِلَّا اللهُ إِذَا جَاءَتْ يَوْمَ الْقِيَامَةِ؟ قَالَ: يَا رَسُولَ اللهِ، اسْتَغْفِرْ لِي. قَالَ: وَكَيْفَ تَصْنَعُ بِلَا إِلَهَ إِلَّا اللهُ إِذَا جَاءَتْ يَوْمَ الْقِيَامَةِ؟ قَالَ: فَجَعَلَ لَا يَزِيْدُهُ عَلَى أَنْ يَقُولَ: كَيْفَ تَصْنَعُ بِلَا إِلَهَ إِلَّا اللهُ إِذَا جَاءَتْ يَوْمَ الْقِيَامَةِ؟

> 'So he ﷺ summoned him and asked him, "Why did you kill him?" He said, "O Messenger of God, he caused pain to the Muslims, and he killed so-and-so and so-and-so, and I attacked him, so when he saw the sword, he said,

---

[1] Narrated by al-Bukhārī in *al-Ṣaḥīḥ*: *Kitāb al-maghāzī* [The Book of Military Expeditions], chapter: 'The Blessed Prophet's Sending of Usāma b. Zayd to the Campsites of the Juhayna Tribe', 4:1555 §4021 and *Kitāb al-diyāt* [The Book of Blood Money], chapter: 'Regarding the Saying of God Most High, "*And Whoever Saves the Life of One Person...*"' [Qur'ān 5:32], 6:2519 §6478; and Ibn Ḥibbān in *al-Ṣaḥīḥ*, 11:56 §4751.

'There is no god but God'!" The Messenger of God ﷺ asked him, "Did you kill him?" When he said, "Yes", he said, "So how will you deal with 'There is no god but God' when the Day of Resurrection comes?" He said, "O Messenger of God, seek forgiveness on my behalf!" He said again: "So how will you deal with 'There is no god but God' when the Day of Resurrection comes?" He then kept saying, without adding anything: "How will you deal with 'There is no god but God' when the Day of Resurrection comes?"'[1]

Miqdād b. Aswad ﷺ said,

قُلْتُ: يَا رَسُولَ اللهِ، أَرَأَيْتَ إِنْ لَقِيتُ رَجُلًا مِنَ الْكُفَّارِ فَقَاتَلَنِي فَضَرَبَ إِحْدَى يَدَيَّ بِالسَّيْفِ، فَقَطَعَهَا، ثُمَّ لَاذَ مِنِّي بِشَجَرَةٍ، فَقَالَ: أَسْلَمْتُ لِلّٰهِ، أَفَأَقْتُلُهُ، يَا رَسُولَ اللهِ، بَعْدَ أَنْ قَالَهَا؟ قَالَ رَسُولُ اللهِ ﷺ: لَا تَقْتُلْهُ. قَالَ: فَقُلْتُ: يَا رَسُولَ اللهِ، إِنَّهُ قَدْ قَطَعَ يَدِي، ثُمَّ قَالَ ذٰلِكَ بَعْدَ أَنْ قَطَعَهَا، أَفَأَقْتُلُهُ؟ قَالَ رَسُولُ اللهِ ﷺ: لَا تَقْتُلْهُ فَإِنْ قَتَلْتَهُ فَإِنَّهُ بِمَنْزِلَتِكَ قَبْلَ أَنْ تَقْتُلَهُ، وَإِنَّكَ بِمَنْزِلَتِهِ قَبْلَ أَنْ يَقُولَ كَلِمَتَهُ الَّتِي قَالَ.

'I said to the Messenger of God, "What do you think, if I meet a man of the disbelievers and we fight and he strikes one of my hands with his sword and cuts it off and then takes refuge from me behind a tree and says, 'I have surrendered to God'? Should I kill him, O Messenger of God, after he has said that?" The Messenger of God ﷺ said, "No. Do not kill him. If you were to kill him, then he would be in your position [i.e., Muslim] before you killed him and you would be in his position [i.e., disbeliever] before he said that word which he said".'[2]

---

[1] Narrated by Muslim in *al-Ṣaḥīḥ*: *Kitāb al-Īmān* [The Book of Faith], chapter: 'On the Prohibition of Killing a Disbeliever when He Says, "There is no god but God"', 1:97 §94–97.

[2] Narrated by al-Bukhārī in *al-Ṣaḥīḥ*: *Kitāb al-maghāzī* [The Book of Military Expeditions], chapter: 'On the Angels Being Present at the Battle of Badr', 4:1474 §3794; and Muslim in *al-Ṣaḥīḥ*: *Kitāb al-Īmān* [The Book of Faith], chapter: 'On the Prohibition of Killing a Disbeliever when He Says, 'There is no

In the light of these merciful and benevolent teachings of the Prophet ﷺ, the brutal and ruthless terrorists, who indiscriminately massacre peaceful Muslims, must ponder over and abandon their misanthropist and barbaric ideologies and dreadful beliefs. If the life of an enemy in the battlefield is protected when he accepts faith, then how odious it is to massacre Muslims in mosques, and how egregious it is to slay them in offices, educational institutes, markets and public buildings!

2.5 BECOMING AN ACCOMPLICE TO TERRORISTS IS ALSO A CRIME

The Prophet ﷺ categorically forbade people to provide help or material support to terrorists. He ordered us to isolate them and deny them any numerical strength, financial assistance and moral support. Abū Hurayra ﷺ reported that the Prophet ﷺ said,

مَنْ أَعَانَ عَلَى قَتْلِ مُؤْمِنٍ بِشَطْرِ كَلِمَةٍ، لَقِيَ اللهَ مَكْتُوبٌ بَيْنَ عَيْنَيْهِ: آيِسٌ مِنْ رَحْمَةِ اللهِ.

> 'If anyone helps in the murder of a believer—even if with only a few words—he will meet God with the words written on his forehead: "hopeless of God's mercy".'[1]

This hadith also indicates that it is not only financial and numerical assistance that must be denied to terrorists, but, according to the expression '*bi shaṭri kalimatin*' ('a few words'), speeches or writings which lend support to the enemies of peace are also condemnable and must be banned. Such support can only deprive us of God's forgiveness and mercy. This hadith contains a strict warning to those who mastermind terrorist acts and misinterpret the Qur'ān by brainwashing youth with glad tidings of Paradise for murdering peaceful civilians.

---

god but God"', 1:95 §95.

[1] Narrated by Ibn Mājah in *al-Sunan*: *Kitāb al-Diyāt* [The Book of Blood Money], chapter: The Gravity of Unjustly Killing a Muslim, 2:874 §2620; al-Rabīʿ in *al-Musnad*, 1:368 §960; and al-Bayhaqī in *al-Sunan al-kubrā*, 8:22 §15646.

2.6 Those Who Attack Mosques Are the Greatest Wrongdoers

Islam not only teaches its adherents to maintain peace and observe tolerance with other communities, but it also instils in them a respect for the beliefs and viewpoints, and norms and rituals of those who do not share their faith and creed. To launch attacks against opponents, their properties and sacred sites on account of religious, ideological or political differences is not only against the express spirit of Islam but is inhumane as well. Those who violate the sanctity of the houses of God and kill peaceful and devout worshippers through bomb explosions and suicide attacks are neither true believers nor people of guidance. Those who hinder people from making mention of God's name in mosques, by spreading terror and intimidation, through violence and terrorism are grave sinners and enemies of peace; the Qur'ān, in fact, declares them the greatest wrongdoers and warns them of an immense suffering in the Hereafter. God says,

﴿وَمَنْ أَظْلَمُ مِمَّن مَّنَعَ مَسَٰجِدَ ٱللَّهِ أَن يُذْكَرَ فِيهَا ٱسْمُهُۥ وَسَعَىٰ فِى خَرَابِهَآ أُو۟لَٰٓئِكَ
مَا كَانَ لَهُمْ أَن يَدْخُلُوهَآ إِلَّا خَآئِفِينَ لَهُمْ فِى ٱلدُّنْيَا خِزْىٌ وَلَهُمْ فِى ٱلْءَاخِرَةِ عَذَابٌ
عَظِيمٌ﴾

> '*And who is more unjust than he who forbids the remembrance of God's name in the places of prostration* [mosques] *and strives to demolish them? It was not proper for them to enter the mosques but in a state of fear* [fearing God]. *For them is disgrace in this world and there is a dreadful torment for them in the Hereafter*'.[1]

Elsewhere, God proclaims that those who maintain the houses of worship are only those who believe in God and the Last Day; it is they who are the guided ones. This implies that those people, who, instead of maintaining the houses of worship, mount attacks on them, believe neither in Islam nor in the Day of Judgement. God says,

---

[1] Qur'ān 2:114.

﴿إِنَّمَا يَعْمُرُ مَسَٰجِدَ ٱللَّهِ مَنْ ءَامَنَ بِٱللَّهِ وَٱلْيَوْمِ ٱلْأَخِرِ وَأَقَامَ ٱلصَّلَوٰةَ وَءَاتَى ٱلزَّكَوٰةَ
وَلَمْ يَخْشَ إِلَّا ٱللَّهَ فَعَسَىٰٓ أُوْلَٰٓئِكَ أَن يَكُونُواْ مِنَ ٱلْمُهْتَدِينَ﴾

'*Only he who believes in God and the Last Day and establishes prayer and pays Zakat and who fears none but God can maintain and frequent the mosques of God. So they alone are expected to be amongst the rightly guided*'.[1]

Consider the life and company of the miscreants who violate the sanctity of mosques and tombs of Muslim saints! With a little thought, one will quickly discover that their ideological and intellectual growth takes place in an atmosphere laden with narrow-mindedness. This narrow-mindedness generates extremism, which further leads to violence and aggression. And aggression takes its logical shape—that being the monstrosity known as terrorism—which is the outcome of hatred, prejudice and violence, which strip us of the qualities of love, peace, moderation and tolerance. Such a person, in the words of the Qur᾿ān, becomes stone-hearted:

﴿ثُمَّ قَسَتْ قُلُوبُكُم مِّنۢ بَعْدِ ذَٰلِكَ فَهِىَ كَٱلْحِجَارَةِ أَوْ أَشَدُّ قَسْوَةً﴾

'*Then* [even] *after this your hearts hardened. So* [in hardness] *they* [have become] *like stones, or even harder*'.[2]

Such a person is the worst embodiment of wretchedness and callous nihilism; he descends to a low level and takes the lives of peaceful people in shops, markets, public places and educational institutions. He sets himself loose on people engaged in worship at mosques, and does not hesitate to tear down places of worship. What do these terroristic acts have to do with Islam? Had there been just a little fear of God and the Afterlife within such people, at least the mosques would have been safe, and the Muslims busy worshipping God would have been in peace. This mindset proves that terrorists have no link with Islam, which is the religion of peace, harmony, safety and tolerance.

---

[1] Ibid., 9:18.

[2] Ibid., 2:74.

2.7 KILLING A MUSLIM IS A GREATER SIN THAN DESTROYING THE WORLD

How can wrongdoers who brutally kill peaceful citizens to realize their vicious objectives claim to be the stalwarts of peace and security? They are engaged in the wanton killing of thousands of non-combatant Muslims through their terrorist activities; however, the Prophet ﷺ declared that killing a Muslim is a greater sin than destroying the whole world.

ʿAbd Allāh b. ʿAmr ؓ reported that the Messenger of God ﷺ said,

لَزَوَالُ الدُّنْيَا أَهْوَنُ عَلَى اللهِ مِنْ قَتْلِ رَجُلٍ مُسْلِمٍ.

> 'Certainly, the passing away of the entire world is less in the sight of God than the murder of a single Muslim'.[1]

ʿAbd Allāh b. Burayda ؓ reported from his father that the Messenger of God ﷺ said,

قَتْلُ الْمُؤْمِنِ أَعْظَمُ عِنْدَ اللهِ مِنْ زَوَالِ الدُّنْيَا.

> 'Killing a believer is a more serious matter in the sight of God than the destruction of the entire world'.[2]

Another report says the killing of a man, without legal authority, is a tragedy more serious than the passing away of the entire world. Al-Barāʾ b. ʿĀzib ؓ reported that the Messenger of God ﷺ said,

---

[1] Narrated by al-Tirmidhī in *al-Sunan*: *Kitāb al-diyāt* [The Book of Blood Money], chapter: 'What Has Come to Us Concerning the Gravity of Killing a Believer', 4:16 §1395; al-Nasāʾī in *al-Sunan*: *Kitāb taḥrīm al-dam* [The Book on the Prohibition of Bloodshed], chapter: 'The Sanctity of Blood', 7:82 §3987; and Ibn Mājah in *al-Sunan*: *Kitāb al-diyāt* [The Book of Blood Money], chapter: 'The Gravity of Killing a Muslim Unjustly', 2:874 §2619.

[2] Narrated by al-Nasāʾī in *al-Sunan*: *Kitāb taḥrīm al-dam* [The Book on the Prohibition of Bloodshed], chapter: 'The Sanctity of Blood', 7:82–83 §§3988–3990; al-Ṭabarānī in *al-Muʿjam al-ṣaghīr*, 1:355 §594; and al-Bayhaqī in *al-Sunan al-kubrā*, 8:22 §15647. Imam al-Ṭabarānī declared this tradition authentic [*ḥasan*].

لَزَوَالُ الدُّنْيَا جَمِيعًا أَهْوَنُ عِنْدَ اللهِ مِنْ سَفْكِ دَمٍ بِغَيْرِ حَقٍّ.

'Certainly, in the estimation of God, the passing away of the whole world is lighter than unjustly shedding the blood of a human being'.[1]

The humiliating punishment of a murderer who intentionally kills a believer can be understood from the verse wherein God mentioned the punishment of Hell for these sinners with phrases such as '*abide for ages*', '*His wrath*', '*curse him*' and '*dreadful torment*'. God says,

﴿وَمَن يَقْتُلْ مُؤْمِنًا مُّتَعَمِّدًا فَجَزَآؤُهُ جَهَنَّمُ خَٰلِدًا فِيهَا وَغَضِبَ ٱللَّهُ عَلَيْهِ وَلَعَنَهُ وَأَعَدَّ لَهُ عَذَابًا عَظِيمًا﴾

'*But he who kills a Muslim deliberately, his recompense will be Hell, wherein will he abide for ages. God will afflict him with His wrath and will curse him. And He has prepared for him a dreadful torment*'.[2]

2.8 The Massacre of Muslims is an Act of Disbelief

The Prophet Muhammad ﷺ declared that shedding the blood of peaceful Muslims and spreading violence and mischief in society are disbelief and cause one to revert from Islam to disbelief, technically known as apostasy, or *irtidād*. Imam al-Bukhārī narrates on the authority of ʿAbd Allāh b. ʿAbbās ﷺ that the Messenger of God ﷺ said,

لَا تَرْتَدُّوا بَعْدِي كُفَّارًا يَضْرِبُ بَعْضُكُمْ رِقَابَ بَعْضٍ.

'Do not revert as disbelievers after me by striking one another's necks!'[3]

---

[1] Narrated by Ibn Abī al-Dunyā in *al-Ahwāl*, p. 190 §183; Ibn Abī ʿĀṣim in *al-Diyāt*, p. 2 §2; and al-Bayhaqī in *Shuʿab al-Īmān*, 4:345 §5344.

[2] Qurʾān 4:93.

[3] Narrated by al-Bukhārī in *al-Ṣaḥīḥ*: *Kitāb al-fitan* [The Book of Tribulations], chapter: 'The Saying of the Prophet ﷺ, "Do Not Revert to Disbelievers after Me, Striking One Another's Necks!"', 6:2594 §6668; and al-Ṭabarānī in *al-Muʿjam al-awsaṭ*, 4:269 §4166.

Therefore, committing murder and killing Muslims is a clear act of disbelief, which bears a likeness to apostasy.

2.9 Like Polytheism, Murder is One of the Greatest Wrongs

Ibn Kathīr interpreted the verse,

﴿وَمَن يَقْتُلْ مُؤْمِنًا مُّتَعَمِّدًا﴾

'But he who kills a Muslim deliberately',[1]

declaring intentional murder a major sin that it is so severe and grave, that God has mentioned it in conjunction with the greatest wrong—that of *shirk*, or idolatry. He writes:

> هَذَا تَهْدِيْدٌ شَدِيْدٌ وَوَعِيْدٌ أَكِيْدٌ لِمَنْ تَعَاطَى هَذَا الذَّنْبَ الْعَظِيْمَ، الَّذِي هُوَ مَقْرُونٌ بِالشِّرْكِ بِاللهِ فِي غَيْرِ مَا آيَةٍ فِي كِتَابِ اللهِ، حَيْثُ يَقُولُ سُبْحَانَهُ فِي سُورَةِ الْفُرْقَانِ: ﴿وَٱلَّذِينَ لَا يَدْعُونَ مَعَ ٱللَّهِ إِلَٰهًا ءَاخَرَ وَلَا يَقْتُلُونَ ٱلنَّفْسَ ٱلَّتِى حَرَّمَ ٱللَّهُ إِلَّا بِٱلْحَقِّ وَلَا يَزْنُونَ﴾ وَقَالَ تَعَالَى: ﴿قُلْ تَعَالَوْاْ أَتْلُ مَا حَرَّمَ رَبُّكُمْ عَلَيْكُمْ أَلَّا تُشْرِكُواْ بِهِ شَيْئًا﴾ إِلَى أَنْ قَالَ: ﴿وَلَا تَقْتُلُواْ ٱلنَّفْسَ ٱلَّتِى حَرَّمَ ٱللَّهُ إِلَّا بِٱلْحَقِّ ذَٰلِكُمْ وَصَّٰكُم بِهِ لَعَلَّكُمْ تَعْقِلُونَ﴾.
>
> This is a stern warning and emphatic Divine threat to those who perpetrate this grievous sin that is connected—in more than one verse in God's Book—with the taking of partners in worship along with God. The Most High says in *Sūra al-Furqān*, '*And* [the believers are] *those who do not worship any other god besides God, or kill a soul unlawfully—except with just cause—or commit adultery*'.[2] And God says, '*Say* [*O Prophet*], "*Come, I will recite to you those things which your Lord has forbidden to you: Do not set up anything as a partner with Him; treat your parents with excellence and do not kill your children owing to poverty. We alone give you sustenance*

---

[1] Qur'ān 4:93.

[2] Ibid., 25:68.

> *and* [will provide for] *them as well. And do not draw near to shameful deeds, be they open or hidden. And do not kill the soul whose* [killing] *God has forbidden, except when it is justified* [legally]. *These are the injunctions He has enjoined upon you so that you may apply reason".'* [Qur'ān 6:151][1]

As he was delivering his Last Sermon on the eve of the Hajj, the Prophet ﷺ made clear the unlawfulness of killing and pointed out its inherent evil. He said,

> إِنَّ دِمَاءَكُمْ وَأَمْوَالَكُمْ وَأَعْرَاضَكُمْ عَلَيْكُمْ حَرَامٌ، كَحُرْمَةِ يَوْمِكُمْ هَذَا، فِي شَهْرِكُمْ هَذَا فِي بَلَدِكُمْ هَذَا، إِلَى يَوْمِ تَلْقَوْنَ رَبَّكُمْ. أَلَا، هَلْ بَلَّغْتُ؟ قَالُوا: نَعَمْ. قَالَ: اَللّٰهُمَّ اشْهَدْ، فَلْيُبَلِّغِ الشَّاهِدُ الْغَائِبَ، فَرُبَّ مُبَلَّغٍ أَوْعَى مِنْ سَامِعٍ، فَلَا تَرْجِعُوا بَعْدِي كُفَّارًا يَضْرِبُ بَعْضُكُمْ رِقَابَ بَعْضٍ.

> 'Indeed your blood and your property are inviolable, like the inviolability of this day of yours and this month of yours and this land of yours, until the day you meet your Lord. Listen, have I conveyed the message?' The Companions replied, 'Yes'. He ﷺ said, 'O God! Bear witness. Let the one present inform those who are absent, for perhaps the one to whom it is conveyed will retain it better than he who hears it [directly]. Do not revert as disbelievers after me, striking each other's necks'.[2]

The Messenger of God ﷺ has clearly given the judgement in this agreed upon hadith that those who shed blood, engage in violence and acts of terrorism, raise arms and kill Muslims are no longer Muslims; they are disbelievers. The Messenger of God ﷺ has removed all doubts about this, using the words, 'Do not revert

[1] Ibn Kathīr, *Tafsīr al-Qur'ān al-ʿAẓīm,* 1:535.

[2] Narrated by al-Bukhārī in *al-Ṣaḥīḥ*: *Kitāb al-Ḥajj* [The Book of Pilgrimage], 2:620 §1654, and *Kitāb al-ʿilm* [The Book of Knowledge], chapter: 'The Saying of the Prophet ﷺ, "Many a Person to Whom Something is Conveyed Retains it Better than the One Who Heard It"', 1:37 §67 and Muslim in *al-Ṣaḥīḥ*, 3:1305–1306 §1679.

as disbelievers after me, striking each other's necks'. This is a clear declaration that those who commit terrorism and mass murder are disbelievers.

Abū Saʿīd al-Khudrī and Abū Hurayra ﷺ reported that the Prophet ﷺ said regarding the murder of a believer,

لَوْ أَنَّ أَهْلَ السَّمَاءِ وَأَهْلَ الْأَرْضِ اشْتَرَكُوا فِي دَمِ مُؤْمِنٍ لَأَكَبَّهُمُ اللهُ فِي النَّارِ.

> 'Even if all the inhabitants of the heavens and the earth gathered together to shed the blood of a single believer, God would cast them all in the Hellfire'.[1]

2.10 Bloodshed is the Greatest of all Crimes

Mass murder, bloodshed, and unjust killing are such grave offences that God Most High will take those who commit them to task before anything else on the Day of Resurrection. ʿAbd Allāh b. Masʿūd ﷺ reported that the Prophet ﷺ said while describing the enormity of shedding blood unlawfully,

أَوَّلُ مَا يُقْضَى بَيْنَ النَّاسِ يَوْمَ الْقِيَامَةِ فِي الدِّمَاءِ.

> 'The first issue that will be judged between people on the Day of Resurrection is that of blood [i.e., murder]'.[2]

ʿAbd Allāh b. ʿUmar ﷺ reported that the Prophet ﷺ warned about the disastrous consequences of fighting and bloodshed and said,

إِنَّ مِنْ وَرَطَاتِ الْأُمُورِ الَّتِي لَا مَخْرَجَ لِمَنْ أَوْقَعَ نَفْسَهُ فِيْهَا سَفْكُ الدَّمِ الْحَرَامِ بِغَيْرِ حِلِّهِ.

> 'Of the serious matters from which no one who brings it

[1] Narrated by al-Tirmidhī in *al-Sunan*: *Kitāb al-diyāt* [The Book of Blood Money], chapter: 'The Legal Ruling Concerning Blood', 4:17 §1398; al-Rabīʿ in *al-Musnad*, 1:292 §757; and al-Daylamī in *Musnad al-firdaws*, 3:361 §5089.

[2] Narrated by al-Bukhārī in *al-Ṣaḥīḥ*: *Kitāb al-diyāt* [The Book of Blood Money], chapter: 'Whoever Kills a Believer Intentionally', 6:2517 §6471; Muslim in *al-Ṣaḥīḥ*, 3:1304 §1678; al-Nasāʾī in *al-Sunan*: *Kitāb taḥrīm al-dam* [The Book on the Prohibition of Bloodshed], chapter: 'The Sanctity of Blood', 7:83 §3994; and Aḥmad b. Ḥanbal in *al-Musnad*, 1:442.

upon himself and falls into it will escape is that of blood that was shed unlawfully'.[1]

Abū Hurayra ﷺ reported that the Messenger of God ﷺ said,

يَتَقَارَبُ الزَّمَانُ، وَيَنْقُصُ الْعِلْمُ، وَيُلْقَى الشُّحُّ، وَتَظْهَرُ الْفِتَنُ، وَيَكْثُرُ الْهَرْجُ. قَالُوا: يَا رَسُولَ اللهِ، أَيُّمَا هُوَ؟ قَالَ: الْقَتْلُ، الْقَتْلُ.

'Time will seem to get shorter and knowledge will diminish. Miserliness will surface and tribulations will rise and *haraj* will abound'. The Companions asked, 'O Messenger of God, what is *haraj*?' He said, 'It is killing. It is killing'.[2]

When peaceful civilians are targets of terrorism, tyranny and barbarism, and are victimized due to doctrinal and ideological differences between the political and religious personalities, the logical consequence is anarchy, chaos, lawlessness and strife. ʿAbd Allāh b. ʿUmar ﷺ said,

كُنَّا قُعُودًا عِنْدَ رَسُولِ اللهِ ﷺ فَذَكَرَ الْفِتَنَ، فَأَكْثَرَ فِي ذِكْرِهَا حَتَّى ذَكَرَ فِتْنَةَ الْأَحْلَاسِ. فَقَالَ قَائِلٌ: يَا رَسُولَ اللهِ! وَمَا فِتْنَةُ الْأَحْلَاسِ؟ قَالَ: هِيَ هَرَبٌ وَحَرْبٌ.

'We were once sitting with the Prophet ﷺ when he described the tribulations. He described them at length, until he mentioned the tribulation of *al-aḥlās*. At that point, someone asked, "O Messenger of God! What is the tribulation of *al-aḥlās*?" The Prophet ﷺ said, "It is chaos and mass killing".'[3]

---

[1] Narrated by al-Bukhārī in *al-Ṣaḥīḥ*: *Kitāb al-diyāt* [The Book of Blood Money], chapter: 'Whoever Kills a Believer Intentionally', 6:2517 §6470 and al-Bayhaqī in *al-Sunan al-kubrā*, 8:21 §15637.

[2] Narrated by al-Bukhārī in *al-Ṣaḥīḥ*: *Kitāb al-fitan* [The Book of Tribulation], chapter: 'The Emergence of Tribulations', 6:2590 §6652; and Muslim in *al-Ṣaḥīḥ*: *Kitāb al-fitan wa ashrāṭ al-sāʿa* [The Book of Tribulations and the Portents of the Final Hour], chapter: 'When Two Muslims Confront Each Other with Their Swords', 4:2215.

[3] Narrated by Abū Dāwūd in *al-Sunan: Kitāb al-fitan wa al-malāḥim* [The Book

2.11 Those Who Subject Muslims to Burning through Explosions and Other Means Belong in the Hellfire

According to the Qur'ān, terrorists who bomb common people, engage in suicide bombings and otherwise kill peaceful people are criminals who are destined to suffer the torments of the Hellfire. The chapter of the Qur'ān, *al-Burūj*, prohibits the burning of common people:

﴿إِنَّ ٱلَّذِينَ فَتَنُوا۟ ٱلْمُؤْمِنِينَ وَٱلْمُؤْمِنَـٰتِ ثُمَّ لَمْ يَتُوبُوا۟ فَلَهُمْ عَذَابُ جَهَنَّمَ وَلَهُمْ عَذَابُ ٱلْحَرِيقِ﴾

> '*Indeed, those who subject the believing men and women to tribulation* [*fatanū*] *and then do not repent, for them is the punishment of Hell, and for them is a burning torment*'.[1]

Some Qur'ānic exegetes interpret the word *fatanū* as 'burning in fire'. This verse implies that those who burn people through bomb blasts are the inhabitants of the Hellfire. Ibn ʿAbbās and Muqātil said, 'The words '*fatanū al-muʾminīna*' (subject the believers to tribulation) mean: "They burnt them (the believers) with fire".'[2] ʿAbd b. Ḥumayd and Ibn al-Mundhir reported that Qatāda said regarding the verse, '*Indeed those who subject the believing men and women to tribulation*', 'This means killing by burning'.[3] Imam al-Qurṭubī and Abū Ḥafṣ al-Ḥanbalī have also given the same interpretation.[4]

Those who deem it lawful to kill the Muslims are out of the fold of Islam, and are liable to the torment of the blazing fire of Hell. ʿAbd Allāh b. Busr ﷺ reported that the Messenger of God ﷺ said,

---

of Tribulations and Battles], chapter: 'Mention of Tribulations', 4:94 §4242.

[1] Qur'ān 85:10.

[2] Al-Rāzī, *al-Tafsīr al-kabīr*, 13:111.

[3] Jalāl al-Dīn al-Suyūṭī, *al-Durr al-manthūr*, 8:466.

[4] Muhammad al-Qurṭubī, *al-Jāmiʿ li aḥkām al-Qurʾān*, 19:295; and Abū Ḥafṣ al-Ḥanbalī, *al-Lubāb fī ʿulūm al-Kitāb*, 20:253.

لَيْسَ مِنِّي ذُو حَسَدٍ وَلَا نَمِيْمَةٍ وَلَا كَهَانَةٍ وَلَا أَنَا مِنْهُ. ثُمَّ تَلَا رَسُولُ اللهِ ﷺ هَذِهِ الْآيَةَ: ﴿وَٱلَّذِينَ يُؤْذُونَ ٱلْمُؤْمِنِينَ وَٱلْمُؤْمِنَٰتِ بِغَيْرِ مَا ٱكْتَسَبُواْ فَقَدِ ٱحْتَمَلُواْ بُهْتَٰنًا وَإِثْمًا مُّبِينًا﴾

'The envious, the calumnious and the soothsayer are not from me, and I am not from them'. Then the Messenger of God ﷺ recited the following verse: '*And those who hurt the believing men and women without their doing anything* [wrong], *surely they bear the burden of slander and clear sin*'. [Qur'ān 33:58][1]

In Imam Fakhr al-Dīn al-Rāzī's exegesis of the Qur'ān, it is written:

إِنَّ كِلَا الْعَذَابَيْنِ يَحْصُلَانِ فِي الْآخِرَةِ، إِلَّا أَنَّ عَذَابَ جَهَنَّمَ وَهُوَ الْعَذَابُ الْحَاصِلُ بِسَبَبِ كُفْرِهِمْ، وَعَذَابُ الْحَرِيْقِ هُوَ الْعَذَابُ الزَّائِدُ عَلَى عَذَابِ الْكُفْرِ بِسَبَبِ أَنَّهُمْ أَحْرَقُوا الْمُؤْمِنِيْنَ.

'Both punishments will occur in the Hereafter; however, the torment of the Hellfire will be on account of their disbelief, and the burning torment will be an additional punishment meted out to them on account of their burning of the believers'.[2]

The authors of the Qur'ānic exegesis, *Tafsīr al-Jalālayn*, also held the same view:

﴿إِنَّ ٱلَّذِينَ فَتَنُواْ ٱلْمُؤْمِنِينَ وَٱلْمُؤْمِنَٰتِ﴾ بِالْإِحْرَاقِ ﴿ثُمَّ لَمْ يَتُوبُواْ فَلَهُمْ عَذَابُ جَهَنَّمَ﴾ بِكُفْرِهِمْ ﴿وَلَهُمْ عَذَابُ ٱلْحَرِيقِ﴾ أَيْ عَذَابُ إِحْرَاقِهِمُ الْمُؤْمِنِيْنَ فِي الْآخِرَةِ.

'"*Indeed, those who subject the believing men and women to tribulation* [*fatanū*]" by burning, "*and then do not repent, for them is the punishment of Hell*" due to their disbelief, "*and for them is a burning torment*",

---

[1] Narrated by al-Mundhirī in *al-Targhīb wa al-tarhīb*, 3:324 §4275; and Ibn ʿAsākir in *Tārīkh Dimashq al-kabīr*, 21:334.

[2] Al-Rāzī, *al-Tafsīr al-kabīr*, 31:111.

in other words, the punishment in the Hereafter for them having burnt the believers'.[1]

2.12 No Act of Worship Performed by a Murderer of a Muslim is Acceptable

No act of worship, whether obligatory or supererogatory, performed by the one who kills the Muslims will be accepted. ʿAbd Allāh b. al-Ṣāmit ﷺ reported that the Messenger of God ﷺ said,

مَنْ قَتَلَ مُؤْمِنًا فَاعْتَبَطَ بِقَتْلِهِ لَمْ يَقْبَلِ اللهُ مِنْهُ صَرْفًا وَلَا عَدْلًا.

'God will not accept any act of worship, obligatory or supererogatory, from the one who attacks a Muslim and kills him'.[2]

Those who perform acts of worship and acts of vigorous religious discipline, but who also commit violence and murders, are unfortunate creatures whose worship will be rejected. Inflicting humiliation upon humans and expecting deliverance by means of pious acts of worship will only earn them the torment of Hell:

﴿فَلَهُمْ عَذَابُ جَهَنَّمَ وَلَهُمْ عَذَابُ ٱلْحَرِيقِ﴾

'*For them is the punishment of Hell, and for them is a burning torment*'.[3]

2.13 Those Who Torture Muslims Will Face the Torment of Hell

Persecuting members of the Muslim community by subjecting

[1] Jalāl al-Dīn al-Suyūṭī and Jalāl al-Dīn al-Maḥallī, *Tafsīr al-Jalālayn*, 1:801.

[2] Narrated by Abū Dāwūd in *al-Sunan*: *Kitāb al-fitan wa al-malāḥim* [The Book of Tribulations and Battles], chapter: 'The Gravity of Killing a Believer', 4:103 §4270; al-Ṭabarānī in *Musnad al-Shāmiyyīn*, 2:266 §1311; al-Mundhirī in *al-Targhīb wa al-tarhīb*, 3:203 §3691; and cited by al-ʿAsqalānī in *al-Dirāya*, 2:259; and al-Shawkānī in *Nayl al-awṭār*, 7:197.

[3] Qurʾān 85:10.

them to violence, tyranny and brutality is strictly forbidden. God has threatened those who do such deeds with a painful torment:

﴿إِنَّ ٱلَّذِينَ فَتَنُواْ ٱلْمُؤْمِنِينَ وَٱلْمُؤْمِنَٰتِ ثُمَّ لَمْ يَتُوبُواْ فَلَهُمْ عَذَابُ جَهَنَّمَ وَلَهُمْ عَذَابُ ٱلْحَرِيقِ﴾

'Indeed those who subject the believing men and women to tribulation [fatanū] and then do not repent, for them is the punishment of Hell, and for them is a burning torment'.[1]

Those who oppress God's creation will face the consequences of their vicious deeds. Hishām b. al-Ḥakīm ﷺ reported that the Messenger of God ﷺ said,

إِنَّ اللهَ يُعَذِّبُ الَّذِينَ يُعَذِّبُونَ النَّاسَ فِي الدُّنْيَا.

'Indeed, God shall inflict His torment upon those who torture people in the life of this world'.[2]

All of the Imams of Qur'ānic exegesis concurred that Hell shall be the abode of those who oppress and torture Muslims. Interpreting this Qur'ānic verse, Imam Fakhr al-Dīn al-Rāzī posited that this applies to 'everyone who does that—and this is more fitting, because both the wording and the ruling are general, and so a specification would entail leaving the apparent meaning without proof'.[3] So, it is just as fitting to apply the ruling in these verses to the so-called 'religious' terrorists of today.[4]

2.14 THE UNLAWFULNESS OF SUICIDE

Suicide is forbidden in Islam. The one who commits suicide defies God and becomes a resident of Hell. Before examining the revealed texts that forbid suicide, let us consider why it is forbidden.

---

1 Ibid.

2 Narrated by Muslim in *al-Ṣaḥīḥ: Kitāb al-birr wa al-ṣila wa al-ādāb* [The Book of Piety, Filial Duty and Good Manners], chapter: 'The Severe Divine Threat for Someone Who Punishes People Unjustly', 4:2018 §2613.

3 Al-Rāzī, *al-Tafsīr al-kabīr*, 13:111.

4 Qur'ān 85:4–10.

Human life is neither owned nor acquired; it is a gift and trust from God. The blessing of life serves as a basis for all other blessings. It is for this reason that Islam directs people to safeguard their lives and forbids suicide. Islam does not allow any human being to take his or her own life. On the contrary, the teachings of Islam emphasize the safety and security of life and body. These teachings aim at preserving human life and ensuring the continuation of humanity.

2.15 The Qur'ānic Texts and Hadith Reports on Suicide

As mentioned earlier, the real owner of life and death is God. So just as murdering a person is akin to murdering all of humanity, so too is suicide considered a despicable act. God says,

﴿وَلَا تُلْقُوا۟ بِأَيْدِيكُمْ إِلَى ٱلتَّهْلُكَةِ وَأَحْسِنُوٓا۟ إِنَّ ٱللَّهَ يُحِبُّ ٱلْمُحْسِنِينَ﴾

'*And do not cast yourselves into destruction with your own hands—and adopt righteousness. Verily, God loves the righteous*'.[1]

Interpreting verse 30 of *Sūra al-Nisā'*, Imam al-Baghawī cited the aforementioned verse and said,

قِيْلَ: أَرَادَ بِهِ قَتْلَ الْمُسْلِمِ نَفْسَهُ.

'It is said that He intended the Muslim who kills himself'.[2]

God also revealed,

﴿يَٰٓأَيُّهَا ٱلَّذِينَ ءَامَنُوا۟ لَا تَأْكُلُوٓا۟ أَمْوَٰلَكُم بَيْنَكُم بِٱلْبَٰطِلِ إِلَّآ أَن تَكُونَ تِجَٰرَةً عَن تَرَاضٍ مِّنكُمْ وَلَا تَقْتُلُوٓا۟ أَنفُسَكُمْ إِنَّ ٱللَّهَ كَانَ بِكُمْ رَحِيمًا. وَمَن يَفْعَلْ ذَٰلِكَ عُدْوَٰنًا وَظُلْمًا فَسَوْفَ نُصْلِيهِ نَارًا وَكَانَ ذَٰلِكَ عَلَى ٱللَّهِ يَسِيرًا﴾

'*O you who believe! Do not devour one another's wealth unlawfully amongst yourselves unless it is a trade by your mutual agreement, and do not kill yourselves. Surely,*

---

1 Ibid., 2:195.

2 Ḥusayn al-Baghawī, *Ma'ālim al-Tanzīl*, 1:418.

> *God is kind to you. But whoever does that through transgression and injustice, We shall soon throw him into the Fire* [of Hell] *and that is easy for God*'.[1]

Interpreting this verse, Imam Fakhr al-Dīn al-Rāzī wrote,

﴿وَلَا تَقْتُلُوْا أَنفُسَكُمْ﴾ يَدُلُّ عَلَى النَّهْيِ عَنْ قَتْلِ غَيْرِهِ وَعَنْ قَتْلِ نَفْسِهِ بِالْبَاطِلِ.

> 'This verse, "*And do not kill yourselves*", proves that it is unlawful for one to kill someone else or oneself unjustly'.[2]

Moreover, Imam al-Baghawī quoted traditions on the prohibition of suicide, as did Ibn Kathīr[3] and al-Thaʿālabī[4] in their respective exegeses. These traditions, which we reproduce here, prove that the notable Imams of Qurʾānic exegesis considered them proofs for the unlawfulness of suicide. The Prophet ﷺ said,

إِنَّ لِجَسَدِکَ عَلَيْکَ حَقًّا، وَإِنَّ لِعَيْنِکَ عَلَيْکَ حَقًّا.

> 'Indeed, your body has a right on you and your eyes also have a right on you'.[5]

This hadith prescribes that we safeguard life and limb and observe the rights of our bodies. Therefore, killing oneself and others through suicide bombing is a grievous sin. How can one possibly imagine that Islam sanctions self-destruction and the taking of life through wanton acts of terror and suicide bombings? The Prophet ﷺ explicitly declared the act of suicide forbidden when he said, 'The one who commits suicide will go to Hell, and will keep falling into it and will abide there forever'.[6]

---

[1] Qurʾān 4:29–30.

[2] Al-Rāzī, *al-Tafsīr al-kabīr*, 10:57.

[3] Ibn Kathīr, *Tafsīr al-Qurʾān al-ʿAẓīm*, 1:481.

[4] ʿAbd al-Raḥmān al-Thaʿālabī, *al-Jawāhir al-ḥisān fī tafsīr al-Qurʾān*, 3:293.

[5] Narrated by al-Bukhārī in *al-Ṣaḥīḥ*: *Kitāb al-Ṣawm* [The Book of Fasting], chapter: 'The Right of the Body while Fasting', 2:697 §1874.

[6] Narrated by al-Bukhārī in *al-Ṣaḥīḥ*: *Kitāb al-ṭibb* [The Book of Medicine], chapter: 'Taking Poison and Using it for Medical Treatment, or Using What May be Dangerous or Impure', 5:2179 §5442.

In the hadith reports from the Messenger of God ﷺ, we find that the one who commits suicide is threatened with a severe torment in the Hereafter. Abū Hurayra ﵁ reported that the Messenger of God ﷺ said,

مَنْ تَرَدَّى مِنْ جَبَلٍ فَقَتَلَ نَفْسَهُ فَهُوَ فِي نَارِ جَهَنَّمَ، يَتَرَدَّى فِيْهِ خَالِدًا مُخَلَّدًا فِيْهَا أَبَدًا. وَمَنْ تَحَسَّى سُمًّا فَقَتَلَ نَفْسَهُ، فَسُمُّهُ فِي يَدِهِ يَتَحَسَّاهُ فِي نَارِ جَهَنَّمَ خَالِدًا مُخَلَّدًا فِيْهَا أَبَدًا. وَمَنْ قَتَلَ نَفْسَهُ بِحَدِيْدَةٍ، فَحَدِيْدَتُهُ فِي يَدِهِ يَجَأُ بِهَا فِي بَطْنِهِ فِي نَارِ جَهَنَّمَ، خَالِدًا مُخَلَّدًا فِيْهَا أَبَدًا.

'Whoever throws himself off a mountain, thereby killing himself, he will throw himself down a mountain in Hell forever. And whoever drinks poison, thereby killing himself, he will hold poison in his hand, eternally drinking it in Hell. And if someone kills himself with iron [stabbing himself], he will eternally stab himself with it in Hell'.[1]

Abū Hurayra ﵁ also reported that the Messenger of God ﷺ said,

اَلَّذِي يَطْعَنُ نَفْسَهُ إِنَّمَا يَطْعَنُهَا فِي النَّارِ، وَالَّذِي يَتَقَحَّمُ فِيْهَا يَتَقَحَّمُ فِي النَّارِ، وَالَّذِي يَخْنُقُ نَفْسَهُ يَخْنُقُهَا فِي النَّارِ.

'Whoever stabs himself to death will continue to stab himself in Hell. And whoever throws himself off a cliff will continue to throw himself off a cliff in Hell. And

[1] Narrated by al-Bukhārī in *al-Ṣaḥīḥ*: *Kitāb al-ṭibb* [The Book of Medicine], chapter: 'Taking Poison and Using it for Medical Treatment, or Using What May be Dangerous or Impure', 5:2179 §5442; Muslim in *al-Ṣaḥīḥ*: *Kitāb al-Īmān* [The Book of Faith], chapter: 'The Strict Forbiddance of Killing Oneself, and if Someone Commits Suicide with Something, He Will be Tormented with the Same Thing in the Hellfire', 1:103 §109; al-Tirmidhī in *al-Sunan*: *Kitāb al-ṭibb* [The Book of Medicine], chapter: 'What Has Come to Us about Someone Who Kills Himself with Poison or Something Else', 4:386 §2044; and Abū Dāwūd in *al-Sunan*: *Kitāb al-ṭibb* [The Book of Medicine], chapter: 'Abhorred Medicines', 4:7 §3872.

whoever hangs himself will continue to hang himself in Hell'.[1]

Thābit b. al-Ḍaḥḥāk ﷺ reported that the Messenger of God ﷺ said,

مَنْ قَتَلَ نَفْسَهُ بِشَيْءٍ عُذِّبَ بِهِ فِي نَارِ جَهَنَّمَ.

'Whoever kills himself with something will be tormented by it in the Hellfire'.[2]

According to these traditions, the method of suicide will continue in Hell as well. That shows the gravity of this sin. Other transgressions will be punished through the torment of Hell, but suicide is such a heinous offence that its method will continue.

2.16 The Condemnation of the Leaders Who Command Others to Commit Suicide

These aforementioned hadith reports forbid suicide in general; however, some hadith reports particularly forbid unlawful obedience to authorities, as that may cause detriment to the lives of others. We hear many youth in their self-made online

---

[1] Narrated by al-Bukhārī in *al-Ṣaḥīḥ*: *Kitāb al-janā'iz* [The Book of Funeral Rites], chapter: 'What Has Come to Us About Someone Who Kills Himself', 1:459 §1299; Aḥmad b. Ḥanbal in *al-Musnad*, 2:435 §9616; al-Ṭabarānī in *Musnad al-Shāmiyyīn*, 4:285 §3311; and al-Bayhaqī in *Shuʿab al-Īmān*, 4:350 §5362.

[2] Narrated by al-Bukhārī in *al-Ṣaḥīḥ*: *Kitāb al-adab* [The Book of Good Manners], chapter: 'If Someone Calls his Brother a Disbeliever Without Any Interpretable Grounds, Then He Himself is What He Said', 5:2264 §5754; Muslim in *al-Ṣaḥīḥ*: *Kitāb al-Īmān* [The Book of Faith], chapter: 'The Strict Forbiddance of Killing Oneself, and if Someone Commits Suicide with Something, He Will be Tormented with the Same in the Hellfire', 1:104 §110; Abū Dāwūd in *al-Sunan*: *Kitāb al-aymān wa al-nudhūr* [The Book of Oaths and Vows], 3:224 §3257; al-Nasā'ī in *al-Sunan*: *Kitāb al-aymān wa al-nudhūr* [The Book of Oaths and Vows], chapter: 'What Has Come to Us Regarding Oaths Taken by Swearing Disavowal of the Religion [if the Person is Lying] or by Adhering to Another Religion other than Islam', 7:5–6 §§3770–3771; and Aḥmad b. Ḥanbal in *al-Musnad*, 4:33–34 §§16434, 16438.

'martyrdom videos' describe their leader's command as the motivation for taking their own lives. They are well-grounded in obedience to their leaders and commanders, but they are unaware of the confines, limits and restraints of obedience. It is extreme foolishness, ignorance and absurdity to destroy the lives of common people in obedience to a leader's command.

ʿAlī b. Abī Ṭālib رضي الله عنه reported,

أَنَّ النَّبِيَّ ﷺ بَعَثَ جَيْشًا وَأَمَّرَ عَلَيْهِمْ رَجُلًا، فَأَوْقَدَ نَارًا، وَقَالَ: ادْخُلُوهَا. فَأَرَادُوا أَنْ يَدْخُلُوهَا، وَقَالَ آخَرُونَ: إِنَّمَا فَرَرْنَا مِنْهَا. فَذَكَرُوا لِلنَّبِيِّ ﷺ، فَقَالَ ﷺ لِلَّذِيْنَ أَرَادُوا أَنْ يَدْخُلُوهَا: لَوْ دَخَلُوهَا لَمْ يَزَالُوا فِيْهَا إِلَى يَوْمِ الْقِيَامَةِ. وَقَالَ لِلْآخَرِيْنَ: لَا طَاعَةَ فِي مَعْصِيَةٍ. إِنَّمَا الطَّاعَةُ فِي الْمَعْرُوفِ.

'The Messenger of God ﷺ dispatched a military force and appointed one of the *Anṣār* as its leader. He then started a fire and said [to them], "Enter it". Some of them were about to enter it, while others amongst them said, "We have only sought to free ourselves from it [by embracing Islam]". When they submitted the episode to the Prophet ﷺ he said to those who had intended to enter the fire, "If they had entered it, they would have remained in it until the Day of Resurrection". Then he said to the others, "There is no obedience in that which is disobedience. Obedience is only in that which is right".'[1]

In another narration of ʿAlī رضي الله عنه found in Imam Muslim's *al-Ṣaḥīḥ*, it reads:

بَعَثَ رَسُولُ اللهِ ﷺ سَرِيَّةً وَاسْتَعْمَلَ عَلَيْهِمْ رَجُلًا مِنَ الْأَنْصَارِ، وَأَمَرَهُمْ أَنْ يَسْمَعُوا لَهُ وَيُطِيْعُوا، فَأَغْضَبُوهُ فِي شَيْءٍ، فَقَالَ: اجْمَعُوا لِي حَطَبًا. فَجَمَعُوا لَهُ، ثُمَّ قَالَ: أَوْقِدُوا نَارًا. فَأَوْقَدُوا، ثُمَّ قَالَ: أَلَمْ يَأْمُرْكُمْ رَسُولُ اللهِ ﷺ أَنْ تَسْمَعُوا لِي وَتُطِيْعُوا؟ قَالُوا: بَلَى. قَالَ: فَادْخُلُوهَا. قَالَ: فَنَظَرَ بَعْضُهُمْ إِلَى بَعْضٍ، فَقَالُوا: إِنَّمَا فَرَرْنَا إِلَى رَسُولِ

[1] Narrated by Muslim in *al-Ṣaḥīḥ*: *Kitāb al-imāra* [The Book of Leadership], chapter: 'The Obligation to Obey the Leaders', 3:1469 § 1840.

اللهِ ﷺ مِنَ النَّارِ. فَكَانُوا كَذَلِكَ، وَسَكَنَ غَضَبُهُ، وَطُفِئَتِ النَّارُ، فَلَمَّا رَجَعُوا، ذَكَرُوا ذَلِكَ لِلنَّبِيِّ ﷺ، فَقَالَ: لَوْ دَخَلُوهَا مَا خَرَجُوا مِنْهَا، إِنَّمَا الطَّاعَةُ فِي الْمَعْرُوفِ.

> 'The Messenger of God ﷺ dispatched a military force and appointed one of the *Anṣār* as its leader. He ordered them [the soldiers] to heed and obey him. The leader became annoyed with the troops on account of something and said, 'Gather firewood for me', and they gathered it. Then he said, 'Kindle the fire', and they kindled the fire. Then he said, "Has the Messenger of God ﷺ not enjoined you to obey me?" They replied, "Of course". The leader said, "Then plunge yourselves into it". The troops started looking at each other [when they intended to enter it]. They said, "We have fled to the Messenger of God ﷺ for the sake of saving ourselves from the Fire". They continued to procrastinate until the fire went out and the leader's anger subsided. When they returned and submitted the episode to the Prophet ﷺ, he said, "If they had entered it, they would have never come out of it. Obedience is only in that which is right".'[1]

Those who are motivated to act as suicide bombers should pay heed to this agreed upon hadith narrated from our master ʿAlī ؓ. If they obey their commander's orders to attack civilians and kill themselves in the process, then they shall be the fuel of Hell.

2.17 Paradise is Forbidden for the One Who Commits Suicide

The masterminds of terrorism who groom and brainwash young people for suicide bombings and encourage them with dreams of Paradise by means of 'martyrdom' should realize that God has

---

[1] Narrated by al-Bukhārī in *al-Ṣaḥīḥ*: *Kitāb al-aḥkām* [The Book of Legal Rulings], chapter: 'The Imam Should be Heeded and Obeyed as Long as it is Not Disobedience', 6:2649 §6830; and Muslim in *al-Ṣaḥīḥ*: *Kitāb al-imāra* [The Book of Leadership], chapter: 'The Obligation to Obey the Leaders', 3:1469 §1840.

decreed a permanent torment in Hell awaiting those who commit suicide. Jundub b. ʿAbd Allāh ﷺ reported that the Prophet ﷺ said,

كَانَ فِيمَنْ كَانَ قَبْلَكُمْ رَجُلٌ بِهِ جُرْحٌ، فَجَزِعَ فَأَخَذَ سِكِّينًا، فَحَزَّ بِهَا يَدَهُ، فَمَا رَقَأَ الدَّمُ حَتَّى مَاتَ. قَالَ اللهُ تَعَالَى: بَادَرَنِي عَبْدِي بِنَفْسِهِ؛ حَرَّمْتُ عَلَيْهِ الْجَنَّةَ.

> 'Amongst those before you was a man who was wounded. Unable to bear the pain, he took a knife, sliced his wounded hand and died due to excessive blood loss. God Most High said, "My slave decided to hasten his own demise, so I made Paradise forbidden for him".'[1]

Al-Ḥasan al-Baṣrī narrates from Jundub b. ʿAbd Allāh ﷺ that the Messenger of God ﷺ said,

إِنَّ رَجُلًا مِمَّنْ كَانَ قَبْلَكُمْ، خَرَجَتْ بِهِ قُرْحَةٌ، فَلَمَّا آذَتْهُ انْتَزَعَ سَهْمًا مِنْ كِنَانَتِهِ، فَنَكَأَهَا، فَلَمْ يَرْقَإِ الدَّمُ حَتَّى مَاتَ. قَالَ رَبُّكُمْ: قَدْ حَرَّمْتُ عَلَيْهِ الْجَنَّةَ.

> 'Certainly, a man before you belonging to the people of the past suffered from a boil. When its pain became too much for him to bear, he drew out an arrow from the quiver and pierced it and the bleeding did not stop until he died. Your Lord said, "I forbid his entrance into Paradise".'[2]

These hadith reports do not grant permission to someone suffering from a trouble or ailment to kill himself in order to be freed from misery; if someone commits suicide, he has earned Hell for himself.

---

[1] Narrated by al-Bukhārī in *al-Ṣaḥīḥ*: *Kitāb al-Anbiyā'* [The Book of the Prophets], chapter: 'What has Been Mentioned About the Children of Israel', 3:1272 §3276; Muslim in *al-Ṣaḥīḥ*: *Kitāb al-Īmān* [The Book ofFaith], chapter: 'The Severe Prohibition of Killing Oneself, and if Someone Commits Suicide with Something, He Will be Tormented with the Same in the Hellfire', 1:107 §113; and Ibn Ḥibbān in *al-Ṣaḥīḥ*, 13:329 §5989.

[2] Narrated by Muslim in *al-Ṣaḥīḥ*: *Kitāb al-Īmān* [The Book of Faith], chapter: 'The Strict Prohibition of Killing Oneself, and if Someone Commits Suicide with Something, He Will be Tormented with the Same in the Fire of Hell', 1:103 §109, 1:107 §113; and Ibn Ḥibbān in *al-Ṣaḥīḥ*, 13:329 §5989.

2.18 He Who Commits Suicide during Jihad Will Enter Hell

According to a hadith narrated in *Ṣaḥīḥ al-Bukhārī*,[1] a Muslim soldier fought gallantly in one of the military expeditions. The Companions reported his valour to the Messenger of God ﷺ, but he informed the Companions of his prophetic knowledge, telling them that he was one of the denizens of Hell. Upon hearing this, they felt astonished. Ultimately, when the man, unable to bear his injuries, committed suicide, they understood the reality of what the Prophet ﷺ said. The one who commits suicide is debarred from Paradise forever, irrespective of his valour and gallant performance as a soldier of God.

Sahl b. Saʿd ؓ said,

إِلْتَقَى النَّبِيُّ ﷺ وَالْمُشْرِكُونَ فِي بَعْضِ مَغَازِيهِ، فَاقْتَتَلُوا، فَمَالَ كُلُّ قَوْمٍ إِلَى عَسْكَرِهِمْ، وَفِي الْمُسْلِمِيْنَ رَجُلٌ لَا يَدَعُ مِنَ الْمُشْرِكِينَ شَاذَّةً وَلَا فَاذَّةً إِلَّا اتَّبَعَهَا، فَضَرَبَهَا بِسَيْفِهِ، فَقِيْلَ: يَا رَسُولَ اللهِ، مَا أَجْزَأَ أَحَدٌ، مَا أَجْزَأَ فُلَانٌ. فَقَالَ ﷺ: إِنَّهُ مِنْ أَهْلِ النَّارِ. فَقَالُوا: أَيُّنَا مِنْ أَهْلِ الْجَنَّةِ إِنْ كَانَ هَذَا مِنْ أَهْلِ النَّارِ! فَقَالَ رَجُلٌ مِنَ الْقَوْمِ: لَأَتَّبِعَنَّهُ، فَإِذَا أَسْرَعَ، وَأَبْطَأَ، كُنْتُ مَعَهُ حَتَّى جُرِحَ، فَاسْتَعْجَلَ الْمَوْتَ، فَوَضَعَ نِصَابَ سَيْفِهِ بِالْأَرْضِ وَذُبَابَهُ بَيْنَ ثَدْيَيْهِ، ثُمَّ تَحَامَلَ عَلَيْهِ، فَقَتَلَ نَفْسَهُ، فَجَاءَ الرَّجُلُ إِلَى النَّبِيِّ ﷺ: فَقَالَ: أَشْهَدُ أَنَّكَ رَسُولُ اللهِ. فَقَالَ: وَمَا ذَاكَ. فَأَخْبَرَهُ. فَقَالَ: إِنَّ الرَّجُلَ لَيَعْمَلُ بِعَمَلِ أَهْلِ الْجَنَّةِ فِيمَا يَبْدُو لِلنَّاسِ، وَإِنَّهُ لَمِنْ أَهْلِ النَّارِ. وَيَعْمَلُ بِعَمَلِ أَهْلِ النَّارِ فِيْمَا يَبْدُو لِلنَّاسِ وَهُوَ مِنْ أَهْلِ الْجَنَّةِ.

'The Prophet ﷺ and the pagans met in battle, and would fight each other and then go back to their troops. There was a man amongst the Muslims who would not leave

[1] Narrated by al-Bukhārī in *al-Ṣaḥīḥ*: *Kitāb al-maghāzī* [The Book of Military Expeditions], chapter: 'The Expedition of Khaybar', 4:1541 §3970; Muslim in *al-Ṣaḥīḥ*: *Kitāb al-Īmān* [The Book of Faith], chapter: 'The Severe Prohibition of Killing Oneself, and if Someone Commits Suicide with Something, He Will be Tormented with the Same in the Hellfire', 1:106 §112; Ibn Manda in *al-Īmān*, 2:663 §644; and ʿAbd b. Ḥumayd in *al-Musnad*, 1:169 §459.

any of the pagans who were separated or alone, save that he would go to them and strike them with his sword. Someone said to the Messenger of God ﷺ, "O Messenger of God! What a great reward that man has! What a great reward indeed!" [Upon hearing] the Messenger of God ﷺ said, "Indeed, he is from the people of the Fire". The Companions said, "If he is from the people of the Fire, then who amongst us is from the people of Paradise?" A man amongst them said, "I will follow him around [and keep an eye on him]". He went out with him and stopped whenever he stopped and hurried with him whenever he hurried. When he was wounded, he hastened his death by placing the hilt of his sword in the earth and its point at his breast and then fell on it and committed suicide. The man [who followed him around] went to the Messenger of God ﷺ and said, "I bear witness that you are the Messenger of God ﷺ!" He ﷺ asked him, "What happened?" The man informed him of what happened, upon which he ﷺ said, "Indeed, a man will do the acts of the people of Paradise—insomuch as it appears to people—even though he is from the denizens of the Fire; and indeed, a man will do the acts of the people of the Fire—insomuch as it appears to people—even though he is from the people of Paradise".'[1]

Abū Hurayra ؓ said,

شَهِدْنَا مَعَ رَسُولِ اللهِ ﷺ حُنَيْنًا، فَقَالَ لِرَجُلٍ مِمَّنْ يُدْعَى بِالْإِسْلَامِ: هَذَا مِنْ أَهْلِ النَّارِ. فَلَمَّا حَضَرْنَا الْقِتَالَ، قَاتَلَ الرَّجُلُ قِتَالًا شَدِيْدًا، فَأَصَابَتْهُ جِرَاحَةٌ. فَقِيْلَ: يَا رَسُولَ اللهِ، الرَّجُلُ الَّذِي قُلْتَ لَهُ آنِفًا إِنَّهُ مِنْ أَهْلِ النَّارِ، فَإِنَّهُ قَاتَلَ الْيَوْمَ قِتَالًا شَدِيْدًا،

[1] Narrated by al-Bukhārī in *al-Ṣaḥīḥ*: *Kitāb al-maghāzī* [The Book of Military Expeditions], chapter: 'The Expedition of Khaybar', 4:1541 §3970; Muslim in *al-Ṣaḥīḥ*: *Kitāb al-Īmān* [The Book of Faith], chapter: 'The Strict Prohibition of Killing Oneself, and if Someone Commits Suicide with Something, He Will be Tormented with the Same in the Fire of Hell', 1:106 §112; Ibn Manda in *al-Īmān* 2:663 §644; and ʿAbd b. Ḥumayd in *al-Musnad*, 1:169 §459.

وَقَدْ مَاتَ. فَقَالَ النَّبِيُّ ﷺ: إِلَى النَّارِ. فَكَادَ بَعْضُ الْمُسْلِمِينَ أَنْ يَرْتَابَ، فَبَيْنَمَا هُمْ عَلَى ذَلِكَ إِذْ قِيلَ: إِنَّهُ لَمْ يَمُتْ وَلَكِنَّ بِهِ جِرَاحًا شَدِيْدًا. فَلَمَّا كَانَ مِنَ اللَّيْلِ لَمْ يَصْبِرْ عَلَى الْجِرَاحِ، فَقَتَلَ نَفْسَهُ، فَأُخْبِرَ النَّبِيُّ ﷺ بِذَلِكَ، فَقَالَ: اللهُ أَكْبَرُ، أَشْهَدُ أَنِّي عَبْدُ اللهِ وَرَسُولُهُ. ثُمَّ أَمَرَ بِلَالًا، فَنَادَى فِي النَّاسِ أَنَّهُ لَا يَدْخُلُ الْجَنَّةَ إِلَّا نَفْسٌ مُسْلِمَةٌ، وَأَنَّ اللهَ يُؤَيِّدُ هَذَا الدِّيْنَ بِالرَّجُلِ الْفَاجِرِ.

'We participated in the Battle of Ḥunayn along with the Messenger of God ﷺ. The Messenger ﷺ said about a man who was considered to be a Muslim, "This man is from the denizens of the Fire". When we were in the thick of the battle, that man fought bravely and was wounded. Later, someone said to the Messenger of God ﷺ, "O Messenger of God! That man whom you earlier said is from the denizens of the Fire fought bravely today and died". The Prophet ﷺ said, "He is doomed to the Fire". Some of the Muslims [not grasping what the Prophet ﷺ said] were on the verge of doubt. As they were in that state, someone said that he did not die [of his wounds] but he is severely wounded. When nightfall came, he did not endure the pain of his wounds and committed suicide. When the Prophet ﷺ was informed of this he said, "God is the Greatest! I bear witness that I am God's servant and Messenger". Then he ordered Bilāl to gather people, and he called out to them, proclaiming that only a Muslim soul will enter Paradise and that God aids this religion by means of a sinful person'.[1]

2.19 The Prophet ﷺ Did Not Offer the Funeral Prayer over People Who Committed Suicide

We can infer the gravity of suicide from the fact that the

---

[1] Narrated by Muslim in *al-Ṣaḥīḥ*: *Kitāb al-Īmān* [The Book of Faith], chapter: 'The Strict Prohibition of Killing Oneself, and if Someone Commits Suicide with Something, He Will be Tormented with the Same in the Fire of Hell', 1:106 §111.

Messenger of God ﷺ did not offer the funeral prayer over those who committed it. Its seriousness can be further inferred from the fact that the Prophet ﷺ would supplicate even for his worst enemies and offer the funeral prayer over avowed hypocrites, until the Divine order was revealed, commanding him to abandon that practice—but he would not offer the funeral prayer over the one who committed suicide.

Imam Muslim reported from Jābir b. Samura ؓ who said,

أُتِيَ النَّبِيُّ ﷺ بِرَجُلٍ قَتَلَ نَفْسَهُ بِمَشَاقِصَ، فَلَمْ يُصَلِّ عَلَيْهِ.

> 'Someone who killed himself with a spear was brought to the Prophet ﷺ but he did not pray over him'.[1]

Imam al-Nasā'ī, Abū Dāwūd and Aḥmad b. Ḥanbal cited the same report in the following words:

عَنِ ابْنِ سَمُرَةَ أَنَّ رَجُلًا قَتَلَ نَفْسَهُ بِمَشَاقِصَ، فَقَالَ رَسُولُ اللهِ ﷺ: أَمَّا أَنَا فَلَا أُصَلِّي عَلَيْهِ.

> 'Ibn Samura ؓ reported that someone killed himself with a spear and the Messenger of God ﷺ said, "As for me, I shall not pray over him".'[2]

A deep study of Islamic teachings and thought reveals that Islam is a religion of peace, security and protection, and the true believers in the sight of God and His Messenger ﷺ are those who embody those qualities. Moreover, they also exemplify the lofty qualities of tolerance, forbearance and moderation.

---

[1] Narrated by Muslim in *al-Ṣaḥīḥ*: *Kitāb al-janā'iz* [The Book of Funeral Processions], chapter: 'On Not Offering Prayer over Someone who Committed Suicide', 2:672 §978.

[2] Narrated by al-Nasā'ī in *al-Sunan: Kitāb al-janā'iz* [The Book of Funeral Processions], chapter: 'On Not Offering Prayer over Someone who Committed Suicide', 4:66 §1964; Abū Dāwūd in *al-Sunan*: *Kitāb al-janā'iz* [The Book of Funeral Processions], chapter: 'The Imam Should Not Offer Prayer over Someone who Committed Suicide', 3:206 §3185; and Aḥmad b. Ḥanbal in *al-Musnad*, 5:92 §20891.

On the other hand, there are people who—in the name of making God's word uppermost—tread the dangerous path of hatred and prejudice, extremism and violence, injustice and oppression. They murder civilians and seize their wealth. Their claims to Islam are null and void. As false bearers of the banner of Islam and self-appointed defenders of faith, they do not have even the remotest link with Islam.

One can gauge the real value Islam attaches to human life and security from the Qur'ān. It declares that the murder of one individual is equal to murdering all of humanity and declares that it must be awarded capital punishment. Those who indiscriminately kill women and children are warned of a painful chastisement in the Hereafter. Since Islam does not allow the unjust killing of any individual, how can it possibly tolerate suicide attacks, bomb blasts, murder and revolt against the authority of the state that is charged with guaranteeing the safety and security of its citizens? Those who sit on the sidelines, passively participating in terrorism by motivating others to commit murder and shed blood, and those who actively commit violence, both have deviated from the straight path of Islam. Their behaviour brings Islam into disrepute.

Chapter 3

The Unlawfulness of Indiscriminately Killing Non-Muslims and Torturing Them

3.1 No Discrimination Between the Killings of Muslim and Non-Muslim Citizens

In the preceding pages, we demonstrated in the light of the Qur'ān and prophetic traditions that Islam is a religion of peace that guarantees the protection of life, property and honour for all members of society, without any discrimination on the basis of caste, colour, race and religion. In this chapter we will establish that the protection of the life, honour and property of non-Muslim citizens living in any Islamic state or any non-Muslim country is a binding duty upon the Muslims in general and the Islamic state in particular.

On the occasion of his Last Sermon, the Prophet ﷺ said, guaranteeing the protection of life, property and honour of the whole humankind,

إِنَّ دِمَاءَكُمْ وَأَمْوَالَكُمْ وَأَعْرَاضَكُمْ عَلَيْكُمْ حَرَامٌ، كَحُرْمَةِ يَوْمِكُمْ هَذَا، فِي شَهْرِكُمْ هَذَا، فِي بَلَدِكُمْ هَذَا، إِلَى يَوْمِ تَلْقَوْنَ رَبَّكُمْ.

> 'Indeed your blood and your property and your honour are inviolable, like the inviolability of this day of yours and this month of yours and this land of yours until the day you meet your Lord'.[1]

Therefore, it is completely forbidden to kill anyone unjustly, or plunder his wealth, or humiliate him or malign his honour.

Following this principle, killing Muslim and non-Muslim citizens—wherever they reside—is strictly prohibited on the basis of equality. It is clearly stated in the Qur'ān,

﴿مَن قَتَلَ نَفْسًا بِغَيْرِ نَفْسٍ أَوْ فَسَادٍ فِى ٱلْأَرْضِ فَكَأَنَّمَا قَتَلَ ٱلنَّاسَ جَمِيعًا﴾

---

[1] Narrated by al-Bukhārī in *al-Ṣaḥīḥ*: *Kitāb al-Ḥajj* [The Book of Pilgrimage], chapter: 'The Sermon During the Days of Mina', 2:620 §1654; and Muslim in *al-Ṣaḥīḥ*, 3:1305–1306 §1679.

> '*Whoever kills a person* [unjustly], *except as a punishment for murder or* [as a prescribed punishment for spreading] *disorder in the land, it is as if he killed all of humanity*'.[1]

This verse uses the word 'person' [*nafs*], which is a general expression that gives the verse a broad-based application. So in other words unjust killing is completely forbidden, no matter what religion, language or citizenship is held by the victim. This is a sin as grave as killing the whole of humanity. Therefore, the killing of non-Muslim citizens living in an Islamic state falls in the same category.

3.2 The Massacre of Civilian Population and Considering it Lawful is an Act of Disbelief

Killing a person is akin to disbelief. Imam Abū Manṣūr al-Māturīdī, one of the Imams of *Ahl al-Sunna*[2] in theology, interpreted the verse:

﴿مَن قَتَلَ نَفْسًا بِغَيْرِ نَفْسٍ أَوْ فَسَادٍ فِى ٱلْأَرْضِ فَكَأَنَّمَا قَتَلَ ٱلنَّاسَ جَمِيعًا﴾

> '*Whoever kills a person* [unjustly], *except as a punishment for murder or* [as a prescribed punishment for spreading] *disorder in the land, it is as if he killed all of humanity*'[3]

declaring that murder can be an act of disbelief. He wrote:

مَنِ اسْتَحَلَّ قَتْلَ نَفْسٍ حَرَّمَ اللهُ قَتْلَهَا بِغَيْرِ حَقٍّ، فَكَأَنَّمَا اسْتَحَلَّ قَتْلَ النَّاسِ جَمِيْعًا، لِأَنَّهُ يَكْفُرُ بِاسْتِحْلَالِهِ قَتْلَ نَفْسٍ مُحَرَّمٍ قَتْلُهَا، فَكَانَ كَاسْتِحْلَالِ قَتْلِ النَّاسِ جَمِيْعًا، لِأَنَّ مَنْ كَفَرَ بِآيَةٍ مِنْ كِتَابِ اللهِ يَصِيْرُ كَافِرًا بِالْكُلِّ. . . .

وَتَحْتَمِلُ الْآيَةُ وَجْهًا آخَرَ، وَهُوَ مَا قِيْلَ: إِنَّهُ يَجِبُ عَلَيْهِ مِنَ الْقَتْلِ مِثْلَمَا أَنَّهُ لَوْ قَتَلَ

---

[1] Qur'ān 5:32.

[2] *Ahl al-Sunna*: Literally, the people of the prophetic practice; the orthodox, Sunni majority, represented by the theological schools of Abū al-Ḥasan al-Ashʿarī and Abū Manṣūr al-Māturīdī and the four Sunni schools of jurisprudence. Ed.

[3] Qur'ān 5:32.

> النَّاسَ جَمِيْعًا. وَوَجْهٌ آخَرُ: أَنَّهُ يَلْزَمُ النَّاسَ جَمِيْعًا دَفْعُ ذَلِكَ عَنْ نَفْسِهِ وَمَعُونَتُهُ لَهُ، فَإِذَا قَتَلَهَا أَوْ سَعَى عَلَيْهَا بِالْفَسَادِ، فَكَأَنَّمَا سَعَى بِذَلِكَ عَلَى النَّاسِ كَافَّةً. . . . وَهَذَا يَدُلُّ أَنَّ الْآيَةَ نَزَلَتْ بِالْحُكْمِ فِي أَهْلِ الْكُفْرِ وَأَهْلِ الْإِسْلَامِ جَمِيْعاً، إِذَا سَعَوْا فِي الْأَرْضِ بِالْفَسَادِ.
>
> Whoever declares lawful the killing of a person whose killing has been forbidden by God (except when there is a valid reason), it is as if he considers it lawful to kill all of humanity. This is because he disbelieves by his declaring lawful the killing of one whose killing is unlawful, which is akin to declaring lawful the killing of humanity entire; because the one who disbelieves in one verse from God's Book disbelieves in the whole of it. . . .
>
> This verse contains another possible angle of interpretation, and it is as has been said: His murder of one person entails the same burden [in the Hereafter] as if he killed humanity entire. Another possible angle of interpretation is that it is necessary for everyone to make a collective effort to help and save the peaceful person from murder. So, when the murderer kills that harmless soul or attempts to harm it, it is as if he is attempting to do that to everyone. . . . This indicates that the verse was revealed as a ruling for the people of disbelief and the people of Islam together, if they sow corruption in the earth.[1]

In his *al-Lubāb fī ʿulūm al-Kitāb*, Abū Ḥafṣ al-Ḥanbalī interpreted the Qurʾānic verse, '*it is as if he killed all of humanity*',[2] and declared that the murder of one individual is comparable to the killing of all of humanity, and he quoted the sayings of different Imams in support of this position.

> قَالَ مُجَاهِدٌ: مَنْ قَتَلَ نَفْساً مُحَرَّمَةً يَصْلَى النَّارَ بِقَتْلِهَا، كَمَا يَصْلَاهَا لَوْ قَتَلَ النَّاسَ

---

[1] Abū Manṣūr al-Māturīdī, *Taʾwilāt Ahl al-Sunna*, 3:501.

[2] Qurʾān 5:32.

جَمِيْعًا. وَقَالَ قَتَادَةُ: أَعْظَمَ اللهُ أَجْرَهَا وَعَظَّمَ وِزْرَهَا، مَعْنَاهُ: مَنِ اسْتَحَلَّ قَتْلَ مُسْلِمٍ بِغَيْرِ حَقِّهِ، فَكَأَنَّمَا قَتَلَ النَّاسَ جَمِيْعًا. وَقَالَ الْحَسَنُ: ﴿فَكَأَنَّمَا قَتَلَ ٱلنَّاسَ جَمِيعًا﴾، يَعْنِي: أَنَّهُ يَجِبُ عَلَيْهِ مِنَ الْقِصَاصِ بِقَتْلِهَا، مِثْلُ الَّذِي يَجِبُ عَلَيْهِ لَوْ قَتَلَ النَّاسَ جَمِيْعًا.

قَوْلُهُ تَعَالَى: ﴿إِنَّمَا جَزَآؤُاْ ٱلَّذِينَ يُحَارِبُونَ ٱللَّهَ وَرَسُولَهُ وَيَسْعَوْنَ فِى ٱلْأَرْضِ فَسَادًا أَن يُقَتَّلُوٓاْ أَوْ يُصَلَّبُوٓاْ أَوْ تُقَطَّعَ أَيْدِيهِمْ وَأَرْجُلُهُم مِّنْ خِلَٰفٍ أَوْ يُنفَوْاْ مِنَ ٱلْأَرْضِ ذَٰلِكَ لَهُمْ خِزْىٌ فِى ٱلدُّنْيَا وَلَهُمْ فِى ٱلْأَخِرَةِ عَذَابٌ عَظِيمٌ. إِلَّا ٱلَّذِينَ تَابُواْ مِن قَبْلِ أَن تَقْدِرُواْ عَلَيْهِمْ فَٱعْلَمُوٓاْ أَنَّ ٱللَّهَ غَفُورٌ رَّحِيمٌ﴾

وَقَوْلُهُ: ﴿يُحَارِبُونَ ٱللَّهَ﴾، أَيْ: يُحَارِبُونَ أَوْلِيَاءَهُ، كَذَا قَدَّرَهُ الْجُمْهُورُ. وَقَالَ الزَّمَخْشَرِيُّ: يُحَارِبُونَ رَسُولَ اللهِ، وَمُحَارَبَةُ الْمُسْلِمِيْنَ فِي حُكْمِ مُحَارَبَتِهِ. نَزَلَتْ هَذِهِ الْآيَةُ فِي قُطَّاعِ الطَّرِيْقِ مِنَ الْمُسْلِمِيْنَ. (وَهَذَا قَوْلُ) أَكْثَرِ الْفُقَهَاءِ.

أَنَّ قَوْلَهُ تَعَالَى: ﴿ٱلَّذِينَ يُحَارِبُونَ ٱللَّهَ وَرَسُولَهُ وَيَسْعَوْنَ فِى ٱلْأَرْضِ فَسَادًا﴾ يَتَنَاوَلُ كُلَّ مَنْ يُوصَفُ بِهَذِهِ، سَوَاءٌ كَانَ مُسْلِمًا أَوْ كَافِرًا، وَلَا يُقَالُ: الْآيَةُ نَزَلَتْ فِي الْكُفَّارِ، لِأَنَّ الْعِبْرَةَ بِعُمُومِ اللَّفْظِ لَا بِخُصُوصِ السَّبَبِ، فَإِنْ قِيْلَ: الْمُحَارِبُونَ هُمُ الَّذِيْنَ يَجْتَمِعُونَ وَلَهُمْ مَنَعَةٌ، وَيَقْصِدُونَ الْمُسْلِمِيْنَ فِي أَرْوَاحِهِمْ وَدِمَائِهِمْ، وَاتَّفَقُوا عَلَى أَنَّ هَذِهِ الصِّفَةَ إِذَا حُصِلَتْ فِي الصَّحْرَاءِ كَانُوا قُطَّاعَ الطَّرِيْقِ، وَأَمَّا إِنْ حُصِلَتْ فِي الْأَمْصَارِ، فَقَالَ الْأَوْزَاعِيُّ وَمَالِكٌ وَاللَّيْثُ بْنُ سَعْدٍ وَالشَّافِعِيُّ: هُمْ أَيْضًا قُطَّاعُ الطَّرِيْقِ، هَذَا الْحَدُّ عَلَيْهِمْ، قَالُوا: وَإِنَّهُمْ فِي الْمُدُنِ يَكُونُونَ أَعْظَمَ ذَنْبًا فَلَا أَقَلَّ مِنَ الْمُسَاوَاةِ، وَاحْتَجُّوا بِالْآيَةِ وَعُمُومِهَا، وَلِأَنَّ هَذَا حَدٌّ فَلَا يَخْتَلِفُ كَسَائِرِ الْحُدُودِ.

Mujāhid said, 'If someone kills a soul unjustly, he will go to Hell due to that murder, just as he would have gone to Hell if he killed humanity entire'. Qatāda said, 'God has made the reward for saving it [a life] tremendous and made the burden of sin [for taking a life unjustly] tremendous, too. This means that whoever declares it lawful for himself to kill a Muslim, it is as if he killed all humanity'. Interpreting the same verse, al-Ḥasan al-Baṣrī said, 'This means that he is liable to legal retribution [*qiṣāṣ*] for killing it [the sinless soul] as would be the person who killed all of humanity'.

God says: '*Indeed, those who wage war against God and His Messenger and remain engaged in creating mischief in the land* [i.e., perpetrate terrorism, robbery and burglary amongst people], *their punishment is that they should be slain, or crucified, or their hands and their feet on opposite sides should be cut off, or that they should be exiled from the land. That is for them a humiliation in this world, and for them there is a terrible torment in the Hereafter—except those who turn to God in repentance before you overpower them. So, know that God is Most Forgiving, Ever-Merciful*'.[1]

The phrase in the verse, '*yuhāribūn Allāh*' ('*wage war against God*'), implies that they wage war against the friends of God. That is the interpretation maintained by the overwhelming majority of scholars. Al-Zamakhsharī said, 'They wage war against the Messenger of God, and waging war against the Muslims takes the same ruling as waging war against him'. This verse was revealed about the brigands [highway robbers: *quṭṭāʿ al-ṭarīq*] amongst the Muslims, and [this position is held] by most of the jurists.[2]

Indeed, God's statement, '*Those who wage war against God and His Messenger and remain engaged in creating mischief in the land*', includes everyone who possesses these traits, whether he is a Muslim or a disbeliever. One cannot object or claim that the verse was revealed regarding the disbelievers, because the point of consideration is the generality of its expression, not the particular circumstance in which it was revealed.[3] If it is

[1] Ibid., 5:33–34.

[2] Ḥusayn al-Baghawī, *Maʿālim al-Tanzīl*, 2:33; and al-Rāzī, *al-Tafsīr al-kabīr*, 11:196.

[3] This is a maxim of Qurʾānic hermeneutics. Ed.

said that those who wage war [*muḥāribūn*] are those who join forces and who possess power and target the Muslims in their lives and wealth, and that they [the scholars] agree that if these traits are found amongst people of the desert wastelands—then they are brigands. And if these traits are adopted by a group residing in cities, al-Awzāʿī, Mālik, Layth b. Saʿd and al-Shāfiʿī all agree that they, too, are considered brigands and that the same prescribed punishment is to be applied against them. They stated that when their crimes take place in populated areas the sin is severer. They inferred this from the aforementioned verse and the generality of its expression, and because it is a prescribed punishment, and therefore it is no different from the other prescribed punishments.[1]

3.3 The Killing of Non-Muslim Citizens Makes Paradise Forbidden for the Killer

The non-Muslim citizens of an Islamic state enjoy the same rights and safeguards as their Muslim counterparts. The first right endowed upon them by the Islamic state is that of protection against external aggression and domestic oppression and encroachments, so they can live their life peacefully, inwardly and outwardly.

Abū Bakra ﵁ reported that the Prophet ﷺ said,

مَنْ قَتَلَ مُعَاهَدًا فِي غَيْرِ كُنْهِهِ، حَرَّمَ اللهُ عَلَيْهِ الْجَنَّةَ.

'Any Muslim who unjustly kills a non-Muslim with whom there is a peace treaty [*muʿāhad*], God will make Paradise forbidden for him'.[2]

---

[1] Abū Ḥafṣ al-Ḥanbalī, *al-Lubāb fī ʿulūm al-Kitāb*, 7:301.

[2] Narrated by al-Nasāʾī in *al-Sunan*: *Kitāb al-qasāma* [The Book of Apportioning Wealth], chapter: 'The Gravity of Killing Non-Muslim Citizens', 8:24 §4747; Abū Dāwūd in *al-Sunan*: *Kitāb al-jihād* [The Book of Sacred Martial Struggle], chapter: 'Fulfilling the Contract of a Non-Muslim Citizen and the Sanctity of His Contract', 3:83 §2760; Aḥmad b. Ḥanbal in *al-Musnad*, 5:36, 38 §§20393, 20419; al-Dārimī in *al-Sunan*, 2:308 §2504; and al-Ḥākim in *al-Mustadrak*, 2:154 §2631. Al-Ḥākim said, 'This is a tradition with a rigorously authentic

ʿAbd Allāh b. ʿUmar ﷺ reported that the Prophet ﷺ said,

مَنْ قَتَلَ مُعَاهَدًا لَمْ يَرِحْ رَائِحَةَ الْجَنَّةِ، وَإِنَّ رِيحَهَا تُوجَدُ مِنْ مَسِيْرَةِ أَرْبَعِيْنَ عَامًا.

> 'Anyone who kills a non-Muslim under treaty [*muʿāhad*] will not smell the fragrance of Paradise, even though its fragrance can be smelt at a distance of forty years'.[1]

Therefore, the one who unjustly murders a non-Muslim citizen will not approach Paradise; rather, he will be kept away from it by a distance of forty years. Commenting on this hadith, Anwar Shāh Kāshmīrī writes in his book *Fayḍ al-Bārī*:

قَوْلُهُ ﷺ: مَنْ قَتَلَ مُعَاهَدًا لَمْ يَرِحْ رَائِحَةَ الْجَنَّةِ، وَمُخُّ الْحَدِيْثِ: إِنَّکَ أَيُّهَا الْمُخَاطَبُ: قَدْ عَلِمْتَ مَا فِي قَتْلِ الْمُسْلِمِ مِنَ الْإِثْمِ، فَإِنَّ شَنَاعَتَهُ بَلَغَتْ مَبْلَغَ الْكُفْرِ، حَيْثُ أَوْجَبَ التَّخْلِيْدَ. أَمَّا قَتْلُ مُعَاهَدٍ، فَأَيْضًا لَيْسَ بِهَيِّنٍ، فَإِنَّ قَاتِلَهُ أَيْضًا لَا يَجِدُ رَائِحَةَ الْجَنَّةِ.

> Regarding his statement ﷺ, 'Anyone who kills a non-Muslim under treaty [*muʿāhad*] will not smell the fragrance of Paradise, even though its fragrance can be smelt at a distance of forty years', the quintessential meaning of it, dear brother, can be expressed as such: You know the gravity of sin for killing a Muslim, for its odiousness has reached the point of disbelief, and it necessitates that [the killer abides in Hell] forever. As for killing a non-Muslim citizen [*muʿāhad*], it is similarly no small matter, for the one who does it will not smell the fragrance of Paradise.[2]

---

chain of transmission'.

[1] Narrated by al-Bukhārī in *al-Ṣaḥīḥ*: *Kitāb al-jizya* [The Book of Taxation for Non-Muslims Living in an Islamic State], chapter: 'The Sin of Someone Who Kills a Non-Muslim Citizen Without His Having Committed a Crime', 3:1155 §2995; Ibn Mājah in *al-Sunan*: *Kitāb al-diyāt* [The Book of Blood Money], chapter: 'Someone Who Kills a Non-Muslim Citizen', 2:896 § 2686; al-Bazzār in *al-Musnad*, 6:368 §2383.

[2] Anwar Shāh Kāshmīrī, *Fayḍ al-Bārī ʿalā Ṣaḥīḥ al-Bukhārī*, 4:288.

3.4 The Unlawfulness of Killing Foreign Delegates and Religious Leaders

Islam teaches peace and tolerance in national and international affairs. According to the teachings of the Qurʾān and hadith, it is forbidden to kill a diplomat hailing from a hostile nation who comes to a Muslim state for the purpose of diplomacy. Many non-Muslim diplomats and delegates would come to the Prophet ﷺ on various occasions and he not only treated them with the utmost respect, but also instructed his Companions to treat them well. It is even recorded that the representatives of Musaylama the liar, a false claimant to prophethood, visited the Prophet ﷺ and confessed to their apostasy, yet the Prophet ﷺ treated them well because they were diplomats. ʿAbd Allāh b. Masʿūd ؓ said,

> إِنِّي كُنْتُ عِنْدَ رَسُولِ اللهِ ﷺ جَالِسًا إِذْ دَخَلَ هَذَا (عَبْدُ اللهِ بْنُ نُوَاحَةَ) وَرَجُلٌ وَافِدَيْنِ مِنْ عِنْدِ مُسَيْلَمَةَ. فَقَالَ لَهُمَا رَسُولُ اللهِ ﷺ: أَتَشْهَدَانِ أَنِّي رَسُولُ اللهِ؟ فَقَالَا لَهُ: نَشْهَدُ أَنَّ مُسَيْلَمَةَ رَسُولُ اللهِ، فَقَالَ: آمَنْتُ بِاللهِ وَرُسُلِهِ، لَوْ كُنْتُ قَاتِلًا وَافِدًا لَقَتَلْتُكُمَا.
>
> 'I was in the presence of God's Messenger ﷺ when this man [ʿAbd Allāh b. Nuwāḥa] and another man came as official representatives of Musaylama (the liar). The Messenger of God ﷺ asked them, "Do you bear witness that I am the Messenger of God?" They said to him, "We bear witness that Musaylama is the Messenger of God!" The Messenger of God ﷺ said to them, "I believe in God and His Messengers. Were I to execute ambassadors, I would have executed both of you".'[1]

See that despite the apostasy and disbelief of Musaylama's followers, extreme tolerance was shown towards them. They were not punished in any way. Because they were diplomats, they were

---

[1] Narrated by al-Dārimī in *al-Sunan*, 2:307 §2503; Aḥmad b. Ḥanbal in *al-Musnad*, 1:404 §3837; al-Nasāʾī in *al-Sunan al-kubrā*, 5:205 §8675; Abū Yaʿlā in *al-Musnad*, 9:31 §5097; and al-Ḥākim in *al-Mustadrak*, 3:54 §4378.

neither imprisoned nor ordered to be killed.

According to a narration in the *Musnad* of Aḥmad b. Ḥanbal,[1] the *Muṣannaf* of ʿAbd al-Razzāq [al-Ṣanʿānī][2] and the *Musnad* of al-Bazzār,[3] it is impermissible to kill either diplomats or their diplomatic staff.

The aforementioned hadith establishes that safeguarding the life of diplomats and foreign representatives is the Sunna of the Prophet ﷺ. ʿAbd Allāh b. Masʿūd ؓ said,

فَجَرَتْ سُنَّةٌ أَنْ لَا يُقْتَلَ الرَّسُولُ.

> 'It is an established Sunna that ambassadors are not to be killed'.[4]

This statement of the Messenger of God ﷺ set the precedent in international law with respect to diplomatic protection. This further illustrates that all the personnel staffed in an embassy on diplomatic assignments are entitled to the same treatment, and it is impermissible to kill them. In recent years in Pakistan and other parts of the world there have been a number of incidents where foreign diplomats and engineers have been kidnapped and killed. Unfortunately, those who commit these actions continue to call themselves *Mujāhidūn* [those who wage martial jihad] despite the fact that their actions completely contravene the teachings of the Prophet ﷺ.

Just as foreign diplomats enjoy sanctity and protection in Islamic law, so too do non-Muslim religious leaders; it is strictly forbidden to kill them. ʿAbd Allāh b. ʿAbbās ؓ said,

كَانَ رَسُولُ اللهِ ﷺ إِذَا بَعَثَ جُيُوشَهُ قَالَ: لَا تَغْدِرُوا، وَلَا تَغُلُّوا، وَلَا تُمَثِّلُوا، وَلَا تَقْتُلُوا الْوِلْدَانَ وَلَا أَصْحَابَ الصَّوَامِعِ.

> 'When the Messenger of God ﷺ would dispatch his troops

[1] Narrated by Aḥmad b. Ḥanbal in *al-Musnad*, 1:390, 396 §3708, 3761.

[2] Narrated by ʿAbd al-Razzāq in *al-Muṣannaf*, 10:196 §18708.

[3] Narrated by al-Bazzār in *al-Musnad*, 5:142 §1733.

[4] Narrated by Aḥmad b. Ḥanbal in *al-Musnad*, 1:390 §3708.

> he would say [to them], "Do not act treacherously, do not steal the spoils of war, do not disfigure the dead bodies, and do not kill children and priests".'[1]

This hadith establishes that, even during times of war—let alone in normal circumstances—it is impermissible to kill religious leaders.

3.5 The Retribution [*Qiṣāṣ*] of Muslims and Non-Muslims is the Same

In Islam, retribution is necessary when someone murders someone else intentionally, whether the victim is Muslim or non-Muslim; however, the payment of monetary compensation [*diya*] is obligatory if it was an accidental killing. God says:

﴿وَلَكُمْ فِي ٱلْقِصَاصِ حَيَوٰةٌ يَٰٓأُوْلِي ٱلْأَلْبَٰبِ لَعَلَّكُمْ تَتَّقُونَ﴾

> '*And there is a* [guarantee of] *life for you in retribution, O wise people, so that you may guard* [against bloodshed and destruction]'.[2]

Regarding unintentional killing, God says,

﴿مَن قَتَلَ مُؤْمِنًا خَطَـًٔا فَتَحْرِيرُ رَقَبَةٍ مُّؤْمِنَةٍ وَدِيَةٌ مُّسَلَّمَةٌ إِلَىٰٓ أَهْلِهِۦٓ إِلَّآ أَن يَصَّدَّقُواْ﴾

> '*Whoever kills a Muslim unintentionally shall* [be liable to] *free a male or female Muslim and pay blood money, to be handed over to the heirs of the person slain, unless they forgo it*'.[3]

In the former verse, retribution, or the command to kill the murderer for his crime of murder, has been described. There is a complete consensus amongst the Muslim community that the unjust killer should be killed by way of retribution, unless the

---

[1] Narrated by Aḥmad b. Ḥanbal in *al-Musnad*, 1:330 §2728; Ibn Abī Shayba in *al-Muṣannaf*, 6:484 §33132; Abū Yaʿlā in *al-Musnad*, 4:422 §2549; and mentioned by Ibn Rushd in *Bidāyat al-mujtahid*, 1:281.

[2] Qurʾān 2:179.

[3] Ibid., 4:92.

heirs of the killed pardon the killer. The latter verse mentions monetary compensation. In Islamic law, if someone accidently and unintentionally kills someone else, he or she is ordered to pay blood money to the heirs of the killed.

ʿAbd al-Raḥmān b. Baylamānī ﷺ said,

أَنَّ رَجُلًا مِنَ الْمُسْلِمِيْنَ قَتَلَ رَجُلًا مِنْ أَهْلِ الْكِتَابِ، فَرُفِعَ إِلَى النَّبِيِّ ﷺ، فَقَالَ رَسُولُ اللهِ ﷺ: أَنَا أَحَقُّ مَنْ وَفَّى بِذِمَّتِهِ، ثُمَّ أَمَرَ بِهِ فَقُتِلَ.

> 'There was a man from the Muslims who killed a man from the People of the Book.[1] The case was presented to the Prophet ﷺ and he said, "I am most responsible of all for fulfilling the rights of those under his care [non-Muslim citizens]". Then he ordered [the killing of the Muslim killer by way of retribution] and he was killed'.[2]

The Prophet ﷺ explained retribution and monetary compensation in the following words:

مَنْ أُصِيْبَ بِقَتْلٍ أَوْ خَبْلٍ، فَإِنَّهُ يَخْتَارُ إِحْدَى ثَلَاثٍ: إِمَّا أَنْ يَقْتَصَّ، وَإِمَّا أَنْ يَعْفُوَ، وَإِمَّا أَنْ يَأْخُذَ الدِّيَةَ. فَإِنْ أَرَادَ الرَّابِعَةَ فَخُذُوا عَلَى يَدَيْهِ ﴿فَمَنِ ٱعْتَدَىٰ بَعْدَ ذَٰلِكَ فَلَهُۥ عَذَابٌ أَلِيمٌ﴾.

> 'If someone's relative is killed, or if one of his extremities is cut off, he may choose one of three options: he may retaliate, forgive or receive compensation. But if he wishes a fourth [something that exceeds the bounds set by the Shariah], you must hold him back [for God says,] "*After this, whoever exceeds the limits shall receive a painful punishment*" [Qurʾān 5:94].'[3]

---

[1] *Ahl al-Kitāb*, or, 'the People of the Book', is a term designating the Jews and the Christians. Ed.

[2] Cited by al-Shāfiʿī in *al-Musnad*, p. 343; narrated by Abū Nuʿaym in *Musnad Abī Ḥanīfa*, p. 104; cited by al-Shaybānī in *al-Mabsūṭ*, 4:488; and narrated by al-Bayhaqī in *al-Sunan al-kubrā*, 8:30 §15696.

[3] Narrated by Abū Dāwūd in *al-Sunan*: *Kitāb al-diyāt* [The Book of Blood Money], chapter: 'The Leader Should Urge Forgiveness in the Matter of Shedding

It is clearly established from these prophetic traditions that Muslims and non-Muslims share an equal status with respect to monetary compensation and retribution. According to one report, ʿAlī b. Abī Ṭālib ﷺ said,

إِذَا قَتَلَ الْمُسْلِمُ النَّصْرَانِيَّ قُتِلَ بِهِ.

> 'If a Muslim kills a Christian, he should be killed in retribution'.[1]

The Prophet ﷺ also granted non-Muslims the same rights with regard to monetary compensation. He ﷺ said,

دِيَةُ الْيَهُودِيِّ وَالنَّصْرَانِيِّ وَكُلِّ ذِمِّيٍّ مِثْلُ دِيَةِ الْمُسْلِمِ.

> 'The blood money for a [peaceful] Jew, a Christian and every non-Muslim citizen is like that of the Muslim [i.e., their heirs receive the same amount of monetary compensation as a Muslim family]'.[2]

Imam Abū Ḥanīfa ﷺ said,

دِيَةُ الْيَهُودِيِّ وَالنَّصْرَانِيِّ وَالْمَجُوسِيِّ مِثْلُ دِيَةِ الْحُرِّ الْمُسْلِمِ.

> 'The blood money for a [peaceful] Jew, Christian or Zoroastrian is equal to that of a free Muslim'.[3]

Imam Ibn Shihāb al-Zuhrī said,

إِنَّ دِيَةَ الْمُعَاهَدِ فِي عَهْدِ أَبِي بَكْرٍ وَعُمَرَ وَعُثْمَانَ ﷺ مِثْلُ دِيَةِ الْحُرِّ الْمُسْلِمِ.

> 'During the reigns of Abū Bakr, ʿUmar, ʿUthmān and ʿAlī ﷺ, the blood money for a non-Muslim citizen was equal to that of a free Muslim'.[4]

Blood', 4:169 §4496; and ʿAbd al-Razzāq in *al-Muṣannaf*, 10:86 §18454.

[1] Cited by al-Shaybānī in *al-Ḥujja*, 4:349; and al-Shāfiʿī in *al-Umm*, 7:320.

[2] Narrated by ʿAbd al-Razzāq in *al-Muṣannaf*, 10:97–98; and cited by Ibn Rushd in *Bidāyat al-mujtahid*, 2:310.

[3] Narrated by Ibn Abī Shayba in *al-Muṣannaf*, 5:407 §27448; and ʿAbd al-Razzāq in *al-Muṣannaf*, 10:95, 97, 99.

[4] Cited by al-Shaybānī in *al-Ḥujja*, 4:351; and al-Shāfiʿī in *al-Umm*, 7:321.

The position of the Ḥanafī school of jurisprudence is that a Muslim should be killed in retribution for killing a non-Muslim citizen. This position is supported by the general import of the texts within the Qurʾān and hadith, which make retribution obligatory. Muslim and non-Muslim blood shares an equal amount of inviolability and sanctity, without any discrimination. Imam al-Nakhaʿī, Ibn Abī Laylā, al-Shaʿbī and ʿUthmān al-Battī also share this view held by the Ḥanafī school.

A doubt may emerge from hearing the saying of the Prophet ﷺ,

لَا يُقْتَلُ مُسْلِمٌ بِكَافِرٍ.

> 'A Muslim is not to be killed in retaliation for murdering a disbeliever'.[1]

So what does it mean? The jurists explained this and said that here the word 'disbeliever' does not imply a peaceful citizen: it signifies a combatant who is killed. There is to be no retribution in this case. This is an international law in effect in all countries of the world and there is no difference of opinion about it.

The great jurist and Qurʾānic exegete, Imam al-Jaṣṣāṣ, stated that in this hadith, 'a disbeliever' means the non-Muslim in a state of war. It does not mean the non-Muslim who is a citizen of an Islamic state or a peaceful non-Muslim citizen of a non-Muslim state.[2]

3.6 The Unlawfulness of Harming a Non-Muslim Citizen out of Revenge

According to the Qurʾān and Sunna, every person is responsible for his or her actions. According to this rule, only the doer of an act of injustice is liable to punishment, and no one else can be held responsible for that. The punishment for his or her crime cannot be awarded to his or her family, friends or tribe. God says,

---

[1] Narrated by al-Bukhārī in *al-Ṣaḥīḥ*: *Kitāb al-ʿilm* [The Book of Knowledge], chapter: 'On Writing Down Knowledge', 1:53 §111.

[2] Cited by Abū Bakr al-Jaṣṣāṣ in *Aḥkām al-Qurʾān*, chapter: 'A Muslim's Murder of a Disbeliever', pp. 140–144.

﴿وَلَا تَكْسِبُ كُلُّ نَفْسٍ إِلَّا عَلَيْهَا وَلَا تَزِرُ وَازِرَةٌ وِزْرَ أُخْرَىٰ ثُمَّ إِلَىٰ رَبِّكُم مَّرْجِعُكُمْ فَيُنَبِّئُكُم بِمَا كُنتُمْ فِيهِ تَخْتَلِفُونَ﴾

'*And whatever* [sin] *each soul earns* [its evil outcome] *falls back upon it. And no bearer of burden will bear another's burden. Then you are to return to your Lord alone, and He will inform you of that wherein you used to differ*'.[1]

Islam does not allow anyone to punish common people for the oppressive actions of oppressors. The Prophet ﷺ said,

لَا يُؤْخَذُ مِنْهُمْ رَجُلٌ بِظُلْمِ آخَرَ.

'No man amongst them [the peaceful non-Muslim citizens] shall be punished as a penalty for the injustice of a coreligionist'.[2]

All of this clearly demonstrates that those who seek to exact revenge by terrorising and killing people from other nations oppose and violate the manifest Qur'ānic injunctions and prophetic traditions.

3.7 The Unlawfulness of Usurping the Wealth of Non-Muslims

In Islam, it is unlawful to usurp the wealth of others. God says,

﴿وَلَا تَأْكُلُوٓاْ أَمْوَالَكُم بَيْنَكُم بِٱلْبَٰطِلِ وَتُدْلُواْ بِهَآ إِلَى ٱلْحُكَّامِ لِتَأْكُلُواْ فَرِيقًا مِّنْ أَمْوَالِ ٱلنَّاسِ بِٱلْإِثْمِ وَأَنتُمْ تَعْلَمُونَ﴾

'*And do not eat up one another's wealth amongst yourselves through injustice, nor take wealth to the authorities* [as a bribe] *so that, this way, you may swallow*

[1] Qur'ān 6:164.

[2] Cited by Abū Yūsuf in *Kitāb al-kharāj*, p. 78; and al-Balādhurī in *Futūḥ al-buldān*, p. 90.

a portion of others' wealth unfairly, while you are aware [that this is a sin]'.[1]

The Prophet ﷺ has also forbidden the pilfering of others' wealth and property. He said,

إِنَّ دِمَاءَكُمْ وَأَمْوَالَكُمْ عَلَيْكُمْ حَرَامٌ.

'Indeed, your blood and your property are unlawful to you'.[2]

Like the life of non-Muslim citizens, the protection of their property is also the responsibility of the Muslim state. There is a consensus amongst the Muslims over this matter. Imam Abū ʿUbayd al-Qāsim b. Sallām, Ibn Zanjawayh, Ibn Saʿd and Abū Yūsuf have all cited the provision of the Prophet's agreement with the Christians of Najran:

وَلِنَجْرَانَ وَحَاشِيَتِهَا جِوَارُ اللهِ وَذِمَّةُ مُحَمَّدٍ رَسُولِ اللهِ ﷺ، عَلَى أَمْوَالِهِمْ وَأَنْفُسِهِمْ وَأَرْضِهِمْ وَمِلَّتِهِمْ، وَغَائِبِهِمْ وَشَاهِدِهِمْ، وَعَشِيرَتِهِمْ وَبِيَعِهِمْ، وَكُلِّ مَا تَحْتَ أَيْدِيهِمْ مِنْ قَلِيلٍ أَوْ كَثِيرٍ.

'Indeed, Najran and her allies are under the protection of God and the guarantee of the Messenger of God ﷺ. They are to be protected in their wealth, lives, lands and religion; this includes those who are present and those who are absent amongst them; and their families, goods and everything in their possession, be it plentiful or scarce'.[3]

The letter ʿUmar wrote to Abū ʿUbayda ؓ, the then Governor of Syria, also contains similar provisions,

---

[1] Qurʾān 2:188.

[2] Narrated by al-Bukhārī in *al-Ṣaḥīḥ*: *Kitāb al-Ḥajj* [The Book of Pilgrimage], chapter: 'The Sermon During the days of Mina', 2:620 §1654.

[3] Cited by Abū Yūsuf in *al-Kharāj*, 78; Abū ʿUbayd al-Qāsim b. Sallām in *Kitāb al-amwāl*, p. 244–245 §503; Ibn Saʿd in *al-Ṭabaqāt al-kubrā*, 1:288, 358; Ibn Zanjawayh in *Kitāb al-amwāl*, pp. 449–450 §732; and al-Balādhurī in *Futūḥ al-buldān*, p. 90.

وَامْنَعِ الْمُسْلِمِيْنَ مِنْ ظُلْمِهِمْ، وَالْإِضْرَارِ بِهِمْ، وَأَكْلِ أَمْوَالِهِمْ إِلَّا بِحِلِّهَا.

'See to it that you prohibit the Muslims [under your command] from oppressing them [the non-Muslim citizens], harming them or illegally plundering their wealth'.[1]

ʿAlī b. Abī Ṭālib ﷺ said,

إِنَّمَا بَذَلُوا الْجِزْيَةَ لِتَكُونَ دِمَاؤُهُمْ كَدِمَائِنَا وَأَمْوَالُهُمْ كَأَمْوَالِنَا.

'The non-Muslim citizens pay the tax[2] so that their blood and property should be as inviolable as ours'.[3]

So much importance has been associated with the life, property and honour of the non-Muslim citizens that the Muslim state has been equally charged with protecting them as it protects the Muslim citizens. In fact, the Muslims have been prohibited from destroying the pork and wine belonging to non-Muslim citizens, and if they do, they must pay a fine. The famous book of Ḥanafī jurisprudence, *al-Durr al-mukhtār*, states,

يَضْمَنُ الْمُسْلِمُ قِيْمَةَ خَمْرِهِ وَخِنْزِيْرِهِ إِذَا أَتْلَفَهُ.

'The Muslim who destroys his [the Christian's] wine and pork is legally responsible for paying its price'.[4]

Islam has forbidden theft and prescribed strict punishment for it. When a woman from the Quraysh tribe committed theft during the time of the Prophet ﷺ, he ordered the prescribed punishment to be imposed on her. When people requested him to soften the punishment he ﷺ said,

وَأَيْمُ اللهِ، لَوْ أَنَّ فَاطِمَةَ بِنْتَ مُحَمَّدٍ سَرَقَتْ، لَقَطَعْتُ يَدَهَا.

---

1 Cited by Abū Yūsuf in *al-Kharāj*, p. 152.

2 A tax levied on the non-Muslim citizens of an Islamic state in lieu of military service. Ed.

3 Cited by Ibn Qudāma in *al-Mughnī*, 9:181; and al-Zaylaʿī in *Naṣb al-rāya*, 3:381.

4 Al-Ḥaṣkafī, *al-Durr al-mukhtār*, 2:223; and al-Shāmī, *Radd al-muḥtār*, 3:273.

> 'By God, had my daughter Fāṭima stolen, I would have applied the prescribed punishment upon her, too'.[1]

Imam Yaḥyā b. Sharaf al-Nawawī writes,

إِنَّ مَالَ الذِّمِّيِّ وَالْمُعَاهَدِ وَالْمُرْتَدِّ فِي هَذَا كَمَالِ الْمُسْلِمِ.

> 'In this context, the wealth of the non-Muslim citizen, the non-Muslim under agreement of protection and the apostate is certainly like the wealth of a Muslim'.[2]

Imam Ibn Qudāma al-Ḥanbalī mentioned that the prescribed punishment should be enforced if the possessions of a non-Muslim are stolen, just as it is imposed when a Muslim's belongings are stolen.[3] Ibn Ḥazm mentioned that there is no disagreement that the prescribed punishment should be applied on the Muslim who steals the possessions of a non-Muslim citizen.[4] Ibn Rushd said that there is a consensus on this point.[5]

The Muslim and non-Muslim citizens are equal in the eyes of Islamic law when it comes to the theft of belongings. If a Muslim steals the belongings of a non-Muslim, the prescribed punishment will be enforced upon him, and if he unlawfully seizes his wealth, a discretionary punishment from the ruler [*taʿzīr*] will be carried out. Islam has given so much importance to the belongings of non-Muslims that every item of their belongings, which they so declare, is to be safeguarded, though it may not fall in the category of belongings in the eyes of the Muslims, such as wine and pork. If anyone destroys the wine belonging to a Muslim, neither a prescribed punishment nor a discretionary punishment will be enforced against him. On the other hand, if a Muslim destroys the wine and pork belonging to a non-Muslim, he will be required to

---

[1] Narrated by al-Bukhārī in *al-Ṣaḥīḥ: Kitāb al-Anbiyā'* [The Book of the Prophets], chapter: 'The Tradition of the Cave', 3:1282 §3288; and Muslim in *al-Ṣaḥīḥ: Kitāb al-ḥudūd* [The Book of Prescribed Punishments], 3:1315 §1688.

[2] Yaḥyā al-Nawawī, *Sharḥ Ṣaḥīḥ Muslim*, 12:7.

[3] Ibn Qudāma al-Maqdisī, *al-Mughnī*, 9:112.

[4] Ibn Ḥazm, *al-Muḥallā*, 10:351.

[5] Ibn Rushd, *Bidāyat al-mujtahid*, 2:299.

pay a fine, because both wine and pork are considered a part of the non-Muslim's belongings.

3.8 Humiliating Non-Muslim Citizens is Forbidden

Just as the humiliation and violation of a Muslim's dignity is forbidden in Islam, it is also forbidden to disgrace and dishonour a non-Muslim citizen. No Muslim is allowed to abuse a non-Muslim, or slander or attribute falsehood to him or her. Islam also restrains its followers from making mention of any flaw in the person of a non-Muslim, which may be associated with his or her self, family or lineage.

Once, the son of ʿAmr b. al-ʿĀṣ, the Governor of Egypt, punished a non-Muslim unjustly. When a complaint of this injustice reached Caliph ʿUmar ﷺ, he made the non-Muslim Egyptian publically exact the same punishment upon the Governor's son, and uttered the historic sentence, which according to some researchers characterized the struggle during the French Revolution:

مَتَى اسْتَعْبَدْتُمُ النَّاسَ وَقَدْ وَلَدَتْهُمْ أُمَّهَاتُهُمْ أَحْرَارًا؟

> 'Since when have you regarded people as your slaves, while their mothers gave birth to them as free men?'[1]

Harming a non-Muslim citizen with one's tongue and hands and abusing him or her is no less forbidden than doing so to a Muslim. In *al-Durr al-mukhtār* it is stated:

يَجِبُ كَفُّ الْأَذَى عَنْهُ وَتَحْرُمُ غِيْبَتُهُ كَالْمُسْلِمِ.

> 'All harm must be kept from him [the non-Muslim citizen] and it is forbidden to backbite him—just as it is for a Muslim'.[2]

Imam Shihāb al-Dīn al-Qarāfī, the famous Mālikī jurist, wrote in his book *al-Furūq* about the rights of non-Muslim citizens:

---

[1] Narrated by al-Hindī in *Kanz al-ʿummāl,* 2:455.

[2] Al-Ḥaṣkafī, *al-Durr al-mukhtār,* 2:223; Ibn ʿĀbidīn al-Shāmī, *Radd al-muḥtār,* 3:273–274.

إِنَّ عَقْدَ الذِّمَّةِ يُوجِبُ لَهُمْ حُقُوقًا عَلَيْنَا، لِأَنَّهُمْ فِي جِوَارِنَا وَفِي خِفَارَتِنَا (حِمَايَتِنَا) وَذِمَّتِنَا وَذِمَّةِ اللهِ تَعَالَى، وَذِمَّةِ رَسُولِ اللهِ ﷺ، وَدِيْنِ الْإِسْلَامِ. فَمَنِ اعْتَدَى عَلَيْهِمْ وَلَوْ بِكَلِمَةِ سُوءٍ أَوْ غِيْبَةٍ، فَقَدْ ضَيَّعَ ذِمَّةَ اللهِ، وَذِمَّةَ رَسُولِهِ ﷺ، وَذِمَّةَ دِيْنِ الْإِسْلَامِ.

The *dhimma* contract for non-Muslims establishes certain rights that they have upon us because they live in proximity to us and are under our protection and care and the care of God and the Messenger of God ﷺ and the religion of Islam. So whoever transgresses against them—even if by an evil word or through backbiting—has neglected the guarantee of God, His Messenger ﷺ and the religion of Islam.[1]

Ibn ʿĀbidīn al-Shāmī writes about the rights of non-Muslim citizens:

لِأَنَّهُ بِعَقْدِ الذِّمَّةِ وَجَبَ لَهُ مَا لَنَا، فَإِذَا حُرِّمَتْ غِيْبَةُ الْمُسْلِمِ حُرِّمَتْ غِيْبَتُهُ، بَلْ قَالُوا: إِنَّ ظُلْمَ الذِّمِّيِّ أَشَدُّ.

That is because due to the contract about non-Muslims, he [a non-Muslim] deserves the same rights as we do; and since it is unlawful to backbite a Muslim, it is also unlawful to backbite him [a non-Muslim]. Nay, they [the jurists] have said that oppression meted out to a non-Muslim citizen is even severer [in sin].[2]

Al-Kāsānī regarded the rights of Muslims and non-Muslims as equal in his book *Badāʾiʿ al-ṣanāʾiʿ*:

لَهُمْ مَا لَنَا وَعَلَيْهِمْ مَا عَلَيْنَا.

'Non-Muslim citizens enjoy the same rights that are enjoyed by us (Muslims), and they have the same responsibilities as we do'.[3]

---

[1] Al-Qarāfī, *al-Furūq*, 3:14.

[2] Ibn ʿĀbidīn al-Shāmī in *Radd al-muḥtār*, 3:273, 274.

[3] Narrated by al-Kāsānī in *Badāʾiʿ al-ṣanāʾiʿ*, 7:111.

The aforementioned sayings of the jurists prove that it is the collective responsibility of all Muslims to protect the honour of non-Muslim citizens.

The Prophet ﷺ enjoined his followers to treat non-Muslim citizens with excellence. It is the duty of the Islamic state to guarantee the protection of the non-Muslim citizens against oppression, wrongs and excesses. If the Islamic state fails to deliver justice and security to its non-Muslim citizens, the Prophet ﷺ declared that he would be the advocate of such oppressed people and that he would restore to them their rights on the Day of Judgment.

The Prophet ﷺ said,

أَلَا مَنْ ظَلَمَ مُعَاهِدًا، أَوِ انْتَقَصَهُ، أَوْ كَلَّفَهُ فَوْقَ طَاقَتِهِ، أَوْ أَخَذَ مِنْهُ شَيْئًا بِغَيْرِ طِيْبِ نَفْسٍ، فَأَنَا حَجِيْجُهُ يَوْمَ الْقِيَامَةِ.

> 'Beware! Whoever wrongs a non-Muslim citizen, or diminishes any of his rights, or imposes on him more than he can bear, or takes anything from him without his consent, I shall plead on his [the latter's] behalf on the Day of Resurrection'.[1]

The goal behind the Prophet's saying was to make the Muslim society realize its responsibility towards the rights of its non-Muslim citizens, so that they do not falter in discharging this duty.

3.9 The Protection of Non-Muslim Citizens from Internal and External Aggression

According to Islamic law, the protection of non-Muslim citizens is one of the duties of the state. If any person—irrespective of his association with any nation, religion or state—commits aggression against a non-Muslim citizen and oppresses him or her, it is the

[1] Narrated by Abū Dāwūd in *al-Sunan*: *Kitāb al-kharāj wa al-imāra wa al-fay'* [The Book on the Land Tax, Leadership and Spoils Acquired without Fighting], 3:170 §3052; al-Bayhaqī in *al-Sunan al-kubrā*, 9:205 §18511; and al-Mundhirī in *al-Targhīb wa al-tarhīb*, 4:7 §4558. Al-ʿAjlūnī said in *Kashf al-khafā'* that the chain of this tradition is good [*ḥasan*] (2:342).

responsibility of the state to protect that non-Muslim citizen, even if such protection entails entering into a war. God says,

﴿وَأَخَذْنَا ٱلَّذِينَ ظَلَمُواْ بِعَذَابٍ بَئِيسٍ بِمَا كَانُواْ يَفْسُقُونَ﴾

> '*And We seized* [the rest of] *the people who committed injustice* [actively or passively] *with a very harsh punishment because they were disobeying*'.[1]

The Qur'ān threatens with torment those who oppress others, but it gives an ever harsher warning to those who allow oppression to go unchallenged.

Islam has laid great emphasis on the protection of non-Muslim citizens against internal violence and oppression and has made their protection the duty of the Islamic state. Islam does not allow any Muslim citizen to encroach upon the rights of non-Muslim citizens or resort to oppression and violence against them, verbally or physically.

There are many Qur'ānic verses and prophetic traditions that reveal the calamitous repercussions and painful results of atrocities and oppression, in this world and in the Hereafter. Special injunctions prohibit oppressing non-Muslim citizens in particular.

A hadith reported in the *Sunan* of Abū Dāwūd has already been mentioned in which the Prophet ﷺ declared that, on the Day of Judgment, he will act as an advocate for the oppressed. Another hadith dealing with the same subject has been reported by ʿAbd Allāh b. Masʿūd ﷺ in which the Prophet ﷺ said,

مَنْ آذَى ذِمِّيًّا فَأَنَا خَصْمُهُ، وَمَنْ كُنْتُ خَصْمَهُ، خَصَمْتُهُ يَوْمَ الْقِيَامَةِ.

> 'Whoever hurts a non-Muslim citizen, I shall be his opponent. And when I am someone's adversary, I shall overcome him on the Day of Resurrection'.[2]

---

[1] Qur'ān 7:165.

[2] Narrated by al-Khaṭīb al-Baghdādī in *Tārīkh Baghdād* with an excellent chain of transmission (8:370); and cited by Badr al-Dīn al-ʿAynī in *ʿUmdat al-qārī*, 15:89.

The contemporary nation-states are responsible for taking all necessary measures to safeguard the lives of their citizens, including Muslims and non-Muslims, against any external aggression or war. Since the government is the repository of legal, political and economic powers coupled with military power, it is obligatory on the governments to take all required steps for their protection against any internal danger. ʿAlī ﷺ, the Leader of the Faithful, said,

إِنَّمَا بَذَلُوا الْجِزْيَةَ لِتَكُونَ دِمَاؤُهُمْ كَدِمَائِنَا وَأَمْوَالُهُمْ كَأَمْوَالِنَا.

> 'The non-Muslim citizens pay the tax so that their blood and property should be as inviolable as ours'.[1]

One of the books of Ḥanbalī jurisprudence, *Maṭālib ūlī al-nuhā*, states,

هَذَا مِنْ وَاجِبَاتِ الدَّوْلَةِ الْإِسْلَامِيَّةِ أَنَّهَا تُوَفِّرُ لِلذِّمِّيِّينَ ضَمَانًا كَامِلًا بِكَوْنِهِمْ سُكَّانَ الدَّوْلَةِ الْإِسْلَامِيَّةِ.

> 'It is the duty of the Muslim government to give complete protection to its non-Muslim citizens against suffering and torture of every kind, because of their being residents in the Islamic state'.[2]

If any external power chooses to flex its military muscle against the non-Muslim citizens of an Islamic state and aims to attack them in any manner, it is incumbent upon the Islamic government to take urgent measures to protect them. In his book *al-Furūq*, Imam al-Qarāfī quoted a saying of Ibn Ḥazm from his book *Marātib al-ijmāʿ*,

وَجَبَ عَلَيْنَا أَنْ نَخْرُجَ لِقِتَالِهِمْ بِالْكُرَاعِ وَالسِّلَاحِ وَنَمُوتَ دُونَ ذَلِكَ.

> 'It is obligatory for us to go out and wage war against them [who aggress against the non-Muslim citizens of an

[1] Cited by Ibn Qudāma al-Maqdisī in *al-Mughnī*, 9:181; and al-Zaylaʿī in *Naṣb al-rāya*, 3:381.

[2] Muṣṭafā b. Saʿd, *Maṭālib ūlī al-nuhā*, 2:602–603.

> Islamic state] with military might, even though we may die in the process'.[1]

This is also the viewpoint of Ibn Taymiyya. When the Mongols occupied Syria, Ibn Taymiyya went to the king for the release of the prisoners. The Mongol leadership showed their willingness to release the Muslim prisoners, but refused to release the non-Muslim citizens. Ibn Taymiyya said, 'We will not be happy unless all the prisoners from amongst the Jews and the Christians are released. They are our non-Muslim citizens and we will not leave any of our prisoners in captivity, whether they belong to the non-Muslim or Muslim population'. When the king saw the force of Ibn Taymiyya's arguments and his unrelenting insistence, he ordered the release of all Muslim and non-Muslim prisoners.[2]

It is clear in the light of the Qur'ānic verses, prophetic traditions and sayings of the jurists that no Muslim has the right to kill a non-Muslim citizen merely on the basis of his being non-Muslim, and it is unlawful to plunder his wealth or dishonour him. In addition, Islam not only guarantees the protection of the life, honour and property of non-Muslim citizens, but it also gives complete protection to their places of worship.

---

[1] Shihāb al-Dīn al-Qarāfī, *al-Furūq*, 3:14–15.

[2] Ibn Taymiyya, *Majmūʿa al-fatāwā*, 28:617–618.

Chapter 4

The Unlawfulness of Terrorism against Non-Muslims—Even During Times of War

4.1 Preliminary Remarks

According to the Islamic laws on war, it is prohibited to wage war against neutral countries, even if there are major ideological disagreements with them. Islam has enjoined upon its followers to remain peaceful with neutral people, because Islam does not approve of needless war or senseless conflict. It respects every human life and ensures that the sanctity and dignity of humanity is upheld at all times. God says in the Qur'ān,

﴿يَـٰٓأَيُّهَا ٱلَّذِينَ ءَامَنُوا۟ كُونُوا۟ قَوَّٰمِينَ لِلَّهِ شُهَدَآءَ بِٱلْقِسْطِ وَلَا يَجْرِمَنَّكُمْ شَنَـَٔانُ قَوْمٍ
عَلَىٰٓ أَلَّا تَعْدِلُوا۟ ٱعْدِلُوا۟ هُوَ أَقْرَبُ لِلتَّقْوَىٰ وَٱتَّقُوا۟ ٱللَّهَ إِنَّ ٱللَّهَ خَبِيرٌۢ بِمَا تَعْمَلُونَ﴾

> 'O *you who believe! Stand firm for God, witness in justice, and do not let the hatred of a people prevent you from being just. Be just; that is closer to righteousness. And fear God. Indeed, God is Well-Informed of what you do*'.[1]

This verse prohibits the believers from exceeding the limits or resorting to oppressive measures in their interactions with other nations, despite the extreme hostility that may be between them. Imam al-Qurṭubī explained this verse, quoting Abū ʿUbayda and al-Farrāʾ, 'This phrase "*lā yajrimannakum* [*do not let . . . prevent you*]" means that you should not let your hatred of a people cause you to transgress the truth and engage in falsehood or swerve from justice to oppression'.[2]

Similarly, with regard to the prohibition of indiscriminate massacre, God says,

﴿لَّا يَنْهَىٰكُمُ ٱللَّهُ عَنِ ٱلَّذِينَ لَمْ يُقَـٰتِلُوكُمْ فِى ٱلدِّينِ وَلَمْ يُخْرِجُوكُم مِّن دِيَـٰرِكُمْ أَن
تَبَرُّوهُمْ وَتُقْسِطُوٓا۟ إِلَيْهِمْ إِنَّ ٱللَّهَ يُحِبُّ ٱلْمُقْسِطِينَ﴾

---

1 Qur'ān 5:8.

2 Muhammad al-Qurṭubī, *al-Jāmiʿ li aḥkām al-Qur'ān*, 6:45.

> *'God does not forbid you of those who do not fight you because of religion and do not expel you from your homes—from being righteous towards them and treating them justly. Indeed, God loves the just'.*[1]

The terrorists who indiscriminately murder people through bomb blasts, suicide bombings and other means of destruction, without any distinction for religion, race, colour and creed, argue that, since the foreign powers are doing their utmost to occupy Muslim lands, and since the Muslims have been subjected to war, they are fully justified in adopting terrorism as a tactic. This is a false argument. The divine injunction, '*do not let the hatred of a people prevent you from being just*', clearly enjoins that no nation or group of people can be allowed to abandon justice and adopt oppression as a policy. According to Imam al-Qurṭubī, it is established from the Qur'ān that Islam orders tolerance, moderation, balance and harmony under all circumstances—so much so that the massacre of peaceful people is strictly prohibited even in times of war.

The condemnation of terrorism and the arguments against it are evident. If we, for a moment, accept the view of the terrorists and extremists who argue that they are waging a jihad against anti-Islamic forces, still their activities are outside of the pale of Islamic laws on war.

4.2 The Unlawfulness of Killing Non-Muslim Women

Many people are killed in non-Muslim countries, in addition to Muslim countries, in the unending wave of terrorism. The terrorists invoke the anti-Islamic actions of non-Muslim countries to justify their terrorism, and contend that since these governments play a role in either killing Muslims or getting them killed through different means, they are justified in killing their citizens in retaliation. This argument is contrary to the fundamental teachings of Islam and contravenes the character of Islam. Islam does not allow the killing of peaceful non-Muslims in times of war—much less in times of peace. Islam's jurisprudential tradition

---

[1] Qur'ān 60:8.

has articulated what is called in the West, the Just War Theory, and has detailed regulations that guide the conduct of its soldiers during war. Thus, the killing of women during war is prohibited.

ʿAbd Allāh b. ʿUmar ﵄ said,

وُجِدَتِ امْرَأَةٌ مَقْتُولَةً فِي بَعْضِ مَغَازِي رَسُولِ اللهِ ﷺ ، فَنَهَى رَسُولُ اللهِ ﷺ عَنْ قَتْلِ النِّسَاءِ وَالصِّبْيَانِ.

> 'A woman was found slain in one of the expeditions. Upon this the Messenger of God ﷺ forbade the killing of women and children'.[1]

Ibn Baṭṭāl and Imam al-Nawawī have both supported this standpoint in *Sharḥ Ṣaḥīḥ al-Bukhārī* (5:186) and *Sharḥ Ṣaḥīḥ Muslim* (12:37), respectively, and declared that killing women is in direct contravention to Islamic teachings. There is also a hadith narrated by ʿAbd al-Razzāq in his *Muṣannaf*, al-Shāfiʿī in his *al-Musnad*, al-Ṭaḥāwī in *Sharḥ maʿānī al-āthār* and al-Bayhaqī in *al-Sunan al-kubrā* from the son of Kaʿb b. Mālik ﵁ who mentioned that when the Prophet ﷺ dispatched an army to Ibn Abī Ḥaqīq, he forbade the killing of women and children.[2] Abū Thaʿlaba said,

نَهَى رَسُولُ اللهِ ﷺ عَنْ قَتْلِ النِّسَاءِ وَالْوِلْدَانِ.

> 'The Messenger of God ﷺ prohibited the murder of women and children'.[3]

---

[1] Narrated by al-Bukhārī in *al-Ṣaḥīḥ*: *Kitāb al-jihād wa al-siyar* [The Book of Martial Jihad and Battles], chapter: 'Killing Women in War', 3:1098 §2852; Muslim in *al-Saḥīḥ: Kitāb al-jihād wa al-siyar* [The Book of Martial Jihad and Battles], chapter: 'The Unlawfulness of Killing Women and Children during War', 3:1364 §1744; al-Tirmidhī in *al-Sunan*: *Kitāb al-siyar* [The Book of Military Expeditions], chapter: 'What Has Come to Us About the Killing of Women and Children', 4:136 §1569; Ibn Mājah in *al-Sunan*: *Kitāb al-jihād* [The Book of Martial Jihad], 2:947 §2841; and Aḥmad b. Ḥanbal in *al-Musnad*, 2:22 §4739.

[2] Narrated by ʿAbd al-Razzāq in *al-Muṣannaf*, 5:202 §9385; al-Shāfiʿī in *al-Musnad*, p. 238; cited by al-Ṭaḥāwī in *Sharḥ maʿānī al-āthār*, 3:221; and by al-Bayhaqī in *al-Sunan al-kubrā*, 9:77 §17865.

[3] Narrated by al-Ṭabarānī in *al-Muʿjam al-awsaṭ*, 7:113 §7011.

4.3 THE UNLAWFULNESS OF KILLING THE CHILDREN OF NON-MUSLIMS

The strict and total prohibition prescribed against killing peaceful non-Muslim children is another humane principle of Islam. Compare and contrast the actions of the self-proclaimed defenders of Islam with those of the Prophet ﷺ; the reality will be laid bare for everyone to see and the intentions of these terrorist elements will become clear. Would that they had held the prophetic traditions in due esteem and felt shame while shaping their destructive designs!

Quoting a letter of Ibn ʿAbbās ؓ, Imam Muslim wrote in his collection:

إِنَّ رَسُولَ اللهِ ﷺ لَمْ يَكُنْ يَقْتُلُ الصِّبْيَانَ، فَلَا تَقْتُلِ الصِّبْيَانَ.

> 'Indeed, the Messenger of God ﷺ did not kill children; so you must not kill them either'.[1]

In another hadith, the Prophet ﷺ forbade the Companions—with very harsh words—from killing the children of non-Muslims, and repeated his prohibition for effect. Aswad b. Sarīʿ ؓ said,

كُنَّا فِي غَزَاةٍ فَأَصَبْنَا ظَفَرًا وَقَتَلْنَا مِنَ الْمُشْرِكِيْنَ، حَتَّى بَلَغَ بِهِمُ الْقَتْلُ إِلَى أَنْ قَتَلُوا الذُّرِّيَّةَ، فَبَلَغَ ذَلِكَ النَّبِيَّ ﷺ، فَقَالَ: مَا بَالُ أَقْوَامٍ بَلَغَ بِهِمُ الْقَتْلُ إِلَى أَنْ قَتَلُوا الذُّرِّيَّةَ؟ أَلَا! لَا تَقْتُلُنَّ ذُرِّيَّةً. أَلَا! لَا تَقْتُلُنَّ ذُرِّيَّةً. قِيْلَ: لِمَ يَا رَسُولَ اللهِ، أَلَيْسَ هُمْ أَوْلَادَ الْمُشْرِكِيْنَ؟ قَالَ: أَوَلَيْسَ خِيَارُكُمْ أَوْلَادَ الْمُشْرِكِيْنَ؟

> 'We were once in a battle and gained the upper hand and killed many of the pagans, including some children. News of this reached the Messenger of God ﷺ and he said, "What is wrong with some people that they went so far as to kill children? Beware! Do not kill children at all! Beware! Do not kill children at all!" Someone asked, "Why, O Messenger of God? Are they not the children of the pagans?" He ﷺ replied, "Are the best amongst you

[1] Narrated by Muslim in *al-Ṣaḥīḥ: Kitāb al-jihād wa al-siyar* [The Book of Martial Jihad and Battles], 3:1444 §1812.

not from the children of pagans?"'[1]

In another narration it reads: 'A man said, "O Messenger of God! They are only the children of the pagans!" He ﷺ replied,

خِيَارُكُمْ أَبْنَاءُ الْمُشْرِكِيْنَ. أَلَا! لَا تُقْتَلُ الذُّرِّيَّةُ.

"The best of you are children of pagans. Beware! Children must not be killed".'[2]

None would know about the need for spiritual excellence in fighting for God's sake more than the Companions of the Prophet ﷺ; these paragons of love and obedience deserve a lasting tribute for having acted upon the instructions of the Prophet ﷺ, and observed the finest details of the laws of war, without transgressing their limits. ʿAṭiya al-Quraẓī ﷺ said,

كُنْتُ فِيْمَنْ حَكَمَ فِيْهِمْ سَعْدُ بْنُ مُعَاذٍ، فَشَكُّوا فِيَّ أَمِنَ الذُّرِّيَّةِ أَنَا أَمْ مِنَ الْمُقَاتِلَةِ؟ فَنَظَرُوا إِلَى عَانَتِي فَلَمْ يَجِدُوهَا نَبَتَتْ، فَأُلْقِيْتُ فِي الذُّرِّيَّةِ، وَلَمْ أُقْتَلْ.

'I was amongst those judged by Saʿd b. Muʿādh [when he was given the authority to decide the fate of the plotters of Banū Qurayẓa], but they were in doubt about me: was I to be counted amongst the children or amongst those who engaged in hostilities? So to find the answer, they examined my pubic regions and saw that I had yet to grow pubic hair [and thus was underage], so they grouped me with the children and I was spared'.[3]

---

[1] Narrated by al-Nasāʾī in *al-Sunan al-kubrā: Kitāb al-siyar* [The Book of Military Expeditions], chapter: 'The Prohibition of Killing the Children of the Pagans', 5:184 §8616; al-Dārimī in *al-Sunan*, 2:294 §2463; al-Ḥākim in *al-Mustadrak*, 2:133–134 §§2566–2567; and al-Ṭabarānī in *al-Muʿjam al-kabīr*, 1:284.

[2] Narrated by Aḥmad b. Ḥanbal in *al-Musnad*, 3:435 §§15626–15627; and al-Bayhaqī in *al-Sunan al-kubrā*, 9:77 §17868.

[3] Narrated by Ibn Ḥibbān in *al-Ṣaḥīḥ: Kitāb al-siyar* [The Book of Military Expeditions], 11:109 §4788; ʿAbd al-Razzāq in *al-Muṣannaf*, 10:179 §18742; al-Ṭabarānī in *al-Muʿjam al-kabīr*, 17:164 §434; and al-Bayhaqī in *al-Sunan al-kubrā*, 6:166 §11098.

Regarding the prohibition of killing non-Muslim women, children and elderly folk during war, the respected Ḥanafī jurist, Imam al-Sarakhsī, wrote in his magnum opus, *al-Mabsūṭ*:

قَالَ ﷺ: وَلَا تَقْتُلُوا وَلِيْدًا وَالْوَلِيْدُ، الْمَوْلُودُ فِي اللُّغَةِ، وَكُلُّ آدَمِيٍّ مَوْلُودٌ، وَلَكِنْ هَذَا اللَّفْظُ إِنَّمَا يُسْتَعْمَلُ فِي الصِّغَارِ عَادَةً. فَفِيْهِ دَلِيْلٌ عَلَى أَنَّهُ لَا يَحِلُّ قَتْلُ الصِّغَارِ مِنْهُمْ، إِذَا كَانُوا لَا يُقَاتِلُونَ. وَقَدْ جَاءَ فِي الْحَدِيْثِ أَنَّ النَّبِيَّ ﷺ نَهَى عَنْ قَتْلِ النِّسَاءِ وَالْوِلْدَانِ. وَقَالَ: اقْتُلُوا شُيُوخَ الْمُشْرِكِيْنَ، وَاسْتَحْيُوا شُرُوخَهُمْ. وَالْمُرَادُ بِالشُّيُوخِ الْبَالِغُونَ وَبِالشُّرُوخِ الْأَتْبَاعُ مِنَ الصِّغَارِ وَالنِّسَاءِ، وَالْإِسْتِحْيَاءُ الْإِسْتِرْقَاقُ. قَالَ اللهُ: ﴿وَٱسْتَحْيُواْ نِسَآءَهُمْ﴾. وَفِي وَصِيَّةِ أَبِي بَكْرٍ ؓ لِيَزِيْدَ بْنِ أَبِي سُفْيَانَ: لَا تَقْتُلْ شَيْخًا ضَرِعًا وَلَا صَبِيًّا ضَعِيفًا، يَعْنِي شَيْخًا فَانِيًا وَصَغِيْرًا لَا يُقَاتِلُ.

The Prophet ﷺ said, 'Do not kill children [*walīd*]'. In the [Arabic] language, the word *walīd* means one who is born [*mawlūd*]; and every human being [*ādamī*] is born; however, customarily this word is only used for young children. Therefore, in it is proof that it is impermissible to kill the young children amongst them [the non-Muslims], as long as they are not fighting. It is mentioned in a hadith that the Prophet ﷺ forbade the killing of women and children, and said, 'Kill the [warring] elders of the pagans [during the state of war] and keep alive their subordinates'. What is meant by 'elders' are the adults amongst them, and what is meant by 'subordinates' are their followers amongst the young and the womenfolk. To 'keep alive' here means to take them as captives. God says, '*And they kept their women alive*'.[1] And it is mentioned in Abū Bakr's ؓ dictated commands to Yazīd b. Abī Sufyān: 'Kill neither a feeble old man nor a fragile young child'; in other words, an elderly man and young child do not fight.[2]

---

[1] Qur'ān 40:25.

[2] Al-Sarakhsī, *al-Mabsūṭ*, 10:5–6.

4.4 The Unlawfulness of Killing Elderly Non-Muslims

Islam has strictly and unequivocally forbidden the killing of the elderly during war. This principle is illustrated in many prophetic traditions.

Imam Abū Dāwūd narrates on the authority of Anas b. Mālik ﷺ that the Prophet ﷺ said,

لَا تَقْتُلُوا شَيْخًا فَانِيًا، وَلَا طِفْلًا، وَلَا صَغِيرًا، وَلَا امْرَأَةً.

> 'Do not kill any feeble old man, or any infant or young child or woman'.[1]

Imam Ibn Abī Shayba narrates on the authority of al-Ḍaḥḥāk ﷺ who said,

كَانَ ﷺ يَنْهَى عَنْ قَتْلِ الْمَرْأَةِ وَالشَّيْخِ الْكَبِيرِ.

> 'The Prophet ﷺ used to forbid the killing of women and feeble old men'.[2]

Imam Ibn Abī Shayba also narrates on the authority of Rāshid b. Saʿd who said,

نَهَى رَسُولُ اللهِ ﷺ عَنْ قَتْلِ النِّسَاءِ وَالذُّرِّيَّةِ وَالشَّيْخِ الْكَبِيرِ الَّذِي لَا حِرَاكَ بِهِ.

> 'The Messenger of God ﷺ forbade the killing of women, children and the infirm'.[3]

Imam al-Bayhaqī narrated a hadith from ʿAlī ﷺ, that when the Prophet ﷺ would dispatch an army, he would advise them,

لَا تَقْتُلُوا وَلِيْدًا طِفْلًا، وَلَا امْرَأَةً، وَلَا شَيْخًا كَبِيرًا، وَلَا تُغَوِّرُنَّ عَيْنًا، وَلَا تَعْقِرُنَّ شَجَرَةً إِلَّا شَجَرًا يَمْنَعُكُمْ قِتَالًا، وَلَا تُمَثِّلُوا بِآدَمِيٍّ وَلَا بَهِيْمَةٍ، وَلَا تَغْدِرُوا وَلَا تَغُلُّوا.

> 'Do not kill a young boy, a woman or an old man. Do

---

[1] Narrated by Abū Dāwūd in *al-Sunan*: *Kitāb al-jihād* [The Book of Martial Jihad], 3:37 §2614; Ibn Abī Shayba in *al-Muṣannaf*, 6:483 §33118; and al-Bayhaqī in *al-Sunan al-kubrā*, 9:90 §17932.

[2] Narrated by Ibn Abī Shayba in *al-Muṣannaf*, 6:484 §33133.

[3] Ibid., §33135.

> not cause fountains to dry up and do not destroy any trees, except those which cause hindrance during war. Mutilate neither a human nor an animal, and do not break a promise or breach a trust'.[1]

Jubayr b. Nufayl said,

> مَرَّ رَجُلٌ بِثَوْبَانَ، فَقَالَ: أَيْنَ تُرِيْدُ؟ قَالَ: أُرِيْدُ الْغَزْوَ فِي سَبِيْلِ اللهِ. قَالَ: وَلَا تَغْلُلْ إِنْ غَنِمْتَ، وَلَا تَقْتُلَنَّ شَيْخًا كَبِيْرًا، وَلَا صَبِيًّا صَغِيْرًا. فَقَالَ لَهُ الرَّجُلُ: مِمَّنْ سَمِعْتَ هَذَا؟ قَالَ: مِنْ رَسُوْلِ اللهِ ﷺ.

> 'A man passed by Thawbān ﷺ, so he [Thawbān] asked him, "Where do you intend to go?" The man said, "I want to wage battle in the path of God". Thawbān then said to him, "If war booty comes your way, do not steal from it, and do not kill an old man or a young boy". Upon hearing this, the man asked him, "From whom did you hear this?" Thawbān replied, "From the Messenger of God ﷺ".'[2]

4.5 The Unlawfulness of Killing the Religious Leaders of Non-Muslims

Islam has forbidden its adherents from killing the religious leaders of non-Muslims during the course of war and after the battles have ceased. There is no justification for fighting against non-Muslim religious leaders and children if they do not engage in war. The perpetrators are putting to shame the great values of Islam and its culture of toleration. Imam Aḥmad b. Ḥanbal quoted Ibn ʿAbbās ﷺ who said that the Prophet ﷺ would issue clear instructions when dispatching an army to go into battle. He ﷺ would say,

> لَا تَغْدِرُوا، وَلَا تَغُلُّوا، وَلَا تُمَثِّلُوا، وَلَا تَقْتُلُوا الْوِلْدَانَ، وَلَا أَصْحَابَ الصَّوَامِعِ.

---

[1] Narrated by al-Bayhaqī in *al-Sunan al-Kubrā*, 9:90 §17934.

[2] Narrated by Ibn ʿAsākir in *Tārīkh Dimashq al-kabīr*, 27:404.

'Break no promise, steal not from the spoils of war and do not mutilate bodies or slay children or monks'.[1]

Imam Ibn Abī Shayba mentions another hadith from Ibn ʿAbbās ﷺ in which the Prophet ﷺ said as he dispatched an army,

لَا تَقْتُلُوا أَصْحَابَ الصَّوَامِعِ.

'Do not kill those who tend to the monasteries'.[2]

Imam Ibn Abī Shayba also quotes Thābit b. Ḥajjāj al-Kilābī, who reported that Abū Bakr ﷺ stood up, praised God and said to people,

أَلَا! لَا يُقْتَلُ الرَّاهِبُ فِي الصَّوْمَعَةِ.

'Beware, no [non-combatant] priest tending to his monastery should be killed'.[3]

Imam al-Bayhaqī narrates that Saʿīd b. al-Musayyab ﷺ reported that Abū Bakr al-Ṣiddīq ﷺ would always say to the Islamic army as he dispatched it for jihad,

لَا تُغْرِقُنَّ نَخْلًا، وَلَا تُحْرِقُنَّهَا، وَلَا تَعْقِرُوا بَهِيْمَةً، وَلَا شَجَرَةً تُثْمِرُ، وَلَا تَهْدِمُوا بِيْعَةً، وَلَا تَقْتُلُوا الْوِلْدَانَ، وَلَا الشُّيُوخَ، وَلَا النِّسَاءَ، وَسَتَجِدُونَ أَقْوَامًا حَبَسُوا أَنْفُسَهُمْ فِي الصَّوَامِعِ فَدَعُوهُمْ، وَمَا حَبَسُوا أَنْفُسَهُمْ لَهُ.

'Do not drown or burn date-palm trees. Do not kill any animal. Do not cut down a fruit-bearing tree. Do not demolish a church. And do not kill any children or old people or women. Soon you shall you come upon people who have secluded themselves in cloisters; you must leave them to engage in that for whose sake they have secluded themselves'.[4]

---

[1] Narrated by Aḥmad b. Ḥanbal in *al-Musnad*, 5:358 §2728.

[2] Narrated by Ibn Abī Shayba in *al-Muṣannaf*, 6:484 §33132; Abū Yaʿlā in *al-Musnad*, 5:59 §2650; al-Ṭaḥāwī in *Sharḥ maʿānī al-āthār*, 3:225; and al-Daylamī in *Musnad al-firdaws*, 5:45 §7410.

[3] Narrated by Ibn Abī Shayba in *al-Muṣannaf*, 6:483 §33127.

[4] Narrated by al-Bayhaqī in *al-Sunan al-kubrā*, 9:85 §17904.

Likewise, another tradition reported by Ṣāliḥ b. Kaysān and narrated by Imam al-Bayhaqī mentions that Abū Bakr al-Ṣiddīq ﷺ said as he was dispatching the Islamic army towards Syria,

> إِنَّكُمْ سَتَجِدُونَ أَقْوَامًا قَدْ حَبَسُوا أَنْفُسَهُمْ فِي هَذِهِ الصَّوَامِعِ، فَاتْرُكُوهُمْ وَمَا حَبَسُوا لَهُ أَنْفُسَهُمْ، وَلَا تَقْتُلُوا كَبِيرًا هَرِمًا، وَلَا امْرَأَةً، وَلَا وَلِيدًا، وَلَا تُخْرِبُوا عُمْرَانًا، وَلَا تَقْطَعُوا شَجَرَةً إِلَّا لِنَفْعٍ، وَلَا تَعْقِرُنَّ بَهِيمَةً إِلَّا لِنَفْعٍ، وَلَا تُحْرِقُنَّ نَخْلًا وَلَا تُغْرِقُنَّهُ، وَلَا تَغْدِرْ، وَلَا تُمَثِّلْ، وَلَا تَجْبُنْ، وَلَا تَغْلُلْ.
>
> 'You shall soon come upon people who have secluded themselves in monasteries; you must leave them to engage in that for whose sake they have secluded themselves. Do not kill an old, feeble man or a woman or a child. Do not damage any populated area. Do not cut down trees needlessly. Do not kill animals unless it is for a benefit [to feed others]. Do not burn down date-palm trees or drown them. Do not commit any treachery. Do not mutilate (anyone). Do not behave cowardly. And do not take anything without right when distributing the spoils of war'.[1]

In the light of these clear injunctions that prohibit killing the religious leaders of non-Muslims, what interpretation can one give to the self-styled and the misplaced religious concepts of those who murder Islamic religious scholars, destroy the mosques of those who adhere to other schools of thought and burn down the shrines of the Sufis? Not only do these people consider these actions justified, but they also invoke religion by claiming to take guidance from the Qur'ān and the Sunna!

4.6 The Unlawfulness of Killing Non-Muslim Traders and Farmers

Islam has given complete protection to farmers, traders and businessmen, and forbade killing them, because they are associated

[1] Ibid., 9:90 §17929.

with the economy and financial survival of humanity. There are several prophetic narrations that speak of this.

Imam Ibn Abī Shayba and Imam al-Bayhaqī narrated on the authority of Jābir b. ʿAbd Allāh ﷺ who said,

كَانُوا لَا يَقْتُلُونَ تُجَّارَ الْمُشْرِكِيْنَ.

> 'They [the Muslim soldiers] did not kill the merchants amongst the pagans'.[1]

Imam Ibn Abī Shayba also narrated on the authority of Zayd b. Wahb that ʿUmar ﷺ sent him a letter in which he said,

لَا تَغُلُّوا وَلَا تَغْدِرُوا، وَلَا تَقْتُلُوا وَلِيْدًا، وَاتَّقُوا اللهَ فِي الْفَلَّاحِيْنَ.

> 'Do not take anything without right when distributing the spoils of war, and do not commit any treachery or kill children. And fear God regarding farmers'.[2]

Imam al-Bayhaqī's version of this report reads,

اِتَّقُوا اللهَ فِي الْفَلَّاحِيْنَ فَلَا تَقْتُلُوهُمْ.

> 'Fear God regarding the farmers and do not kill them'.[3]

Ibn al-Qayyim said,

إِنَّ أَصْحَابَ النَّبِيِّ ﷺ لَمْ يَقْتُلُوهُمْ حِيْنَ فَتَحُوا الْبِلَادَ، وَلِأَنَّهُمْ لَا يُقَاتِلُونَ، فَأَشْبَهُوا الشُّيُوخَ وَالرُّهْبَانَ.

> 'Indeed, when the Companions of the Prophet ﷺ conquered the various lands, they did not kill them [farmers and merchants] because the latter did not fight [against them], and so in that sense they [the civilians] resembled the elderly and the religious leaders'.[4]

---

[1] Narrated by Ibn Abī Shayba in *al-Muṣannaf*, 6:484 §33129; al-Bayhaqī in *al-Sunan al-kubrā*, 9:91 §17939; and cited by Ibn Ādam al-Qurashī in *al-Kharāj*, 1:52 §133.

[2] Narrated by Ibn Abī Shayba in *al-Muṣannaf*, 6:483 §33120; and cited by Ibn Ādam al-Qurashī in *Kitāb al-Kharāj*, 1:52 §132.

[3] Narrated by al-Bayhaqī in *al-Sunan al-kubrā*, 9:91 §17938.

[4] Ibn al-Qayyim, *Aḥkām ahl al-dhimma*, 1:165.

Imam al-Awzāʿī took a similar view and said,

لَا يُقْتَلُ الْحَرَّاثُ إِذَا عُلِمَ أَنَّهُ لَيْسَ مِنَ الْمُقَاتِلَةِ.

'Farmers are not to be killed [during war] if it is known that they are not from the combatants'.[1]

And Ibn Qudāma al-Maqdisī stated,

أَمَّا الْفَلَّاحُ الَّذِي لَا يُقَاتِلُ فَيَنْبَغِي أَلَّا يُقْتَلَ، لِمَا رُوِيَ عَنْ عُمَرَ بْنِ الْخَطَّابِ ﷺ أَنَّهُ قَالَ: اتَّقُوا اللهَ فِي الْفَلَّاحِيْنَ، الَّذِيْنَ لَا يَنْصُبُونَ لَكُمْ فِي الْحَرْبِ.

'As for the farmer who is a non-combatant, he should not be killed, because it was narrated from ʿUmar b. al-Khaṭṭāb ﷺ that he said, "Fear God regarding the farmers who do not wage war against you".'[2]

4.7 The Unlawfulness of Killing Non-Muslim Service Personnel

Islamic laws are to regulate the conduct of the Muslim soldiers during the course of war and restrain them from killing non-Muslim professionals and those tasked with the delivery of services. Rabāḥ b. Rabīḥ ﷺ said,

كُنَّا مَعَ رَسُولِ اللهِ ﷺ فِي غَزْوَةٍ، فَرَأَى النَّاسَ مُجْتَمِعِيْنَ عَلَى شَيْءٍ، فَبَعَثَ رَجُلًا فَقَالَ: انْظُرْ عَلَى مَا اجْتَمَعَ هَؤُلَاءِ؟ فَجَاءَ، فَقَالَ: عَلَى امْرَأَةٍ قَتِيْلٍ. فَقَالَ: مَا كَانَتْ هَذِهِ لِتُقَاتِلَ. قَالَ: وَعَلَى الْمُقَدَّمَةِ خَالِدُ بْنُ الْوَلِيْدِ. فَبَعَثَ رَجُلًا فَقَالَ: قُلْ لِخَالِدٍ: لَا يَقْتُلَنَّ امْرَأَةً وَلَا عَسِيفًا. وَفِي رِوَايَةٍ: لَا تَقْتُلَنَّ ذُرِّيَّةً وَلَا عَسِيفًا.

'We were with the Messenger of God ﷺ in one of the battle expeditions, when he saw some people gathered around something. He sent a man out, saying, "Go and see what they are gathering around". The man returned and informed him, saying, "They are gathering around

[1] Ibid.

[2] Ibn Qudāma al-Maqdisī, *al-Mughnī*, 9:251.

a slain woman". The Prophet ﷺ said, "She was not amongst those who fight!" At the head of the group was Khālid b. Walīd, so the Prophet sent a man to go and inform Khālid: "Neither an [idolatrous] woman nor a hired servant should be killed".' [In one report:] 'Do not kill children or hired servants'.[1]

In fact, non-Muslim employees working in the households of non-Muslim employers in the conquered areas are not to be killed and no kind of tax can be imposed upon them. Ibn al-Qayyim stated the same thing, quoting ʿAbd Allāh b. ʿUmar ﷺ:

إِنَّ الْعَبْدَ مَحْقُونُ الدَّمِ فَأَشْبَهَ النِّسَاءَ وَالصِّبْيَانَ.

'The blood of a servant is inviolable, and is thereby similar to that of women and children'.[2]

Likewise, Ibn al-Mundhir cited a consensus amongst the scholars that, like the unemployed, the old, the sick, the destitute and women and children of non-Muslims—no tax can be levelled on the servants under their responsibility and care.[3]

4.8 The Unlawfulness of Killing Non-Muslims Who are Non-Combatants

Islam holds that the sanctity of life is superior to the sanctity of the Kaʿba. That is why shedding blood unjustly has been condemned in the harshest possible terms. The only enemies who are allowed to be killed are those who actively take part in combat. A large part of population, which is non-combatant, including children, women, the old, the sick and the disabled, have been excluded

---

[1] Narrated by Abū Dāwūd in *al-Sunan*: *Kitāb al-jihād* [The Book of Martial Jihad], chapter: 'The Killing of Women', 3:53 §2669; Ibn Mājah in *al-Sunan*: *Kitāb al-jihād* [The Book of Martial Jihad], 2:948 §2842; Aḥmad b. Ḥanbal in *al-Musnad*, 3:488 §16035; al-Nasāʾī in *al-Sunan al-kubrā*, 5:186–187 §§8625, 8627; and al-Ḥākim in *al-Mustadrak*, 2:133 §2565.

[2] Ibn Qayyim al-Jawziyya, *Aḥkām ahl al-dhimma*, 1:172.

[3] Ibid.

from this. On the day of the conquest of Mecca, the Prophet ﷺ ordered that those who were not fighting should run away to save their lives, and shut their doors, and he ordered that those who were injured should not be attacked.

Imam Muslim narrated on the authority of Abū Hurayra ؓ that the Messenger of God ﷺ said on the day of the conquest of Mecca,

مَنْ دَخَلَ دَارَ أَبِي سُفْيَانَ فَهُوَ آمِنٌ، وَمَنْ أَلْقَى السِّلَاحَ فَهُوَ آمِنٌ، وَمَنْ أَغْلَقَ بَابَهُ فَهُوَ آمِنٌ.

> 'Whoever enters Abū Sufyān's house is safe, and whoever lays down his weapon is safe and whoever shuts his door is safe'.[1]

All of these steps convey the message of peace and protection.

It is reported in ʿAbd al-Razzāq's *Muṣannaf* that ʿAlī b. Abī Ṭālib ؓ said,

لَا يُذَفَّفُ عَلَى جَرِيْحٍ، وَلَا يُقْتَلُ أَسِيرٌ، وَلَا يُتْبَعُ مُدْبِرٌ.

> 'The injured person or prisoner should not be killed, and the one who flees should not be pursued'.[2]

According to another narration recorded by ʿAbd al-Razzāq, Juwaybir reported that a woman from the tribe of Banū Asad told him that she heard ʿAmmār ؓ declare after ʿAlī ؓ had finished the Battle of the Camel,[3]

لَا تُذَفِّفُوا عَلَى جَرِيْحٍ، وَلَا تَدْخُلُوا دَارًا. مَنْ أَلْقَى السِّلَاحَ فَهُوَ آمِنٌ، وَمَنْ أَغْلَقَ بَابَهُ فَهُوَ آمِنٌ.

---

1 Narrated by Muslim in *al-Ṣaḥīḥ: Kitāb al-jihād wa al-siyar* [The Book of Martial Jihad and Military Expeditions], chapter: 'The Conquest of Mecca', 3:1407 §1780; Abū Dāwūd in *al-Sunan*: *Kitāb al-kharāj wa al-imāra wa al-fayʾ* [The Book of Land Tax, Leadership and the Spoils Acquired without Fighting], 3:162 §3021; and al-Bazzār in *al-Musnad*, 4:122 §1292.

2 Narrated by ʿAbd al-Razzāq in *al-Muṣannaf*, 10:123 §18590.

3 A battle that took place in 656 CE. ED.

> 'Do not kill an injured person and do not enter the house of someone who has laid down his arms, for he is considered safe. Similarly, the one who shuts his door is considered safe'.[1]

4.9 The Unlawfulness of Waging Night Offensives against Non-Muslims

The military code of conduct enshrined in the Shariah holds that enemies should not be attacked at night. Military forces should wait until dawn when launching their offensives so that non-combatants, such as women, children, the old and the sick, do not become frightened and have their sleep disturbed.

Imam al-Bukhārī and Imam Muslim narrated on the authority of Anas b. Mālik ﵁ who said,

أَنَّ رَسُولَ اللهِ ﷺ أَتَى خَيْبَرَ لَيْلًا، وَكَانَ إِذَا أَتَى قَوْمًا بِلَيْلٍ لَمْ يُغِرْ بِهِمْ حَتَّى يُصْبِحَ.

> 'The Messenger of God ﷺ came to Khaybar at night, and when he came to a people [a force] at night, he would not attack them until daybreak'.[2]

Contrast the prophetic laws concerning war with the methods of the modern-day terrorists who bomb populated areas without any care for peaceful life.

4.10 The Unlawfulness of Burning Non-Muslims

In the pre-Islamic days of ignorance, a man would go to such extremes in revenge and enmity against his opponents during war that he would burn them alive. The Prophet ﷺ forbade Muslims from resorting to this barbaric tactic.

---

[1] Narrated by ʿAbd al-Razzāq in *al-Muṣannaf*, 10:124 §18591.

[2] Narrated by al-Bukhārī in *al-Ṣaḥīḥ*: *Kitāb al-maghāzī* [The Book of Military Expeditions], chapter: 'The Campaign of Khaybar', 4:1538 §3961; Muslim in *al-Ṣaḥīḥ*: *Kitāb al-jihād wa al-siyar* [The Book of Martial Jihad and Expeditions], chapter: 'The Campaign of Khaybar', 3:1427 §1365; and al-Tirmidhī in *al-Sunan*: *Kitāb al-siyar* [The Book of Military Expeditions], 4:121 §1550.

ʿAbd al-Raḥmān b. ʿAbd Allāh quoted his father as saying that once they were on a journey and the Prophet ﷺ went to relieve himself. After he left, the Companions saw a sparrow with two of her young hatchlings. When they took the hatchlings, the sparrow, greatly upset, came and began to spread out her wings. When the Prophet ﷺ returned he said,

مَنْ فَجَعَ هَذِهِ بِوَلَدِهَا؟ رُدُّوا وَلَدَهَا إِلَيْهَا.

> 'Who has tormented this bird by taking her young ones? Give them back to her'.[1]

In another report the Prophet ﷺ saw an anthill that was burned and declared,

إِنَّهُ لَا يَنْبَغِي أَنْ يُعَذِّبَ بِالنَّارِ إِلَّا رَبُّ النَّارِ.

> 'It is not fitting that anyone but the Lord of the fire should punish with the fire'.[2]

If Islam has forbidden the burning of ants, how can it allow the burning of human beings? Likewise, when the Prophet ﷺ sent his Companions for war, he ordered them to avoid burning their enemies.[3] But in the wake of the recent bomb blasts and suicide attacks that burn the harmless people and tear them to pieces, the so-called Muslim terrorist groups that accept responsibility for these attacks convey to the world that the Muslims' concept of jihad is barbaric and oppressive. The opposite, however, is true and Islam has nothing to do with any of this.

---

[1] Narrated by Abū Dāwūd in *al-Sunan*: *Kitāb al-jihād* [The Book of Martial Jihad], chapter: 'The Abhorrence of Burning the Enemy', 3:55 §2675.

[2] Narrated by Abū Dāwūd in *al-Sunan*: *Kitāb al-jihād* [The Book of Martial Jihad], chapter: 'The Abhorrence of Burning the Enemy', 3:55 §2675.

[3] Narrated by al-Bukhārī in *al-Ṣaḥīḥ*: *Kitāb al-jihād wa al-siyar* [The Book of Martial Jihad and Expeditions], chapter: 'May He Not Suffer the Chastisement of God', 3:1098 §2853; al-Tirmidhī in *al-Sunan*: *Kitāb al-siyar* [The Book of Military expeditions], chapter 20, 4:137 §1571; Abū Dāwūd in *al-Sunan*: *Kitāb al-jihād* [The Book of Martial Jihad], chapter: 'The Abhorrence of Burning the Enemy', 3:54 §2674.

4.11 THE UNLAWFULNESS OF BREAKING INTO ENEMY HOMES AND LOOT THEM

Muslim forces are strictly forbidden from forcibly entering the houses of their enemies. Islam has emphasized the sanctity of the honour and property of others—even in times of war—and it forbade soldiers from beating children or women or eating the food of others without their permission.

It is reported in Abū Dāwūd's *al-Sunan* that ʿIrbāḍ b. Sāriya al-Sulamī ﷺ said, 'We disembarked at Khaybar with the Prophet ﷺ and many of his Companions were with him. One of the fighters of Khaybar who was arrogant and contentious came to the Prophet ﷺ and asked, "Is it fair that you slaughter our donkeys, eat our fruits and beat our women?" The Prophet ﷺ became annoyed and said, "O Ibn ʿAwf! Ride on your steed and declare that Paradise is only for the believers, and that they should gather for prayer". When they all gathered together, he stood up and said,

> أَيَحْسَبُ أَحَدُكُمْ مُتَّكِئًا عَلَى أَرِيكَتِهِ قَدْ يَظُنُّ أَنَّ اللهَ لَمْ يُحَرِّمْ شَيْئًا إِلَّا مَا فِي هَذَا الْقُرْآنِ؟ أَلَا وَإِنِّي وَاللهِ، قَدْ وَعَظْتُ، وَأَمَرْتُ، وَنَهَيْتُ عَنْ أَشْيَاءَ، إِنَّهَا لَمِثْلُ الْقُرْآنِ أَوْ أَكْثَرُ. وَإِنَّ اللهَ لَمْ يُحِلَّ لَكُمْ أَنْ تَدْخُلُوا بُيُوتَ أَهْلِ الْكِتَابِ إِلَّا بِإِذْنٍ، وَلَا ضَرْبَ نِسَائِهِمْ، وَلَا أَكْلَ ثِمَارِهِمْ.
>
> "Does any of you recline on his couch and imagine that God has not forbidden anything save that which has been mentioned in the Qurʾān? Beware, by God, I have exhorted, issued commands and forbade various matters. They are as numerous as what is found in the Qurʾān, or more. God has not permitted you to enter the houses of the People of the Book without permission, or to beat their women, or to eat their fruit".'[1]

---

[1] Narrated by Abū Dāwūd in *al-Sunan*: *Kitāb al-kharāj wa al-imāra wa al-fay*ʾ [The Book of Land Tax, Leadership and the Spoils Acquired without Fighting], 3:170 §3050; al-Bayhaqī in *al-Sunan al-kubrā*, 9:204 §18508; and cited by Ibn ʿAbd al-Barr in *al-Tamhīd*, 1:149.

During the pre-Islamic days of ignorance, the Arab warriors would initiate war for the sole purpose of forcibly acquiring wealth and belongings through pillage and plunder. Plundering the trading caravans had become a business of many tribes, but Islam eliminated this oppressive practice. When some people wanted to loot a caravan of travellers in one of the battles, the Prophet ﷺ forbade them.

It is reported by Muʿādh b. Anas ؓ that he was blessed to be with the Prophet ﷺ in one of the sacred battles. Some people started looting some travellers and when the Prophet ﷺ came to know of this, he sent one of the Companions to declare:

أَنَّ مَنْ ضَيَّقَ مَنْزِلًا أَوْ قَطَعَ طَرِيْقًا فَلَا جِهَادَ لَهُ.

> 'There is no jihad for the one who breaks into the houses of others or loots people on the road'.[1]

Thus, when those fighting in the way of God resort to plunder and looting, and harass people and become a source of trouble for them, God rejects their emotional appeals to jihad and declares their acts unlawful.

4.12 The Unlawfulness of Destroying the Cattle, Crops and Properties of the Enemy

Islam neither allows the unjust shedding of blood, nor does it approve of the scorched earth policy of total war. Islam calls for reform and peace. Therefore, it takes care that those fighting for its sake do not destroy crops and fruit-bearing trees, or burn down properties.

Imam al-Tirmidhī quoted the following saying of the First Rightly Guided Caliph in this regard:

نَهَى أَبُو بَكْرٍ الصِّدِّيْقُ ؓ أَنْ يَقْطَعَ شَجَرًا مُثْمِرًا أَوْ يُخَرِّبَ عَامِرًا، وَعَمِلَ بِذَلِكَ الْمُسْلِمُونَ بَعْدَهُ.

---

[1] Narrated by Abū Dāwūd in *al-Sunan*: *Kitāb al-jihād* [The Book of Martial Jihad], 3:41 §2629.

> 'Abū Bakr al-Ṣiddīq ﵁ forbade people from cutting down fruit-bearing trees or destroying buildings [during war]—and the Muslims abided by his instructions after that'.[1]

Many traditions have been reported by Imam Mālik, ʿAbd al-Razzāq, Ibn Abī Shayba and al-Bayhaqī to this effect. According to these traditions, the Prophet ﷺ strictly forbade cutting down trees. Yaḥyā b. Saʿīd states that he was told that while seeing off the Muslim forces for Syria, Abū Bakr al-Ṣiddīq ﵁ came to Yazīd b. Abī Sufyān and told him,

> إِنِّي أُوصِيكَ بِعَشْرٍ: لَا تَقْتُلَنَّ صَبِيًّا وَلَا امْرَأَةً، وَلَا كَبِيرًا هَرِمًا، وَلَا تَقْطَعَنَّ شَجَرًا مُثْمِرًا، وَلَا تُخَرِّبَنَّ عَامِرًا، وَلَا تَعْقِرَنَّ شَاةً وَلَا بَعِيْرًا إِلَّا لِمَأْكَلَةٍ، وَلَا تُحْرِقَنَّ نَخْلًا، وَلَا تُغْرِقَنَّهُ، وَلَا تَغْلُلْ، وَلَا تَجْبُنْ.

> 'I command you to observe ten things: Do not kill a young child, a woman or an elderly infirm man. Do not cut down fruit-bearing trees or demolish buildings. Do not slaughter a sheep or camel except for food. Do not drown or burn date-palm trees. And do not steal from the war booty or show cowardice'.[2]

Ibn Abī Shayba quotes a tradition reported by Mujāhid who said,

> لَا يُقْتَلُ فِي الْحَرْبِ الصَّبِيُّ، وَلَا امْرَأَةٌ وَلَا الشَّيْخُ الْفَانِي، وَلَا يُحْرَقُ الطَّعَامُ، وَلَا النَّخْلُ، وَلَا تُخْرَبُ الْبُيُوتُ، وَلَا يُقْطَعُ الشَّجَرُ الْمُثْمِرُ.

> 'Young children, women and infirm elderly men should not be killed in war. Food and date-palm trees should not be burned, houses should not be demolished and fruit-

---

[1] Narrated by al-Tirmidhī in *al-Sunan*: *Kitāb al-siyar* [The Book of Military Expeditions], 4:122 §1552.

[2] Narrated by Mālik in *al-Muwaṭṭa*: *Kitāb al-jihād* [The Book of Martial Jihad], chapter: 'The Unlawfulness of Killing Women and Children During Military Expeditions', 2:447 §965; ʿAbd al-Razzāq in *al-Muṣannaf*, 5:199 §9375; Ibn Abī Shayba in *al-Muṣannaf*, 6:483 §33121; al-Bayhaqī in *al-Sunan al-kubrā*, 9:89–90 §§17927, 17929; and al-Marwazī in *Musnad Abī Bakr,* pp. 69–72 §21.

bearing trees should not be cut'.[1]

ʿAbd Allāh b. ʿUmar ﷺ stated in one narration that when Abū Bakr al-Ṣiddīq ﷺ dispatched the Muslim troops to Syria, he walked with them for two miles and addressed them, saying,

أُوصِيْكُمْ بِتَقْوَى اللهِ، لَا تَعْصُوا وَلَا تَغُلُّوا، وَلَا تَجْبُنُوا، وَلَا تُغْرِقُوا نَخْلًا، وَلَا تُحْرِقُوا زَرْعًا، وَلَا تَحْبَسُوا بَهِيْمَةً، وَلَا تَقْطَعُوا شَجَرَةً مُثْمِرَةً، وَلَا تَقْتُلُوا شَيْخًا كَبِيْرًا، وَلَا صَبِيًّا صَغِيْرًا.

'I enjoin you to fear God. Do not disobey [the military commander] or show cowardice. Do not drown date-palm trees or set crops on fire. Do not hobble animals and do not cut down fruit-bearing trees. Do not kill an old man or a young child'.[2]

ʿĀṣim b. Kulayb narrated on the authority of his father that one of the *Anṣār* related, 'We set out on a journey with the Prophet ﷺ. The people were suffering hunger and were in need, so they forcibly took some goats and slaughtered them. The pots were boiling when the Prophet ﷺ came over with his back resting against a bow, and he started turning our pans upside down with the bow and mixing the meat with the soil. Then he said,

إِنَّ النُّهْبَةَ لَيْسَتْ بِأَحَلَّ مِنَ الْمَيْتَةِ.

"Eating stolen food is not any more lawful than eating carrion!".'[3]

What a lofty demonstration of conduct and commitment to ethical principles! Whether in the theatre of war, or during a state of extreme hunger in a long, tiresome journey, no military leader, religious figure or spiritual mentor can demonstrate this level of pious, exalted and strong character. It was the influence

---

[1] Narrated by Ibn Abī Shayba in *al-Muṣannaf*, 6:483 §33122.

[2] Narrated by al-Marwazī in *Musnad Abī Bakr*, pp. 69–72 §21.

[3] Narrated by Abū Dāwūd in *al-Sunan*: *Kitāb al-jihād* [The Book of Martial Jihad], 3:66 §2705; and al-Bayhaqī in *al-Sunan al-kubrā*, 9:61 §17789.

of the Prophet's training of the Companions that when the pans containing cooked meat were mixed into the dust in front of them, though they were seized with extreme hunger at that time, these embodiments of patience totally submitted themselves before the Prophet ﷺ.

The words spoken by the Prophet ﷺ on that occasion are a valuable gift for humanity. His describing stolen food as viler than the flesh of an un-slaughtered dead animal should give pause to those who feel no compunction in robbing banks and stealing from people to finance their terrorist activities.

4.13 Summary

In the light of the aforementioned explanations, it is evident that even when war is imposed on Islam, and the Muslims are made victims of external aggression and the Islamic state is compelled to order its armies to fight in defence, children, women and the elderly cannot be killed. Furthermore, damaging crops, destroying buildings, properties and places of worship are also strictly forbidden. How can Islam, which does not allow these practices during jihad, condone and approve the killing of non-combatants who are not directly involved in the aggression and who are going about their daily routines? It is abundantly clear that such activities are in direct contravention of the teachings of the Qur᾽ān and hadith.

Chapter 5

On the Protection of the Non-Muslims' Lives, Properties and Places of Worship

5.1 The Protection of Non-Muslim Citizens during the Time of the Prophet Muhammad ﷺ

The blessed period of the Messenger of God ﷺ was an unparalleled time in history. There is no comparable era in which the rights of non-Muslim citizens were so well protected. The Prophet ﷺ provided a constitutional and legal status to this protection through his agreements, accords, contracts and commands. The agreement worked out with the people of Najran is a notable example in which all their rights and freedoms—in particular religious freedoms—were guaranteed. Imam Abū ʿUbayd al-Qāsim b. al-Sallām, Imam Ḥumayd b. Zanjawayh, Ibn Saʿd and al-Balādhūrī have cited a hadith in which the Prophet ﷺ dictated:

> وَلِنَجْرَانَ وَحَاشِيَتِهَا ذِمَّةُ اللهِ وَذِمَّةُ مُحَمَّدٍ النَّبِيِّ رَسُولِ اللهِ، عَلَى دِمَائِهِمْ وَأَنْفُسِهِمْ وَمِلَّتِهِمْ وَأَرْضِهِمْ وَأَمْوَالِهِمْ وَمِلَّتِهِمْ وَرَهْبَانِيَّتِهِمْ وَأَسَاقِفَتِهِمْ وَغَائِبِهِمْ وَشَاهِدِهِمْ وَغَيْرِهِمْ وَبَعْثِهِمْ وَأَمْثِلَتِهِمْ، لَا يُغَيَّرُ مَا كَانُوا عَلَيْهِ، وَلَا يُغَيَّرُ حَقٌّ مِنْ حُقُوقِهِمْ وَأَمْثِلَتِهِمْ، لَا يُفْتَنُ أُسْقُفٌ مِنْ أُسْقُفِيَّتِهِ، وَلَا رَاهِبٌ مِنْ رَهْبَانِيَّتِهِ، وَلَا وَاقِفٌ مِنْ وَقَافِيَّتِهِ، عَلَى مَا تَحْتَ أَيْدِيهِمْ مِنْ قَلِيلٍ أَوْ كَثِيرٍ، وَلَيْسَ عَلَيْهِمْ رَهَقٌ.

> ‘Indeed, Najran and her allies are under the protection of God and the guarantee of the Messenger of God ﷺ. They are to be protected in their wealth, lives, lands and religion. This includes their priests, monks, those who are present amongst them and those who are absent and others amongst them, and their delegations and the like. They shall not be forced to change that (faith) which they are upon and no right of theirs is to be forfeited. No monk, priest or attendant amongst them should lose that which is in his possession, be it plentiful or scarce, and no fear or danger will threaten them’.[1]

---

[1] Cited by Abū Yūsuf in *al-Kharāj*, 78; Abū ʿUbayd al-Qāsim b. Sallām in *Kitāb*

Imam Ḥumayd b. Zanjawayh states that this agreement remained in force during the reign of Abū Bakr al-Ṣiddīq ﷺ after the passing of the Messenger of God ﷺ. Certain amendments were incorporated in it due to the changing circumstances during the reign of ʿUmar and ʿUthmān ﷺ, but the responsibility for protecting the rights of the non-Muslims, which was the main highlight of the agreement, remained intact.

Likewise, the Prophet ﷺ issued a declaration about the properties and belongings of the Jews during the conquest of Khaybar. This was reported by Imam Aḥmad, Imam Abū Dāwūd, Imam al-Ṭabarānī and other Imams of hadith. Khālid b. al-Walīd ﷺ said,

غَزَوْنَا مَعَ رَسُولِ اللهِ ﷺ غَزْوَةَ خَيْبَرَ، فَأَسْرَعَ النَّاسُ فِي حَظَائِرِ يَهُودَ، فَأَمَرَنِي أَنْ أُنَادِيَ: الصَّلَاةُ. . . . ثُمَّ قَالَ ﷺ: أَيُّهَا النَّاسُ، إِنَّكُمْ قَدْ أَسْرَعْتُمْ فِي حَظَائِرِ يَهُودَ. أَلَا! لَا تَحِلُّ أَمْوَالُ الْمُعَاهَدِينَ إِلَّا بِحَقِّهَا.

> 'We fought in the Battle of Khaybar with the Messenger of God ﷺ and [as victory loomed] some people hastened to enter the compounds of the Jews. The Prophet ﷺ then ordered me to deliver the call to prayer . . . then he ﷺ said, "O people! You have hastened to enter the compounds of the Jews, but beware, the property of the non-Muslim citizens is not lawful to you except that which is due".'[1]

The same narration has been reported with the following wording as well:

أَلَا! وَإِنِّي أُحَرِّمُ عَلَيْكُمْ أَمْوَالَ الْمُعَاهَدِيْنَ بِغَيْرِ حَقِّهَا.

---

al-amwāl, pp. 244–245 §503; Ibn Saʿd in *al-Ṭabaqāt al-kubrā*, 1:288, 358; Ibn Zanjawayh in *Kitāb al-amwāl*, pp. 449–450 §732; and al-Balādhurī in *Futūḥ al-buldān*, p. 90.

[1] Narrated by Aḥmad b. Ḥanbal in *al-Musnad*, 4:89 §16862; Abū Dāwūd in *al-Sunan*: *Kitāb al-aṭʿima* [The Book of Foodstuffs], chapter: 'The Unlawfulness of Eating Beasts of Prey', 3:356 §3806; and Ibn Zanjawayh in *Kitāb al-amwāl*, p. 379 §618.

> 'Beware! I forbid you from the property of the non-Muslim citizens, except that which is due'.[1]

Imam al-Dāraquṭnī reported the same hadith in a different wording, where Khālid b. al-Walīd ﷺ said,

حَرَّمَ رَسُولُ اللهِ ﷺ يَوْمَ خَيْبَرَ أَمْوَالَ الْمُعَاهَدِيْنَ.

> 'On the day of Khaybar the Messenger of God ﷺ forbade taking the wealth of the non-Muslim citizens'.[2]

From the assorted agreements, documents and declarations, we see that the non-Muslim citizens of the prophetic period enjoyed the following rights:

1. They enjoy equal treatment under the law
2. The protection of their religion from any harm
3. Their honour, life and property are protected
4. The Islamic government can appoint them to the highest administrative positions, provided they possess the necessary qualifications
5. They have the authority to appoint their religious representatives and office-holders without any interference
6. Their places of worship are sacred and enjoy complete protection

5.2 The Protection of Non-Muslim Citizens during the Reign of Abū Bakr al-Ṣiddīq ﷺ

The protection afforded to the life, honour and property of non-Muslim citizens was not confined to the life of the Prophet ﷺ. The Rightly Guided Caliphs who succeeded the Prophet ﷺ also continued to give the non-Muslim citizens full recognition.

During the caliphate of Abū Bakr al-Ṣiddīq, the non-Muslim citizens had similar rights as their Muslim counterparts. Whenever an Islamic army would leave for a military expedition, Abū Bakr would give special instructions to the commander:

---

[1] Narrated by al-Ṭabarānī in *al-Muʿjam al-kabīr*, 4:111 §3828; and Ibn Zanjawayh in *Kitāb al-amwāl*, p. 380 §619.

[2] Narrated by al-Dāraquṭnī in *al-Sunan*, 4:287 §63.

لَا تُفْسِدُوا فِي الْأَرْضِ وَلَا تَعْصُوا مَا تُؤْمَرُونَ . . . وَلَا تُغْرِقُنَّ نَخْلًا وَلَا تُحْرِقُنَّهَا، وَلَا تَعْقِرُوا بَهِيْمَةً وَلَا شَجَرَةً تُثْمِرُ، وَلَا تَهْدِمُوا بِيْعَةً، وَلَا تَقْتُلُوا الْوِلْدَانَ وَلَا الشُّيُوخَ وَلَا النِّسَاءَ. وَسَتَجِدُونَ أَقْوَامًا حَبَسُوا أَنْفُسَهُمْ فِي الصَّوَامِعِ، فَدَعُوهُمْ، وَمَا حَبَسُوا أَنْفُسَهُمْ لَهُ.

'Do not spread corruption in the earth and do not disobey orders. . . . Do not drown or burn date-palm trees. Do not kill any animal. Do not cut down a fruit-bearing tree. Do not demolish a church. Do not kill any children, old people or women. Soon you shall come upon people who have secluded themselves in cloisters; leave them to engage in that for whose sake they have secluded themselves'.[1]

Ḥusām al-Dīn al-Hindī mentioned an additional wording to this report in his *Kanz al-ʿummāl*,

وَلَا مَرِيْضًا وَلَا رَاهِبًا.

'And [do] not [kill] a sick person or a monk'.[2]

When Abū Bakr ﷺ sent Yazīd b. Abī Sufyān to Syria, he said,

لَا تَهْدِمُوا بِيْعَةً . . . وَلَا تَقْتُلُوا شَيْخًا كَبِيْرًا، وَلَا صَبِيًّا وَلَا صَغِيْرًا، وَلَا امْرَأَةً.

'Do not demolish any place of worship . . . and do not kill an old, feeble man or an infant or a child or a woman'.[3]

Thābit b. al-Ḥajjāj al-Kilābī reported that Abū Bakr al-Ṣiddīq ﷺ said while delivering his address,

أَلَا! لَا يُقْتَلُ الرَّاهِبُ فِي الصَّوْمَعَةِ.

'Beware! A priest should not be killed in his church'.[4]

---

[1] Narrated by al-Bayhaqī in *al-Sunan al-kubrā*, 9:85; Mālik in *al-Muwaṭṭa*, 2:448 §966; ʿAbd al-Razzāq in *al-Muṣannaf*, 5:199 §9375; al-Hindī in *Kanz al-ʿummāl*, 1:296; and cited by Ibn Qudāma in *al-Mughnī*, 8:451–452, 477.

[2] Narrated by al-Hindī in *Kanz al-ʿummāl*, 4:474 §11409.

[3] Narrated by al-Bayhaqī in *al-Sunan al-kubrā*, 9:90 §17929.

[4] Narrated by Ibn Abī Shayba in *al-Muṣannaf*, 6:483 §33127; and al- Hindī in

When Khālid b. al-Walīd, under the command of the Abū Bakr al-Ṣiddīq ﷺ, returned to Iraq and Iran from the borders of Syria, he concluded an agreement with the non-Muslim inhabitants there that their churches and convents will not be demolished, that they can beat their wooden clapper [*nāqūs*] without any restriction—except for the times of the five daily prayers—and that they can take out their crucifixes on the occasion of their Eid.[1]

5.3 The Protection of Non-Muslim Citizens during the Reign of ʿUmar b. al-Khaṭṭāb ﷺ

During the caliphate of ʿUmar b. al-Khaṭṭāb ﷺ, the respect, dignity and esteem for the non-Muslim citizens of the conquered areas increased so much that they considered themselves more secure and free during that period than before. Montgomery Watt, a renowned orientalist, admitted this in his book *Islamic Political Thought: The Basic Concepts*. He said, 'The Christians were probably better off as *dhimmis* under Muslim-Arab rulers than they had been under the Byzantine Greeks'.[2]

The level of protection and respect shown towards the non-Muslim citizens during ʿUmar's caliphate can be gauged from his letter to Abū ʿUbayda ﷺ, the then Governor of Syria, in which he said,

وَامْنَعِ الْمُسْلِمِيْنَ مِنْ ظُلْمِهِمْ وَالإِضْرَارِ بِهِمْ وَأَكْلِ أَمْوَالِهِمْ إِلَّا بِحِلِّهَا.

> 'You must prohibit the Muslims from wronging and harming their non-Muslim citizens and consuming their wealth illegally'.[3]

It was the standard practice of ʿUmar ﷺ that whenever a non-Muslim delegation from the Islamic territories would come to call on him, he would ask them about the conditions of the non-Muslim citizens of their locality, lest some Muslims had created problems for them. To this, they would say, 'We can only say that

---

Kanz al-ʿummāl, 4:472.

[1] Cited by Abū Yūsuf in *Kitāb al-kharāj*, p. 158.

[2] Montgomery Watt, *Islamic Political Thougtht: The Basic Concepts*, p. 51.

[3] Cited by Abū Yūsuf in *Kitāb al-kharāj*, p. 152.

every Muslim has fulfilled his commitment that is present between the Muslims and ourselves'.[1]

ʿUmar remained mindful of the rights of the minorities till the last moment of his life. Despite his impending martyrdom at the hands of a member of a minority group, he said,

أُوصِي الْخَلِيْفَةَ مِنْ بَعْدِي بِذِمَّةِ اللهِ وَذِمَّةِ رَسُولِهِ ﷺ: أَنْ يُوفَى لَهُمْ بِعَهْدِهِمْ، وَأَنْ يُقَاتَلَ مِنْ وَرَائِهِمْ، وَأَنْ لَا يُكَلَّفُوا فَوْقَ طَاقَتِهِمْ.

> 'I advise my successor to fulfil the contract of the non-Muslim citizens who are under the protection of God and His Messenger ﷺ. I enjoin him to fight for them if the need arises and not to burden them with more than they can bear'.[2]

5.3.1 ʿUmar's Relaxation of Tax Collection from the Non-Muslim Citizens

ʿUmar ؓ instructed his officials to deal with the non-Muslim subjects in an excellent manner and advised them to give concessions to them in levying and collecting taxes. Aslam, a freed slave of ʿUmar ؓ, stated,

إِنَّ عُمَرَ كَتَبَ إِلَى أُمَرَاءِ الْأَجْنَادِ: أَنْ لَا يَضْرِبُوا الْجِزْيَةَ عَلَى النِّسَاءِ، وَلَا عَلَى الصِّبْيَانِ.

> 'ʿUmar ؓ wrote a letter to the military commanders stating that they should not impose tax on non-Muslim women or children'.[3]

Imam Ibn Qudāma stated,

---

[1] Narrated by al-Ṭabarī in *Tārīkh al-umam wa al-mulūk*, 2:503.

[2] Narrated by al-Bukhārī in *al-Ṣaḥīḥ*: *Kitāb al-janāʾiz* [The Book of Funerals], chapter: 'What Has Come Regarding the Grave of the Prophet ﷺ', 1:469 §1328; Ibn Abī Shayba in *al-Muṣannaf*, 7:436 §37059; al-Bayhaqī in *al-Sunan al-kubrā*, 8:150; and Ibn Saʿd in *al-Ṭabaqāt*, 3:339.

[3] Narrated by ʿAbd al-Razzāq in *al-Muṣannaf*, 6:85 §10009; and al-Bayhaqī in *al-Sunan al-kubrā*, 9:195 §18463.

فَإِنَّ عُمَرَ ﷺ أُتِيَ بِمَالٍ كَثِيرٍ، قَالَ أَبُو عُبَيْدٍ: وَأَحْسِبُهُ مِنَ الْجِزْيَةِ. فَقَالَ: إِنِّي لَأَظُنُّكُمْ قَدْ أَهْلَكْتُمُ النَّاسَ، قَالُوا: لَا، وَاللهِ، مَا أَخَذْنَا إِلَّا عَفْوًا صَفْوًا. قَالَ: بِلَا سَوْطٍ وَلَا نَوْطٍ؟ قَالُوا: نَعَمْ. قَالَ: الْحَمْدُ لِلّٰهِ الَّذِي لَمْ يَجْعَلْ ذَلِكَ عَلَى يَدَيَّ وَلَا فِي سُلْطَانِي.

'A large amount of wealth was brought to ʿUmar, and Abū ʿUbayd said, "I believe it was money collected from tax". ʿUmar said, "For certain, you have destroyed the people!" They [the tax collectors] said, "No, by God! We have only taken with tenderness and ease". ʿUmar inquired, "Was it acquired without recourse to a whip or coercion?" They replied, "Yes". He said, "All praise is due to God, Who did not put that on my hands or during my rule".'[1]

During his journey to Syria, ʿUmar saw that the tax officials were making the non-Muslim citizens stand out in the sun as their taxes were collected. Upon seeing this, he said,

دَعُوهُمْ، لَا تُكَلِّفُوهُمْ مَا لَا يُطِيقُونَ، فَإِنِّي سَمِعْتُ رَسُولَ اللهِ ﷺ يَقُولُ: لَا تُعَذِّبُوا النَّاسَ، فَإِنَّ الَّذِينَ يُعَذِّبُونَ النَّاسَ فِي الدُّنْيَا يُعَذِّبُهُمُ اللهُ يَوْمَ الْقِيَامَةِ.

'Spare them from this and do not burden them with more than they can bear. Indeed, I heard the Messenger of God ﷺ say, "Do not torture people, for those who torture people in this life will be tortured by God on the Day of Resurrection".'[2]

Upon hearing this, the tax official let them go.

Hishām b. al-Ḥakīm saw ʿIyāḍ b. Ghanam, a government officer of Homs, make a Copt stand out in the sun during the time of tax collection. He reprimanded him and said that he heard the Prophet ﷺ say,

[1] Ibn Qudāma al-Maqdisī, *al-Mughnī*, 9:290.

[2] Cited by Abū Yūsuf in *Kitāb al-kharāj*, p. 135.

إِنَّ اللهَ يُعَذِّبُ الَّذِيْنَ يُعَذِّبُونَ النَّاسَ فِي الدُّنْيَا.

> 'Indeed, God shall torment those who torment others in the life of this world'.[1]

5.3.2 Stipends for the Handicapped, Old and Poor Non-Muslim Citizens

Such was the excellent treatment towards the non-Muslim citizens during the reign of Caliph ʿUmar ﵁ that the old, disabled and the weak non-Muslim citizens were not only exempted from the tax, but were also given stipends from the government treasury for the maintenance of their households.

Imam Abū ʿUbayd al-Qāsim b. Sallām writes in *Kitāb al-amwāl*,

إِنَّ أَمِيْرَ الْمُؤْمِنِيْنَ عُمَرَ ﵁ مَرَّ بِشَيْخٍ مِنْ أَهْلِ الذِّمَّةِ يَسْأَلُ عَلَى أَبْوَابِ النَّاسِ،
فَقَالَ: مَا أَنْصَفْنَاكَ أَنْ كُنَّا أَخَذْنَا مِنْكَ الْجِزْيَةَ فِي شَبِيْبَتِكَ، ثُمَّ ضَيَّعْنَاكَ فِي كِبَرِكَ.
قَالَ: ثُمَّ أَجْرَى عَلَيْهِ مِنْ بَيْتِ الْمَالِ مَا يُصْلِحُهُ.

> 'The Commander of the Faithful, ʿUmar ﵁, passed by an elderly man amongst the non-Muslim citizens who was begging at people's doors. ʿUmar said to him, "We have not been fair to you if we have taken the tax from you when you were younger but left you in helplessness in your old age". After that, ʿUmar issued instructions for the man to receive enough money from the public treasury that would take care of his needs'.[2]

Imam Abū Yūsuf described the same report in *Kitāb al-kharāj* in the following words:

---

[1] Narrated by Muslim in *al-Ṣaḥīḥ*: *Kitāb al-birr wa al-ṣila wa al-ādāb* [The Book of Piety, Filial Duty and Good Manners], chapter: 'The Severe Divine Threat to the One Who Punishes People Unjustly', 4:2018 § 2613; Abū Dāwūd in *al-Sunan*: *Kitāb al-kharāj* [The Book of Land Taxation], chapter: 'On Being Harsh', 3:106 §3045; Aḥmad b. Ḥanbal in *al-Musnad*, 3:403, 404, 468; and al-Nasāʾī in *al-Sunan al-kubrā*, 5:236 §8771.

[2] Narrated by Abū ʿUbayd al-Qāsim b. Sallām in *Kitāb al-amwāl*, p. 57 §119.

مَرَّ عُمَرُ بْنُ الْخَطَّابِ ﷺ بِبَابِ قَوْمٍ وَعَلَيْهِ سَائِلٌ يَسْأَلُ، شَيْخٌ كَبِيْرٌ ضَرِيْرُ الْبَصَرِ، فَضَرَبَ عَضُدَهُ مِنْ خَلْفِهِ، وَقَالَ: مِنْ أَيِّ أَهْلِ الْكِتَابِ أَنْتَ؟ فَقَالَ: يَهُودِيٌّ. قَالَ: فَمَا أَلْجَأَكَ إِلَى مَا أَرَى؟ قَالَ أَسْأَلُ الْجِزْيَةَ وَالْحَاجَةَ وَالسِّنَّ. قَالَ: فَأَخَذَ عُمَرُ بِيَدِهِ وَذَهَبَ إِلَى مَنْزِلِهِ فَرَضَخَ لَهُ بِشَيْءٍ مِنَ الْمَنْزِلِ. ثُمَّ أَرْسَلَ إِلَى خَازِنِ بَيْتِ الْمَالِ، فَقَالَ: انْظُرْ هَذَا وَضُرَبَاءَهُ، فَوَاللهِ، مَا أَنْصَفْنَاهُ أَنْ أَكَلْنَا شَبِيْبَتَهُ، ثُمَّ نَخْذُلُهُ عِنْدَ الْهَرَمِ ﴿إِنَّمَا ٱلصَّدَقَٰتُ لِلْفُقَرَآءِ وَٱلْمَسَٰكِينِ﴾ وَالْفُقَرَاءُ هُمُ الْمُسْلِمُونَ، وَهَذَا مِنَ الْمَسَاكِيْنِ مِنْ أَهْلِ الْكِتَابِ. وَوَضَعَ عَنْهُ الْجِزْيَةَ وَعَنْ ضُرَبَائِهِ.

'ʿUmar b. al-Khaṭṭāb ﷺ passed by the door of some people and there was an elderly blind man there, begging. ʿUmar put his hand on his arm from behind and asked, "From which group amongst the People of the Book do you belong?" The man replied, "I am a Jew". ʿUmar then asked him, "So why are you begging?" "I am begging for money", the man said, "so I can pay the tax and fulfil my needs, because I am too old to earn money". ʿUmar took him by the hand and led him to his home and gave him a few things, then he sent him to the treasurer of the public treasury and said, "Take care of him and those like him, for by God, we have not treated him fairly if we benefited from him in his younger days but left him helpless in his old age! "[Then he recited the verse,] '*Charity is only for the poor and indigent*"[1] and the poor are amongst the Muslims and this one is from the indigent amongst the People of the Book". So ʿUmar exempted him and those like him from payment of taxes'.[2]

ʿAbd Allāh b. Ḥadrad al-Aslamī said,

لَمَّا قَدِمْنَا مَعَ عُمَرَ بْنِ الْخَطَّابِ الْجَابِيَةَ، إِذَا هُوَ بِشَيْخٍ مِنْ أَهْلِ الذِّمَّةِ يَسْتَطْعِمُ، فَسَأَلَ عَنْهُ، فَقُلْنَا: يَا أَمِيرَ الْمُؤْمِنِيْنَ، هَذَا رَجُلٌ مِنْ أَهْلِ الذِّمَّةِ كَبُرَ وَضَعُفَ. فَوَضَعَ

[1] Qurʾān 9:60.

[2] Abū Yūsuf, *Kitāb al-kharāj*, p. 136.

عَنْهُ عُمَرُ الْجِزْيَةَ الَّتِي فِي رَقَبَتِهِ. وَقَالَ: كَلَّفْتُمُوهُ الْجِزْيَةَ حَتَّى إِذَا ضَعُفَ تَرَكْتُمُوهُ يَسْتَطْعِمُ. فَأَجْرَى عَلَيْهِ مِنْ بَيْتِ الْمَالِ عَشَرَةَ دَرَاهِمَ، وَكَانَ لَهُ عِيَالٌ.

'When we reached al-Jābiya with ʿUmar b. al-Khaṭṭāb there was an elderly man from the non-Muslim citizens who was begging others and asking for food. ʿUmar inquired about him and we said, "O Commander of the Faithful! This is a man from the non-Muslim citizens. He is elderly and weak". Upon learning of this, ʿUmar exempted him from the tax that was due from him and said, "You burdened him with the payment of the tax and when he became weak you left him to beg!" Then ʿUmar provided him with ten dirhams [monthly] from the public treasury because he had his family'.[1]

5.4 The Protection of Non-Muslim Citizens during the Reign of ʿUthmān b. ʿAffān ﷺ

The third phase of the Rightly Guided Caliphate started with a heart-wrenching tragedy. A non-Muslim assassinated ʿUmar b. al-Khaṭṭāb ﷺ, making him a martyr. ʿUbayd Allāh b. ʿUmar was so enraged at the assassination that he killed three people who were involved in the conspiracy: two of whom were Christians and one of whom was a Muslim. After this, ʿUbayd Allāh was detained and soon after assuming the role of the third Caliph, ʿUthmān b. ʿAffān ﷺ sought the opinion of the Companions regarding his status. The consensus of the Companions was that ʿUbayd Allāh b. ʿUmar should be killed in retribution. Had the heirs of those killed not reconciled and forgiven him in lieu of blood money, ʿUbayd Allāh would most certainly have been killed. After the reconciliation was reached, the blood money was evenly distributed amongst the victims' families.[2] Imam Abū ʿUbayd, Imam Ḥumayd b. Zanjawayh and al-Balādhurī have cited the following words of ʿUthmān's ﷺ official order:

[1] Ibn ʿAsākir, *Tārīkh Dimashq al-kabīr*, 27:334.

[2] Ibn Saʿd, *al-Ṭabaqāt*, 5:17.

إِنِّي أُوصِيكَ بِهِمْ خَيْرًا، فَإِنَّهُمْ قَوْمٌ لَهُمُ الذِّمَّةُ.

> 'I hereby command you to deal with the non-Muslim citizens in an excellent manner, for they are a folk with a complete guarantee [of protection and rights]'.[1]

This establishes that the blood of Muslims and non-Muslims is of equal sanctity.

5.5 The Protection of Non-Muslim Citizens during the Reign of ʿAlī b. Abī Ṭālib ﷺ

During the caliphate of ʿAlī b. Abī Ṭālib ﷺ, non-Muslim citizens continued to enjoy the same rights and protections they had during the prophetic period and that of the three preceding Rightly Guided Caliphs.

A Muslim who had killed a non-Muslim was presented in the court of ʿAlī ﷺ. After the proof of his crime was furnished and found valid, ʿAlī ﷺ ordered him to be killed in retribution. The heirs of the killer managed to get the brother of the victim to pardon him in return for a blood money payment. When ʿAlī learned of this he said to one of the heirs of the victim,

لَعَلَّهُمْ فَزَّعُوكَ أَوْ هَدَّدُوكَ؟

> 'Did they [the heirs of the killer] scare you or threaten you in any way?'

He replied in the negative and said that his brother would not come back, even if the killer was killed in retribution, and that since the heirs of the killer would be paying the blood money, which would take care of the needs of his brother's [the victim's] family, he agreed to the reconciliation out of his own will without any pressure. Upon hearing this, ʿAlī ﷺ said that the final decision rested with him, for he knew better what to do; however, the operative principle of the Shariah is that

[1] Cited by Ibn Saʿd in *al-Ṭabaqāt*, 1:360; Abū Yūsuf in *Kitāb al-kharāj*, p. 80; Abū ʿUbayd al-Qāsim b. Sallām in *Kitāb al-amwāl*, p. 246 §505; Ibn Zanjawayh in *Kitāb al-amwāl*, p. 451 §732; and al-Balādhurī in *Futūḥ al-buldān*, p. 91.

مَنْ كَانَ لَهُ ذِمَّتُنَا، فَدَمُهُ كَدَمِنَا، وَدِيَتُهُ كَدِيَتِنَا.

> 'Whoever is under our guarantee of protection, then his blood is like our blood, and the blood money due to him is like the blood money due to us'.[1]

According to another tradition, our master ʿAlī ﷺ said,

إِذَا قَتَلَ الْمُسْلِمُ النَّصْرَانِيَّ قُتِلَ بِهِ.

> 'If a Muslim kills a Christian, he should be killed in retribution'.[2]

5.6 The Protection of Non-Muslim Citizens during the Reign of ʿUmar b. ʿAbd al-ʿAzīz ﷺ

In strict accordance with the teachings and conduct of the Prophet ﷺ and the practice of the Rightly Guided Caliphs, ʿUmar b. ʿAbd al-ʿAzīz ﷺ would always instruct his officials, saying,

لَا تَهْدِمُوا كَنِيْسَةً وَلَا بِيْعَةً وَلَا بَيْتَ نَارٍ.

> 'Do not demolish any church, cloister or Zoroastrian temple'.[3]

There is a famous incident in which an Umayyad ruler, Walīd b. ʿAbd al-Mālik, seized a piece of property belonging to the Church of Damascus and made it a part of a mosque. When news of this reached ʿUmar b. ʿAbd al-ʿAzīz, he ordered the demolishment of that portion of the mosque and instructed that it be returned to the Christians. One report about this incident reads:

لَمَّا اسْتَخْلَفَ عُمَرُ بْنُ عَبْدِ الْعَزِيْزِ ﷺ، شَكَى النَّصَارَى إِلَيْهِ مَا فَعَلَ الْوَلِيْدُ بِهِمْ فِي كَنِيْسَتِهِمْ، فَكَتَبَ إِلَى عَامِلِهِ يَأْمُرُهُ بِرَدِّ مَا زَادَهُ فِي الْمَسْجِدِ.

---

[1] Narrated by al-Bayhaqī in *al-Sunan al-kubrā*, 8:34; al-Shāfiʿī in *al-Musnad*, 1:344; and cited by al-Shaybanī in *Kitāb al-ḥujja ʿalā Ahl al-Madīna*, 4:355.

[2] Cited by al-Shaybānī in *Kitāb al-ḥujja ʿala Ahl al-Madīna*, 4:349; and al-Shāfiʿī in *al-Umm*, 7:320.

[3] Cited by Ibn Qayyim al-Jawziyya in *Aḥkām ahl al-dhimma*, 3:1200.

> 'When ʿUmar b. ʿAbd al-ʿAzīz ﵀ became the Caliph, the Christians complained to him about al-Walīd's seizure of Church property. He dictated orders to his governor there, commanding him to return to them the portion that was added to the mosque'.[1]

ʿUmar b. ʿAbd al-ʿAzīz ﵀ said to one of his governors,

إِنْ كَانَتْ مِنَ الْخَمْسِ عَشَرَةَ كَنِيْسَةً الَّتِي فِي عَهْدِهِمْ فَلَا سَبِيْلَ لَكَ إِلَيْهَا.

> 'If it [their Church] was from amongst the fifteen Churches that were extant during their reign, then it is off limits to you'.[2]

It is also reported that ʿUmar b. ʿAbd al-ʿAzīz ﵀ wrote to the governor about a Muslim in his territory who had killed a non-Muslim citizen. He ordered him to hand that Muslim over to the guardian of the victim, who was then given the choice to either pardon him or have him. The governor handed the killer over to the guardian of the victim, and the former was subjected to capital punishment.[3]

Whether during the prophetic period or the period of the Rightly Guided Caliphs and those after them, Islamic history is replete with the examples of excellent treatment towards non-Muslim citizens of the Islamic state. The members of other nations and religions would live a peaceful and comfortable life there to the extent that they regarded Islamic rule preferable to the rule of others. Their places of worship were afforded complete protection and security, and they were free to follow and practise their religion. All of their economic needs were met from the *bayt al-māl* (public treasury). People were so impressed by the Muslims' excellent manners and character that millions of non-Muslim citizens chose to embrace Islam willingly out of their own volition.

---

[1] Cited by al-Balādhūrī in *Futūḥ al-buldān,* p. 150.

[2] Cited by Abū ʿUbayd al-Qāsim b. Sallām in *Kitāb al-amwāl,* p. 201 §426; and Ibn Zanjawayh in *Kitāb al-amwāl,* p. 387 §635.

[3] Narrated by ʿAbd al-Razzāq in *al-Muṣannaf,* 10:101 §18518.

It is disconcerting to see that Muslims—let alone non-Muslims—are not safe from the terrorist activities of the modern-day extremists. The peace of society is shattered, blood is shed with reckless abandon and properties and infrastructures are subject to wanton destruction. The conduct of today's terrorists defaces the 1400-year history of Islam's excellent treatment of non-Muslim citizens. The acts of terrorism committed today do not champion the cause of Islam; rather, they malign its good name.

Chapter 6

The Unlawfulness of Forcing One's Belief upon Others and Destroying Places of Worship

6.1 Preliminary Statement

Islam gives complete religious freedom to non-Muslims, and the Islamic government is not to interfere in their religious affairs. Islam also guarantees the protection of their places of worship and other religious sites, as well as their life, honour and property. In short, Islam presents an unprecedented model of tolerance, harmony and peaceful co-existence. The Qur'ān fostered feelings of harmony amongst religions and ensured their freedom to the point that it forbade the believers from insulting the false gods of other faith traditions. God says in the Qur'ān,

﴿وَلَا تَسُبُّوا۟ ٱلَّذِينَ يَدْعُونَ مِن دُونِ ٱللَّهِ فَيَسُبُّوا۟ ٱللَّهَ عَدْوًا بِغَيْرِ عِلْمٍ﴾

> '*And do not insult those whom they worship besides God, lest they insult God wrongfully and out of ignorance*'.[1]

There can be no better example of interfaith tolerance than this.

6.2 The Complete Freedom to Practise One's Religion

There is no room for coercion in Islam and no one can be forced to convert. Islam gives complete religious freedom to all non-Muslim citizens to adhere to their respective faith traditions and to freely practise their teachings. God says,

﴿لَآ إِكْرَاهَ فِى ٱلدِّينِ قَد تَّبَيَّنَ ٱلرُّشْدُ مِنَ ٱلْغَىِّ﴾

> '*There is no compulsion in religion. Surely, right guidance is clearly distinguished from error*'.[2]

Ibn Kathīr explained this verse in the following words:

> 'Do not coerce anyone to embrace the religion of Islam, for its proofs and evidence are clear, obvious and

---

[1] Qur'ān 6:108.

[2] Ibid., 2:256.

manifest. There is no need for anyone to be coerced into embracing it'.[1]

God also says in the Qur'ān,

﴿أَفَأَنتَ تُكْرِهُ ٱلنَّاسَ حَتَّىٰ يَكُونُواْ مُؤْمِنِينَ﴾

'*So will you coerce people until they become believers?*'[2]

God has strictly forbidden the Muslims from coercing others to embrace Islam. Therefore, no non-Muslim can be compelled to become a Muslim, because Islam is not merely the profession of faith or the performance of bodily rituals; it requires the confirmation and conviction of the heart; and in matters of the heart, there is no scope for coercion.

When ʿUmar ﷺ granted security and protection to the people of Jerusalem, his treaty formed the constitution of religious freedom available for non-Muslims in an Islamic society. He wrote:

هَذَا مَا أَعْطَى عَبْدُ اللهِ عُمَرُ أَمِيْرُ الْمُؤْمِنِيْنَ أَهْلَ إِيْلِيَاءَ مِنَ الْأَمَانِ. أَعْطَاهُمْ أَمَانًا لِأَنْفُسِهِمْ وَأَمْوَالِهِمْ وَلِكَنَائِسِهِمْ وَصُلْبَانِهِمْ، وَسَقِيْمِهَا وَبَرِيْئِهَا وَسَائِرِ مِلَّتِهَا، أَنَّهُ لَا تُسْكَنُ كَنَائِسُهُمْ وَلَا تُهْدَمُ، وَلَا يُنْتَقَصُ مِنْهَا وَلَا مِنْ حَيِّزِهَا، وَلَا مِنْ صَلِيْبِهِمْ، وَلَا مِنْ شَيْءٍ مِنْ أَمْوَالِهِمْ، وَلَا يُكْرَهُونَ عَلَى دِيْنِهِمْ، وَلَا يُضَارُّ أَحَدٌ مِنْهُمْ، وَلَا يَسْكُنُ بِإِيْلِيَاءَ مَعَهُمْ أَحَدٌ مِنَ الْيَهُودِ.

'This is the covenant of security from the servant of God, ʿUmar, the Commander of the Faithful, to the people of Jerusalem. He grants them security in their lives, properties, churches, crucifixes and to their ill and their healthy and their entire religious community. Their churches are not to be occupied, demolished or decreased in number. Their churches or crucifixes should not be desecrated, or anything else of their property. They are not to be coerced to abandon their faith, and no one

[1] Ibn Kathīr, *Tafsīr al-Qur'ān al-ʿAẓīm*, 1:310.

[2] Qur'ān 10:99.

> amongst them is to be harmed in any way. And none of the Jews are to reside with them in Jerusalem [due to the severe enmity between them in those days].[1]

Professor Philip K. Hitti writes, 'They [non-Muslims] were allowed the jurisdiction of their own canon laws as administered by the respective heads of their religious communities. This state of partial autonomy, recognized later by the Sultans of Turkey, has been retained by the Arab successor states'.[2] Further on he writes, 'All non-Moslems were allowed autonomy under their own religious heads.[3] ... Syria as a whole remained largely Christian until the third Moslem century. ... In fact Lebanon remained Christian in faith and Syriac in speech for centuries after the conquest'.[4]

The opinion of Hitti and other non-Muslim orientalists testifies to the fact that the Islamic governments did not resort to coercion or pressure to change the religion of the non-Muslim citizens in their territories. Non-Muslims were given complete freedom and protection to practise their religions and hold fast to their faith traditions. Despite the Muslim conquests of these areas, the Christians held firm to their religion and the Muslim governments neither interfered with their faith nor hindered its practice. This demonstrates the benevolence of Islam, which has been duly appreciated by many non-Muslim researchers and historians.

6.3 The Unlawfulness of Killing a Non-Muslim and Destroying His or Her Property Due to Religious Differences

The diversities and differences between the various faith traditions cannot be a basis for killing others and seizing their wealth. It is unequivocally forbidden to oppress others through torture,

---

[1] Narrated by al-Ṭabarī in *Tārīkh al-umam wa al-mulūk*, 2:449.

[2] Philip K. Hitti, *History of the Arabs*, p. 170.

[3] Ibid., p. 225.

[4] Ibid., p. 231.

slander or false accusations—no matter what their race, religion or region. There is a recompense for every excess as God says,

﴿يَٰٓأَيُّهَا ٱلَّذِينَ ءَامَنُواْ كُتِبَ عَلَيۡكُمُ ٱلۡقِصَاصُ فِي ٱلۡقَتۡلَى﴾

'*O you who believe! Retribution* [*qiṣāṣ*] *is prescribed for you in cases where one is unjustly killed*'.[1]

Here, the word *qatlā* has been used, which encompasses both Muslims and non-Muslims, and then there is the order of 'a life for a life' in retribution. This can include the life of both a Muslim and a non-Muslim. Elsewhere in the Qur'ān God says,

﴿وَكَتَبۡنَا عَلَيۡهِمۡ فِيهَآ أَنَّ ٱلنَّفۡسَ بِٱلنَّفۡسِ وَٱلۡعَيۡنَ بِٱلۡعَيۡنِ وَٱلۡأَنفَ بِٱلۡأَنفِ وَٱلۡأُذُنَ بِٱلۡأُذُنِ وَٱلسِّنَّ بِٱلسِّنِّ وَٱلۡجُرُوحَ قِصَاصٞ﴾

'*And We prescribed for them in it* [the Torah] *retribution: a life for a life, an eye for an eye, a nose for a nose, an ear for an ear, a tooth for a tooth and for injuries*'.[2]

Likewise, if a Muslim steals from a non-Muslim, the prescribed punishment [*ḥadd*] can be enforced against him. Ibn Rushd reports that there is a consensus amongst the Muslims on this matter.[3] This illustrates that differences in religious doctrine do not justify killing or stealing from others.

6.4 It is a Sunna of the Prophet ﷺ to Safeguard the Non-Muslims' Places of Worship

The Prophet ﷺ allowed non-Muslims to retain their places of worship. Detailing the Prophet's practice ﷺ, Ibn al-Qayyim mentioned that the Prophet ﷺ allowed the places of worship belonging to the non-Muslims to remain intact after the conquest of Khaybar and did not allow them to be demolished. When other areas became part of the Islamic empire, the Rightly Guided

---

1 Qur'ān 2:178.

2 Ibid., 5:45.

3 Ibn Rushd, *Bidāyat al-mujtahid*, 2:299.

Caliphs and Companions followed the Prophet's orders and did not demolish them.[1]

6.5 It is a Religious Obligation to Safeguard the Non-Muslims' Places of Worship

According to the Qur'ān and prophetic hadith, it is binding upon the Islamic state to safeguard the sanctity of the religious sites and places of worship belonging to other religions, and to afford them complete protection. God says in the Qur'ān,

﴿وَلَوْلَا دَفْعُ ٱللَّهِ ٱلنَّاسَ بَعْضَهُم بِبَعْضٍ لَّهُدِّمَتْ صَوَٰمِعُ وَبِيَعٌ وَصَلَوَٰتٌ وَمَسَٰجِدُ يُذْكَرُ فِيهَا ٱسْمُ ٱللَّهِ كَثِيرًا﴾

> '*And had God not repelled one group of people from another, the cloisters, synagogues, churches and mosques in which God's name is mentioned in abundance would have been ruined*'.[2]

In his commentary on this verse, Imam Abū Bakr al-Jaṣṣāṣ quoted the words of Imam al-Ḥasan al-Baṣrī:

يَدْفَعُ عَنْ هَدْمِ مُصَلَّيَاتِ أَهْلِ الذِّمَّةِ بِالْمُؤْمِنِيْنَ.

> 'God uses the believers as a means of preventing the destruction of the places of worship belonging to the non-Muslim citizens'.[3]

Al-Jaṣṣāṣ continued:

فِي الْآيَةِ دَلِيْلٌ عَلَى أَنَّ هَذِهِ الْمَوَاضِعَ الْمَذْكُورَةَ لَا يَجُوزُ أَنْ تُهْدَمَ عَلَى مَنْ كَانَ لَهُ ذِمَّةٌ أَوْ عَهْدٌ مِنَ الْكُفَّارِ.

> 'Within this verse there is a proof that it is impermissible to destroy the aforementioned places of worship belonging

[1] Ibn Qayyim al-Jawziyya, *Aḥkām ahl al-dhimma*, 3:1199.

[2] Qur'ān 22:40.

[3] Abū Bakr al-Jaṣṣāṣ, *Aḥkām al-Qur'ān*, 5:83; and Ibn al-Qayyim, *Aḥkām ahl al-dhimma*, 3:1169.

> to those of the non-Muslims who are citizens or under a guarantee of protection'.[1]

Al-Akhfash stated in his interpretation of the same verse that the places of worship belonging to the non-Muslims should not be demolished at all. So in other words, it is the responsibility of the Islamic state to provide them complete protection in all circumstances. Every community safeguards its own values and culture and it is their right to do so. So the Muslims have been ordered to protect the places of worship belonging to the non-Muslims, despite religious differences.

Ibn al-Qayyim writes in *Aḥkām ahl al-dhimma*,

> يَدْفَعُ عَنْ مَوَاضِعِ مُتَعَبَّدَاتِهِمْ بِالْمُسْلِمِيْنَ. . . . كَمَا يُحِبُّ الدَّفْعَ عَنْ أَرْبَابِهَا وَإِنْ كَانَ يُبْغِضُهُمْ، وَهَذَا الْقَوْلُ هُوَ الرَّاجِحُ، وَهُوَ مَذْهَبُ ابْنِ عَبَّاسٍ.

> 'God uses the believers to defend their places of worship. . . . Moreover, it is obligatory for him [the believer] to defend their objects of worship, even though he detests them. This is the correct position and it is the view of Ibn ʿAbbās'.[2]

6.6 The Unlawfulness of Destroying the Non-Muslims' Places of Worship Located in Muslim-Majority Areas

Islam has strictly forbidden the Muslims from destroying the places of worship that belong to non-Muslims—even if they are located in Muslim-majority areas. The Islamic state is constitutionally responsible for the protection and safeguarding of these sites. Imam Abū Bakr al-Jaṣṣāṣ quoted Muhammad b. al-Ḥasan al-Shaybānī, who said,

> فِي أَرْضِ الصُّلْحِ إِذَا صَارَتْ مِصْرًا لِلْمُسْلِمِيْنَ، لَمْ يُهْدَمْ مَا كَانَ فِيْهَا مِنْ بِيْعَةٍ أَوْ كَنِيْسَةٍ أَوْ بَيْتِ نَارٍ.

---

1 Abū Bakr al-Jaṣṣāṣ, *Aḥkām al-Qurʾān*, 5:83.

2 Ibn Qayyim al-Jawziyya, *Aḥkām ahl al-dhimma*, 3:1169.

> 'When a territory under treaty becomes a territory of the Muslims, no church, sanctuary or Zoroastrian temple that was there before should be demolished'.[1]

All of these quotes and texts establish that Islam orders the Muslims to safeguard the places of worship that belong to the non-Muslim citizens of the Islamic lands. Furthermore, Islam grants them complete freedom to practise their religion without any interference. Considering all this, how is it possible that a person who claims to be a Muslim can shamelessly murder people engaged in worship and destroy their places of worship?

---

[1] Abū Bakr al-Jaṣṣāṣ, *Aḥkām al-Qurʾān*, 5:83.

Chapter 7

Legal Maxims Concerning the Basic Rights of the Non-Muslim Citizenry of an Islamic State

7.1 Legal Maxims

As demonstrated by the Qur'ān, the hadith reports and the practical examples of the Prophet ﷺ and the Rightly Guided Caliphs, we see that Islam not only endows non-Muslim citizens with the same rights as their Muslim counterparts, but also offers them equal protection. Islamic history is replete with examples of this. In the light of the revealed texts and precedents of the Rightly Guided Caliphs which we have mentioned in the previous chapters, many legal maxims can be derived concerning the fundamental rights of the non-Muslim citizens in an Islamic state. Of them:

1. It is the responsibility of the Islamic state to protect the life, honour and property of its non-Muslim citizens from internal aggression
2. It is the responsibility of the Islamic state to protect its non-Muslim citizens from external aggression
3. In the Islamic state, Muslims and non-Muslims are equal with respect to blood money and retribution
4. The sanctity of the blood of a Muslim and a non-Muslim is the same
5. In the Islamic state, Muslim and non-Muslim citizens enjoy the same general rights and responsibilities
6. In the Islamic state, its non-Muslim citizens enjoy complete freedom to adhere to their faith
7. In the Islamic state, its non-Muslim citizens enjoy complete religious freedom to perform their rituals of worship
8. It is the Islamic state's responsibility to provide security to non-Muslim diplomats
9. It is the Islamic state's responsibility to arrange for the security of the religious leaders and places of worship of non-Muslims
10. It is the Islamic state's responsibility to care for the disabled, elderly and poor non-Muslim citizens
11. It is the Islamic state's responsibility to ensure that the sanctity of all religions in its territory is respected

Chapter 8

The Unlawfulness of Rebelling Against the Muslim State, Administration and Authority

8.1 What is Rebellion and Who is a Rebel?—Terms, Definitions and Signs

In the preceding pages we described the Islamic teachings pertaining to the prohibition of torturing Muslims, killing non-Muslims and bringing harm to the non-combatants of an enemy nation—including their properties and crops. This chapter seeks to determine the magnitude and heinousness of rebellion and terrorism in an Islamic state. Since this chapter deals exclusively with rebellion, we must first explain the meanings of words 'rebellion' and 'terrorism', and identify the signs of those who engage in them.

8.2 The Lexical Definition of Rebellion

The Arabic equivalent of the word 'rebellion' is derived from the word '*baghyun*', which sometimes implies demand and sometimes oppression and excess. According to the jurists, rebellion means to disobey the commands of a lawful government and launch armed struggle against it.

The philologist Ibn Fāris said:

بَغْيٌ: اَلْبَاءُ وَالْغَيْنُ وَالْيَاءُ، أَصْلَانِ: أَحَدُهُمَا طَلَبُ الشَّيْءِ، وَالثَّانِي: جِنْسٌ مِنَ الْفَسَادِ . . . وَالْأَصْلُ الثَّانِي: قَوْلُهُمْ بَغَى الْجَرْحُ، إِذَا تَرَامَى إِلَى فَسَادٍ . . . ثُمَّ يُشْتَقُّ مِنْ هَذَا مَا بَعْدَهُ، فَالْبَغْيُ الْفَاجِرَةُ . . . وَمِنْهُ أَنْ يَبْغِيَ الْإِنْسَانُ عَلَى الْآخَرِ . . . وَإِذَا كَانَ ذَا بَغْيٍ فَلَا بُدَّ أَنْ يَقَعَ مِنْهُ فَسَادٌ . . . وَالْبَغْيُ: اَلظُّلْمُ.

> The origin of the word *baghyun* is from the letters *bā*ʾ, *ghayn* and *yā*ʾ, and it has two primary meanings: [one] to seek something, and [two] a type of depravity. . . . Regarding the second meaning, it is found in their statement, that 'the wound got septic (*baghā*) or it deteriorated. . . . Then, after this, the other words are derived from it; so it is said that *baghyun* is an adulteress

> because she transgresses the limits of chastity and commits fornication. . . . And that *baghyun* from the same origin also implies oppression committed by one against the other. . . When it becomes someone's habit then mischief generates from his behaviour. That is why *baghyun* is also used to imply violence and oppression.[1]

Ibn Nujaym defined rebellion in the following words:

> اَلْبُغَاةُ جَمْعُ بَاغٍ، مِنْ بَغَى عَلَى النَّاسِ ظَلَمَ وَاعْتَدَى، وَبَغْيٌ سَعْيٌ بِالْفَسَادِ، وَمِنْهُ الْفِرْقَةُ الْبَاغِيَةُ لِأَنَّهَا عُدِلَتْ عَنِ الْقَصْدِ . . . وَفِئَةٌ بَاغِيَةٌ خَارِجَةٌ عَنْ طَاعَةِ الْإِمَامِ الْعَادِلِ.

> The word *bughāt* is the plural of *bāgh* (rebel). He who 'transgressed [*baghā*] against people' is the one who oppressed and committed excess. It also means that he spread mischief. From it comes the term *al-firqa al-bāghiya* (the rebellious sect), because it deviated from the middle path . . . and the *fi'a bāghiya* (the rebellious group) is one that does not obey the writ of the state.[2]

---

[1] Ibn Fāris, *Muʿjam maqāyīs al-lugha*, p. 144; and Ibn Manẓūr, *Lisān al-ʿArab*, 14:75–78.

[2] Ibn Nujaym, *al-Baḥr al-rāʾiq*, 5:150.
In Islamic literature, such as hadith books, Qurʾānic exegeses and works pertaining to jurisprudence and doctrine, we find that the terms used for the Islamic state are *jamāʿa* [congregation] or Emirate, and that for the ruler, the terms caliph, emir or imam are used. The Prophet ﷺ used the words *jamāʿa* and imam when he said, 'Stick to the congregation of the Muslims and their Imam'. (al-Bukhārī in *al-Ṣaḥīḥ: Kitāb al-fitan* [The Book of Tribulations], chapter: 'What Should be Done when There is no Congregation', 2:2595 §2273; and Ibn Mājah in *al-Sunan: Kitāb al-fitan* [The Book of Tribulations], chapter: 'On Seclusion', 2:1317 §2979.)

Ibn Khaldūn elaborates on the concept of imamate in the following words: 'The caliphate and emirate refer to the successorship of the possessor of the Sacred Law [the Prophet ﷺ] in safeguarding the religion and the affairs of the world'. (Ibn Khaldūn, *al-Muqaddima*, p. 134.) In contemporary times we have new terms for all sciences, so we have translated some common Islamic terms into the contemporary legal language. The word 'imam' has been translated as 'government', 'Muslim government' and 'Muslim state', and 'obedience' [*ṭāʿa, riyāsa*] have been translated as the administration of the state and authority.

Al-Ḥaṣkafī said about rebellion,

اَلْبَغْيُ لُغَةً: الطَّلَبُ، وَمِنْهُ: ﴿ذَالِكَ مَا كُنَّا نَبْغِ﴾. وَعُرْفًا: طَلَبُ مَا لَا يَحِلُّ مِنْ جَوْرٍ وَظُلْمٍ.

> 'Lexically, the word *baghyun* means to seek or demand something. An example of this meaning is in the verse, "*That is what we were seeking* [*nabghi*]" [Qur'ān 18:46]. Conventionally, it means to seek that which is unlawful, such as oppression, tyranny and terror'.[1]

These semantic details are given in lexicons such as *Tahdhīb al-lugha*, *al-Ṣiḥāḥ* and *Lisān al-ʿArab*. These lexical definitions prove that the word 'rebellion' means 'excess' and 'oppression'. Furthermore, it also refers to the breach of all legal, constitutional and Islamic limits to spread strife, mischief and chaos in society.

8.3 The Legal Definition of Rebellion

The lexicologists have provided various definitions for rebellion, all of which converge on the same root meaning. Likewise, numerous legal definitions have also been mentioned by the different schools of Islamic jurisprudence.

8.3.1 Rebellion According to the Ḥanafī School of Jurisprudence

The name of Ibn Humām figures prominently in the Ḥanafī school. He spelled out the most comprehensive definition of rebellion in his book, *Fatḥ al-Qadīr*, and described the different kinds of rebels. He said:

اَلْبَاغِي فِي عُرْفِ الْفُقَهَاءِ: الْخَارِجُ عَنْ طَاعَةِ إِمَامِ الْحَقِّ. وَالْخَارِجُونَ عَنْ طَاعَتِهِ أَرْبَعَةُ أَصْنَافٍ:

أَحَدُهَا: الْخَارِجُونَ بِلَا تَأْوِيلٍ بِمَنَعَةٍ وَبِلَا مَنَعَةٍ، يَأْخُذُونَ أَمْوَالَ النَّاسِ وَيَقْتُلُونَهُمْ وَيُخِيفُونَ الطَّرِيْقَ، وَهُمْ قُطَّاعُ الطَّرِيْقِ.

وَالثَّانِي: قَومٌ كَذَلِکَ إِلَّا أَنَّهُمْ لَا مَنَعَةَ لَهُمْ لَكِنْ لَهُمْ تَأْوِيْلٌ. فَحُكْمُهُمْ حُكْمُ قُطَّاعِ

[1] Al-Ḥaṣkafī, *al-Durr al-mukhtār*, 4:261.

الطَّرِيْقِ. إِنْ قَتَلُوا قُتِلُوا وَصُلِبُوا. وَإِنْ أَخَذُوا مَالَ الْمُسْلِمِيْنَ قُطِعَتْ أَيْدِيْهِمْ وَأَرْجُلِهِمْ عَلَى مَا عُرِفَ.

وَالثَّالِثُ: قَوْمٌ لَهُمْ مَنَعَةٌ وَحَمِيَّةٌ خَرَجُوا عَلَيْهِ بِتَأْوِيْلٍ يَرَوْنَ أَنَّهُ عَلَى بَاطِلٍ كُفْرٍ أَوْ مَعْصِيَةٍ. يُوجِبُ قِتَالَهُ بِتَأْوِيْلِهِمْ. وَهَؤُلَاءِ يُسَمَّوْنَ بِالْخَوَارِجِ يَسْتَحِلُّوْنَ دِمَاءَ الْمُسْلِمِيْنَ وَأَمْوَالَهُمْ، وَيسْبُونَ نِسَاءَهُمْ وَيُكَفِّرُونَ أَصْحَابَ رَسُولِ اللهِ ﷺ. وَحُكْمُهُمْ عِنْدَ جَمْهُورِ الْفُقَهَاءِ وَجَمْهُورِ أَهْلِ الْحَدِيْثِ حُكْمُ الْبُغَاةِ. . . .

وَالرَّابِعُ: قَوْمٌ مُسْلِمُونَ خَرَجُوا عَلَى إِمَامٍ وَلَمْ يَسْتَبِيْحُوا مَا اسْتَبَاحَهُ الْخَوَارِجُ، مِنْ دِمَاءِ الْمُسْلِمِيْنَ وَسَبْيِ ذَرَارِيْهِمْ وَهُمُ الْبُغَاةُ.

According to the conventional usage amongst the jurists, the word *bāghī* [rebel] denotes the one who rebels against the authority of the government. Those who challenge the writ of the state are four kinds:

[1] Those who rebel without any incorrect interpretation [*ta'wīl*]—whether they have a force of arms or not—and who seize the wealth of people, murder them and terrorise travellers on the road. They are brigands.

[2] A folk who are just like the aforementioned group. They *do not* have a force of arms, but *do* have an incorrect interpretation. The legal ruling upon this group is that they are considered brigands: if they fight they are to be killed and crucified, and if they steal the wealth of the Muslims the prescribed punishment has to be given to them, in the manner that is well-known [in Islamic law].

[3] A folk who have a force of arms and protection, and who rebel against the writ of the government with an incorrect interpretation and believe that the government is based on falsehood, disbelief or disobedience, and that according to their incorrect interpretation it is obligatory to rebel against it; this group is called Kharijites. They declare lawful the blood and wealth of the Muslims, capture their womenfolk and declare the Companions of God's Messenger ﷺ apostates. According to the majority

of the jurists and the traditionists [*ahl al-ḥadīth*] they are given the same ruling as that of the rebels [*bughāt*]. . . .

[4] A group of Muslims who rebelled against the government, but did not declare lawful what the Kharijites declared lawful, such as shedding the blood of the Muslims and capturing their children. This group is considered amongst the rebels [*bughāt*].[1]

Zayn al-Dīn b. Nujaym al-Ḥanafī defined rebels as:

قَوْمٌ مُسْلِمُونَ خَرَجُوا عَلَى الإِمَامِ الْعَدْلِ، وَلَمْ يَسْتَبِيْحُوا مَا اسْتَبَاحَهُ الْخَوَارِجُ مِنْ دِمَاءِ الْمُسْلِمِيْنَ وَسَبْيِ ذَرَارِيْهِمْ.

'A group of Muslims who rebelled against a legitimate government, but did not declare lawful what the Kharijites declared lawful, such as shedding the blood of Muslims and capturing their children'.[2]

Ibn ʿĀbidīn al-Shāmī defined rebellion in *Radd al-muḥtār* in the following words:

أَهْلُ الْبَغْيِ: كُلُّ فِئَةٍ لَهُمْ مَنَعَةٌ. يَتَغَلَّبُونَ وَيَجْتَمِعُونَ وَيُقَاتِلُونَ أَهْلَ الْعَدْلِ بِتَأْوِيْلٍ. يَقُولُونَ: "اَلْحَقُّ مَعَنَا" وَيَدَّعُونَ الْوِلَايَةَ.

'The people of rebellion include every faction that possesses force of arms and seeks to gain power; they fight the people of justice on the basis of an incorrect interpretation, and argue that "the truth is with us" and that they are the true authorities'.[3]

In *al-Durr al-mukhtār*, al-Ḥaṣkafī described three different kinds of rebels:

ثُمَّ الْخَارِجُونَ عَنْ طَاعَةِ الإِمَامِ ثَلَاثَةٌ: قُطَّاعُ طَرِيْقٍ . . . وَبُغَاةٌ . . . وَخَوَارِجُ وَهُمْ

---

[1] Ibn Humām, *Fatḥ al-Qadīr*, 5:334.

[2] Ibn Nujaym, *al-Baḥr al-rāʾiq*, 5:151.

[3] Ibn ʿĀbidīn al-Shāmī, *Radd al-muḥtār*, 4:262; al-Dasūqī, *al-Ḥāshiya*, 4:261; and Badr al-Dīn al-ʿAynī in *al-Bināya sharḥ al-Hidāya*, 5:888.

قَوْمٌ لَهُمْ مَنَعَةٌ خَرَجُوا عَلَيْهِ بِتَأْوِيلٍ يَرَوْنَ أَنَّهُ عَلَى بَاطِلٍ كُفْرٍ أَوْ مَعْصِيَةٍ، تُوجِبُ قِتَالَهُ بِتَأْوِيلِهِمْ. وَيَسْتَحِلُّونَ دِمَاءَنَا وَأَمْوَالَنَا، وَيَسْبُونَ نِسَاءَنَا وَيُكَفِّرُونَ أَصْحَابَ نَبِيِّنَا ﷺ. وَحُكْمُهُمْ حُكْمُ الْبُغَاةِ بِإِجْمَاعِ الْفُقَهَاءِ كَمَا حَقَّقَهُ فِي الْفَتْحِ.

Furthermore, those who rebel against the government and spread mischief are three types: brigands [*quṭṭāʿ al-ṭarīq*], . . . rebels [*bughāt*] . . . and Kharijites. As for the Kharijites, they are a folk possessing a force of arms who rebel against the government on the basis of an incorrect interpretation by which they believe it is based on falsehood, disbelief or disobedience, and who believe, according to their incorrect interpretation, that it is obligatory to engage in militancy against the state. They declare lawful the shedding of our blood and the seizure of our wealth, and they capture our womenfolk and declare our Prophet's ﷺ Companions disbelievers. According to the consensus of the jurists, they take the same judgement as the rebels, as he [Ibn Humām] verified in *al-Fatḥ* [*Fatḥ al-Qadīr*].[1]

8.3.2 Rebellion According to the Mālikī School of Jurisprudence

Imam Muhammad b. Ahmad b. al-Juzayy al-Kalbī, one of the notable jurists of the Mālikī school, wrote:

اَلْبُغَاةُ هُمُ الَّذِيْنَ يُقَاتِلُونَ عَلَى التَّأْوِيلِ، وَالَّذِيْنَ يَخْرُجُونَ عَلَى الْإِمَامِ، أَوْ يَمْتَنِعُونَ مِنَ الدُّخُولِ فِي طَاعَتِهِ، أَوْ يَمْنَعُونَ حَقًّا وَجَبَ عَلَيْهِمْ كَالزَّكَاةِ وَشَبَهِهَا.

The rebels are those who fight on the basis of a self-styled interpretation, and who refuse to accept the authority of the state, or who, by force of arms, refuse to obey it, or who refuse to fulfil a duty that is incumbent upon them, such as Zakat and the like.[2]

Imam al-Dasūqī writes in his marginalia on *al-Sharḥ al-kabīr* in the chapter titled, 'The Section on Rebellion and Related Matters':

---

[1] Al-Ḥaṣkafī, *al-Durr al-mukhtār*, 4:262–263.

[2] Ibn Juzayy al-Kalbī, *al-Qawānīn al-fiqhiyya*, p. 364.

هُوَ لُغَةً التَّعَدِّي وَبَغَى فُلَانٌ عَلَى فُلَانٍ: اسْتَطَالَ عَلَيْهِ. وَشَرْعًا قَالَ ابْنُ عَرَفَةَ: هُوَ الْإِمْتِنَاعُ مِنْ طَاعَةِ مَنْ ثَبَتَتْ إِمَامَتُهُ فِي غَيْرِ مَعْصِيَةٍ بِمُغَالَبَةٍ وَلَوْ تَأَوُّلًا.

'Lexically, it means to transgress. It is said "so-and-so *baghā* against so-and-so" if he went against him. Legally, it is, as Ibn ʿArafa said, "To employ force—even if through a self-styled interpretation—while refusing lawful obedience to a lawfully established government".'

8.3.3 Rebellion According to the Shāfiʿī School of Jurisprudence

Imam al-Nawawī penned an entire chapter on fighting rebels in his book *Rawḍat al-ṭālibīn*. He defined the term rebel, saying,

اَلْبَاغِي فِي اصْطِلَاحِ الْعُلَمَاءِ هُوَ الْمُخَالِفُ لِلإِمَامِ الْعَدْلِ، الْخَارِجُ عَنْ طَاعَتِهِ بِامْتِنَاعِهِ مِنْ أَدَاءِ وَاجِبٍ عَلَيْهِ أَوْ غَيْرِهِ بِشَرْطٍ.

'In the technical nomenclature of the scholars, the term "rebel" denotes the one who goes against the Muslim government, defies and conditionally withholds that which he or others are duty-bound to fulfil'.[1]

Zakariyyā al-Anṣārī al-Shāfiʿī defined rebels, saying:

اَلْبُغَاةُ هُمْ مُخَالِفُو إِمَامٍ بِتَأْوِيلٍ بَاطِلٍ ظَنًّا وَشَوْكَةٍ لَهُمْ، وَيَجِبُ قِتَالُهُمْ. وَأَمَّا الْخَوَارِجُ: وَهُمْ قَوْمٌ يُكَفِّرُونَ مُرْتَكِبَ كَبِيرَةٍ وَيَتْرُكُونَ الْجَمَاعَاتِ، فَلَا يُقَاتَلُونَ مَا لَمْ يُقَاتِلُوا.

Rebels are those who, possessing strength, go against the government on the basis of a speculative and false interpretation. It is obligatory to fight them [to crush their revolt]. As for the Kharijites, they are a folk who declare those who commit enormities to be disbelievers, and they abandon the community [*jamāʿa*]; they are not to be fought as long as they do not fight.[2]

---

1 Yaḥyā al-Nawawī, *Rawḍat al-ṭālibīn*, 10:50.

2 Zakariyyā al-Anṣārī, *Manhaj al-ṭullāb*, 1:123.

Imam al-Shirbīnī said in *al-Iqnāʿ*:

> اَلْبُغَاةُ جَمْعُ بَاغٍ. وَالْبَغْيُ اَلظُّلْمُ وَمُجَاوَزَةُ الْحَدِّ. سُمُّوا بِذَلِكَ لِظُلْمِهِمْ وَعُدُولِهِمْ عَنِ الْحَقِّ. وَالْأَصْلُ فِيْهِ آيَةٌ: ﴿وَإِن طَآئِفَتَانِ مِنَ ٱلْمُؤْمِنِينَ ٱقْتَتَلُواْ﴾. وَلَيْسَ فِيْهَا ذِكْرُ الْخُرُوجِ عَلَى الإِمَامِ صَرِيْحًا لَكِنَّهَا تَشْمَلُهُ بِعُمُومِهَا أَوْ تَقْتَضِيْهِ، لِأَنَّهُ إِذَا طُلِبَ الْقِتَالُ لَبَغَى طَائِفَةٌ عَلَى طَائِفَةٍ فَلِلْبَغْيِ عَلَى الإِمَامِ أَوْلَى. وَهُمْ مُسْلِمُونَ مُخَالِفُو إِمَامٍ وَلَوْ جَائِرًا، بِأَنْ خَرَجُوا عَنْ طَاعَتِهِ بِعَدَمِ انْقِيَادِهِمْ لَهُ أَوْ مَنْعِ حَقٍّ تَوَجَّهَ عَلَيْهِمْ كَزَكَاةٍ بِالشُّرُوطِ الْآتِيَةِ. وَيُقَاتَلُ أَهْلُ الْبَغْيِ وُجُوبًا كَمَا اسْتُفِيْدَ مِنَ الْآيَةِ الْمُتَقَدِّمَةِ.

> The word '*bughāt*' is the plural of *bāgh*, and *baghyun* is oppression and going beyond the bounds. They [the rebels] are given this name because of their oppression and departure from the truth. The basis for this is found in the verse, '*And if two parties amongst the believers fight each other . . .*'[1] [Qurʾān 49:9] There is no explicit mention here of rebellion against the Muslim government, but its general import does include it or imply it, because if it is ordered to fight the rebellious of two contending parties, then it is ordered—*a fortiori*—to fight against the one who rebels against the government. These are the anti-government Muslims, even if the government is oppressive. They revolt against the writ of the government through disobeying it or withholding rights due upon them, such as the payment of Zakat with previously mentioned conditions. It is obligatory to fight the rebels, as is inferred from the aforementioned verse.[2]

Imam al-Shirbīnī has also described the same detail in his other work, *Mughnī al-muḥtāj* (4:123).

---

[1] The complete verse is: '*And if two parties amongst the believers fight each other then make peace between them. And if one party goes against [baghat] the other, then all of you together fight the contentious party until they all submit to the command of God*'. ED.

[2] al-Shirbīnī, *al-Iqnāʿ*, 2:547.

8.3.4 Rebellion According to the Ḥanbalī School of Jurisprudence

Ibn Hubayra al-Ḥanbalī described rebellion in the following words:

وَاتَّفَقُوا عَلَى أَنَّهُ إِذَا خَرَجَ عَلَى إِمَامِ الْمُسْلِمِيْنَ طَائِفَةٌ ذَاتُ شَوْكَةٍ بِتَأْوِيْلٍ مُشْتَبَهٍ، فَإِنَّهُ يُبَاحُ قِتَالُهُمْ حَتَّى يَفِيْئُوا.

'They [the jurists] all concurred that if a party possessing strength rebels against the writ of the Muslim government, with self-styled and mistaken interpretations, it is permissible to fight them until they submit to the writ of the state'.[1]

Imam Ibn Qudāma al-Maqdisī defined rebels as:

قَوْمٌ مِنْ أَهْلِ الْحَقِّ خَرَجُوا عَلَى الْإِمَامِ بِتَأْوِيْلٍ سَائِغٍ، وَرَامُوا خَلْعَهُ، وَلَهُمْ مَنَعَةٌ وَشَوْكَةٌ.

'A folk from the people of truth [i.e., the Muslims] that rebel against the writ of the state due to some alluring interpretation, and that seek to overthrow the government with the force of arms and strength'.[2]

Muhammad b. Mufliḥ al-Maqdisī al-Ḥanbalī wrote in *al-Furūʿ*:

أَهْلُ الْبَغْيِ: وَهُمُ الْخَارِجُونَ عَلَى الْإِمَامِ بِتَأْوِيْلٍ سَائِغٍ. وَلَهُمْ شَوْكَةٌ لَا جَمْعٌ يَسِيْرٌ خِلَافًا لِأَبِي بَكْرٍ. وَإِنْ فَاتَ شَرْطٌ فَقُطَّاعُ طَرِيْقٍ. وَفِي التَّرْغِيْبِ لَا تَتِمُّ الشَّوْكَةُ إِلاَّ وَفِيْهِمْ وَاحِدٌ مُطَاعٌ. وَأَنَّهُ يُعْتَبَرُ كَوْنُهُمْ فِي طَرَفِ وِلَايَتِهِ.

The rebels are those who rise against the state due to some apparently alluring interpretation, and who possess power; they are not a small group—contrary to the view of Abū Bakr [al-Marwazī]—even if they do not fit the conditions for being considered brigands [*quṭṭāʿ al-ṭarīq*].

---

[1] Ibn Hubayra, *al-Ifṣāḥ*, p. 402.

[2] Ibn Qudāma al-Maqdisī, *al-Kāfī*, 4:147; al-Shirbīnī, *Mughnī al-muḥtāj*, 4:123–124; and al-Qarāfī, *al-Dhakhīra*, 5:512.

> In *al-Targhīb* it is mentioned: 'They are not considered to have power unless there is one person amongst them who is obeyed [as a leader]'. And they can also be considered [rebels] if they apply their force in any part [of the Islamic state's jurisdiction].[1]

Imam Ibrāhīm b. Muḥammad b. ʿAbd Allāh b. Mufliḥ al-Ḥanbalī writes in *al-Mubdiʿ*,

> اَلْبَغْيُ مَصْدَرُ بَغَى يَبْغِي بَغْيًا إِذَا اعْتَدَى. وَالْمُرَادُ هُنَا الظَّلَمَةُ الْخَارِجُونَ عَنْ طَاعَةِ الْإِمَامِ الْمُعْتَدُونَ عَلَيْهِ.

> '*Baghyun* is the verbal noun of the verb *baghā/yabghī*. It is said that someone "*baghā*" if he transgressed. In this context it means the oppressors who rebel and transgress against the Muslim government'.[2]

Marʿī b. Yūsuf al-Ḥanbalī wrote in *Ghāyat al-muntahā*:

> هُمُ الْخَارِجُونَ عَلَى إِمَامٍ وَلَوْ غَيْرِ عَدْلٍ، بِتَأْوِيلٍ سَائِغٍ وَلَهُمْ شَوْكَةٌ، وَلَوْ لَمْ يَكُنْ فِيهِمْ مُطَاعٌ وَيَحْرُمُ الْخُرُوجُ عَلَى الْإِمَامِ وَلَوْ غَيْرِ عَدْلٍ.

> They are the ones who, with an apparently appealing interpretation, rebel against the Muslim government, even if it is unjust. And they possess power, even if they have no central leader who is obeyed. It is unlawful to rebel against the writ of the government, even if it is unjust.[3]

Al-Buhūtī al-Ḥanbalī wrote in *Kashshāf al-qināʿ ʿan matn al-iqnāʿ*, in the chapter on fighting rebels,

> هُوَ مَصْدَرُ بَغَى يَبْغِي إِذَا اعْتَدَى، وَالْمُرَادُ هُنَا الظَّلَمَةُ الْخَارِجُونَ عَنْ طَاعَةِ الْإِمَامِ الْمُعْتَدُونَ عَلَيْهِ.

---

1 Ibn Mufliḥ, *al-Furūʿ*, 6:147.

2 Ibn Mufliḥ, *al-Mubdiʿ*, 9:159–160.

3 Marʿī b. Yūsuf al-Karmī, *Ghāyat al-muntahā*, 3:348.

> 'It [*baghyun*] is the verbal noun of the verb *baghā/yabghī*. It is said that someone "*baghā*" if he transgressed. In this context it refers to the oppressive rebels who revolt and transgress against the writ of the state'.[1]

8.3.5 Rebellion According to the Jaʿfarī School of Jurisprudence

Abū Jaʿfar Muhammad b. Ḥusayn al-Ṭūsī, the Jaʿfarī jurist, penned an entire chapter in his book *al-Iqtiṣād al-hādī ilā ṭarīq al-rashād*, describing the prescriptions against rebels. He said:

> اَلْبَاغِي هُوَ كُلُّ مَنْ خَرَجَ عَلَى إِمَامٍ عَادِلٍ وَشَقَّ عَصَاهُ، فَإِنَّ عَلَى الْإِمَامِ أَنْ يُقَاتِلَهُمْ. وَيَجِبُ عَلَى كُلِّ مَنْ يَسْتَنْهِضُهُ الْإِمَامُ أَنْ يَنْهَضَ مَعَهُ وَيُعَاوِنُهُ عَلَى قِتَالِهِمْ، وَلَا يَجُوزُ لِغَيْرِ الْإِمَامِ قِتَالُهُمْ بِغَيْرِ إِذْنِهِ. فَإِذَا قُوتِلُوا لَا يُرْجَعُ عَنْهُمْ إِلاَّ أَنْ يَفِيئُوا إِلَى الْحَقِّ أَوْ يُقْتَلُوا، وَلَا يُقْبَلُ مِنْهُمْ عِوَضٌ وَلَا جِزْيَةٌ.
>
> وَالْبُغَاةُ عَلَى ضَرْبَيْنِ: أَحَدُهُمَا: مَنْ لَهُ رَئِيسٌ يَرْجِعُونَ إِلَيْهِ. فَهَؤُلَاءِ يَجُوزُ أَنْ يُجْتَازَ عَلَى جَرَاحَاتِهِمْ وَيُتْبَعَ مُدْبِرُهُمْ وَيُقْتَلَ أَسِيْرُهُمْ. وَالْآخَرُ: لَا يَكُونُ لَهُمْ فِيْهِ رَئِيْسٌ، فَهَؤُلَاءِ لَا يُجَازُ عَلَى جَرِيْحِهِمْ وَلَا يُقْتَلُ أَسِيْرُهُمْ.

> The word rebel denotes everyone who rebels and revolts against a Muslim government. It is the duty of the government to fight them, and it is obligatory upon everyone whom the government drafts [to fight them] to go with it or help it in fighting them. It is impermissible for someone other than the government to fight them—unless it is by its permission. When they are fought, there must be no turning back unless they return to the truth or are killed. Neither tax [in lieu of fealty] nor compensation is accepted from them.
>
> There are two types of rebels. The first type is a group that has a leader to whom they defer. It is permissible to finish off their wounded, pursue those of them who

---

[1] Al-Buhūtī, *Kashshāf al-qināʿ ʿan matn al-Iqnāʿ*, 6:158.

> flee [in battle] and kill those of them who are captured. The second type is a group that does not have a leader to whom they defer; their wounded and captured ones are not to be killed.[1]

The Jaʿfarī jurist and Qurʾānic exegete, al-Faḍl b. al-Ḥasan al-Ṭabarsī, defined the term 'rebel' in *al-Muʾtalif min al-mukhtalif*,

اَلْبَاغِي هُوَ الَّذِي يَخْرُجُ عَلَى إِمَامٍ عَادِلٍ وَيُقَاتِلُهُ، وَيَمْنَعُ مِنْ تَسْلِيمِ الْحَقِّ إِلَيْهِ.

> 'A rebel is the one who revolts and fights against a Muslim state, and refuses to give it his rightful due'.[2]

These quotes demonstrate that the renowned and the distinguished scholars of the Muslim world have described rebellion in much the same way, and with little variation, despite their different eras, doctrines and schools of jurisprudence. It is important for us to know the conclusions of the various jurisprudential traditions so we may assimilate them into one single definition.

All of the esteemed jurists interpreted the term 'rebels' as a group whose actions spring from extremism and who challenge the authority of the government on the basis of their self-styled interpretations. The terrorism we are facing today belongs to the same category and deserves the same treatment meted out to the terrorists of the past. If enforced, the aforementioned legal precepts would uproot terrorism.

8.3.6 Rebellion According to Contemporary Jurists

The sixteenth session of the Muslim World League was held in the Islamic Academy of Jurisprudence in Mecca, from January 5 to January 10, 2002, under the supervision of King Fahd bin Abdul Aziz, the Custodian of the two Sanctuaries. After five days of deliberation, the 'Makka Declaration' defined terrorism:

اَلْإِرْهَابُ هُوَ الْعُدْوَانُ الَّذِي يُمَارِسُهُ أَفْرَادٌ أَوْ جَمَاعَاتٌ أَوْ دُوَلٌ بَغْيًا عَلَى الْإِنْسَانِ: دِيْنِهِ، وَدَمِهِ، وَعَقْلِهِ، وَمَالِهِ، وَعِرْضِهِ. وَيَشْمَلُ صُنُوفَ التَّخْوِيْفِ وَالْأَذَى وَالتَّهْدِيْدِ

---

[1] Al-Ṭūsī, *al-Iqtiṣād al-hādī ilā ṭarīq al-rashād*, p. 315.

[2] Al-Ṭabarsī, *al-Muʾtalif min al-mukhtalif*, 2:377.

وَالْقَتْلِ بِغَيْرِ حَقٍّ وَمَا يَتَّصِلُ بِصُوَرِ الْحَرَابَةِ وَإِخَافَةِ السَّبِيْلِ وَقَطْعِ الطَّرِيْقِ، وَكُلِّ فِعْلٍ مِنْ أَفْعَالِ الْعُنْفِ أَوِ التَّهْدِيْدِ، يَقَعُ تَنْفِيْذًا لِمَشْرُوعٍ إِجْرَامِيٍّ فَرْدِيٍّ أَوْ جَمَاعِيٍّ، وَيَهْدِفُ إِلَى إِلْقَاءِ الرُّعْبِ بَيْنَ النَّاسِ، أَوْ تَرْوِيْعِهِمْ بِإِيْذَائِهِمْ، أَوْ تَعْرِيْضِ حَيَاتِهِمْ أَوْ حُرِيَّتِهِمْ أَوْ أَمْنِهِمْ أَوْ أَحْوَالِهِمْ لِلْخَطَرِ، وَمِنْ صُنُوفِهِ إِلْحَاقُ الضَّرَرِ بِالْبِيْئَةِ أَوْ بِأَحَدِ الْمَرَافِقِ وَالْأَمْلَاكِ الْعَامَّةِ أَوِ الْخَاصَّةِ، أَوْ تَعْرِيْضِ أَحَدِ الْمَوَارِدِ الْوَطَنِيَّةِ، أَوِ الطَّبِيْعِيَّةِ لِلْخَطَرِ، فَكُلُّ هَذَا مِنْ صُوَرِ الْفَسَادِ فِي الْأَرْضِ الَّتِي نَهَى اللهُ سُبْحَانَهُ وَتَعَالَى الْمُسْلِمِيْنَ عَنْهَا: ﴿وَلَا تَبْغِ ٱلْفَسَادَ فِى ٱلْأَرْضِ إِنَّ ٱللَّهَ لَا يُحِبُّ ٱلْمُفْسِدِينَ﴾. وَقَدْ شَرَعَ اللهُ الْجَزَاءَ الرَّادِعَ لِلْإِرْهَابِ وَالْعُدْوَانِ وَالْفَسَادِ، وَعَدَّهُ مُحَارَبَةَ اللهِ وَرَسُولِهِ ﷺ: ﴿إِنَّمَا جَزَٰٓؤُاْ ٱلَّذِينَ يُحَارِبُونَ ٱللَّهَ وَرَسُولَهُۥ وَيَسْعَوْنَ فِى ٱلْأَرْضِ فَسَادًا أَن يُقَتَّلُوٓاْ أَوْ يُصَلَّبُوٓاْ أَوْ تُقَطَّعَ أَيْدِيهِمْ وَأَرْجُلُهُم مِّنْ خِلَٰفٍ أَوْ يُنفَوْاْ مِنَ ٱلْأَرْضِ ذَٰلِكَ لَهُمْ خِزْىٌ فِى ٱلدُّنْيَا وَلَهُمْ فِى ٱلْأَخِرَةِ عَذَابٌ عَظِيمٌ﴾

وَلَا تُوجَدُ فِي أَيِّ قَانُونٍ بَشَرِيٍّ عُقُوبَةٌ بِهَذِهِ الشِّدَّةِ نَظَرًا لِخُطُورَةِ هَذَا الْاِعْتِدَاءِ، الَّذِي يُعَدُّ فِي الشَّرِيْعَةِ الْإِسْلَامِيَّةِ حَرْبًا ضِدَّ حُدُودِ اللهِ، وَضِدَّ خَلْقِهِ. وَيُؤَكِّدُ الْمَجْمَعُ أَنَّ مِنْ أَنْوَاعِ الْإِرْهَابِ: إِرْهَابَ الدَّوْلَةِ، وَمِنْ أَوْضَحِ صُوُرِهِ وَأَشَدِّهَا شَنَاعَةَ الْإِرْهَابَ الَّذِي يُمَارِسُهُ الْيَهُودُ فِي فِلَسْطِيْنَ، وَمَا مَارَسَهُ الصَّرْبُ فِي كُلٍّ مِنَ الْبَوْسَنَةِ وَالْهَرْسَكِ وَكَوْسَوْفَا، وَرَأَى الْمَجْمَعُ أَنَّ هَذَا النَّوْعَ مِنَ الْإِرْهَابِ مِنْ أَشَدِّ أَنْوَاعِهِ خَطَرًا عَلَى الْأَمْنِ وَالسَّلَامِ فِي الْعَالَمِ، وَعَدَّ مُوَاجَهَتَهُ مِنْ قُبَيْلِ الدِّفَاعِ عَنِ النَّفْسِ، وَالْجِهَادِ فِي سَبِيْلِ اللهِ.

Terrorism is aggression perpetrated by individuals, groups or states in a spirit of oppression against one's religion, blood, reason, wealth or honour. It comprises all types of fear-inducing behaviours, harms and threats, including armed burglary, the spreading of fear amongst travellers and acts of highway robbery. It covers all acts of violence or threats to commit individual or group crimes for the sake of striking fear amongst people or terrifying them through threats of causing harm to them or endangering their lives, freedom, security or general conditions. Included in the types of terrorism is the endangering of national or natural resources or the damaging of public utilities or private properties. All of the above are types of mischief on earth which God prohibited Muslims from committing when He said in the Qur'ān: '*And seek not mischief in the earth. Indeed, God does not like those who spread mischief*'.[1] God has legislated a rigorous punishment for terrorism, aggression and corruption and regarded them as acts of war against God and His Messenger ﷺ: '*Indeed, those who wage war against God and His Messenger* [i.e., perpetrate terrorism, robbery and burglary amongst people], *and remain engaged in creating mischief in the land, their punishment is that they should be slain, or crucified, or their hands and their feet on opposite sides should be cut off, or that they should be exiled from the land. That is for them a humiliation in this world, and for them there is a terrible torment in the Hereafter*'.[2]

There is not to be found any man-made law that prescribes such a severe punishment that is commensurate with the severity of this crime—a crime that the Shariah considers as war against the limits set by God, and against His creation. This council reiterates its stance that state-terrorism is a type of terrorism, and that its clearest examples are the acts of terror perpetrated by the Jews in Palestine and the Serbs in Bosnia Herzegovina and Kosovo. It is the view of this council that state-terror is the most dangerous form of terror threatening world security and peace, and it is this council's view that countering this state-terror is self-defence and jihad in the path of God.

---

[1] Qur'ān 28:77.

[2] Ibid., 5:33.

8.4 The Legal Definition of 'Unlawful Warfare' and 'Illegal Fighters'

Some religious scholars have used the word 'rebel' to mean 'illegal fighter' [*muḥārib*] and others have differentiated between a rebel and an illegal fighter and described different ways of dealing with both. Imam Ibn Humām said,

> بِأَنَّهُمُ الْخَارِجُونَ بِلَا تَأْوِيْلٍ بِمَنَعَةٍ وَبِلَا مَنَعَةٍ يَأْخُذُونَ أَمْوَالَ النَّاسِ، وَيَقْتُلُونَهُمْ وَيُخِيْفُونَ الطَّرِيْقَ.

> 'They [*muḥāribūn*] are those who rebel without a self-styled interpretation [justifying it on religious grounds], with or without force of arms, and who steal people's wealth, kill them and spread terror on the road'.[1]

Imam Ibn ʿAbd al-Barr also defined robbers, brigands and illegal fighters as those who shed blood and violate the dignity and honour of others. He said,

> كُلُّ مَنْ قَطَعَ السُّبُلَ وَأَخَافَهَا، وَسَعَى فِي الْأَرْضِ فَسَادًا بِأَخْذِ الْمَالِ، وَاسْتِبَاحَةِ الدِّمَاءِ، وَهَتْكِ مَا حَرَّمَ اللهُ هَتْكَهُ مِنَ الْمَحَارِمِ فَهُوَ مُحَارِبٌ.

> 'Every individual who blocks the roads, spreads fear, sows corruption on the earth by seizing wealth and shedding blood and violates those whose honour God has made inviolable [i.e., chaste women] is an illegal fighter [*muḥārib*]'.[2]

8.5 The Distinguishing Characteristics of Rebels

Imam al-Kāsānī, one of the notable jurists of the Ḥanafī school, said:

> اَلْبُغَاةُ هُمُ الْخَوَارِجُ. وَهُمْ قَوْمٌ مِنْ رَأْيِهِمْ أَنَّ كُلَّ ذَنْبٍ كُفْرٌ كَبِيْرَةً كَانَتْ أَوْ صَغِيْرَةً،

[1] Ibn Humām, *Fatḥ al-Qadīr*, 6:99; al-Māwardī, *al-Iqnāʿ*, p. 143.

[2] Ibn ʿAbd al-Barr, *al-Kāfī fī fiqh Ahl al-Madīna*, 2:1087; al-Dardīr, *al-Sharḥ al-ṣaghīr*, 4:492–493.

يَخْرُجُونَ عَلَى إِمَامِ أَهْلِ الْعَدْلِ. وَيَسْتَحِلُّونَ الْقِتَالَ وَالدِّمَاءَ وَالْأَمْوَالَ بِهَذَا التَّأْوِيلِ وَلَهُمْ مَنَعَةٌ وَقُوَّةٌ.

The rebels [*bughāt*] are the Kharijites, and they are a folk who believe that every sin is disbelief, whether it is a major or a minor sin. They rebel against the Muslim state, and with this self-styled interpretation they believe it is lawful to kill, shed blood and seize wealth; and they possess force and strength.[1]

In his well-known marginalia, *Ḥāshiya al-Bujayrimī,* Sulaymān b. ʿUmar b. Muhammad al-Shāfiʿī wrote:

أَمَّا الْخَوَارِجُ: وَهُمْ صِنْفٌ مِنَ الْمُبْتَدِعَةِ. قَائِلُونَ: بِأَنَّ مَنْ أَتَى كَبِيرَةً كَفَرَ وَحَبِطَ عَمَلُهُ وَخُلِّدَ فِي النَّارِ وَأَنَّ دَارَ الْإِسْلَامِ بِظُهُورِ الْكَبَائِرِ بِهَا تَصِيرُ دَارَ كُفْرٍ.

As for the Kharijites, they are a group from the innovators who assert that when someone commits a grave sin, he has disbelieved, his good deeds are null, and that he will abide eternally in Hell. They also believe that the lands of Islam become lands of disbelief when enormities are committed in them.[2]

In his book *al-Mughnī*, Imam Ibn Qudāma al-Maqdisī penned a chapter on the subject of fighting rebels. Referring to verses nine and ten of *Sūra al-Ḥujurāt*, he described the religious prescription regarding rebels and described the various kinds of Kharijites:

الْخَارِجُونَ عَنْ قَبْضَةِ الْإِمَامِ أَصْنَافٌ أَرْبَعَةٌ:

أَحَدُهَا: قَوْمٌ امْتَنَعُوا مِنْ طَاعَتِهِ وَخَرَجُوا عَنْ قَبْضَتِهِ بِغَيْرِ تَأْوِيلٍ، فَهَؤُلَاءِ قُطَّاعُ طَرِيقٍ سَاعُونَ فِي الْأَرْضِ بِالْفَسَادِ.

الثَّانِي: قَوْمٌ لَهُمْ تَأْوِيلٌ إِلاَّ أَنَّهُمْ نَفَرٌ يَسِيرٌ لَا مَنَعَةَ لَهُمْ كَالْوَاحِدِ وَالْاِثْنَيْنِ وَالْعَشْرَةِ وَنَحْوِهِمْ. فَهَؤُلَاءِ قُطَّاعُ طَرِيقٍ فِي قَوْلِ أَكْثَرِ أَصْحَابِنَا، وَهُوَ مَذْهَبُ الشَّافِعِيِّ لِأَنَّ

---

[1] Al-Kāsānī, *Badāʾiʿ al-ṣanāʾiʿ*, 7:140.

[2] Sulaymān al-Bujayrimī, *al-Ḥāshiya*, 4:201.

ابْنَ مُلْجِمٍ لَمَّا جَرَحَ عَلِيًّا ﵁ قَالَ لِلْحَسَنِ: إِنْ بَرِئْتُ رَأَيْتُ رَأْيِي، وَإِنْ مُتُّ فَلَا تُمَثِّلُوا بِهِ.

اَلثَّالِثُ: اَلْخَوَارِجُ الَّذِيْنَ يُكَفِّرُونَ بِالذَّنْبِ وَيُكَفِّرُونَ عُثْمَانَ وَعَلِيًّا وَطَلْحَةَ وَالزُّبَيْرَ وَكَثِيْرًا مِنَ الصَّحَابَةِ وَيَسْتَحِلُّونَ دِمَاءَ الْمُسْلِمِيْنَ وَأَمْوَالَهُمْ إِلاَّ مَنْ خَرَجَ مَعَهُمْ.

اَلرَّابِعُ: قَوْمٌ مِنْ أَهْلِ الْحَقِّ يَخْرُجُونَ عَنْ قَبْضَةِ الْإِمَامِ وَيَرُومُونَ خَلْعَهُ لِتَأْوِيْلٍ سَائِغٍ، وَفِيْهِمْ مَنَعَةٌ يَحْتَاجُ فِي كَفِّهِمْ إِلَى جَمْعِ الْجَيْشِ. فَهَؤُلَاءِ الْبُغَاةُ الَّذِيْنَ نَذْكُرُ فِي هَذَا الْبَابِ حُكْمَهُمْ وَوَاجِبٌ عَلَى النَّاسِ مَعُونَةُ إِمَامِهِمْ فِي قِتَالِ الْبُغَاةِ . . . لِأَنَّهُمْ لَوْ تَرَكُوا مَعُونَتَهُ لَقَهَرَهُ أَهْلُ الْبَغْيِ وَظَهَرَ الْفَسَادُ فِي الْأَرْضِ.

Those who are outside of the writ of the government and its authority are four categories:

[1] The first category is of those who refuse to obey the writ of the government and who rebel against it without a self-styled interpretation. They are brigands who spread mischief in the land.

[2] The second category is of those who have a self-styled interpretation, but they are a miniscule party without power, such as one or two people, or ten and the like. According to the position of most of our [Ḥanbalī] colleagues [and the position of al-Shāfiʿī], they are brigands, because when Ibn Muljam[1] stabbed ʿAlī, [ʿAlī] said to al-Ḥasan, 'If I recover from this I will decide about him, and if I die do not mutilate his corpse'.

[3] The third category is of those who are Kharijites: those who declare [others] disbelievers because of sins, and who declare ʿUthmān, ʿAlī, Ṭalḥa, Zubayr and many of the Companions disbelievers. And they believe that it is lawful to shed the blood of the Muslims and seize their wealth—except those of them who rebel along with them.

[4] The fourth category is of a folk from the people of truth [i.e., the Muslims] that rebel against the Muslim

[1] ʿAbd al-Raḥmān b. Muljam al-Murādī, the Kharijite who assassinated ʿAlī ﵁. ED.

> government due to a self-styled interpretation, and they seek, with force of arms and strength, to overthrow the government.[1]

Just as the jurists concur on the definition of rebels, so too they agree on their distinguishing characteristics. Their first characteristic is that they declare Muslims disbelievers and justify extremism through their erroneous interpretation of the religion, issuing verdicts of disbelief against the Muslims and the corrupt rulers in the Muslim lands. Their characteristics are similar to those of the Kharijites. Thus, the judgment of the fourth Caliph, ʿAlī ﷺ, against the Kharijites of his day is equally applicable to their modern counterparts.

---

[1] Ibn Qudāma al-Maqdisī, *al-Mughnī*, 9:3, 5.

Chapter 9

Rebellion: Its Gravity and Punishment

9.1 Why is Rebellion a Grave Crime?

We see from the previously mentioned definitions and details that those who revolt and commit acts of terrorism against Muslim citizens and governments do not deserve any concessions, because the power, strength, stability and survival of any nation depends on unity and community cohesion, which these terrorists attempt to destroy. The gravity and magnitude of rebellion against Muslim governments can be gauged from the following commandment of God Almighty,

﴿إِنَّمَا جَزَٰٓؤُاْ ٱلَّذِينَ يُحَارِبُونَ ٱللَّهَ وَرَسُولَهُۥ وَيَسْعَوْنَ فِى ٱلْأَرْضِ فَسَادًا أَن يُقَتَّلُوٓاْ أَوْ يُصَلَّبُوٓاْ أَوْ تُقَطَّعَ أَيْدِيهِمْ وَأَرْجُلُهُم مِّنْ خِلَٰفٍ أَوْ يُنفَوْاْ مِنَ ٱلْأَرْضِ ذَٰلِكَ لَهُمْ خِزْىٌ فِى ٱلدُّنْيَا وَلَهُمْ فِى ٱلْأَخِرَةِ عَذَابٌ عَظِيمٌ﴾

'*Indeed, those who wage war against God and His Messenger and remain engaged in creating mischief in the land* [i.e., perpetrate terrorism, robbery and burglary], *their punishment is that they should be slain, or crucified, or their hands and their feet on opposite sides should be cut off, or that they should be exiled from the land. That is for them a humiliation in this world, and for them there is a terrible torment in the Hereafter*'.[1]

This verse indicates that it is binding on the state to eliminate those who terrorise society through militancy and violence, irrespective of their faith that they claim to uphold. Explaining the aforementioned verse, Ibn ʿAbbās ﵄ said,

مَنْ شَهَرَ السِّلَاحَ فِي فِئَةِ الْإِسْلَامِ وَأَخَافَ السَّبِيْلَ، ثُمَّ ظَفِرَ بِهِ وَقَدَرَ عَلَيْهِ، فَإِمَامُ الْمُسْلِمِيْنَ فِيْهِ بِالْخِيَارِ إِنْ شَاءَ قَتَلَهُ وَإِنْ شَاءَ صَلَبَهُ وَإِنْ شَاءَ قَطَعَ يَدَهُ وَرِجْلَهُ.

1 Qurʾān 5:33.

> 'Whoever takes up arms against the community of Islam, terrorises the roads and is subsequently captured and apprehended, it is the discretion of the government to kill him, crucify him or cut off his hands and feet from opposite sides'.[1]

Imam al-Ṭabarī and Ibn Kathīr reported that Saʿīd b. al-Musayyab, Mujāhid, ʿAṭāʾ, al-Ḥasan al-Baṣrī, Ibrāhīm al-Nakhaʿī and al-Ḍaḥḥāk all shared the same position. Imam al-Suyūṭī narrated the same view in *al-Durr al-manthūr*. Imam al-Qurṭubī mentioned in his exegesis that this verse was revealed in connection with a group in the time of the Prophet ﷺ. They murdered peaceful people and plundered wealth, and in turn received a severe punishment.

This verse also indicates that capital punishment is lawful. Al-Qāḍī Thanāʾ Allāh Pānīpatī wrote:

> أَجْمَعُوا عَلَى أَنَّ الْمُرَادَ بِالْمُحَارِبِيْنَ الْمُفْسِدِيْنَ فِي هَذِهِ الْآيَةِ قُطَّاعُ الطَّرِيْقِ، سَوَاءٌ كَانُوا مُسْلِمِيْنَ أَوْ مِنْ أَهْلِ الذِّمَّةِ. وَاتَّفَقُوا عَلَى أَنْ مَنْ بَرَزَ وَشَهَرَ السِّلَاحَ مُخِيْفًا مُغِيْرًا خَارِجَ الْمِصْرِ بِحَيْثُ لَا يُدْرِكُهُ الْغَوْثُ، فَهُوَ مُحَارِبٌ قَاطِعٌ لِلطَّرِيْقِ جَارِيَةٌ عَلَيْهِ أَحْكَامُ هَذِهِ الْآيَةِ. . . . وَقَالَ الْبَغَوِيُّ: اَلْمُكَابِرُونَ فِي الْأَمْصَارِ دَاخِلُونَ فِي حُكْمِ هَذِهِ الْآيَةِ.

> They [the jurists] concurred that 'those who wage war and sow corruption in the earth' mentioned in the verse are the brigands, whether they are Muslims or from the non-Muslim citizens. They also agreed that the one who takes up arms for the purpose of spreading fear on the roads outside of the urban areas—as no help can reach there—is an unlawful combatant [*muḥārib*] and brigand who is subject to the rulings contained in this verse. . . . Al-Baghawī said, 'Those who rebel within the urban areas are also subject to the ruling contained in this verse'.[2]

---

[1] Ibn Kathīr, *Tafsīr al-Qurʾān al-ʿAẓīm*, 2:51; al-Ṭabarī, *Jāmiʿ al-bayān*, 6:214.

[2] Al-Qāḍī Thanāʾ Allāh Pānīpatī, *al-Tafsīr al-mazharī*, 3:86.

Al-Zamakhsharī interpreted this verse, saying,

يُحَارِبُونَ رَسُولَ اللهِ، وَمُحَارَبَةُ الْمُسْلِمِيْنَ فِي حُكْمِ مُحَارَبَتِهِ.

'They wage war against the Messenger of God ﷺ, and waging war against the Muslims takes the same legal ruling as waging war against him ﷺ'.[1]

Citing this exact quote from al-Zamakhsharī, Abū Ḥafṣ al-Ḥanbalī commented:

أَنَّ الْمَقْصُوْدَ أَنَّهُمْ يُحَارِبُونَ رَسُولَ اللهِ ﷺ وَإِنَّمَا ذَكَرَ اسْمَ اللهِ – تَبَارَكَ وَتَعَالَى – تَعْظِيْمًا وَتَفْخِيْمًا لِمَنْ يُحَارَبُ، كَقَوْلِهِ تَعَالَى: ﴿إِنَّ ٱلَّذِينَ يُبَايِعُونَكَ إِنَّمَا يُبَايِعُونَ ٱللَّهَ﴾.

What is meant here is that they wage war against the Messenger of God ﷺ—and God's name was only mentioned in exaltation and esteem for the one against whom war is waged, similar to the statement of God Most High, '*Indeed, those who pledge fealty to you are only pledging fealty to God*'. [Qurʾān 48:10][2]

Speaking on this verse, Imam Ibn Humām said that terrorism is tantamount to waging war against God, the Messenger ﷺ and the general body of Muslims:

سُمِّيَ قَاطِعُ الطَّرِيْقِ مُحَارِبًا لِلّٰهِ لِأَنَّ الْمُسَافِرَ مُعْتَمِدٌ عَلَى اللهِ تَعَالَى. فَالَّذِي يُزِيْلُ أَمْنَهُ مُحَارِبٌ لِمَنْ اعْتَمَدَ عَلَيْهِ فِي تَحْصِيْلِ الْأَمْنِ. وَأَمَّا مُحَارَبَتُهُ لِرَسُولِهِ ﷺ فَإِمَّا بِاعْتِبَارِ عِصْيَانِ أَمْرِهِ وَإِمَّا بِاعْتِبَارِ أَنَّ الرَّسُولَ ﷺ هُوَ الْحَافِظُ لِطَرِيْقِ الْمُسْلِمِيْنَ وَالْخُلَفَاءُ وَالْمُلُوكُ بَعْدَهُ نُوَّابُهُ. فَإِذَا قُطِعَ الطَّرِيْقُ الَّتِي تَوَلَّى حِفْظَهَا بِنَفْسِهِ وَنَائِبِهِ فَقَدْ حَارَبَهُ. أَوْ هُوَ عَلَى حَذْفِ مُضَافٍ أَي يُحَارِبُونَ عِبَادَ اللهِ.

The brigand is called one who wages war against God, because the traveller relies upon God Most High; so

[1] Jār Allāh al-Zamakhsharī, *al-Kashshāf ʿan ḥaqāʾiq ghawāmiḍ al-Tanzīl*, 1:661.

[2] Abū Ḥafṣ al-Ḥanbalī, *al-Lubāb fī ʿulūm al-Kitāb*, 7:303.

> the one who spoils his security wages war against the one in whom the traveller trusts for the obtainment of security. As for his waging war against His Messenger ﷺ, it is either because he disobeys him ﷺ, or because the Messenger ﷺ is the one who safeguards the paths of the Muslims, and the caliphs and kings after him are his deputies. So he who acts as a highway bandit on the roads that the Messenger ﷺ and his deputies took upon themselves to safeguard has waged war against him. On the other hand, the phrase can be understood as one in which the first particle of the construction is omitted, so in other words it means those who wage war against the servants of God.[1]

These aforementioned quotes prove that those who engage in terrorism are engaged in war against God and His Messenger ﷺ and the Muslim community entire.

9.2 AN IMPORTANT POINT

Highway robbers and bandits are also declared rebels and must be put to death according to the verse of *Sūra al-Māʾida* and its subsequent exegeses. Highway robbers block roads and cause misery to God's creation. In the present-day scenario, this crime also includes incidents where terrorists hold people hostage by taking over buildings, schools or mosques by force.

Terrorism is a form of social disruption that causes peaceful people to die a tormenting death and suffer from psychological distress and mental disorders. Terrorism has plagued the entire society with fear. Since terrorists attempt to mislead people by baseless and specious interpretations, their activities are a form of religious strife. This is also the reason why God declared them killers of humanity, or worse, those who wage war against God and His Messenger ﷺ. The Almighty has declared these mischief-mongers and terrorists the killers of humanity or the perpetrators of even a bigger sin. God's words are clear,

---

[1] Ibn Humām, *Fatḥ al-Qadīr*, 5:177.

﴿وَٱلْفِتْنَةُ أَشَدُّ مِنَ ٱلْقَتْلِ﴾

'And tribulation [fitna] is worse than killing'.[1]

9.3 THE PROPHET'S ﷺ CONDEMNATION OF ARMED UPRISING AGAINST THE MUSLIM COMMUNITY

The Prophet ﷺ vehemently condemned the forces of dissention and declared them outside the pale of Islam, saying, 'they are not from me'. They deviate from the right path, indiscriminately kill peaceful people, and rise in revolt against the state and society at large. Our Prophet ﷺ, the one who gave us the Shariah, prescribed severe punishments against rebels and mischief-makers, and the jurists followed suit with legal edicts in their respective periods.

The Prophet ﷺ severely warned against rebellion,

مَنْ خَرَجَ مِنَ الطَّاعَةِ وَفَارَقَ الْجَمَاعَةَ فَمَاتَ، مَاتَ مِيْتَةً جَاهِلِيَّةً، وَمَنْ قَاتَلَ تَحْتَ رَايَةٍ عِمِّيَّةٍ يَغْضَبُ لِعَصَبَةٍ أَوْ يَدْعُو إِلَى عَصَبَةٍ أَوْ يَنْصُرُ عَصَبَةً فَقُتِلَ فَقِتْلَةٌ جَاهِلِيَّةٌ، وَمَنْ خَرَجَ عَلَى أُمَّتِي يَضْرِبُ بَرَّهَا وَفَاجِرَهَا وَلَا يَتَحَاشَى مِنْ مُؤْمِنِهَا وَلَا يَفِي لِذِي عَهْدٍ عَهْدَهُ فَلَيْسَ مِنِّي وَلَسْتُ مِنْهُ.

'Whoever rebels against the writ of the Muslim state [and challenges its authority] and separates himself from the community [*jamāʿa*] and then dies, he dies the death of one in a state of *jāhilīya* [pre-Islamic time of ignorance]. And whoever fights under a blind banner, becomes angry for the sake of ignorant bigotry, calls to ignorant bigotry and gives support to blind bigotry and is then killed, his death is one of *jāhilīyya*. And whoever secedes from my nation [and rebels against the state, raising legions and troops], killing its righteous and sinful members and feels no compunction [in killing] its believers and does not fulfil the oath of the one from whom an oath is taken, then he is not from me and I am not from him'.[2]

---

[1] Qurʾān 2:191.

[2] Narrated by Muslim in *al-Ṣaḥīḥ*: *Kitāb al-imāra* [The Book of Leadership],

In this hadith, the Prophet ﷺ declared that the blind pursuit of war and fighting is lethal against the community cohesion. If someone fights against the main body of the Muslim *Umma*, or attempts to foment hostilities on the basis of extremism, the Prophet ﷺ has not only declared his death one in a state of gross ignorance, but he has also expelled him from the *Umma*.

The Prophet ﷺ also said,

مَنْ خَلَعَ يَدًا مِنْ طَاعَةٍ لَقِيَ اللهَ يَوْمَ الْقِيَامَةِ لَا حُجَّةَ لَهُ، وَمَنْ مَاتَ وَلَيْسَ فِي عُنُقِهِ بَيْعَةٌ مَاتَ مِيْتَةً جَاهِلِيَّةً.

> 'Whoever withdraws his obedience [to the rightful ruler] shall meet God on the Day of Resurrection bereft of any argument; and whoever dies the death of a rebel against the Muslim state dies the death of pre-Islamic ignorance [*jāhiliyya*]'.[1]

The odiousness of unjust rebellion can be gauged from a unique hadith report found in Imam al-Bayhaqī's *Shuʿab al-Īmān*, from our master ʿAbd Allāh b. ʿAbbās ﷺ who said,

لَوْ بَغَى جَبَلٌ عَلَى جَبَلٍ لَجَعَلَ اللهُ الْبَاغِيَ مِنْهُمَا دَكًّا.

> 'If one mountain rebelled against another mountain, God would have surely pulverised the rebellious one'.[2]

Speaking about the punishment that should be meted out to rebel groups, Imam al-Kāsānī wrote in *Badāʾiʿ al-ṣanāʾiʿ*:

إِنْ عَلِمَ الْإِمَامُ أَنَّ الْخَوَارِجَ يَشْهَرُونَ السِّلَاحَ وَيَتَأَهَّبُونَ لِلْقِتَالِ، فَيَنْبَغِي لَهُ أَنْ يَأْخُذَهُمْ

---

chapter: 'The Obligation to Stick to the Main Body of the Muslims in the Time of Trials', 3:1476, 1477 §1848; al-Nasāʾī in *al-Sunan*: *Kitāb taḥrīm al-dam* [The Book on the Prohibition of Bloodshed], 7:123 §4114; and Aḥmad b. Ḥanbal in *al-Musnad*, 2:296 §488.

[1] Narrated by Muslim in *al-Ṣaḥīḥ: Kitāb al-imāra* [The Book of Leadership], chapter: 'The Obligation to Stick to the Main Body of the Muslims in the Time of Trials', 3:1478 §1851; and al-Bayhaqī in *al-Sunan al-kubrā*, 8:156.

[2] Narrated by al-Bayhaqī in *Shuʿab al-Īmān*, 5:291 §6693; and cited by al-Dhahabī in *al-Kabāʾir*, 1:603; and al-Suyūṭī in *al-Durr al-manthūr*, 4:353.

وَيَحْبِسَهُمْ حَتَّى يَقْلَعُوا عَنْ ذَلِكَ وَيُحْدِثُوا تَوْبَةً. لِأَنَّهُ لَوْ تَرَكَهُمْ لَسَعَوا فِي الْأَرْضِ بِالْفَسَادِ فَيَأْخُذُهُمْ عَلَى أَيْدِيهِمْ. وَلَا يَبْدَؤُهُمُ الْإِمَامُ بِالْقِتَالِ حَتَّى يَبْدَؤُوهُ لِأَنَّ قِتَالَهُمْ لِدَفْعِ شَرِّهِمْ لَا لِشَرِّ شِرْكِهِمْ. لِأَنَّهُمْ مُسْلِمُونَ فَمَا لَمْ يَتَوَجَّهِ الشَّرُّ مِنْهُمْ لَا يُقَاتِلُهُمْ. وَإِنْ لَمْ يَعْلَمِ الْإِمَامُ بِذَلِكَ حَتَّى تَعَسْكَرُوا وَتَأَهَّبُوا لِلْقِتَالِ، فَيَنْبَغِي لَهُ أَنْ يَدْعُوَهُمْ إِلَى الْعَدْلِ وَالرُّجُوعِ إِلَى رَأْيِ الْجَمَاعَةِ أَوَّلًا لِرَجَاءِ الْإِجَابَةِ وَقَبُولِ الدَّعْوَةِ كَمَا فِي حَقِّ أَهْلِ الْحَرْبِ. وَكَذَا رُوِيَ أَنَّ سَيِّدَنَا عَلِيًّا ﵁ لَمَّا خَرَجَ عَلَيْهِ أَهْلُ حَرُورَاءَ نَدَبَ إِلَيْهِمْ عَبْدَ اللهِ بْنَ عَبَّاسٍ ﵄ لِيَدْعُوَهُمْ إِلَى الْعَدْلِ. فَدَعَاهُمْ وَنَاظَرَهُمْ فَإِنْ أَجَابُوا كَفَّ عَنْهُمْ وَإِنْ أَبَوْا قَاتَلَهُمْ لِقَوْلِهِ تَعَالَى: ﴿فَإِنۢ بَغَتْ إِحْدَىٰهُمَا عَلَى ٱلْأُخْرَىٰ فَقَـٰتِلُوا۟ ٱلَّتِى تَبْغِى حَتَّىٰ تَفِىٓءَ إِلَىٰٓ أَمْرِ ٱللَّهِ﴾ وَكَذَا قَاتَلَ سَيِّدُنَا عَلِيٌّ ﵁ أَهْلَ حَرُورَاءَ بِالنَّهْرَوَانِ بِحَضْرَةِ الصَّحَابَةِ ﵃.

If the government learns that the Kharijites [terrorists] are wielding weapons and preparing for battle, it must seize them and detain them until they desist and repent. If the government were to leave them, they would most certainly spread more terrorism on the earth. Hence it should apprehend them but not fight them until they initiate hostilities, because fighting them is for the sake of repelling their *evil*, not the evil of their polytheism [as it is for the pagans], for they are Muslims; and so long as their evil is not directed to others they are not to be fought. Therefore the government should first invite them to observe justice and return to the view of the greater community [*jamāʿa*], in hopes that they will respond and accept the invitation—as is the practice with the people with whom there are hostilities [*ahl al-ḥarb*]. On this note, it is reported that when the Ḥarūriyya rebelled against our master ʿAlī ﵁, he sent ʿAbd Allāh b. ʿAbbās ﵄ to invite them to justice. He attempted to persuade them and debated them. Those amongst them who responded positively were left alone and those amongst them who refused were fought, as per the words of the Most High,

> *'So if one group rebels against the other then fight, all of you together, against the rebellious one until it returns to the command of God'.*[1] And similarly, ʿAlī ﵁, along with the Companions, fought against the Ḥarūriyya at Nahrawan.[2]

Those who see some inkling of jihad within the current anti-state activities of terrorists should know with certainty that taking the lives of peaceful Muslims is no jihad at all. Rather, such acts malign the exalted concept of jihad. It is a part of faith to consider rebellion both unlawful and anti-social.

9.4 THE THREAT OF HELL AWAITS THOSE WHO FOMENT REBELLION

No Muslim is allowed to rebel against the Muslim polity. Muslims are commanded to stay away from those groups of rebels and terrorists who provoke sedition and militancy against the collective order of a Muslim state. Imam al-Bukhārī and Muslim narrated from Ḥudhayfa b. al-Yamān ﵁ who said,

> كَانَ النَّاسُ يَسْأَلُونَ رَسُولَ اللهِ ﷺ عَنِ الْخَيْرِ، وَكُنْتُ أَسْأَلُهُ عَنِ الشَّرِّ مَخَافَةَ أَنْ يُدْرِكَنِي. فَقُلْتُ: يَا رَسُولَ اللهِ، إِنَّا كُنَّا فِي جَاهِلِيَّةٍ وَشَرٍّ فَجَاءَنَا اللهُ بِهَذَا الْخَيْرِ، فَهَلْ بَعْدَ هَذَا الْخَيْرِ شَرٌّ؟ قَالَ: نَعَمْ. فَقُلْتُ: هَلْ بَعْدَ ذَالِكَ الشَّرِّ مِنْ خَيْرٍ؟ قَالَ: نَعَمْ، وَفِيْهِ دَخَنٌ. قُلْتُ: وَمَا دَخَنُهُ؟ قَالَ: قَوْمٌ يَسْتَنُّونَ بِغَيْرِ سُنَّتِي وَيَهْدُونَ بِغَيْرِ هَدْيِي تَعْرِفُ مِنْهُمْ وَتُنْكِرُ. فَقُلْتُ: هَلْ بَعْدَ ذَالِكَ الْخَيْرِ مِنْ شَرٍّ؟ قَالَ: نَعَمْ، دُعَاةٌ عَلَى أَبْوَابِ جَهَنَّمَ مَنْ أَجَابَهُمْ إِلَيْهَا قَذَفُوهُ فِيْهَا. فَقُلْتُ: يَا رَسُولَ اللهِ، صِفْهُمْ لَنَا. قَالَ: نَعَمْ قَوْمٌ مِنْ جِلْدَتِنَا وَيَتَكَلَّمُونَ بِأَلْسِنَتِنَا. قُلْتُ: يَا رَسُولَ اللهِ، فَمَا تَرَى إِنْ أَدْرَكَنِي ذَالِكَ؟ قَالَ: تَلْزَمُ جَمَاعَةَ الْمُسْلِمِيْنَ وَإِمَامَهُمْ. فَقُلْتُ: فَإِنْ لَمْ تَكُنْ لَهُمْ جَمَاعَةٌ وَلَا إِمَامٌ؟ قَالَ: فَاعْتَزِلْ تِلْكَ الْفِرَقَ كُلَّهَا، وَلَوْ أَنْ تَعَضَّ عَلَى أَصْلِ شَجَرَةٍ حَتَّى يُدْرِكَكَ الْمَوْتُ وَأَنْتَ عَلَى ذَلِكَ.

---

[1] Qurʾān 29:9.

[2] Al-Kāsānī, *Badāʾiʿ al-ṣanāʾiʿ*, 7:120.

> 'The people used to ask the Messenger of God ﷺ about the good, but I would ask him about evil for fear that it would overtake me. I said, "O Messenger of God! We were in a state of extreme ignorance and evil and then God brought us this good. Tell me, will there be any evil after this good?" He ﷺ said, "Yes". I then asked, "And will there be any good after that evil?" He ﷺ said, "Yes, but it will be mixed". I asked, "So what is this mixture?" He ﷺ replied, "There will come a people who will follow a way other than my Sunna and a path different from my guidance. You will see some things from them that you will approve of, and other things that you detest". I asked him, "Will there be any evil after that good?" He ﷺ replied, "Yes. There will be people who invite to the gates of Hell; whoever responds to their invitation shall be cast by them into it". I asked, "O Messenger of God! Describe them for us". He ﷺ said, "Of course. They are a folk from our race and who speak our language [i.e., the language of the Muslims]". I said, "O Messenger of God! What do you think I should do if that time comes upon me?" He ﷺ replied, "Stick to the general body of the Muslims [*jamāʿa*] and their ruler". I asked, "But what if there is neither a general body nor a righteous ruler?" He replied, "Then steer clear of all those groups completely, even if you must bite firmly onto a tree trunk until death overtakes you".'[1]

This hadith mentions several important points related to the subject under discussion. It mentions that in the final days there will appear dissention and tribulation in the Muslim *Umma*, and that those who instigate rebellion will lead others to Hell instead of Paradise. Their language, colour, appearance and demeanour will

---

[1] Narrated by al-Bukhārī in *al-Ṣaḥīḥ*: *Kitāb al-manāqib* [The Book of Exemplary Virtues], chapter: 'The Signs of Prophethood in Islam', 3:1319 §3411; and Muslim in *al-Ṣaḥīḥ: Kitāb al-imāra* [The Book of Leadership], Chapter: 'The Obligation to Stick to the Main Body of the Muslims in the Time of Tribulation, 3:1475 §1847.

outwardly be that of the Prophet ﷺ but they will show hostility to the majority of mainstream Muslims. Furthermore, they will rise in revolt against the Muslim governments or invite others to revolt. We also learn from this hadith that avoiding these evil people and associating with the main body of Muslims will guarantee that our faith is protected. And finally, we see that the way of terrorism and armed rebellion against the Muslim government contravenes the law of Islam and that those who respond to this call will go to Hell.

Commenting on this hadith, Qāḍī ʿIyāḍ said,

أَحَادِيْثُ مُسْلِمٍ الَّتِي أَدْخَلَ فِي الْبَابِ كُلُّهَا حُجَّةٌ فِي مَنْعِ الْخُرُوجِ عَلَى الْأُمَرَاءِ الْجَوَرَةِ وَلُزُومِ طَاعَتِهِمْ.

> 'All the hadith reports of [*Ṣaḥīḥ*] Muslim placed in this chapter are proofs that it is forbidden to rebel against unjust rulers and disobey them'.[1]

This means that all legal, constitutional, democratic and peaceful means can be used against injustice, excess and state oppression, and the methods which have been strictly prohibited are those of terrorism, rebellion and armed struggle.

It is important to understand that there is a vast distinction between enjoining the good and forbidding the evil [*al-amr bi al-maʿrūf wa al-nahī ʿan al-munkar*] and armed struggle. The Shariah has clearly spelled out rules and regulations for both. It is reported by Abū al-Bukhtarī that it was said to Ḥudhayfa b. al-Yamān ﷺ,

أَلَا نَأْمُرُ بِالْمَعْرُوفِ وَنَنْهَى عَنِ الْمُنْكَرِ؟ قَالَ: إِنَّهُ لَحَسَنٌ وَلَكِنْ لَيْسَ مِنَ السُّنَّةِ أَنْ تَرْفَعَ السِّلَاحَ عَلَى إِمَامِكَ.

> 'Should we not enjoin good and forbid evil?' He said, 'That is good; however, it is not from the Sunna to take up arms against your government [i.e., it is terrorism and rebellion and no way "bidding good and forbidding evil]".'[2]

---

[1] Qāḍī ʿIyāḍ, *Ikmāl al-muʿlim bi fawāʾid Muslim*, 6:256–257.

[2] Narrated by Ibn Abī Shayba in *al-Muṣannaf*, 7:508 §37613; and al-Bayhaqī

The method of enjoining good and forbidding evil must be peaceful, and not even an iota of violence is permissible in its enforcement.

9.5 The Unlawfulness of Using Slogans to Incite Hatred and Violence

The jurists have declared it a duty of the government to eliminate miscreants and terrorists who kill peaceful people and raise bigoted slogans. Ibn ʿAlāʾ al-Andarītī writes in *al-Fatāwā al-tātārkhānīyya*:

> إِذَا أَظْهَرَتْ جَمَاعَةٌ مِنْ أَهْلِ الْقِبْلَةِ رَأْيًا وَدَعَتْ إِلَيْهِ، وَقَاتَلَتْ عَلَيْهِ وَصَارَتْ لَهُمْ مَنَعَةٌ وَشَوْكَةٌ وَقُوَّةٌ. فَإِنْ كَانَ ذَلِكَ لِظُلْمِ السُّلْطَانِ فِي حَقِّهِمْ، فَيَنْبَغِي أَنْ لَا يَظْلِمَهُمْ. فَإِنْ كَانَ لَا يَمْتَنِعُ مِنَ الظُّلْمِ فَقَاتَلَتْ تِلْكَ الطَّائِفَةُ السُّلْطَانَ. فَلَا يَنْبَغِي لِلنَّاسِ أَنْ يُعِينُوهُمْ وَلَا أَنْ يُعِينُوا السُّلْطَانَ وَإِنْ لَمْ يَكُنْ لِأَجْلِ أَنَّهُ ظَلَمَهُمْ وَلَكِنَّهُمْ قَالُوا: "اَلْحَقُّ مَعَنَا" وَادَّعُوا الْوِلَايَةَ: فَلِلسُّلْطَانِ أَنْ يُقَاتِلَهُمْ وَلِلنَّاسِ أَنْ يُعِينُوهُ.

> Supposing that a group from the people of the *qibla* [i.e., Muslims] appear, raising a banner [i.e., slogan] and calling to it and killing for its sake, and supposing they gain strength, force and power—if that is due to the ruler's oppression of them, he should not oppress them; and if he ceases to desist from oppressing them and that group continues to fight against the ruler, then the people should neither assist them nor the ruler. And if that group's fighting is not due to the ruler's oppression of them, and rather they say, 'The truth is with us', and they claim independent authority, then the ruler must fight them to establish the writ of the government and the people must assist him.[1]

9.6 Killing Due to Sectarian Differences is Blameworthy

Whatever misguided interpretations terrorists put forth, their major

in *Shuʿab al-Īmān*, 6:62–63.

[1] Ibn al-ʿAlāʾ al-Andarītī, *al-Fatāwā al-tātārkhāniyya*, 4:172.

claim is that they alone are the representatives of truth. To present it legally and religiously, they also raise the slogan, 'the truth is on our side'. The extremists of today believe that their view alone represents true Islam and true faith according to the Qur'ān and Sunna. In their minds the rest of the Muslims, who do not approve of their ideas, and all Muslim rulers and governments not governing completely in accordance with Islamic law and who are, in reality, a mixture of good and evil, are disbelievers and polytheists, or at least misguided. These extremists regard democratic institutions and elections as an embodiment of disbelief and believe that it is jihad to fight against them. Due to this ideology, they declare that it is lawful to kill government officials and the masses of people who participate in voting. They also believe that theft and robbery are lawful because, in their minds, they are engaged in a jihad against disbelief and disbelievers. Thus, in their minds, everything they do to achieve their objectives is fair, including suicide bombing, mass killing and wanton acts of violence. The fact remains that all they say and do is misguidance, terrorism and revolt. On that note, the Prophet ﷺ said,

> إِنَّمَا أَتَخَوَّفُ عَلَيْكُمْ رَجُلٌ قَرَأَ الْقُرْآنَ حَتَّى إِذَا رُئِيَتْ عَلَيْهِ بَهْجَتُهُ. وَكَانَ رِدْئًا لِلْإِسْلَامِ غَيَّرَهُ إِلَى مَا شَاءَ اللهُ، فَانْسَلَخَ مِنْهُ وَنَبَذَهُ وَرَاءَ ظَهْرِهِ. وَسَعَى عَلَى جَارِهِ بِالسَّيْفِ وَرَمَاهُ بِالشِّرْكِ. قَالَ: قُلْتُ: يَا نَبِيَّ اللهِ! أَيُّهُمَا أَوْلَى بِالشِّرْكِ؟ اَلْمَرْمِيُّ أَمِ الرَّامِي؟ قَالَ: بَلِ الرَّامِي.
>
> 'The only thing I fear for you is a man who recites the Qur'ān until you see its beauty upon him, and who supports Islam until God willed, until he abandons it and casts it behind his back and attacks his neighbour [a Muslim] with a sword and accuses him of polytheism [*shirk*]'. [The narrator of this hadith said,] 'O Messenger of God! Which of the two is closer to polytheism, the accuser or the accused?' The Messenger of God ﷺ responded, 'Of course, it is the accuser'.[1]

---

[1] Narrated by Ibn Ḥibbān in *al-Ṣaḥīḥ*, 1:282 §81; and al-Bazzār in *al-Musnad*, 7:220 §2793.

The worst manifestation of sectarianism that the Muslim *Umma* faces, and over which Muslims across the world remain worried and divided, is the escalating tendency of accusing others of polytheism. The majority of the Muslims in Europe, the US, the Middle East and the Indian Subcontinent are weathering the storm of allegations from a particular brand of extremists who regard everyone as disbelievers except themselves. In their warped view, the Sufis and saints who rendered excellent service to the faith and spread it during the 1400-year history of Islam did nothing but foster polytheism. They think that they alone have been rightly guided and that the elders and saints of the past generations were ignoramuses, polytheists and innovators.

In truth, many non-Muslims around the world have developed strong hatred towards Islam due to their extremist activities, while the Muslims have come to blows, tearing apart the unity of the *Umma*. The aforementioned hadith is a clear illustration of their misplaced arrogance and false assumptions.

Chapter 10

The Legal Status of Fighting Against a Corrupt Government

10.1 The Unlawfulness of Rebelling against a Government that is not Explicitly Idolatrous

The Shariah has made it crystal clear that armed struggle against a Muslim government is impermissible, even if the government is sinful and corrupt, unless it makes an open declaration of disbelief, or there is a complete and absolute consensus in the *Umma* that the rulers have become disbelievers, or the rulers declare lawful that which is forbidden or vice versa, or they stop the believers from offering their prayers. This has been called *kufr bawāḥ* [manifest disbelief] and is proven from the following agreed upon hadith of al-Bukhārī and Muslim. Junāda b. Abī Umayya said,

> دَخَلْنَا عَلَى عُبَادَةَ بْنِ الصَّامِتِ وَهُوَ مَرِيْضٌ، قُلْنَا: أَصْلَحَكَ اللهُ، حَدِّثْ بِحَدِيثٍ يَنْفَعُكَ اللهُ بِهِ سَمِعْتَهُ مِنَ النَّبِيِّ ﷺ. قَالَ: دَعَانَا النَّبِيُّ ﷺ فَبَايَعْنَاهُ. فَقَالَ: فِيْمَا أَخَذَ عَلَيْنَا أَنْ بَايَعَنَا عَلَى السَّمْعِ وَالطَّاعَةِ، فِي مَنْشَطِنَا وَمَكْرَهِنَا، وَعُسْرِنَا وَيُسْرِنَا، وَأَثَرَةً عَلَيْنَا، وَأَنْ لَا نُنَازِعَ الْأَمْرَ أَهْلَهُ إِلَّا أَنْ تَرَوْا كُفْرًا بَوَاحًا عِنْدَكُمْ مِنَ اللهِ فِيْهِ بُرْهَانٌ.

> 'We went to see ʿUbāda b. al-Ṣāmit when he was sick and we said to him, "May God improve your condition! Narrate to us a hadith that God benefitted you with and you heard of from the Prophet ﷺ". He said, "The Prophet ﷺ called us forward and we pledged fealty to him. In our pledge of fealty, he made us commit to hearing and obeying both when energetic and tired, and in difficulty and ease, and that we [as he ﷺ said] 'do not come into conflict with the leaders that are over you unless you witness manifest disbelief for which you have proof with God'."'[1]

---

[1] Narrated by al-Bukhārī in *al-Ṣaḥīḥ*: *Kitāb al-fitan* [The Book of Tribulations], chapter: 'The Saying of the Prophet ﷺ "After My Departure, You Will Observe

The hadith commentators have explained the phrase 'manifest disbelief' and stated that it must be so explicit that it leaves no room for an alternative interpretation [*ta'wīl*].

Ibn Ḥajar al-ʿAsqalānī said,

وَوَقَعَ عِنْدَ الطَّبَرَانِيِّ مِنْ رِوَايَةِ أَحْمَدَ بْنِ صَالِحٍ عَنِ ابْنِ وَهْبٍ فِي هَذَا الْحَدِيْثِ: كُفْرًا صَرَّاحًا.

> 'And in a variant of this report with al-Ṭabarānī from the narration of Aḥmad b. Ṣāliḥ from Ibn Wahb, the phrase, "explicit disbelief", [*kufr ṣarāḥ*] occurs'.[1]

Commenting on the phrase, 'for which you have proof with God', Ibn Ḥajar stated,

مُقْتَضَاهُ أَنَّهُ لَا يَجُوزُ الْخُرُوجُ عَلَيْهِمْ مَا دَامَ فِعْلُهُمْ يَحْتَمِلُ التَّأْوِيْلَ.

> 'The import of this is that it is impermissible to rebel against them [the rulers] so long as their actions have room for an alternative interpretation'.[2]

This means that revolt against the government would be legally permissible according to the Shariah when there is complete and absolute consensus on the disbelief of the government and no scope for any alternative interpretation for their actions. Ibn Ḥajar explained further,

قَالَ ابْنُ بَطَّالٍ: فِي الْحَدِيْثِ حُجَّةٌ فِي تَرْكِ الْخُرُوجِ عَلَى السُّلْطَانِ وَلَوْ جَارَ.

> 'Ibn Baṭṭāl said, "This hadith contains a proof that the government should not be rebelled against, even if it is oppressive".'[3]

Things that You Will Dislike"', 6:2588 §6647; and Muslim in *al-Ṣaḥīḥ*: *Kitāb al-imāra* [The Book of Leadership], chapter: 'The Obligation to Obey the Rulers in that which Does not Entail Disobedience, and the Prohibition of Disobeying Their Orders', 3:1470 §1709.

[1] Ibn Ḥajar al-ʿAsqalānī, *Fatḥ al-Bārī*, 13:8.

[2] Ibid., 13:11.

[3] Ibid., 13:7.

So despite a government being unjust and unfair, armed rebellion against it is strictly prohibited; however, peaceful, constitutional, democratic and legal means can be used to effect a change.

Imam Badr al-Dīn al-ʿAynī commented on the word 'proof' used in the hadith and stated,

قَوْلُهُ: بُرْهَانٌ أَيْ: نَصُّ آيَةٍ أَوْ خَبَرٌ صَحِيْحٌ لَا يَحْتَمِلُ التَّأْوِيْلَ.

> 'His statement ﷺ, "proof", means a definitive text [*naṣṣ*] from a Qurʾānic verse or a rigorously authentic report that does not carry the possibility of an alternative interpretation'.[1]

Imam al-Qasṭalānī maintained the same view in his commentary, *Irshād al-sārī*.[2]

Shabbīr Aḥmad ʿUthmānī described the same view in *Fatḥ al-Mulhim* under the heading 'The issue of Rebelling against the Unjust Rulers'. He says,

بِهَذَا الْحَدِيْثِ اسْتَدَلَّ جَمْهُورُ الْعُلَمَاءِ عَلَى أَنَّهُ لَا يَجُوزُ الْخُرُوجُ عَلَى السُّلْطَانِ الْجَائِرِ أَوِ الْفَاسِقِ، إِلاَّ أَنْ يَظْهَرَ مِنْهُ كُفْرٌ صَرِيْحٌ.

> 'The majority of scholars infer from this hadith that it is impermissible to rebel against the unjust or corrupt ruler, unless he manifests explicit disbelief'.[3]

10.2 Raising Arms against Muslims is an Act of Disbelief

The Prophet ﷺ stated that those who take up arms against the Muslims do not belong to the Muslim *Umma*. It is narrated by ʿAbd Allāh b. ʿUmar ؓ that the Prophet ﷺ said,

مَنْ حَمَلَ عَلَيْنَا السِّلَاحَ فَلَيْسَ مِنَّا.

> 'He who raises arms against us is not from us'.[4]

---

[1] Badr al-Dīn al-ʿAynī, *ʿUmdat al-qārī*, 16:33.

[2] Aḥmad al-Qasṭalānī, *Irshād al-sārī*, 15:9.

[3] Shabbīr Aḥmad ʿUthmānī, *Fatḥ al-Mulhim*, 3:184.

[4] Narrated by al-Bukhārī in *al-Ṣaḥīḥ*: *Kitāb al-fitan* [The Book of Tribulations],

Islam not only prohibits the taking up of arms, initiation of armed struggle and revolt against the Muslims in an Islamic government, but also brands these actions as disbelief. Islam declares these actions as sedition and corruption on the earth. No good can come from them and they will always lead to civil strife and disorder. Therefore, contrary to resorting to terrorism and rebellion, one should always use peaceful means to struggle against oppression and injustice. If one has insight and understands this point, one will realize that there is no contradiction between the command to enjoin the good and forbid the evil, and the prohibition of armed revolt against the rulers.

10.3 The Legal and Constitutional Way of Changing a Corrupt Government

Even if the rulers of an Islamic government are corrupt and unjust, armed rebellion against them is not allowed. However, the prohibition of armed struggle against an oppressive and corrupt government does not mean that the government has a license to continue with its injustice, corruption and atrocious policies. Islam has not only permitted but also commanded the Muslims to raise every possible voice against the unjust, nefarious and illegal deeds of the government, and to condemn and pressure it to mend its ways and reform. Islam has also recommended that the government be replaced if it refuses to listen to sound counsel and rejects reform. However, such replacement and transition should be a smooth, peaceful and just process void of any violence, bloodshed

---

chapter: 'The Saying of the Prophet ﷺ, "He Who Raises Arms against Us is not from Us",' 6:2591 §6659; Muslim in *al-Ṣaḥīḥ*: *Kitāb al-Īmān* [The Book of Faith], chapter: 'The Saying of the Prophet ﷺ, "He Who Raises Arms against Us is not from Us",' 1:98 §98; Aḥmad b. Ḥanbal in *al-Musnad*, 2:3 §4467; al-Tirmidhī in *al-Sunan*: *Kitāb al-ḥudūd* [The Book of Prescribed Punishments], chapter: 'What Has Come to Us Regarding One Who Brandishes a Weapon', 4:59 §1459; al-Nasā'ī in *al-Sunan*: *Kitāb taḥrīm al-dam* [The Book on Prohibition of Bloodshed], chapter: 'Concerning the One Who Brandishes His Sword and then Thrusts it amongst People', 7:117 §4100; and Ibn Mājah in *al-Sunan*: *Kitāb al-ḥudūd* [The Book of Prescribed Punishments], chapter: 'Concerning the One who Brandishes His Sword', 2:860 §2575.

or killing. This is the correct meaning of jihad against corrupt rulers. Therefore, killing people on the pretext of preventing evil and promoting truth and justice cannot be declared permissible.

The Prophet ﷺ said,

إِنَّ أَفْضَلَ الْجِهَادِ كَلِمَةُ حَقٍّ عِنْدَ سُلْطَانٍ جَائِرٍ.

> 'Indeed, the best jihad is a just word in the presence of an unjust ruler'.[1]

Speaking out against the oppression of the rulers falls under our duty. It is part of enjoining the good and forbidding the evil. It is not disallowed; on the contrary, those who abstain from it are regarded as wrongdoers. The difference is that Islam has ordered us to use constitutional, legal and democratic means to effect a change, and commanded that the entire struggle be peaceful. This hadith does not permit killing, armed rebellion and terrorism. Seizing some parts of the land and imposing one's view on others, shedding blood and committing acts of terrorism are all absolutely forbidden and are tantamount to disbelief. Wanton murder and mischief-mongering create chaos, disorder and anarchy in the *Umma*, and as a result, foreign powers get a chance to interfere in the internal affairs of the Muslim states. That is why the Shariah has ruled that rebellion should be put down firmly.

Umm Salama, the Mother of the Believers ﵂, reported:

قَالَ النَّبِيُّ ﷺ: إِنَّهُ يُسْتَعْمَلُ عَلَيْكُمْ أُمَرَاءُ، فَتَعْرِفُونَ وَتُنْكِرُونَ، فَمَنْ كَرِهَ فَقَدْ بَرِيءَ، وَمَنْ أَنْكَرَ فَقَدْ سَلِمَ، وَلَكِنْ مَنْ رَضِيَ وَتَابَعَ. قَالُوا: يَا رَسُولَ اللهِ، أَلَا نُقَاتِلُهُمْ؟ قَالَ: لَا، مَا صَلَّوْا، أَيْ مَنْ كَرِهَ بِقَلْبِهِ وَأَنْكَرَ بِقَلْبِهِ.

[1] Narrated by Aḥmad b. Ḥanbal in *al-Musnad*, 3:19 §11159; al-Tirmidhī in *al-Sunan*: *Kitāb al-fitan* [The Book of Tribulations], chapter: 'What Has Come to Us Concerning the Fact That the Best Jihad is a Just Word in the Presence of an Unjust Ruler', 4:471 §2174; Abū Dāwūd in *al-Sunan: Kitāb al-malāḥim* [The Book of Tumultuous Battles], chapter: 'Enjoining the Good and Forbidding the Evil', 4:124 §4324; al-Nasāʾī in *al-Sunan*: *Kitāb al-bayʿa* [The Book on the Pledge of Fealty], chapter: 'Concerning the One Who Utters a True Word in front of an Unjust Ruler', 7:161 §1209; and Ibn Mājah in *al-Sunan: Kitāb al-fitan* [The Book of Tribulations], chapter: 'Enjoining the Good and Forbidding the Evil', 2:1329 §4011.

> The Prophet ﷺ said, 'Indeed, rulers will be appointed over you, and you find some things with them agreeable and other things disagreeable. So, whoever detests their bad deeds will be absolved of blame and whoever censures their bad deeds will find safety; but whoever is pleased with their bad deeds and follows them [will not find safety or be absolved of blame]'. The Companions said, 'O Messenger of God! Should we not fight them?' He ﷺ replied, 'Do not fight them as long as they observe the prayer [i.e., are Muslims. "Hating and disapproving" refer to disliking from the heart]'.[1]

Interpreting this hadith, Qāḍī ʿIyāḍ writes in *Ikmāl al-muʿlim bi fawāʾid Muslim*:

قَوْلُهُ: أَفَلَا نُقَاتِلُهُمْ؟ قَالَ: لَا، مَا صَلُّوا عَلَى مَا تَقَدَّمَ مِنْ مَنْعِ الْخُرُوجِ عَلَى الْأَئِمَّةِ، وَالْقِيَامِ عَلَيْهِمْ مَا دَامُوا عَلَى كَلِمَةِ الْإِسْلَامِ، وَلَمْ يُظْهِرُوا كُفْرًا بَيِّنًا، وَهُوَ الْإِشَارَةُ هَاهُنَا: مَا صَلُّوا، أَيْ مَا كَانَ لَهُمْ حُكْمُ أَهْلِ الْقِبْلَةِ وَالصَّلَاةِ، وَلَمْ يَرْتَدُّوا وَيُبَدِّلُوا الدِّيْنَ وَيَدْعُوا إِلَى غَيْرِهِ. وَالْإِشَارَةُ أَيْضًا بِقَوْلِهِ: عَبْدًا حَبَشِيًّا يَقُودُكُمْ بِكِتَابِ اللهِ، أَيْ بِالْإِسْلَامِ وَحُكْمِ كِتَابِ اللهِ وَإِنْ جَارَ.

> The part, 'Should we not fight them?' He ﷺ replied, 'Do not fight them as long as they observe the prayer', further establishes what was mentioned before, in that it is prohibited to rebel against the rulers and revolt against them so long as they continue to hold to the phrase of Islam ['There is no god but God'] and do not manifest evident disbelief. This is indicated here in the phrase, 'Do not fight them as long as they observe the prayer'. In other words, they are not to be fought so long as they continue to receive the rulings of the people of the *qibla* [Muslims] and prayer and do not apostate and alter the religion and call to another one besides it. This point

[1] Narrated by Muslim in *al-Ṣaḥīḥ*: *Kitāb al-imāra* [The Book of Leadership], 3:1481 §1854; and Abū ʿAwāna in *al-Musnad*, 4:417–418 §7162.

is further indicated in his statement, 'Even if he is an Abyssinian slave who leads you with the Book of God': meaning Islam and the rulings of God's Book, even if he is oppressive [you are not allowed to rebel agains him].[1]

He further explained:

قَوْلُهُ ﷺ: وَلَكِنْ مَنْ رَضِيَ وَتَابَعَ مَعْنَاهُ: وَلَكِنَّ الْإِثْمَ وَالْعُقُوبَةَ عَلَى مَنْ رَضِيَ وَتَابَعَ، وَفِيْهِ دَلِيْلٌ عَلَى أَنَّ مَنْ عَجزَ عَنْ إِزَالَةِ الْمُنْكَرِ، لَا يَأْثَمُ بِمُجَرَّدِ السُّكُوتِ، بَلْ إِنَّمَا يَأْثَمُ بِالرِّضَى بِهِ، أَوْ بِأَنْ لَا يَكْرَهَهُ بِقَلْبِهِ، أَوْ بِالْمُتَابَعَةِ عَلَيْهِ. وَأَمَّا قَوْلُهُ: أَفَلَا نُقَاتِلُهُمْ؟ قَالَ: لَا مَا صَلُّوا فَفِيْهِ مَعْنَى مَا سَبَقَ، أَنَّهُ لَا يَجُوزُ الْخُرُوجُ عَلَى الْخُلَفَاءِ بِمُجَرَّدِ الظُّلْمِ أَوِ الْفِسْقِ مَا لَمْ يُغَيِّرُوا شَيْئًا مِنْ قَوَاعِدِ الْإِسْلَامِ.

His statement ﷺ, 'but whoever is pleased with their bad deeds and follows them', means rather sin and punishment will be earned by the one who is pleased and goes along [with them]. This contains a proof that the one who is incapable of removing an evil is not considered sinful by his mere silence; rather, he will only earn sin by being pleased with him [an unjust ruler] or not hating him in his heart, or by following him. As for the part, 'Should we not fight them?' He ﷺ replied, 'Do not fight them as long as they observe the prayer'. This contains the same meaning as what preceded, that it is prohibited to rebel against the rulers merely on account of oppression or corruption, so long as they do not alter anything from the principles of Islam.[2]

ʿAwf b. Mālik ؓ reported that the Prophet ﷺ said:

خِيَارُ أَئِمَّتِكُمُ الَّذِيْنَ تُحِبُّونَهُمْ وَيُحِبُّونَكُمْ، وَيُصَلُّونَ عَلَيْكُمْ وَتُصَلُّونَ عَلَيْهِمْ، وَشِرَارُ أَئِمَّتِكُمُ الَّذِينَ تُبْغِضُونَهُمْ وَيُبْغِضُونَكُمْ، وَتَلْعَنُونَهُمْ وَيَلْعَنُونَكُمْ. قِيْلَ: يَا رَسُولَ اللهِ، أَفَلَا نُنَابِذُهُمْ بِالسَّيْفِ؟ فَقَالَ: لَا مَا أَقَامُوا فِيْكُمُ الصَّلَاةَ، وَإِذَا رَأَيْتُمْ مِنْ وُلَاتِكُمْ

---

1 Qāḍī ʿIyāḍ, *Ikmāl al-muʿlim bi fawāʾid Muslim,* 6:264–265.

2 Ibid., 6:264.

شَيْئًا تَكْرَهُونَهُ فَاكْرَهُوا عَمَلَهُ، وَلَا تَنْزِعُوا يَدًا مِنْ طَاعَةٍ.

> 'The best of your rulers are those whom you love and who love you, who invoke God's blessings upon you and upon whom you invoke His blessings. And the worst of your rulers are those whom you hate and who hate you, and whom you curse and who curse you'. It was asked, 'O Messenger of God! Should we not overthrow them with the help of the sword [i.e., arms]?' He said, 'No, as long as they establish prayer amongst you. If you then find anything detestable in a ruler, you should hate his action, but do not withdraw from his writ and authority'.[1]

The scholars of hadith have interpreted this hadith and said that the phrase, 'but do not withdraw from his writ and authority', means that unless the rulers order you to disbelieve, it is strictly forbidden to rebel against them. The Prophet's saying 'as long as they establish prayer amongst you' describes them as Muslims metaphorically, so the implicit meaning is, 'as long as they are Muslims'. It does not necessarily mean that they offer prayers regularly five times a day and are pious and God-fearing. The reason why it does not mean that they literally establish the five daily prayers is because the same hadith has already declared them the worst of the rulers. It is apparent that since the Muslims would hate them, they would dislike the Muslims and would be called the worst rulers due to their oppression, evil deeds and injustice. We cannot expect them to be staunch Muslims who regularly offer prayers and fast. Had that been so, they would not have been given the pejorative 'the worst of rulers'. In spite of this, the Prophet ﷺ said that as long as they continue to offer prayers amongst you—implying that they are called Muslims, even if in word and not in deed—armed rebellion should not be undertaken against them.

Imam al-Qurṭubī has explained these words in *al-Mufhim li ma ushkila min talkhīṣ kitāb Muslim*, a commentary on Muslim's

---

[1] Narrated by Muslim in *al-Ṣaḥīḥ*: *Kitāb al-imāra* [The Book of Leadership], chapter: 'The Best and the Worst of the Leaders', 3:1481 §1855; and Ibn Ḥibbān in *al-Ṣaḥīḥ*, 10:449 §4589.

Ṣaḥīḥ. He said, 'Just as he described those who pray as Muslims, as he ﷺ said, "I have been forbidden from killing those who pray", meaning the Muslims'.[1] Therefore, this legal meaning would also apply here as well.

Imam al-Tirmidhī narrated this hadith from Umm Salama ؓ on his own authority:

> قَالَ النَّبِيُّ ﷺ: إِنَّهُ سَيَكُونُ عَلَيْكُمْ أَئِمَّةٌ تَعْرِفُونَ وَتُنْكِرُونَ، فَمَنْ أَنْكَرَ فَقَدْ بَرِيءَ، وَمَنْ كَرِهَ فَقَدْ سَلِمَ، وَلَكِنْ مَنْ رَضِيَ وَتَابَعَ. فَقِيلَ: يَا رَسُولَ اللهِ، أَفَلَا نُقَاتِلُهُمْ؟ قَالَ: لَا مَا صَلَّوْا.

> 'The Prophet ﷺ said, 'Indeed, rulers will be appointed over you, and you find some things with them agreeable and other things disagreeable. So, whoever detests their bad deeds will be absolved of blame and whoever censures their bad deeds will find safety; but whoever is pleased with their bad deeds and follows them [will not find safety or be absolved of blame]'. It was said, 'O Messenger of God! Should we not fight them?' He ﷺ replied, 'Do not fight them as long as they observe the prayer [i.e., are Muslims]'.[2]

ʿAbd al-Raḥmān Mubārakpūrī wrote regarding this hadith,

> أَفَلَا نُقَاتِلُهُمْ؟ قَالَ: لَا أَيْ: لَا تُقَاتِلُوهُمْ مَا صَلَّوْا. إِنَّمَا مَنَعَ عَنْ مُقَاتَلَتِهِمْ مَا دَامُوا يُقِيمُونَ الصَّلَاةَ، الَّتِي هِيَ عُنْوَانُ الْإِسْلَامِ حَذَرًا مِنْ هَيْجِ الْفِتَنِ وَاخْتِلَافِ الْكَلِمَةِ.

> 'The question "Should we not fight them?" and the Prophet's reply, "Do not fight them as long as they observe the prayer" mean that they were forbidden from fighting them as long as they establish the prayer—the distinguishing mark of Islam—for fear of discord and disunity'.[3]

---

1 Al-Qurṭubī, *al-Mufhim li ma ushkila min talkhīṣ Kitāb Muslim*, 4:66.

2 Narrated by al-Tirmidhī in *al-Sunan*: *Kitāb al-fitan* [The Book of Tribulation], chapter:78, 4:529 §2265.

3 ʿAbd al-Raḥmān Mubārakpūrī, *Tuḥfat al-aḥwadhī*, 6:138.

This means that permission has been granted to the Muslims to carry out their democratic and constitutional struggle through peaceful means by demonstrating patience over the injustice of the rulers, so as to avoid mischief, bloodshed and massacre amongst the Muslim *Umma*. Armed rebellion and war were ruled out.

In the *Sunan* of Abū Dāwūd there is a narration in which Ḍabba b. Miḥṣan through Umm Salama, the Mother of the Believers ﷺ, reported:

قَالَ النَّبِيُّ ﷺ: سَتَكُونُ عَلَيْكُمْ أَئِمَّةٌ تَعْرِفُونَ مِنْهُمْ وَتُنْكِرُونَ، فَمَنْ أَنْكَرَ قَالَ أَبُو دَاوُدَ: قَالَ هِشَامٌ: بِلِسَانِهِ فَقَدْ بَرِئَ، وَمَنْ كَرِهَ بِقَلْبِهِ فَقَدْ سَلِمَ، وَلَكِنْ مَنْ رَضِيَ وَتَابَعَ. فَقِيْلَ: يَا رَسُولَ اللهِ، أَفَلَا نَقْتُلُهُمْ؟ قَالَ ابْنُ دَاوُدَ: أَفَلَا نُقَاتِلُهُمْ؟ قَالَ: لَا، مَا صَلَّوْا.

> 'The Prophet ﷺ said, "Indeed, rulers will be appointed over you, and you find some things with them agreeable and other things disagreeable. So, whoever detests their bad deeds [Abū Dāwūd said, 'Hishām said, "With his tongue"'] will be absolved of blame, and whoever detests their bad deeds with his heart will find safety; but whoever is pleased with their bad deeds and follows them [will not find safety or be absolved of blame]". It was said, "O Messenger of God! Should we not fight them?" He ﷺ replied, "Do not fight them as long as they observe the prayer [i.e., are Muslims]".'[1]

These hadith reports and their commentaries illustrate two points in particular: firstly, armed revolt is prohibited against the Muslim rulers despite their corruption, deviation, oppression and injustice, and that is because of the fear of disruption, mass killing and bloodshed. There are several peaceful ways to bring these erring governments back to the right path. Secondly, it is impermissible to engage in armed revolt against the rulers unless they commit and demonstrate manifest disbelief. If a group

---

[1] Narrated by Abū Dāwūd in *al-Sunan*: *Kitāb al-Sunna* [The Book of the Sunna], chapter: 'On Fighting the Kharijites', 4:242 §4760.

launches an armed struggle in the name of enforcing the Shariah, it becomes necessary, nay mandatory, for the state to crush it with all its might.

Chapter 11

Legal Verdicts and Statements from the Four Imams and Eminent Authorities of the *Umma* against Terrorism and Rebellion

AFTER HAVING PRODUCED EVIDENCE FROM THE HADITH LITERATURE, we present here the views of the Four Imams of jurisprudence. The objective is to make it clear that the *Umma* has been unanimous on this issue for the last fourteen centuries and that there has been no departure or deviation from the mainstream.

11.1 Imam Abū Ḥanīfa

Imam Abū Ḥanīfa has said in his book, *al-Fiqh al-absaṭ*, regarding fighting the terrorists:

> فَقَاتِلْ أَهْلَ الْبَغْيِ بِالْبَغْيِ لَا بِالْكُفْرِ. وَكُنْ مَعَ الْفِئَةِ الْعَادِلَةِ. وَلَا تَكُنْ مَعَ أَهْلِ الْبَغْيِ. فَإِنْ كَانَ فِي أَهْلِ الْجَمَاعَةِ فَاسِدُونَ ظَالِمُونَ، فَإِنَّ فِيْهِمْ أَيْضًا صَالِحِيْنَ يُعِيْنُونَكَ عَلَيْهِمْ، وَإِنْ كَانَتِ الْجَمَاعَةُ بَاغِيَةً فَاعْتَزِلْهُمْ وَاخْرُجْ إِلَى غَيْرِهِمْ. قَالَ اللهُ تَعَالَى: ﴿أَلَمْ تَكُنْ أَرْضُ ٱللَّهِ وَاسِعَةً فَتُهَاجِرُواْ فِيهَا﴾، ﴿إِنَّ أَرْضِى وَاسِعَةٌ فَإِيَّٰىَ فَٱعْبُدُونِ﴾.
>
> So fight against rebels on account of their rebellion, not because of disbelief. Be with the just and moderate group and do not be with the people of rebellion. If there is to be found oppressors and corrupt individuals amongst the mainstream majority group [*jamāʿa*], then there are also righteous people amongst them who will help you against them. If the *jamāʿa* is itself in a state of rebellion, withdraw yourself from them and go to others. God Most High says, '*Was God's earth not spacious enough for you to migrate therein?*' [Qurʾān 4:97] and, '*Indeed, My earth is vast so worship Me alone*'. [Qurʾān 29:52][1]

11.2 Imam al-Ṭaḥāwī

The eminent imam of the Ḥanafī juridical school, Imam Abū Jaʿfar al-Ṭaḥāwī said,

[1] Abū Ḥanīfa, *al-Fiqh al-absaṭ* (cited by Zāhid al-Kawtharī in his *Majmūʿat al-ʿaqīda wa ʿilm al-kalām*), pp. 606–607.

لَا نَرَى السَّيْفَ عَلَى أَحَدٍ مِنْ أُمَّةِ مُحَمَّدٍ إِلاَّ مَنْ وَجَبَ عَلَيْهِ السَّيْفُ، وَلَا نَرَى الْخُرُوجَ عَلَى أَئِمَّتِنَا وَوُلَاةِ أُمُورِنَا، وَإِنْ جَارُوا، وَلَا نَدْعُو عَلَيْهِمْ، وَلَا نَنْزِعُ يَدًا مِنْ طَاعَتِهِمْ.

> We do not approve [the use of the sword] against any of the *Umma*, except him against whom the sword is deemed necessary. And we do not approve of rebellion against our rulers and those in charge of our affairs, even if they are unjust. We do not supplicate against them or withdraw obedience from them.[1]

Interpreting this statement of Imam al-Ṭaḥāwī, Ibn Abī al-ʿIzz al-Ḥanafī quoted a hadith narrated in *Ṣaḥīḥ Muslim* from ʿAwf b. Mālik, in which the Prophet ﷺ said, 'If you then find anything detestable in a ruler, you should hate his action, but do not disobey him'. Ibn Abī al-ʿIzz also mentioned the prophetic command, 'do not withdraw obedience to them'. He explained:

فَقَدْ دَلَّ الْكِتَابُ وَالسُّنَّةُ عَلَى وُجُوبِ طَاعَةِ أُولِي الْأَمْرِ مَا لَمْ يَأْمُرُوا بِمَعْصِيَةٍ. فَتَأَمَّلْ قَوْلَهُ تَعَالَى: ﴿يَٰٓأَيُّهَا ٱلَّذِينَ ءَامَنُوٓاْ أَطِيعُواْ ٱللَّهَ وَأَطِيعُواْ ٱلرَّسُولَ وَأُوْلِى ٱلْأَمْرِ مِنكُمْ﴾ لِأَنَّ أُولِي الْأَمْرِ لَا يُفْرَدُونَ بِالطَّاعَةِ، بَلْ يُطَاعُونَ فِيْمَا هُوَ طَاعَةُ اللهِ وَرَسُولِهِ. وَأَعَادَ الْفِعْلَ مَعَ الرَّسُولِ ﷺ، لِأَنَّهُ هُوَ مَعْصُومٌ. "وَأُولُو الْأَمْرِ" لَا يُطَاعُ إِلاَّ فِيْمَا هُوَ طَاعَةُ اللهِ وَرَسُولِهِ. وَإِمَّا لُزُومُ طَاعَتِهِمْ (وَإِنْ جَارُوا) فَلِأَنَّهُ يَتَرَتَّبُ عَلَى الْخُرُوجِ عَنْ طَاعَتِهِمْ مِنَ الْمَفَاسِدِ أَضْعَافُ مَا يَحْصُلُ مِنْ جَوْرِهِمْ.

> The Book and the Sunna both prove that it is obligatory to obey those in authority as long as they do not order that which is disobedience. So contemplate the words of the Most High, '*Obey God and obey the Messenger and those of authority amongst you*'. See how He said, '*obey the Messenger*' and did not say '*and obey those of authority amongst you*', because the people of authority are not obeyed for their own sake, but are obeyed in

[1] Al-Ṭaḥāwī, *al-ʿAqīda al-ṭaḥāwīyya*, §§71, 72.

that which is obedience to God and His Messenger. The command verb is repeated for the Messenger ﷺ because he is infallible [*ma*ᶜ*ṣūm*], and the people of authority are only obeyed in that which is obedience to God and His Messenger. As for obeying them 'even if they are unjust', it is because the harms associated with rebelling against them far outweigh than what occurs with their injustice.[1]

11.3 Imam Mālik

Imam Saḥnūn recorded in *al-Mudawwana*:

قَالَ مَالِكٌ فِي الْإِبَاضِيَّةِ، وَالْحَرُورِيَّةِ، وَأَهْلِ الْأَهْوَاءِ كُلِّهِمْ: أَرَى أَنْ يُسْتَتَابُوا، فَإِنْ تَابُوا، وَإِلاَّ قُتِلُوا. قَالَ ابْنُ الْقَاسِمِ: وَقَالَ مَالِكٌ فِي الْحَرُورِيَّةِ وَمَا أَشْبَهَهُمْ: إِنَّهُمْ يُقْتَلُونَ إِذَا لَمْ يَتُوبُوا إِذَا كَانَ الْإِمَامُ عَدْلًا. فَهَذَا يَدُلُّكَ عَلَى أَنَّهُمْ إِنْ خَرَجُوا عَلَى إِمَامٍ عَدْلٍ وَهُمْ يُرِيْدُونَ قِتَالَهُ وَيَدْعُونَ إِلَى مَا هُمْ عَلَيْهِ دُعُوا إِلَى الْجَمَاعَةِ وَالسُّنَّةِ، فَإِنْ أَبَوْا قُتِلُوا. قَالَ: وَلَقَدْ سَأَلْتُ مَالِكًا عَنْ أَهْلِ الْعَصَبِيَّةِ الَّذِيْنَ كَانُوا بِالشَّامِ، قَالَ مَالِكٌ: أَرَى لِلْإِمَامِ أَنْ يَدْعُوَهُمْ إِلَى الرُّجُوعِ، وَإِلَى مُنَاصَفَةِ الْحَقِّ بَيْنَهُمْ، فَإِنْ رَجَعُوا وَإِلاَّ قُوتِلُوا.

Mālik said regarding the Ibadis, the Ḥarūriyya and the people of vain desires, 'I am of the view that repentance should be sought from all of them. If they repent [well and good], otherwise they should be killed'. Ibn al-Qāsim said, 'And Mālik said regarding the Ḥarūriyya and their ilk, "They should be killed if they do not repent [of their destructive activities]—provided it is a Muslim state".' This shows you that if they rebel against a just ruler and desire to kill him, and call to their way of understanding, they should be invited to the community [*jamā*ᶜ*a*] and the correct belief [Sunna], and if they refuse they should be killed. And I asked Mālik about the biased partisans who were present in the Levant and he said, 'I am of the view that the government should invite them to return

[1] Ibn Abī al-ᶜIzz al-Ḥanafī, *Sharḥ al-*ᶜ*aqīda al-ṭaḥāwiyya*, p. 282.

and deal justly between themselves, and if they return [well and good], otherwise they should be fought'.[1]

11.4 IMAM AL-SHĀFIʿĪ

Imam al-Shāfiʿī said about terrorists:

لَوْ أَنَّ قَوْمًا كَانُوا فِي مِصْرٍ أَوْ صَحْرَاءَ فَسَفَكُوا الدِّمَاءَ وَأَخَذُوا الْأَمْوَالَ، كَانَ حُكْمُهُمْ كَحُكْمِ قُطَّاعِ الطَّرِيْقِ، وَسَوَاءٌ كَانَتِ الْمُكَابَرَةُ فِي الْمِصْرِ أَوِ الصَّحْرَاءِ، وَلَوِ افْتَرَقَا كَانَتِ الْمُكَابَرَةُ فِي الْمِصْرِ أَعْظَمَهُمَا.

فَإِذَا دُعِيَ أَهْلُ الْبَغْيِ فَامْتَنَعُوا مِنَ الْإِجَابَةِ فَقَاتِلُوا. . . . فَإِنَّمَا أُبِيحَ قِتَالُ أَهْلِ الْبَغْيِ ما كَانُوا يُقَاتِلُونَ، وَهُمْ لَا يَكُونُونَ مُقَاتِلِيْنَ أَبَدًا إِلَّا مُقْبِلِيْنَ مُمْتَنِعِيْنَ مُرِيْدِيْنَ. فَمَتَى زَايَلُوا هَذِهِ الْمَعَانِيَ فَقَدْ خَرَجُوا مِنَ الْحَالِ الَّتِي أُبِيحَ بِهَا قِتَالُهُمْ، وَهُمْ لَا يَخْرُجُونَ مِنْهَا أَبَدًا إِلَّا إِلَى أَنْ تَكُونَ دِمَاؤُهُمْ مُحَرَّمَةً كَهِيَ قَبْلُ.

If there is a group of people who are shedding blood and seizing wealth in either populated areas or barren wastelands, they take the same legal ruling as highway robbers. The gravity of their crime is equal whether it takes place in a populated area or a barren wasteland; but if they split up, then the crime that takes place in the populated areas is the severer of the two.[2]

If rebels are invited [to lay down their arms] but refuse to comply they are to be fought. . . . It is only permissible to fight rebels when they are engaged in fighting; and they are never seen as fighters unless they are pressing forward, withholding obedience and doing so resolutely. So whenever these qualities are absent they are no longer in the state in which it is permissible to fight them; and never do they abandon these things except that their blood is considered inviolable as it was before [their rebellion].[3]

---

[1] Saḥnūn, *al-Mudawwana al-kubrā*, 3:94.

[2] Al-Shāfiʿī, *al-Umm*, 4:218.

[3] Ibid.

11.5 Imam Aḥmad b. Ḥanbal

The illustrious Imams have always taught moderation, self-control, tolerance and harmony to save people from mischief, terrorism and bloodshed. Despite immense pressures and severe hardships, including imprisonment and lashing, Imam Aḥmad b. Ḥanbal did not provoke the Muslim masses against the government of his day. He suffered his trials due to a well-known controversial issue in Islamic doctrine regarding the createdness or uncreatedness of the Qurʾān. Declaring God's Speech, the Qurʾān, created was the single most dangerous tribulation the *Umma* had faced.

The belief in the createdness of the Qurʾān was a product of the extremist beliefs of the Mutazilites and had completely engulfed the rulers of that time. The Mutazilites, who were the intellectual heirs of the Kharijites, were highly influential in the government. It was for this reason that many of the notable personalities of the Muslim world suffered serious opposition and oppressive measures taken by the government against them.

Imam Aḥmad b. Ḥanbal was amongst those who suffered the most during this tribulation. He was lashed and tortured, but, despite all the oppression he suffered, he dissuaded people from armed revolt and rebellion against the government. Examples of his forbearance and perseverance have been chronicled in many famous books. Of them, Abū Bakr al-Khalāl's *al-Sunna* presents many accounts of his life and surrounding events. Abū al-Ḥārith narrated that he asked Imam Aḥmad b. Ḥanbal about the rebellion movement launched against the government in Baghdad. The Abbasid rulers, under the influence of the Mutazilites, were causing serious troubles to the common Muslims, but when Imam Aḥmad b. Ḥanbal was requested to join and support a rebellious movement against the government, he said,

سُبْحَانَ اللهِ، الدِّمَاءَ، الدِّمَاءَ، لَا أَرَى ذَلِكَ، وَلَا آمُرُ بِهِ، اَلصَّبْرُ عَلَى مَا نَحْنُ فِيهِ
خَيْرٌ مِنَ الْفِتْنَةِ يُسْفَكُ فِيْهَا الدِّمَاءُ، وَيُسْتَبَاحُ فِيْهَا الأَمْوَالُ، وَيُنْتَهَكُ فِيهَا الْمَحَارِمُ.

'Glorified is God! In no way do I consider it lawful to shed blood, nor do I command it. For us to be patient in

> these circumstances is better than tribulation in which blood is shed and in which wealth is seized and people's honour is violated'.[1]

Some people still insisted and said, 'Are we not faced with a situation that necessitates jihad in order to annihilate it?' Hearing that, he replied, 'Certainly, it is a disruption that will die in some days, but if swords are drawn then massacre will be the outcome, and the doors to peace and piety will close'.

When the rebellion gained momentum in the days of Caliph al-Wāthiq Billāh, the Islamic jurists collectively approached Imam Aḥmad b. Ḥanbal and mentioned the rapidly deteriorating situation. He inquired as to what they wanted and all of them submitted that they had come to him to seek his guidance and counsel, as they were fed up with the government's stance. They wanted to join the uprising and overthrow the Caliph's rule. Imam Aḥmad advised them to be patient, saying, 'Although the circumstances are worsening, you must change your mind and not challenge the government's authority'. He also said,

عَلَيْكُمْ بِالنَّكِرَةِ بِقُلُوبِكُمْ، وَلَا تَخْلَعُوا يَدًا مِنْ طَاعَةٍ، وَلَا تَشُقُّوا عَصَا الْمُسْلِمِيْنَ، وَلَا تَسْفِكُوا دِمَاءَكُمْ وَدِمَاءَ الْمُسْلِمِيْنَ مَعَكُمْ. أُنْظُرُوا فِي عَاقِبَةِ أَمْرِكُمْ، وَاصْبِرُوا حَتَّى يَسْتَرِيْحَ بَرٌّ، أَوْ يُسْتَرَاحَ مِنْ فَاجِرٍ. لَا، هَذَا خِلَافُ الْآثَارِ الَّتِي أُمِرْنَا فِيْهَا بِالصَّبْرِ.

> See to it that you detest [these things] in your hearts but do not challenge the writ and authority of the government or cause a split in Muslim unity. Do not shed your own blood or the blood of the Muslims with you. Consider the consequences of your actions and observe patience until a pious person enjoys comfort or comfort is enjoyed at the demise of a criminal. This [idea to rebel against the government] is against the reports that command us to observe patience.[2]

---

[1] Narrated by al-Khalāl in *al-Sunna*, p. 132 §89. This narration has an authentic chain of transmission.

[2] Ibid., p. 133 §90.

11.6 Imam Sufyān al-Thawrī

Someone approached Imam Sufyān al-Thawrī for an edict in favour of armed struggle against Caliph Hārūn al-Rashīd, but he exhorted him to observe patience and avoid turmoil. He said,

كَفَيْتُكَ هَذَا الأَمْرَ، وَنَقَّرْتُ لَكَ عَنْهُ. اجْلِسْ فِي بَيْتِكَ.

> 'I have sufficed you from this matter and explained it, so sit in your home [and avoid this turmoil]'.[1]

11.7 Imam al-Māwardī

Imam al-Māwardī took a detailed account of the commands pertaining to rebels and terrorists and maintained that the rebels must be fought back until they submit to the authority of the government. He derived this decree from the verse nine of *Sūra al-Ḥujurāt*:

﴿وَإِن طَآئِفَتَانِ مِنَ ٱلْمُؤْمِنِينَ ٱقْتَتَلُواْ فَأَصْلِحُواْ بَيْنَهُمَا فَإِنۢ بَغَتْ إِحْدَىٰهُمَا عَلَى ٱلْأُخْرَىٰ فَقَٰتِلُواْ ٱلَّتِى تَبْغِى حَتَّىٰ تَفِىٓءَ إِلَىٰٓ أَمْرِ ٱللَّهِ فَإِن فَآءَتْ فَأَصْلِحُواْ بَيْنَهُمَا بِٱلْعَدْلِ وَأَقْسِطُوٓاْ إِنَّ ٱللَّهَ يُحِبُّ ٱلْمُقْسِطِينَ﴾

> '*And if two parties amongst the believers fight each other, then make peace between them. And if one party goes against the other, then all of you together fight the contentious party until they all submit to the command of God. And if they submit, then make peace between them with fairness and behave justly. Indeed, God loves the just*'.[2]

Imam al-Māwardī said:

فِي قَوْلِهِ ﴿فَإِنْ بَغَتْ إِحْدَىٰهُمَا عَلَى ٱلْأُخْرَىٰ﴾ وَجْهَانِ: أَحَدُهُمَا بَغَتْ بِالتَّعَدِّي فِي الْقِتَالِ؛ وَالثَّانِي بَغَتْ بِالْعُدُولِ عَنِ الصُّلْحِ. وَقَوْلُهُ ﴿فَقَٰتِلُواْ ٱلَّتِى تَبْغِى﴾ يَعْنِي بِالسَّيْفِ رَدْعًا عَنِ الْبَغْيِ وَزَجْرًا عَنِ الْمُخَالَفَةِ. وَفِي قَوْلِهِ تَعَالَى: ﴿حَتَّىٰ تَفِىٓءَ إِلَىٰ

[1] Ibid., p. 137 §96.

[2] Qurʾān 49:9.

أَمْرِ ٱللَّهِ﴾ حَتَّى تَرْجِعَ إِلَى الصُّلْحِ الَّذِي أَمَرَ اللهُ تَعَالَى بِهِ، وَهُوَ قَوْلُ سَعِيْدِ بْنِ جُبَيْرٍ.
﴿فَإِن فَآءَتْ﴾ أَي رَجَعَتْ عَنِ الْبَغْيِ.

The phrase, '*And if one party goes against the other*', has two angles of interpretation. One of them is that '*goes against*' [*baghat*] means to transgress by fighting, and the second angle is that '*goes against*' means to avoid reconciliation. His statement, '*then all of you together fight the contentious party . . .*', means that they should be fought with the sword so as to dissuade them from rebellion and discourage them from opposition. And His statement, '*until they all submit to the command of God*', means that they should be fought until they return and make peace, as God Most High ordered them. And this is the view of Saʿīd b. Jubayr. '*And if they submit*' means that they give up rebellion.[1]

11.8 IMAM AL-SARAKHSĪ

Imam al-Sarakhsī, a well-known authority in Ḥanafī jurisprudence, ruled that it is lawful to crush rebels. He said,

فَحِيْنَئِذٍ يَجِبُ عَلَى مَنْ يَقْوَى عَلَى الْقِتَالِ أَنْ يُقَاتِلَ مَعَ إِمَامِ الْمُسْلِمِيْنَ الْخَارِجِيْنَ لِقَوْلِهِ تَعَالَى: ﴿فَإِنْ بَغَتْ إِحْدَٰهُمَا عَلَى ٱلْأُخْرَىٰ فَقَٰتِلُوا۟ ٱلَّتِى تَبْغِى﴾. وَالْأَمْرُ حَقِيْقَةً لِلْوُجُوبِ، وَلِأَنَّ الْخَارِجِيْنَ قَصَدُوا أَذَى الْمُسْلِمِيْنَ وَإِمَاطَةَ الْأَذَى مِنْ أَبْوَابِ الدِّيْنِ، وَخُرُوجُهُم مَعْصِيَةٌ فَفِي الْقِيَامِ بِقِتَالِهِمْ نَهْيٌ عَنِ الْمُنْكَرِ وَهُوَ فَرْضٌ وَلِأَنَّهُمْ يُهَيْجُونَ الْفِتْنَةَ. قَالَ ﷺ: اَلْفِتْنَةُ نَائِمَةٌ، لَعَنَ اللهُ مَنْ أَيْقَظَهَا. فَمَنْ كَانَ مَلْعُونًا عَلَى لِسَانِ صَاحِبِ الشَّرْعِ – صَلَوَاتُ اللهِ عَلَيْهِ – يُقَاتَلُ مَعَهُ.

So under those circumstances it is incumbent upon an able-bodied man to fight with the government of the Muslims against those who rebel. This is due to the statement of the Most High, '*And if one party goes against the other, then all of you together fight the contentious party until*

[1] Al-Māwardī, *al-Aḥkām al-sulṭāniyya*, p. 59.

they all submit to the command of God'. This command is indicative of obligation, and furthermore, those who rebel intend to harm the Muslims and removing harm is a part of the religion[1] and their rebellion is disobedience. So fighting against them is a part of forbidding the evil, which is obligatory. Moreover, they are to be fought because they instigate turmoil. The Prophet ﷺ said, 'Tribulation is sleeping; may God curse the one who awakens it'. Anyone who is cursed upon the tongue of the Prophet ﷺ should be fought.[2]

11.9 IMAM AL-KĀSĀNĪ

Imam al-Kasānī, the author of the famous book of Ḥanafī jurisprudence, *Badāʾiʿ al-ṣanāʾiʿ*, ruled that terrorists must be killed in order to eliminate mischief and strife. He wrote:

لِأَنَّهُمْ سَاعُونَ فِي الْأَرْضِ بِالْفَسَادِ، فَيقْتُلُونَ دَفْعًا لِلْفَسَادِ عَلَى وَجْهِ الْأَرْضِ. وَإِنْ قَاتَلَهُمْ قَبْلَ الدَّعْوَةِ لَا بَأْسَ بِذَلِكَ، لِأَنَّ الدَّعْوَةَ قَدْ بَلَغَتْهُمْ لِكَوْنِهِمْ فِي دَارِ الْإِسْلَامِ، وَمِنَ الْمُسْلِمِيْنَ أَيْضًا. وَيَجِبُ عَلَى كُلِّ مَنْ دَعَاهُ الْإِمَامُ إِلَى قِتَالِهِمْ أَنْ يُجِيْبَهُ إِلَى ذَلِكَ، وَلَا يَسَعُهُ التَّخَلُّفُ إِذَا كَانَ عِنْدَهُ غِنًا وَقُدْرَةٌ لِأَنَّ طَاعَةَ الْإِمَامِ فِيْمَا لَيْسَ بِمَعْصِيَةٍ فَرْضٌ، فَكَيْفَ فِيْمَا هُوَ طَاعَةٌ.

Because they spread corruption on the earth, they should be fought in order to prevent that. And if the government fights them before inviting them [to change their ways], there is no harm in that, since the invitation has already reached them on account of their being in the lands in which Islam is dominant [*Dār al-Islam*] and being Muslims. It is incumbent upon all who are ordered by the government to fight against them to obey and it is not

[1] As indicated in the hadith, 'Faith has over seventy branches. The loftiest of them is the statement, "There is no god but God", and the lowest of them is removing harm from the street; and modesty is a branch of faith'. [*Ṣaḥīḥ Muslim*] ED.

[2] Al-Sarakhsī, *al-Mabsūṭ*, 10:124.

permitted for the individual fighter to lag behind if he has sufficient provisions and capability. This is because it is obligatory to obey the authority of the government in that which does not entail disobedience—so even more so if the command entails obedience![1]

11.10 Imam al-Marghīnānī

An important question on this topic is how long an operation against terrorists should last; Imam al-Marghīnānī spoke about this, saying:

إِذَا تَغَلَّبَ قَوْمٌ مِنَ الْمُسْلِمِيْنَ عَلَى بَلَدٍ، وَخَرَجُوا مِنْ طَاعَةِ الْإِمَامِ، دَعَاهُمْ إِلَى الْعَوْدِ إِلَى الْجَمَاعَةِ، وَكَشَفَ عَنْ شُبْهَتِهِمْ لِأَنَّ عَلِيًّا ﷺ فَعَلَ ذَلِكَ بِأَهْلِ حَرُورَاءَ قَبْلَ قِتَالِهِمْ، وَلِأَنَّهُ أَهْوَنُ الْأَمْرَيْنِ وَلَعَلَّ الشَّرَّ يَنْدَفِعُ بِهِ، فَيَبْدَأُ بِهِ وَلَا يَبْدَأُ بِقِتَالٍ حَتَّى يَبْدَؤُوهُ، فَإِنْ بَدَؤُوهُ قَاتَلَهُمْ حَتَّى يُفَرِّقَ جَمْعَهُمْ.

When a group of Muslims overtake an area and rebel against the authority of the Muslim government, it is to invite them to return to the main body and refute their specious arguments', just as ʿAlī ﷺ did with the people of Ḥārūrā before they were fought. Moreover, this is the easier of the two options, and perhaps evil will be averted because of it. So he is to first invite them back and should not fight against them until they initiate hostilities. But when they initiate hostilities, he should fight them and scatter their forces [and crush their power].[2]

11.11 Imam Ibn Qudāma al-Maqdisī

In his magnum opus, *al-Mughnī*, Imam Ibn Qudāma al-Maqdisī penned a section on fighting against rebels. He cited the views of the hadith scholars and stated,

ذَهَبَتْ طَائِفَةٌ مِنْ أَهْلِ الْحَدِيْثِ إِلَى أَنَّهُمْ كُفَّارٌ مُرْتَدُّونَ، حُكْمُهُمْ حُكْمُ الْمُرْتَدِّيْنَ

---

[1] Al-Kāsānī, *Badāʾiʿ al-ṣanāʾiʿ*, 7:140.

[2] Al-Marghīnānī, *al-Hidāya*, p. 573.

وَتُبَاحُ دِمَاؤُهُمْ وَأَمْوَالُهُمْ. فَإِنْ تَحَيَّزُوا فِي مَكَانٍ وَكَانَتْ لَهُمْ مَنَعَةٌ وَشَوْكَةٌ، صَارُوا أَهْلَ حَرْبٍ كَسَائِرِ الْكُفَّارِ، وَإِنْ كَانُوا فِي قَبْضَةِ الْإِمَامِ اسْتَتَابَهُمْ كَاسْتِتَابَةِ الْمُرْتَدِّينَ. فَإِنْ تَابُوا وَإِلَّا ضُرِبَتْ أَعْنَاقُهُمْ، وَكَانَتْ أَمْوَالُهُمْ فَيْئًا لَا يَرِثُهُمْ وَرَثَتُهُمُ الْمُسْلِمُونَ.

A group amongst the traditionists [hadith scholars] were of the opinion that the rebels are disbelievers and apostates, and that they take the same ruling as apostates in that their blood and wealth are lawful. If they confine themselves to a particular location and possess power and force, they become people of war [*ahl al-ḥarb*] like the other disbelievers. And if they are in the custody of the government, repentance is to be sought from them just as repentance is sought from the apostates. If they repent [good and well], otherwise they are to be executed and their wealth will be considered *fay*ʾ (spoils acquired without fighting) and their Muslim heirs will not inherit from them.[1]

11.12 Imam al-Nawawī

Imam al-Nawawī mentioned that there is a consensus amongst the Companions that rebels are to be fought.

قَالَ الْعُلَمَاءُ: وَيَجِبُ قِتَالُ الْبُغَاةِ وَلَا يُكَفَّرُونَ بِالْبَغْيِ، وَإِذَا رَجَعَ الْبَاغِي إِلَى الطَّاعَةِ قُبِلَتْ تَوْبَتُهُ وَتُرِكَ قِتَالُهُ، وَأَجْمَعَتِ الصَّحَابَةُ ﷺ عَلَى قِتَالِ الْبُغَاةِ.

The scholars state, 'It is obligatory to fight rebels and they are not declared disbelievers on account of their rebellion. And if a rebel returns to obedience [to the government], his repentance is to be accepted and he should not be killed. The Companions ﷺ were unanimous in their view that rebels should be eliminated'.[2]

Imam al-Nawawī also described the stance of the scholarly majority with regard to declaring rebels disbelievers. He said,

---

1 Ibn Qudāma al-Maqdisī, *al-Mughnī*, 9:4.

2 Yaḥyā al-Nawawī, *Rawḍat al-ṭālibīn*, 10:50.

أَطْلَقَ الْبَغَوِيُّ أَنَّهُمْ إِنْ قَاتَلُوا فَهُمْ فَسَقَةٌ وَأَصْحَابُ بَهْتٍ، فَحُكْمُهُمْ حُكْمُ قُطَّاعِ الطَّرِيْقِ. فَهَذَا تَرْتِيْبُ الْمَذْهَبِ وَالْمَنْصُوصِ، وَمَا قَالَهُ الْجَمْهُورُ. وَحَكَى الْإِمَامُ فِي تَكْفِيْرِ الْخَوَارِجِ وَجْهَيْنِ. قَالَ: فَإِن لَمْ نُكَفِّرْهُمْ فَلَهُمْ حُكْمُ الْمُرْتَدِّيْنَ، وَقِيْلَ حُكْمُ الْبُغَاةِ. فَإِنْ قُلْنَا كَالْمُرْتَدِّيْنَ لَمْ تَنْفُذْ أَحْكَامُهُمْ.

Imam al-Baghawī stated that they are considered reprobates and bearers of calumny if they fight, and that the legal ruling upon them is the same as the ruling upon highway robbers. This is according to the dictates of the legal school and what is textually stated, and it is the view of the scholarly majority. The Imam [al-Baghawī] cited two views with regard to declaring the Kharijites disbelievers. He said, 'If we do not charge them with disbelief they will be treated with the rulings reserved for apostates. It has also been said that they are treated with the rulings reserved for rebels. And if we say like apostates their rulings will not be carried out'.[1]

11.13 ʿĀlim b. al-ʿAlāʾ al-Andarītī al-Dihlawī

ʿĀlim b. al-ʿAlāʾ al-Andarītī al-Dihlawī writes,

يَجِبُ أَنْ يُعْلَمَ أَنَّ أَهْلَ الْبَغْيِ قَوْمٌ مِنَ الْمُسْلِمِيْنَ، يَخْرُجُونَ عَلَى الْإِمَامِ الْعَدْلِ وَيَمْتَنِعُونَ عَنْ أَحْكَامِ أَهْلِ الْعَدْلِ، فَالْحُكْمُ فِيْهِمْ أَنَّهُمْ إِذَا تَجَهَّزُوا وَاجْتَمَعُوا حَلَّ لِإِمَامِ أَهْلِ الْعَدْلِ أَنْ يُقَاتِلَهُمْ، وَعَلَى كُلِّ مَنْ يَقْدِرُ عَلَى الْقِتَالِ أَنْ يَقُومَ بِنُصْرَةِ إِمَامِ أَهْلِ الْعَدْلِ.

It must be known that the people of rebellion are a folk amongst the Muslims who rebel against the government and refuse the jurisdiction of the people of justice. The ruling regarding them is that it is permissible for the government to fight them if they take up arms and assemble a force. And everyone who is capable of fighting must assist the ruler of the people of justice.[2]

---

[1] Ibid., 10:51–52.

[2] ʿĀlim b. al-ʿAlāʾ al-Andarītī al-Dihlawī, *al-Fatāwā al-tātārkhāniyya*, 4:172.

11.14 Imam Ibn Mufliḥ al-Ḥanbalī

Like Imam al-Nawawī, Imam Ibrāhīm b. Mufliḥ al-Ḥanbalī also ruled that rebels must be fought. He said,

> أَصْلُ مَنْ كَفَّرَ أَهْلَ الْحَقِّ وَالصَّحَابَةَ وَاسْتَحَلَّ دِمَاءَ الْمُسْلِمِيْنَ فَهُمْ بُغَاةٌ فِي قَوْلِ الْجَمَاهِيْرِ، تَتَعَيَّنُ اسْتِتَابَتُهُمْ، فَإِنْ تَابُوا وَإِلَّا قُتِلُوا عَلَى إِفْسَادِهِمْ لَا عَلَى كُفْرِهِمْ.
>
> Those who impute the people of truth and the Companions with disbelief and declare lawful the shedding of Muslim blood are considered rebels [*bughāt*], according the view of the scholarly majority. It is obligatory to demand their repentance. If they repent [well and good], otherwise they are to be killed as punishment for their crimes, not because of disbelief.[1]

He continued:

> فَإِنْ فَاؤُوا وَإِلَّا قَاتَلَهُمْ وَعَلَى رَعِيَّتِهِ مَعُونَتُهُ عَلَى حَرْبِهِمْ، فَإِنِ اسْتَنْظَرُوهُ مُدَّةً رَجَا فَلَا يُمْكِنُ ذَلِكَ فِي حَقِّهِمْ، فَإِنْ أَبَوْا الرَّجُوعَ وَعِظْهُمْ وَخَوِّفْهُمُ الْقِتَالَ لِأَنَّ الْمَقْصُودَ دَفْعُ شَرِّهِمْ لَا قَتْلُهُمْ، فَإِنْ فَاؤُوا أَيْ رَجَعُوا إِلَى الطَّاعَةِ وَإِلَّا قَاتِلْهُمْ أَي يَلْزَمُ عَلَى الْقَادِرِ قِتَالُهُمْ لِإِجْمَاعِ الصَّحَابَةِ عَلَى ذَلِكَ.
>
> If they submit [that is well and good]; otherwise the government should fight them. And the subjects are duty-bound to assist the government in fighting against them. If they [the rebels] seek a cessation of hostilities for a time, that is not possible for them. If they refuse to return [to the main body], the government is to exhort them and warn them of impending fighting, because the objective is to repel their evil and not to kill them. If they submit to the authority of the state [well and good]; otherwise he is to fight them. So in other words, the one who is capable must fight them due to the consensus of the Companions to that effect.[2]

---

[1] Ibn Mufliḥ, *al-Mubdiʿ*, 9:160.

[2] Ibid., 9:161.

11.15 IMAM ZAYN AL-DĪN B. AL-NUJAYM

Imam Zayn al-Dīn b. Nujaym, one of the notable jurists of the Ḥanafī school and author of a commentary on the legal manual *Kanz al-daqāʾiq*, said:

قَوْلُهُ: خَرَجَ قَوْمٌ مُسْلِمُونَ عَنْ طَاعَةِ الْإِمَامِ وَغَلَبُوا عَلَى بَلَدٍ دَعَاهُمْ إِلَيْهِ وَكَشَفَ شُبْهَتَهُمْ بِأَنْ يَسْأَلَهُمْ عَنْ سَبَبِ خُرُوجِهِمْ، فَإِنْ كَانَ لِظُلْمٍ مِنْهُ أَزَالَهُ وَإِنْ قَالُوا الْحَقُّ مَعَنَا وَالْوِلَايَةُ لَنَا، فَهُمْ بُغَاةٌ، لِأَنَّ عَلِيًّا ﷺ فَعَلَ ذَلِكَ بِأَهْلِ حَرُورَاءَ قَبْلَ قِتَالِهِمْ وَلِأَنَّهُ أَهْوَنُ الْأَمْرَيْنِ. وَلَعَلَّ الشَّرَّ يَنْدَفِعُ بِهِ، فَيَبْدَأُ بِهِ اسْتِحْبَابًا لَا وُجُوبًا. فَإِنَّ أَهْلَ الْعَدْلِ لَوْ قَاتَلُوهُمْ مِنْ غَيْرِ دَعْوَةٍ إِلَى الْعَوْدِ إِلَى الْجَمَاعَةِ، لَمْ يَكُنْ عَلَيْهِمْ شَيْءٌ، لِأَنَّهُمْ عَلِمُوا مَا يُقَاتِلُونَ عَلَيْهِ، فَحَالُهُمْ كَالْمُرْتَدِّينَ وَأَهْلِ الْحَرْبِ بَعْدَ بُلُوغِ الدَّعْوَةِ.

> His statement, 'a folk from the Muslims revolt against the authority of the government and overtake a territory', (implies) the ruler is to invite them and refute their specious arguments by asking them their reasons for revolt. If it is due to some oppression that he is committing he should remove it, and if they say, 'The truth is on our side and we are in authority', they are considered rebels [*bughāt*], because ʿAlī ﷺ did that with the people of Ḥarūrā before fighting them, and it is the easier of the two options, for perhaps evil can be averted through it. It is recommended for him [the ruler] to initiate this, but it is not obligatory; for if the people of justice fought them without inviting them to return to the community [*jamāʿa*] there would be no sin upon them because they [the rebels] know that for which sake they are fighting, so their condition is like that of the apostates and the people of war [*ahl al-ḥarb*] after the invitation has reached them.[1]

11.16 ʿABD AL-RAḤMĀN AL-JAZĪRĪ

Supporting the majority opinion in his book on comparative jurisprudence, *al-Fiqh ʿalā al-madhāhib al-ʿarbaʿa,* ʿAbd al-

[1] Ibn Nujaym, *al-Baḥr al-rāʾiq*, 5:151.

Raḥmān al-Jazīrī held that war is obligatory against rebels. He wrote:

لَوْ خَرَجَ جَمَاعَةٌ عَلَى الْإِمَامِ وَمَنَعُوا حَقًّا لِلّٰهِ أَوْ لِآدَمِيٍّ، أَوْ أَبَوْا طَاعَتَهُ يُرِيْدُونَ عَزْلَهُ، وَلَوْ كَانَ جَائِرًا، فَيَجِبُ عَلَى الْإِمَامِ أَنْ يُنْذِرَ هَؤُلَاءِ الْبُغَاةَ، وَيَدْعُوهُمْ لِطَاعَتِهِ، فَإِنْ هُمْ عَادُوا إِلَى الْجَمَاعَةِ تَرَكَهُمْ، وَإِنْ لَمْ يُطِيْعُوا أَمْرَهُ قَاتَلَهُمْ بِالسَّيْفِ.

> If a group revolts against the Muslim government and withholds a right of God or a human being, or refuses to obey the writ of the government and seeks to overthrow it—even if it is unjust—it is obligatory upon the government to warn these rebels and call them to obey it. If they then return to the fold of the community [*jamāʿa*], it should leave them be, but if they refuse to obey the writ of the state, it must fight them with the sword.[1]

11.17 CONCLUDING REMARKS

These citations from the illustrious imams and jurists of the four legal schools amply demonstrate that they were in unanimous agreement regarding the impermissibility of rebelling against the Muslim government. It is the responsibility of the government to assert its authority and jurisdiction, and the citizens of the Muslim state must provide full support to the government in crushing armed rebellion.

---

1 ʿAbd al-Raḥmān al-Jazarī, *al-Fiqh ʿalā al-madhāhib al-ʿarbaʿa*, 5:419.

Chapter 12

Statements from Contemporary Salafi Scholars Against Terrorists

Religious scholars of every school of thought have rejected the wanton murder and destruction of terrorists. The renowned contemporary Salafi scholars have clearly stated in their rulings and edicts that killing Muslims, branding them as disbelievers and subjecting them to oppression are behaviours of the Kharijites, and that those who perform such heinous deeds are subject to the same rulings that apply to the Kharijites.

12.1 Shaykh Muhammad Nāṣir al-Dīn al-Albānī: The Terrorists are the Kharijites of Our Era

The renowned Salafi scholar of the Arab world, Shaykh Muhammad Nāṣir al-Dīn al-Albānī, described his viewpoint about terrorists in the following words:

وَالْمَقْصُودُ أَنَّهُمْ سَنُّوا فِي الْإِسْلَامِ سُنَّةً سَيِّئَةً، وَجَعَلُوا الْخُرُوجَ عَلَى حُكَّامِ الْمُسْلِمِيْنَ دِيْنًا عَلَى مَرِّ الزَّمَانِ وَالْأَيَّامِ، رَغْمَ تَحْذِيرِ النَّبِيِّ ﷺ مِنْهُمْ فِي أَحَادِيْثَ كَثِيْرَةٍ، مِنْهَا قَوْلُهُ ﷺ: اَلْخَوَارِجُ كِلَابُ النَّارِ. وَرَغْمَ أَنَّهُمْ لَمْ يَرَوْا كُفْرًا بَوَاحًا مِنْهُمْ، وَإِنَّمَا مَا دُونَ ذَلِكَ مِنْ ظُلْمٍ وَفُجُورٍ وَفِسْقٍ.

وَالْيَوْمُ وَالتَّارِيْخُ يُعِيْدُ نَفْسَهُ كَمَا يَقُولُوْنَ، فَقَدْ نَبَتَتْ نَابِتَةٌ مِنَ الشَّبَابِ الْمُسْلِمِ لَمْ يَتَفَقَّهُوا فِي الدِّيْنِ إِلَّا قَلِيْلًا. وَرَأَوْا أَنَّ الْحُكَّامَ لَا يَحْكُمُونَ بِمَا أَنْزَلَ اللهُ إِلَّا قَلِيْلًا، فَرَأَوُا الْخُرُوجَ عَلَيْهِمْ دُونَ أَنْ يَسْتَشِيْرُوا أَهْلَ الْعِلْمِ وَالْفِقْهِ وَالْحِكْمَةِ مِنْهُمْ بَلْ رَكِبُوا رُؤُوسَهُمْ أَثَارُوا فِتَنًا عَمْيَاءَ وَسَفَكُوا الدِّمَاءَ فِي مِصْرَ، وَسُورِيَا، وَالْجَزَائِرِ وَقَبْلَ ذَلِكَ فِتْنَةُ الْحَرَمِ الْمَكِّيِّ فَخَالَفُوا بِذَلِكَ هَذَا الْحَدِيْثَ الصَّحِيْحَ الَّذِي جَرَى عَلَيْهِ عَمَلُ الْمُسْلِمِيْنَ سَلَفًا وَخَلَفًا إِلَّا الْخَوَارِجَ.

The point here is that they instituted an evil practice in Islam and made revolt against the Muslim rulers an act of faith through the ages, despite the Prophet's ﷺ warning against them in many hadith reports such as this statement, 'The Kharijites are the dogs of Hell'. [And they made revolt against the rulers an act of faith,] despite the fact that they did not observe any clear-cut disbelief from them [the rulers], but rather, all they saw were things less than that, such as oppression, injustice and corruption.

So today—and as they say, 'History repeats itself'—there has emerged a faction from the Muslim youth that has gained only a small amount of religious knowledge, and they believe that the rulers do not rule by what God has revealed but a little. So as a result, they believe that it is permissible to revolt against them without seeking the counsel of the people of knowledge, understanding and wisdom. Nay, they spread blind sedition and shed blood in Egypt, Syria, Algeria and before that in the Meccan Sanctuary. By all of this they have opposed this rigorously authentic hadith that has been the basis of action for all the Muslims—from the times of the predecessors to those after them—except the Kharijites.[1]

12.2 Shaykh Ibn Bāz: Declaring Muslims to be Disbelievers is a Sign of the Kharijites

On his official website, Shaykh ʿAbd al-ʿAzīz b. ʿAbd Allāh b. Bāz, the former Grand Mufti of Saudi Arabia, was asked, 'We know that these words represent a fundamental from the fundamentals of the people of the Sunna and the community, but unfortunately there are some youth from *Ahl al-Sunna wa al-Jamāʿa* who believe that this is a defeatist mentality and a type of cowardice. This has been expressed, which is why they encourage the youth to adopt violence in effecting a change'.

Shaykh Ibn Bāz responded:

هَذَا غَلَطٌ مِنْ قَائِلِهِ، وَقِلَّةُ فَهْمٍ؛ لِأَنَّهُمْ مَا فَهِمُوا السُّنَّةَ وَلَا عَرَفُوهَا كَمَا يَنْبَغِي، وَإِنَّمَا
تَحْمِلُهُمُ الْحَمَاسَةُ وَالْغَيْرَةُ لِإِزَالَةِ الْمُنْكَرِ عَلَى أَنْ يَقَعُوا فِيمَا يُخَالِفُ الشَّرْعَ كَمَا

[1] Muhammad Nāsir al-Dīn al-Albānī, *Silsilat al-aḥādīth al-ṣaḥīḥa*, pp. 1240–1243.

وَقعَتِ الْخَوَارِجُ، حَمَلَهُم حُبُّ نَصْرِ الْحَقِّ أَوِ الْغَيْرَةُ لِلْحَقِّ، حملَهُمْ ذَلِكَ عَلَى أَنْ وَقعُوا فِي الْبَاطِلِ حَتَّى كَفَّرُوا الْمُسْلِمِيْنَ بِالْمَعَاصِي كَمَا فَعلَتِ الْخَوَارِجُ، فَالْخَوَارِجُ كَفَّرُوا بِالْمَعَاصِيْ، وَخَلَّدُوا الْعُصَاةَ فِي النَّارِ.

وَالَّذِي عَلَيْهِ أَهْلُ السُّنَّةِ – وَهُوَ الْحَقُّ – أَنَّ الْعَاصِيَ لَا يُكَفَّرُ بِمَعْصِيَتِهِ مَا لَمْ يَسْتَحِلَّهَا فَإِذَا زَنَا لَا يَكْفُرُ، وَإِذَا سَرَقَ لَا يَكْفُرُ، وَإِذَ شَرِبَ الْخَمْرَ لَا يَكْفُرُ، وَلَكِنْ يَكُونُ عَاصِيًا ضَعِيْفَ الْإِيْمَانِ فَاسِقًا تُقَامُ عَلَيْهِ الْحُدُودُ، وَلَا يُكَفَّرُ بِذَلِكَ إِلَّا إِذَا اسْتَحَلَّ الْمَعْصِيَةَ وَقَالَ: إِنَّهَا حَلَالٌ. وَمَا قَالَهُ الْخَوَارِجُ فِي هَذَا بَاطِلٌ، وَتَكْفِيْرُهُمْ لِلنَّاسِ بَاطِلٌ؛ وَلِهَذَا قَالَ فِيْهِمُ النَّبِيُّ ﷺ: إِنَّهُمْ يَمْرُقُونَ مِنَ الدِّيْنِ، مُرُوقَ السَّهْمِ مِنَ الرَّمِيَّةِ، ثُمَّ لَا يَعُودُونَ إِلَيْهِ. يُقَاتِلُونَ أَهْلَ الْإِسْلَامِ وَيَدَعُونَ أَهْلَ الْأَوْثَانِ.

هَذِهِ حَالُ الْخَوَارِجِ بِسَبَبِ غُلُوِّهِمْ وَجَهْلِهِمْ وَضَلَالِهِمْ، فَلَا يَلِيْقُ بِالشَّبَابِ وَلَا غَيْرِ الشَّبَابِ أَنْ يُقَلِّدُوا الْخَوَارِجَ، بَلْ يَجِبُ أَنْ يَسِيْرُوا عَلَى مَذْهَبِ أَهْلِ السُّنَّةِ وَالْجَمَاعَةِ عَلَى مُقْتَضَى الْأَدِلَّةِ الشَّرْعِيَّةِ، فَيَقِفُوا مَعَ النُّصُوصِ كَمَا جَاءَتْ، وَلَيْسَ لَهُمُ الْخُرُوجُ عَلَى السُّلْطَانِ مِنْ أَجْلِ مَعْصِيَةٍ أَوْ مَعَاصٍ وَقَعَتْ مِنْهُ، بَلْ عَلَيْهِمُ الْمُنَاصَحَةُ بِالْمُكَاتَبَةِ وَالْمُشَافَهَةِ، بِالطُّرُقِ الطَّيِّبَةِ الْحَكِيْمَةِ، وَبِالْجِدَالِ بِالَّتِي هِيَ أَحْسَنُ، حَتَّى يَنْجَحُوا، وَحَتَّى يَقِلَّ الشَّرُّ أَوْ يَزُولَ وَيَكْثُرَ الْخَيْرُ.

This is a mistake from the speaker and shows a deficiency of understanding. This is because they did not know or understand the Sunna as they should, and it was only their zealousness and eagerness to remove evil that caused them to fall into that which opposes the Shariah—as occurred with the Kharijites. Their love for supporting the truth and their zealousness for the truth motivated them, but their inability to differentiate between honour and rebellion caused them to fall into falsehood to the point that they accused the Muslims of disbelief on account of disobedience, as did the Kharijites who declared others disbelievers on account of disobedience and believed that they would abide eternally in Hell. . . .

The position of *Ahl al-Sunna*—which is the truth—is that a disobedient person is not to be declared a disbeliever on account of his disobedience so long as he does not declare it lawful. So if he fornicates, for instance, he is not declared a disbeliever; if he steals, he is not declared a disbeliever; and if he drinks alcohol, he is not declared a disbeliever. However, in those cases he will be considered a disobedient person with weak faith, a reprobate against whom the prescribed punishments should be applied. He is not to be declared a disbeliever for any of these things, unless he declares disobedience lawful and states that it is lawful. The view of the Kharijites on this issue is false and their charges of disbelief against people are false. For this reason, the Prophet ﷺ said concerning them, 'They shall pass through the religion just as an arrow passes through a hunted game. They will not return. They kill the people of Islam and leave the idolaters'.

This condition of the Kharijites is due to their extremism, ignorance and misguidance. Therefore, it is not fitting for the youth—or anyone else for that matter—to blindly follow the Kharijites. Nay, it is obligatory upon them to follow the way of *Ahl al-Sunna wa al-Jamāʿa* in accordance with the legal proofs. They must stop where the revealed texts stop. It is impermissible for them to revolt against the ruler due to one or several acts of disobedience he commits; rather, they must see to it that they deliver advice verbally or in writing, and with goodly and wise methods, and by arguing in a way that is best: that they may be successful and in order to minimize or eliminate evil and increase goodness.[1]

12.3 Shaykh Ṣāliḥ al-Fawzān: The Terrorists of Today Are a Group of Ignorant Folk

The renowned Salafi scholar of Saudi Arabia, Shaykh Ṣāliḥ al-

[1] See: www.binbaz.org.sa:mat:1934 (accessed May 24, 2010).

Fawzān, was asked: 'Some people say that the government and religious scholars have suspended jihad, which is tantamount to rejecting God's rulings. What is your opinion about that?' To this, he replied:

> هَذَا كَلَامُ جَاهِلٍ، يَدُلُّ عَلَى أَنَّهُ مَا عِنْدَهُ بَصِيْرَةٌ وَلَا عِلْمٌ وَأَنَّهُ يُكَفِّرُ النَّاسَ، وَهَذَا رَأْيُ الْخَوَارِجِ وَالْمُعْتَزِلَةِ، نَسْأَلُ اللهَ الْعَافِيَةَ، لَكِنْ مَا نُسِيْءُ الظَّنَّ بِهِمْ، نَقُولُ: هَؤُلَاءِ جُهَّالٌ، يَجِبُ عَلَيْهِمْ أَنْ يَتَعَلَّمُوا قَبْلَ أَنْ يَتَكَلَّمُوا، أَمَّا إِنْ كَانَ عِنْدَهُمْ عِلْمٌ وَيَقُولُونَ بِهَذَا الْقَوْلِ، فَهَذَا رَأْيُ الْخَوَارِجِ وَأَهْلِ الضَّلَالِ.
>
> These are the words of an ignorant person, and they show that he lacks insight and knowledge and that he is imputing people with disbelief. This is the view of the Kharijites and the Mutazilites—may God give us well-being. That said, we should not think bad of such people; we should rather say, 'These people are ignorant and they must learn before speaking'. On the other hand, if they possess knowledge and say this, then this is the view of the Kharijites and the people of misguidance.[1]

When asked if people with the mindset of the Kharijites still exist today, he replied,

> سُبْحَانَ اللهِ، وَهَذَا الْمَوْجُودُ، أَلَيْسَ هُوَ فِعْلُ الْخَوَارِجِ، وَهُوَ تَكْفِيْرُ الْمُسْلِمِيْنَ، وَأَشَدُّ مِنْ ذَلِكَ قَتْلُ الْمُسْلِمِيْنَ وَالْاِعْتِدَاءُ عَلَيْهِمْ. هَذَا مَذْهَبُ الْخَوَارِجِ. وَهُوَ يَتَكَوَّنُ مِنْ ثَلَاثَةِ أَشْيَاءَ: أَوَّلًا: تَكْفِيْرُ الْمُسْلِمِيْنَ. ثَانِيًا: اَلْخُرُوجُ عَنْ طَاعَةِ وَلِيِّ الْأَمْرِ. ثَالِثًا: اِسْتِبَاحَةُ دِمَاءِ الْمُسْلِمِيْنَ. هَذِهِ مِنْ مَذْهَبِ الْخَوَارِجِ، حَتَّى لَوِ اعْتَقَدَ بِقَلْبِهِ وَلَا تَكَلَّمَ وَلَا عَمِلَ شَيْئًا، صَارَ خَارِجِيًّا فِي عَقِيْدَتِهِ وَرَأْيِهِ الَّذِي مَا أَفْصَحَ عَنْهُ.
>
> God is exalted above all imperfections! Is it not present—the act of the Kharijites, declaring the Muslims disbelievers; and more severe than that, killing Muslims and transgressing against them? This is the way of the Kharijites. Their way is composed of three elements:

[1] Ṣaliḥ al-Fawzān, *al-Jihād wa ḍawābiṭuhu al-sharʿiyya*, p. 49.

> Declaring the Muslims disbelievers, revolting against the ruler and declaring lawful the blood of the Muslims. These three things are from the way of the Kharijites. If someone merely believed these things in his heart and did not speak about them or act upon them he would still be considered a Kharijite in his belief and view that he left unarticulated.[1]

12.4 Mufti Nadhīr Ḥusayn al-Dihlawī: Terrorist Activities Are Not Jihad

Speaking about jihad, Mufti Nadhīr Ḥusayn al-Dihlawī, one of the Salafi *Ahl al-Ḥadīth* scholars of the Indian Subcontinent, wrote:

> But there are many conditions for jihad and unless they are fulfilled, there will be no jihad. Firstly, there should be a ruler of the Muslims. The evidence for this is that, in the Qur'ān, God Most High described a story of one of the Prophets of old who told his people that they should have a ruler or head to wage jihad:
>
> ﴿أَلَمْ تَرَ إِلَى ٱلْمَلَإِ مِنْ بَنِىٓ إِسْرَآءِيلَ مِنْ بَعْدِ مُوسَىٰٓ إِذْ قَالُوا۟ لِنَبِىٍّ لَّهُمُ ٱبْعَثْ لَنَا مَلِكًا نُّقَٰتِلْ فِى سَبِيلِ ٱللَّهِ﴾
>
> '*Have you not seen the group from the Children of Israel who came after Moses? When they said to their Prophet, "Appoint for us a king so that we may fight in the cause of God* [under his command]".'[2]

This verse clearly shows that there is no jihad without a ruler, because had there been jihad without a ruler, they would not have felt any need to say that. And it has been mentioned in a hadith that the ruler is a shield and one should fight behind it and save oneself through it. Abū Hurayra ﷺ reported that the Messenger of God ﷺ said,

[1] Fahd al-Ḥuṣayn, *al-Fatāwā al-sharʿiyya fī al-qaḍāyā al-ʿaṣrīyya.*

[2] Qur'ān 2:246.

إِنَّمَا الْإِمَامُ جُنَّةٌ. يُقَاتَلُ مِنْ وَرَائِهِ وَيُتَّقَى بِهِ. الْحَدِيْثُ، رَوَاهُ الْبُخَارِيُّ وَمُسْلِمٌ.

'Indeed, the ruler is a shield. One fights behind him and is protected by him'.[1] Narrated by al-Bukhārī and Muslim.

This clearly states that jihad can only be waged if it is led by a ruler. Secondly, there should be a sufficient amount of logistical support with which one can face the disbelievers in combat. God Most High states in the Qur'ān:

﴿وَأَعِدُّوا۟ لَهُم مَّا ٱسْتَطَعْتُم مِّن قُوَّةٍ وَمِن رِّبَاطِ ٱلْخَيْلِ تُرْهِبُونَ بِهِۦ عَدُوَّ ٱللَّهِ وَعَدُوَّكُمْ وَءَاخَرِينَ مِن دُونِهِمْ﴾

'And prepare against them as much might as you can as well as war steeds, thereby striking fear into God's enemies and your enemies'.[2]

Imam al-Baghawī said in his exegesis of this verse,

الْإِعْدَادُ اتِّخَاذُ الشَّيْءِ بِوَقْتِ الْحَاجَةِ مِنْ قُوَّةٍ أَيْ مِنَ الْآلَاتِ الَّتِي تَكُونُ لَكُمْ قُوَّةً عَلَيْهِمْ مِنَ الْخَيْلِ وَالسِّلَاحِ.

'Preparation is to take something of power during a time of need, such as the tools that will be a source of strength for you against them, including steeds and weaponry'.

God also says,

﴿يَـٰٓأَيُّهَا ٱلَّذِينَ ءَامَنُوا۟ خُذُوا۟ حِذْرَكُمْ فَٱنفِرُوا۟ ثُبَاتٍ أَوِ ٱنفِرُوا۟ جَمِيعًا﴾

'O you who believe! Take your precautions; set out as separate units or go out all together'.[3]

---

[1] Narrated by al-Bukhārī in *al-Ṣaḥīḥ*: *Kitāb al-jihād wa al-siyar* [The Book of Martial Jihad and Expeditions], chapter: 'Fighting behind the Ruler and Seeking His Protection', 3:1080 §2797; and Muslim in *al-Ṣaḥīḥ*: *Kitāb al-imāra* [The Book of Leadership], chapter: 'Fighting behind the Ruler and Seeking His Protection', 3:1080 §2797.

[2] Qur'ān 8:60.

[3] Ibid., 4:71.

The hadith master and reviver of the Sunna said in his exegesis of this verse, 'In other words, your military preparation and weaponry'. Traditions also tell us their significance, and it is evident that nothing can be accomplished without weapons.

Thirdly, there should be a citadel, nation, or hub of peace for the Muslims to look forward to. Regarding the word 'might', ʿIkrima said, '"Might" means the fortresses'. This was cited in al-Baghawī's *Maʿālim al-tanzīl*. Jihad was not made obligatory until the Prophet ﷺ immigrated to Medina and it became a centre of peace. This clearly proves that it is necessary to have a place of peace.

Fourthly, the Muslims should have sufficient numerical strength to fight the disbelievers, and it should not be less than half of the enemy army. God says,

﴿ٱلْـَٰٔنَ خَفَّفَ ٱللَّهُ عَنكُمْ وَعَلِمَ أَنَّ فِيكُمْ ضَعْفًا فَإِن يَكُن مِّنكُم مِّائَةٌ صَابِرَةٌ يَغْلِبُوا۟ مِائَتَيْنِ وَإِن يَكُن مِّنكُمْ أَلْفٌ يَغْلِبُوٓا۟ أَلْفَيْنِ بِإِذْنِ ٱللَّهِ وَٱللَّهُ مَعَ ٱلصَّٰبِرِينَ﴾

'God has now lightened the burden upon you, and He knows there is some weakness amongst you. So if there are one hundred resolute and steadfast men, they will overcome two hundred; and if there are one thousand, they will triumph over two thousand by God's command. And God is with the steadfast'.[1]

This verse clearly states that the Muslims should fight against two times more than their number and not more than that. In my view, none of these conditions for jihad are fulfilled today. Jihad, therefore, is not possible under these circumstances. . . .

عَنْ أَنَسٍ أَنَّ رَسُولَ اللهِ ﷺ قَالَ: لِكُلِّ غَادِرٍ لِوَاءٌ يَوْمَ الْقِيَامَةِ يُعْرَفُ بِهِ. رَوَاهُ الشَّيْخَانُ.

عَنِ ابْنِ عُمَرَ أَنَّ رَسُولَ اللهِ ﷺ قَالَ: إِنَّ الْغَادِرَ يُنْصَبُ لَهُ لِوَاءٌ يَوْمَ الْقِيَامَةِ، فَيُقَالُ: هَذِهِ غَدْرَةُ فُلَانِ بْنِ فُلَانٍ. رَوَاهُ الشَّيْخَانِ.

---

[1] Ibid., 8:66.

Anas ﷺ reported that the Prophet ﷺ said, 'On the Day of Resurrection, every violator of trusts will have a banner by which he will be known'. Narrated by al-Bukhārī and Muslim.

Ibn ʿUmar ﷺ reported that the Messenger of God ﷺ said, 'On the Day of Rising, a banner will be fixed for a mischief-monger, and it will be proclaimed, "This is a sign of mischief of so-and-so".' Narrated by al-Bukhārī and Muslim.

12.5 Summary

We have seen from the Qurʾān, the Sunna, the commentaries of the jurists, the explanations of the hadith scholars and the various religious edicts and research works, that rebels are those who initiate armed revolt against the Muslim polity and have the strength to do so. They refuse to submit themselves to the authority of the government and they declare an open war against it by brandishing weapons—regardless if their rebellion is against a corrupt government or a just one. Whether their struggle is based on an incorrect religious interpretation or a purely worldly pursuit, their acts clearly designate them as rebels and terrorists. As long as they take up arms and fight against the legitimate Muslim government, the government should launch military operations against them until they lay down their arms, submit to its sovereignty, completely give up their terrorist activities and make a commitment to act as peaceful citizens and support legal and democratic means for getting their demands fulfilled.

Chapter 13

The Tribulation of the Kharijites and Modern-Day Terrorists

13.1 The Beliefs, Doctrines and Blameworthy Innovations of the Kharijites

Islam is a religion of balance and moderation. God Almighty mentions about the Muslim *Umma*:

﴿وَكَذَٰلِكَ جَعَلْنَٰكُمْ أُمَّةً وَسَطًا﴾

'And likewise We have made you a moderate nation'.[1]

Some people have rendered the phrase '*ummatan wasaṭan*' as the middle, medium or impartial nation, but in reality, it signifies moderation, balance and equilibrium. This moderation is in both doctrine and behaviour. That is the chief attribute of Islam. Those who eschew moderation have drifted away from the true spirit of Islam. Throughout the ages there emerged amongst the Muslims various groups that have embraced extremism, and were shunned as a consequence even though they manifested Islam, performed acts of religious devotion and adopted the outward trappings of Islam. At the forefront of these extremist groups are the Kharijites.

The Kharijites first appeared in the days of the Prophet ﷺ and their ideas gained momentum during the caliphate of ʿUthmān ﷺ, until it emerged as a full-fledged and organized group during the caliphate of our master ʿAlī ﷺ. God Most High alluded to the Kharijites in the Qurʾān and there are many prophetic hadith reports that explain their signs, beliefs, doctrines and practices.

In general, the Kharijites committed acts of terrorism and carried out atrocities in the name of Islam. Due to their extreme and specious religious arguments, they would declare it permissible to shed the blood of Muslims. In this chapter we shall examine the relationship between the beliefs and actions of the Kharijites of old and the terrorists of today.

---

[1] Qurʾān 2:143.

13.2 THE DEFINITION OF A KHARIJITE

Before examining the signs, beliefs and doctrines of the Kharijites, let us cite some of the definitions that the classical scholars have given for them. Imam Muhammad b. ʿAbd al-Karīm al-Shahrastānī said in his famous book of heresiology, *al-Milal wa al-niḥal*:

كُلُّ مَنْ خَرَجَ عَنِ الْإِمَامِ الْحَقِّ الَّذِي اتَّفَقَتِ الْجَمَاعَةُ عَلَيْهِ يُسَمَّى خَارِجِيًّا، سَوَاءٌ كَانَ الْخُرُوجُ فِي أَيَّامِ الصَّحَابَةِ عَلَى الْأَئِمَّةِ الرَّاشِدِيْنَ أَوْ كَانَ بَعْدَهُمْ عَلَى التَّابِعِيْنَ بِإِحْسَانٍ وَالْأَئِمَّةِ فِي كُلِّ زَمَانٍ.

> Anyone who revolts against the Muslim government that enjoys the support of the community [*jamāʿa*] is called a Kharijite—whether this revolt was against the Rightly Guided Caliphs during the time of the Companions or against those after them who followed them with excellence [the second generation, *al-Tābiʿīn*], or the Muslim rulers of every subsequent era.[1]

Imam al-Nawawī said:

اَلْخَوَارِجُ صِنْفٌ مِنَ الْمُبْتَدِعَةِ يَعْتَقِدُونَ أَنَّ مَنْ فَعَلَ كَبِيْرَةً كَفَرَ، وَخُلِّدَ فِي النَّارِ، وَيَطْعَنُونَ لِذَلِكَ فِي الْأَئِمَّةِ وَلَا يَحْضُرُونَ مَعَهُمُ الْجُمُعَاتِ وَالْجَمَاعَاتِ.

> The Kharijites are a group of blameworthy innovators who believe that a person who commits a grave sin falls into disbelief and will eternally reside in Hell. For this reason, they defame the rulers and do not participate in the congregational prayers or the Friday prayers with them.[2]

Ibn Taymiyya stated:

كَانُوا أَهْلَ سَيْفٍ وَقِتَالٍ، ظَهَرَتْ مُخَالَفَتُهُمْ لِلْجَمَاعَةِ؛ حِيْنَ كَانُوا يُقَاتِلُونَ النَّاسَ. وَأَمَّا الْيَوْمَ فَلَا يَعْرِفُهُمْ أَكْثَرُ النَّاسِ . . . وَمُرُوقُهُمْ مِنَ الدِّيْنِ خُرُوجُهُمْ بِاسْتِحْلَالِهِمْ دِمَاءَ الْمُسْلِمِيْنَ وَأَمْوَالَهُمْ.

---

[1] Al-Shahrastānī, *al-Milal wa al-niḥal*, p. 114.

[2] Yaḥyā al-Nawawī, *Rawḍat al-ṭālibīn*, 10:51.

> Since they were armed and inclined to fight, their opposition to the community [*jamāʿa*] manifested when they started killing the people. However, as for today, most people [due to their religious garb and appearance] do not know of them. . . . [A]nd their 'passing through the religion' is their leaving it because of their having declared lawful the blood and wealth of the Muslims.[1]

Elsewhere he stated:

> وَهَؤُلَاءِ الْخَوَارِجُ لَيْسُوا ذَلِكَ الْمُعَسْكَرَ الْمَخْصُوصَ الْمَعْرُوفَ فِي التَّارِيْخِ، بَلْ يَخْرُجُونَ إِلَى زَمَنِ الدَّجَّالِ. وَتَخْصِيْصُهُ ﷺ لِلْفِئَةِ الَّتِي خَرَجَتْ فِي زَمَنِ عَلِيِّ بْنِ أَبِي طَالِبٍ، إِنَّمَا هُوَ لِمَعَانٍ قَامَتْ بِهِمْ، وَكُلُّ مَنْ وُجِدَتْ فِيْهِ تِلْكَ الْمَعَانِي أُلْحِقَ بِهِمْ، لِأَنَّ التَّخْصِيْصَ بِالذِّكْرِ لَمْ يَكُنْ لِاخْتِصَاصِهِمْ بِالْحُكْمِ، بَلْ لِحَاجَةِ الْمُخَاطَبِيْنَ فِي زَمَنِهِ ﷺ إِلَى تَعْيِيْنِهِمْ.

> And these Kharijites are not only the armed group that was known in history [during the caliphate of ʿAlī]; rather, they are the ones who will appear time and time again until the time of the Anti-Christ [al-Dajjāl].[2] The Prophet's particular mention of the group that appeared during the time of ʿAlī b. Abī Ṭālib was due to the many traits found in them. Anyone in whom these traits are found is counted amongst them, for the particular mention of them [by the Prophet ﷺ] was not because the ruling applied to them alone, but rather it was because those who were addressed during the Prophet's time ﷺ needed to fix their identity in the times to come.[3]

Ibn Ḥajar states,

> اَلْخَوَارِجُ فَهُمْ جَمْعُ خَارِجَةٍ أَيْ طَائِفَةٍ، وَهُمْ قَوْمٌ مُبْتَدِعُونَ. سُمُّوا بِذَلِكَ لِخُرُوجِهِمْ عَنِ الدِّيْنِ، وَخُرُوجِهِمْ عَلَى خِيَارِ الْمُسْلِمِيْنَ.

---

1 Ibn Taymiyya, *al-Nubuwwāt*, p. 222.

2 Ibn Taymiyya, *Majmūʿa al-fatāwā*, 28:495–496.

3 Ibid., 28:476–477.

'The word "Kharijites" is the plural of *khārija* ["he who went out"], which means a faction. They are a group of blameworthy innovators, and are called rebels because of their leaving the religion and rebelling against the best of the Muslims'.[1]

Imam Badr al-Dīn al-ʿAynī commented:

طَائِفَةٌ خَرَجُوا عَنِ الدِّيْنِ وَهُمْ قَوْمٌ مُبْتَدِعُونَ سُمُّوا بِذَلِكَ لِأَنَّهُمْ خَرَجُوا عَلَى خِيَارِ الْمُسْلِمِيْنَ.

'They are a faction that has left the religion, and they are a group of blameworthy innovators. They are called that because they rebelled against the best of the Muslims'.[2]

Ibn Nujaym al-Ḥanafī stated,

اَلْخَوَارِجُ قَوْمٌ لَهُمْ مَنَعَةٌ وَحَمِيَّةٌ خَرَجُوا عَلَيْهِ بِتَأْوِيْلٍ يَرَوْنَ أَنَّهُ عَلَى بَاطِلٍ كُفْرٍ أَوْ مَعْصِيَةٍ، تُوجِبُ قِتَالَهُ بِتَأْوِيْلِهِمْ يَسْتَحِلُّونَ دِمَاءَ الْمُسْلِمِيْنَ وَأَمْوَالَهُمْ.

The Kharijites are a folk possessing strength and zealotry, who revolt against the government due to a self-styled interpretation. They believe that government is upon falsehood, disbelief or disobedience that necessitates it being fought against, and they declare lawful the blood and wealth of the Muslims.[3]

This is a basic outline and definition of the Kharijites. Let us now review the Qurʾānic exegeses, hadith commentaries and other sources to know the meanings of the Qurʾānic verses and prophetic hadith that condemn the atrocities and terrorism committed by the Kharijites against Muslims and non-Muslims.

---

[1] Ibn Ḥajar al-ʿAsqalānī, *Fatḥ al-Bārī,* 12:283.

[2] Badr al-Dīn al-ʿAynī, *ʿUmdat al-qārī*, 24:84.

[3] Ibn Nujaym, *al-Baḥr al-rāʾiq*, 2:234.

13.3 THE TRIBULATION OF THE KHARIJITES AS ARTICULATED IN THE QUR'ĀN

The Qur'ān has strongly rejected, in numerous places, the heinous act of murder, especially murder on a mass scale that spreads terror and mischief on earth. According to the Qur'ān, those who commit such deeds are considered brigands and rebels (which we already discussed). A thorough study of the Qur'ān will shed light on the many signs and blameworthy innovations of the Kharijites. Here we present some of these Qur'ānic verses.

13.3.1 THE KHARIJITES POSSESS DEVIATION IN THEIR HEARTS

God says in the Qur'ān,

﴿هُوَ ٱلَّذِىٓ أَنزَلَ عَلَيْكَ ٱلْكِتَٰبَ مِنْهُ ءَايَٰتٌ مُّحْكَمَٰتٌ هُنَّ أُمُّ ٱلْكِتَٰبِ وَأُخَرُ
مُتَشَٰبِهَٰتٌ فَأَمَّا ٱلَّذِينَ فِى قُلُوبِهِمْ زَيْغٌ فَيَتَّبِعُونَ مَا تَشَٰبَهَ مِنْهُ ٱبْتِغَآءَ ٱلْفِتْنَةِ وَٱبْتِغَآءَ
تَأْوِيلِهِۦ وَمَا يَعْلَمُ تَأْوِيلَهُۥٓ إِلَّا ٱللَّهُ وَٱلرَّٰسِخُونَ فِى ٱلْعِلْمِ يَقُولُونَ ءَامَنَّا بِهِۦ كُلٌّ مِّنْ عِندِ
رَبِّنَا وَمَا يَذَّكَّرُ إِلَّآ أُو۟لُوا۟ ٱلْأَلْبَٰبِ﴾

> '*He is the One Who has revealed to you the Book comprising some firm and solid verses* [i.e., literally clear and precise in meaning]; *they are the foundation of [commandments] of the Book. And other verses are figurative* [i.e., containing abstract and allusive meaning]. *So, those who have deviation in their hearts follow only its figurative verses [just] under the urge to create disruption and with the motive to supply them self-seeking interpretation instead of their true interpretation. But none knows its true interpretation apart from God. And those who are perfectly firm in knowledge say: 'We believe in it. The whole (Book) has been revealed by our Lord'. And direction and guidance is the share of only those who possess wisdom and insight'.*[1]

Interpreting this verse, Imam Ibn Abī Ḥātim wrote,

---

[1] Qur'ān 3:7.

عَنْ أَبِي أُمَامَةَ عَنْ رَسُولِ اللهِ ﷺ: أَنَّهُمُ الْخَوَارِجُ.

'Abū Umāma reported that the Messenger of God ﷺ said, "They are the Kharijites".'[1]

Ibn Kathīr cited a hadith in which the Prophet ﷺ said,

﴿فَأَمَّا ٱلَّذِينَ فِى قُلُوبِهِمْ زَيْغٌ فَيَتَّبِعُونَ مَا تَشَٰبَهَ﴾: هُمُ الْخَوَارِجُ.

'"*As for those who possess deviation in their hearts, they seek to follow what is unclear thereof*" are none else but the Kharijites'.[2]

Imam al-Khāzin mentioned in his exegesis the various people of deviation and included the Kharijites amongst them.[3] The hadith of Abū Umāma cited by Abū Ḥafṣ al-Ḥanbalī in his exegesis is revealing and deserves mention. Abū Ḥafṣ al-Ḥanbalī wrote:

قَالَ الْحَسَنُ: هُمُ الْخَوَارِجُ، وَكَانَ قَتَادَةُ إِذَا قَرَأَ هَذِهِ الآيَةَ ﴿فَأَمَّا ٱلَّذِينَ فِى قُلُوبِهِمْ زَيْغٌ﴾ قَالَ: إِنْ لَمْ يَكُونُوا الْحَرُورِيَّةَ فَلَا أَدْرِي مَنْ هُمْ. . . . وَعَنْ أَبِي غَالِبٍ قَالَ: كُنْتُ أَمْشِي مَعَ أَبِي أُمَامَةَ، وَهُوَ عَلَى حِمَارٍ حَتَّى إِذَا انْتَهَى إِلَى دَرَجِ مَسْجِدِ دِمَشْقَ، فَقَالَ أَبُو أُمَامَةَ: كِلَابُ النَّارِ، كِلَابُ النَّارِ، كِلَابُ النَّارِ، شَرُّ قَتْلَى تَحْتَ ظِلِّ السَّمَاءِ، طُوبَى لِمَنْ قَتَلَهُمْ وَقَتَلُوهُ – يَقُولُهَا ثَلَاثًا. ثُمَّ بَكَى، فَقُلْتُ: مَا يُبْكِيكَ يَا أَبَا أُمَامَةَ؟ قَالَ: رَحْمَةً لَهُمْ. إِنَّهُمْ كَانُوا مِنْ أَهْلِ الْإِسْلَامِ (فَصَارُوا كُفَّارًا) فَخَرَجُوا مِنْهُ. فَقُلْتُ: يَا أَبَا أُمَامَةَ، هُمْ هَؤُلَاءِ؟ قَالَ: نَعَمْ، قُلْتُ: أَشَيْءٌ تَقُولُهُ بِرَأْيِكَ، أَمْ شَيْءٌ سَمِعْتَهُ مِنْ رَسُولِ اللهِ ﷺ؟ فَقَالَ: إِنِّي إِذَنْ لَجَرِيءٌ، إِنِّي إِذًا لَجَرِيءٌ، بَلْ سَمِعْتُهُ مِنْ رَسُولِ اللهِ ﷺ غَيْرَ مَرَّةٍ وَلَا مَرَّتَيْنِ، وَلَا ثَلَاثٍ، وَلَا أَرْبَعٍ، وَلَا خَمْسٍ، وَلَا سِتٍّ، وَلَا سَبْعٍ، وَوَضَعَ أُصْبُعَيْهِ فِي أُذُنَيْهِ، قَالَ: وَإِلَّا فَصُمَّتَا – قَالَهَا ثَلَاثًا.

Al-Ḥasan said, 'They [who have deviation in their hearts] are the Kharijites'. And when Qatāda recited this verse,

[1] Ibn Abī Ḥātim al-Rāzī, *Tafsīr al-Qur'ān al-ʿAẓīm*, 2:594.

[2] Ibn Kathīr, *Tafsīr al-Qur'ān al-ʿAẓīm*, 1:347.

[3] Al-Khāzin, *Lubāb al-ta'wīl*, 1:217.

> '*So as for those who possess deviation in their hearts* . . .', he would say, 'If they are not the Ḥarūriyya [i.e., Kharijites] then I do not know who they are. . . .' It is reported from Abū Ghālib who said, 'I was once walking with Abū Umāma as he rode a donkey. When he finally reached the door of the Mosque of Damascus he said thrice, "They are the dogs of Hellfire. They are the most evil of those slain under the heavens. Glad tidings to the one who kills them and the one who is killed by them", then he wept. I said, "O Abū Umāma, what causes you to cry?" He replied, "Out of pity for them. They were from the people of Islam [and became disbelievers] and left its fold". I asked, "O Abū Umāma! Are these [the Kharijites] the ones you are referring to?" He replied, "Yes". I then asked, "Is this something you say from your own opinion, or is it something you heard from the Messenger of God ﷺ?" He replied, "I would be most foolhardy if I said this from my own opinion; rather, I heard it from the Messenger of God not once, twice, thrice, or four times, five times, six times or seven times, but several times". Then he inserted his fingers into his ears and said thrice, "If what I say is untrue, let both of my ears go deaf".'[1]

Imam al-Suyūṭī also narrated this hadith in his exegesis and explained that the Prophet ﷺ meant the Kharijites.[2] Al-Naḥās has also narrated from ʿĀʾisha who reported that ʿAbd Allāh b. ʿAbbās said that the people of deviation mentioned in the verse were the Kharijites.[3]

13.3.2 The Kharijites Are Apostates Whose Faces Will Be Darkened

God says in the Qurʾān,

---

[1] Abū Ḥafṣ al-Ḥanbalī, *al-Lubāb fī ʿulūm al-Kitāb*, 3:437.

[2] Jalāl al-Dīn al-Suyūṭī, *al-Durr al-manthūr*, 2:148.

[3] Al-Naḥās, *Maʿānī al-Qurʾān al-Karīm*, 1:349.

﴿يَوْمَ تَبْيَضُّ وُجُوهٌ وَتَسْوَدُّ وُجُوهٌ فَأَمَّا ٱلَّذِينَ ٱسْوَدَّتْ وُجُوهُهُمْ أَكَفَرْتُم بَعْدَ إِيمَٰنِكُمْ
فَذُوقُواْ ٱلْعَذَابَ بِمَا كُنتُمْ تَكْفُرُونَ﴾

'On the Day when many faces will be bright and many others will be dark, the ones with dark faces [will be asked], *"Did you reject faith after you had believed? So taste the torment for the disbelief you had been committing".'*[1]

Interpreting this verse, Imam Ibn Abī Ḥātim narrated from Abū Umāma that the Prophet ﷺ said, '[In this verse] they [who rejected faith after believing] are the Kharijites'.[2] Ibn Kathīr also referred to the Kharijites in his interpretation of this verse.[3] Ibn Mardawayh narrated the same report via Abū Ghālib and Abū Umāma. Imam Aḥmad narrated it in his *Musnad*, Imam al-Ṭabarānī in his *al-Muʿjam al-kabīr* and Imam Ibn Abī Ḥātim narrated it in his exegesis from Abū Ghālib's chain of transmission. In his exegesis of this verse, Imam al-Suyūṭī also referred to the Kharijites.[4]

13.3.3 The Kharijites are People of Sedition and Ruin

God says in the Qurʾān,

﴿يَٰٓأَيُّهَا ٱلَّذِينَ ءَامَنُواْ لَا تَتَّخِذُواْ بِطَانَةً مِّن دُونِكُمْ لَا يَأْلُونَكُمْ خَبَالًا وَدُّواْ مَا عَنِتُّمْ
قَدْ بَدَتِ ٱلْبَغْضَآءُ مِنْ أَفْوَٰهِهِمْ وَمَا تُخْفِى صُدُورُهُمْ أَكْبَرُ قَدْ بَيَّنَّا لَكُمُ ٱلْأَيَٰتِ إِن
كُنتُمْ تَعْقِلُونَ﴾

'O believers! Do not confide in those who are not from amongst you. They will never miss [any] *chance to cause you mischief. They wish you severe torture. As for their malice, that has become evident from their utterances, and* [the hostility] *that they have concealed in their hearts*

---

[1] Qurʾān 3:106.

[2] Ibn Abī Ḥātim al-Rāzī, *Tafsīr al-Qurʾān al-ʿAẓīm*, 2:594.

[3] Ibn Kathīr, *Tafsīr al-Qurʾān al-ʿAẓīm*, 1:347.

[4] Jalāl al-Dīn al-Suyūṭī, *al-Durr al-manthūr*, 2:148.

is [even] *greater. We have made the Signs manifest to you, if you would use your intellect'.*[1]

Imam Ibn Abī Ḥātim said in his exegesis of this verse,

عَنْ أَبِي أُمَامَةَ، عَنْ رَسُولِ اللهِ ﷺ، أَنَّهُ قَالَ: هُمُ الْخَوَارِجُ.

'Abū Umāma reported that the Messenger of God ﷺ said, "They are the Kharijites".'[2]

Imam al-Qurṭubī commented in his exegesis of this verse that it indicates the Kharijites, and he mentioned that they will continually cause strife and use trickery and deceit.[3]

13.3.4 The Kharijites are at War with God and His Messenger ﷺ and Must be Killed

God says in the Qur'ān,

﴿إِنَّمَا جَزَٰٓؤُاْ ٱلَّذِينَ يُحَارِبُونَ ٱللَّهَ وَرَسُولَهُۥ وَيَسْعَوْنَ فِى ٱلْأَرْضِ فَسَادًا أَن يُقَتَّلُوٓاْ أَوْ يُصَلَّبُوٓاْ أَوْ تُقَطَّعَ أَيْدِيهِمْ وَأَرْجُلُهُم مِّنْ خِلَٰفٍ أَوْ يُنفَوْاْ مِنَ ٱلْأَرْضِ ذَٰلِكَ لَهُمْ خِزْىٌ فِى ٱلدُّنْيَا وَلَهُمْ فِى ٱلْأَخِرَةِ عَذَابٌ عَظِيمٌ﴾

'*Indeed, those who wage war against God and His Messenger and remain engaged in creating mischief in the land* [i.e., perpetrate terrorism, robbery and burglary amongst the Muslims], *their punishment is that they should be slain, or crucified, or their hands and their feet on opposite sides should be cut off, or that they should be exiled from the land* [either by banishment or by imprisonment]. *That is for them a humiliation in this world, and for them there is a terrible torment in the Hereafter'.*[4]

Ibn 'Abbās ﷺ said in his interpretation of this verse,

---

1 Qur'ān 3:118.

2 Ibn Abī Ḥātim al-Rāzī, *Tafsīr al-Qur'ān al-'Aẓīm*, 3:742.

3 Muhammad al-Qurṭubī, *al-Jāmi' li aḥkām al-Qur'ān*, 4:179.

4 Qur'ān 5:33.

مَنْ شَهَرَ السِّلَاحَ فِي فِئَةِ الْإِسْلَامِ، وَأَخَافَ السَّبِيْلَ ثُمَّ ظَفِرَ بِهِ، وَقَدَرَ عَلَيْهِ فَإِمَامُ الْمُسْلِمِيْنَ فِيْهِ بِالْخِيَارِ، إِنْ شَاءَ قَتَلَهُ وَإِنْ شَاءَ صَلَبَهُ وَإِنْ شَاءَ قَطَعَ يَدَهُ وَرِجْلَهُ.

> Whoever takes up arms against the Muslims and spreads fear on the roads, and is subsequently apprehended and caught, his fate is at the discretion of the ruler of the Muslims; if he so decides he may kill him, and if he so decides he may crucify him or cut off his hands and feet from opposite sides.[1]

This interpretation was also mentioned by Imam al-Ṭabarī and Ibn Kathīr, and reported from Saʿīd b. al-Musayyab, Mujāhid, ʿAṭāʾ, al-Ḥasan al-Baṣrī, Ibrāhīm al-Nakhaʿī and al-Ḍaḥḥāk.[2] Imam al-Qurṭubī narrated in his exegesis that this verse was revealed about a group during the time of the Prophet ﷺ. This group committed terrorism and violence outside of Medina, and as a result, were subjected to a severe punishment. Al-Zamakhsharī interpreted this verse, saying,

يُحَارِبُونَ رَسُولَ اللهِ، وَمُحَارَبَةُ الْمُسْلِمِيْنَ فِي حُكْمِ مُحَارَبَتِهِ.

> 'They wage war against the Messenger of God ﷺ, and waging war against the Muslims takes the same legal ruling as waging war against him ﷺ'.[3]

Citing this exact quote from al-Zamakhsharī, Abū Ḥafṣ al-Ḥanbalī wrote:

أَنَّ الْمَقْصُودَ أَنَّهُمْ يُحَارِبُونَ رَسُولَ اللهِ ﷺ وَإِنَّمَا ذَكَرَ اسْمَ اللهِ تَبَارَكَ وَتَعَالَى تَعْظِيْمًا وَتَفْخِيْمًا لِمَنْ يُحَارَبُ، كَقَوْلِهِ تَعَالَى: ﴿إِنَّ ٱلَّذِينَ يُبَايِعُونَكَ إِنَّمَا يُبَايِعُونَ ٱللَّهَ﴾.

> What is meant here is that they wage war against the Messenger of God ﷺ—and God's name was only

---

[1] Ibn Jarīr al-Ṭabarī, *Jāmiʿ al-bayān*, 6:214; and Ibn Kathīr, *Tafsīr al-Qurʾān al-ʿAẓīm*, 2:51.

[2] Ibid.

[3] Jār Allāh al-Zamakhsharī, *al-Kashshāf ʿan ḥaqāʾiq ghawāmiḍ al-Tanzīl*, 1:661.

> mentioned in exaltation and esteem for the one against whom war is waged, similar to the statement of God Most High, '*Indeed, those who pledge fealty to you are only pledging fealty to God*'. [Qur'ān 48:10][1]

This verse also implies that it is permissible to kill brigands. Al-Qāḍī Thanā' Allāh Pānīpatī said:

> أَجْمَعُوا عَلَى أَنَّ الْمُرَادَ بِالْمُحَارِبِيْنَ الْمُفْسِدِيْنَ فِي هَذِهِ الآيَةِ قُطَّاعُ الطَّرِيْقِ، سَوَاءٌ كَانُوا مُسْلِمِيْنَ أَوْ مِنْ أَهْلِ الذِّمَّةِ. وَاتَّفَقُوا عَلَى أَنَّ مَنْ بَرَزَ وَشَهَرَ السِّلَاحَ مُخِيْفًا مُغِيْرًا خَارِجَ الْمِصْرِ بِحَيْثُ لَا يُدْرِكُهُ الْغَوْثُ فَهُوَ مُحَارِبٌ قَاطِعٌ لِلطَّرِيْقِ جَارِيَةٌ عَلَيْهِ أَحْكَامُ هَذِهِ الآيَةِ. . . . وَقَالَ الْبَغَوِيُّ: اَلْمُكَابِرُونَ فِي الْأَمْصَارِ دَاخِلُونَ فِي حُكْمِ هَذِهِ الآيَةِ.

> They [the jurists] concurred that 'those who wage war and sow corruption in the earth' mentioned in the verse are the brigands, whether they are Muslims or from the non-Muslim citizens. They also agreed that the one who takes up arms for the purpose of spreading fear on the roads outside of the urban areas—as no help can reach there—is an unlawful combatant [*muḥārib*] and brigand who is subject to the rulings contained in this verse. . . . Al-Baghawī said, 'Those who rebel within the urban areas are also subject to the ruling contained in this verse'.[2]

What we gather from this verse and the interpretations of the exegetes is that those who spread terror within an Islamic state must be eliminated, and those who challenge the authority of the state and take up arms against it will be subject to painful punishments in this life and the Hereafter.

13.3.5 The Kharijites are Cursed

God says in the Qur'ān:

---

[1] Abū Ḥafṣ al-Ḥanbalī, *al-Lubāb fī ʿulūm al-Kitāb*, 7:303.

[2] Al-Qāḍī Thanā' Allāh Pānīpatī, *Tafsīr al-mazharī*, 3:86.

﴿وَيُفْسِدُونَ فِى ٱلْأَرْضِ أُوْلَٰٓئِكَ لَهُمُ ٱللَّعْنَةُ وَلَهُمْ سُوٓءُ ٱلدَّارِ﴾

> '*And those who spread corruption on the earth; for them is the curse and the worst abode*'.[1]

This verse refers to the Kharijites, as evidenced by the interpretation of the great Companion, Saʿd b. Abī Waqqāṣ ﷺ, who said,

وَاللهِ الَّذِي لَا إِلَهَ إِلَّا هُوَ! إِنَّهُمُ الْحَرُورِيَّةُ.

> 'By the One besides whom there is no other god, they are the Ḥarūriyya [i.e., Kharijites]!'[2]

The phrase '*corruption on the earth*' implies the killing of peaceful citizens and the destruction of wealth and property. Abū Ḥafṣ al-Ḥanbalī reported,

قَالَ: ﴿وَيُفْسِدُونَ فِى ٱلْأَرْضِ﴾ إِمَّا بِالدُّعَاءِ إِلَى غَيْرِ دِيْنِ اللهِ، وَإِمَّا بِالظُّلْمِ كَمَا فِي النُّفُوسِ وَالْأَمْوَالِ وَتَخْرِيْبِ الْبِلَادِ.

> 'As for His statement "... *and those who spread corruption on the earth*": that is either by inviting to something other than God's religion or committing oppression, such as taking lives, destroying wealth and laying waste the land'.[3]

This interpretation by Abū Ḥafṣ al-Ḥanbalī (which was also reiterated by al-Rāzī in *al-Tafsīr al-kabīr*) details that in addition to taking peaceful life and plundering wealth, corruption on the earth includes calling people to heretical beliefs at odds with Islam.

13.3.6 The Kharijites Presume That They Are Pious

The Kharijites of old were fervent in their prayers, fasting and recitation of the Qurʾān, and exceeded the Prophet's Companions in these things. The modern-day Kharijites are no different from

---

1 Qurʾān 13:25.

2 Al-Qurṭubī, *al-Jāmiʿ li aḥkām al-Qurʾān*, 9:314.

3 Abū Ḥafṣ al-Ḥanbalī, *al-Lubāb fī ʿulūm al-Kitāb*, 9:425.

their predecessors in this regard. They also appear outwardly pious, and are seemingly observant of Islamic Law. Inwardly, however, they are prey to evils like extremism, radicalism and erroneous beliefs that are detrimental to the Muslim *Umma*, which lead to fighting and killing that badly damage Islam's reputation.

God says,

﴿قُلْ هَلْ نُنَبِّئُكُم بِٱلْأَخْسَرِينَ أَعْمَٰلًا. ٱلَّذِينَ ضَلَّ سَعْيُهُمْ فِى ٱلْحَيَوٰةِ ٱلدُّنْيَا وَهُمْ يَحْسَبُونَ أَنَّهُمْ يُحْسِنُونَ صُنْعًا﴾

'*Say, "Shall We inform you of those who are the greatest losers with respect to their deeds? It is those whose entire struggle is wasted in the life of this world, but they presume they are doing good".*'[1]

Imam al-Ṭabarī mentioned in his exegesis that this verse was revealed regarding the People of the Book who abandoned their faith, adopted an evil path and added blameworthy innovations to their religion. A second view mentioned by al-Ṭabarī states that these losers are the Kharijites, because when Ibn al-Kawāʾ the Kharijite asked ʿAlī ﷺ about these losers, ʿAlī replied, 'You and your ilk'. One report mentions that Abū al-Ṭufayl said, 'Ibn al-Kawāʾ the Kharijite asked ʿAlī, "Who are the greatest losers with respect to their deeds?" ʿAlī replied, "You, O Ḥarūriyya!"'[2]
Al-Samarqandī says about the same verse,

قَالَ عَلِيُّ بْنُ أَبِي طَالِبٍ: هُمُ الْخَوَارِجُ.

'ʿAlī b. Abī Ṭālib said, "They are the Kharijites".'[3]

God also says,

﴿وَإِذَا قِيلَ لَهُمْ لَا تُفْسِدُوا۟ فِى ٱلْأَرْضِ قَالُوٓا۟ إِنَّمَا نَحْنُ مُصْلِحُونَ. أَلَآ إِنَّهُمْ هُمُ ٱلْمُفْسِدُونَ وَلَٰكِن لَّا يَشْعُرُونَ﴾

---

[1] Qurʾān 18:103–104.

[2] Ibn Jarīr al-Ṭabarī, *Jāmiʿ al-bayān*, 16:33–34.

[3] Al-Samarqandī, *Baḥr al-ʿulūm*, 2:364.

> ‘*And when it is said to them, “Do not spread corruption on the earth”, they say, “We are only reformers”. Beware, it is they who truly spread corruption, although they perceive it not*’,[1]

and,

﴿أَفَمَن زُيِّنَ لَهُۥ سُوٓءُ عَمَلِهِۦ فَرَءَاهُ حَسَنًا﴾

> ‘*So* [what about him] *whose evil action has been made attractive to him and he considers it good?*’[2]

Abū Ḥafṣ al-Ḥanbalī said,

قَالَ قَتَادَةُ: مِنْهُمُ الْخَوَارِجُ الَّذِيْنَ يَسْتَحِلُّونَ دِمَاءَ الْمُسْلِمِيْنَ وَأَمْوَالَهُمْ.

> ‘Qatāda said, “Amongst them are the Kharijites who declare lawful the blood and wealth of the Muslims”.’[3]

13.4 The Appearance of the Kharijites During the Time of the Prophet ﷺ

The turmoil of the Kharijites began during the time of the Prophet ﷺ. Abū Saʿīd al-Khudrī ﷺ said,

بَيْنَا النَّبِيُّ ﷺ يَقْسِمُ ذَاتَ يَوْمٍ قِسْمًا فَقَالَ ذُوالْخُوَيْصِرَةِ، رَجُلٌ مِنْ بَنِي تَمِيْمٍ: يَا رَسُولَ اللهِ، اعْدِلْ. قَالَ: وَيْلَكَ، مَنْ يَعْدِلُ إِذَا لَمْ أَعْدِلْ! فَقَالَ عُمَرُ: اِئْذَنْ لِي فَلْأَضْرِبْ عُنُقَهُ، قَالَ: لَا، إِنَّ لَهُ أَصْحَابًا يَحْقِرُ أَحَدُكُمْ صَلَاتَهُ مَعَ صَلَاتِهِمْ، وَصِيَامَهُ مَعَ صِيَامِهِمْ، يَمْرُقُونَ مِنَ الدِّيْنِ كَمُرُوقِ السَّهْمِ مِنَ الرَّمِيَّةِ.

> ‘When the Prophet ﷺ was apportioning the war booty, Dhū al-Khuwayṣira, a man from Banū Tamīm, said, “O Messenger of God! Be just!” The Prophet ﷺ said, “Woe to you! Who will be just if I am not just?” ʿUmar b. al-Khaṭṭāb ﷺ said, “[O Messenger of God!] Give me permission to strike his neck!” The Prophet ﷺ said,

---

[1] Qurʾān 2:11–12.

[2] Ibid., 35:8.

[3] Abū Ḥafṣ al-Ḥanbalī, *al-Lubāb fī ʿulūm al-Kitāb*, 13:175.

> "Leave him, for he has compatriots; and you will belittle your prayers and fasting in comparison to theirs, but they shall pass through the religion just as an arrow passes through a hunted game".'[1]

13.5 The Legacy of the Kharijites Began with Disrespect to the Prophet ﷺ

It was Dhū al-Khuwayṣira's disrespect to the Prophet ﷺ that laid the foundation for one of the worst trials faced by the *Umma*. And the militants and rebels who revolted against the authority of ʿUthmān and ʿAlī were a continuation of the evil precedent set by Dhū al-Khuwayṣira.

Imam Abū Bakr al-Ājurrī wrote about this issue in his book *Kitāb al-sharīʿa* and penned a chapter called, 'On the Condemnation of the Kharijites and Their Evil Way, and the Permissibility of Killing them, and the Reward for the One Who Either Kills them or is Killed By Them'. In it he stated:

أَوَّلُ قَرْنٍ طَلَعَ مِنْهُمْ عَلَى عَهْدِ رَسُولِ اللهِ ﷺ: هُوَ رَجُلٌ طَعَنَ عَلَى النَّبِيِّ ﷺ، وَهُوَ يَقْسِمُ الْغَنَائِمَ بِالْجِعْرَانَةِ، فَقَالَ: اعْدِلْ يَا مُحَمَّدُ، فَمَا أَرَاکَ تَعْدِلُ، فَقَالَ ﷺ: وَيْلَکَ، فَمَنْ يَعْدِلُ إِذَا لَمْ أَكُنْ أَعْدِلُ؟

> The first of them to appear was during the time of the Messenger of God ﷺ, and he was a man who accused the Prophet ﷺ of injustice as he apportioned the war booty at Jaʿrāna. He said, 'O Muhammad! Be just, for I don't think you are acting fairly'. So the Messenger of God ﷺ replied, 'Woe to you! Who will be just if I am not just?'

---

[1] Narrated by al-Bukhārī in *al-Ṣaḥīḥ*: *Kitāb al-adab* [The Book of Good Manners], chapter: 'What Has Come to Us About Someone Saying, "Woe to you!"', 5:2281 §5811, and *Kitāb istitāba al-murtaddīn wa al-muʿānidīn wa qitālihim* [The Book on Demanding the Repentance of the Apostates and Reprobates, and Fighting Them], chapter: 'On the One Who Refrains from Fighting the Kharijites for the Sake of Drawing Hearts Near and so People Will Not Flee', 6:2540 §6534; and Muslim in *al-Ṣaḥīḥ*: *Kitāb al-Zakāt* [The Book of Zakat], chapter: 'On the Kharijites and Their Qualities', 2:744 §1064.

Ibn Ḥajar al-ʿAsqalānī mentioned a report from ʿAbd al-Razzāq al-Ṣanʿānī who said,

ذُوالْخُوَيْصِرَةِ التَّمِيْمِيُّ وَهُوَ حُرْقُوصُ بْنُ زُهَيْرٍ، أَصْلُ الْخَوَارِجِ.

> 'Dhū al-Khuwayṣira al-Tamīmī's real name was Ḥurqūṣ b. Zuhayr and he was the founder of the Kharijites'.[1]

Thus, the later-day Kharijites had the same mindset as their founder. Badr al-Dīn al-ʿAynī writes,

قَالَ الذَّهَبِيُّ: ذُو الْخُوَيْصِرَةِ الْقَائِلُ، فَقَالَ: يَا رَسُولَ اللهِ، إِعْدِلْ. يُقَالُ هُوَ حُرْقُوصُ بْنُ زُهَيْرٍ، رَأْسُ الْخَوَارِجِ، قُتِلَ فِي الْخَوَارِجِ يَوْمَ النَّهْرِ. . . . وَفِي تَفْسِيْرِ الثَّعَالِبِيِّ: بَيْنَا رَسُولُ اللهِ ﷺ يَقْسِمُ غَنَائِمَ هَوَازِنَ، جَاءَهُ ذُو الْخُوَيْصِرَةِ التَّمِيْمِيُّ، أَصْلُ الْخَوَارِجِ.

> Al-Dhahabī said, 'Dhu al-Khuwayṣira, the one who said, "O Messenger of God! Be just", is said to be Ḥurqūṣ b. Zuhayr, and he was the head of the Kharijites and was amongst the Kharijites who were slain during the Battle of al-Nahr. . . .[2] In the exegesis of al-Thaʿlabī it is mentioned that 'when the Messenger of God ﷺ was apportioning the war booty of Hawāzin, Dhū al-Khuwayṣira al-Tamīmī, the head of the Kharijites, came to him. . .'[3]

13.6 The Ideological Development of the Kharijites During the Reign of ʿUthmān b. ʿAffān ﵁

Many disruptions erupted in the *Umma* after the passing of the Prophet ﷺ. They include false claims to prophethood, apostasy, refusal to pay Zakat and rejection of several other basic teachings of Islam. Those who embraced the beliefs of the Kharijites promoted their warped understanding, exploited these disruptions and began organizing themselves. Those who actively hatched the conspiracy against ʿUthmān, and ultimately killed him in the final

---

1 Ibn Ḥajar al-ʿAsqalānī, *Fatḥ al-Bārī*, 12:292; and *al-Iṣāba fī tamyīz al-Ṣaḥāba*, 2:49.

2 Badr al-Dīn al-ʿAynī in *ʿUmdat al-qārī*, 15:62.

3 Ibid., 16:142.

days of his rule, were composed of those who held the extremist beliefs of the Kharijites. The most prominent of them was one ʿAbd Allāh b. Sabā. This was the first time an extremist and terrorist group challenged the authority of the Islamic state.

Imam al-Ḥākim mentioned an episode of Ḥusayn b. Khārija, who said,

لَمَّا كَانَتِ الْفِتْنَةُ الْأُولَى أُشْكِلَتْ عَلَيَّ فَقُلْتُ: اَللّٰهُمَّ أَرِنِي أَمْرًا مِنْ أَمْرِ الْحَقِّ أَتَمَسَّكُ بِهِ. قَالَ: فَأُرِيْتُ الدُّنْيَا وَالْآخِرَةَ وَبَيْنَهُمَا حَائِطٌ غَيْرُ طَوِيْلٍ، وَإِذَا أَنَا بِجَائِزٍ فَقُلْتُ: لَوْ تَشَبَّثْتُ بِهَذَا الْجَائِزِ لَعَلِّي أَهْبِطُ إِلَى قَتْلَى أَشْجَعَ لِيُخْبِرُونِي. قَالَ: فَهَبَطْتُ بِأَرْضٍ ذَاتِ شَجَرٍ وَإِذَا أَنَا بِنَفَرٍ جُلُوسٍ فَقُلْتُ: أَنْتُمُ الشُّهَدَاءُ؟ قَالُوْا: لَا نَحْنُ الْمَلَائِكَةُ. قُلْتُ: فَأَيْنَ الشُّهَدَاءُ؟ قَالُوا: تَقَدَّمْ إِلَى الدَّرَجَاتِ الْعُلَى إِلَى مُحَمَّدٍ ﷺ، فَتَقَدَّمْتُ فَإِذَا أَنَا بِدَرَجَةِ اللهِ أَعْلَمُ مَا هِيَ السَّعَةُ وَالْحُسْنُ. فَإِذَا أَنَا بِمُحَمَّدٍ ﷺ وَإِبْرَاهِيْمَ عَلَيْهِ السَّلَامُ وَهُوَ يَقُولُ لِإِبْرَاهِيْمَ عَلَيْهِ السَّلَامُ: اسْتَغْفِرْ لِأُمَّتِي. فَقَالَ لَهُ إِبْرَاهِيْمُ عَلَيْهِ السَّلَامُ: إِنَّكَ لَا تَدْرِي مَا أَحْدَثُوا بَعْدَكَ؟ أَرَاقُوا دِمَاءَهُمْ وَقَتَلُوا إِمَامَهُمْ، أَلَا فَعَلُوا كَمَا فَعَلَ خَلِيْلِي سَعْدٌ. قُلْتُ: أَرَانِي قَدْ أُرِيْتُ أَذْهَبُ إِلَى سَعْدٍ، فَأَنْظُرُ مَعَ مَنْ هُوَ، فَأَكُونُ مَعَهُ فَأَتَيْتُهُ، فَقَصَصْتُ عَلَيْهِ الرُّؤْيَا، فَمَا أَكْثَرَ بِهَا فَرَحًا. وَقَالَ: قَدْ شَقِيَ مَنْ لَمْ يَكُنْ لَهُ إِبْرَاهِيْمُ عَلَيْهِ السَّلَامُ خَلِيْلًا. قُلْتُ: فِي أَيِّ الطَّائِفَتَيْنِ أَنْتَ؟ قَالَ: لَسْتُ مَعَ وَاحِدٍ مِنْهُمَا. قُلْتُ: فَكَيْفَ تَأْمُرُنِي؟ قَالَ: أَلَكَ مَاشِيَةٌ؟ قُلْتُ: لَا. قَالَ: فَاشْتَرِ مَاشِيَةً وَاعْتَزِلْ فِيْهَا حَتَّى تَنْجَلِيَ.

'During the first outbreak of turmoil, I was confused, so I said, "O God! Show me something of the truth that I may hold fast to it". So I was shown the world and the Hereafter [in a dream], and there was a wall between the two that was not very tall and suddenly I was over it. I said, "If I continue to be suspended over this, I might fall upon those slain at Ashjaʿ, so they can inform me". So I descended on to a land, green and fresh with vegetation, and there was a group sitting, whom I asked, "Are you martyrs?" They said, "No, we are angels". I said, "So where are the martyrs?" They said, "Go towards the higher levels up to the Prophet Muhammad ﷺ". Then I advanced until I reached a level, and its beauty and vastness was indescribable. Upon reaching this level, suddenly I saw the Prophet Muhammad ﷺ and Abraham ﷺ and he [Muhammad ﷺ] was saying to Abraham, "Seek forgiveness for my *Umma*". Abraham said to him, "You do not know what blameworthy things they did after you. They shed their blood and killed their ruler; why don't they do what my friend Saᶜd did?" I said to myself that what God has shown me leads me to visit Saᶜd. So I went to him and told him my dream. He felt glad and said, "Wretched is he who does not have Abraham as a friend!" I asked him, "So to which of the two factions do you belong?" He replied, "I am with neither". Then I asked him, "So what is your advice to me?" He said, "Do you have any cattle?" I said, "No". He said, "Go and buy some cattle and withdraw until things become clear".'[1]

In Ibn ᶜAbd al-Barr's *al-Tamhīd*[2] and Ibn Ḥajar's *al-Iṣāba*[3] there is described what has been called the 'first tribulation', which is the turmoil that ensued when ᶜUthmān ﷺ was assassinated. The people of sedition divided into two groups and were the ones who initiated bloodshed and added blameworthy innovations to the religion. It was that band of extremists who laid down the foundation for the Kharijites after the Battle of Ṣiffīn during the reign of ᶜAlī ﷺ.

13.7 The Kharijites During the Reign of ᶜAlī b. Abi Ṭālib ﷺ

The major objective of the Kharijites is to destabilize the foundations of the Muslim state in the name of the religion. When

---

[1] Narrated by al-Ḥākim in *al-Mustadrak*, 4:499 §8394; and cited by Ibn ᶜAbd al-Barr in *al-Tamhīd*, 19:222; and al-Dhahabī in *Siyar aᶜlām al-nubalāʾ*, 1:120.

[2] Cited by Ibn ᶜAbd al-Barr in *al-Tamhīd*, 19:222.

[3] Ibn Ḥajar al-ᶜAsqalānī, *al-Iṣāba fī tamyīz al-Ṣaḥāba*, 2:172 §1979.

we look critically at the history of the Kharijites, we see that theirs was a violent movement that was against dialogue and peaceful settlement of disputes, such as the policy that ʿAlī ﷺ, the fourth Rightly Guided Caliph, adopted in the form of arbitration before the Battle of Ṣiffīn. As long as the clamour of war prevailed, the Kharijite elements in ʿAlī's army were active, but the moment he decided to seek arbitration for the sake of avoiding further bloodshed, they rejected his decision and deserted his troops. Calling him a disbeliever, they organized a terrorist rebellion group and rose against him and the Muslim *Umma* in the name of jihad. When they organized themselves, their motto and call was, 'There is no judgement but for God'. When ʿAlī heard their slogan he said,

كَلِمَةُ حَقٍّ أُرِيْدَ بِهَا بَاطِلٌ.

'A word of truth by which falsehood is intended'.[1]

In some collections ʿAlī is reported to have said,

إِنْ سَكَتُوا غَمَمْنَاهُمْ، وَإِنْ تَكَلَّمُوا حَجَجْنَاهُمْ، وَإِنْ خَرَجُوا عَلَيْنَا قَاتَلْنَاهُمْ.

'If they are quiet we will overwhelm them, and if they speak we will talk to them with logic, and if they rebel against us we will fight them'.[2]

The Kharijites initiated an armed rebellion against ʿAlī and based themselves in Ḥarūrā, located on the Iraqi border. They accused him of polytheism and blameworthy innovations and declared him a disbeliever and rebelled against him. This would prove to be the start of their mass killing and terrorism. They argued,

تُحَكِّمُونَ فِي أَمْرِ اللهِ الرِّجَالَ؟ لَا حُكْمَ إِلَّا لِلّٰهِ!

---

[1] Narrated by Muslim in *al-Ṣaḥīḥ*: *Kitāb al-Zakāt* [The Book of Zakat], chapter: 'The Encouragement to Kill the Kharijites', 2:749 §1066; al-Nasāʾī in *al-Sunan al-kubrā*, 5:160 §8562; Ibn Abī Shayba in *al-Muṣannaf*, 7:557 §37907; and al-Bayhaqī in *al-Sunan al-kubrā*, 8:171 §16478.

[2] Ibn al-Athīr, *al-Kāmil fī al-tārīkh*, 3:212–213; al-Ṭabarī, *Ṭārīkh al-umam wa al-mulūk*, 3:114.

> 'Do you seek judgment from men in that which is God's command? There is no judgment but for God!'[1]

A leader of Kharijites, Yazīd b. ʿĀṣim al-Muḥāribī, delivered a sermon, saying,

> اَلْحَمْدُ لِلّٰهِ غَيْرَ مُوَدَّعٍ رَبَّنَا وَلَا مُسْتَغْنٍ عَنْهُ. اَللّٰهُمَّ إِنَّا نَعُوذُ بِكَ مِنْ إِعْطَاءِ الدَّنِيَّةِ فِي دِيْنِنَا، فَإِنَّ إِعْطَاءَ الدَّنِيَّةِ فِي الدِّيْنِ إِدْهَانٌ فِي أَمْرِ اللهِ، وَذُلٌّ رَاجِعٌ بِأَهْلِهِ إِلَى سَخَطِ اللهِ. يَا عَلِيُّ، أَبِالْقَتْلِ تُخَوِّفُنَا؟ أَمَا وَاللهِ، إِنِّي لَأَرْجُو أَنْ نَضْرِبَكُمْ بِهَا عَمَّا قَلِيْلٍ غَيْرِ مُصَفَّحَاتٍ، ثُمَّ لَتَعْلَمُ أَيَّنَا أَوْلَى بِهَا صَلِيًّا.

> 'All praise is for God alone. We cannot give it up. O God! We seek refuge from any weakness or fawning flattery in matters of the religion, because that brings humiliation, which will lead to God's wrath. O ʿAlī! Would you have us fear death? Beware! By God, I hope that we will kill you with the edge of the sword. Then, you will come to know who amongst us deserves torment the most!'[2]

Similarly, another leader of the Kharijites said in his sermon,

> أُخْرُجُوا بِنَا مِنْ هَذِهِ الْقَرْيَةِ الظَّالِمِ أَهْلُهَا إِلَى بَعْضِ كُوَرِ الْجِبَالِ أَوْ إِلَى بَعْضِ هَذِهِ الْمَدَائِنِ مُنْكِرِيْنَ لِهَذِهِ الْبِدَعِ الْمُضِلَّةِ.

> 'Leave with us and let us abandon this city of oppressors and head for the mountains or some of the other cities, while detesting these blameworthy and misguided innovations'.[3]

When the prominent leaders of the Kharijites gathered in the house of Shurayḥ b. Awfā al-ʿAbasī, Ibn Wahb said, addressing the gathering,

> إِشْخَصُوا بِنَا إِلَى بَلْدَةٍ نَجْتَمِعُ فِيْهَا لِإِنْفَاذِ حُكْمِ اللهِ، فَإِنَّكُمْ أَهْلُ الْحَقِّ.

---

[1] Ibn al-Athīr, *al-Kāmil fī al-tārīkh*, 3:196.

[2] Ibid., 3:313.

[3] Ibid., 3:313–314.

> 'Let us come together and head for a land where we will carry out the law of God, for you are the people of the truth'.[1]

In their response to ʿAlī's letter addressed to them, the Kharijites wrote,

> إِنَّكَ لَمْ تَغْضَبْ لِرَبِّكَ وَإِنَّمَا غَضِبْتَ لِنَفْسِكَ، فَإِنْ شَهِدْتَ عَلَى نَفْسِكَ بِالْكُفْرِ وَاسْتَقْبَلْتَ التَّوْبَةَ، نَظَرْنَا فِيْمَا بَيْنَنَا وَبَيْنَكَ، وَإِلَّا فَقَدْ نَبَذْنَاكَ عَلَى سَوَاءٍ أَنَّ اللهَ لَا يُحِبُّ الْخَائِنِيْنَ.
>
> 'Indeed, you were not angry for the sake of your Lord; you were angry for the sake of your ego. Now, if you confess that you fell into disbelief and repent, we will look into the matter that is between you and us; otherwise, we reject you, and indeed, God does not love the deceitful'.[2]

This letter and the sermons by the Kharijites indicate that, in their opposition to ʿAlī, they considered themselves to be the paragons of righteousness and truth and considered ʿAlī a purveyor of polytheism and blameworthy innovation (and God's refuge is sought from such a notion!). They were so earnest in their hatred of polytheism and blameworthy innovation that they deserted ʿAlī's city and claimed that it was an abode of disbelief. They would take to the mountains and wastelands and ambush travelers and they would catch hold of their opponents and torture them to death.

Later, ʿAlī formed an army of Companions to launch military offensives against them in order to eliminate them completely and restore peace and security and establish the authority of the government. They were finally defeated as the Prophet ﷺ had prophesied and ordered. Imam Muslim and others reported from Zayd b. Wahb al-Juhanī, who was amongst ʿAlī's army that fought against the Kharijites:

---

[1] Ibid.

[2] Ibid., 3:217.

قَالَ عَلِيٌّ ﷺ: أَيُّهَا النَّاسُ، إِنِّي سَمِعْتُ رَسُولَ اللهِ ﷺ يَقُولُ: يَخْرُجُ قَوْمٌ مِنْ أُمَّتِي يَقْرَءُونَ الْقُرْآنَ لَيْسَ قِرَاءَتُكُمْ إِلَى قِرَاءَتِهِمْ بِشَيْءٍ، وَلَا صَلَاتُكُمْ إِلَى صَلَاتِهِمْ بِشَيْءٍ، وَلَا صِيَامُكُمْ إِلَى صِيَامِهِمْ بِشَيْءٍ، يَقْرَءُونَ الْقُرْآنَ يَحْسِبُونَ أَنَّهُ لَهُمْ وَهُوَ عَلَيْهِمْ، لَا تُجَاوِزُ صَلَاتُهُمْ تَرَاقِيَهُمْ، يَمْرُقُونَ مِنَ الْإِسْلَامِ كَمَا يَمْرُقُ السَّهْمُ مِنَ الرَّمِيَّةِ. لَوْ يَعْلَمُ الْجَيْشُ الَّذِينَ يُصِيبُونَهُمْ مَا قُضِيَ لَهُمْ عَلَى لِسَانِ نَبِيِّهِمْ ﷺ لَاتَّكَلُوا عَنِ الْعَمَلِ وَآيَةُ ذَلِكَ أَنَّ فِيهِمْ رَجُلًا لَهُ عَضُدٌ وَلَيْسَ لَهُ ذِرَاعٌ عَلَى رَأْسِ عَضُدِهِ مِثْلُ حَلَمَةِ الثَّدْيِ عَلَيْهِ شَعَرَاتٌ بِيضٌ. فَتَذْهَبُونَ إِلَى مُعَاوِيَةَ وَأَهْلِ الشَّامِ وَتَتْرُكُونَ هَؤُلَاءِ يَخْلُفُونَكُمْ فِي ذَرَارِيِّكُمْ وَأَمْوَالِكُمْ، وَاللهِ، إِنِّي لَأَرْجُو أَنْ يَكُونَ هَؤُلَاءِ الْقَوْمَ فَإِنَّهُمْ قَدْ سَفَكُوا الدَّمَ الْحَرَامَ وَأَغَارُوا فِي سَرْحِ النَّاسِ فَسِيرُوا عَلَى اسْمِ اللهِ.

قَالَ سَلَمَةُ بْنُ كُهَيْلٍ فَنَزَّلَنِي زَيْدُ بْنُ وَهْبٍ مَنْزِلًا حَتَّى قَالَ مَرَرْنَا عَلَى قَنْطَرَةٍ فَلَمَّا الْتَقَيْنَا وَعَلَى الْخَوَارِجِ يَوْمَئِذٍ عَبْدُ اللهِ بْنُ وَهْبٍ الرَّاسِبِيُّ فَقَالَ لَهُمْ: أَلْقُوا الرِّمَاحَ وَسُلُّوا سُيُوفَكُمْ مِنْ جُفُونِهَا فَإِنِّي أَخَافُ أَنْ يُنَاشِدُوكُمْ كَمَا نَاشَدُوكُمْ يَوْمَ حَرُورَاءَ، فَرَجَعُوا فَوَحَّشُوا بِرِمَاحِهِمْ وَسَلُّوا السُّيُوفَ وَشَجَرَهُمُ النَّاسُ بِرِمَاحِهِمْ. قَالَ: وَقُتِلَ بَعْضُهُمْ عَلَى بَعْضٍ وَمَا أُصِيبَ مِنَ النَّاسِ مِنْ أَصْحَابِ عَلِيٍّ يَوْمَئِذٍ إِلَّا رَجُلَانِ. فَقَالَ عَلِيٌّ ﷺ: الْتَمِسُوا فِيهِمُ الْمُخْدَجَ فَالْتَمَسُوهُ فَلَمْ يَجِدُوهُ، فَقَامَ عَلِيٌّ ﷺ بِنَفْسِهِ حَتَّى أَتَى نَاسًا قَدْ قُتِلَ بَعْضُهُمْ عَلَى بَعْضٍ قَالَ: أَخِّرُوهُمْ فَوَجَدُوهُ مِمَّا يَلِي الْأَرْضَ فَكَبَّرَ، ثُمَّ قَالَ: صَدَقَ اللهُ، وَبَلَّغَ رَسُولُهُ. قَالَ: فَقَامَ إِلَيْهِ عُبَيْدَةُ السَّلْمَانِيُّ فَقَالَ: يَا أَمِيرَ الْمُؤْمِنِينَ! هُوَ اللهُ الَّذِي لَا إِلَهَ إِلَّا هُوَ لَسَمِعْتَ هَذَا الْحَدِيثَ مِنْ رَسُولِ اللهِ ﷺ، فَقَالَ: أَي وَاللهِ الَّذِي لَا إِلَهَ إِلَّا هُوَ! حَتَّى اسْتَحْلَفَهُ ثَلَاثًا، وَهُوَ يَحْلِفُ لَهُ.

'ʿAlī said, "O people! Indeed, I heard God's Messenger ﷺ say, 'There shall be a folk that comes from my *Umma* and they will recite the Qurʾān—your recitation will not be comparable to theirs, or your prayers or your fasting to theirs. They will recite the Qurʾān and believe it supports them but [in reality] it is against them. Their prayers will not go past their throats, and they shall exit from the religion just as an arrow exits from a hunted game. If only the army who encounters them knew what has been decreed for them upon the tongue of their Prophet ﷺ, they would rely on it [and cease doing other deeds]. Their [i.e., the Kharijites'] distinctive sign is that there is a man amongst them, one of whose arms is like a woman's breast, or a piece of meat palpitating and with some white hairs'. [ʿAli continued:] You will be marching towards Muʿāwiya and the inhabitants of the Levant and will leave these folk behind amongst your children and properties! By God, I most certainly hope that they are these people [mentioned in the hadith], for they have shed inviolable blood and raided the people's belongings. So go forth [against them] in the name of God".'

Salama b. Kuhayl said, "Zayd b. Wahb took me to a place in which to stay until we crossed the bridge. ʿAbd Allāh b. Wahb al-Rāsibī was the head of the Kharijites on that day and he said to his army, 'Cast down your spears and unsheathe your swords, for I fear that they will attack you as they attacked you on the Day of Ḥārūrā".' So they cast down their spears, drew their swords, and people fought them with spears until they were killed. Only two soldiers of ʿAlī's army were killed on that day. ʿAlī ﷺ said, 'Search for the maimed one [Dhū al-Khuwayṣira] amongst the slain'. They searched but did not find him. ʿAlī then stood up and [walked] until he came upon a pile of bodies from the enemy. He ordered, 'Search them'. They removed the bodies and found him at the bottom of the pile. ʿAlī ﷺ then cried out, 'God is the Greatest! God spoke the truth and His Messenger conveyed the message!' Then there stood before him ʿUbayda al-Salmānī who said, 'O Commander of the Faithful! By God, besides whom there is no other god. Did you hear this [description] from the Messenger of God ﷺ?' ʿAlī replied, 'Yes, by God, besides whom there is no other god'. ʿUbayda sought an oath from him three times and each time he swore by God".'

There are other related hadith reports that describe this man's handicap as a distinguishing mark. In one report it mentions that he would be of dark complexion and have a hand like a women's breast. In that report it states that when our master ʿAlī defeated them, he said, 'Search for the one with this sign'. When they continued to look and could not find him, ʿAlī said twice or thrice, 'By my Lord! I have neither lied nor been told something false'. The people eventually found the body in a barren place and brought it before ʿAlī. ʿUbayd Allāh—the narrator—said, 'I was with ʿAlī the entire time and his statement was regarding the Kharijites'.[1]

Jundub b. ʿAbd Allāh ﵄ said,

لَمَّا فَارَقَتِ الْخَوَارِجُ عَلِيًّا ﵁ خَرَجَ فِي طَلَبِهِمْ وَخَرَجْنَا مَعَهُ، فَانْتَهَيْنَا إِلَى عَسْكَرِ الْقَوْمِ فَإِذَا لَهُمْ دَوِيٌّ كَدَوِيِّ النَّحْلِ مِنْ قِرَاءَةِ الْقُرْآنِ، وَفِيْهِمْ أَصْحَابُ الثَّفِنَاتِ وَأَصْحَابُ الْبَرَانِسِ، فَلَمَّا رَأَيْتُهُمْ دَخَلَنِي مِنْ ذَلِكَ شِدَّةٌ، فَتَنَحَّيْتُ فَرَكَزْتُ رُمْحِي وَنَزَلْتُ عَنْ فَرَسِي وَوَضَعْتُ بُرْنُسِي، فَنَشَرْتُ عَلَيْهِ دِرْعِي، وَأَخَذْتُ بِمِقْوَدِ فَرَسِي فَقُمْتُ أُصَلِّي إِلَى رُمْحِي وَأَنَا أَقُولُ فِي صَلَاتِي: اَللَّهُمَّ إِنْ كَانَ قِتَالُ هَؤُلَاءِ الْقَوْمِ لَكَ طَاعَةً، فَأْذَنْ لِي فِيْهِ، وَإِنْ كَانَ مَعْصِيَةً فَأَرِنِي بَرَاءَتَكَ. فَأَنَا كَذَلِكَ إِذَا أَقْبَلَ عَلِيُّ بْنُ أَبِي طَالِبٍ ﵁ عَلَى بَغْلَةِ رَسُولِ اللهِ ﷺ. فَلَمَّا حَاذَانِي قَالَ: تَعَوَّذْ بِاللهِ يَا جُنْدُبُ، مِنْ شَرِّ الشَّكِّ. فَجِئْتُ أَسْعَى إِلَيْهِ، وَنَزَلَ، فَقَامَ يُصَلِّي إِذَا أَقْبَلَ رَجُلٌ عَلَى بِرْذَوْنٍ يَقْرُبُ بِهِ. فَقَالَ: يَا أَمِيْرَ الْمُؤْمِنِيْنَ. قَالَ: مَا شَأْنُكَ؟ قَالَ: حَاجَةٌ فِي الْقَوْمِ. قَالَ: وَمَا ذَاكَ؟ قَالَ: قَدْ قَطَعُوا النَّهْرَ، فَذَهَبُوا، قُلْتُ: اَللهُ أَكْبَرُ. فَقَالَ عَلِيٌّ ﵁: مَا قَطَعُوهُ، ثُمَّ جَاءَ آخَرُ يَسْتَحْضِرُ بِفَرَسِهِ. فَقَالَ: يَا أَمِيْرَ الْمُؤْمِنِيْنَ. قَالَ: مَا تَشَاءُ؟ قَالَ: أَلَكَ حَاجَةٌ فِي الْقَوْمِ؟ قَالَ وَمَا ذَاكَ؟ قَالَ: قَدْ قَطَعُوا النَّهْرَ. فَقَالَ عَلِيٌّ ﵁: مَا قَطَعُوهُ

[1] Narrated by Muslim in *al-Ṣaḥīḥ*: *Kitāb al-Zakāt* [The Book of Zakat], chapter: 'The Encouragement to Kill the Kharijites', 2:748 §1066; Abū Dāwūd in *al-Sunan*: *Kitāb al-Sunna*, chapter: 'On Fighting the Kharijites', 4:244 §4768; al-Nasāʾī in *al-Sunan al-kubrā*, 5:163 §8571; Aḥmad b. Ḥanbal in *al-Musnad*, 1:91 §706; ʿAbd al-Razzāq in *al-Muṣannaf*, 10:147; and al-Bazzār in *al-Musnad*, 2:197 §581.

وَلَا يَقْطَعُوهُ، وَلْيَقْتُلَنَّ دُونَهُ عَهْدٌ مِنَ اللهِ تَعَالَى وَرَسُولِهِ ﷺ. ثُمَّ رَكِبَ، فَقَالَ لِي: يَا جُنْدُبُ، أَمَّا أَنَا فَأَبْعَثُ إِلَيْهِمْ رَجُلًا يَقْرَأُ الْمُصْحَفَ، يَدْعُو إِلَى كِتَابِ رَبِّهِمْ وَسُنَّةِ نَبِيِّهِمْ، فَلَا يُقْبِلُ عَلَيْنَا بِوَجْهِهِ حَتَّى يَرْشُقُوهُ بِالنَّبْلِ، يَا جُنْدُبُ، أَمَّا أَنَّهُ لَا يُقْتَلُ مِنَّا عَشَرَةٌ وَلَا يَنْجُو مِنْهُمْ عَشَرَةٌ. ثُمَّ قَالَ: مَنْ يَأْخُذُ هَذَا الْمُصْحَفَ فَيَمْشِي بِهِ إِلَى هَؤُلَاءِ الْقَوْمِ فَيَدْعُوهُمْ إِلَى كِتَابِ رَبِّهِمْ وَسُنَّةِ نَبِيِّهِمْ وَهُوَ مَقْتُولٌ وَلَهُ الْجَنَّةُ؟ فَلَمْ يُجِبْهُ إِلَّا شَابٌّ مِنْ بَنِي عَامِرِ بْنِ صَعْصَعَةَ. فَقَالَ لَهُ عَلِيٌّ رضي الله عنه: خُذْ. فَأَخَذَ الْمُصْحَفَ، فَقَالَ: أَمَا إِنَّكَ مَقْتُولٌ، وَلَسْتَ تُقْبِلُ عَلَيْنَا بِوَجْهِكَ حَتَّى يَرْشُقُوكَ بِالنَّبْلِ. فَخَرَجَ الشَّابُّ يَمْشِي بِالْمُصْحَفِ إِلَى الْقَوْمِ، فَلَمَّا دَنَا مِنْهُمْ حَيْثُ سَمِعُوا قَامُوا وَنَشَبُوا الْقِتَالَ قَبْلَ أَنْ يَرْجِعَ، قَالَ: فَرَمَاهُ إِنْسَانٌ، فَأَقْبَلَ عَلَيْنَا بِوَجْهِهِ، فَقَعَدَ فَقَالَ عَلِيٌّ رضي الله عنه: دُونَكُمُ الْقَوْمُ. قَالَ جُنْدُبٌ: فَقَتَلْتُ بِكَفِّي هَذِهِ ثَمَانِيَةً قَبْلَ أَنْ أُصَلِّيَ الظُّهْرَ وَمَا قُتِلَ مِنَّا عَشَرَةٌ وَلَا نَجَا مِنْهُمْ عَشَرَةٌ.

'When the Kharijites seceded from ʿAlī, he went out in pursuit of them and we went with him. When we reached their troops, we heard a loud recitation of the Qurʾān that sounded like the buzzing of bees. Amongst them were some wearing loin cloths and mantles, and seeing them in that state [of ostensible piety], I had mixed feelings about fighting against them. I stuck my spear into the ground, dismounted from my steed, took off my mantle and spread it out and placed my armour on it. I then took my steed by the reigns and started praying towards my spear [as a barrier]. During my prayer I said, "O God! If it is obedience to You to fight these folk, then give me permission to do it; and if it is disobedience, then show me a sign of Your disapproval". As I was in that state of entreaty, suddenly, ʿAlī b. Abī Ṭālib came, riding the Prophet's mule. After he came close to me he said, "O Jundub! Seek refuge with God from the evil of doubt!" I then hastened to come closer to him, but he dismounted and began to pray. Suddenly, someone on a galloping horse approached and said, "O Commander of

> the Faithful!" ʿAlī said, "What is the matter?" The rider said, "They have all crossed the stream and got away". I said, "God is the Greatest". ʿAlī said, "They have not crossed it, and will not do it. It is the promise of God and His Messenger that they will be killed". Then he mounted his steed and said, "O Jundub! I shall send someone to them who will recite the Qurʾān to them and invite them to the Book of their Lord and the Sunna of their Prophet ﷺ. He will not turn to us [to signal the attack] until they shoot arrows at him. O Jundub! Less than ten will be slain amongst us and less than ten will survive amongst them". Then he said, "So who will take this copy of the Qurʾān to those folk and invite them to the Book of their Lord and the Sunna of their Prophet ﷺ and get killed and earn Paradise?" No one responded to his call except a young man from Banū ʿĀmir b. Ṣaʿṣaʿ. ʿAlī said to him, "Take [this copy of the Qurʾān]". And so the young man took it and ʿAlī said to him, "You will be killed and will not turn to us until they shoot you with arrows". The young man walked towards the encampment of the folk, carrying a copy of the Qurʾān. When he reached a place where they could hear, one of them shot him with an arrow. He then turned towards us and sat down. ʿAlī then said, "Now attack them". I killed eight of them with this hand of mine before I prayed the Afternoon Prayer and less than ten amongst us were slain and less than ten amongst them survived'.[1]

As you see, Jundub was affected by the ostensible piety, asceticism and worship of the Kharijites. Despite that, all their distinguishing marks that ʿAlī told of proved true.

Ṭāriq b. Ziyād said,

خَرَجْنَا مَعَ عَلِيٍّ رضي الله عنه إِلَى الْخَوَارِجِ فَقَتَلَهُمْ، ثُمَّ قَالَ: انْظُرُوا فَإِنَّ نَبِيَّ اللهِ ﷺ قَالَ:

---

[1] Narrated by al-Ṭabarānī in *al-Muʿjam al-awsaṭ*, 4:227 §4051; and cited by al-Haythamī in *Majmaʿ al-zawāʾid*, 4:227; Ibn Ḥajar al-ʿAsqalānī in *Fatḥ al-Bārī*, 12:296; and al-Shawkānī in *Nayl al-awṭār*, 7:349.

إِنَّهُ سَيَخْرُجُ قَومٌ يَتَكَلَّمُونَ بِالْحَقِّ لَا يُجَاوِزُ حَلْقَهُمْ، يَخْرُجُونَ مِنَ الْحَقِّ كَمَا يَخْرُجُ السَّهْمُ مِنَ الرَّمِيَّةِ، سِيْمَاهُمْ أَنَّ فِيْهِمْ رَجُلًا أَسْوَدَ مُخْدَجَ الْيَدِ، فِي يَدِهِ شَعَرَاتٌ سُودٌ، إِنْ كَانَ هُوَ فَقَدْ قَتَلْتُمْ شَرَّ النَّاسِ وَإِن لَّمْ يَكُنْ هُوَ فَقَدْ قَتَلْتُمْ خَيرَ النَّاسِ. فَبَكَيْنَا. ثُمَّ قَالَ: اطْلُبُوا. فَطَلَبْنَا، فَوَجَدْنَا الْمُخْدَجَ، فَخَرَرْنَا سُجُودًا وَخَرَّ عَلِيٌّ ﷺ مَعَنَا.

'We went out with ʿAlī ﷺ to pursue the Kharijites and he slew them. Then he said, "Take a close look, for the Prophet of God ﷺ said, 'There shall emerge a folk who speak the truth but it will not pass their throats. They shall leave the truth just as an arrow exits a hunted game. Their distinguishing trait is that there is amongst them a man of dark complexion with a deformed hand with black hairs on it'. If it is him, then you have killed the most evil of the people, and if it is not, then you have killed the best of the people". We then began to cry and then he said, "Look for him". We looked for him and found him with a deformed hand, so we fell into prostration [in gratitude] and ʿAlī ﷺ prostrated with us'.[1]

13.8 The Beliefs of the Kharijites

The preceding discussion has shown us that sometimes crooked and short-sighted people emerge in society with compound ignorance concerning the wisdom and vision of the religion. They strictly observe the outward religious acts, which in turn instil them with the conceited belief that they are staunch Muslims and true embodiments of Islam. They feel themselves near to God and consider all others either disbelievers or disobedient. They believe it is their right to force others to adhere to the path of righteousness and they forget God's words,

﴿ٱدْعُ إِلَىٰ سَبِيلِ رَبِّكَ بِٱلْحِكْمَةِ وَٱلْمَوْعِظَةِ ٱلْحَسَنَةِ﴾

---

[1] Narrated by al-Nasāʾī in *al-Sunan al-kubrā*, 5:161 §8566; Aḥmad b. Ḥanbal in *al-Musnad*, 1:107 §848, and *Faḍāʾil al-Ṣaḥāba*, 2:714 §1224; and cited by al-Khaṭīb al-Baghdādī in *Tārīkh Baghdād*, 14:362 §7689; and al-Marwazī in *Taʿẓīm qadr al-ṣalāh*, 1:256 §247.

'Invite to the path of your Lord with wisdom and goodly invitation',[1]

and,

﴿لَآ إِكْرَاهَ فِى ٱلدِّينِ﴾

'There is no compulsion in the religion'.[2]

Satan plants the seeds of arrogance in their hearts, which in turn cause them to see themselves as pure Muslims and others as impure, if Muslims at all. They believe that it is their right to force others to believe what they believe, and because Satan has moulded them and shaped them with the idea that they are peerless, they are convinced that they are free to use whatever means at their disposal to either bring wayward Muslims back to the right path or eliminate them.

This mindset allows them to kill people, spread terror and plunder wealth and property without fear of sin. According to their warped understanding, whatever crimes they do are jihad. The Qur'ān informs us that they will be the greatest of losers in the Hereafter:

﴿قُلْ هَلْ نُنَبِّئُكُم بِٱلْأَخْسَرِينَ أَعْمَٰلاً. ٱلَّذِينَ ضَلَّ سَعْيُهُمْ فِى ٱلْحَيَوٰةِ ٱلدُّنْيَا وَهُمْ يَحْسَبُونَ أَنَّهُمْ يُحْسِنُونَ صُنْعًا﴾

'Say, "Shall We inform you of those who are the greatest losers with respect to their deeds? It is those whose entire struggle is wasted in the life of this world, but they presume they are doing good".'[3]

Imam al-Shahrastānī said about the false beliefs and ideologies of Kharijites:

كِبَارُ فِرَقِ الْخَوَارِجِ سِتَّةٌ: اَلْأَزَارِقَةُ وَالنَّجَدَاتُ وَالْعِجَارَةُ وَالثَّعَالِبَةُ وَالْإِبَاضِيَّةُ وَالصَّفْرِيَّةُ

---

1 Qur'ān 16:125.

2 Ibid., 2:256.

3 Ibid., 18:103–104.

وَالْبَاقُونَ فُرُوعُهُمْ، وَيَرَوْنَ الْخُرُوجَ عَلَى الْإِمَامِ إِذَا خَالَفَ السُّنَّةَ حَقًّا وَاجِبًا. . . . هُمُ الَّذِينَ خَرَجُوا عَلَى أَمِيرِ الْمُؤْمِنِينَ عَلِيٍّ ﷺ حِينَ جَرَى أَمْرُ الْحَكَمَيْنِ وَاجْتَمَعُوا بِحَرُورَاءَ مِنْ نَاحِيَةِ الْكُوفَةِ وَرَئِيسُهُمْ عَبْدُ اللهِ بْنُ الْكَوَّاءِ وَعَتَّابُ بْنُ الْأَعْوَرِ وَعَبْدُ اللهِ بْنُ وَهْبٍ الرَّاسِبِيُّ وَعُرْوَةُ بْنُ جَرِيرٍ وَيَزِيدُ بْنُ عَاصِمٍ الْمُحَارِبِيُّ وَحُرْقُوصُ بْنُ زُهَيْرٍ الْبَجَلِيُّ الْمَعْرُوفُ بِذِي الثُّدَيَّةِ، وَكَانُوا يَوْمَئِذٍ فِي اثْنَي عَشَرَ أَلْفَ رَجُلٍ أَهْلِ صَلَاةٍ وَصِيَامٍ أَعْنِي يَوْمَ النَّهْرَوَانِ . . . وَهُمُ الَّذِينَ أَوَّلُهُمْ ذُو الْخُوَيْصِرَةِ وَآخِرُهُمْ ذُو الثُّدَيَّةِ.

The major factions of the Kharijites are six: al-Azāriqa, al-Najdāt, al-ʿIjāra, al-Thaʿāliba, al-Ibāḍiyya and al-Ṣafriyya. The remaining factions are but offshoots of these. They believe that it is right and obligatory to revolt against the government if it goes against the Sunna. . . . They are the ones who rebelled against the Commander of the Faithful, ʿAlī ﷺ, when the process of arbitration was underway. They gathered at Ḥārūrā in the region of Kufa. Their leaders were ʿAbd Allāh b. al-Kawāʾ, ʿAtāb b. al-Aʿwar, ʿAbd Allāh b. Wahb al-Rābisī, ʿUrwa b. Jarīr, Yazīd b. ʿĀṣim and Ḥurqūṣ b. Zuhayr, better known as Dhū al-Thaddīya. In those days they totalled twelve thousand men dedicated to prayer and fasting—meaning on the day of the Battle of Nahrawan. . . . The first of them was known as Dhū al-Khuwayṣira and the last of them [in the first organized revolt] was known as Dhū al-Thadīyya.[1]

Ibn Ḥajar al-ʿAsqalānī said:

قَالَ الْقَاضِي أَبُو بَكْرِ بْنُ الْعَرَبِيِّ: اَلْخَوَارِجُ صِنْفَانِ: أَحَدُهُمَا يَزْعَمُ أَنَّ عُثْمَانَ وَعَلِيًّا ﷺ وَأَصْحَابَ الْجَمَلِ وَصِفِّينَ وَكُلَّ مَنْ رَضِيَ بِالتَّحْكِيمِ كُفَّارٌ. وَالْآخَرُ يَزْعَمُ أَنَّ كُلَّ مَنْ أَتَى كَبِيرَةً فَهُوَ كَافِرٌ مُخَلَّدٌ فِي النَّارِ أَبَدًا، وَزَادَ نَجْدَةُ عَلَى مُعْتَقَدِ الْخَوَارِجِ أَنَّ مَنْ لَمْ يَخْرُجْ وَيُحَارِبِ الْمُسْلِمِينَ فَهُوَ كَافِرٌ، وَلَوِ اعْتَقَدَ مُعْتَقَدَهُمْ.

[1] ʿAbd al-Karīm al-Shahrastānī, *al-Milal wa al-niḥal*, p. 115.

> Al-Qāḍī Abū Bakr Ibn al-ʿArabī said, 'The Kharijites are two types: Those who claim that ʿUthmān, ʿAlī and those present at the Battle of al-Jamal and Ṣiffīn, and all who were pleased with the arbitration, were disbelievers; and those who claim that anyone who commits a grave sin is a disbeliever who will abide eternally in Hell. Najda [b. ʿĀmir] had added a belief not held by the other Kharijites, namely that the one who does not march out and wage war against the Muslims is himself a disbeliever—even if he held the belief of the Kharijites'.[1]

Ibn Taymiyya spoke about the blasphemous beliefs of the Kharijites and their oppressive behaviour against the Muslims,

> كَانُوا كَمَا نَعَتَهُمُ النَّبِيُّ ﷺ: يَقْتُلُونَ أَهْلَ الْإِسْلَامِ وَيَدَعُونَ أَهْلَ الْأَوْثَانِ وَكَفَّرُوا عَلِيَّ بْنَ أَبِي طَالِبٍ وَعُثْمَانَ بْنَ عَفَّانَ وَمَنْ وَالَاهُمَا. وَقَتَلُوا عَلِيَّ بْنَ أَبِي طَالِبٍ مُسْتَحِلِّيْنَ لِقَتْلِهِ. قَتَلَهُ عَبْدُ الرَّحْمَنِ بْنُ مُلْجِمٍ الْمُرَادِيُّ مِنْهُمْ، وَكَانَ هُوَ وَغَيْرُهُ مِنَ الْخَوَارِجِ مُجْتَهِدِيْنَ فِي الْعِبَادَةِ، لَكِنْ كَانُوا جُهَّالًا فَارَقُوا السُّنَّةَ وَالْجَمَاعَةَ، فَقَالَ هَؤُلَاءِ: مَا النَّاسُ إِلاَّ مُؤْمِنٌ أَوْ كَافِرٌ؛ وَالْمُؤْمِنُ مَنْ فَعَلَ جَمِيْعَ الْوَاجِبَاتِ وَتَرَكَ جَمِيْعَ الْمُحَرَّمَاتِ: فَمَنْ لَّمْ يَكُنْ كَذَلِكَ فَهُوَ كَافِرٌ: مُخَلَّدٌ فِي النَّارِ. ثُمَّ جَعَلُوا كُلَّ مَنْ خَالَفَ قَوْلَهُمْ كَذَلِكَ. فَقَالُوا: إِنَّ عُثْمَانَ وَعَلِيًّا وَنَحْوَهُمَا حَكَمُوا بِغَيْرِ مَا أَنْزَلَ اللهُ، وَظَلَمُوا فَصَارُوا كُفَّارًا.

> As the Prophet ﷺ described them, they would 'kill the people of Islam and leave the idolaters'. They declared ʿAlī b. Abī Ṭālib and ʿUthmān b. ʿAffān disbelievers, as well as those who allied with them. They killed ʿAlī b. Abī Ṭālib, believing that it was lawful. The killer was ʿAbd al-Raḥmān b. Muljam al-Murādī. He, along with the other Kharijites, was devout in their worship; however, they were grossly ignorant [of religious logic and wisdom] and abandoned the Sunna and the community [*jamāʿa*]. They said, 'There is only the believer and the disbeliever; the

---

[1] Ibn Ḥajar al-ʿAsqalānī, *Fatḥ al-Bārī*, 12:283, 285.

> believer is he who performs every single obligation and abstains from every single prohibition. So whoever does not fit that description is a disbeliever who will abide eternally in the Fire'. Furthermore, they applied this to anyone who objected to them, and said, 'ʿUthmān and ʿAlī and their ilk have judged by other than what God has revealed and committed oppression therefore they are disbelievers'.[1]

Describing the known features of the Kharijites, Ibn Taymiyya said:

> لَهُمْ خَاصَّتَانِ مَشْهُورَتَانِ فَارَقُوا بِهِمَا جَمَاعَةَ الْمُسْلِمِيْنَ وَأَئِمَّتَهُمْ، أَحَدُهُمَا: خُرُوجُهُمْ عَنِ السُّنَّةِ، وَجَعْلُهُمْ مَا لَيْسَ بِسَيِّئَةٍ سَيِّئَةً، أَوْ مَا لَيْسَ بِحَسَنَةٍ حَسَنَةً. اَلْفَرْقُ الثَّانِي فِي الْخَوَارِجِ وَأَهْلِ الْبِدَعِ: إِنَّهُمْ يُكَفِّرُونَ بِالذُّنُوبِ وَالسَّيِّئَاتِ. وَيَتَرَتَّبُ عَلَى تَكْفِيْرِهِمْ بِالذُّنُوبِ اسْتِحْلَالُ دِمَاءِ الْمُسْلِمِيْنَ وَأَمْوَالِهِمْ، وَإِنَّ دَارَ الْإِسْلَامِ دَارُ حَرْبٍ، وَدَارُهُمْ هِيَ دَارُ الْإِيْمَانِ.

> There are two well-known and exclusive traits by which they parted from the community of Muslims and the Islamic state: their abandonment of the Sunna and the act of declaring sinful that which is not a sin or declaring as good that which is not good. The second difference between the Kharijites and the remaining people of blameworthy innovation is that they declare people disbelievers over sins and misdeeds. Their imputation of disbelief on account of sins results in their making lawful the blood and wealth of the Muslims and declaring the abode of Islam [*Dār al-Islām*] an abode of war [*Dār al-Ḥarb*] and only the land in their control the abode of faith.[2]

The reason why the Kharijites are also called Ḥarūriyya is because the first group of Kharijites emerged from the area of

---

[1] Ibn Taymiyya, *Majmūʿa al-fatāwā*, 7:481.

[2] Ibid., 19:72–73.

Ḥārūrā in the days of ʿAlī's caliphate. Shabbīr Aḥmad ʿUthmānī said:

> قَوْلُهُ ﷺ عَنِ الْحَرُورِيَّةِ إِلَخْ: هُمُ الْخَوَارِجُ، جَمْعُ خَارِجَةٍ، أَيْ طَائِفَةٌ، وَهُمْ قَوْمٌ مُبْتَدِعُونَ سُمُّوا بِذَلِكَ، لِخُرُوجِهِمْ عَنِ الدِّيْنِ، وَخُرُوجِهِمْ عَلَى خِيَارِ الْمُسْلِمِيْنَ، وَأَصْلُ ذَلِكَ أَنَّ بَعْضَ أَهْلِ الْعِرَاقِ أَنْكَرُوا سِيْرَةَ بَعْضِ أَقَارِبِ عُثْمَانَ ﷺ، فَطَعَنُوا عَلَى عُثْمَانَ ﷺ بِذَلِكَ، وَكَانَ يُقَالُ لَهُمْ: الْقُرَّاءُ، لِشِدَّةِ اجْتِهَادِهِمْ فِي التِّلَاوَةِ وَالْعِبَادَةِ، إِلَّا أَنَّهُمْ كَانُوا يَتَأَوَّلُونَ الْقُرْآنَ عَلَى غَيْرِ الْمُرَادِ مِنْهُ، وَيَسْتَبِدُّونَ بِرَأْيِهِمْ، وَيَتَنَطَّعُونَ فِي الزُّهْدِ وَالْخُشُوعِ وَغَيْرِ ذَلِكَ، فَلَمَّا قُتِلَ عُثْمَانُ ﷺ قَاتَلُوا مَعَ عَلِيٍّ ﷺ، وَاعْتَقَدُوا كُفْرَ عُثْمَانَ ﷺ وَمَنْ تَابَعَهُ، وَاعْتَقَدُوا إِمَامَةَ عَلِيٍّ ﷺ وَكُفْرَ مَنْ قَاتَلَهُ مِنْ أَهْلِ الْجَمَلِ. (فَأَنْكَرُوا التَّحْكِيمَ، فَتَرَكُوهُ بِصِفِّيْنَ وَصَارُوا خَوَارِجَ).
>
> The Prophet's statement regarding 'the Ḥarūriyya' is regarding the Kharijites, which is from the word '*khārija*', which means 'those who went out'. They are a folk from the blameworthy innovators and were given that name because of their separation from the religion and the best of the Muslims. The start of all this lies with some of the people of Iraq who objected to the behaviour of some of ʿUthmān's relatives [who were in power], so as a result they defamed ʿUthmān. They used to be called 'the reciters' because of their dedication to recitation and worship; however, they would incorrectly interpret the Qurʾān, force others to adopt their views and go to extremes in asceticism, humility and so on. So after ʿUthmān was killed they fought alongside ʿAlī, believing that ʿUthmān and those who followed him were disbelievers. They believed in the imamate of ʿAlī and held that those who fought against him during the Battle of al-Jamal were disbelievers. However, when he chose arbitration, they censured him and left him at Ṣiffīn and became secessionists [Kharijites].[1]

---

[1] Shabbīr Aḥmad ʿUthmānī, *Fatḥ al-Mulhim*, 5:158.

هُمْ ثَمَانِيَةُ آلاَفٍ. وَقِيلَ: كَانُوا أَكْثَرَ مِنْ عَشَرَةِ آلاَفٍ. . . . فَتَنَادَوا مِنْ جَوَانِبِ الْمَسْجِدِ: لَا حُكْمَ إِلَّا لِلَّهِ، فَقَالَ: كَلِمَةُ حَقٍّ يُرَادُ بِهَا بَاطِلٌ، فَقَالَ لَهُمْ: لَكُمْ عَلَيْنَا ثَلَاثَةٌ: أَنْ لَا نَمْنَعُكُمْ مِنَ الْمَسَاجِدِ، وَلَا مِنْ رِزْقِكُمْ مِنَ الْفَيْءِ، وَلَا نَبْدَؤُكُمْ بِقِتَالٍ مَا لَمْ تُحْدِثُوا فَسَادًا، وَخَرَجُوا شَيْئًا بَعْدَ شَيْءٍ إِلَى أَنِ اجْتَمَعُوا بِالْمَدَائِنِ، . . . فَأَصَرُّوا عَلَى الْإِمْتِنَاعِ حَتَّى يَشْهَدَ عَلِيٌّ ﵁ نَفْسَهُ بِالْكُفْرِ لِرِضَاهُ بِالتَّحْكِيمِ، . . . ثُمَّ اجْتَمَعُوا عَلَى أَنَّ مَنْ لَا يَعْتَقِدُ مُعْتَقَدَهُمْ يُكَفَّرُ وَيُبَاحُ دَمُهُ وَمَالُهُ وَأَهْلُهُ، . . . فَقَتَلُوا مَنِ اجْتَازَ بِهِمْ مِنَ الْمُسْلِمِينَ.

They were eight thousand in number, although it was said that they were over ten thousand. . . . [When ʿAlī was making an address] they issued calls from around the mosque, saying, 'There is no judgement but for God'. ʿAlī said, 'A true word by which falsehood is intended'. He also said to them, 'There are three rights you have over us: that we do not prevent you from the mosques, that we do not withhold from you your provision from the *fay*ʾ (spoils acquired without fighting), and that we do not initiate fighting against you so long as you do not spread corruption'. They seceded, bit by bit, until they gathered in Madāʾin . . . and they began withholding obedience [from ʿAlī, saying they would continue] until ʿAlī confessed to disbelief for having preferred arbitration. . . . Then they concurred amongst themselves that whoever does not believe as they do is to be declared a disbeliever whose blood, wealth and family are lawful. . . . Then they killed any of the Muslims who passed their way.[1]

هَذَا مُلَخَّصُ أَوَّلِ أَمْرِهِمْ، فَكَانُوا مُخْتَفِينَ فِي خِلَافَةِ عَلِيٍّ ﵁ حَتَّى كَانَ مِنْهُمْ عَبْدُ الرَّحْمَنِ بْنُ مُلْجِمٍ الَّذِي قَتَلَ عَلِيًّا ﵁ بَعْدَ أَنْ دَخَلَ عَلِيٌّ ﵁ فِي صَلَاةِ الصُّبْحِ. . . . فَظَهَرَ الْخَوَارِجُ حِينَئِذٍ بِالْعِرَاقِ مَعَ نَافِعِ بْنِ الْأَزْرَقِ، وَبِالْيَمَامَةِ مَعَ نَجْدَةَ بْنِ عَامِرٍ، وَزَادَ نَجْدَةُ عَلَى مُعْتَقَدِ الْخَوَارِجِ أَنَّ مَنْ لَمْ يَخْرُجْ وَيُحَارِبِ الْمُسْلِمِينَ فَهُوَ

---

[1] Ibid.

كَافِرٌ، وَلَوِ اعْتَقَدَ مُعْتَقَدَهُمْ. . . . وَكَفَّرُوا مَنْ تَرَكَ الْأَمْرَ بِالْمَعْرُوفِ وَالنَّهْيَ عَنِ الْمُنْكَرِ إِنْ كَانَ قَادِرًا، وَإِنْ لَمْ يَكُنْ قَادِرًا فَقَدِ ارْتَكَبَ كَبِيرَةً، وَحُكْمُ مُرْتَكِبِ الْكَبِيرَةِ عِنْدَهُمْ حُكْمُ الْكَافِرِ. قَالَ أَبُو مَنْصُورٍ الْبَغْدَادِيُّ فِي "الْمَقَالَاتِ": عِدَّةُ فِرَقِ الْخَوَارِجِ عِشْرُونَ فِرْقَةً.

This is a synopsis of their origin. They were concealed within the ranks during the caliphate of ʿAlī ﷺ, until ʿAbd al-Raḥmān b. Muljam killed ʿAlī after having approached him during the Dawn Prayer. . . . During that time the Kharijites emerged from Iraq with Nāfiʿ b. al-Azraq, and in Yamama with Najda b. ʿĀmir, and Najda had added a belief not held by the other Kharijites, namely that the one who does not march out and wage war against the Muslims is himself a disbeliever—even if he held the belief of the Kharijites. They imputed disbelief upon those who neglected to enjoin the good and forbid the evil—if they were able to do so and still neglected it. And if they were unable, it was believed that they committed a grave sin, and according to them, the one who commits a major sin is a disbeliever. Abū Manṣūr al-Baghdādī said in *al-Maqālāt*, 'The factions of the Kharijites are over twenty in number'.[1]

13.9 The Psychological Traits of the Kharijites

Commenting on the Kharijites and their activities, Imam Ibn al-Athīr wrote:

ثُمَّ إِنَّ الْخَوَارِجَ لَقِيَ بَعْضُهُمْ بَعْضًا وَاجْتَمَعُوا فِي مَنْزِلِ عَبْدِ اللهِ بْنِ وَهْبٍ الرَّاسِبِيِّ، فَخَطَبَهُمْ فَزَهَّدَهُمْ فِي الدُّنْيَا وَأَمَرَهُمْ بِالْأَمْرِ بِالْمَعْرُوفِ وَالنَّهْيِ عَنِ الْمُنْكَرِ، ثُمَّ قَالَ: اخْرُجُوا بِنَا مِنْ هَذِهِ الْقَرْيَةِ الظَّالِمِ أَهْلُهَا إِلَى بَعْضِ كُوَرِ الْجِبَالِ أَوْ إِلَى بَعْضِ هَذِهِ الْمَدَائِنِ مُنْكِرِيْنَ لِهَذِهِ الْبِدَعِ الْمُضِلَّةِ. ثُمَّ اجْتَمَعُوا فِي مَنْزِلِ شُرَيْحِ بْنِ أَوْفَى الْعَبَسِيِّ، فَقَالَ ابْنُ وَهْبٍ: اِشْخَصُوا بِنَا إِلَى بَلْدَةٍ نَجْتَمِعُ فِيهَا لِإِنْفَاذِ حُكْمِ اللهِ

[1] Ibid.

فَإِنَّكُمْ أَهْلُ الْحَقِّ. قَالَ شُرَيْحٌ: نَخْرُجُ إِلَى الْمَدَائِنِ فَنَنْزِلُهَا وَنَأْخُذُهَا بِأَبْوَابِهَا وَنُخْرِجُ مِنْهَا سُكَّانَهَا.

Then the Kharijites joined forces and gathered in the home of ʿAbd Allāh b. Wahb al-Rāsibī, where he addressed them and encouraged them to abstain from the delights of the world and to enjoin the good and to forbid the evil. Then he said, 'Leave with us and let us abandon this city of oppressors and head for the mountains or some of the other cities, while detesting these blameworthy and misguided innovations'. Then they gathered in the house of Shurayḥ b. Awfā al-ʿAbasī. Ibn Wahb said, addressing the gathering, 'Let us come together and head for a land where we will carry out the law of God, for you are the people of the truth'. Shurayḥ said, 'We would go to the various towns, enter them and expel their inhabitants'.[1]

One particularly heinous event occured when the Kharijites brutally slaughtered ʿAbd Allāh b. Khabbāb and his wife for refusing to declare ʿUthmān and ʿAlī disbelievers. Imam al-Ṭabarī, Ibn al-Athīr and Ibn Kathīr narrated:

أَضْجَعُوهُ، فَذَبَحُوهُ، فَسَالَ دَمُهُ فِي الْمَاءِ، وَأَقْبَلُوا إِلَى الْمَرْأَةِ. فَقَالَتْ: أَنَا امْرَأَةٌ، أَلَا تَتَّقُونَ اللهَ؟ فَبَقَرُوا بَطْنَهَا، وَقَتَلُوا ثَلَاثَ نِسْوَةٍ مِنْ طَيْءٍ.

They put him on the ground and slaughtered him, causing his blood to flow into the water. Then they advanced towards his wife and she said, 'I am a woman! Do you not fear God?' Then, they sliced open her stomach and killed three other women from Ṭayʾ [because they sympathized with her].[2]

When ʿAlī learnt about the murder of ʿAbd Allāh b. Khabbāb, he dispatched al-Ḥārith b. Murra al-ʿAbdī to the Kharijites to investigate the incident. When he reached the Kharijites and asked

---

[1] Ibn al-Athīr, *al-Kāmil fī al-tārīkh*, 3:213–214.

[2] Ibid., 3:219, 7:288; al-Ṭabarī, *Tārīkh al-umam wa al-mulūk*, 3:119.

why they murdered ʿAbd Allāh, they killed him as well.

Ibn Kathīr mentioned that after this, the Kharijites wrote to ʿAlī, saying,

كُلُّنَا قَتَلَ إِخْوَانَكُمْ، وَنَحْنُ مُسْتَحِلُّونَ دِمَاءَهُمْ وَدِمَاءَكُمْ.

> 'All of us have killed your brothers, and we believe that both their blood and your blood are lawful'.[1]

When ʿAlī dispatched Qays b. Saʿd b. ʿUbāda al-Anṣārī to go and negotiate with the Kharijites, he addressed them, saying,

عِبَادَ اللهِ، أَخْرِجُوا إِلَيْنَا طَلْبَتَنَا مِنْكُمْ، وَادْخُلُوا فِي هَذَا الْأَمْرِ الَّذِي خَرَجْتُمْ مِنْهُ . . .

فَإِنَّكُمْ رَكِبْتُمْ عَظِيْمًا مِنَ الْأَمْرِ تَشْهَدُونَ عَلَيْنَا بِالشِّرْكِ وَتَسْفِكُونَ دِمَاءَ الْمُسْلِمِيْنَ.

> 'O servants of God! Hand over those of you whom we want, and obey the authority of the state that you have challenged. . . . For indeed, you have committed a grievous crime; you accuse us of polytheism and shed the blood of the Muslims'.[2]

Similarly, as ʿAlī's representative, Abū Ayyūb al-Anṣārī also tried to convince the Kharijites. He said,

عِبَادَ اللهِ، إِنَّا وَإِيَّاكُمْ عَلَى الْحَالِ الْأُولَى الَّتِي كُنَّا عَلَيْهَا، لَيْسَتْ بَيْنَنَا وَبَيْنَكُمْ عَدَاوَةٌ، فَعَلَامَ تُقَاتِلُونَنَا؟

> 'O servants of God! Certainly, we and you are in the same state as we were before. There is no hostility as such between you and us, so why do you fight against us?'[3]

Their terrorist and rebellious state of mind is also revealed in the address ʿAlī made to the Kharijites:

بَيِّنُوا لَنَا بِمَ تَسْتَحِلُّونَ قِتَالَنَا وَالْخُرُوجَ عَنْ جَمَاعَتِنَا، وَتَضَعُونَ أَسْيَافَكُمْ عَلَى عَوَاتِقِكُمْ، ثُمَّ تَسْتَعْرِضُونَ النَّاسَ تَضْرِبُونَ رِقَابَهُمْ، إِنَّ هَذَا لَهُوَ الْخُسْرَانُ الْمُبِيْنُ، وَاللهِ لَو قَتَلْتُمْ

[1] Ibn Kathīr, *al-Bidāya wa al-nihāya*, 7:288–289.

[2] Ibn al-Athīr, *al-Kāmil fī al-tārīkh*, 3:219.

[3] Ibid.

عَلَى هَذَا دَجَاجَةً لَعَظُمَ عِنْدَ اللهِ قَتْلُهَا، فَكَيْفَ بِالنَّفْسِ الَّتِي قَتْلُهَا عِنْدَ اللهِ حَرَامٌ.

'Explain to us: by what justification do you declare it lawful to kill us and rebel against the authority of the state and take up arms? And then you go out and slay people! Indeed, this is most surely a clear loss. I swear by God, it would be seen as grievous in the sight of God that you even kill a chicken with this intention, so what about a harmless soul that is considered inviolable in His sight?'[1]

When ʿAlī ﷺ presented the banner of peace to Abū Ayyūb al-Anṣārī ﷺ, he went out and said,

مَنْ جَاءَ تَحْتَ هَذِهِ الرَّايَةِ فَهُوَ آمِنٌ، وَمَنْ لَمْ يَقْتُلْ وَلَمْ يَسْتَعْرِضْ فَهُوَ آمِنٌ، وَمَنِ انْصَرَفَ مِنْكُمْ إِلَى الْكُوفَةِ أَوْ إِلَى الْمَدَائِنِ وَخَرَجَ مِنْ هَذِهِ الْجَمَاعَةِ فَهُوَ آمِنٌ.

'Whoever takes refuge under this banner is safe; whoever abstains from fighting and killing will be safe; and whoever amongst you heads to Kufa or to the other towns and abandons this group is safe'.[2]

These citations clearly show that the Kharijites declared the Prophet's Companions and the common Muslims disbelievers and polytheists and considered it not only lawful to kill them, but religiously mandated.

13.10 How the Kharijites Roused Religious Sentiments

The Kharijites would base their call for religion on the Qurʾān. Expressing their religious zealotry, they would rouse extremist sentiments in some of the hapless and ignorant Muslims, and misinterpreting jihad, they would incite them to commit mass murder. To motivate them further, they would mention the rewards of Paradise, so as to mentally prepare their followers to

---

[1] Ibn al-Athīr, *al-Kāmil fī al-tārīkh*, 3:220; Ibn Kathīr, *al-Bidāya wa al-nihāya*, 7:226.

[2] Ibn al-Athīr, *al-Kāmil fī al-tārīkh*, 3:221.

kill and be killed. Ibn Kathīr recounted a sermon delivered to the Kharijites by one Zayd b. Ḥiṣn al-Ṭāʾī al-Sanbasī.

> اجْتَمَعُوا أَيْضًا فِي بَيْتِ زَيْدِ بْنِ حِصْنٍ الطَّائِيِّ السَّنْبَسِيِّ فَخَطَبَهُمْ وَحَثَّهُمْ عَلَى الْأَمْرِ بِالْمَعْرُوفِ وَالنَّهْيِ عَنِ الْمُنْكَرِ، وَتَلَا عَلَيْهِم آيَاتٍ مِنَ الْقُرْآنِ مِنْهَا قَولُهُ تَعَالَى: ﴿يَٰدَاوُۥدُ إِنَّا جَعَلْنَٰكَ خَلِيفَةً فِى ٱلْأَرْضِ فَٱحْكُم بَيْنَ ٱلنَّاسِ بِٱلْحَقِّ وَلَا تَتَّبِعِ ٱلْهَوَىٰ فَيُضِلَّكَ عَن سَبِيلِ ٱللَّهِ﴾، وَقَوْلُهُ تَعَالَى: ﴿وَمَن لَّمْ يَحْكُم بِمَآ أَنزَلَ ٱللَّهُ فَأُوْلَٰٓئِكَ هُمُ ٱلْكَٰفِرُونَ﴾، وَكَذَا الَّتِي بَعْدَهَا وَبَعْدَهَا الظَّالِمُونَ الْفَاسِقُونَ. ثُمَّ قَالَ: فَأَشْهَدُ عَلَى أَهْلِ دَعْوَتِنَا مِنْ أَهْلِ قِبْلَتِنَا أَنَّهُمْ قَدِ اتَّبَعُوا الْهَوَى، وَنَبَذُوا حُكْمَ الْكِتَابِ، وَجَارُوا فِي الْقَولِ وَالْأَعْمَالِ، وَأَنَّ جِهَادَهُمْ حَقٌّ عَلَى الْمُؤْمِنِيْنَ. فَبَكَى رَجُلٌ مِنْهُمْ يُقَالُ لَهُ عَبْدُ اللهِ بْنُ سَخْبَرَةَ السُّلَمِيُّ، ثُمَّ حَرَّضَ أُولَئِكَ عَلَى الْخُرُوجِ عَلَى النَّاسِ، وَقَالَ فِي كَلَامِهِ: وَاضْرِبُوا وُجُوهَهُمْ وَجِبَاهَهُمْ بِالسُّيُوفِ حَتَّى يُطَاعَ الرَّحْمَنُ الرَّحِيْمُ، فَإِنْ أَنْتُمْ ظَفَرْتُمْ وَأُطِيْعَ اللهُ كَمَا أَرَدْتُمْ أَثَابَكُمْ ثَوَابُ الْمُطِيْعِيْنَ لَهُ الْعَامِلِيْنَ بِأَمْرِهِ، وَإِنْ قُتِلْتُمْ فَأَيُّ شَيْءٍ أَفْضَلُ مِنَ الْمَصِيْرِ إِلَى رِضْوَانِ اللهِ وَجَنَّتِهِ.

> They also gathered in the house of Zayd b. Ḥiṣn al-Ṭāʾī al-Sanbasī. He addressed them and encouraged them to enjoin the good and forbid the evil. He recited to them some select verses from the Qurʾān, such as the statement of the Most High, '*O David! Indeed, We have made you a vicegerent on the earth, so judge between people with truth and do not follow vain desires, lest they lead you astray from the path of God*' [Qurʾān 38:36], and His statement, '*And whoever does not judge by what God has revealed, then they are the disbelievers*'. He went on to recite the similar verses that mention '*they are the oppressors*' and '*they are the corrupt*'. Then he said, 'I call the people of our call and *qibla* to bear witness that they [ʿAlī and the community] have followed vain desires and cast the ruling of the Book [Qurʾān] aside and acted unjustly in their words and deeds. And I call you to bear witness that it is incumbent upon the believers to wage jihad against them'. Upon hearing

> this, a man amongst them by the name of ʿAbd Allāh b. Sakhbara al-Sulamī began to weep, then he [Zayd b. Ḥiṣn] started to rouse them to revolt and said, 'Strike their faces and sides with swords until the Most Compassionate and Merciful is obeyed. If you are victorious and God is obeyed as you wish, He will reward you with the recompense of those who obey Him and act upon His commands. And if you are killed, then what could be better than God's good pleasure and Paradise?'[1]

If we analyse the methodology and activities of modern-day terrorists, we see that they are mentally immature, young and brainwashed, and have the same modus operandi as the Kharijites of old. Their warped view of Islam is plain to see; on the one hand they are very devout in their worship, and on the other hand they have no compunction in killing peaceful Muslims. Ibn Kathīr reported that once the branch of a date palm fell during a journey and one of the Kharijites picked up a date from it and put it in his mouth. A fellow Kharijite objected and reminded him that he did not have the owner's permission. Immediately, the man spit it out.[2]

Similarly, Imam Ibn al-Athīr related that once, when a pig owned by one of the non-Muslim citizens passed by a member of the Kharijites, he killed it with his sword. A fellow Kharijite condemned him for killing it, and when its owner came, he begged his pardon, paid its price and made the man happy.[3]

Look at the apparent religiosity of the Kharijites on the one hand and their terrorism, barbarism and ruthlessness on the other. Ibn Kathīr reported,

> وَمَعَ هَذَا قَدَّمُوا عَبْدَ اللهِ بْنَ خَبَّابٍ فَذَبَحُوهُ، وَجَاؤُوا إِلَى امْرَأَتِهِ فَقَالَتْ: إِنِّي امْرَأَةٌ حُبْلَى، أَلَا تَتَّقُونَ اللهَ، فَذَبَحُوهَا وَبَقَرُوا بَطْنَهَا عَنْ وَلَدِهَا، فَلَمَّا بَلَغَ النَّاسَ هَذَا مِنْ صَنِيْعِهِمْ خَافُوا إِنْ هُمْ ذَهَبُوا إِلَى الشَّامِ وَاشْتَغَلُوا بِقِتَالِ أَهْلِهِ أَنْ يُخْلِفَهُمْ هَؤُلَاءِ فِي

---

[1] Ibn Kathīr, *al-Bidāya wa al-nihāya*, 7:286.

[2] Ibid., 7:288.

[3] Ibn al-Athīr, *al-Kāmil fī al-tārīkh*, 3:218.

ذَرَارِيْهِمْ وَدِيَارِهِمْ بِهَذَا الصَّنْعِ، فَخَافُوا غَائِلَتَهُمْ، وَأَشَارُوا عَلَى عَلِيٍّ ﵁ بِأَنْ يَبْدَأَ بِهَؤُلَاءِ، ثُمَّ إِذَا فَرَغَ مِنْهُمْ ذَهَبَ إِلَى أَهْلِ الشَّامِ بَعْدَ ذَلِكَ وَالنَّاسُ آمِنُونَ مِنْ شَرِّ هَؤُلَاءِ فَاجْتَمَعَ الرَّأْيُ عَلَى هَذَا وَفِيْهِ خَيْرَةٌ عَظِيْمَةٌ لَهُمْ وَلِأَهْلِ الشَّامِ أَيْضًا. فَأَرْسَلَ عَلِيٌّ ﵁ إِلَى الْخَوَارِجِ رَسُولًا مِنْ جِهَتِهِ وَهُوَ الْحَرْبُ بْنُ مُرَّةَ الْعَبْدِيُّ، فَقَالَ: أَخْبِرْ لِي خَبَرَهُمْ، وَاعْلَمْ لِي أَمْرَهُمْ وَاكْتُبْ إِلَيَّ بِهِ عَلَى الْجَلِيَّةِ، فَلَمَّا قَدِمَ عَلَيْهِمْ قَتَلُوهُ وَلَمْ يَنْظُرُوهُ، فَلَمَّا بَلَغَ ذَلِكَ عَلِيًّا ﵁ عَزَمَ عَلَى الذَّهَابِ إِلَيْهِمْ أَوَّلًا قَبْلَ أَهْلِ الشَّامِ. فَبَعَثُوا إِلَى عَلِيٍّ ﵁ يَقُولُونَ: كُلُّنَا قَتَلَ إِخْوَانَكُمْ وَنَحْنُ مُسْتَحِلُّونَ دِمَاءَهُمْ وَدِمَاءَكُمْ. فَتَقَدَّمَ إِلَيْهِمْ قَيْسُ بْنُ سَعْدِ بْنِ عُبَادَةَ فَوَعَظَهُمْ فِيْمَا ارْتَكَبُوهُ مِنَ الْأَمْرِ الْعَظِيْمِ، وَالْخَطْبِ الْجَسِيْمِ، فَلَمْ يَنْفَعْ وَكَذَلِكَ أَبُو أَيُّوبَ الْأَنْصَارِيُّ وَتَقَدَّمَ أَمِيْرُ الْمُؤْمِنِيْنَ عَلِيُّ بْنُ أَبِي طَالِبٍ إِلَيْهِمْ، فَإِنَّكُمْ قَدْ سَوَّلَتْ لَكُمْ أَنْفُسُكُمْ أَمْرًا تَقْتُلُونَ عَلَيْهِ الْمُسْلِمِيْنَ، وَاللهِ لَو قَتَلْتُمْ عَلَيْهِ دَجَاجَةً لَكَانَ عَظِيْمًا عِنْدَ اللهِ، فَكَيْفَ بِدِمَاءِ الْمُسْلِمِيْنَ.

So along with this, they brought ʿAbd Allāh b. Khabbāb forward and slaughtered him. Then they approached his wife and she said, 'I am pregnant; do you not fear God?' Then they slaughtered her and sliced open her stomach and killed her unborn child. When news of their deed reached people, they were afraid; if they went to the Levant to fight them they would leave their wives and children at risk of suffering the same fate. They were afraid for their families and suggested to ʿAlī that he should first fight them, and then go confront the people of the Levant after he is done with them; that way, the people will be safe from their evil. There was a unanimous opinion that fighting them was the best course, and that was a tremendous good for both them and the people of the Levant. ʿAlī dispatched a messenger to them, one Ḥārith b. Murra al-ʿAbdī, and said to him, 'Keep me well-informed about them and write to me'. When Ḥārith reached them they killed him and did not even

> give him a chance to speak. When news of this reached ᶜAlī, he was resolute in his decision to fight them first before the people of the Levant. The Kharijites soon sent him a message, saying, 'All of us killed your brothers and we declare lawful their blood and yours'. Qays b. Saᶜd b. ᶜUbāda went to them and exhorted them, denouncing them for their grievous crime, but it was of no avail. Similarly, Abū Ayyūb al-Anṣārī went to them, as did the Commander of the Faithful, ᶜAlī b. Abī Ṭālib, who said to them, 'Your vain desires have made pleasing to you that for which you kill the Muslims! I swear by God, it would be seen as grievous in the sight of God that you even kill a chicken with this intention, so what about the blood of the Muslims?'[1]

These historical records prove that the Kharijites considered blood a cheap commodity. They had no reservations about killing people and cared not one iota for those who were brought up with the Prophet's spiritual training.

Since the Prophet ﷺ made it categorically clear that these people would continue to emerge, time and time again, it is easy to recognize the modern-day Kharijites, for they share the same traits of those of old. They too shed the blood of people; they too brutally slaughter women and children and challenge the authority of the state; they too attack mosques, murder peaceful people engaged in worship and target them in the marketplaces; and they too call their dastardly deeds jihad. All the current acts of terrorism committed by the so-called '*Mujāhidūn*' are but a continuation of the Kharijite doctrine and ideology.

13.11 The Blameworthy Religious Innovations of the Kharijites

From the previous sections we learnt that the Kharijites held many baseless positions and added numerous heretical innovations in the religion. They would give self-made interpretations of the

---

[1] Ibn Kathīr, *al-Bidāya wa al-nihāya*, 7:288.

Qurʾān and hadith and, on that basis, declare lawful the blood of Muslims. The Prophet ﷺ foretold many of their innovations. He foretold that they would kill the Muslims and spare the idolaters;[1] he stated that they would consider it lawful to murder non-Muslim minorities;[2] he said that they would be extreme in worship;[3] he informed us that they would declare the perpetrators of enormities as permanent residents of Hell and hold that their lives and properties are lawful; he said that they would believe that the one who disobeys the Qurʾān in his practice and opinion is a disbeliever; and finally, he foretold that they would believe it is obligatory to revolt and rebel against oppressive and corrupt governments.[4] Ibn Umar ﷺ mentioned that they would take the Qurʾānic verses revealed about the disbelievers and apply them to the believers.[5]

Early history reveals that the Kharijites were so extreme in their beliefs, ideologies and innovations that they even regarded the Prophet's Companions as disbelievers. Imam al-Shahrastānī writes in *al-Milal wa al-niḥal* that Ziyād b. Umayya asked the Kharijite, ʿUrwa b. Udayya [or Udhayna], 'What do you think of Abū Bakr and ʿUmar?' He said, 'They were good'. Then he asked about ʿUthmān. He said, 'I took him as my friend in the first six years of his caliphate, but when he introduced new things and made innovations, I stepped aside, because he disbelieved in the end'. Then he asked about ʿAlī. He replied, 'He too was good in the beginning, but when he initiated arbitration, he turned into a disbeliever. So, I got away from him too'. And when he asked

---

[1] Ibid., *Kitāb al-tawḥīd* [The Book of Divine Unity], chapter: 'God's saying, *"The angels and the Spirit Ascend to Him"*' [Qurʾān 70:4], 6:2702 §6995.

[2] Narrated by al-Ḥākim in *al-Mustadrak*, 2:166 §2657.

[3] Narrated by Abū Yaʿlā in *al-Musnad*, 1:90 §90.

[4] ʿAbd al-Qāhir al-Baghdādī, *al-Farq bayn al-firaq*, p. 73; Ibn Taymiyya, *Majmūʿa al-fatāwā*, 13:31.

[5] Narrated by al-Bukhārī in *al-Ṣaḥīḥ*: *Kitāb istitāba al-murtaddīn wa al-muʿānidīn wa qitālihim* [The Book on Demanding the Repentance of the Apostates and Reprobates, and Fighting Them], chapter: 'On Fighting the Kharijites and the Heretics after Establishing the Evidence against Them', 6:2539.

about Muʿāwiya, he reviled and condemned him as well.[1] Imam al-Shahrastānī also commented that the Kharijites used to declare the Muslims disbelievers, including the eminent Companions such as ʿUthmān, Ṭālḥa, Zubayr, ʿĀʾisha and ʿAbd Allāh b. ʿAbbās ﵃.[2]

13.12 THE RESEARCH OF IMAM ABŪ BAKR AL-ĀJURRĪ

Imam Abū Bakr al-Ājurrī wrote about the Kharijites in his book *Kitāb al-sharīʿa* and penned a chapter called, 'On the Condemnation of the Kharijites and Their Evil Way, and the Permissibility of Killing them, and the Reward for the One Who Either Kills them or is Killed By Them'. He stated,

لَمْ يَخْتَلِفِ الْعُلَمَاءُ قَدِيمًا وَحَدِيثًا أَنَّ الْخَوَارِجَ قَوْمُ سُوءٍ، عُصَاةٌ لِلّٰهِ وَلِرَسُولِهِ ﷺ، وَإِنْ صَلُّوا وَصَامُوا، وَاجْتَهَدُوا فِي الْعِبَادَةِ، فَلَيْسَ ذَلِكَ بِنَافِعٍ لَهُمْ، وَإِنْ أَظْهَرُوا الْأَمْرَ بِالْمَعْرُوفِ وَالنَّهْيَ عَنِ الْمُنْكَرِ، وَلَيْسَ ذَلِكَ بِنَافِعٍ لَهُمْ، لِأَنَّهُمْ قَوْمٌ يَتَأَوَّلُونَ الْقُرْآنَ عَلَى مَا يَهْوَوْنَ، وَيُمَوِّهُونَ عَلَى الْمُسْلِمِينَ. وَقَدْ حَذَّرَنَا اللهُ مِنْهُمْ، وَحَذَّرَنَا النَّبِيُّ ﷺ، وَحَذَّرَنَاهُمُ الْخُلَفَاءُ الرَّاشِدُونَ بَعْدَهُ، وَحَذَّرَنَاهُمُ الصَّحَابَةُ ﵃ وَمَنْ تَبِعَهُمْ بِإِحْسَانٍ رَحْمَةُ اللهِ تَعَالَى عَلَيْهِمْ.

اَلْخَوَارِجُ هُمُ الشُّرَاةُ الْأَنْجَاسُ الْأَرْجَاسُ، وَمَنْ كَانَ عَلَى مَذْهَبِهِمْ مِنْ سَائِرِ الْخَوَارِجِ، يَتَوَارَثُونَ هَذَا الْمَذْهَبَ قَدِيمًا وَحَدِيثًا، وَيَخْرُجُونَ عَلَى الْأَئِمَّةِ وَالْأُمَرَاءِ وَيَسْتَحِلُّونَ قَتْلَ الْمُسْلِمِينَ. وَأَوَّلُ قَرْنٍ طَلَعَ مِنْهُمْ عَلَى عَهْدِ رَسُولِ اللهِ ﷺ: هُوَ رَجُلٌ طَعَنَ عَلَى النَّبِيِّ ﷺ، وَهُوَ يَقْسِمُ الْغَنَائِمَ بِالْجِعْرَانَةِ، فَقَالَ: اعْدِلْ يَا مُحَمَّدُ، فَمَا أَرَاكَ تَعْدِلُ، فَقَالَ ﷺ: وَيْلَكَ، فَمَنْ يَعْدِلُ إِذَا لَمْ أَكُنْ أَعْدِلُ؟ فَأَرَادَ عُمَرُ ﵁ قَتْلَهُ، فَمَنَعَهُ النَّبِيُّ ﷺ مِنْ قَتْلِهِ، وَأَخْبَرَ عَلَيْهِ الصَّلَاةُ وَالسَّلَامُ: أَنَّ هَذَا وَأَصْحَابًا لَهُ يَحْقِرُ أَحَدُكُمْ صَلَاتَهُ مَعَ صَلَاتِهِمْ، وَصِيَامَهُ مَعَ صِيَامِهِمْ، يَمْرُقُونَ مِنَ الدِّينِ كَمَا يَمْرُقُ السَّهْمُ مِنَ الرَّمِيَّةِ.

وَأَمَرَ عَلَيْهِ الصَّلَاةُ وَالسَّلَامُ فِي غَيْرِ حَدِيثٍ بِقِتَالِهِمْ، وَبَيَّنَ فَضْلَ مَنْ قَتَلَهُمْ أَوْ قَتَلُوهُ. ثُمَّ إِنَّهُمْ بَعْدَ ذَلِكَ خَرَجُوا مِنْ بُلْدَانٍ شَتَّى، وَاجْتَمَعُوا وَأَظْهَرُوا الْأَمْرَ

---

[1] Al-Shahrastānī, *al-Milal wa al-niḥal*, 1:118.

[2] Ibid., 1:121.

بِالْمَعْرُوفِ وَالنَّهْيَ عَنِ الْمُنْكَرِ، حَتَّى قَدِمُوا الْمَدِيْنَةَ، فَقَتَلُوا عُثْمَانَ بْنَ عَفَّانَ ﵁. وَقَدِ اجْتَهَدَ أَصْحَابُ رَسُولِ اللهِ ﷺ مِمَّنْ كَانَ فِي الْمَدِيْنَةِ فِي أَنْ لَا يُقْتَلَ عُثْمَانُ، فَمَا أَطَاقُوا ذَلِكَ. ثُمَّ خَرَجُوا بَعْدَ ذَلِكَ عَلَى أَمِيرِ الْمُؤْمِنِيْنَ عَلِيِّ بْنِ أَبِي طَالِبٍ ﵁، وَلَمْ يَرْضَوْا بِحُكْمِهِ، وَأَظْهَرُوا قَوْلَهُمْ. وَقَالُوا: لَا حُكْمَ إِلَّا لِلّٰهِ، فَقَالَ عَلِيٌّ ﵁: كَلِمَةُ حَقٍّ أَرَادُوا بِهَا الْبَاطِلَ، فَقَاتَلَهُمْ عَلِيٌّ ﵁ فَأَكْرَمَهُ اللهُ بِقَتْلِهِمْ، وَأَخْبَرَ النَّبِيُّ ﷺ بِفَضْلِ مَنْ قَتَلَهُمْ أَوْ قَتَلُوهُ، وَقَاتَلَ مَعَهُ الصَّحَابَةُ ﵃. فَصَارَ سَيْفُ عَلِيِّ بْنِ أَبِي طَالِبٍ فِي الْخَوَارِجِ سَيْفَ حَقٍّ إِلَى أَنْ تَقُومَ السَّاعَةُ.

فَلَا يَنْبَغِي لِمَنْ رَأَى اجْتِهَادَ خَارِجِيٍّ قَدْ خَرَجَ عَلَى إِمَامٍ، عَادِلًا كَانَ الْإِمَامُ أَمْ جَائِرًا، فَخَرَجَ وَجَمَعَ جَمَاعَةً وَسَلَّ سَيْفَهُ، وَاسْتَحَلَّ قِتَالَ الْمُسْلِمِيْنَ ، فَلَا يَنْبَغِي لَهُ أَنْ يَغْتَرَّ بِقِرَاءَتِهِ لِلْقُرْآنِ، وَلَا بِطُولِ قِيَامِهِ فِي الصَّلَاةِ، وَلَا بِدَوَامِ صِيَامِهِ، وَلَا بِحُسْنِ أَلْفَاظِهِ فِي الْعِلْمِ إِذَا كَانَ مَذْهَبُهُ مَذْهَبَ الْخَوَارِجِ.

All the scholars of the past and the present agree that the Kharijites are an evil folk who disobey God, the Exalted and Sublime, and His Messenger ﷺ—even if they pray and fast and strive in worship. None of that will avail them, despite their show of enjoining the good and forbidding the evil. That is because they interpret the Qurʾān according to their vain desires and pass it off on the Muslims. God, the Exalted and Sublime, the Prophet ﷺ and the Rightly Guided Caliphs after the Prophet ﷺ warned us of them, as did the Companions and those who followed them in excellence—may God have mercy upon them.

The Kharijites are a vile and despicable folk, as are the other sects that adhere to their doctrine and inherit their way, from those of the past to the present day. They revolt against the governments and declare lawful the murder of Muslims. The first of them to appear was during the time of the Messenger of God, and he was a man who accused the Prophet ﷺ of injustice as he apportioned the war booty at Jaʿrāna. He said, ‘O Muhammad! Be just,

> for I don't think you are acting fairly'. So the Messenger of God ﷺ replied, 'Woe to you! Who will be just if I am not just?' ʿUmar wanted to kill him but the Prophet ﷺ forbade him and said, 'Leave him, for he has compatriots. You will belittle your prayers and fasting in comparison to theirs, but they shall pass through the religion just as an arrow passes through a hunted game'.
>
> In several hadith reports the Prophet ﷺ ordered that they be fought, and explained the virtue of the one who either kills or is killed by them. After their appearance they abandoned the various cities and gathered together, enjoining the good and forbidding the evil, until they reached Medina and killed ʿUthmān b. ʿAffān ﵁. The Prophet's Companions who were in Medina tried to prevent ʿUthmān's murder but were unsuccessful. Afterwards, the same people revolted against the Commander of the Faithful, ʿAlī b. Abī Ṭālib ﵁, because they were displeased with his judgement, and raised their slogan, 'There is no judgement but for God'. In response, ʿAlī said, 'A word of truth by which falsehood is intended'. Then ʿAlī fought against them and God honoured him with slaying them. The Prophet ﷺ informed us about the virtue of the one who either kills them or is killed by them. The Companions fought alongside ʿAlī, and as a result, ʿAlī's sword against the Kharijites became a sword of truth until the Final Hour.
>
> Therefore, if a Kharijite revolts against the government—whether the government is just or not—and gathers forces and unsheathes his sword, no one should be deceived by his efforts in reciting the Qurʾān, praying lengthy prayers, engaging in constant fasts or his uttering of fine words regarding Sacred Knowledge, since his doctrine is that of the Kharijites.

Some of the most well-known reports about the Kharijites were narrated by Imam al-Ājurrī in his chapter about the reward of those who fight agaisnt them and either kill them or get killed by them. ʿAbd Allāh b. Masʿūd ﷺ reported:

قَالَ رَسُولُ اللهِ ﷺ: يَخْرُجُ فِي آخِرِ الزَّمَانِ قَوْمٌ أَحْدَاثُ الْأَسْنَانِ سُفَهَاءُ الْأَحْلَامِ يَقُولُونَ مِنْ خَيْرِ قَوْلِ النَّاسِ، يَمْرُقُونَ مِنَ الْإِسْلَامِ كَمَا يَمْرُقُ السَّهْمُ مِنَ الرَّمِيَّةِ، مَنْ لَقِيَهُمْ فَلْيَقْتُلْهُمْ، فَإِنَّ قَتْلَهُمْ أَجْرٌ عِنْدَ اللهِ.

> The Messenger of God ﷺ said, 'At the end of time there shall appear a folk, young in age and foolish. They will utter the best of words spoken by people, but they shall pass through Islam just as an arrow passes through a hunted game. Whoever encounters them [during war] should kill them, for killing them will be rewarded by God'.[1]

Abū Umāma ﷺ reported that the Prophet ﷺ said,

طُوبَى لِمَنْ قَتَلَهُمْ وَقَتَلُوهُمْ.

> 'Glad tidings of Paradise to those who kill them or are killed by them'.[2]

Abū Umāma ﷺ also reported that the Prophet ﷺ said thrice, 'They are the dogs of the Hellfire; they are the dogs of the Hellfire; they are the dogs of the Hellfire'. Then he ﷺ said,

---

[1] Narrated by al-Bukhārī in *al-Ṣaḥīḥ*: *Kitāb istitāba al-murtaddīn wa al-muʿānidīn wa qitālihim* [The Book on Demanding the Repentance of the Apostates and Reprobates, and Fighting Them], chapter: 'On Fighting the Kharijites and the Heretics after Establishing the Evidence against Them', 6:2539 §6531; Muslim in *al-Ṣaḥīḥ*: *Kitāb al-Zakāt* [The Book of Zakat], chapter: 'The Encouragement to Kill the Kharijites', 2:746 §1066; and al-Tirmidhī in *al-Sunan*: *Kitāb al-fitan* [The Book of Tribulations], chapter: 'Concerning the Trait of Renegades [*al-māriqa*]', 4:481 §2188. After having narrated this tradition in *al-Sunan*, Imam al-Tirmidhī said, 'This tradition is reported by ʿAlī, Abū Saʿīd and Abū Dharr ﷺ, and it is a fine sound tradition'.

[2] Narrated by Abū Dāwūd in *al-Sunan*: *Kitāb al-Sunna*, 4:243 §4765; Aḥmad b. Ḥanbal in *al-Musnad*, 3:224 §13362; and al-Ḥākim in *al-Mustadrak*, 2:161 §2649.

شَرُّ قَتْلَى قُتِلُوا تَحْتَ ظِلِّ السَّمَاءِ ، وَخَيْرُ قَتْلَى الَّذِيْنَ قَتَلُوهُمْ.

'They are the most evil of those slain under the heavens, and the best of those slain are the ones killed by them'.[1]

ʿAlī ﷺ said,

أَيْنَمَا لَقِيْتُمُوهُمْ فَاقْتُلُوهُمْ، فَإِنَّ قَتْلَهُمْ أَجْرٌ لِمَنْ قَتَلَهُمْ يَوْمَ الْقِيَامَةِ.

'Wherever you encounter them [during war], slay them, for whoever slays them will be granted a reward on the Day of Resurrection'.[2]

ʿĀʾisha ﷺ said,

ذَكَرَ رَسُولُ اللهِ ﷺ الْخَوَارِجَ، فَقَالَ: هُمْ شِرَارُ أُمَّتِي يَقْتُلُهُمْ خِيَارُ أُمَّتِي.

'The Messenger of God ﷺ mentioned the Kharijites and said, "They are the worst of my *Umma* and shall be killed by the best of my *Umma*".'

---

[1] Narrated by Ibn Mājah in *al-Sunan*: 'Introduction', section: 'On the Kharijites', 1:62 §176; and al-Ḥākim in *al-Mustadrak*, 2:163 §2654.

[2] Narrated by al-Bukhārī in *al-Ṣaḥīḥ*: *Kitāb istitāba al-murtaddīn wa al-muʿānidīn wa qitālihim* [The Book on Demanding the Repentance of the Apostates and Reprobates, and Fighting Them], chapter: 'On Fighting the Kharijites and the Heretics after Establishing the Evidence against Them', 6:2539 §6531; and Muslim in *al-Ṣaḥīḥ*: *Kitāb al-Zakāt* [The Book of Zakat], chapter: 'The Encouragement to Kill the Kharijites', 2:746 §1066.

Chapter 14

The Prophetic Sayings Regarding the Kharijite Terrorists

EXTREMISM AND TERRORISM ARE COSTING US DEARLY. ON THE ONE hand they create doubts about Islam and its teachings, and on the other hand they result in the loss of lives and destruction of property. Peace and harmony guarantee prosperity, development, tranquillity and pleasure, whereas violence and strife cause turmoil and destruction. For this reason, the Prophet ﷺ blocked all the passages and doors through which disaster and destruction could enter. He encouraged softness, kindness, mutual affection and clemency. ʿĀʾisha ؓ reported that the Prophet ﷺ said,

إِنَّ اللهَ رَفِيْقٌ وَيُحِبُّ الرِّفْقَ وَيُعْطِي عَلَى الرِّفْقِ مَا لَا يُعْطِي عَلَى الْعُنْفِ.

> 'Indeed, God is gentle and He loves gentleness. He bestows for the sake of gentleness that which He does not bestow for harshness'.[1]

Gentleness and affability are constructive, but harshness and violence are destructive. Softness and moderation are signs of well-wishing, while extremism and fanaticism represent hatred and violence. Extremism does not bring good in this life or the Hereafter, while violence perpetrated in the name of religion is more dangerous than violence done for the sake of worldly matters. Violence and aggression stem from extremism. The Prophet ﷺ said,

إِيَّاكُمْ وَالْغُلُوَّ فِي الدِّينِ، فَإِنَّهُ أَهْلَكَ مَنْ كَانَ قَبْلَكُمُ الْغُلُوُّ فِي الدِّينِ.

> 'Beware of extremism in the religion, for that is what destroyed those before you'.[2]

---

[1] Narrated by Muslim in *al-Ṣaḥīḥ*: *Kitāb al-birr wa al-ṣila wa al-ādāb* [The Book of Piety, Filial Duty and Good Manners], chapter: 'The Virtue of Gentleness', 4:2003 §2593; Abū Dāwūd in *al-Sunan*: *Kitāb al-adab* [The Book of Good Manners], chapter: 'On Gentleness', 4:254 §4807; and by Aḥmad b. Ḥanbal in *al-Musnad*, 1:112 §902.

[2] Narrated by Ibn Mājah in *al-Sunan*: *Kitāb al-manāsik* [The Book of Pilgrimage Rites], 2:1008 §3029; al-Shaybanī in *al-Sunna*, p. 46 §98; and Ibn Abī Shayba

The beloved Messenger of God ﷺ beheld the state of affairs until the Day of Resurrection and also foretold of terrorism that would be committed in the name of religion. Therefore, he not only distinguished jihad from murder, but also warned the Muslim *Umma* of those who would perpetrate violence and bloodshed in the name of religion. He clearly described the behaviour patterns and signs of these so-called *Mujāhidūn*, so as to remove all doubts about their heinous designs and evil intentions, that the *Umma* might not get deceived by their pious appearance and abundant worship and recitation of the Qurʾān. He urged the *Umma* to stay away from turmoil and ordered them to excise the cancerous growth of the Kharijites from the body of the *Umma*.

14.1 The Kharijite Terrorists Will Appear Extremists in Religious Matters

According to the prophetic traditions, the Kharijites will appear religious. They will look more constant in their prayers, fasting and other acts of worship than the rest of the Muslims. They will also seem stricter than others in their observance of the legal commands. The Messenger of God ﷺ said,

إِنَّهُ يَخْرُجُ مِنْ ضِئْضِىءِ هَذَا قَوْمٌ يَتْلُونَ كِتَابَ اللهِ رَطْبًا لَا يُجَاوِزُ حَنَاجِرَهُمْ، يَمْرُقُونَ مِنَ الدِّيْنِ كَما يَمْرُقُ السَّهْمُ مِنَ الرَّمِيَّةِ.

> 'Indeed, from the offspring of this man there shall emerge a folk whose tongues shall be moist from reciting God's Book, but it shall not go past their throats. They shall pass through the religion just as an arrow passes through a hunted game'.[1]

Abū Saʿīd al-Khudrī ﷺ reported that the Prophet ﷺ said,

in *al-Muṣannaf*, 3:248 §13909.

[1] Narrated by al-Bukhārī in *al-Ṣaḥīḥ*: *Kitāb al-maghāzī* [The Book of Military Expeditions], chapter: 'The Dispatch of ʿAlī b. Abī Ṭālib and Khālid b. al-Walīd to Yemen before the Farewell Pilgrimage', 4:1581 §4094; Muslim in *al-Ṣaḥīḥ*: *Kitāb al-Zakāt* [The Book of Zakat], Chapter: 'On the Kharijites and their Qualities', 2:742 §1064; and Aḥmad b. Ḥanbal in *al-Musnad*, 3:4 §11021.

إِنَّ لَهُ أَصْحَابًا يَحْقِرُ أَحَدُكُمْ صَلَاتَهُ مَعَ صَلَاتِهِمْ، وَصِيَامَهُ مَعَ صِيَامِهِمْ.

> '[H]e has compatriots; you will belittle your prayers and fasting in comparison to theirs'.[1]

It is reported from Abū Salama and ʿAṭāʾ b. Yasār ﷺ that they went to Abū Saʿīd al-Khudrī ﷺ and asked him about the Ḥarūriyya. They asked, 'Did you hear the Prophet ﷺ say anything about them?' Abū Saʿīd replied, 'I don't know about the Ḥarūriyya, but the Prophet ﷺ said,

يَخْرُجُ فِي هَذِهِ الْأُمَّةِ – وَلَمْ يَقُلْ مِنْهَا – قَوْمٌ تَحْقِرُونَ صَلَاتَكُمْ مَعَ صَلَاتِهِمْ يَقْرَءُونَ الْقُرْآنَ لَا يُجَاوِزُ حُلُوقَهُمْ أَوْ حَنَاجِرَهُمْ يَمْرُقُونَ مِنَ الدِّيْنِ مُرُوقَ السَّهْمِ مِنَ الرَّمِيَّةِ.

> "There shall appear a folk *in* this *Umma*", and he did not say "*from* it", "and you will belittle your prayers in comparison to theirs; they will read the Qurʾān but it shall not pass their throats or larynxes. They shall pass through the religion just as an arrow passes through a hunted game".'[2]

In his commentary on this hadith, Ibn Ḥajar al-ʿAsqalānī wrote:

قَوْلُهُ: يَخْرُجُ فِي هَذِهِ الْأُمَّةِ وَلَمْ يَقُلْ "مِنْهَا" قَوْمٌ لَمْ تَخْتَلِفِ الطُّرُقُ الصَّحِيْحَةُ عَلَى أَبِي سَعِيْدٍ فِي ذَلِكَ، . . . وَأَمَّا مَا أَخْرَجَهُ الطَّبَرِيُّ مِنْ وَجْهٍ آخَرَ عَنْ أَبِي سَعِيْدٍ بِلَفْظِ

---

[1] Narrated by al-Bukhārī in *al-Ṣaḥīḥ*: *Kitāb al-adab* [The Book of Good Manners], chapter: 'What Has Come to Us About Someone Saying, "Woe to you!"', 5:2281 §5811, and *Kitāb istitāba al-murtaddīn wa al-muʿānidīn wa qitālihim* [The Book on Demanding the Repentance of the Apostates and Reprobates, and Fighting Them], chapter: 'On the One Who Refrains from Fighting the Kharijites for the Sake of Drawing Hearts Near and so People Will Not Flee', 6:2540 §6534; and Muslim in *al-Ṣaḥīḥ*: *Kitāb al-Zakāt* [The Book of Zakat], chapter: 'On the Kharijites and Their Qualities', 2:744 §1064.

[2] Narrated by al-Bukhārī in *al-Ṣaḥīḥ*: *Kitāb istitāba al-murtaddīn wa al-muʿānidīn wa qitālihim* [The Book on Demanding the Repentance of the Apostates and Reprobates, and Fighting Them], chapter: 'On Fighting the Kharijites and Heretics after Establishing the Evidence against Them', 6:2540 §6532; Muslim in *al-Ṣaḥīḥ*: *Kitāb al-Zakāt* [The Book of Zakat], chapter: 'On the Kharijites and Their Qualities', 2:743 §1064.

مِنْ أُمَّتِي فَسَنَدُهُ ضَعِيْفٌ، لَكِنْ وَقَعَ عِنْدَ مُسْلِمٍ مِنْ حَدِيْثِ أَبِي ذَرٍّ بِلَفْظِ سَيَكُونُ بَعْدِي مِنْ أُمَّتِي قَوْمٌ وَلَهُ مِنْ طَرِيْقِ زَيْدِ بْنِ وَهْبٍ عَنْ عَلِيٍّ: يَخْرُجُ قَوْمٌ مِنْ أُمَّتِي وَيُجْمَعُ بَيْنَهُ وَبَيْنَ حَدِيْثِ أَبِي سَعِيْدٍ بِأَنَّ الْمُرَادَ بِالْأُمَّةِ فِي حَدِيْثِ أَبِي سَعِيْدٍ: أُمَّةُ الْإِجَابَةِ، وَفِي رِوَايَةِ غَيْرِهِ: أُمَّةُ الدَّعْوَةِ. قَالَ النَّوَوِيُّ: وَفِيْهِ دَلَالَةٌ عَلَى فِقْهِ الصَّحَابَةِ وَتَحْرِيْرِهِمُ الْأَلْفَاظَ، وَفِيْهِ إِشَارَةٌ مِنْ أَبِي سَعِيْدٍ إِلَى تَكْفِيْرِ الْخَوَارِجِ، وَأَنَّهُمْ مِنْ غَيْرِ هَذِهِ الْأُمَّةِ.

There is no discrepancy in any of the rigorously authentic chains from Abū Saʿīd regarding his statement, 'and he did not say "*from* it".' . . . As for the other wording narrated by al-Ṭabarī from Abū Saʿīd, 'from my *Umma*', its chain is weak; however, there does appear in the hadith of Abū Dharr in Muslim the wording, 'There shall be a folk after me from my *Umma*'. And he also has another report from the route of Zayd b. Wahb, from ʿAlī, which reads, 'There shall come a folk from my *Umma*'. This hadith is reconciled with Abū Saʿīd's by stating that the meaning of *Umma* in the hadith of Abū Saʿīd is the *Umma* of Response, and the meaning of *Umma* in the others' narrations is the *Umma* of Invitation. Al-Nawawī—may God have mercy upon him—said, 'This hadith indicates the deep understanding of the Companions and their exactitude in words. It also contains an indication from Abū Saʿīd that the Kharijites are charged with disbelief and are not from this *Umma*'.[1]

Ibn Ḥajar al-ʿAsqalānī further writes,

وَصَفَ عَاصِمٌ أَصْحَابَ نَجْدَةَ الْحَرُورِيِّ: بِأَنَّهُمْ يَصُومُونَ النَّهَارَ، وَيَقُومُونَ اللَّيْلَ، وَيَأْخُذُونَ الصَّدَقَاتِ عَلَى السُّنَّةِ. أَخْرَجَهُ الطَّبَرِيُّ. وَعِنْدَهُ مِنْ طَرِيْقِ سُلَيْمَانَ التَّيْمِيِّ

[1] The '*Umma* of Response' refers to those who have accepted the message of the Prophet ﷺ and embraced Islam, whereas the '*Umma* of Invitation' refers to the 'potential *Umma*', those who are invited to the religion, but have yet to embrace it. ED.

عَنْ أَنَسٍ ذُكِرَ عَنْ رَسُولِ اللهِ ﷺ قَالَ: إِنَّ فِيكُمْ قَوْمًا يَدْأَبُونَ وَيَعْمَلُونَ حَتَّى يُعْجِبُوا النَّاسَ وُتُعْجِبُهُمْ أَنْفُسُهُمْ، وَمِنْ طَرِيْقِ حَفْصِ بْنِ أَخِي أَنَسٍ عَنْ عَمِّهِ بِلَفْظٍ: يَتَعَمَّقُونَ فِي الدِّيْنِ. وَفِي حَدِيْثِ ابْنِ عَبَّاسٍ عِنْدَ الطَّبَرَانِيِّ فِي قِصَّةِ مُنَاظَرَتِهِ لِلْخَوَارِجِ قَالَ: فَأَتَيْتُهُمْ فَدَخَلْتُ عَلَى قَوْمٍ لَمْ أَرَ أَشَدَّ اجْتِهَادًا مِنْهُمْ. أَيْدِيْهِمْ كَأَنَّهَا ثَفِنُ الْإِبِلِ، وَوُجُوهُهُمْ مُعَلَّمَةٌ مِنْ آثَارِ السُّجُودِ. وَأَخْرَجَ ابْنُ أَبِي شَيْبَةَ عَنِ ابْنِ عَبَّاسٍ أَنَّهُ ذُكِرَ عِنْدَهُ الْخَوَارِجُ وَاجْتِهَادُهُمْ فِي الْعِبَادَةِ، فَقَالَ: لَيْسُوا أَشَدَّ اجْتِهَادًا مِنَ الرُّهْبَانِ.

ʿĀṣim described the traits of Najda al-Ḥarūrī, saying 'they fast through the day and pray through the night and collect the alms according to the Sunna'. This was narrated by al-Ṭabarī, who has another report from the route of Sulaymān al-Taymī from Anas who mentioned that the Messenger of God ﷺ said, 'Amongst you are a folk who persevere and strive until they amaze people and their own egos amaze themselves'. This is reported from the route of Ḥafṣ, Anas' nephew, from his uncle, with the wording: 'They will absorb themselves deeply in the religion [*yataʿammaqūn*]'. Al-Ṭabarānī narrates the story of Ibn ʿAbbās' debate with the Kharijites, in which Ibn ʿAbbās said, 'I went to them and I had never seen a people more assiduous in their efforts. Their hands resembled the feet of camels [thick and rough] and the marks of prostration were prominent upon their faces'. Ibn Abī Shayba narrated that when someone mentioned the Kharijites and their efforts in the presence of Ibn ʿAbbās, he said, 'They are not as hard working as the monks!'[1]

Shabbīr Aḥmad ʿUthmānī has also included this research in his *Fatḥ al-Mulhim* (5:159).

According to the description given in the traditions, the first denigrator of the beloved Messenger of God ﷺ, ʿAbd Allāh b. Dhī al-Khuwayṣira al-Tamīmī, the chief of the extremists, had a mark

[1] Ibn Ḥajar al-ʿAsqalānī, *Fatḥ al-Bārī*, 12:289.

of prostration on his face and signs of extensive worship, and had thick, coarse beard.[1]

Zayd b. Wahb al-Juhanī reported that he was amongst those in the army who were allied with ʿAlī. ʿAlī said,

أَيُّهَا النَّاسُ، إِنِّي سَمِعْتُ رَسُولَ اللهِ ﷺ يَقُولُ: يَخْرُجُ قَوْمٌ مِنْ أُمَّتِي يَقْرَءُونَ الْقُرْآنَ لَيْسَ قِرَاءَتُكُمْ إِلَى قِرَاءَتِهِمْ بِشَيْءٍ، وَلَا صَلَاتُكُمْ إِلَى صَلَاتِهِمْ بِشَيْءٍ، وَلَا صِيَامُكُمْ إِلَى صِيَامِهِمْ بِشَيْءٍ، يَقْرَءُونَ الْقُرْآنَ يَحْسِبُونَ أَنَّهُ لَهُمْ، وَهُوَ عَلَيْهِمْ لَا تُجَاوِزُ صَلَاتُهُمْ تَرَاقِيَهُمْ. يَمْرُقُونَ مِنَ الْإِسْلَامِ كَمَا يَمْرُقُ السَّهْمُ مِنَ الرَّمِيَّةِ.

> 'O people! Indeed, I heard the Messenger of God ﷺ say, "There shall be a folk that comes from my *Umma* and they will recite the Qurʾān—your recitation will not be comparable to theirs, or your prayers or fasting to theirs. They will recite the Qurʾān and believe it supports them but [in reality] it is against them. Their prayers will not go past their throats. They will exit from the religion just as an arrow exits from a hunted game".'[2]

Shabbīr Aḥmad ʿUthmānī commented:

قَوْلُهُ ﷺ: يَحْسِبُونَ أَنَّهُ لَهُمْ إلخ؛ أَيْ: هُمْ يَحْسِبُونَ أَنَّ الْقُرْآنَ حُجَّةٌ لَهُمْ فِي إِثْبَاتِ دَعَاوِيْهِمُ الْبَاطِلَةِ، وَلَيْسَ كَذَلِكَ، بَلْ هُوَ حُجَّةٌ عَلَيْهِمْ عِنْدَ اللهِ تَعَالَى. وَفِيْهِ إِشَارَةٌ إِلَى أَنَّ مِنَ الْمُسْلِمِيْنَ مَنْ يَخْرُجُ مِنَ الدِّيْنِ مِنْ غَيْرِ أَنْ يَقْصِدَ الْخُرُوجَ مِنْهُ، وَمِنْ غَيْرِ أَنْ يَخْتَارَ دِيْنًا عَلَى دِيْنِ الْإِسْلَامِ.

---

[1] Narrated by al-Bukhārī in *al-Ṣaḥīḥ*: *Kitāb al-maghāzī* [The Book of Military Expeditions], chapter: 'The Dispatch of ʿAlī b. Abī Ṭālib and Khālid b. al-Walīd to Yemen before the Farewell Pilgrimage', 4:1581 §4094; and Muslim in *al-Ṣaḥīḥ*: *Kitāb al-Zakāt* [The Book of Zakat], chapter: 'The Encouragement to Kill the Kharijites', 2:742–743 §1064.

[2] Narrated by Muslim in *al-Ṣaḥīḥ*: *Kitāb al-Zakāt* [The Book of Zakat], chapter: 'The Encouragement to Kill the Kharijites', 2:748 §1066; Abū Dāwūd in *al-Sunan*: *Kitāb al-Sunna*, chapter: 'On Fighting the Kharijites', 4:244 §4768; al-Nasāʾī in *al-Sunan al-kubrā*, 5:163 §8571; Aḥmad b. Ḥanbal in *al-Musnad*, 1:91 §706; and ʿAbd al-Razzāq in *al-Muṣannaf*, 10:147.

The Prophet's statement, '. . . and believe it supports them . . .', means that they believe that the Qur'ān is a proof for them in affirming their false claim, whereas that is not the case. Rather, it is a proof against them in the sight of God Most High. This also indicates that there are some amongst the Muslims who exit the religion without intending to do so, and without consciously choosing another religion over Islam.[1]

14.2 The Slogans of the Kharijites Will Seem True and Appealing to the Common Man

The Kharijites will pay lip service to the religion and raise 'Islamic' slogans, but their intentions will be evil. No one should be fooled by their pro-Islamic rhetoric and outward appearance; their aim will be to create disunity within the Muslim *Umma*, spread misconceptions and foment turmoil. ʿAlī ﷺ reported that the Messenger of God ﷺ said,

يَقُولُونَ مِنْ خَيْرِ قَوْلِ الْبَرِيَّةِ.

'They will speak the words of the best of people [just to mislead people]'.[2]

Ibn Ḥajar al-ʿAsqalānī says in his commentary upon this hadith,

أَيْ: مِنَ الْقُرْآنِ، وَكَانَ أَوَّلَ كَلِمَةٍ خَرَجُوا بِهَا قَوْلُهُمْ: لَا حُكْمَ إِلاَّ لِلّهِ، وَانْتَزَعُوهَا مِنَ الْقُرْآنِ، وَحَمَلُوهَا عَلَى غَيْرِ مَحْمَلِهَا.

'[These words imply that the Kharijites will cite] the Qur'ān [to validate their stance]. And the first phrase they used to justify their rebellion was, "There is no

---

[1] Shabbīr Aḥmad ʿUthmānī, *Fatḥ al-Mulhim*, 5:167.

[2] Narrated by al-Bukhārī in *al-Ṣaḥīḥ*: *Kitāb istitāba al-murtaddīn wa al-muʿānidīn wa qitālihim* [The Book on Demanding the Repentance of the Apostates and Reprobates, and Fighting Them], chapter: 'On Fighting the Kharijites and the Heretics after Establishing the Evidence against Them', 6:2539 §6531; and Muslim in *al-Ṣaḥīḥ*: *Kitāb al-Zakāt* [The Book of Zakat], chapter: 'The Encouragement to Kill the Kharijites', 2:746 §1066.

> judgement but for God [they put across their manifesto in the garb of Islam]", and they drew this from the Qur'ān and interpreted it incorrectly'.[1]

A similar commentary was mentioned by ʿAbd al-Raḥmān Mubārakpūrī in his commentary on al-Tirmidhī's *Sunan* called *Tuḥfat al-aḥwadhī*.[2]

ʿUbayd Allāh b. Abī Rāfiʿ, the freed bondsman of the Messenger of God ﷺ, reported:

> أَنَّ الْحَرُورِيَّةَ لَمَّا خَرَجَتْ وَهُوَ مَعَ عَلِيِّ بْنِ أَبِي طَالِبٍ رضي الله عنه، قَالُوا: لَا حُكْمَ إِلَّا لِلَّهِ. قَالَ عَلِيٌّ: كَلِمَةُ حَقٍّ أُرِيْدَ بِهَا بَاطِلٌ، إِنَّ رَسُولَ اللهِ ﷺ وَصَفَ نَاسًا إِنِّي لَأَعْرِفُ صِفَتَهُمْ فِي هَؤُلَاءِ يَقُولُونَ الْحَقَّ بِأَلْسِنَتِهِمْ لَا يَجُوزُ هَذَا مِنْهُمْ وَأَشَارَ إِلَى حَلْقِهِ، مِنْ أَبْغَضِ خَلْقِ اللهِ إِلَيْهِ مِنْهُمْ أَسْوَدُ إِحْدَى يَدَيْهِ طُبْيُ شَاةٍ أَوْ حَلَمَةُ ثَدْيٍ، فَلَمَّا قَتَلَهُمْ عَلِيُّ بْنُ أَبِي طَالِبٍ رضي الله عنه قَالَ: انْظُرُوا، فَنَظَرُوا فَلَمْ يَجِدُوا شَيْئًا. فَقَالَ: ارْجِعُوا فَوَاللهِ، مَا كَذَبْتُ وَلَا كُذِبْتُ مَرَّتَيْنِ أَوْ ثَلَاثًا ثُمَّ وَجَدُوهُ فِي خَرِبَةٍ فَأَتَوْا بِهِ حَتَّى وَضَعُوهُ بَيْنَ يَدَيْهِ. قَالَ عُبَيْدُ اللهِ: وَأَنَا حَاضِرٌ. ذَلِكَ مِنْ أَمْرِهِمْ وَقَوْلِ عَلِيٍّ فِيهِمْ.

> 'When the Kharijites started their rebellion, I was with ʿAlī when they uttered, "There is no judgment but for God". He reported that ʿAlī said, "A word of truth by which falsehood is intended. Indeed, the Messenger of God ﷺ described some people, and I certainly recognize their qualities in these folk. They speak the truth with their tongues but it does not pass this from them (and he pointed at his throat). They are from the most despised of creation in the sight of God. Amongst them is a man of dark complexion who has a hand like the teat of a goat or like a nipple of a breast". When ʿAlī b. Abī Ṭālib رضي الله عنه killed them he said, "Go look for him [his corpse]", and so they looked but did not find anything. He then said twice or thrice, "Go back, for by God, I have neither lied

---

1 Ibn Ḥajar al-ʿAsqalānī, *Fatḥ al-Bārī*, 6:619.

2 Abd al-Raḥmān Mubārakpūrī, *Tuḥfat al-aḥwadhī*, 6:354.

> nor been lied to". Afterwards they found his body in a heap and brought it to ʿAlī, placing it right in front of him. I witnessed all this: from his command until the time they found him'.[1]

Imam al-Nawawī mentioned on the above narration,

مَعْنَاهُ أَنَّ الْكَلِمَةَ أَصْلُهَا صِدْقٌ، قَالَ اللهُ تَعَالَى: ﴿إِنِ ٱلْحُكْمُ إِلَّا لِلَّهِ﴾ لَكِنَّهُمْ أَرَادُوا بِهَا الْإِنْكَارَ عَلَى عَلِيٍّ ﷺ فِي تَحْكِيمِهِ.

> 'What this means is that the phrase is based on the truth, as God Most High said "*Indeed, the judgement is for God alone*";[2] however, their intention with this phrase was to censure ʿAlī ﷺ for his arbitration'.[3]

A similar explanation was mentioned by Shabbīr Aḥmad ʿUthmānī in his commentary, *Fatḥ al-Mulhim* (5:169).

Ṭāriq b. Ziyād said,

خَرَجْنَا مَعَ عَلِيٍّ ﷺ إِلَى الْخَوَارِجِ فَقَتَلَهُمْ، ثُمَّ قَالَ: انْظُرُوا فَإِنَّ نَبِيَّ اللهِ ﷺ قَالَ: إِنَّهُ سَيَخْرُجُ قَوْمٌ يَتَكَلَّمُونَ بِالْحَقِّ لَا يُجَاوِزُ حَلْقَهُمْ.

> 'We went out with ʿAlī ﷺ to fight against the Kharijites. After he killed them he said, "Observe, the Prophet of God ﷺ said, 'There shall appear a folk who speak the truth but it will not pass their throats'".'[4]

These traditions prove that the Kharijites raise their slogans to accomplish their extremist designs, and that behind them are nefarious objectives for which they must be exposed so that people do not go astray.

---

[1] Narrated by Muslim in *al-Ṣaḥīḥ*: *Kitāb al-Zakāt* [The Book of Zakat], chapter: 'The Encouragement to Kill the Kharijites', 2:749 §1066; al-Nasāʾī in *al-Sunan al-kubrā*, 5:160 §8562; and Ibn Ḥibbān in *al-Ṣaḥīḥ*, 15:387 §6939.

[2] Qurʾān 6:57.

[3] Yaḥyā al-Nawawī, *Sharḥ Ṣaḥīḥ Muslim*, 7:173–174.

[4] Narrated by al-Nasāʾī in *al-Sunan al-kubrā*, 5:161 §8566; and by Aḥmad b. Ḥanbal in *al-Musnad*, 1:107 §848.

14.3 The Kharijites will Brainwash Young People and Use Them for Terrorist Activities

The Prophet ﷺ mentioned that the Kharijites would be young in age and use brainwashed youth to carry out their evil designs. ʿAlī ؓ reported that he heard the Messenger of God ﷺ say,

سَيَخْرُجُ قَوْمٌ فِي آخِرِ الزَّمَانِ، أَحْدَاثُ الْأَسْنَانِ، سُفَهَاءُ الْأَحْلَامِ، يَقُولُونَ مِنْ خَيْرِ قَوْلِ الْبَرِيَّةِ، لَا يُجَاوِزُ إِيْمَانُهُمْ حَنَاجِرَهُمْ، يَمْرُقُونَ مِنَ الدِّيْنِ كَمَا يَمْرُقُ السَّهْمُ مِنَ الرَّمِيَّةِ، فَأَيْنَمَا لَقِيْتُمُوهُمْ فَاقْتُلُوهُمْ، فَإِنَّ فِي قَتْلِهِمْ أَجْرًا لِمَنْ قَتَلَهُمْ يَوْمَ الْقِيَامَةِ.

> 'At the end of time there shall appear a folk, young in age and foolish. They will speak the words of the best of people [just to mislead people], but their faith will not pass their throats. They shall pass through Islam just as an arrow passes through a hunted game. Kill them wherever you find them [during war], for the one who kills them will be rewarded on the Day of Resurrection'.[1]

Imam al-Tirmidhī narrated from Ibn Masʿūd ؓ in *al-Sunan*:

يَخْرُجُ فِي آخِرِ الزَّمَانِ قَوْمٌ أَحْدَاثُ الْأَسْنَانِ، سُفَهَاءُ الْأَحْلَامِ، يَقرَءُونَ الْقُرْآنَ، لَا يُجَاوِزُ تَرَاقِيَهُمْ. يَقُولُونَ مِنْ قَوْلِ خَيْرِ الْبَرِيَّةِ. يَمْرُقُونَ مِنَ الدِّيْنِ كَمَا يَمْرُقُ السَّهْمُ مِنَ الرَّمِيَّةِ.

> 'At the end of time there shall appear a folk, young in age and foolish [so their brainwashing will not pose any

[1] Narrated by al-Bukhārī in *al-Ṣaḥīḥ*: *Kitāb istitāba al-murtaddīn wa al-muʿānidīn wa qitālihim* [The Book on Demanding the Repentance of the Apostates and Reprobates, and Fighting Them], chapter: 'On Fighting the Kharijites and the Heretics after Establishing the Evidence against Them', 6:2539 §6531; Muslim in *al-Ṣaḥīḥ*: *Kitāb al-Zakāt* [The Book of Zakat], chapter: 'The Encouragement to Kill the Kharijites', 2:746 §1066; Aḥmad b. Ḥanbal in *al-Musnad*, 1:81, 113–131 §§§616, 912, 1086; al-Nasāʾī in *al-Sunan*: *Kitāb taḥrīm al-dam* [The Book on the Prohibition of Bloodshed], chapter: 'Regarding the One Who Unsheathes His Sword and Wields it amongst People', 7:119 §4102; and Ibn Mājah in *al-Sunan*: 'Introduction', section: 'Mention of the Kharijites', 1:59 §168.

> problem]. They will recite the Qurʾān but it will not pass their throats. They will speak the words of the best of people [just to mislead people], but they shall pass through Islam just as an arrow passes through a hunted game'.[1]

The phrases '*aḥdāth al-asnān*' and '*sufahāʾ al-aḥlām*' used in the two hadith reports indicate that the Kharijites will be young and use young people for their heinous acts of terrorism. Similarly, the Qurʾān also calls the foolish '*sufahāʾ*'. God says,

﴿وَلَا تُؤْتُوا۟ ٱلسُّفَهَآءَ أَمْوَٰلَكُمُ ٱلَّتِى جَعَلَ ٱللَّهُ لَكُمْ قِيَـٰمًا﴾

> '*And do not give the foolish your wealth that God has made a means of support for you*'.[2]

Ibn Ḥajar al-ʿAsqalānī said,

قَوْلُهُ ﷺ: أَحْدَاثٌ، وَالْحَدَثُ هُوَ الصَّغِيْرُ السِّنِّ، هَكَذَا فِي أَكْثَرِ الرِّوَايَاتِ، وَوَقَعَ هُنَا لِلْمُسْتَمْلِي، وَالسَّرَخْسِيِّ حُدَّاثٌ قَالَ فِي الْمَطَالِعِ: مَعْنَاهُ شَبَابٌ. قَوْلُهُ ﷺ: سُفَهَاءُ الْأَحْلَامِ وَالْمَعْنَى أَنَّ عُقُولَهُمْ رَدِيْئَةٌ.

> The Prophet's statement, '*aḥdāth*', means someone who is young in age—and this is how it appears in most of the narrations. In the version of al-Mustamlī and al-Sarakhsī, it reads '*ḥuddāth*', and the author of *al-Maṭāliʿ* said that it means youth.'... 'The Prophet's statement ﷺ, '*sufahāʾ al-aḥlām*', means that those intellects [who are engaged in brutal terrorist activities] are deficient in intellects.[3]

Badr al-Dīn al-ʿAynī said:

قَوْلُهُ ﷺ: حُدَّاثُ الْأَسْنَانِ هَكَذَا فِي رِوَايَةِ الْمُسْتَمْلِي وَالسَّرَخْسِيِّ. وَفِي أَكْثَرِ

---

1 Narrated by Aḥmad b. Ḥanbal in *al-Musnad*, 5:36, §44; al-Ḥākim in *al-Mustadrak*, 2:159 §2645; Ibn Abī ʿĀṣim in *al-Sunna*, 2:456 §937; al-Bayhaqī in *al-Sunan al-kubrā*, 8:187; and al-Daylamī in *Musnad al-firdaws*, 2:322 §3460.

2 Qurʾān 4:5.

3 Ibid.

الرِّوَايَاتِ: أَحْدَاثُ الْأَسْنَانِ، وَهُوَ صَغِيْرُ السِّنِّ. وَقَالَ ابْنُ الْأَثِيْرِ: حَدَاثَةُ السِّنِّ كِنَايَةٌ عَنِ الشَّبَابِ، وَأَوَّلُ الْعُمْرِ. وَالْمُرَادُ بِالْأَسْنَانِ الْعُمْرُ يَعْنِي أَنَّهُمْ شَبَابٌ. قَوْلُهُ ﷺ: سُفَهَاءُ الْأَحْلَامِ يَعْنِي عُقُولُهُمْ رَدِيْئَةٌ.

The Prophet's statement, '*ḥuddāth al-asnān*', is how it appears in the narration of al-Mustamlī and al-Sarakhsī, but in most narrations it says '*aḥdāth al-asnān*', which means someone who is young in age. Ibn al-Athīr said, '"*ḥadātha al-sinn*" is a metonym that implies young age and adolescence, and "*asnān*" means age, so in other words they are youth'. The phrase, '*sufahāʾ al-aḥlām*', implies mentally deficient are the brainwashed.[1]

ʿAbd al-Raḥmān Mubārakpūrī also held the position that '*aḥdāth al-asnān*' denotes youth.[2] Shabbīr Aḥmad ʿUthmānī said,

قَوْلُهُ: أَحْدَاثُ الْأَسْنَانِ إِلَخْ: وَالْحَدَثُ هُوَ: الصَّغِيْرُ السِّنِّ، هَكَذَا فِي أَكْثَرِ الرِّوَايَاتِ، وَوَقَعَ فِي بَعْضِهَا حُدَّاثٌ. قَالَ فِي الْمَطَالِعِ: مَعْنَاهُ شَبَابٌ. . . . وَالْأَسْنَانُ جَمْعُ سِنٍّ، وَالْمُرَادُ بِهِ الْعُمْرُ، وَالْمُرَادُ: أَنَّهُمْ شَبَابٌ.

Regarding the phrase, '*aḥdāth al-asnān*', the word *ḥadath* means the one who is young in age—and this is how the word appears in most narrations. In some variations, however, it reads, '*ḥuddāth*'. The author of *al-Maṭāliʿ* said that it means youth. . . . And *al-asnān* is the plural of *sinn*, which means age; and so the phrase means that they [who perpetrate terrorism] are young.

These explanations by the hadith scholars illustrate that *aḥdāth al-asnān* and *sufahāʾ al-aḥlām* are not people who suffer from insanity, properly speaking, but rather they are brainwashed, immature youth. If we observe the current upsurge of terrorism committed in the name of Islam, we will realize that the prophecy of God's Messenger ﷺ has become a tangible reality.

---

[1] Badr al-Dīn al-ʿAynī, *ʿUmdat al-qārī*, 16:208–209.

[2] Abd al-Raḥmān Mubārakpūrī, *Tuḥfat al-aḥwadhī*, 6:353.

14.4 The Kharijites Will Appear from the East

The Prophet ﷺ also prophesied that the Kharijites would emerge from the east. Abū Saʿīd al-Khudrī ﷺ reported that the Prophet ﷺ said,

> يَخْرُجُ نَاسٌ مِنْ قِبَلِ الْمَشْرِقِ وَيَقْرَءُونَ الْقُرْآنَ. لَا يُجَاوِزُ تَرَاقِيَهُمْ. يَمْرُقُونَ مِنَ الدِّيْنِ كَمَا يَمْرُقُ السَّهْمُ مِنَ الرَّمِيَّةِ، ثُمَّ لَا يَعُودُونَ فِيْهِ حَتَّى يَعُودَ السَّهْمُ إِلَى فُوقِهِ.

> 'A people shall appear from the east; they shall recite the Qurʾān but it will not pass their throats. They shall pass through the religion just as an arrow passes through a hunted game, never to return until an arrow returns to its bowstring'.[1]

Yusayr b. ʿAmr ﷺ asked Sahl b. Ḥunayf ﷺ, 'Did you ever hear the Messenger of God ﷺ say anything about the Kharijites?' Sahl replied,

> سَمِعْتُهُ – وَأَشَارَ بِيَدِهِ نَحْوَ الْمَشْرِقِ – قَوْمٌ يَقْرَءُونَ الْقُرْآنَ بِأَلْسِنَتِهِمْ لَا يَعْدُو تَرَاقِيَهُمْ، يَمْرُقُونَ مِنَ الدِّيْنِ كَمَا يَمْرُقُ السَّهْمُ مِنَ الرَّمِيَّةِ.

> 'Yes, I heard him, and he pointed towards the east [and said], "There shall appear a folk who will recite the Qurʾān with their tongues but it will not pass their throats. They shall pass through the religion just as an arrow passes through a hunted game".'[2]

ʿAbd Allāh b. ʿUmar ﷺ said, 'I once heard the Messenger of God say, while standing upon the pulpit,

---

[1] Narrated by al-Bukhārī in *al-Ṣaḥīḥ*: *Kitāb al-tawḥīd* [The Book of Divine Unity], chapter: 'The Recitation, Articulation and Reading of the Reprobate and Hypocrite [Reading the Qurʾān] Does Not Pass Beyond Their Throats', 6:2748 §7123; Aḥmad b. Ḥanbal in *al-Musnad*, 3:64 §11632; Ibn Abī Shayba in *al-Muṣannaf*, 7:563 §37397; Abū Yaʿlā in *al-Musnad*, 2:408 §1193; and al-Ṭabarānī in *al-Muʿjam al-kabīr*, 6:91 §5609.

[2] Narrated by Muslim in *al-Ṣaḥīḥ*: *Kitāb al-Zakāt* [The Book of Zakat], chapter: 'The Kharijites are the Worst of Creation', 2:750 §1068.

أَلَا إِنَّ الْفِتْنَةَ هَا هُنَا – يُشِيْرُ إِلَى الْمَشْرِقِ – مِنْ حَيْثُ يَطْلُعُ قَرْنُ الشَّيْطَانِ.

"Beware, the tribulation shall appear from here [and he pointed to the east]; from there the horn [i.e., generation] of Satan shall rise".'[1]

Besides being told of the impending appearance of the Kharijites, the Companions were also informed of the region and location from where they would emerge. In another hadith reported by ʿAbd Allāh b. ʿUmar, the Messenger ﷺ also disclosed the name of this eastern region. Ibn ʿUmar said,

ذَكَرَ النَّبِيُّ ﷺ: اَللّٰهُمَّ بَارِکْ لَنَا فِي شَامِنَا، اَللّٰهُمَّ بَارِکْ لَنَا فِي يَمَنِنَا. قَالُوا: يَا رَسُولَ اللهِ، وَفِي نَجْدِنَا؟ قَالَ: اَللّٰهُمَّ بَارِکْ لَنَا فِي شَامِنَا، اَللّٰهُمَّ بَارِکْ لَنَا فِي يَمَنِنَا. قَالُوا: يَا رَسُولَ اللهِ، وَفِي نَجْدِنَا؟ فَأَظُنُّهُ قَالَ فِي الثَّالِثَةِ: هُنَاکَ الزَّلَازِلُ وَالْفِتَنُ، وَبِهَا يَطْلُعُ قَرْنُ الشَّيْطَانِ.

'The Prophet ﷺ said, "O God! Bless for us our Levant. O God! Bless for us our Yemen". Some people said, "O Messenger of God! And our Najd?" The Prophet ﷺ said, "O God! Bless for us our Levant. O God! Bless for us our Yemen". Some people said [once more], "O Messenger of God! And our Najd?" I think the third time around he said, "There [in Najd] shall occur the earthquakes and tribulations, and there shall rise the horn [i.e., generation] of Satan".'[2]

---

[1] Narrated by al-Bukhārī in *al-Ṣaḥīḥ*: *Kitāb al-manāqib* [The Book of Exemplary Virtues], chapter: 'On the Ascription of Yemen to Ishmael ﷺ', 3:1293 §3320; Muslim in *al-Ṣaḥīḥ*: *Kitāb al-fitan wa ashrāṭ al-sāʿa* [The Book of Tribulations and the Portents of the Final Hour], chapter: 'Tribulation is from the East and from There the Horn of Satan Shall Rise', 4:2229 §2905; Mālik in *al-Muwaṭṭā*: *Kitāb al-istiʾdhān* [The Book on Seeking Permission], chapter: 'What Has Come to Us Regarding the East', 2:975 §1757; and Aḥmad b. Ḥanbal in *al-Musnad*, 2:73 §5428.

[2] Narrated by al-Bukhārī in *al-Ṣaḥīḥ*: *Kitāb al-fitan* [The Book of Tribulation], chapter: 'The Saying of the Prophet ﷺ, "Tribulation Shall Appear from the East"', 6:2598 §6681; al-Tirmidhī in *al-Sunan*: *Kitāb al-manāqib* [The Book of Exemplary Virtues], chapter: 'The Virtues of the Levant and Yemen', 5:733

The meaning of this narration materialized during the reign of our master, ʿAlī, when the first faction of the Kharijites came from Najd and Ḥarūrā, east of the Sacred Sanctuaries [of Mecca and Medina]. From there they started the blameworthy trend of terrorism, and the Prophet ﷺ informed us that they would appear in every era.

Geographically, Pakistan is also situated east of the Sacred Sanctuaries and its direction of prayer [*qibla*] lies in the west as it is east of the Kaʿba. The term 'east' has been used in the traditions in a general sense, and so its application may not be fixed in particular. The terrorists who are active in Pakistan possess all the traits of the Kharijites and have wreaked havoc in the land through bloodshed, suicide bombings and indiscriminate carnage.

14.5 The Kharijites Will Continue to Appear until the Emergence of the Anti-Christ

Sharīk b. Shihāb ؓ said,

كُنْتُ أَتَمَنَّى أَنْ أَلْقَى رَجُلًا مِنْ أَصْحَابِ النَّبِيِّ ﷺ أَسْأَلُهُ عَنِ الْخَوَارِجِ، فَلَقِيْتُ أَبَا بَرْزَةَ فِي يَومِ عِيْدٍ فِي نَفَرٍ مِنْ أَصْحَابِهِ، فَقُلْتُ لَهُ: هَلْ سَمِعْتَ رَسُولَ اللهِ ﷺ يَذْكُرُ الْخَوَارِجَ؟ فَقَالَ: نَعَمْ، سَمِعْتُ رَسُولَ اللهِ ﷺ بِأُذُنِي وَرَأَيْتُهُ بِعَيْنِي، أُتِيَ رَسُولُ اللهِ ﷺ بِمَالٍ فَقَسَمَهُ، فَأَعْطَى مَنْ عَنْ يَمِيْنِهِ وَمَنْ عَنْ شِمَالِهِ، وَلَمْ يُعْطِ مَنْ وَرَاءَهُ شَيْئًا، فَقَامَ رَجُلٌ مِنْ وَرَائِهِ، فَقَالَ: يَا مُحَمَّدُ، مَا عَدَلْتَ فِي الْقِسْمَةِ، رَجُلٌ أَسْوَدُ مَطْمُومُ الشَّعْرِ، عَلَيْهِ ثَوْبَانِ أَبْيَضَانِ، فَغَضِبَ رَسُولُ اللهِ ﷺ غَضَبًا شَدِيْدًا، وَقَالَ: وَاللهِ، لَا تَجِدُونَ بَعْدِي رَجُلًا هُوَ أَعْدَلُ مِنِّي. ثُمَّ قَالَ: يَخْرُجُ فِي آخِرِ الزَّمَانِ قَوْمٌ كَأَنَّ هَذَا مِنْهُمْ، يَقْرَءُونَ الْقُرْآنَ لَا يُجَاوِزُ تَرَاقِيَهُمْ، يَمْرُقُونَ مِنَ الْإِسْلَامِ كَمَا يَمْرُقُ السَّهْمُ مِنَ الرَّمِيَّةِ، سِيْمَاهُمُ التَّحْلِيْقُ، لَا يَزَالُونَ يَخْرُجُونَ حَتَّى يَخْرُجَ آخِرُهُمْ مَعَ الْمَسِيْحِ الدَّجَّالِ، فَإِذَا لَقِيْتُمُوهُمْ فَاقْتُلُوهُمْ، هُمْ شَرُّ الْخَلْقِ وَالْخَلِيْقَةِ.

---

§3953; Aḥmad b. Ḥanbal in *al-Musnad*, 2:118 §5987; and Ibn Ḥibbān in *al-Ṣaḥīḥ*, 16:290 §7301.

> 'For the longest I was eager to meet a man from the Companions so I could ask him about the Kharijites. Finally, I met Abū Burza during the day of Eid as he was with a group of his associates. I asked him, "Did you ever hear the Messenger of God ﷺ mention the Kharijites?" He replied, "Yes. I heard the Messenger of God ﷺ with my own ears and saw him with my own eyes. One time some wealth was brought to the Messenger of God ﷺ, so he apportioned it. He gave to those on his right and those on his left, but he did not give any to those who were behind him. Suddenly, a man stood up behind him and said, "O Muhammad! You have not acted justly in your apportioning". He was a man of dark complexion with a large head of hair, wearing two white garments. The Messenger of God ﷺ became severely angry and said, "By God! You shall not find any after me who is more just than I". Then he ﷺ said, "At the end of time there will appear a folk—and this one was from them. They shall recite the Qurʾān but it will not pass their throats. They shall pass through the religion just as an arrow passes through a hunted game. Their notable feature is shaven heads. They shall continue to appear until the last of them appears with the Anti-Christ [al-Dajjāl]; so you should kill them when you encounter them [in the battlefield]. They are the most evil of the creation".'[1]

ʿAbd Allāh b. ʿAmr b. al-ʿĀṣ رضي الله عنهما reported that the Prophet ﷺ said,

سَيَخْرُجُ أُنَاسٌ مِنْ أُمَّتِي مِنْ قِبَلِ الْمَشْرِقِ يَقْرَءُونَ الْقُرْآنَ لَا يُجَاوِزُ تَرَاقِيَهُمْ، كُلَّمَا خَرَجَ مِنْهُمْ قَرْنٌ قُطِعَ كُلَّمَا خَرَجَ مِنْهُمْ قَرْنٌ قُطِعَ حَتَّى عَدَّهَا زِيَادَةً عَلَى عَشْرَةِ مَرَّاتٍ، كُلَّمَا خَرَجَ مِنْهُمْ قَرْنٌ قُطِعَ حَتَّى يَخْرُجَ الدَّجَّالُ فِي بَقِيَّتِهِمْ.

---

[1] Narrated by Aḥmad b. Ḥanbal in *al-Musnad*, 4:421; al-Nasāʾī in *al-Sunan*: *Kitāb taḥrīm al-dam* [The Book on the Prohibition of Bloodshed], chapter: 'Regarding the One Who Unsheathes His Sword and Wields it amongst People', 7:119 §4103; al-Nasāʾī in *al-Sunan al-kubrā*, 2:312 §3566; al-Bazzār in *al-Musnad*, 9:294 §3846; and al-Ṭayālisī in *al-Musnad*, 1:124 §923.

> 'There shall appear a group of people from my *Umma* in the direction of the east. They will recite the Qur'ān but it will not pass their throats. Every time a generation of them appears it will be cut down, every time a generation of them appears it will be cut down, every time a generation of them appears it will be cut down [ᶜAbd Allāh said, 'He said that more than ten times']—until the Anti-Christ appears from their last remnants'.[1]

When the Prophet ﷺ said, 'they shall continue to appear', he eliminated all possible doubts that the Kharijites would appear only once. The first appearance of the Kharijites during the reign of our master ᶜAlī was but their vanguard. Whenever and wherever they rise, they take up arms against the Muslim states and massacre peaceful citizens. Terrorism is their mark of distinction, and the word *qarn* [generation] has been used in the traditions to refer to a well organized group of people in a generation. Lexically, however, *qarn* also denotes a horn. Animals with horns use them as weapons against an enemy or threat. Metaphorically, *qarn* refers to armed rebellion. *Qarn al-Shayṭān* means that weapons will be used to fulfil evil objectives, as taking peaceful life and fomenting turmoil are two of the most sought-after goals of Satan.

ᶜAbd Allāh b. ᶜUmar ﷺ reported that the Messenger of God ﷺ said,

كُلَّمَا خَرَجَ قَرْنٌ قُطِعَ، أَكْثَرَ مِنْ عِشْرِينَ مَرَّةً، حَتَّى يَخْرُجَ فِي عِرَاضِهِمُ الدَّجَّالُ.

> 'Every time a generation of them appears it will be cut down—this will occur over twenty times—until the Anti-Christ appears in their last remnant'.[2]

---

[1] Narrated by Aḥmad b. Ḥanbal in *al-Musnad*, 2:198 §6871; al-Ḥākim in *al-Mustadrak*, 4:533 §8497; Nuᶜaym b. Ḥammād in *al-Fitan*, 2:532; Ibn Rāshid in *al-Jāmiᶜ*, 11:377; and al-Ājurrī in *al-Sharīᶜa*, p. 113 §260.

[2] Narrated by Ibn Mājah in *al-Sunan*: 'Introduction', section, 'Mention of the Kharijites', 1:61 §174.

14.6 The Kharijites will Exit from the Religion

ʿAlī ﷺ said, 'I heard the Messenger of God ﷺ say,

يَمْرُقُونَ مِنَ الدِّيْنِ كَمَا يَمْرُقُ السَّهْمُ مِنَ الرَّمِيَّةِ.

"They shall pass through the religion just as an arrow passes through a hunted game".'[1]

Imam al-Tirmidhī narrates in *al-Sunan* from ʿAbd Allāh b. Masʿūd ﷺ who reported that the Messenger of God ﷺ said,

يَمْرُقُونَ مِنَ الْإِسْلَامِ كَمَا يَمْرُقُ السَّهْمُ مِنَ الرَّمِيَّةِ.

'They shall pass through Islam just as an arrow passes through a hunted game'.[2]

Interpreting this hadith, Badr al-Dīn al-ʿAynī said:

قَوْلُهُ ﷺ: يَمْرُقُونَ مِنَ الدِّيْنِ مِنَ الْمُرُوقِ وَهُوَ الْخُرُوجُ. يُقَالُ: مَرَقَ مِنَ الدِّيْنِ مُرُوقًا خَرَجَ مِنْهُ بِبِدْعَتِهِ وَضَلَالَتِهِ. وَفِي رِوَايَةِ سُوَيْدِ بْنِ غَفَلَةَ عِنْدَ النَّسَائِيِّ وَالطَّبَرِيِّ: يَمْرُقُونَ مِنَ الْإِسْلَامِ، وَفِي رِوَايَةٍ لِلنَّسَائِيِّ: يَمْرُقُونَ مِنَ الْحَقِّ.

The Prophet's statement ﷺ, 'They shall pass through the religion', uses the word *murūq*, which is to exit. It is said, 'So-and-so exited the religion [*maraqa*],' when he left it due to his blameworthy innovation and misguidance. In the narration of Suwayd b. Ghafla in the collections of

[1] Narrated by al-Bukhārī in *al-Ṣaḥīḥ*: *Kitāb istitāba al-murtaddīn wa al-muʿānidīn wa qitālihim* [The Book on Demanding the Repentance of the Apostates and Reprobates, and Fighting Them], chapter: 'On Fighting the Kharijites and the Heretics after Establishing the Evidence against Them', 6:2539 §6531; Muslim in *al-Ṣaḥīḥ*: *Kitāb al-Zakāt* [The Book of Zakat], chapter: 'The Encouragement to Kill the Kharijites', 2:746 §1066; al-Nasāʾī in *al-Sunan*: *Kitāb taḥrīm al-dam* [The Book on the Prohibition of Bloodshed], chapter: 'Regarding the One Who Unsheathes His Sword and Wields it amongst People', 7:119 §4102; Ibn Mājah in *al-Sunan*: 'Introduction', section: 'On Mention of the Kharijites', 1:59 §168; and Aḥmad b. Ḥanbal in *al-Musnad*, 1:81, 113, 131 §§§616, 912, 1086.

[2] Narrated by al-Tirmidhī in *al-Sunan*: *Kitāb al-fitan* [The Book of Tribulations], chapter: 'Concerning the Trait of Renegades [*al-māriqa*]', 4:481 §2188.

> al-Nasāʾī and al-Ṭabarī, it says, 'They shall pass through Islam. . . .' and in al-Nasāʾī's narration it reads, 'They shall pass through the truth'.[1]

In addition, Anwar Shāh Kāshmīrī said in his commentary,

> اَلْمُرُوقُ هُوَ الْخُرُوجُ مِنْ حَيْثُ لَا يَدْرِي.
>
> '*Murūq* is to unknowingly exit something'.[2]

14.7 The Kharijites will be the Dogs of Hell

The Messenger of God ﷺ declared the Kharijites the dogs of Hell. Abū Ghālib reported that Abū Umāma ﷺ said,

> كِلَابُ النَّارِ شَرُّ قَتْلَى تَحْتَ أَدِيْمِ السَّمَاءِ خَيْرُ قَتْلَى مَنْ قَتَلُوهُ ثُمَّ قَرَأَ: ﴿يَوْمَ تَبْيَضُّ وُجُوهٌ وَتَسْوَدُّ وُجُوهٌ﴾ إِلَى آخِرِ الْآيَةِ. قُلْتُ لِأَبِي أُمَامَةَ: أَنْتَ سَمِعْتَهُ مِنْ رَسُولِ اللهِ ﷺ؟ قَالَ: لَوْ لَمْ أَسْمَعْهُ إِلَّا مَرَّةً أَوْ مَرَّتَيْنِ أَوْ ثَلَاثًا أَوْ أَرْبَعًا حَتَّى عَدَّ سَبْعًا، مَا حَدَّثْتُكُمُوهُ.
>
> 'They are the dogs of Hell. They are the most evil of those slain under the heavens, and the best of those killed are those killed at their hands'. Then he recited the verse, '*On the Day when many faces will be bright and many will be dark. . . .* '.[3] I asked Abū Umāma, 'Did you hear that from the Messenger of God ﷺ?' He replied, 'Had I not heard it once, twice, thrice, four times, five times, six times or seven times, I would not have narrated it to you all'.[4]

---

[1] Badr al-Dīn al-ʿAynī, *ʿUmdat al-qārī*, 16:209.

[2] Shabbīr Aḥmad ʿUthmānī, *Fatḥ al-Mulhim*, 5:168.

[3] Qurʾān 3:106.

[4] Narrated by al-Tirmidhī in *al-Sunan*: *Kitāb tafsīr al-Qurʾān* [The Book of Qurʾānic Exegesis], chapter: 'From *Sūra Āl ʿImrān*', 5:226 §3000; Aḥmad b. Ḥanbal in *al-Musnad*, 5:256 §22262; al-Ḥākim in *al-Mustadrak*, 2:163 §2655; al-Bayhaqī in *al-Sunan al-kubrā*, 8:188; and al-Ṭabarānī in *Musnad al-Shāmiyyīn*, 2:248 §1279.

Imam Ibn Abī Shayba, al-Bayhaqī and al-Ṭabarānī narrated from Abū Ghālib that Abū Umāma ﷺ said about the Kharijites,

كِلَابُ جَهَنَّمَ، شَرُّ قَتْلَى قُتِلُوا تَحْتَ ظِلِّ السَّمَاءِ، وَمَنْ قَتَلُوا خَيْرُ قَتْلَى تَحْتَ السَّمَاءِ.

'They are the dogs of the Hellfire, the most evil of those slain under the shade of the heavens. Whoever is killed by them is the best of those slain under the heavens. . . .'[1]

Saʿīd b. Juhmān said,

كَانَتِ الْخَوَارِجُ قَدْ تَدْعُونِي حَتَّى كِدْتُ أَنْ أَدْخُلَ فِيْهِمْ، فَرَأَتْ أُخْتُ أَبِي بِلَالٍ فِي النَّوْمِ أَنَّ أَبَا بِلَالٍ كَلْبٌ أَهْلَبُ أَسْوَدُ عَيْنَاهُ تَذْرِفَانِ. فَقَالَتْ: بِأَبِي أَنْتَ يَا أَبَا بِلَالٍ مَا شَأْنُكَ أَرَاكَ هَكَذَا؟ فَقَالَ: جُعِلْنَا بَعْدَكُمْ كِلَابَ أَهْلِ النَّارِ، وَكَانَ أَبُو بِلَالٍ مِنْ رُؤُوسِ الْخَوَارِجِ.

'The Kharijites used to invite me to their way until I almost joined them, until the sister of Abū Bilāl (one of the leaders of the Kharijites) beheld him in a dream vision in the form of a shaggy black dog whose eyes were moist with tears. She said to him, "May my father be sacrificed for you, Abū Bilāl! What is wrong with you, that I see you in this state?" He replied, "After you, we were turned into the dogs of the inhabitants of the Fire".'[2]

14.8 The Outward Religious Appearance of the Kharijites should not Fool Anyone

The Kharijites would adhere to a strict regimen of Qurʾānic recitation, ritual prayers and fasting. They would speak extensively about asceticism, the transience of the world, fear of God and the

[1] Narrated by Ibn Abī Shayba in *al-Muṣannaf*, 7:554 §37892; al-Ṭabarānī in *al-Muʿjam al-kabīr*, 8:267–268 §§8034, 8035; and al-Bayhaqī in *al-Sunan al-kubrā*, 8:188.

[2] Narrated by Ibn Abī Shayba in *al-Muṣannaf*, 7:555 §37895; and ʿAbd Allāh b. Aḥmad in *al-Sunna*, 2:634 §1509.

duty of enjoining good and forbidding evil—all outward signs of pious people. Ibn Mājah and Aḥmad b. Ḥanbal narrated from Abū Salama who said,

قُلْتُ لِأَبِي سَعِيْدٍ الْخُدْرِيِّ ﷺ: هَلْ سَمِعْتَ رَسُولَ اللهِ ﷺ يَذْكُرُ فِي الْحَرُورِيَّةِ شَيْئًا؟ فَقَالَ: سَمِعْتُهُ يَذْكُرُ قَوْمًا يَتَعَبَّدُونَ (وَفِي رِوَايَةِ أَحْمَدَ: يَتَعَمَّقُونَ فِي الدِّيْنِ) يَحْقِرُ أَحَدُكُمْ صَلَاتَهُ مَعَ صَلَاتِهِمْ وَصَوْمَهُ مَعَ صَوْمِهِمْ.

'I said to Abū Saʿīd al-Khudrī ﷺ, "Did you hear the Messenger of God ﷺ mention anything about the Ḥarūriyya [i.e., Kharijites]?" He replied, "I heard him mention a folk who engage in much worship [and in the narration of Aḥmad, 'they absorbed themselves deeply in the religion']; you will belittle your prayers and fasting in comparison to theirs".'[1]

These outward displays of piety struck the Companions as ironic and confusing. In one narration reported by Imam al-Ḥākim and al-Nasāʾī, Ibn ʿAbbās ﷺ mentioned that he had not seen anyone as ascetic and outwardly devout as them. He said,

فَأَتَيْتُهُمْ وَهُمْ مُجْتَمِعُونَ فِي دَارِهِمْ قَائِلُونَ، فَسَلَّمْتُ عَلَيْهِمْ. فَقَالُوا: مَرْحَبًا بِكَ يَا ابْنَ عَبَّاسٍ. قَالَ ابْنُ عَبَّاسٍ: وَأَتَيْتُ قَوْمًا لَمْ أَرَ قَوْمًا قَطُّ أَشَدَّ اجْتِهَادًا مِنْهُمْ. مُسْهَمَةٌ وُجُوهُهُمْ مِنَ السَّهَرِ كَأَنَّ أَيْدِيَهُمْ وَرُكَبَهُمْ تُثْنَى عَلَيْهِمْ.

'So I went to see them [as he represented ʿAlī ﷺ] and they were gathered together in their home as they were speaking to one another. I greeted them with the salutations of peace [*al-salām ʿalaykum*], and they replied, "Welcome, O son of ʿAbbās!" [They did not wish peace to the Prophet's Companions.] I never saw a people more devout [outwardly] than them. Due to their prolonged nights of sleeplessness [in the night vigil prayer], their

[1] Narrated by Ibn Mājah in *al-Sunan*: 'Introduction', section: 'Mention of the Kharijites', 1:60 §169; Aḥmad b. Ḥanbal in *al-Musnad*, 3:33 §11309; and Ibn Abī Shayba in *al-Muṣannaf*, 7:557 §37909.

faces bore marks [of prostration] and their hands and knees were calloused'.[1]

Jundub b. ʿAbd Allāh ﷺ said,

لَمَّا فَارَقَتِ الْخَوَارِجُ عَلِيًّا خَرَجَ فِي طَلَبِهِمْ وَخَرَجْنَا مَعَهُ، فَانْتَهَيْنَا إِلَى عَسْكَرِ الْقَوْمِ فَإِذَا لَهُمْ دَوِيٌّ كَدَوِيِّ النَّحْلِ مِنْ قِرَاءَةِ الْقُرْآنِ، وَفِيْهِمْ أَصْحَابُ الثَّفِنَاتِ وَأَصْحَابُ الْبَرَانِسِ، فَلَمَّا رَأَيْتُهُمْ دَخَلَنِي مِنْ ذَلِكَ شِدَّةٌ فَتَنَحَّيْتُ فَرَكَزْتُ رُمْحِي وَنَزَلْتُ عَنْ فَرَسِي وَوَضَعْتُ بُرْنُسِي، فَنَشَرْتُ عَلَيْهِ دِرْعِي، وَأَخَذْتُ بِمِقْوَدِ فَرَسِي فَقُمْتُ أُصَلِّي إِلَى رُمْحِي وَأَنَا أَقُولُ فِي صَلَاتِي: اَللّٰهُمَّ إِنْ كَانَ قِتَالُ هَؤُلَاءِ الْقَوْمِ، لَكَ طَاعَةً فَائْذَنْ لِي فِيْهِ، وَإِنْ كَانَ مَعْصِيَةً فَأَرِنِي بَرَاءَتَكَ.

'When the Kharijites seceded from ʿAlī, he went out in pursuit of them and we went with him. When we reached their troops, we heard a loud recitation of the Qurʾān that sounded like the buzzing of bees. Amongst them were some wearing loin cloths and mantles, and seeing them in that state [of ostensible piety], I had mixed feelings about fighting against them. I stuck my spear into the ground, dismounted from my steed, took off my mantle, spreading it out and placing my armour on it. I then took my steed by the reigns and started praying towards my spear [as a barrier]. During my prayer I said, "O God! If it is obedience to You to fight these folk, then give me permission to do it; and if it is disobedience, then show me a sign of Your disapproval".'[2]

Jundub was so influenced by the apparent piety, asceticism and worship of the Kharijites that he was reluctant to fight them. Then he heard the prophetic traditions about them from our master ʿAlī

---

[1] Narrated by al-Ḥākim in *al-Mustadrak*, 2:164 §2656; al-Nasāʾī in *al-Sunan al-kubrā*, 5:165 §8575; ʿAbd al-Razzāq in *al-Muṣannaf*, 10:146; al-Ṭabarānī in *al-Muʿjam al-kabīr*, 10:257 §10598; and al-Bayhaqī in *al-Sunan al-kubrā*, 8:179.

[2] Narrated by al-Ṭabarānī in *al-Muʿjam al-awsaṭ*, 4:227 §4051; and cited by al-Haythamī in *Majmaʿ al-zawāʾid*, 4:227; Ibn Ḥajar al-ʿAsqalānī in *Fatḥ al-Bārī*, 12:296; and al-Shawkānī in *Nayl al-awṭār*, 7:349.

which proved true. That expanded his heart, gave him insight and strengthened his belief that they should be killed and eliminated.

The modern Kharijites appear to be pious and righteous servants of God; however, due to their inner states, anti-Islamic activities, unjust killings and terrorism, they are called the worst of creation. No doubt, they recite the Qur'ān, but they take the verses revealed about the disbelievers and apply them to the Muslims and declare them disbelievers. On the basis of their so-called doctrine, they justify the murder of peaceful people.

14.9 The Kharijites are the Worst of Creation

The Messenger of God ﷺ, his Companions and their followers all declared the Kharijites the worst of creation. Al-Bukhārī narrated in his collection, in the chapter heading for the section, 'The Statement of God Most High, "*God will not lead a people astray after having guided them until He makes clear to them that which they should avoid*"' [Qur'ān 9:115], that Ibn ʿUmar ؓ believed that they [the Kharijites] were the worst of God's creation. He said, 'They took the verses revealed about the disbelievers and applied them to the believers'.

Ibn Ḥajar al-ʿAsqalānī said in *al-Fatḥ*:

وَصَلَهُ الطَّبَرِيُّ فِي مُسْنَدِ عَلِيٍّ مِنْ تَهْذِيْبِ الْآثَارِ مِنْ طَرِيْقِ بُكَيْرِ بْنِ عَبْدِ اللهِ بْنِ الْأَشَجِّ: أَنَّهُ سَأَلَ نَافِعًا: كَيْفَ كَانَ رَأْيُ ابْنِ عُمَرَ فِي الْحَرُورِيَّةِ؟ قَالَ: كَانَ يَرَاهُمْ شِرَارَ خَلْقِ اللهِ، انْطَلَقُوا إِلَى آيَاتِ الْكُفَّارِ فَجَعَلُوهَا فِي الْمُؤْمِنِيْنَ.

قُلْتُ: وَسَنَدُهُ صَحِيْحٌ، وَقَدْ ثَبَتَ فِي الْحَدِيْثِ الصَّحِيْحِ الْمَرْفُوعِ عِنْدَ مُسْلِمٍ مِنْ حَدِيْثِ أَبِي ذَرٍّ ؓ فِي وَصْفِ الْخَوَارِجِ: هُمْ شِرَارُ الْخَلْقِ وَالْخَلِيْقَةِ. وَعِنْدَ أَحْمَدَ بِسَنَدٍ جَيِّدٍ عَنْ أَنَسٍ مَرْفُوعًا مِثْلَهُ.

وَعِنْدَ الْبَزَّارِ مِنْ طَرِيْقِ الشَّعْبِيِّ عَنْ عَائِشَةَ ؓ قَالَتْ: ذَكَرَ رَسُولُ اللهِ ﷺ الْخَوَارِجَ فَقَالَ: هُمْ شِرَارُ أُمَّتِي، يَقْتُلُهُمْ خِيَارُ أُمَّتِي. وَسَنَدُهُ حَسَنٌ.

وَعِنْدَ الطَّبَرَانِيِّ مِنْ هَذَا الْوَجْهِ مَرْفُوعًا: هُمْ شِرَارُ الْخَلْقِ وَالْخَلِيْقَةِ يَقْتُلُهُمْ خَيْرُ الْخَلْقِ وَالْخَلِيْقَةِ. وَفِي حَدِيْثِ أَبِي سَعِيْدٍ ؓ عِنْدَ أَحْمَدَ: هُمْ شَرُّ الْبَرِيَّةِ.

وَفِي حَدِيْثِ عَبْدِ اللهِ بْنِ خَبَّابٍ ﵁ يَعْنِي عَنْ أَبِيْهِ عِنْدَ الطَّبَرَانِيِّ: شَرُّ قَتْلَى أَظَلَّتْهُمُ السَّمَاءُ وَأَقَلَّتْهُمُ الْأَرْضُ. وَفِي حَدِيْثِ أَبِي أُمَامَةَ ﵁ نَحْوَهُ.

وَفِي رِوَايَةِ عُبَيْدِ اللهِ بْنِ أَبِي رَافِعٍ عَنْ عَلِيٍّ ﵁ عِنْدَ مُسْلِمٍ: مِنْ أَبْغَضِ خَلْقِ اللهِ إِلَيْهِ.

وَعِنْدَ أَحْمَدَ وَابْنِ أَبِي شَيْبَةَ مِنْ حَدِيْثِ أَبِي بَرْزَةَ مَرْفُوعًا فِي ذِكْرِ الْخَوَارِجِ: شَرُّ الْخَلْقِ وَالْخَلِيْقَةِ يَقُوْلُهَا ثَلَاثًا. وَعِنْدَ ابْنِ أَبِي شَيْبَةَ مِنْ طَرِيْقِ عُمَيْرِ بْنِ إِسْحَاقَ عَنْ أَبِي هُرَيْرَةَ ﵁: هُمْ شَرُّ الْخَلْقِ. وَهَذَا مِمَّا يُؤَيِّدُ قَوْلَ مَنْ قَالَ بِكُفْرِهِمْ.

In *Musnad ʿAlī* al-Ṭabarī traced it back to Bukayr b. ʿAbd Allāh b. al-Ashajj from *Tahdhīb al-āthār*. He asked Nāfiʿ, 'What was Ibn ʿUmar's view regarding the Ḥarūriyya?' Nāfiʿ replied, 'He believed that they were the worst of God's creation. They took the verses revealed about the disbelievers and applied them to the believers'.

I [al-ʿAsqalānī] say: This chain is rigorously authentic, and it was affirmed in the rigorously authentic traceable [*marfūʿ*] report with [Imam] Muslim from the hadith of Abū Dharr, describing the Kharijites: 'They are the worst of creation'. And there is a report from Anas traced to its ultimate source with a similar wording found in Aḥmad's collection, with a fine chain of narration.

Al-Bazzār has a report from the route of al-Shaʿbī from ʿĀʾisha ﵂ who said, 'The Messenger of God ﷺ mentioned the Kharijites and said, "They are the worst of my *Umma* and shall be killed by the best of my *Umma*".' This has a fine chain.

There is a report traced to its ultimate source, similar to this, with al-Ṭabarānī: 'They are the worst of the creation and shall be killed by the best of creation'. And in the hadith of Abū Saʿīḍ [al-Khudrī] found in the collection of Aḥmad, it reads: 'They are the worst of humanity'.

In the narration of ʿUbayd Allāh b. Abī Rāfiʿ from ʿAlī, which is found in the collection of Muslim, it reads:

'They are the most despised of creation in the sight of God'. And in the hadith of al-Ṭabarānī from ʿAbd Allāh b. Khabbāb ﷺ, from his father: 'They are the worst of those slain who are shaded by the heavens and carried by the earth'. And in the hadith of Abū Umāma ﷺ there is a similar wording.

In the report of Abū Barza, traced to its ultimate source, concerning the Kharijites, which is narrated by Aḥmad and Ibn Abī Shayba: 'He said thrice, "They are the worst of creation".' In a report with Ibn Abī Shayba from the route of ʿUmayr b. Isḥāq, from Abū Hurayra ﷺ, it reads: 'They are the most evil of creation'. The above report gives support to the view of those who held that they [the Kharijites] were disbelievers.[1]

Ḥudhayfa ﷺ reported that the Messenger of God ﷺ said,

إِنَّ مَا أَتَخَوَّفُ عَلَيْكُمْ رَجُلٌ قَرَأَ الْقُرْآنَ حَتَّى إِذَا رُئِيَتْ بَهْجَتُهُ عَلَيْهِ وَكَانَ رِدْئًا لِلْإِسْلَامِ غَيَّرَهُ إِلَى مَا شَاءَ اللهُ فَانْسَلَخَ مِنْهُ وَنَبَذَهُ وَرَاءَ ظَهْرِهِ وَسَعَى عَلَى جَارِهِ بِالسَّيْفِ وَرَمَاهُ بِالشِّرْكِ قَالَ: قُلْتُ: يَا نَبِيَّ اللهِ، أَيُّهُمَا أَوْلَى بِالشِّرْكِ: الْمَرْمِيُّ أَمِ الرَّامِي؟ قَالَ: بَلِ الرَّامِي.

'The only thing I fear for you is a man who recites the Qurʾān until you see its beauty upon him, and who

---

[1] Narrated by al-Bukhārī in *al-Ṣaḥīḥ: Kitāb istitāba al-murtaddīn wa al-muʿānidīn wa qitālihim* [The Book on Demanding the Repentance of the Apostates and Reprobates, and Fighting Them], chapter: 'On Fighting the Kharijites and the Heretics after Establishing the Evidence against Them', 6:2539; Muslim in *al-Ṣaḥīḥ: Kitāb al-Zakāt* [The Book of Zakat], chapter: 'The Kharijites Are the Most Evil of Creation', 2:750 §1067; Abū Dāwūd in *al-Sunan*: *Kitāb al-Sunna* [The Book of the Sunna], chapter: 'On Fighting the Kharijites', 4:243 §4765; al-Nasāʾī in *al-Sunan*: *Kitāb taḥrīm al-dam* [The Book on the Prohibition of Bloodshed], chapter: 'Regarding the One Who Unsheathes His Sword and Wields it amongst People', 7:119–120 §4103; Aḥmad b. Ḥanbal in *al-Musnad*, 3:15 §11133; Ibn Abī Shayba in *al-Muṣannaf*, 7:557, 559 §37905; al-Bazzār in *al-Musnad*, 9:294, 305 §3846; and al-Ṭabarānī in *al-Muʿjam al-awsaṭ*, 6:186 §6142, 7:335 §7660, and in *al-Muʿjam al-ṣaghīr*, 1:42 §33.

> supports Islam until God wills, until he abandons it and casts it behind his back and attacks his neighbour with a sword and accuses him of polytheism [*shirk*]'. Ḥudhayfa said, 'O Messenger of God! Which of the two is closer to polytheism, the accuser or the accused?' The Messenger of God ﷺ responded, 'Of course, it is the accuser'.[1]

14.10 A Noteworthy Point

Ṣafwān b. Muḥarraz narrated from Jundub b. ʿAbd Allāh رضي الله عنه that he passed by a group who were reciting the Qurʾān. Jundub remarked,

لَا يَغُرَّنَّکَ هَؤُلَاءِ؛ إِنَّهُمْ يَقْرَأُونَ الْقُرْآنَ الْيَوْمَ، وَيَتَجَالَدُونَ بِالسُّيُوفِ غَدًا.

> 'Do not be deceived by them; today they are reciting the Qurʾān, but tomorrow they will be fighting [the Muslims] with their weapons'.[2]

Ḥarb b. Ismāʿīl al-Kirmānī reported that Aḥmad b. Ḥanbal said,

اَلْخَوَارِجُ قَوْمُ سُوءٍ. لَا أَعْلَمُ فِي الْأَرْضِ قَوْمًا شَرًّا مِنْهُمْ، وَقَالَ: صَحَّ الْحَدِيثُ فِيهِمْ عَنِ النَّبِيِّ ﷺ، وَمِنْ عَشَرَةِ وُجُوهٍ.

> 'The Kharijites are an evil folk. I know of no one else on the earth more evil than them. The Prophet's hadith ﷺ about them is authentic from ten different angles [chains of narration]'.[3]

Yūsuf b. Mūsā reported that Imam Aḥmad was asked if the Kharijites were disbelievers. He said, 'They have passed through the religion'. He was again asked, 'Are they disbelievers?' He said again, 'They have passed through the religion'.[4]

---

[1] Narrated by Ibn Ḥibbān in *al-Ṣaḥīḥ*, 1:282 §81; and al-Bazzār in *al-Musnad*, 7:220 §2793.

[2] Narrated by al-Ṭabarānī in *al-Muʿjam al-kabīr*, 2:167 §1685; al-Mundhirī in *al-Targhīb wa al-tarhīb*, 3:166 §3513; al-Daylamī in *Musnad al-firdaws*, 4:134 §6419; and al-Haythamī in *Majmaʿ al-zawāʾid*, 6:231.

[3] Al-Khalāl, *al-Sunna*, p. 145 §110.

[4] Ibid., §111.

Chapter 15

The Prophetic Decree That the Turmoil of the Kharijites Must be Eliminated

IN THE PRECEDING CHAPTERS WE PRESENTED THE QUR'ĀNIC VERSES AND hadith reports that mention the beliefs, ideologies, signs and blameworthy innovations of the Kharijites. Let us now consider the Prophet's orders to eliminate them.

15.1 It is Obligatory to Eliminate the Kharijites

ʿAlī ﷺ reported that he heard the Messenger of God ﷺ say,

سَيَخْرُجُ قَومٌ فِي آخِرِ الزَّمَانِ: أَحْدَاثُ الْأَسْنَانِ سُفَهَاءُ الْأَحْلَامِ، يَقُولُونَ مِنْ خَيْرِ قَوْلِ الْبَرِيَّةِ، لَا يُجَاوِزُ إِيْمَانُهُمْ حَنَاجِرَهُمْ، يَمْرُقُونَ مِنَ الدِّيْنِ كَمَا يَمْرُقُ السَّهْمُ مِنَ الرَّمِيَّةِ، فَأَيْنَمَا لَقِيْتُمُوهُمْ فَاقْتُلُوهُمْ، فَإِنَّ فِي قَتْلِهِمْ أَجْرًا لِمَنْ قَتَلَهُمْ يَوْمَ الْقِيَامَةِ.

> 'At the end of time there shall appear a folk, young in age and foolish. They will speak the words of the best of people, but their faith will not pass their throats. They shall pass through Islam just as an arrow passes through a hunted game. Kill them wherever you find them [during war], for the one who kills them will be rewarded on the Day of Resurrection'.[1]

After narrating this hadith from ʿAbd Allāh b. Masʿūd ﷺ, Imam al-Tirmidhī stated that it was narrated from ʿAlī, Abū Saʿīd and Abū Dharr ﷺ. And this a good hadith. Abū Saʿīd al-Khudrī ﷺ reported that the Messenger of God ﷺ said,

---

[1] Narrated by al-Bukhārī in *al-Ṣaḥīḥ*: *Kitāb istitāba al-murtaddīn wa al-muʿānidīn wa qitālihim* [The Book on Demanding the Repentance of the Apostates and Reprobates, and Fighting Them], chapter: 'On Fighting the Kharijites and the Heretics after Establishing the Evidence against Them', 6:2539 §6531; Muslim in *al-Ṣaḥīḥ*: *Kitāb al-Zakāt* [The Book of Zakat], chapter: 'The Encouragement to Kill the Kharijites', 2:746 §1066; Aḥmad b. Ḥanbal in *al-Musnad*, 1:81, 113, 131 §§§616, 912, 1086; al-Nasāʾī in *al-Sunan*: *Kitāb taḥrīm al-dam* [The Book on the Prohibition of Bloodshed], chapter: 'Regarding the One Who Unsheathes His Sword and Wields it amongst People', 7:119 §4102; and Ibn Mājah in *al-Sunan*: 'Introduction', section: 'Mention of the Kharijites', 1:59 §168.

إِنَّهُ يَخْرُجُ مِنْ ضِئْضِىءِ هَذَا قَوْمٌ . . . لَئِنْ أَدْرَكْتُهُمْ لَأَقْتُلَنَّهُمْ قَتْلَ ثَمُودَ.

> 'There shall emerge from the offspring of this man [Dhū al-Khuwayṣira al-Tamīmī] a folk. . . . If I were to encounter them, I would slay them like the people of Thamūd!'[1]

In another narration, Abū Saʿīd al-Khudrī ﷺ reported that the Messenger of God ﷺ said,

إِنَّ مِنْ ضِئْضِىءِ هَذَا قَوْمًا يَقْرَءُونَ الْقُرْآنَ لَا يُجَاوِزُ حَنَاجِرَهُمْ، يَمْرُقُونَ مِنَ الْإِسْلَامِ مُرُوقَ السَّهْمِ مِنَ الرَّمِيَّةِ، يَقْتُلُونَ أَهْلَ الْإِسْلَامِ وَيَدَعُونَ أَهْلَ الْأَوْثَانِ، لَئِنْ أَدْرَكْتُهُمْ لَأَقْتُلَنَّهُمْ قَتْلَ عَادٍ.

> 'There shall emerge from the offspring of this man [Dhū al-Khuwayṣira al-Tamīmī] a folk who will recite the Qurʾān but it will not pass their throats. They shall pass through Islam just as an arrow passes through a hunted game. . . . They kill the Muslims but leave the disbelievers. If I were to encounter them, I would slay them like the people of ʿĀd!'[2]

---

[1] Narrated by al-Bukhārī in *al-Ṣaḥīḥ*: *Kitāb al-maghāzī* [The Book of Military Expeditions], chapter: 'The Dispatch of ʿAlī b. Abī Ṭālib and Khālid b. al-Walīd to Yemen before the Farewell Pilgrimage', 4:1581 §4094; Muslim in *al-Ṣaḥīḥ*: *Kitāb al-Zakāt* [The Book of Zakat], chapter: 'On the Kharijites and their Qualities', 2:742, 743 §1064; Aḥmad b. Ḥanbal in *al-Musnad*, 3:4 §11021; Ibn Khuzayma in *al-Ṣaḥīḥ*, 4:71 §2373; Ibn Ḥibbān in *al-Ṣaḥīḥ*, 1:205 §25; and Abū Yaʿlā in *al-Musnad*, 2:390 §1163.

[2] Narrated by al-Bukhārī in *al-Ṣaḥīḥ*: *Kitāb al-tawḥīd* [The Book of Divine Unity], chapter: 'God's saying, "*The angels and the Spirit ascend to Him*"' [Qurʾān 70:4], 6:2702 §6995, and in *Kitāb al-Anbiyāʾ* [The Book of the Prophets], chapter: 'On God's Saying, "*And as for ʿĀd, they were destroyed by a fierce roaring wind*"' [Qurʾān 69:6], 3:1219 §3166; Muslim in *al-Ṣaḥīḥ*: *Kitāb al-Zakāt* [The Book of Zakat], chapter: 'On the Kharijites and Their Traits', 2:741 §1064; Abū Dāwūd in *al-Sunan*: *Kitāb al-Sunna* [The Book of the Sunna], chapter: 'On Fighting the Kharijites', 4:243 §4764; and al-Nasāʾī in *al-Sunan*: *Kitāb taḥrīm al-dam* [The Book on the Prohibition of Bloodshed], chapter: 'Regarding the One Who Unsheathes His Sword and Wields it amongst People', 7:118 §4101, and in *Kitāb al-Zakāt* [The Book of Zakat], chapter: 'Those Whose Hearts are Drawn Near', 5:87 §2578.

Interpreting this hadith, Ibn Ḥajar al-ʿAsqalānī wrote,

قَوْلُهُ ﷺ: يَقْتُلُونَ أَهْلَ الْإِسْلَامِ إِلَخْ. وَهُوَ مِمَّا أَخْبَرَ بِهِ ﷺ مِنَ الْمُغَيَّبَاتِ، فَوَقَعَ كَمَا قَالَ.

'The Prophet's statement ﷺ, "They will kill the people of Islam" is from the unseen matters that he informed about, and it occurred just as he said'.[1]

Shabbīr Aḥmad ʿUthmānī said in his commentary,

قَالَ الْأُبَيُّ: وَمِنْ عَجِيبِ أَمْرِهِمْ مَا يَأْتِي أَنَّهُمْ حِيْنَ خَرَجُوا مِنَ الْكُوفَةِ مُنَابِذِيْنَ لِعَلِيٍّ عليه السلام: لَقُوا فِي طَرِيْقِهِمْ مُسْلِمًا وَكَافِرًا، فَقَتَلُوا الْمُسْلِمَ.

'Ubayy [b. Kaʿb] said, "One of the bewildering aspects of the Kharijites is that when they left Kufa and revolted against ʿAlī عليه السلام, they encountered a Muslim and a disbeliever on the road, and killed the Muslim [but spared the disbeliever]".'[2]

Imam Aḥmad, Abū Dāwūd and Ibn Mājah narrated from Abū Saʿīd al-Khudrī and Anas b. Mālik رضي الله عنهما that the Prophet ﷺ said,

سَيَكُونُ فِي أُمَّتِي اخْتِلَافٌ وَفُرْقَةٌ قَوْمٌ يُحْسِنُونَ الْقِيْلَ وَيُسِيْئُونَ الْفِعْلَ . . . هُمْ شَرُّ الْخَلْقِ وَالْخَلِيْقَةِ، طُوبَى لِمَنْ قَتَلَهُمْ وَقَتَلُوهُ، يَدْعُونَ إِلَى كِتَابِ اللهِ وَلَيْسُوا مِنْهُ فِي شَيْءٍ، مَنْ قَاتَلَهُمْ كَانَ أَوْلَى بِاللهِ مِنْهُمْ. قَالُوا: يَا رَسُولَ اللهِ مَا سِيْمَاهُمْ؟ قَالَ: التَّحْلِيْقُ.

'My nation shall soon fall prey to dissention and disunity. There shall be a folk whose words are good but whose actions are bad. . . . They are the most evil of the creation. Glad tidings [of Paradise] for the one who kills them and who is killed by them. They will invite to God's Book but they have nothing to do with it. Whoever fights them will be nearer to God than they are'. The Companions

[1] Ibn Ḥajar al-ʿAsqalānī, *Fatḥ al-Bārī*, 8:69.

[2] Shabbīr Aḥmad ʿUthmānī, *Fatḥ al-Mulhim*, 5:151.

said, 'O Messenger of God! What is their distinguishing feature?' He replied, 'Shaven heads'.[1]

Imam Aḥmad also reported that Abū Saʿīd al-Khudrī ﷺ said,

أَنَّ أَبَا بَكْرٍ ﷺ جَاءَ إِلَى رَسُولِ اللهِ ﷺ، فَقَالَ: يَا رَسُولَ اللهِ، إِنِّي مَرَرْتُ بِوَادٍ كَذَا وَكَذَا فَإِذَا رَجُلٌ مُتَخَشِّعٌ، حَسَنُ الْهَيْئَةِ، يُصَلِّي. فَقَالَ لَهُ النَّبِيُّ ﷺ: إِذْهَبْ إِلَيْهِ، فَاقْتُلْهُ. قَالَ: فَذَهَبَ إِلَيْهِ أَبُوبَكْرٍ، فَلَمَّا رَآهُ عَلَى تِلْكَ الْحَالِ كَرِهَ أَنْ يَقْتُلَهُ، فَرَجَعَ إِلَى رَسُولِ اللهِ ﷺ. قَالَ: فَقَالَ النَّبِيُّ ﷺ لِعُمَرَ: إِذْهَبْ فَاقْتُلْهُ. فَذَهَبَ عُمَرُ فَرَآهُ عَلَى تِلْكَ الْحَالِ الَّتِي رَآهُ أَبُوبَكْرٍ قَالَ: فَكَرِهَ أَنْ يَقْتُلَهُ. قَالَ: فَرَجَعَ. فَقَالَ: يَا رَسُولَ اللهِ، إِنِّي رَأَيْتُهُ يُصَلِّي مُتَخَشِّعًا فَكَرِهْتُ أَنْ أَقْتُلَهُ. قَالَ ﷺ: يَا عَلِيُّ! اذْهَبْ فَاقْتُلْهُ. قَالَ: فَذَهَبَ عَلِيٌّ، فَلَمْ يَرَهُ فَرَجَعَ عَلِيٌّ، فَقَالَ: يَا رَسُولَ اللهِ، إِنَّهُ لَمْ يَرَهُ. قَالَ: فَقَالَ النَّبِيُّ ﷺ: إِنَّ هَذَا وَأَصْحَابَهُ يَقْرَءُونَ الْقُرْآنَ لَا يُجَاوِزُ تَرَاقِيَهُمْ، يَمْرُقُونَ مِنَ الدِّيْنِ كَمَا يَمْرُقُ السَّهْمُ مِنَ الرَّمِيَّةِ ثُمَّ لَا يَعُودُونَ فِيْهِ حَتَّى يَعُودَ السَّهْمُ فِي فُوقِهِ فَاقْتُلُوهُمْ هُمْ شَرُّ الْبَرِيَّةِ.

'Abū Bakr ﷺ went to the Messenger of God ﷺ and said, "O Messenger of God! I passed through a particular valley, and lo and behold, there was a humble-looking man of pleasant appearance offering prayers". The Prophet ﷺ said, "Go to him and kill him". So Abū Bakr went back to that man, and when he saw him in that state [of humble worship], he hated to kill him, and so he went back to the Messenger of God ﷺ. The Prophet ﷺ then said to ʿUmar ﷺ, "Go and kill him", so ʿUmar went out and when he saw the man in the state in which Abū Bakr saw him, he hated to kill him, and so he went

[1] Narrated by Abū Dāwūd in *al-Sunan*: *Kitāb al-Sunna* [The Book of the Sunna], chapter: 'On Fighting the Kharijites', 4:243 §4765; Ibn Mājah in *al-Sunan*: 'Introduction', section: 'Discussion of the Kharijites', 1:60 §169; Aḥmad b. Ḥanbal in *al-Musnad*, 3:224 §13362; al-Ḥākim in *al-Mustadrak*, 2:161 §2649; al-Bayhaqī in *al-Sunan al-kubrā*, 8:171; al-Maqdisī in *al-Aḥādīth al-mukhtāra*, 7:15 §2391–2392 (and he declared its chain of transmission sound); and Abū Yaʿlā in *al-Musnad*, 5:426 §3117.

back to the Messenger of God ﷺ. He said, "O Messenger of God! I saw him offering prayers in a most humble manner, and so I hated to kill him". The Prophet ﷺ called out, "O ʿAlī! Go out and kill him!" ʿAlī went out to kill him but could not find him, so he returned and said, "O Messenger of God! I did not see him". The Prophet ﷺ said, "Indeed, that man and his compatriots recite the Qurʾān but it does not go past their throats. They shall pass through the religion just as an arrow passes through a hunted game, never to return until an arrow returns to its bowstring. Slay them [whenever you encounter them during war], for they are the worst of creation".'[1]

Imam Ibn ʿAbd al-Barr narrated that ʿAdī b. ʿAdī wrote to ʿUmar b. ʿAbd al-ʿAzīz ﷺ and complained that the Kharijites were insulting him. ʿUmar replied,

إِنْ سَبُّونِي فَسُبُّوهُمْ أَوِ اعْفُوا عَنْهُمْ، وَإِنْ شَهَرُوا السِّلَاحَ فَاشْهَرُوا عَلَيْهِمْ، وَإِنْ ضَرَبُوا فَاضْرِبُوا.

'If they insult me then either retaliate or pardon them, and if they take up arms then take up arms against them, and if they fight then fight them back'.[2]

15.2 Important Commentaries from the Imams of Hadith

Qāḍī ʿIyāḍ said in *Ikmāl al-muʿlim bi fawāʾid Muslim*:

أَجْمَعَ الْعُلَمَاءُ عَلَى أَنَّ الْخَوَارِجَ وَأَشْبَاهَهُمْ مِنْ أَهْلِ الْبِدَعِ وَالْبَغْيِ مَتَى خَرَجُوا وَخَالَفُوا رَأْيَ الْجَمَاعَةِ، وَشَقُّوا عَصَا الْمُسْلِمِينَ، وَنَصَبُوا رَايَةَ الْخِلَافِ. إِنَّ قِتَالَهُمْ وَاجِبٌ بَعْدَ إِنْذَارِهِمْ وَالْإِعْذَارِ إِلَيْهِمْ. قَالَ اللهُ تَعَالَى: ﴿فَقَٰتِلُواْ ٱلَّتِى تَبْغِى حَتَّىٰ تَفِىٓءَ إِلَىٰٓ أَمْرِ ٱللَّهِ﴾. وَهَذَا إِذَا كَانَ بَغْيُهُمْ لِأَجْلِ بِدْعَةٍ يُكَفَّرُونَ بِهَا، وَإِنْ كَانَ بَغْيُهُمْ لِغَيْرِ ذَلِكَ

[1] Narrated by Aḥmad b. Ḥanbal in *al-Musnad*, 3:15 §11133; al-Haythamī in *Majmaʿ al-zawāʾid*, 6:225; and cited by al-ʿAsqalānī in *Fatḥ al-Bārī*, 12:229.

[2] Ibn ʿAbd al-Barr, *al-Tamhīd*, 23:338–339.

لِعَصَبِيَّةٍ، أَوْ طَلَبِ رِئَاسَةٍ دُونَ بِدْعَةٍ، فَلَا يُحْكَمُ فِي هَؤُلَاءِ حُكْمُ الْكُفَّارِ بِوَجْهٍ، وَحُكْمُهُمْ أَهْلُ الْبَغْيِ مُجَرَّدًا عَلَى الْقَوْلِ الْمُتَقَدِّمِ.

The scholars have unanimously agreed that when the Kharijites and their ilk from the people of blameworthy innovation and rebellion revolt against the view of the community [*jamāʿa*], split the unity of the Muslims and raise the banner of dissention, it is obligatory [for the Muslims] to fight them after exhorting and warning them. God Most High says, '*Then all of you together fight the contentious party until they all submit to the command of God*'.[1] Now this is in the case where their rebellion stems from a blameworthy innovation by which they declare others to be disbelievers. If their rebellion was for some other reason that is not an innovation, such as bigoted allegiance [to a group or tribe] or pursuit of leadership, they are not given the same judgement reserved for the disbelievers in any way. According to the aforementioned view, they are given the ruling of the people of rebellion only.[2]

Imam al-Nawawī stated in his commentary on *Ṣaḥīḥ Muslim*:

قَوْلُهُ ﷺ: فَإِذَا لَقِيتُمُوهُمْ فَاقْتُلُوهُمْ فَإِنَّ فِي قَتْلِهِمْ أَجْرًا. هَذَا تَصْرِيحٌ بِوُجُوبِ قِتَالِ الْخَوَارِجِ وَالْبُغَاةِ وَهُوَ إِجْمَاعُ الْعُلَمَاءِ، قَالَ الْقَاضِي: أَجْمَعَ الْعُلَمَاءُ عَلَى أَنَّ الْخَوَارِجَ وَأَشْبَاهَهُم مِنْ أَهْلِ الْبِدَعِ وَالْبَغْيِ مَتَى خَرَجُوا عَلَى الْإِمَامِ، وَخَالَفُوا رَأْيَ الْجَمَاعَةِ وَشَقُّوا الْعَصَا، وَجَبَ قِتَالُهُمْ بَعْدَ إِنْذَارِهِمْ وَالْإِعْتِذَارِ إِلَيْهِمْ.

وَهَذَا كُلُّهُ مَا لَمْ يُكَفِّرُوا بِبِدْعَتِهِمْ، فَإِنْ كَانَتْ بِدْعَةٌ مِمَّا يُكَفَّرُونَ بِهِ جَرَتْ عَلَيْهِمْ أَحْكَامُ الْمُرْتَدِّيْنَ، وَأَمَّا الْبُغَاةُ الَّذِيْنَ لَا يُكَفَّرُونَ فَيَرِثُونَ وَيُورَثُونَ وَدَمُهُمْ فِي حَالِ الْقِتَالِ هَدْرٌ، وَكَذَا أَمْوَالُهُمُ الَّتِي تُتْلَفُ فِي الْقِتَالِ، وَالْأَصَحُّ أَنَّهُمْ لَا يَضْمَنُونَ أَيْضًا مَا أَتْلَفُوهُ عَلَى أَهْلِ الْعَدْلِ فِي حَالِ الْقِتَالِ مِنْ نَفْسٍ وَمَالٍ.

---

[1] Qurʾān 49:9.

[2] Qāḍī ʿIyāḍ, *Ikmāl al-muʿlim bi fawāʾid Muslim*, 3:613–614.

The Prophet's statement ﷺ, 'Kill them wherever you find them [during war], for the one who kills them will be rewarded on the Day of Resurrection', is an explicit declaration of the obligation to fight the Kharijites and rebels, and this is the consensus of the scholars. Qāḍī [ᶜIyāḍ] said, 'The scholars have unanimously agreed that when the Kharijites and their ilk from the people of blameworthy innovation and rebellion revolt against the view of the community [*jamāᶜa*], split the unity [of the Muslims] and raise the banner of dissention, it is obligatory [for the Muslim state] to fight them after exhorting them and warning them'.

Now that applies so long as their innovation is not one that entails disbelief. If their innovation is one that makes them disbelievers, then the rules that pertain to apostates are applied to them. As for the rebels who do not disbelieve, they may inherit and others may inherit from them, although during times of fighting their blood is lawful, as is their wealth that is destroyed [at the hands of the Muslim government] during the fighting. The most correct view is that they are not liable to receive compensation from the people of justice for the lives and wealth that were destroyed during the time of fighting.[1]

Shabbīr Aḥmad ᶜUthmānī wrote in *Fatḥ al-Mulhim*:

قَوْلُهُ ﷺ: فَإِنَّ فِي قَتْلِهِمْ أَجْرًا إِلَخْ: أَيْ أَجْرًا عَظِيْمًا. قَالَ النَّوَوِيُّ: هَذَا تَصْرِيْحٌ بِوُجُوبِ قِتَالِ الْخَوَارِجِ وَالْبُغَاةِ، وَهُوَ إِجْمَاعُ الْعُلَمَاءِ. قَالَ الْقَاضِي: أَجْمَعَ الْعُلَمَاءُ عَلَى أَنَّ الْخَوَارِجَ وَأَشْبَاهَهُمْ مِنْ أَهْلِ الْبِدَعِ وَالْبَغْيِ مَتَى خَرَجُوا عَلَى الْإِمَامِ، وَخَالَفُوا رَأْيَ الْجَمَاعَةِ، وَشَقُّوا الْعَصَا: وَجَبَ قِتَالُهُمْ بَعْدَ إِنْذَارِهِمْ وَالْإِعْتِذَارِ إِلَيْهِمْ.

The Prophet's statement ﷺ, 'for the one who kills them will be rewarded on the Day of Resurrection', means that this person will receive a tremendous reward. Al-Nawawī stated that this 'is an explicit declaration of

[1] Yaḥyā al-Nawawī, *Sharḥ Ṣaḥīḥ Muslim*, 7:170.

> the obligation to fight the Kharijites and rebels, and this is the consensus of the scholars'. Qāḍī [ʿIyāḍ] said, 'The scholars have unanimously agreed that when the Kharijites and their ilk from the people of blameworthy innovation and rebellion revolt against the view of the community [*jamāʿa*], split the unity [of the Muslims] and raise the banner of dissention, it is obligatory to fight them after exhorting them and warning them'.[1]

These commentaries further prove that this is obligatory to take action against the Kharijites and terrorists at the state level and eliminate them completely. Whenever the Kharijites and their ilk appear, the only guarantee of peace and security is their total annihilation. The history of Muslim *Umma* bears witness that whenever these elements raised their heads they were eliminated.

15.3 The Significance of Comparing the Kharijites to the People of ʿĀd and Thamūd

Some of the prophetic traditions about the Kharijites mention the people of ʿĀd and Thamūd. The import of these traditions is that the Kharijites should be uprooted and wiped out just as the people of ʿĀd and Thamūd were destroyed. Before that, however, it is our duty to teach them the truth and provide them the opportunity to take the right path, turn to God and abandon their evil designs. Concerning the people of ʿĀd and their destruction, God revealed,

﴿وَأَمَّا عَادٌ فَأُهْلِكُوا۟ بِرِيحٍ صَرْصَرٍ عَاتِيَةٍ. سَخَّرَهَا عَلَيْهِمْ سَبْعَ لَيَالٍ وَثَمَٰنِيَةَ أَيَّامٍ حُسُومًا
فَتَرَى ٱلْقَوْمَ فِيهَا صَرْعَىٰ كَأَنَّهُمْ أَعْجَازُ نَخْلٍ خَاوِيَةٍ. فَهَلْ تَرَىٰ لَهُم مِّنۢ بَاقِيَةٍ﴾

> *'And as for the people of ʿĀd, they were destroyed by a violently cold and roaring wind. God imposed it upon them for seven nights and eight days in succession, so you would see people felled therein as if they were hollow trunks of palm trees. Then do you see of them any remains?'*[2]

---

[1] Shabbīr Aḥmad ʿUthmānī, *Fatḥ al-Mulhim*, 5:166–167.

[2] Qurʾān 69:6–8.

In another verse, God revealed,

﴿فَلَمَّا رَأَوْهُ عَارِضًا مُّسْتَقْبِلَ أَوْدِيَتِهِمْ قَالُواْ هَٰذَا عَارِضٌ مُّمْطِرُنَا بَلْ هُوَ مَا ٱسْتَعْجَلْتُم بِهِۦ رِيحٌ فِيهَا عَذَابٌ أَلِيمٌ. تُدَمِّرُ كُلَّ شَيْءٍ بِأَمْرِ رَبِّهَا فَأَصْبَحُواْ لَا يُرَىٰٓ إِلَّا مَسَٰكِنُهُمْ كَذَٰلِكَ نَجْزِى ٱلْقَوْمَ ٱلْمُجْرِمِينَ﴾

'So when they saw it as a cloud approaching their valleys, they said, "This a cloud bringing us rain!" Rather, it is that for which you were impatient: a wind containing a grievous punishment. It will destroy everything by the command of its Lord. And they became so that nothing was seen of them, save their dwellings. Thus do We recompense the criminals'.[1]

Ibn Ḥajar al-ʿAsqalānī wrote in his commentary on the Prophet's statement ﷺ that he would kill the Kharijites like the people of ʿĀd and Thamūd: 'The Prophet's statement ﷺ, "If I were to encounter them I would slay them like the people of ʿĀd", means a general killing and elimination [during war], as God Most High said, "*Then do you see of them any remains?*"'[2]

Imam Abū al-ʿAbbās al-Qurṭubī, who preceded al-ʿAsqalānī, commented,

قَوْلُهُ ﷺ: لَئِنْ أَدْرَكْتُهُمْ لَأَقْتُلَنَّهُمْ قَتْلَ عَادٍ، وَفِي الْأُخْرَى: قَتْلَ ثَمُودَ، وَمَعْنَى هَذَا: لَئِنْ أَدْرَكَهُمْ لَيَقْتُلَنَّهُمْ قَتْلًا عَامًّا؛ بِحَيْثُ لَا يُبْقِي مِنْهُمْ أَحَدًا فِي وَقْتٍ وَاحِدٍ، لَا يُؤَخِّرُ قَتْلَ بَعْضِهِمْ عَنْ بَعْضٍ، وَلَا يُقِيلُ أَحَدًا مِنْهُمْ، كَمَا فَعَلَ اللهُ بِعَادٍ؛ حَيْثُ أَهْلَكَهُمْ بِالرِّيحِ الْعَقِيمِ، وَبِثَمُودَ حَيْثُ أَهْلَكَهُمْ بِالصَّيْحَةِ.

The Prophet's statement ﷺ 'If I were to encounter them I would slay them like the people of ʿĀd', and in another wording, 'like the people of Thamūd'. This means that if he were to encounter them, he would kill them all, in the sense that not a single one of them would remain at one given time, and none of them would be left for another

[1] Ibid., 46:24–25.

[2] Ibn Ḥajar al-ʿAsqalānī, *Fatḥ al-Bārī*, 2:377.

> day—just as God dealt with ʿĀd, destroying them with a grievous wind, and destroying Thamūd with the dreadful shriek.[1]

Imam al-Nawawī said,

> قَوْلُهُ ﷺ: لَئِنْ أَدْرَكْتُهُمْ لَأَقْتَلَنَّهُمْ قَتْلَ عَادٍ. أَيْ قَتْلًا عَامًّا مُسْتَأْصِلًا كَمَا قَالَ تَعَالَى: ﴿فَهَلْ تَرَىٰ لَهُم مِّنْ بَاقِيَةٍ﴾.
>
> 'His statement ﷺ, "If I were to encounter them I would slay them like the people of ʿĀd", means he would have killed them all, just as God says, "*Then do you see of them any remains?*"'[2]

Imam al-Qasṭalānī writes in *Irshād al-sārī*,

> لَئِنْ أَدْرَكْتُهُمْ لَأَقْتُلَنَّهُمْ قَتْلَ عَادٍ لَأَسْتَأْصِلَنَّهُمْ بِحَيْثُ لَا أُبْقِي مِنْهُمْ أَحَدًا كَاسْتِئْصَالِ عَادٍ، وَالْمُرَادُ لَازِمُهُ وَهُوَ الْهَلَاكُ.
>
> The phrase, 'If I were to encounter them I would slay them like the people of ʿĀd', means 'I would most certainly annihilate them so that none of them remain, just as ʿĀd were annihilated'. What is meant is the implication of that, which is their total destruction.[3]

Shabbīr Aḥmad ʿUthmānī agreed with this explanation in *Fatḥ al-Mulhim* and stated,

> أَيْ: قَتْلًا عَامًّا مُسْتَأْصِلًا، بِحَيْثُ لَا يَبْقَى مِنْهُمْ أَحَدٌ، كَمَا قَالَ تَعَالَى: ﴿فَهَلْ تَرَىٰ لَهُم مِّنْ بَاقِيَةٍ﴾.
>
> 'In other words, it means a general killing and annihilation, in the sense that none of them remains, as God Most High said, "*Then do you see of them any remains?*"'[4]

---

[1] Muhammad al-Qurṭubī, *al-Mufhim*, 3:110.

[2] Yaḥyā al-Nawawī, *Sharḥ Ṣaḥīḥ Muslim*, 7:162.

[3] Aḥmad al-Qasṭalānī, *Irshād al-sārī*, 10:398.

[4] Shabbīr Aḥmad ʿUthmānī, *Fatḥ al-Mulhim*, 5:151.

Imam Badr al-Dīn al-ʿAynī has also written similar interpretation in *ʿUmdat al-qārī*:

قَوْلُهُ ﷺ: قَتْلَ عَادٍ، وَقَوْلُهُ ﷺ: قَتْلَ ثَمُودَ. وَلَا تَعَارُضَ لِأَنَّ الْغَرَضَ مِنْهُ الْإِسْتِئْصَالُ بِالْكُلِّيَّةِ، وَعَادٌ وَثَمُودُ سَوَاءٌ فِيْهِ.

'The Prophet's statements ﷺ, "like the people of ʿĀd" and "like the people of Thamūd" are not mutually contradictory, because his intent was that they should be completely annihilated, and ʿĀd and Thamūd are the same in that regard'.[1]

Speaking of Thamūd, God revealed,

﴿وَأَخَذَ ٱلَّذِينَ ظَلَمُواْ ٱلصَّيْحَةُ فَأَصْبَحُواْ فِى دِيَٰرِهِمْ جَٰثِمِينَ. كَأَن لَّمْ يَغْنَوْاْ فِيهَآ أَلَآ إِنَّ ثَمُودَاْ كَفَرُواْ رَبَّهُمْ أَلَا بُعْدًا لِّثَمُودَ﴾

'*And the dreadful shriek seized those who had wronged, and so when morning came they were* [dead] *lying prone in their homes as if they had never prospered therein. Beware, Thamūd disbelieved in their Lord—so away with Thamūd*'.[2]

The Prophet ﷺ has commanded the Muslim state to kill the Kharijites like the killing of ʿĀd and Thamūd, because they too have transgressed like the perished nations of old. Another reason is that if some terrorists are killed and others are left alive or left to engage in negotiations, their leaders will take that time to regroup and prepare for more turmoil. Imam Aḥmad, al-Nasāʾī, al-Ḥākim and others narrated that the Prophet ﷺ said,

لَا يَزَالُونَ يَخْرُجُونَ حَتَّى يَخْرُجَ آخِرُهُمْ مَعَ الْمَسِيْحِ الدَّجَّالِ.

'They shall continue to appear until the last of them appears with the Anti-Christ [al-Dajjāl]'.[3]

---

[1] Badr al-Dīn al-ʿAynī, *ʿUmdat al-qārī*, 25:122.

[2] Qurʾān 11:67–68.

[3] Narrated by Aḥmad b. Ḥanbal in *al-Musnad*, 4:421 §19798; al-Nasāʾī in

Aware of the peculiar mentality and strategy of the Kharijites, the Prophet ﷺ taught us how to deal with them. When an operation is launched against them, it must continue unabated until they are decimated. Otherwise, if they are given reprieve or granted the opportunity to regroup, they will launch fresh attacks with renewed vigour and inflict losses on the Muslim state and its citizenry. This is why the Prophet ﷺ ordained the elimination of evil elements from society once and for all, as was done in the case of ʿĀd and Thamūd. This prophetic war strategy is designed to eliminate turmoil and danger in one fell swoop. Comparatively, the Prophet Noah ﷺ supplicated to God, asking for the wholesale destruction of his rebellious people. God says, quoting Prophet Noah ﷺ,

﴿إِنَّكَ إِنْ تَذَرْهُمْ يُضِلُّوا۟ عِبَادَكَ وَلَا يَلِدُوٓا۟ إِلَّا فَاجِرًا كَفَّارًا﴾

> '*Surely, if You leave them they will continue leading Your servants astray and will give birth to none but disbelieving criminals*'.[1]

The complete annihilation of evil forces is a Divine strategy and the Kharijites must suffer it in order to remove their danger. In the Qur'ān God mentions that the people of Thamūd were seized with a torment unexpectedly and ruined completely:

﴿إِنَّآ أَرْسَلْنَا عَلَيْهِمْ صَيْحَةً وَاحِدَةً فَكَانُوا۟ كَهَشِيمِ ٱلْمُحْتَظِرِ﴾

> '*Indeed, We sent upon them one shriek and they became like the dry twig fragments of an animal pen*'.[2]

These Qur'ānic verses and prophetic traditions make it amply clear that negotiations with militant terrorist groups give them time to reorganize for renewed terrorist activities. Taking such a detrimental step amounts to disobedience of the Messenger of

---

al-Sunan: *Kitāb taḥrīm al-dam* [The Book on the Prohibition of Bloodshed], chapter: 'Regarding the One Who Unsheathes His Sword and Wields it amongst People', 7:119 §4103; and al-Ḥākim in *al-Mustadrak*, 2:160 §2647.

[1] Qur'ān 71:27.

[2] Ibid., 54:31.

God ﷻ, which ruins one not only in this life but in the Hereafter as well.

15.4 THE GREAT REWARD FOR FIGHTING THE KHARIJITES

The great reward promised for those who kill the Kharijites has been repeatedly mentioned in the sound prophetic traditions. Imam Aḥmad b. Ḥanbal narrated that Abū Bakra ﷺ reported that the Messenger of God ﷺ said,

> سَيَخْرُجُ قَوْمٌ أَحْدَاثٌ أَحِدَّاءُ أَشِدَّاءُ، ذَلِقَةٌ أَلْسِنَتُهُمْ بِالْقُرْآنِ، يَقْرَءُونَهُ لَا يُجَاوِزُ تَرَاقِيَهُمْ. فَإِذَا لَقِيْتُمُوهُمْ فَأَنِيْمُوهُمْ، ثُمَّ إِذَا لَقِيْتُمُوهُمْ فَاقْتُلُوهُمْ، فَإِنَّهُ يُؤْجَرُ قَاتِلُهُمْ.

> 'There shall soon appear a folk who are young in age, sharp-witted and severe. They will recite the Qur'ān distinctly and clearly but it will not pass their throats. So extinguish [their turmoil] if you encounter them, and if you encounter them [again] slay them, for the one who slays them will be rewarded'.[1]

ʿAbd Allāh b. Rabāḥ al-Anṣārī ﷺ reported that he heard Kaʿb [b. Mālik] ﷺ say,

> لِلشَّهِيْدِ نُورٌ وَلِمَنْ قَاتَلَ الْحَرُورِيَّةَ عَشْرَةُ أَنْوَارٍ (وَفِي رِوَايَةٍ لِابْنِ أَبِي شَيْبَةَ: فَضْلُ ثَمَانِيَةِ أَنْوَارٍ عَلَى نُورِ الشُّهَدَاءِ) وَكَانَ يَقُولُ لِجَهَنَّمَ سَبْعَةُ أَبْوَابٍ ثَلَاثَةٌ مِنْهَا لِلْحَرُورِيَّةِ.

> 'The martyr has a light, and the one who fights against the Ḥarūriyya [i.e., Kharijites] shall have ten lights [and in another narration in Ibn Abī Shayba's *Muṣannaf*, "eight lights in addition to the light of the martyr"].' ʿAbd Allāh said, 'He [Kaʿb] used to say that the Hellfire has seven gates, three of which are reserved for the Ḥarūriyya [i.e., Kharijites]'.[2]

---

[1] Narrated by Aḥmad b. Ḥanbal in *al-Musnad*, 5:36 §44; al-Ḥākim in *al-Mustadrak*, 2:159 §2645; Ibn Abī ʿĀṣim in *al-Sunna*, 2:456 §937; and ʿAbd Allāh b. Aḥmad in *al-Sunna*, 2:637 §1519. The transmitters in Aḥmad's tradition are sound. Ibn Abī ʿĀṣim and al-Ḥākim also declared it a sound tradition.

[2] Narrated by ʿAbd al-Razzāq in *al-Muṣannaf*, 10:155; and Ibn Abī Shayba in *al-Muṣannaf*, 7:557 §37911.

15.5 A Comprehensive Description of the Kharijites and Their Signs

If we gather all of hadith reports and statements of the Companions and scholars concerning the Kharijites, we can develop a composite image and comprehensive description of them.

1. أَحْدَاثُ الْأَسْنَانِ.

They will be young in age.[1]

2. سُفَهَاءُ الْأَحْلَامِ.

They will be brainwashed.[2]

3. كَثُّ اللِّحْيَةِ.

They will have thick, unkempt beards.[3]

4. مُشَمِّرُ الْإِزَارِ.

They will wear their lower garments high upon their legs.[4]

5. يَخْرُجُ نَاسٌ مِنْ قِبَلِ الْمَشْرِقِ.

They will emerge from the east [of sanctuaries].[5]

---

[1] Narrated by al-Bukhārī in *al-Ṣaḥīḥ*: *Kitāb istitāba al-murtaddīn wa al-muʿānidīn wa qitālihim* [The Book on Demanding the Repentance of the Apostates and Reprobates, and Fighting Them], chapter: 'On Fighting the Kharijites and the Heretics after Establishing the Evidence against Them', 6:2539 §6531; and Muslim in *al-Ṣaḥīḥ*: *Kitāb al-Zakāt* [The Book of Zakat], chapter: 'The Encouragement to Kill the Kharijites', 2:746 §1066.

[2] Ibid.

[3] Narrated by al-Bukhārī in *al-Ṣaḥīḥ*: *Kitāb al-maghāzī* [The Book of Military Expeditions], chapter: 'The Dispatch of ʿAlī b. Abī Ṭālib and Khālid b. al-Walīd to Yemen before the Farewell Pilgrimage', 4:1581 §4094; and Muslim in *al-Ṣaḥīḥ*: *Kitāb al-Zakāt* [The Book of Zakat], Chapter: 'On the Kharijites and their Qualities', 2:742 §1064.

[4] Ibid.

[5] Narrated by al-Bukhārī in *al-Ṣaḥīḥ*: *Kitāb al-tawḥīd* [The Book of Divine

6. لَا يَزَالُوْنَ يَخْرُجُوْنَ حَتَّى يَخْرُجَ آخِرُهُمْ مَعَ الْمَسِيْحِ الدَّجَّالِ.

They will continue to appear until the last of them appears with the Anti-Christ [which implies that they will continue to emerge in every generation].[1]

7. لاَ يُجَاوِزُ إِيْمَانُهُمْ حَنَاجِرَهُمْ.

Their faith will not pass their throats [which implies that their faith is shallow and skin-deep, and that the qualities of true faith will not be visible from their conduct].[2]

8. يَتَعَمَّقُوْنَ وَيَتَشَدَّدُوْنَ فِي الدِّيْنِ.

They will be extremists in religious matters.[3]

9. يَحْقِرُ أَحَدُكُمْ صَلَاتَهُ مَعَ صَلَاتِهِمْ وَصِيَامَهُ مَعَ صِيَامِهِمْ.

The believer will consider his own prayers and fasting insignificant in comparison to theirs [i.e., Kharijites].[4]

Unity], chapter: 'The Recitation, Articulation and Reading of the Reprobate and Hypocrite [Reading the Qur'ān] Does Not Pass Beyond Their Throats', 6:2748 §7123.

[1] Narrated by al-Nasā'ī in *al-Sunan*: *Kitāb taḥrīm al-dam* [The Book on the Prohibition of Bloodshed], chapter: 'Regarding the One Who Unsheathes His Sword and Wields it amongst People', 7:119 §4103.

[2] Narrated by al-Bukhārī in *al-Ṣaḥīḥ*: *Kitāb istitāba al-murtaddīn wa al-muʿānidīn wa qitālihim* [The Book on Demanding the Repentance of the Apostates and Reprobates, and Fighting Them], chapter: 'On Killing the Kharijites and the Heretics after Establishing the Evidence against Them', 6:2539 §6531; Muslim in *al-Ṣaḥīḥ*: *Kitāb al-Zakāt* [The Book of Zakat], chapter: 'The Encouragement to Kill the Kharijites', 2:746 §1066.

[3] Narrated by Abū Yaʿlā in *al-Musnad*, 1:90 §90; and ʿAbd al-Razzāq in *al-Muṣannaf*, 10:155 §18673.

[4] Narrated by al-Bukhārī in *al-Ṣaḥīḥ*: *Kitāb al-adab* [The Book of Good Manners], chapter: 'What Has Come to Us About Someone Saying, "Woe to you!"', 5:2281 §5811, and *Kitāb istitāba al-murtaddīn wa al-muʿānidīn wa qitālihim* [The Book on Demanding the Repentance of the Apostates and Reprobates, and Fighting Them], chapter: 'On the One Who Refrains from Fighting the Kharijites for the Sake of Drawing Hearts Near and so People Will

10. لاَ تُجَاوِزُ صَلَاتُهُمْ تَرَاقِيَهُمْ.

Their prayers will not pass their throats [which implies that their prayers will not leave any effect upon their character or conduct].[1]

11. يَقْرَءُوْنَ الْقُرْآنَ لَيْسَ قِرَاءَتُكُمْ إِلَى قِرَاءَتِهِمْ بِشَيْءٍ.

They will recite the Qur'ān but the believers' recitation will not resemble theirs.[2]

12. يَقْرَءُوْنَ الْقُرْآنَ لَا يُجَاوِزُ حُلُوْقَهُمْ.

They shall recite the Qur'ān but it will not pass their throats [which implies that it will have no effect upon their hearts].[3]

13. يَقْرَءُوْنَ الْقُرْآنَ يَحْسَبُوْنَ أَنَّهُ لَهُمْ، وَهُوَ عَلَيْهِمْ.

They shall quote the Qur'ān believing that it is for them although in reality it is against them.[4]

14. يَدْعُوْنَ إِلَى كِتَابِ اللهِ وَلَيْسُوْا مِنْهُ فِي شَيْءٍ.

They will apparently invite the people to God's Book

Not Flee', 6:2540 §6534; and Muslim in *al-Ṣaḥīḥ*: *Kitāb al-Zakāt* [The Book of Zakat], chapter: 'On the Kharijites and Their Qualities', 2:744 §1064.

[1] Narrated by Muslim in *al-Ṣaḥīḥ*: *Kitāb al-Zakāt* [The Book of Zakat], chapter: 'The Encouragement to Kill the Kharijites', 2:748 §1066.

[2] Ibid.

[3] Narrated by al-Bukhārī in *al-Ṣaḥīḥ*: *Kitāb istitāba al-murtaddīn wa al-muʿānidīn wa qitālihim* [The Book on Demanding the Repentance of the Apostates and Reprobates, and Fighting Them], chapter: 'On Killing the Kharijites and Heretics after Establishing the Evidence against Them', 6:2540 §6532; and Muslim in *al-Ṣaḥīḥ: Kitāb al-Zakāt* [The Book of Zakat], chapter: 'On the Kharijites and Their Qualities', 2:743 §1064.

[4] Narrated by Muslim in *al-Ṣaḥīḥ*: *Kitāb al-Zakāt* [The Book of Zakat], chapter: 'The Encouragement to Kill the Kharijites', 2:748 §1066.

although they have nothing to do with it.[1]

15. يَقُوْلُوْنَ مِنْ قَوْلِ خَيْرِ الْبَرِيَّةِ.

They will speak the words of the best of people [which implies that they will raise religious slogans and make Islamic demands].[2]

16. يَقُوْلُوْنَ مِنْ أَحْسَنِ النَّاسِ قَوْلاً.

Their slogans and pretentious talks will be better than others' and moving.[3]

17. يُسِيْئُوْنَ الْفِعْلَ.

They will be extremely oppressive, blood-thirsty and violent.[4]

18. هُمْ شَرُّ الْخَلْقِ وَالْخَلِيقَةِ.

They will be the most evil of the creation.[5]

19. يَطْعَنُوْنَ عَلَى أُمَرَائِهِمْ وَيَشْهَدُوْنَ عَلَيْهِمْ بِالضَّلَالَةِ.

They will defame their rulers and charge them with misguidance.[6]

---

[1] Narrated by Abū Dāwūd in *al-Sunan*: *Kitāb al-Sunna* [The Book of the Sunna], chapter: 'On Fighting the Kharijites', 4:243 §4765.

[2] Narrated by al-Bukhārī in *al-Ṣaḥīḥ*: *Kitāb istitāba al-murtaddīn wa al-muʿānidīn wa qitālihim* [The Book on Demanding the Repentance of the Apostates and Reprobates, and Fighting Them], chapter: 'On Fighting the Kharijites and the Heretics after Establishing the Evidence against Them', 6:2539 §6531; and Muslim in *al-Ṣaḥīḥ*: *Kitāb al-Zakāt* [The Book of Zakat], chapter: 'The Encouragement to Kill the Kharijites', 2:746 §1066.

[3] Narrated by al-Ṭabarānī in *al-Muʿjam al-awsaṭ*, 6:186 §6142.

[4] Narrated by Abū Dāwūd in *al-Sunan*: *Kitāb al-Sunna* [The Book of the Sunna], chapter: 'On Killing the Kharijites', 4:243 §4765.

[5] Narrated by Muslim in *al-Ṣaḥīḥ: Kitāb al-Zakāt* [The Book of Zakat], chapter: 'The Kharijites Are the Most Evil of Creation', 2:750 §1067.

[6] Narrated by Ibn Abū ʿĀṣim in *al-Sunna*, 2:455 §934; and al-Haythamī in

20. يَخْرُجُوْنَ عَلَى حِيْنِ فُرْقَةٍ مِّنَ النَّاسِ.

They will appear during a time in which there is disunity.[1]

21. يَسْفِكُوْنَ الدَّمَ الْحَرَامَ.

They will shed blood that is inviolable [which implies that they will believe it is permissible to kill Muslims and non-Muslims].[2]

22. يَقْطَعُونَ السَّبِيْلَ وَيَسْفِكُوْنَ الدِّمَاءَ بِغَيْرِ حَقٍّ مِّنَ اللهِ وَيَسْتَحِلُّونَ أَهْلَ الذِّمَّةِ (من كلام عائشة ﵂).

They will block the roads, shed blood without any authorization from God, and they will declare lawful the blood of the non-Muslim citizens [taken from the words of ʿĀʾisha ﵂].[3]

23. يُؤْمِنُوْنَ بِمُحْكَمِهِ وَيَهْلِكُوْنَ عِنْدَ مُتَشَابِهِهِ (قول ابن عباس ﵄).

They will believe in the clear-cut verses of the Qurʾān but fall into destruction when it comes to their interpretation of the ambiguous verses [taken from the words of Ibn ʿAbbās ﵄].[4]

24. يَقُوْلُوْنَ الْحَقَّ بِأَلْسِنَتِهِمْ لَا يُجَاوِزُ حُلُوقَهُمْ (قول علي ﵁).

They will make truthful demands with their tongues but

Majmaʿ al-Zawāʾid, 6:228. And he said that its transmitters are those of a sound tradition.

[1] Narrated by al-Bukhārī in *al-Ṣaḥīḥ: Kitāb al-Manāqib* [The Book of Virtues], chapter: 'The Signs of Prophethood in Islam', 3:1321 §3414; and Muslim in *al-Ṣaḥīḥ: al-Zakāt* [The Alms-due], chapter: Discussion of the Kharijites and their Qualities, 2:744 §1064.

[2] Narrated by Muslim in *al-Ṣaḥīḥ*: *Kitāb al-Zakāt* [The Book of Zakat], chapter: 'The Encouragement to Kill the Kharijites', 2:748 §1066.

[3] Narrated by al-Ḥākim in *al-Mustadrak*, 2:166 §2657.

[4] Narrated by al-Ṭabarī in *Jāmiʿ al-Bayān fī Tafsīr al-Qurʾān*, 3:181; and al-ʿAsqalānī, *Fatḥ al-Bārī*, 12:300.

they will not pass beyond their throats [taken from the words of ʿAlī ﷺ].[1]

25. يَنْطَلِقُوْنَ إِلَى آيَاتٍ نَزَلَتْ فِي الْكُفَّارِ فَيَجْعَلُوْهَا عَلَى الْمُؤْمِنِيْنَ (من قول ابن عمر ﷺ).

They will take the verses revealed about the disbelievers and apply them to the believers [taken from the words of Ibn ʿUmar ﷺ].[2]

26. يَمْرُقُوْنَ مِنَ الدِّيْنِ كَما يَمْرُقُ السَّهْمُ مِنَ الرَّمِيَّةِ.

They shall pass through the religion just as an arrow passes through a hunted game.[3]

27. اَلْأَجْرُ الْعَظِيْمُ لِمَنْ قَتَلَهُمْ.

Those who fight against them will earn a great reward.[4]

28. خَيْرُ قَتْلَى مَنْ قَتَلُوْهُ.

The one who is killed by them is the best person killed.[5]

---

[1] Narrated by Muslim in *al-Ṣaḥīḥ*: *Kitāb al-Zakāt* [The Book of Zakat], chapter: 'The Encouragement to Kill the Kharijites', 2:749 §1066.

[2] Narrated by al-Bukhārī in *al-Ṣaḥīḥ*: *Kitāb istitāba al-murtaddīn wa al-muʿānidīn wa qitālihim* [The Book on Demanding the Repentance of the Apostates and Reprobates, and Fighting Them], chapter: 'On Killing the Kharijites and the Heretics after Establishing the Evidence against Them', 6:2539.

[3] Narrated by al-Bukhārī in *al-Ṣaḥīḥ*: *Kitāb istitāba al-murtaddīn wa al-muʿānidīn wa qitālihim* [The Book on Demanding the Repentance of the Apostates and Reprobates, and Fighting Them], chapter: 'On Fighting the Kharijites and the Heretics after Establishing the Evidence against Them', 6:2539 §6531; and Muslim in *al-Ṣaḥīḥ*: *Kitāb al-Zakāt* [The Book of Zakat], chapter: 'The Encouragement to Kill the Kharijites', 2:746 §1066.

[4] Narrated by Muslim in *al-Ṣaḥīḥ*: *Kitāb al-Zakāt* [The Book of Zakat], chapter: 'The Encouragement to Kill the Kharijites', 2:748 §1066.

[5] Narrated by al-Tirmidhī in *al-Sunan*: *Kitāb tafsīr al-Qurʾān* [The Book of Qurʾānic Exegesis], chapter: 'From *Sūra Āl ʿImrān*', 5:226 §3000.

29. شَرُّ قَتْلَى تَحْتَ أَدِيْمِ السَّمَاءِ.

They are the worst of those slain under the heavens.[1]

30. إِنَّهُمْ كِلاَبُ النَّارِ.

They would be made the dogs of Hell [in the Hereafter].[2]

31. They will declare it obligatory to wage armed rebellion against an oppressive and corrupt government.[3]
32. They will declare that the one who commits a major sin is a disbeliever.
33. They will declare lawful the blood and wealth of someone who commits a major sin.
34. They will seize a particular area and make it a centre of terrorist activity—as they did when they took Ḥarūrā as their base.
35. They will reject negotiations with the people [their opponents].

---

[1] Ibid.

[2] Ibid.

[3] Narrated by ʿAbd al-Qāhir al-Baghdādī, *al-Farq bayn al-firaq*, p. 73; and Ibn Taymiyya, *Majmūʿa al-fatāwā*, 13:31.

Chapter 16

Mention of the Imams Who Charged the Kharijites with Disbelief and Ordered Their Elimination

THE SCHOLARS HAVE TWO DIFFERENT OPINIONS ABOUT CHARGING THE Kharijites with disbelief, but there is no difference of opinion about fighting them, for the Prophet ﷺ has given clear instructions in this regard that no Muslim can oppose. The authority to eliminate the Kharijites is taken from his many statements, such as: 'If I were to encounter them, I would slay them like the people of Thamūd', and 'Kill them wherever you find them', and so on. This was understood by the hadith scholars who worded their chapter headings accordingly. Imam al-Bukhārī penned one chapter of his collection, 'On Fighting the Kharijites and the Heretics after Establishing the Evidence against Them'. In his *al-Ṣaḥīḥ*, Imam Muslim penned one chapter named, 'The Encouragement to Kill the Kharijites'. In his commentary, al-Nawawī stated:

> قَوْلُهُ ﷺ: فَإِذَا لَقِيْتُمُوهُمْ فَاقْتُلُوهُمْ، فَإِنَّ فِي قَتْلِهِمْ أَجْرًا. هَذَا تَصْرِيْحٌ بِوُجُوبِ قِتَالِ الْخَوَارِجِ وَالْبُغَاةِ، وَهُوَ إِجْمَاعُ الْعُلَمَاءِ. قَالَ الْقَاضِي: أَجْمَعَ الْعُلَمَاءُ عَلَى أَنَّ الْخَوَارِجَ وَأَشْبَاهَهُمْ مِنْ أَهْلِ الْبِدَعِ وَالْبَغْيِ مَتَى خَرَجُوا عَلَى الْإِمَامِ، وَخَالَفُوا رَأْيَ الْجَمَاعَةِ، وَشَقُّوا الْعَصَا، وَجَبَ قِتَالُهُمْ بَعْدَ إِنْذَارِهِمْ وَالْإِعْتِذَارِ إِلَيْهِمْ. وَهَذَا كُلُّهُ مَا لَمْ يُكَفِّرُوا بِبِدْعَتِهِمْ، فَإِنْ كَانَتِ الْبِدْعَةُ مِمَّا يُكَفَّرُونَ بِهِ جَرَتْ عَلَيْهِمْ أَحْكَامُ الْمُرْتَدِّيْنَ، وَأَمَّا الْبُغَاةُ الَّذِيْنَ لَا يُكَفَّرُونَ فَيَرِثُونَ وَيُورَثُونَ وَدَمُهُمْ فِي حَالِ الْقِتَالِ هَدْرٌ، وَكَذَا أَمْوَالُهُمُ الَّتِي تُتْلَفُ فِي الْقِتَالِ.

> The Prophet's statement ﷺ, 'Kill them wherever you find them, for the one who kills them will be rewarded [on the Day of Resurrection]', is an explicit declaration of the obligation to fight the Kharijites and rebels, and this is the consensus of the scholars. Qāḍī [Abū Bakr b. al-ʿArabī] said, 'The scholars have unanimously agreed that when the Kharijites and their ilk from the people of blameworthy innovation and rebellion revolt against the view of the community [*jamāʿa*], split the unity [of

the Muslims] and take up arms, it is obligatory to fight them after exhorting them and warning them'. Now, that applies so long as their innovation does not entail disbelief. If their innovation is one that makes them disbelievers, then the rules that pertain to apostates are applied to them. As for the rebels who do not disbelieve, they may inherit and others may inherit from them, although during times of fighting their blood is lawful, as is their wealth that is destroyed during the fighting.[1]

Qāḍī ʿIyāḍ said in *al-Shifā*:

وَاخْتَلَفَ قَوْلُ مَالِكٍ وَأَصْحَابِهِ فِي ذَلِكَ، وَلَمْ يَخْتَلِفُوا فِي قِتَالِهِمْ إِذَا تَحَيَّزُوا فِئَةً، وَأَنَّهُمْ يُسْتَتَابُونَ، فَإِنْ تَابُوا وَإِلَّا قُتِلُوا، وَإِنَّمَا اخْتَلَفُوا فِي الْمُنْفَرِدِ مِنْهُمْ. وَهَذَا قَوْلُ مُحَمَّدِ بْنِ الْمَوَّازِ فِي الْخَوَارِجِ، وَعَبْدِ الْمَلِكِ بْنِ الْمَاجِشُونِ، وَقَوْلُ سُحْنُونٍ، وَبِهِ فُسِّرَ قَوْلُ مَالِكٍ فِي الْمُوَطَّإِ، وَمَا رَوَاهُ عَنْ عُمَرَ بْنِ عَبْدِ الْعَزِيزِ: يُسْتَتَابُونَ، فَإِنْ تَابُوا وَإِلَّا قُتِلُوا. وَقَالَ عِيسَى، عَنِ ابْنِ الْقَاسِمِ: فَإِنْ تَابُوا وَإِلَّا قُتِلُوا، وَمِثْلُهُ لَهُ فِي الْمَبْسُوطِ، قَالَ: وَهُمْ مُسْلِمُونَ، وَإِنَّمَا قُتِلُوا لِرَأْيِهِمُ السُّوءِ، وَبِهَذَا عَمِلَ عُمَرُ بْنُ عَبْدِ الْعَزِيزِ. وَابْنُ حَبِيبٍ، وَغَيْرُهُ مِنْ أَصْحَابِنَا يَرَى تَكْفِيرَهُمْ.

وَقَوْلُهُ ﷺ فِي الْخَوَارِجِ: هُمْ مِنْ شَرِّ الْبَرِيَّةِ، وَهَذِهِ صِفَةُ الْكُفَّارِ. وَقَالَ ﷺ: شَرُّ قَبِيلٍ تَحْتَ أَدِيْمِ السَّمَاءِ، طُوبَى لِمَنْ قَتَلَهُمْ أَوْ قَتَلُوهُ. وَقَالَ: فَإِذَا وَجَدْتُمُوهُمْ فَاقْتُلُوهُمْ قَتْلَ عَادٍ. وَظَاهِرُ هَذَا الْكُفْرُ لَاسِيَّمَا مَعَ تَشْبِيْهِهِمْ بِعَادٍ، فَيَحْتَجُّ بِهِ مَنْ يَرَى تَكْفِيرَهُمْ، فَيَقُولُ لَهُ الْآخَرُ: إِنَّمَا ذَلِكَ مِنْ قَتْلِهِمْ لِخُرُوجِهِمْ عَلَى الْمُسْلِمِيْنَ، وَبَغْيِهِمْ عَلَيْهِمْ بِدَلِيْلِهِ مِنَ الْحَدِيْثِ نَفْسِهِ: يَقْتُلُونَ أَهْلَ الْإِسْلَامِ، فَقَتْلُهُمْ هَاهُنَا حَدٌّ لَا كُفْرٌ. وَذِكْرُ عَادٍ تَشْبِيْهٌ لِلْقَتْلِ وَحِلِّهِ، لَا لِلْمَقْتُولِ، وَلَيْسَ كُلُّ مَنْ حُكِمَ بِقَتْلِهِ يُحْكَمُ بِكُفْرِهِ. وَكَذَلِكَ قَوْلُهُ ﷺ: يَمْرُقُونَ مِنَ الدِّيْنِ مُرُوقَ السَّهْمِ مِنَ الرَّمِيَّةِ، ثُمَّ لَا يَعُودُونَ إِلَيْهِ حَتَّى يَعُودَ السَّهْمُ عَلَى فُوقِهِ. وَبِقَوْلِهِ: سَبَقَ الْفَرْثَ وَالدَّمَ يَدُلُّ عَلَى أَنَّهُ لَمْ يَتَعَلَّقْ مِنَ الْإِسْلَامِ بِشَيْءٍ.

[1] Al-Nawawī, *Sharḥ Ṣaḥīḥ Muslim*, 7:169–170.

The view of Mālik and his companions regarding the Kharijites varies concerning this, but they did not disagree about killing those who do this if they form a separate group. Repentance should be sought from them, and if they repent [well and good], otherwise they are to be killed. They only disagreed about an isolated individual who does this. . . . This is what Muhammad b. al-Mawwāz, ʿAbd al-Mālik b. Mājishūn and Imam Saḥnūn said concerning the Kharijites. The statement of Mālik in his *al-Muwaṭṭā* and the report narrated from ʿUmar b. ʿAbd al-ʿAzīz explains,[1] 'Repentance is to be sought from them. If they repent [well and good], otherwise they are to be killed'. Imam ʿĪsā narrates from Imam Ibn al-Qāsim, 'If they repent [well and good], otherwise they should be killed'. Something similar was mentioned in *al-Mabsūṭ*. He said, 'They are Muslims, but should be killed for their evil opinion'. This was the practice of ʿUmar b. ʿAbd al-ʿAzīz. On the other hand, Ibn Ḥabīb and others amongst our companions [in the Mālikī legal school] saw that they should be charged with disbelief.

[. . .] The Prophet ﷺ called the Kharijites 'the most evil of creation', and this is the quality of the disbelievers. He ﷺ also said, 'They are the most evil group under the heavens. Glad tidings to the one who kills them or the one killed by them'. He ﷺ also said, 'So wherever you find them, slay them [through an operation] like the people of ʿĀd'. The apparent meaning of these statements is that they are disbelievers—especially in the light of their comparison to the people of ʿĀd. Those who believe that they should be charged with disbelief infer their position from this hadith. Those who adopt the opposing viewpoint retort, 'That is only due to their having gone out against the Muslims and transgressed against them. This is indicated in the hadith itself: "They will kill the people

[1] An early sect that believed in absolute free will and that man is the creator of his own acts. ED.

of Islam. . . ." So their killing is a prescribed punishment and not because of their alleged disbelief. The mention of the people of ʿĀd is a simile which signifies killing them and its lawfulness, not the state of the one killed. Not everyone given a death sentence is charged with disbelief'. Furthermore [those who believe that the Kharijites are disbelievers infer their view] from the hadith, 'They shall pass through the religion just as an arrow passes through a hunted game, never to return until an arrow returns to its bowstring', and his saying, 'It [the arrow] went too fast to be smeared with dung and blood', which indicates that he had no connection with Islam at all.[1]

16.1 THE TWO POSITIONS OF THE IMAMS ON THE DISBELIEF OF THE KHARIJITES

The Imams of hadith, jurisprudence and Quranic exegesis have generally presented two positions regarding the disbelief of the Kharijites. Ibn Taymiyya said:

إِنَّ الْأُمَّةَ مُتَّفِقُونَ عَلَى ذَمِّ الْخَوَارِجِ وَتَضْلِيْلِهِمْ، وَإِنَّمَا تَنَازَعُوا فِي تَكْفِيْرِهِمْ عَلَى قَوْلَيْنِ مَشْهُورَيْنِ، فِي مَذْهَبِ مَالِكٍ وَأَحْمَدَ، وَفِي مَذْهَبِ الشَّافِعِيِّ أَيْضًا نِزَاعٌ فِي كُفْرِهِمْ وَلِهَذَا كَانَ فِيْهِمْ قَوْلَانِ. أَحَدُهُمَا: أَنَّهُمْ كُفَّارٌ كَالْمُرْتَدِّيْنَ، وَمَنْ قُدِرَ عَلَيْهِ مِنْهُمْ أُسْتُتِيْبَ فَإِنْ تَابَ وَإِلَّا قُتِلَ. وَالثَّانِي: أَنَّهُمْ بُغَاةٌ (وَلَا خِلَافَ فِي جَوَازِ قَتْلِهِمْ كَمَا ذُكِرَ مِنْ قَبْلُ).

The *Umma* is unanimous in its condemnation of the Kharijites and in declaring them misguided; their only contention was regarding whether they are charged with disbelief [or not]. There are two well-known opinions in the legal school of Mālik and Aḥmad concerning this, and there is also dispute about their disbelief in the legal school of al-Shāfiʿī. For this reason, there are two opinions regarding them: [One] that they are disbelievers

[1] Qāḍī ʿIyāḍ, *al-Shifā*, pp. 842–843.

like apostates, and that repentance is to be sought from whomever amongst them is apprehended; and if he repents [well and good], otherwise he is to be killed. [Two] that they are rebels (as was mentioned earlier; there is no disagreement that it is permissible to kill them).[1]

16.2 The First Position: The Kharijites Are Disbelievers

A large group of scholars took the position that the Kharijites are disbelievers. They inferred their belief from numerous prophetic traditions about the Kharijites, most of which we have mentioned earlier, such as the Prophet's statement ﷺ,

سَيَخْرُجُ قَوْمٌ فِي آخِرِ الزَّمَانِ. أَحْدَاثُ الْأَسْنَانِ، سُفَهَاءُ الْأَحْلَامِ. يَقُولُونَ مِنْ خَيْرِ قَوْلِ الْبَرِيَّةِ. لَا يُجَاوِزُ إِيْمَانُهُمْ حَنَاجِرَهُمْ. يَمْرُقُونَ مِنَ الدِّيْنِ كَمَا يَمْرُقُ السَّهْمُ مِنَ الرَّمِيَّةِ، فَأَيْنَمَا لَقِيْتُمُوهُمْ فَاقْتُلُوهُمْ، فَإِنَّ فِي قَتْلِهِمْ أَجْرًا لِمَنْ قَتَلَهُمْ يَوْمَ الْقِيَامَةِ.

'At the end of time there shall appear a folk, young in age and foolish. They will speak the words of the best of people, but they shall pass through Islam just as an arrow passes through a hunted game. Wherever you encounter them, kill them [following the legal procedure], for killing them will be rewarded [by God] on the Day of Resurrection'.[2]

Here, the prophetic command to kill them and the mention of Divine reward establish that the Kharijites are disbelievers. Another proof for this position is the narration of Sufyān b. ʿUyayna who reported from Abū Ghālib that Abū Umāma ؓ said,

---

[1] Ibn Taymiyya, *Majmūʿā al-fatāwā*, 28:518.

[2] Narrated by al-Bukhārī in *al-Ṣaḥīḥ*: *Kitāb istitāba al-murtaddīn wa al-muʿānidīn wa qitālihim* [The Book on Demanding the Repentance of the Apostates and Reprobates, and Fighting Them], chapter: 'On Fighting the Kharijites and the Heretics after Establishing the Evidence against Them', 6:2539 §6531; Muslim in *al-Ṣaḥīḥ*: *Kitāb al-Zakāt* [The Book of Zakat], chapter: 'The Encouragement to Kill the Kharijites', 2:746 §1066; and al-Tirmidhī in *al-Sunan*: *Kitāb al-fitan* [The Book of Tribulations], chapter: 'Concerning the Trait of Renegades [*al-māriqa*]', 4:481 §2188.

شَرُّ قَتْلَى قُتِلُوا تَحْتَ أَدِيْمِ السَّمَاءِ، وَخَيْرُ قَتِيْلٍ مَنْ قَتَلُوا. كِلَابُ أَهْلِ النَّارِ، قَدْ كَانَ هَؤُلَاءِ مُسْلِمِيْنَ فَصَارُوا كُفَّارًا.

'They are the most evil of those slain under the heavens, and the best of those killed is the one whom they kill. They are the dogs of Hell; they were Muslims and then [due to rebellion and revolt] became disbelievers'.[1]

This narration is explicit, for it states that the Kharijites were previously Muslims, and then became disbelievers due to their self-made false beliefs.

16.2.1 Imam al-Bukhārī's Position

The great scholar of hadith, Imam al-Bukhārī, penned a chapter in his *Ṣaḥīḥ* collection in which he sought to prove that the Kharijites are disbelievers. Ibn Ḥajar al-ʿAsqalānī commented:

جُمْلَةٌ مِنَ الْعُلَمَاءِ الَّذِيْنَ قَالُوا بِتَكْفِيْرِ الْخَوَارِجِ كَالْبُخَارِيِّ، حَيْثُ قَرَنَهُمْ بِالْمُرْتَدِّيْنَ وَأَفْرَدَ عَنْهُمُ الْمُتَأَوِّلِيْنَ بِتَرْجَمَةٍ قَالَ فِيْهِ: بَابُ مَنْ تَرَكَ قِتَالَ الْخَوَارِجِ لِلتَّأَلُّفِ وَلِئَلَّا يَنْفِرَ النَّاسُ عَنْهُ.

A large body of scholars said that the Kharijites are to be charged with disbelief, such as al-Bukhārī, who compared them to apostates and heretics, and only singled out individuals [amongst them] who were subject to faulty interpretations, mentioning them in a separate chapter: 'On the One Who Refrains from Fighting the Kharijites for the Sake of Drawing Hearts Near and so People Will Not Flee'.[2]

16.2.2 Imam Ibn Jarīr al-Ṭabarī's Position

The early Qurʾānic exegete and historian, Imam al-Ṭabarī, said:

إِنَّهُ لَا يَجُوزُ قِتَالُ الْخَوَارِجِ وَقَتْلُهُمْ إِلَّا بَعْدَ إِقَامَةِ الْحُجَّةِ عَلَيْهِمْ، بِدُعَائِهِمْ إِلَى الرُّجُوعِ

---

[1] Narrated by Ibn Mājah in *al-Sunan:* 'Introduction', section: 'Mention of the Kharijites', 1:62 §176.

[2] Ibn Ḥajar al-ʿAsqalānī, *Fatḥ al-Bārī*, 12:313.

إِلَى الْحَقِّ، وَالْإِعْذَارِ إِلَيْهِمْ، وَإِلَى ذَلِكَ أَشَارَ الْبُخَارِيُّ فِي التَّرْجَمَةِ بِالْآيَةِ الْمَذْكُورَةِ فِيْهَا، وَاسْتَدَلَّ بِهِ لِمَنْ قَالَ بِتَكْفِيرِ الْخَوَارِجِ، وَهُوَ مُقْتَضَى صَنِيعِ الْبُخَارِيِّ، حَيْثُ قَرَنَهُمْ بِالْمُلْحِدِيْنَ، وَأَفْرَدَ عَنْهُمُ الْمُتَأَوِّلِيْنَ بِتَرْجَمَةٍ.

It is impermissible to fight or kill the Kharijites before the evidence is established against them by inviting them to return to the truth and warning them. This was alluded to by al-Bukhārī in his chapter heading in which he mentioned the aforementioned verse. This is the proof used by those who believe that the Kharijites are to be charged with disbelief—and that is the implication of al-Bukhārī's action, for he compared them to heretics and singled out individuals [amongst them] who were subject to faulty interpretations, mentioning them in a separate chapter.[1]

Ibn Ḥajar al-ʿAsqalānī explained al-Ṭabarī's viewpoint, commenting:

مِمَّنْ جَنَحَ إِلَى بَعْضِ هَذَا الْبَحْثِ: الطَّبَرِيُّ فِي تَهْذِيْبِهِ، فَقَالَ بَعْدَ أَنْ سَرَدَ أَحَادِيْثَ الْبَابِ: فِيْهِ الرَّدُّ عَلَى قَوْلِ مَنْ قَالَ: لَا يَخْرُجُ أَحَدٌ مِنَ الْإِسْلَامِ مِنْ أَهْلِ الْقِبْلَةِ بَعْدَ اسْتِحْقَاقِهِ حُكْمَهُ، إِلَّا بِقَصْدِ الْخُرُوجِ مِنْهُ عَالِمًا، فَإِنَّهُ مُبْطِلٌ لِقَوْلِهِ فِي الْحَدِيْثِ: يَقُولُونَ الْحَقَّ، وَيَقْرَؤُونَ الْقُرْآنَ، وَيَمْرُقُونَ مِنَ الْإِسْلَامِ، وَلَا يَتَعَلَّقُونَ مِنْهُ بِشَيْءٍ.

Al-Ṭabarī was of those who inclined to some of the views presented here. He said in *al-Tahdhīb*, after having mentioned some of the same hadith in this chapter: 'This is a refutation of those who said that no one can leave the fold of Islam from the people of the *qibla*, after its ruling is established for him, except with his full knowledge and intent. This contradicts [the Prophet's] saying in the hadith, "They will speak the truth and recite the Qurʾān, but they will exit from Islam and grasp nothing of it".'[2]

---

[1] Ibid., 12:299.

[2] Ibid., 12:300.

16.2.3 Imam Abū Ḥāmid al-Ghazālī's Position

The Proof of Islam, Imam Abū Ḥāmid al-Ghazālī, held that the Kharijites are disbelievers. Ibn Ḥajar al-ʿAsqalānī said,

قَالَ الْغَزَالِيُّ فِي "الْوَسِيْطِ": تَبْعًا لِغَيْرِهِ فِي حُكْمِ الْخَوَارِجِ وَجْهَانِ، أَحَدُهُمَا: أَنَّهُ كَحُكْمِ أَهْلِ الرِّدَّةِ، وَالثَّانِي: أَنَّهُ كَحُكْمِ أَهْلِ الْبَغْيِ، وَرَجَّحَ الرَّافِعِيُّ الْأَوَّلَ.

'In *al-Wasīṭ*, al-Ghazālī said (following others): There are two positions regarding the judgment on Kharijites: "They take the ruling of apostates or the ruling of rebels", and al-Rāfiʿī declared the first view preponderant'.[1]

16.2.4 Al-Qāḍī Abū Bakr Ibn al-ʿArabī's Position

Al-Qāḍī Abū Bakr Muhammad b. ʿAbd Allāh b. al-ʿArabī al-Mālikī is considered one of the most prominent Islamic scholars of Andalusia. He obtained his learning from eminent scholars like Imam al-Ghazālī and wrote *ʿĀriḍat al-aḥwadhī*, a magisterial commentary on al-Tirmidhī's collection. Ibn Ḥajar mentioned that he also believed that the Kharijites were disbelievers:

بِذَلِكَ صَرَّحَ الْقَاضِي أَبُو بَكْرِ بْنُ الْعَرَبِيِّ فِي شَرْحِ التِّرْمِذِيِّ فَقَالَ: اَلصَّحِيْحُ أَنَّهُمْ كُفَّارٌ لِقَوْلِهِ ﷺ: يَمْرُقُونَ مِنَ الْإِسْلَامِ وَلِقَوْلِهِ: لَأَقْتُلَنَّهُمْ قَتْلَ عَادٍ، وَفِي لَفْظٍ: قَتْلَ ثَمُودَ، وَكُلٌّ مِنْهُمَا إِنَّمَا هَلَكَ بِالْكُفْرِ، وَبِقَوْلِهِ: هُمْ شَرُّ الْخَلْقِ وَلَا يُوصَفُ بِذَلِكَ إِلَّا الْكُفَّارُ، وَلِقَوْلِهِ: إِنَّهُمْ أَبْغَضُ الْخَلْقِ إِلَى اللهِ تَعَالَى، وَلِحُكْمِهِمْ عَلَى كُلِّ مَنْ خَالَفَ مُعْتَقَدَهُمْ بِالْكُفْرِ وَالتَّخْلِيْدِ فِي النَّارِ، فَكَانُوا هُمْ أَحَقَّ بِالْإِسْمِ مِنْهُمْ.

This was explicitly stated by al-Qāḍī Abū Bakr b. al-ʿArabī in his commentary on al-Tirmidhī's [collection]. He said, 'The correct position is that they are disbelievers, due to the Prophet's statements ﷺ, "They shall pass through Islam" and "I would slay them like the people of ʿĀd", and in another wording, "like the people of Thamūd". Both ʿĀd and Thamūd were destroyed because of disbelief. The Prophet ﷺ also said, "They are the worst

[1] Ibn Ḥajar al-ʿAsqalānī, *Fatḥ al-Bārī*, 12:285.

of creation", and none but the disbelievers are described like that. He also said, "They are the most detested of creation in the sight of God Most High". And because they ruled that everyone who opposed their belief was guilty of disbelief and would abide eternally in the Fire, they were more deserving of that than those whom they charged'.[1]

16.2.5 Qāḍī ʿIyāḍ's Position

Qāḍī ʿIyāḍ, the renowned author of *al-Shifā*, one of the most famous and authentic books detailing the exalted rank of the Prophet Muhammad ﷺ, was also of the opinion that the Kharijites are disbelievers. He said in his commentary on *Ṣaḥīḥ Muslim*:

قَالَ بَعْضُ شُيُوخِنَا: قَالَ أَبُو سَعِيْدٍ الْخُدْرِيُّ ﵁: سَمِعْتُ رَسُولَ اللهِ ﷺ يَقُولُ: يَخْرُجُ فِي هَذِهِ الْأُمَّةِ – وَلَمْ يَقُلْ مِنْهَا – قَوْمٌ تَحْقِرُونَ صَلَاتَكُمْ مَعَ صَلَاتِهِمْ. قَالَ الْإِمَامُ (الْمَازِرِيُّ وَنَقَلَهُ النَّوَوِيُّ): هَذَا مِنْ أَدَلِّ الشَّوَاهِدِ عَلَى سَعَةِ فِقْهِ الصَّحَابَةِ ﵃، وَتَحْرِيْرِهِمُ الْأَلْفَاظَ وَفَرْقِهِمْ بَيْنَ مَدْلُولَاتِهَا الْخَفِيَّةِ لِأَنَّ لَفْظَةَ "مِنْ" تَقْتَضِي كَوْنَهُمْ مِنَ الْأُمَّةِ لَا كُفَّارًا بِخِلَافِ "فِي"، وَفِي تَنْبِيْهِ الْخُدْرِيِّ عَلَى التَّفْرِيْقِ بَيْنَ "فِي" وَ "مِنْ" إِشَارَةٌ حَسَنَةٌ إِلَى الْقَوْلِ بِتَكْفِيْرِ الْخَوَارِجِ، لِأَنَّهُ أَفْهَمَ، بِأَنَّهُ لَمَّا لَمْ يَقُلْ مِنْهَا، دَلَّ عَلَى أَنَّهُمْ لَيْسُوا مِنْ أُمَّةِ مُحَمَّدٍ ﷺ، وَإِنْ كَانَ قَدْ رَوَى أَبُو ذَرٍّ بَعْدَ هَذَا فَقَالَ: قَالَ ﷺ: إِنَّ مِنْ بَعْدِي مِنْ أُمَّتِي، أَوْ سَيَكُونُ مِنْ بَعْدِي مِنْ أُمَّتِي الْحَدِيْثُ. وَفِي رِوَايَةِ عَلِيٍّ ﵁: يَخْرُجُ مِنْ أُمَّتِي.

Some of our teachers reported, 'Abū Saʿīd al-Khudrī ﵁ said, "I heard the Messenger of God ﷺ say, 'There shall appear a folk *in* this *Umma*', and he did not say '*from* it', 'and you will belittle your prayers in comparison to theirs. . . .'"' The Imam [al-Māzirī] said [and Imam al-Nawawī has quoted it], 'This is one of the most telling testimonies to the deep understanding of the Companions and their exactitude in words and discrimination between

---

[1] Ibid., 12:299.

> subtle indications. That is because the expression "from" implies that they are from the *Umma* and not disbelievers, contrary to the expression "in". Al-Khudrī's notice regarding the distinction between "from" and "in" is a fine allusion to the view that the Kharijites are to be charged with disbelief, because he explained that since he ﷺ did not say "from the *Umma*", it indicates that they are not from the *Umma* of Muhammad ﷺ—even though Abū Dharr narrated after this statement: "He ﷺ said, 'Indeed there shall be some from my *Umma* after me' or 'There shall be some from my *Umma* after me'." And in the narration of ʿAlī ؓ it reads, "There shall appear from my *Umma*".'[1]

Seeking to reconcile between these two seemingly contradictory narrations, Ibn Ḥajar said, 'This hadith is reconciled with Abū Saʿīd's by stating that the meaning of *Umma* in the hadith of Abū Saʿīd is the *Umma* of Response, and the meaning of *Umma* in the others' narrations is the *Umma* of Invitation'.[2]

It should be kept in mind that the *Umma* of Response is the Muslim *Umma* proper, whereas the *Umma* of Invitation is all of humanity to whom the Prophet ﷺ brought his message, whether they accept it or not. Imam al-Nawawī explained further:

فِيْهِ إِشَارَةٌ مِنْ أَبِي سَعِيْدٍ إِلَى تَكْفِيْرِ الْخَوَارِجِ، وَأَنَّهُمْ مِنْ غَيْرِ هَذِهِ الْأُمَّةِ، وَفِي حَدِيْثِ الْخَوَارِجِ مِنْ أَخْبَارِهِ ﷺ عَنِ الْغُيُوبِ مَا يَعْظُمُ مَوْقِعُهُ، مِنْهَا: إِشَارَتُهُ ﷺ إِلَى مَا يَكُونُ بَعْدَهُ مِنَ اخْتِلَافِ الْأُمَّةِ فِي تَكْفِيْرِهِمْ.

> In this hadith there is an allusion from Abū Saʿid al-Khudrī that the Kharijites are to be charged with disbelief and that they are not from this *Umma*. And the hadith about the Kharijites contains news of the unseen from the Prophet ﷺ regarding momentous events, such as his allusion to the disagreement the *Umma* would have about charging them [the Kharijites] with disbelief.[3]

[1] Qāḍī ʿIyāḍ, *Ikmāl al-muʿlim bi fawāʾid Muslim*, 3:612.

[2] Ibn Ḥajar al-ʿAsqalānī, *Fatḥ al-Bārī*, 12:289.

[3] Ibid.

16.2.6 Imam al-Qurṭubī's Position

Imam Abū al-ʿAbbās Aḥmad b. ʿUmar b. Ibrāhīm al-Anṣārī al-Qurṭubī al-Mālikī was one of the eminent Islamic scholars of Córdoba. Although famous for his Qurʾānic exegesis, he was also the author of an authoritative and oft-quoted commentary on *Ṣaḥīḥ Muslim*. In it, he declared the Kharijites disbelievers.

قَوْلُ الْقَائِلِ فِي قِسْمَةِ النَّبِيِّ ﷺ: "هَذِهِ قِسْمَةٌ مَا أُرِيْدَ بِهَا وَجْهُ اللهِ، أَوْ: مَا عُدِلَ فِيْهَا"، قَوْلُ جَاهِلٍ بِحَالِ النَّبِيِّ ﷺ غَلِيْظِ الطَّبْعِ، حَرِيْصٍ، مُنَافِقٍ. وَكَانَ حَقُّهُ أَنْ يُقْتَلَ؛ لِأَنَّهُ آذَى رَسُولَ اللهِ ﷺ، وَقَدْ قَالَ اللهُ تَعَالَى: ﴿وَٱلَّذِينَ يُؤْذُونَ رَسُولَ ٱللَّهِ لَهُمْ عَذَابٌ أَلِيمٌ﴾. فَالْعَذَابُ فِي الدُّنْيَا هُوَ: الْقَتْلُ، لَكِنْ لَمْ يَقْتُلْهُ النَّبِيُّ ﷺ لِلْمَعْنَى الَّذِي قَالَهُ، وَهُوَ مِنْ حَدِيْثِ جَابِرٍ: لَا يَتَحَدَّثُ النَّاسُ: أَنَّ مُحَمَّدًا يَقْتُلُ أَصْحَابَهُ، وَلِهَذِهِ الْعِلَّةِ امْتَنَعَ النَّبِيُّ ﷺ مِنْ قَتْلِ الْمُنَافِقِيْنَ، مَعَ عِلْمِهِ بِأَعْيَانِ كَثِيْرٍ مِنْهُمْ، وَبِنِفَاقِهِمْ. وَقَدْ أُمِنَتْ تِلْكَ الْعِلَّةُ بَعْدَ رَسُولِ اللهِ ﷺ، فَلَا نِفَاقَ بَعْدَهُ، وَإِنَّمَا هُوَ الزَّنْدَقَةُ، وَهَذَا هُوَ الْحَقُّ وَالصَّوَابُ.

The statement of the one who said when the Prophet ﷺ was apportioning the war booty, 'This apportioning is not for the sake of God', or 'is unjust', is the statement of one ignorant of the Prophet's state ﷺ. It is the statement of one who is coarse in nature, covetous and a hypocrite. He deserved to be put to death because he annoyed the Messenger of God, and God Most High said, '*And those who annoy the Messenger of God will have a painful punishment*'.[1] The punishment in this life is death; however, the Prophet ﷺ did not kill him for the reason mentioned in the hadith of Jābir, 'Lest the people say that Muhammad kills his Companions'. This is the rationale for the Prophet prohibiting the killing of the hypocrites, even though he knew the identities and hypocrisy of many of them. That rationale no longer applies after the

[1] Qurʾān 9:61.

> Messenger of God ﷺ. There is no hypocrisy after him; only heresy—and this is the truth and what is correct.[1]

In the light of the aforementioned Qurʾānic verse, annoying the Messenger of God ﷺ is an act of blasphemy, which some scholars held was enough to charge the Kharijites with disbelief. Elsewhere, al-Qurṭubī said:

> لَئِنْ أَدْرَكْتُهُمْ لَأَقْتُلَنَّهُمْ قَتْلَ عَادٍ، وَفِي الْأُخْرَى: قَتْلَ ثَمُودَ، وَمَعْنَى هَذَا: لَئِنْ أَدْرَكَهُمْ لَيَقْتُلَنَّهُمْ قَتْلًا عَامًّا، بِحَيْثُ لَا يُبْقِي مِنْهُمْ أَحَدًا فِي وَقْتٍ وَاحِدٍ، لَا يُؤَخِّرُ قَتْلَ بَعْضِهِمْ عَنْ بَعْضٍ، وَلَا يُقِيلُ أَحَدًا مِنْهُمْ، كَمَا فَعَلَ اللهُ بِعَادٍ؛ حَيْثُ أَهْلَكَهُمْ بِالرِّيحِ الْعَقِيمِ، وَبِثَمُودَ حَيْثُ أَهْلَكَهُمْ بِالصَّيْحَةِ. قُلْتُ: وَمَقْصُودُ هَذَا التَّمْثِيلِ: أَنَّ هَذِهِ الطَّائِفَةَ خَرَجَتْ مِنْ دِيْنِ الْإِسْلَامِ، وَلَمْ يَتَعَلَّقْ بِهَا مِنْهُ شَيْءٌ، كَمَا خَرَجَ هَذَا السَّهْمُ مِنْ هَذِهِ الْمَرْمِيَّةِ الَّذِي لِشِدَّةِ النَّزْعِ، وَسُرْعَةِ السَّهْمِ، سَبَقَ خُرُوجُهُ خُرُوجَ الدَّمِ، بِحَيْثُ لَا يَتَعَلَّقُ بِهِ شَيْءٌ ظَاهِرٌ، كَمَا قَالَ: سَبَقَ الْفَرْثَ وَالدَّمَ. وَبِظَاهِرِ هَذَا التَّشْبِيْهِ تَمَسَّكَ مَنْ حَكَمَ بِتَكْفِيرِهِمْ مِنْ أَئِمَّتِنَا، وَقَدْ تَوَقَّفَ فِي تَكْفِيرِهِمْ كَثِيْرٌ مِنَ الْعُلَمَاءِ لِقَوْلِهِ ﷺ: فَيَتَمَارَى فِي الْفُوقِ، وَهَذَا يَقْضِي بِأَنَّهُ يَشُكُّ فِي أَمْرِهِمْ فَيَتَوَقَّفُ فِيْهِمْ، وَكَأَنَّ الْقَوْلَ الْأَوَّلَ أَيْ بِالتَّكْفِيرِ، أَظْهَرُ مِنَ الْحَدِيْثَ.

> [The Prophet's ﷺ statement,] 'If I were to encounter them I would slay them like the people of ʿĀd', and in another wording, 'like the people of Thamūd', means that if he were to encounter them he would kill them all, in the sense that not a single one of them would remain at one given time, and none of them would be left for another day—just as God dealt with ʿĀd, destroying them with a grievous wind, and destroying Thamūd with the dreadful shriek. I say: The intent behind this simile is that this group has left the religion of Islam and are not connected with it in any way, just as this arrow exited from that hunted game which, due to the severity of its draw and its speed, exited [the body] before blood came out and

[1] Muhammad al-Qurṭubī, *al-Mufhim*, 3:107.

> nothing was attached to it. This is just as he said, 'too fast to be smeared with blood or dung'. Our imams who ruled that the Kharijites are to be charged with disbelief held to the import of this simile, although many scholars hesitated in charging them with disbelief due to the Prophet's saying ﷺ [at the end of the aforementioned hadith], 'It is doubtful that anything will hang on to it', which implies that there is a degree of doubt regarding them, and thus there is hesitation with respect to their ruling. It seems that the first view, that of charging them with disbelief, is more apparent in the hadith.[1]

Ibn Ḥajar al-ʿAsqalānī commented on al-Qurṭubī's words:

> **يُؤَيِّدُ الْقَوْلُ بِتَكْفِيرِهِمُ التَّمْثِيلَ الْمَذْكُورَ فِي حَدِيثِ أَبِي سَعِيدٍ، فَإِنَّ ظَاهِرَ مَقْصُودِهِ أَنَّهُمْ خَرَجُوا مِنَ الْإِسْلَامِ، وَلَمْ يَتَعَلَّقُوا مِنْهُ بِشَيْءٍ، كَمَا خَرَجَ السَّهْمُ مِنَ الرَّمِيَّةِ لِسُرْعَتِهِ وَقُوَّةِ رَامِيهِ، بِحَيْثُ لَمْ يَتَعَلَّقْ مِنَ الرَّمِيَّةِ بِشَيْءٍ.**
>
> The simile within the hadith of Abū Saʿīd supports the view that they are to be charged with disbelief, for its apparent meaning is that they have left the fold of Islam and have no connection with it whatsoever, just as an arrow exits from a hunted game due to its speed and the strength of the archer, leaving no trace of the game on it.[2]

16.2.7 Shaykh Ibn Taymiyya's Position

Shaykh Ibn Taymiyya believed that the Kharijites were disbelievers. Writing about their emergence, beliefs and appearance, he said:

> **اَلْمَقْصُودُ هُنَا أَنَّ الْخَوَارِجَ ظَهَرُوا فِي الْفِتْنَةِ، وَكَفَّرُوا عُثْمَانَ وَعَلِيًّا ﵄ وَمَنْ وَالَاهُمَا. . . . وَكَانُوا كَمَا وَصَفَهُمُ النَّبِيُّ ﷺ: يَقْتُلُونَ أَهْلَ الْإِسْلَامِ وَيَدَعُونَ أَهْلَ الْأَوْثَانِ. وَكَانُوا أَعْظَمَ النَّاسِ صَلَاةً وَصِيَامًا وَقِرَاءَةً، كَمَا قَالَ النَّبِيُّ ﷺ: يَحْقِرُ أَحَدُكُمْ صَلَاتَهُ مَعَ صَلَاتِهِمْ، وَصِيَامَهُ مَعَ صِيَامِهِمْ، وَقِرَاءَتَهُ مَعَ قِرَاءَتِهِمْ، يَقْرَءُونَ الْقُرْآنَ لَا يُجَاوِزُ**

---

[1] Ibid., 3:110.

[2] Ibn Ḥajar al-ʿAsqalānī, *Fatḥ al-Bārī*, 12:300.

حَنَاجِرَهُمْ، يَمْرُقُونَ مِنَ الْإِسْلَامِ كَمَا يَمْرُقُ السَّهْمُ مِنَ الرَّمِيَّةِ. وَمُرُوقُهُمْ مِنْهُ: خُرُوجُهُمْ، بِاسْتِحْلَالِهِمْ دِمَاءَ الْمُسْلِمِيْنَ وَأَمْوَالَهُمْ. فَإِنَّهُ قَدْ ثَبَتَ عَنْهُ ﷺ فِي الصَّحِيْحِ، أَنَّهُ ﷺ قَالَ: اَلْمُسْلِمُ مَنْ سَلِمَ الْمُسْلِمُونَ مِنْ لِسَانِهِ وَيَدِهِ. . . . وَهُمْ بَسَطُوا فِي الْمُسْلِمِيْنَ أَيْدِيَهُمْ وَأَلْسِنَتَهُمْ فَخَرَجُوا مِنْهُ (أَي مِنَ الْإِسْلَامِ).

> The point here is to state that the Kharijites emerged during a time of tribulation and declared ʿUthmān and ʿAlī disbelievers, as well as those who allied with them. . . . As the Prophet ﷺ described them, they would 'kill the people of Islam and leave the idol worshippers'. The Prophet ﷺ said they were the most assiduous of people when it came to prayers, fasting and recitation: 'You will consider your prayers, fasting and recitation insignificant in comparison to theirs. They shall recite the Qurʾān but it will not pass their throats. They shall exit from Islam just as an arrow exits a hunted game'. Their 'exiting' from it means their leaving it due to their belief that it is lawful to shed the blood of the Muslims and seize their wealth. It is established in the rigorously authentic collection [of al-Bukhārī] that he ﷺ said, 'The Muslim is he from whose tongue and hand the Muslims are safe' . . . and they [on the other hand] extended their hands, harming the Muslims with their hands [through armed struggle and terrorist activities] and tongues [declaring them infidels], and so they left it [i.e., Islam].[1]

16.2.8 Imam Taqī al-Dīn al-Subkī's Position

Imam Taqī al-Dīn Abū al-Ḥasan ʿAlī b. ʿAbd al-Kāfī al-Subkī was one of the eminent latter-day scholars and jurists and author of *Shifā al-siqām*, a well-known book about seeking means through the person of the Prophet ﷺ and undertaking journeys to visit him at his tomb. In his collection of formal legal verdicts, he declared the Kharijites disbelievers. Ibn Ḥajar al-ʿAsqalānī said:

---

[1] Ibn Taymiyya, *al-Nubuwwāt*, p. 225.

مِمَّنْ جَنَحَ إِلَى ذَلِكَ مِنْ أَئِمَّةِ الْمُتَأَخِّرِيْنَ الشَّيْخُ تَقِيُّ الدِّيْنِ السُّبْكِيُّ فَقَالَ فِي فَتَاوِيْهِ: اِحْتَجَّ مَنْ كَفَّرَ الْخَوَارِجَ وَغُلَاةَ الرَّوَافِضِ بِتَكْفِيْرِهِمْ أَعْلَامَ الصَّحَابَةِ لِتَضَمُّنِهِ تَكْذِيْبَ النَّبِيِّ ﷺ فِي شَهَادَتِهِ لَهُمْ بِالْجَنَّةِ، قَالَ: وَهُوَ عِنْدِي احْتِجَاجٌ صَحِيْحٌ.

Shaykh Taqī al-Dīn al-Subkī was of the latter-day imams who inclined to that view. He said in his collection of legal verdicts, 'Those who charged the Kharijites and the extremist Shiites with disbelief argued that they were disbelievers because they charged the notable Companions with disbelief, for that entails belying the Prophet ﷺ in his testimony that they are in Paradise. And as I see it, this argument is valid'.[1]

It should be pointed out that someone can be from the Kharijites without necessarily charging the Companions with disbelief. The great Ḥanafī jurist, Ibn ʿĀbidīn al-Shāmī stated,

يُكَفِّرُونَ أَصْحَابَ نَبِيِّنَا ﷺ، عَلِمْتُ أَنَّ هَذَا غَيْرُ شَرْطٍ فِي مُسَمَّى الْخَوَارِجِ، بَلْ هُوَ بَيَانٌ لِمَنْ خَرَجُوا عَلَى سَيِّدِنَا عَلِيٍّ رضي الله عنه، وَإِلاَّ فَيَكْفِي فِيْهِمُ اعْتِقَادُهُمْ كُفْرَ مَنْ خَرَجُوا عَلَيْهِ.

'They charged the Companions of our Prophet ﷺ with disbelief; but you should know that this is not a prerequisite for the term Kharijite; rather, it is but an explanation regarding those who rebelled against our master ʿAlī رضي الله عنه. Otherwise, it suffices that they believe the one whom they rebel against is a disbeliever'.[2]

16.2.9 Imam Abū Isḥāq al-Shāṭibī's Position

The great jurist and legal theorist of the Mālikī school, Imam al-Shāṭibī, said about the Kharijites:

أَلَا تَرَى أَنَّ الْخَوَارِجَ كَيْفَ خَرَجُوا عَنِ الدِّيْنِ كَمَا يَخْرُجُ السَّهْمُ مِنَ الصَّيْدِ الْمَرْمِيِّ؟

---

[1] Ibn Ḥajar al-ʿAsqalānī, *Fatḥ al-Bārī*, 12:299–300.

[2] Ibn ʿĀbidīn, *Radd al-muḥtār*, 4:262.

لِأَنَّ رَسُولَ اللهِ ﷺ وَصَفَهُمْ بِأَنَّهُمْ يَقْرَؤُونَ الْقُرْآنَ لَا يُجَاوِزُ تَرَاقِيَهُمْ، أَنَّهُمْ لَا يَتَفَقَّهُونَ بِهِ حَتَّى يَصِلَ إِلَى قُلُوبِهِمْ. . . . فَإِنَّهُ إِذَا عَرَفَ الرَّجُلُ فِيْمَا نَزَلَتِ الْآيَةُ، أَوِ السُّورَةُ عَرَفَ مَخْرَجَهَا وَتَأْوِيْلَهَا وَمَا قَصَدَ بِهَا، . . . وَإِذَا جَهِلَ فِيْمَا أُنْزِلَتِ احْتَمَلَ النَّظَرُ فِيْهَا أَوْجَهًا. . . . وَلَيْسَ عِنْدَهُمْ مِنَ الرُّسُوخِ فِي الْعِلْمِ، مَا يَهْدِيْهِمْ إِلَى الصَّوَابِ أَوْ يَقِفُ بِهِمْ دُونَ اقْتِحَامِ حِمَى الْمُشْكَلَاتِ. فَلَمْ يَكُنْ بُدٌّ مِنَ الْأَخْذِ بِبَادِي الرَّأْيِ أَوِ التَّأْوِيْلِ بِالتَّخَرُّصِ الَّذِي لَا يُغْنِي مِنَ الْحَقِّ شَيْئًا إِذْ لَا دَلِيْلَ عَلَيْهِ مِنَ الشَّرِيْعَةِ فَضَلُّوا وَأَضَلُّوا.

وَمِمَّا يُوَضِّحُ ذَلِكَ مَا خَرَّجَهُ ابْنُ وَهْبٍ عَنْ بُكَيْرٍ أَنَّهُ سَأَلَ نَافِعًا: كَيْفَ رَأَى ابْنُ عُمَرَ فِي الْحَرُورِيَّةِ؟ قَالَ: يَرَاهُمْ شِرَارَ خَلْقِ اللهِ. إِنَّهُمُ انْطَلَقُوا إِلَى آيَاتٍ أُنْزِلَتْ فِي الْكُفَّارِ فَجَعَلُوهَا عَلَى الْمُؤْمِنِيْنَ. فَسُرَّ سَعِيْدُ بْنُ جُبَيْرٍ مِنْ ذَلِكَ، فَقَالَ: مِمَّا يَتْبَعُ الْحَرُورِيَّةَ مِنَ الْمُتَشَابِهِ قَوْلُ اللهِ تَعَالَى: ﴿وَمَن لَّمْ يَحْكُم بِمَآ أَنزَلَ ٱللَّهُ فَأُوْلَٰٓئِكَ هُمُ ٱلْكَٰفِرُونَ﴾. وَيَقْرِنُونَ مَعَهَا: ﴿ثُمَّ ٱلَّذِينَ كَفَرُواْ بِرَبِّهِمْ يَعْدِلُونَ﴾. رَأَوُا الْإِمَامَ يَحْكُمُ بِغَيْرِ الْحَقِّ. قَالُوا: قَدْ كَفَرَ وَمَنْ كَفَرَ عَدَلَ بِرَبِّهِ فَقَدْ أَشْرَكَ فَهَذِهِ الْأُمَّةُ مُشْرِكُونَ، فَيَخْرُجُونَ، فَيَقْتُلُونَ، مَا رَأَيْتُ لِأَنَّهُمْ يَتَأَوَّلُونَ هَذِهِ الْآيَةَ. فَهَذَا مَعْنَى الرَّأْيِ الَّذِي نَبَّهَ عَلَيْهِ ابْنُ عَبَّاسٍ وَهُوَ النَّاشِئُ عَنِ الْجَهْلِ بِالْمَعْنَى الَّذِي نَزَلَ فِيْهِ الْقُرْآنُ. وَقَالَ نَافِعٌ: إِنَّ ابْنَ عُمَرَ ﵄ كَانَ إِذَا سُئِلَ عَنِ الْحَرُورِيَّةِ، قَالَ: يُكَفِّرُونَ الْمُسْلِمِيْنَ وَيَسْتَحِلُّونَ دِمَاءَهُمْ وَأَمْوَالَهُمْ.

Do you not see how the Kharijites exited from the religion just as an arrow exits from a hunted game? That is because the Messenger of God ﷺ described them, saying that they will recite the Qurʾān but it will not pass their throats; that is because they do not gain a deep understanding of it, which would allow it to reach their hearts. . . . So when someone knows the circumstances behind the revelation of a Qurʾānic verse, or the chapter, he will know its context, interpretation and what was meant by it. . . . [A]nd when he is ignorant of the circumstances behind its revelation, the mind will consider multiple possibilities. They do not have grounding in knowledge that would guide them to what is correct or prevent them from trespassing beyond the boundaries of problematic areas. For that reason it is inevitable that a shallow opinion is taken or that there is a baseless interpretation founded on conjecture that does not suffice for the truth, for there is no evidence in support of it in the Sacred Law. As a consequence of this, they went astray and led others astray.

This is further explained by the report narrated by Wahb from Bukayr, who mentioned that he asked Nāfiᶜ, 'What was Ibn ᶜUmar's view regarding the Ḥarūriyya?' Nāfiᶜ replied, 'He believed that they were the worst of God's creation. They took the verses revealed about the disbelievers and applied them to the believers'. Saᶜīd b. Jubayr explained that and said, 'Of the ambiguous verses that the Ḥarūriyya follow is God's words: '*And whoever does not judge by what God has revealed, then they are the disbelievers*' [Qurʾān 5:44], juxtaposed with the verse, '*Yet those who disbelieve hold others as equal with their Lord*' [Qurʾān 6:1]. When they see the ruler judge unjustly they proclaim, "He has disbelieved, and whoever disbelieves has held [himself] equal with his Lord and is therefore an idolater, hence the *Umma*, too, are idolaters!" Then they revolt and kill. As far as I see it, it is because they [falsely] interpret this verse'. This is the meaning of 'opinion' that Ibn ᶜAbbās ﷺ mentioned: One that stems from ignorance of the meaning with which the Qurʾān was revealed. Nāfiᶜ said, 'When Ibn ᶜUmar ﷺ was asked about Ḥarūriyya he would reply, "They charge the Muslims with disbelief and declare their blood and wealth lawful".'[1]

16.2.10 Imam Ibn al-Bazzāz al-Kurdarī's Position

Imam Ḥāfiẓ al-Dīn Ibn al-Bazzāz al-Kurdarī, a renowned Ḥanafī authority of the ninth century, said in his collection of legal

---

[1] Abū Isḥāq al-Shāṭibī, *al-Iᶜtiṣām*, 4:182–184.

verdicts,

يَجِبُ إِكْفَارُ الْخَوَارِجِ فِي إِكْفَارِهِمْ جَمِيْعَ الْأُمَّةِ سِوَاهُمْ.

'It is obligatory to charge the Kharijites with disbelief due to their having charged everyone of the *Umma* but themselves with disbelief'.[1]

16.2.11 Imam Badr al-Dīn al-ʿAynī's Position

Imam Badr al-Dīn al-ʿAynī writes in his commentary on *Ṣaḥīḥ al-Bukhārī*:

قَوْلُهُ ﷺ: يَمْرُقُونَ مِنَ الدِّيْنِ، مِنَ الْمُرُوقِ وَهُوَ الْخُرُوجُ. يُقَالُ: مَرَقَ مِنَ الدِّيْنِ مُرُوقًا، خَرَجَ مِنْهُ بِبِدْعَتِهِ وَضَلَالَتِهِ. وَفِي رِوَايَةِ سُوَيْدِ بْنِ غَفَلَةَ عِنْدَ النَّسَائِيِّ وَالطَّبَرِيِّ: يَمْرُقُونَ مِنَ الْإِسْلَامِ.

The Prophet's statement ﷺ, 'They shall pass through the religion', uses the word *murūq*, which is to exit. It is said, 'So-and-so exited the religion [*maraqa*]' when he left it due to his blameworthy innovation and misguidance. In the narration of Suwayd b. Ghafla in the collections of al-Nasāʾī and al-Ṭabarī it says, 'They shall pass through Islam'.[2]

16.2.12 Imam Aḥmad b. Muhammad al-Qasṭalānī's Position

Imam Aḥmad b. Muhammad al-Qasṭalānī said in his commentary on *Ṣaḥīḥ al-Bukhārī*:

يَخْرُجُ فِي هَذِهِ الْأُمَّةِ الْمُحَمَّدِيَّةِ، وَلَمْ يَقُلْ مِنْهَا، فِيْهِ ضَبْطٌ لِلرِّوَايَةِ وَتَحْرِيْرٌ لِمَوَاقِعِ الْأَلْفَاظِ وَإِشْعَارٌ بِأَنَّهُمْ لَيْسُوا مِنْ هَذِهِ الْأُمَّةِ فَظَاهِرُهُ أَنَّهُ يَرَى إِكْفَارَهُمْ لَكِنْ فِي مُسْلِمٍ مِنْ حَدِيْثِ أَبِي ذَرٍّ: سَيَكُونُ بَعْدِي مِنْ أُمَّتِي قَوْمٌ فَيُجْمَعُ بَيْنَهُ وَبَيْنَ حَدِيْثِ أَبِي سَعِيْدٍ بِأَنَّ الْمُرَادَ فِي حَدِيْثِ أَبِي سَعِيْدٍ بِالْأُمَّةِ أُمَّةُ الْإِجَابَةِ وَفِي غَيْرِهِ أُمَّةُ الدَّعْوَةِ.

---

1 Ibn al-Bazzāz, *al-Fatāwā al-bazzāziyya ʿalā hāmish al-fatāwā al-ʿālamghīriyya*, 6:318.

2 Badr al-Dīn al-ʿAynī, *ʿUmdat al-qārī*, 16:209.

The report, 'There shall appear in this [Muhammadan] *Umma*. . .' 'and he did not say, 'from this *Umma*', is a case of exactitude in the narration and clarity in expression. It gives the impression that they are not from this *Umma*. The apparent wording shows that he believed that they are to be charged with disbelief; however, in Muslim's narration from the hadith of Abū Dharr it reads, 'There shall appear a folk from my *Umma* after me'. This hadith is reconciled with the hadith of Abū Saʿīd by stating that the *Umma* in Abū Saʿīd's narration is the *Umma* of Response, and the *Umma* in Abū Dharr's narration is the *Umma* of Invitation.[1]

16.2.13 Mullā ʿAlī al-Qārī's Position

Mullā ʿAlī al-Qārī said in *Mirqāt al-mafātīḥ*,

يَحْتَمِلُ أَنْ يُقَالَ لَهُمْ شَبَهٌ بِأَهْلِ الْحَقِّ لِغُلُوِّهِمْ فِي تَكْفِيرِ أَهْلِ الْمَعْصِيَةِ، وَلَكِنَّهُمْ أَهْلُ الْبَاطِلِ لِمُخَالَفَتِهِمُ الْإِجْمَاعَ.

'It could be said that with their charges of disbelief against disobedient people they bear a resemblance to the people of truth [Muslims]; however, they are the people of falsehood [disbelief] because of their opposition to scholarly consensus'.[2]

16.2.14 Shaykh ʿAbd al-Ḥaqq al-Dihlawī's Position

The renowned Indian scholar, Shaykh ʿAbd al-Ḥaqq al-Dihlawī, said, 'The correct position is that fighting the Kharijites in every age is an act for which one earns reward, as our master ʿAlī ﵁ ordered that they be fought due to their transgression, and this is the well-known position. And the Kharijites believed that even the person who commits sins is a disbeliever—both major and minor sins'.[3]

---

[1] Aḥmad al-Qasṭalānī, *Irshād al-sārī*, 10:85–86.

[2] Al-Qārī, *Mirqāt al-mafātīḥ sharḥ mishkāt al-maṣābīḥ*, 7:107.

[3] ʿAbd al-Ḥaqq al-Dihlawī, *Ashʿat al-lamaʿāt*, 3:254.

16.2.15 Shāh ʿAbd al-ʿAzīz al-Dihlawī's Position

According to Shāh ʿAbd al-ʿAzīz al-Dihlawī, the disbelief of the Kharijites is agreed upon. He said, 'Indeed, it is a point of scholarly consensus that all who fought against ʿAlī out of enmity and hatred are considered disbelievers'.[1]

16.2.16 Imam Ibn ʿĀbidīn al-Shāmī's Position

Ibn ʿĀbidīn al-Shāmī said:

> يُكَفِّرُونَ أَصْحَابَ نَبِيِّنَا ﷺ، عَلِمْتُ أَنَّ هَذَا غَيْرُ شَرْطٍ فِي مُسَمَّى الْخَوَارِجِ، بَلْ هُوَ بَيَانٌ لِمَنْ خَرَجُوا عَلَى سَيِّدِنَا عَلِيٍّ رضي الله عنه، وَإِلَّا فَيَكْفِي فِيْهِمْ اعْتِقَادُهُمْ كُفْرَ مَنْ خَرَجُوا عَلَيْهِ. . . . حُكْمُ الْخَوَارِجِ عِنْدَ جُمْهُورِ الْفُقَهَاءِ وَالْمُحَدِّثِيْنَ حُكْمُ الْبُغَاةِ، وَذَهَبَ بَعْضُ الْمُحَدِّثِيْنَ إِلَى كُفْرِهِمْ.

> They charged the Companions of our Prophet ﷺ with disbelief; but know that this is not a pre-requisite for the term Kharijites; rather, it is but an explanation regarding those who rebelled against our master ʿAlī رضي الله عنه. Otherwise, it suffices that they believe the one whom they rebel against is a disbeliever [for their disbelief]. . . . According to the majority of the jurists and hadith scholars, the Kharijites are judged as rebels, and some of the hadith scholars took the position that they are disbelievers.[2]

16.2.17 Shaykh ʿAbd al-Raḥmān Mubārakpūrī's Position

The famous hadith scholar of India, ʿAbd al-Raḥmān Mubārakpūrī, said,

> "إِنَّمَا هُمُ الْخَوَارِجُ" جَمْعُ خَارِجَةٍ، وَهُمْ قَوْمٌ مُبْتَدِعُونَ سُمُّوا بِذَلِكَ لِخُرُوجِهِمْ عَنِ الدِّيْنِ وَخُرُوجِهِمْ عَلَى خِيَارِ الْمُسْلِمِيْنَ. وَمِمَّنْ ذَهَبَ إِلَى تَكْفِيْرِهِمْ أَيْضًا الْحَسَنُ بْنُ مُحَمَّدِ بْنِ عَلِيٍّ وَرِوَايَةٌ عَنِ الْإِمَامِ الشَّافِعِيِّ وَرِوَايَةٌ عَنِ الْإِمَامِ مَالِكٍ وَطَائِفَةٌ مِنْ أَهْلِ الْحَدِيْثِ.

---

[1] ʿAbd al-ʿAzīz al-Dihlawī, *Tuḥfat ithnā ashʿariyya*, p. 795.

[2] Ibn ʿĀbidīn, *Radd al-muḥtār*, 4:262.

'They are but Kharijites': [*Khawārij*] is the plural of '*khārija*' ['he who went out'], and they are a group of blameworthy innovators given that name because of their having left the religion and the best of the Muslims. Those who held that they are to be charged with disbelief include al-Ḥasan b. Muhammad b. ʿAlī, and there is also a narration to that effect from Imam al-Shāfiʿī, Imam Mālik and a group from the traditionists [*ahl al-ḥadīth*].[1]

16.3 The Second Position: The Kharijites Are Rebels

Another group of scholars observed caution and did not charge the Kharijites with disbelief. Instead, they labelled them as rebels and agreed that they should be fought. Furthermore, the scholars who charged the Kharijites with disbelief also held that they are rebels and should be fought. So although there is a difference of opinion regarding the disbelief of the Kharijites, there is a consensus that they are to be fought against. Imam Ibn Qudāma al-Maqdisī said:

اَلْخَوَارِجُ الَّذِينَ يُكَفِّرُونَ بِالذَّنْبِ، وَيُكَفِّرُونَ عُثْمَانَ وَعَلِيًّا وَطَلْحَةَ وَالزُّبَيْرَ، وَكَثِيرًا مِنَ الصَّحَابَةِ، وَيَسْتَحِلُّونَ دِمَاءَ الْمُسْلِمِينَ، وَأَمْوَالَهُمْ، إِلَّا مَنْ خَرَجَ مَعَهُمْ، فَظَاهِرُ قَوْلِ الْفُقَهَاءِ مِنْ أَصْحَابِنَا الْمُتَأَخِّرِينَ أَنَّهُمْ بُغَاةٌ، حُكْمُهُمْ حُكْمُ الْبُغَاةِ، وَلَا خِلَافَ فِي قَتْلِهِمْ فَإِنَّهُ حُكْمٌ مَنْصُوصٌ عَلَيْهِ بِأَمْرِ النَّبِيِّ ﷺ. وَهَذَا قَوْلُ أَبِي حَنِيفَةَ، وَالشَّافِعِيِّ، وَجُمْهُورِ الْفُقَهَاءِ، وَكَثِيرٍ مِنْ أَهْلِ الْحَدِيثِ.

The Kharijites are those who declare [others] disbelievers on account of sins, and who declare ʿUthmān, ʿAlī, Ṭalḥa, Zubayr and many of the Companions disbelievers. And they believe it is lawful to shed the blood of the Muslims and to seize their wealth—except those of them who rebel along with them. The apparent view of the jurists from our latter-day colleagues is that they are rebels. They take the same ruling as the rebels and there is no disagreement about killing them, for it is a ruling that is textually stated in the Prophet's command ﷺ. This is also the opinion

---

1 Abd al-Raḥmān Mubārakpūrī, *Tuḥfat al-aḥwadhī*, 6:354.

of Abū Ḥanīfa, al-Shāfiʿī, the majority of the jurists and many of the traditionists [*ahl al-ḥadīth*].[1]

The following is a list of scholars and jurists who only considered the Kharijites as rebels. It is worth noting that the responsibility of fighting rebels falls on the state; Islam does not allow vigilantism, no matter how noble the intention behind it.

16.3.1 IMAM ABŪ ḤANĪFA

Imam Abū Ḥanīfa ruled that the Kharijites are rebels that should be fought.

عَنْ أَبِي مُطِيْعٍ، قَالَ: قُلْتُ لِأَبِي حَنِيْفَةَ: مَا تَقُولُ فِي الْخَوَارِجِ الْمُحْكِمَةِ؟ قَالَ: هُمْ أَخْبَثُ الْخَوَارِجِ. قُلْتُ لَهُ: أَنُكَفِّرُهُمْ؟ قَالَ: لَا. وَلَكِنْ نُقَاتِلُهُمْ عَلَى مَا قَاتَلَهُمُ الْأَئِمَّةُ مِنْ أَهْلِ الْخَيْرِ: عَلِيٌّ وَعُمَرُ بْنُ عَبْدِ الْعَزِيْزِ. قُلْتُ: فَإِنَّ الْخَوَارِجَ يُكَبِّرُونَ وَيُصَلُّونَ وَيَتْلُونَ الْقُرْآنَ. قَالَ: أَمَا تَذْكُرُ حَدِيْثَ أَبِي أُمَامَةَ ﷺ حِيْنَ دَخَلَ مَسْجِدَ دِمَشْقَ، فَقَالَ لِأَبِي غَالِبِ الْحِمْصِيِّ: هَؤُلَاءِ كِلَابُ أَهْلِ النَّارِ، هَؤُلَاءِ كِلَابُ أَهْلِ النَّارِ، وَهُمْ شَرُّ قَتْلَى تَحْتَ أَدِيْمِ السَّمَاءِ. (ثُمَّ ذَكَرَ حَدِيثًا طَوِيْلًا.) قَالَ لَهُ: أَشَيْءٌ تَقُولُهُ بِرَأْيِكَ أَمْ سَمِعْتَهُ مِنْ رَسُولِ اللهِ ﷺ؟ قَالَ: إِنِّي لَوْ لَمْ أَسْمَعْهُ مِنْهُ إِلَّا مَرَّةً أَوْ مَرَّتَيْنِ أَوْ ثَلَاثَ مَرَّاتٍ إِلَى سَبْعِ مَرَّاتٍ لَمَا حَدَّثْتُكُمُوهُ.

Abū Muṭīʿ said, 'I said to Abū Ḥanīfa, "What do you say regarding the *Muḥkama* faction of the Kharijites?" He replied, "They are the vilest of the Kharijites". I then asked him, "Should we charge them with disbelief?" He replied, "No; however, we fight them for the same reasons the Imams of goodness—ʿAlī and ʿUmar b. ʿAbd al-ʿAzīz—fought them". I then said, "But the Kharijites cry out with the *takbīr* [saying, '*Allāh akbar*' (God is the Greatest)], offer prayers and recite the Qurʾān". He retorted, "Don't you remember the hadith of Abū Umāma ﷺ? He entered the Mosque of Damascus and said to Abū Ghālib al-Ḥimṣī, 'They are the dogs of Hellfire, they are

[1] Ibn Qudāma al-Maqdisī, *al-Mughnī*, 9:4.

> the dogs of the Hellfire. They are the most evil of those slain under the heavens. . . .' Abū Ghālib asked Abū Umāma, 'Did you give your own opinion or did you hear that from the Messenger of God ﷺ?' He replied, 'Had I not heard it once, twice, thrice, four times, five times, six times or seven times, I would not have narrated it to you all'".'[1]

16.3.2 IMAM SHAMS AL-DĪN AL-SARAKHSĪ

The renowned jurist of the Ḥanafī school, Shams al-Dīn al-Sarakhsī, held that it is lawful to seek the aid and assistance of non-Muslim citizens [*ahl al-dhimma*] against the Kharijites:

> لَا بَأْسَ بِأَنَّ يَسْتَعِيْنَ أَهْلُ الْعَدْلِ بِقَوْمٍ مِنْ أَهْلِ الْبَغْيِ وَأَهْلِ الذِّمَّةِ عَلَى الْخَوَارِجِ . . . لِأَنَّهُمْ يُقَاتِلُونَ لِإِعْزَازِ الدِّيْنِ.

> 'There is no harm in the people of justice seeking the aid of some people from the rebels and non-Muslim citizens against the Kharijites . . . because they are fighting for the sake of promoting the religion'.[2]

16.3.3 IBN ḤAJAR AL-ʿASQALĀNĪ

Ibn Ḥajar said in his commentary on *Ṣaḥīḥ al-Bukhārī*

> فِي الْحَدِيْثِ الْكَفُّ عَنْ قَتْلِ مَنْ يَعْتَقِدُ الْخُرُوجَ عَلَى الْإِمَامِ مَا لَمْ يَنْصَبْ لِذَلِكَ حَرْبًا، أَوْ يَسْتَعِدُّ لِذَلِكَ، لِقَوْلِهِ ﷺ: فَإِذَا خَرَجُوا فَاقْتُلُوهُمْ. وَحَكَى الطَّبَرِيُّ الْإِجْمَاعَ عَلَى ذَلِكَ فِي حَقِّ مَنْ لَا يُكَفَّرُ بِاعْتِقَادِهِ، وَأُسْنِدَ عَنْ عُمَرَ بْنِ عَبْدِ الْعَزِيْزِ أَنَّهُ كَتَبَ فِي الْخَوَارِجِ بِالْكَفِّ عَنْهُمْ مَا لَمْ يَسْفِكُوا دَمًا حَرَامًا، أَوْ يَأْخُذُوا مَالًا، فَإِنْ فَعَلُوا فَقَاتِلُوهُمْ، وَلَوْ كَانُوا وُلْدِي. وَمِنْ طَرِيْقِ ابْنِ جُرَيْجٍ: قُلْتُ لِعَطَاءٍ: مَا يُحِلُّ لِي قِتَالَ الْخَوَارِجِ؟ قَالَ: إِذَا قَطَعُوا السَّبِيْلَ، وَأَخَافُوا الْأَمْنَ. وَأَسْنَدَ الطَّبَرِيُّ عَنِ الْحَسَنِ: أَنَّهُ سَئَلَ عَنْ رَجُلٍ كَانَ يَرَى رَأْيَ الْخَوَارِجِ وَلَمْ يَخْرُجْ، فَقَالَ: اَلْعَمَلُ أَمْلَكُ بِالنَّاسِ مِنَ الرَّأْيِ.

---

[1] Muhammad Zāhid al-Kawtharī, *Majmūʿat al-ʿaqīda wa ʿilm al-kalām*, pp. 603–604.

[2] Shams al-Dīn al-Sarakhsī, *Kitāb al-mabsūṭ*, 10:134.

وَذَهَبَ أَكْثَرُ أَهْلِ الْأُصُولِ مِنْ أَهْلِ السُّنَّةِ إِلَى أَنَّ الْخَوَارِجَ فُسَّاقٌ. إِنَّمَا فُسِّقُوا بِتَكْفِيْرِهِمِ الْمُسْلِمِينَ مُسْتَنِدِيْنَ إِلَى تَأْوِيْلٍ فَاسِدٍ، وَجَرَّهُمْ ذٰلِكَ إِلَى اسْتِبَاحَةِ دِمَاءِ مُخَالِفِيْهِمْ وَأَمْوَالِهِمْ وَالشَّهَادَةِ عَلَيْهِمْ بِالْكُفْرِ وَالشِّرْكِ. رَوَى الْخَلَّالُ فِي السُّنَّةِ بِإِسْنَادِهِ، فَقَالَ: أَخْبَرَنِي يُوسُفُ بْنُ مُوسَى، أَنَّ أَبَا عَبْدِ اللهِ (أَيْ أَحْمَدَ بْنَ مُحَمَّدِ بْنِ حَنْبَلٍ) قِيْلَ لَهُ: أَكَفَرَ الْخَوَارِجُ؟ قَالَ: هُمْ مَارِقَةٌ، قِيْلَ: أَكُفَّارٌ هُمْ؟ قَالَ: هُمْ مَارِقَةٌ مَرَقُوا مِنَ الدِّيْنِ.

This hadith indicates that those who believe in revolting against the government should not be killed so long as they do not wage a war on that basis or make preparations for it—this is due to the Prophet's statement ﷺ, 'and kill them if they revolt'. Al-Ṭabarī cited a consensus about this with respect to the one whose beliefs do not entail disbelief, and traced a report that ʿUmar b. ʿAbd al-ʿAzīz wrote [to his governors] ordering 'that the Kharijites be left alone unharmed so long as they do not shed blood unlawfully or seize wealth. And if they do that, then launch military operation against them at state level, even if they are my own progeny'. And in one route of transmission from Jurayj it is mentioned that he said to ʿAṭāʾ, 'What makes it lawful for me to kill the Kharijites?' ʿAṭāʾ replied, 'When they act as brigands on the roads and threaten security'. And al-Ṭabarī traced a report from al-Ḥasan in which he was asked about a man who held the beliefs of the Kharijites but did not revolt. Al-Ḥasan replied, 'People regard action more valuable than opinion'.[1]

And most of the scholars of legal theory [*uṣūl*] from *Ahl al-Sunna* held that the Kharijites were criminals because of their charges of disbelief levelled against the Muslims—charges that were based on corrupt, self-styled interpretations that led them to declare lawful the blood and wealth of their opponents, and charge them with

[1] Ibn Ḥajar al-ʿAsqalānī, *Fatḥ al-Bārī*, 12:299.

disbelief and polytheism. Al-Khalāl narrated in *al-Sunna* with his chain of transmission: 'Yūsuf b. Mūsā informed me that Abū ʿAbd Allāh [i.e., Imam Aḥmad b. Ḥanbal] was asked, "Did the Kharijites disbelieve?" He said, "They are renegades [*māriqa*]". He was then asked, "Are they disbelievers?" He replied, "They are renegades; they passed through the religion".'[1]

16.3.4 Imam Aḥmad Riḍā Khān

Imam Aḥmad Riḍā Khān said about the Kharijites, 'The people of Nahrawan, who rebelled against ʿAlī and declared him a disbeliever, were corrupt reprobates and arrogant rebels. They struggled under the banner of a new sect named the Kharijites, and the many disruptions that spread in the *Umma*—till today—were because of them'.[2]

16.4 The Rationale behind the Ruling to Eliminate the Kharijites

We see from the aforementioned quotes that the scholars differed about whether the Kharijites should be charged with disbelief or not. All of the jurists, no matter what opinion they took, agreed that they should be fought and eliminated.

In the hadith of Sharīk b. Shihāb ﷺ, the Prophet ﷺ said, 'They shall pass through the religion just as an arrow passes through a hunted game. Their notable feature is shaven heads. They shall continue to appear until the last of them appears with the Anti-Christ [al-Dajjāl]; so you should kill them when you encounter them [during war]. They are the most evil of the creation'.[3] ʿAbd Allāh b. ʿUmar ﷺ reported that the Messenger of God ﷺ said,

---

[1] Ibid., 12:300.

[2] Aḥmad Riḍā Khān, *al-ʿAṭāyā al-Nabawiyya fī al-fatāwā al-riḍawiyya*, 29:363.

[3] Narrated by Aḥmad b. Ḥanbal in *al-Musnad*, 4:421; al-Nasāʾī in *al-Sunan*: *Kitāb taḥrīm al-dam* [The Book on the Prohibition of Bloodshed], chapter: 'Regarding the One Who Unsheathes His Sword and Wields it amongst People', 7:119 §4103; al-Nasāʾī in *al-Sunan al-kubrā*, 2:312 §3566; al-Bazzār in *al-Musnad*, 9:294 §3846; and al-Ṭayālisī in *al-Musnad*, 1:124 §923.

كُلَّمَا خَرَجَ قَرْنٌ قُطِعَ، أَكْثَرَ مِنْ عِشْرِينَ مَرَّةً، حَتَّى يَخْرُجَ فِي عِرَاضِهِمُ الدَّجَّالُ.

'Every time a generation of them appears it will be cut down—this will occur over twenty times—until the Anti-Christ appears in their last remnant'.[1]

Ibn Hubayra al-Ḥanbalī said,

فِي الْحَدِيْثِ أَنَّ قِتَالَ الْخَوَارِجِ أَوْلَى مِنْ قِتَالِ الْمُشْرِكِيْنَ، وَالْحِكْمَةُ فِيْهِ: أَنَّ فِي قِتَالِهِمْ حِفْظُ رَأْسِ مَالِ الْإِسْلَامِ، وَفِي قِتَالِ أَهْلِ الشِّرْكِ طَلَبَ الرِّبْحِ، وَحِفْظُ رَأْسِ الْمَالِ أَوْلَى.

The hadith mentions that fighting the Kharijites is more important than fighting the pagans. The wisdom behind fighting them first is that it safeguards the capital of Islam's wealth, whereas fighting the pagans is a pursuit of profit: and protecting one's capital is more important than seeking profit.[2]

Ibn Taymiyya held that there is consensus on waging war against Kharijites to eliminate them:

كَانَ قِتَالُهُمْ ثَابِتًا بِالسُّنَّةِ الصَّحِيْحَةِ الصَّرِيْحَةِ وَبِاتِّفَاقِ الصَّحَابَةِ. . . . وَالْبُغَاةُ الْمَأْمُورُ بِقِتَالِهِمْ هُمُ الَّذِيْنَ بَغوا بَعْدَ الْاِقْتِتَالِ، وَامْتَنَعُوا مِنَ الْإِصْلَاحِ الْمَأْمُورِ بِهِ؛ فَصَارُوا بُغَاةً مُقَاتِلِيْنَ. وَالْبُغَاةُ إِذَا ابْتَدَأُوا بِالْقِتَالِ جَازَ قِتَالُهُمْ بِالْاِتِّفَاقِ؛ كَمَا يَجُوزُ قِتَالُ الْغُوَاةِ قُطَّاعِ الطَّرِيْقِ إِذَا قَاتَلُوا بِاتِّفَاقِ النَّاسِ.

So fighting against them is established in the authentic and explicit Sunna, and is the agreement of the Companions. . . . The rebels against whom fighting is ordered are those who rebel after fighting erupts, and who refuse to follow the command of making peace and who become militant. By the agreement of the scholars, it is permissible to fight

[1] Narrated by Ibn Mājah in *al-Sunan*: 'Introduction', section, 'Mention of the Kharijites', 1:61 §174.

[2] Ibn Ḥajar al-ʿAsqalānī, *Fatḥ al-Bārī*, 5:157.

against rebels when they initiate fighting, just as everyone agrees that it is permissible to fight the highway brigands when they fight.[1]

Ibn Ḥajar al-ʿAsqalānī said:

فِي رِوَايَةِ أَبِي إِسْحَاقَ عَنْ سُوَيْدِ بْنِ غَفَلَةَ عِنْدَ النَّسَائِيِّ وَالطَّبَرِيِّ: يَمْرُقُونَ مِنَ الْإِسْلَامِ. وَكَذَا فِي حَدِيْثِ ابْنِ عُمَرَ فِي الْبَابِ، وَعِنْدَ النَّسَائِيِّ مِنْ رِوَايَةِ طَارِقِ بْنِ زِيَادٍ عَنْ عَلِيٍّ يَمْرُقُونَ مِنَ الْحَقِّ وَبِقَوْلِهِ ﷺ: فَأَيْنَمَا لَقِيْتُمُوهُمْ فَاقْتُلُوهُمْ، فَإِنَّ فِي قَتْلِهِمْ أَجْرًا لِمَنْ قَتَلَهُمْ يَوْمَ الْقِيَامَةِ.

In the narration of Abū Isḥāq from Suwayd b. Ghafla in the collection of al-Nasāʾī and al-Ṭabarī: 'They shall pass through Islam'. Likewise, in the hadith of Ibn ʿUmar in the same section and recorded by al-Nasāʾī from the narration of Ṭāriq b. Ziyād from ʿAlī: 'They shall pass through the truth', and: 'So kill them wherever you find them for the one who kills them shall receive a reward on the Day of Resurrection'.[2]

16.5 The Great Reward Awaiting Those Who Fight the Kharijites

Ibn Ḥajar al-ʿAsqalānī said:

فِي رِوَايَةِ زَيْدِ بْنِ وَهْبٍ: لَوْ يَعْلَمُ الْجَيْشُ الَّذِيْنَ يُصِيْبُونَهُمْ مَا قُضِيَ لَهُمْ عَلَى لِسَانِ نَبِيِّهِمْ لَنَكَلُوا عَنِ الْعَمَلِ. وَأَخْرَجَ أَحْمَدُ نَحْوَ هَذَا الْحَدِيْثِ عَنْ عَلِيٍّ وَزَادَ فِي آخِرِهِ: قِتَالُهُمْ حَقٌّ عَلَى كُلِّ مُسْلِمٍ. وَقَوْلُهُ ﷺ: صَلَاتَكُمْ مَعَ صَلَاتِهِمْ. زَادَ فِي رِوَايَةِ الزُّهْرِيِّ عَنْ أَبِي سَلَمَةَ كَمَا فِي الْبَابِ بَعْدَهُ وَصِيَامَكُمْ مَعَ صِيَامِهِمْ. وَفِي رِوَايَةِ عَاصِمِ بْنِ شُمَيْخٍ عَنْ أَبِي سَعِيْدٍ: تَحْقِرُونَ أَعْمَالَكُمْ مَعَ أَعْمَالِهِمْ، وَوَصَفَ عَاصِمٌ أَصْحَابَ نَجْدَةَ الْحَرُورِيِّ بِأَنَّهُمْ، يَصُومُونَ النَّهَارَ وَيَقُومُونَ اللَّيْلَ وَيَأْخُذُونَ الصَّدَقَاتِ عَلَى السُّنَّةِ. أَخْرَجَهُ الطَّبَرِيُّ.

---

[1] Ibn Taymiyya, *al-Nubuwwāt*, pp. 223–225.

[2] Ibn Ḥajar al-ʿAsqalānī, *Fatḥ al-Bārī*, 12:288.

وَمِثْلُهُ عِنْدَهُ مِنْ رِوَايَةِ يَحْيَى بْنِ أَبِي كَثِيرٍ عَنْ أَبِي سَلَمَةَ. وَفِي رِوَايَةِ مُحَمَّدِ بْنِ عَمْرٍو عَنْ أَبِي سَلَمَةَ عِنْدَهُ يَتَعَبَّدُونَ يَحْقِرُ أَحَدُكُمْ صَلَاتَهُ وَصِيَامَهُ مَعَ صَلَاتِهِمْ وَصِيَامِهِمْ. وَمِثْلُهُ مِنْ رِوَايَةِ أَنَسٍ عَنْ أَبِي سَعِيْدٍ وَزَادَ فِي رِوَايَةِ الْأَسْوَدِ بْنِ الْعَلَاءِ عَنْ أَبِي سَلَمَةَ وَأَعْمَالَكُمْ مَعَ أَعْمَالِهِمْ. وَفِي رِوَايَةِ سَلَمَةَ بْنِ كُهَيْلٍ عَنْ زَيْدِ بْنِ وَهْبٍ عَنْ عَلِيٍّ: لَيْسَتْ قِرَاءَتُكُمْ إِلَى قِرَاءَتِهِمْ شَيْئًا وَلَا صَلَاتُكُمْ إِلَى صَلَاتِهِمْ شَيْئًا. أَخْرَجَهُ مُسْلِمٌ وَالطَّبَرِيُّ وَعِنْدَهُ مِنْ طَرِيْقِ سُلَيْمَانَ التَّيْمِيِّ عَنْ أَنَسٍ: ذُكِرَ لِي عَنْ رَسُولِ اللهِ ﷺ، قَالَ: إِنَّ فِيْكُمْ قَوْمًا يَدْأَبُونَ وَيَعْمَلُونَ حَتَّى يُعْجِبُوا النَّاسَ وَتُعْجِبُهُمْ أَنْفُسُهُمْ.

وَمِنْ طَرِيْقِ حَفْصِ بْنِ أَخِي أَنَسٍ عَنْ عَمِّهِ بِلَفْظِ "يَتَعَمَّقُونَ فِي الدِّيْنِ". وَفِي حَدِيْثِ ابْنِ عَبَّاسٍ عِنْدَ الطَّبَرَانِيِّ فِي قِصَّةِ مُنَاظَرَتِهِ لِلْخَوَارِجِ، قَالَ: فَأَتَيْتُهُمْ فَدَخَلْتُ عَلَى قَوْمٍ لَمْ أَرَ أَشَدَّ اجْتِهَادًا مِنْهُمْ أَيْدِيْهِمْ كَأَنَّهَا ثَفِنُ الْإِبِلِ وَوُجُوهُهُمْ مُعْلَمَةٌ مِنْ آثَارِ السُّجُودِ. وَأَخْرَجَ ابْنُ أَبِي شَيْبَةَ عَنِ ابْنِ عَبَّاسٍ رضي الله عنه أَنَّهُ ذُكِرَ عِنْدَهُ الْخَوَارِجُ وَاجْتِهَادُهُمْ فِي الْعِبَادَةِ، فَقَالَ: لَيْسُوا أَشَدَّ اجْتِهَادًا مِنَ الرُّهْبَانِ.

In the narration of Zayd b. Wahb: 'If only the Muslim army who encounters them knew what has been decreed for them upon the tongue of their Prophet ﷺ, they would rely on it [and cease doing other deeds]'. Aḥmad narrated a similar hadith from ʿAlī with the additional wording at the end: 'It is the duty upon every Muslim to fight them [in the operation at the state level]'. [We must not relax and procrastinate in fighting and eliminating the Kharijites due to their apparent religiosity, because of] the Prophet's statement ﷺ: '[You will deem] your prayers [insignificant] in comparison to their prayers'. Al-Zuhrī's narration has an additional wording reported by Abū Salama—as is in the chapter after it: 'and [you will deem] your fasting [insignificant] in comparison to their fasting'. And in the narration of ʿĀṣim b. Shumaykh from Abū Saʿīd: 'You will deem your deeds insignificant in comparison to their deeds'. ʿĀṣim also described the people of Najda al-Ḥarūrā, saying, 'They fast during the day and pray during the night and collect the alms according to the Sunna'. This was narrated by al-Ṭabarī.

A similar report is found in his [al-Ṭabarī's] collection from the narration of Yaḥyā b. Abī Kathīr from Abū Salama, and in a narration from Muhammad b. ʿAmr from Abū Salama: 'They will be devout in their worship; one of you will deem his prayers and fasting insignificant in comparison to theirs'. And there is a similar report from the narration of Anas from Abū Saʿīd, and in the narration of Aswad b. al-ʿAlāʾ from Abū Salama, there is the additional wording: 'You will deem your deeds insignificant in comparison to theirs'. And in the narration of Salama b. Kuhayl from Zayd b. Wahb, from ʿAlī: 'Your recitation will not be comparable to theirs, nor your prayers to theirs'. This was narrated by Muslim and al-Ṭabarī, the latter of whom narrated from the route of Sulaymān al-Taymī from Anas: 'It was mentioned to me that the Messenger of God ﷺ said, "Amongst you are a folk who persevere and strive [in good deeds] until they amaze people and their own egos amaze themselves".'

This report has an additional wording from the route of Ḥafṣ, Anas' nephew, from his uncle: 'They will absorb themselves deeply in the religion [*yataʿammaqūn*]'. Al-Ṭabarānī narrates the story of Ibn ʿAbbās' debate with the Kharijites, in which Ibn ʿAbbās said, 'I went to them, and I have never seen a people more assiduous in their efforts. Their hands resembled the feet of camels [thick and rough] and the marks of prostration were prominent upon their faces'. Ibn Abī Shayba narrated that when someone mentioned the Kharijites and their efforts in the presence of Ibn ʿAbbās, he said, 'They are not as hard working as the monks!'[1]

---

[1] Ibid., 12:288–289.

16.6 The Views of Anwar Shāh Kāshmīrī and Shabbīr Aḥmad ʿUthmānī on the Kharijites

Anwar Shāh Kāshmīrī and Shabbīr Aḥmad ʿUthmānī, two well-known scholars from the Deobandi school of thought of the Indian Subcontinent, spoke in detail about the Kharijites and other rebellious groups. ʿUthmānī penned a small research in his book, *Fatḥ al-Mulhim*, with the title: 'A Noble Research Concerning the Charge of Disbelief Applied to the Kharijites and Others from the Ḥarūrīs and Heretics, and Whether They are to be Fought, and if so, When'. He quoted the statements of Ibn Ḥajar al-ʿAsqalānī in which he labelled them corrupt rebels who should be fought, as per the Prophet's command ﷺ: 'Kill them when they revolt against the state'.

Then Shabbīr Aḥmad ʿUthmānī paraphrased the views of Qāḍī ʿIyāḍ, al-Qurṭubī and al-Subkī on the disbelief of the Kharijites, and quoted Kāshmīrī in *Fatḥ al-Mulhim* (5:154):

وَالْحَقُّ أَنَّ حَدِيْثَ الْمُرُوقِ يَدُلُّ عَلَى أَنَّ الْمَارِقَةَ أَقْرَبُ إِلَى الْكُفْرِ مِنَ الْإِيْمَانِ، وَمِنْ أَصْرَحِ مَا وَجَدْتُ فِيْهِ مَا عِنْدَ ابْنِ مَاجه عَنْ أَبِي أُمَامَةَ: قَدْ كَانَ هَؤُلَاءِ مُسْلِمِيْنَ، فَصَارُوا كُفَّارًا. قُلْتُ: يَا أَبَا أُمَامَةَ، هَذَا شَيْءٌ تَقُولُهُ؟ قَالَ: بَلْ سَمِعْتُهُ مِنْ رَسُولِ اللهِ ﷺ. قَالَ الْحَافِظُ مُحَمَّدُ بْنُ إِبْرَاهِيْمَ الْيَمَانِيُّ فِي "إِيْثَارِ الْحَقِّ (ص/ ٤٢١)": وَإِسْنَادُهُ حَسَنٌ. وَحَسَّنَهُ التِّرْمِذِيُّ مُخْتَصَرًا.

> The truth of the matter is that the hadith which mentions 'passing' [*murūq*] proves that those who 'pass' are closer to disbelief than faith. The most explicit text I have found stating this is the narration of Ibn Mājah from Abū Umāma, who said, 'They were Muslims and then became disbelievers'. [Abū Ghālib, the narrator, said:] 'I asked, "Is this something you say from your own opinion, or is it something you heard from the Messenger of God ﷺ?" He replied, ". . . I heard it from the Messenger of God".' Al-Ḥāfiẓ Muhammad b. Ibrāhīm al-Yamānī said in *Īthār al-ḥaqq*, 'Its chain of transmission is authentic, as declared by al-Tirmidhī in summarized form'. (p. 421)

ʿUthmānī commented:

> يُؤَيِّدُ الْقَوْلُ الْمَذْكُورُ الْأَمْرَ بِقَتْلِهِمْ مَعَ مَا تَقَدَّمَ مِنْ حَدِيْثِ ابْنِ مَسْعُودٍ: لَا يَحِلُّ قَتْلُ امْرِءٍ مُسْلِمٍ إِلاَّ بِإِحْدَى ثَلَاثٍ وَفِيْهِ: التَّارِكُ لِدِيْنِهِ؛ الْمُفَارِقُ لِلْجَمَاعَةِ وَوَرَدَ فِي بَعْضِ الرِّوَايَاتِ الصَّحِيْحَةِ: الْمَارِقُ مِنَ الدِّيْنِ، التَّارِكُ لِلْجَمَاعَةِ.
>
> The aforementioned view is buttressed by the command to kill them, in addition to the hadith of Ibn Masʿūd mentioned earlier: 'It is impermissible to kill a Muslim except for one of three reasons. . .' In that hadith it mentions: 'the one who leaves the religion and separates himself from the community [*jamāʿa*]'. In some rigorously authentic narrations of the same report, it mentions, 'the one who passes through the religion [*māriq*], and the one who separates himself from the community'.[1]

ʿUthmānī continued, elaborating the position of the Ḥanbalī school on fighting the Kharijites:

> اَلظَّاهِرُ عِنْدِي دِرَايَةً وَرِوَايَةً قَوْلُ أَهْلِ الْحَدِيْثِ، أَمَّا رِوَايَةً: فَقَوْلُهُ ﷺ: فَأَيْنَ لَقِيْتُمُوهُمْ فَاقْتُلُوهُمْ وَأَمَّا قَوْلُ عَلِيٍّ رضي الله عنه: فَمَعْنَاهُ أَنَّ الْإِنْكَارَ عَلَى الْإِمَامِ وَالطَّعْنِ فِيْهِ لَا يُوجِبُ قَتْلًا، حَتَّى يَنْزِعَ يَدَهُ مِنَ الطَّاعَةِ، فَيَكُونُ بَاغِيًا، أَوْ قَاطِعَ الطَّرِيْقِ.
>
> It seems apparent to me, considering the narrations and their meanings, that the correct view on this is the one held by the traditionists [*ahl al-ḥadīth*]. As for the narrations, consider the statement of the Prophet ﷺ, 'So kill them wherever you find them'. And as for ʿAlī's statement, it means that censuring the ruler and defaming him does not call for fighting; only when such a person challenges the writ of the government and becomes either a rebel or a brigand.[2]

---

[1] Shabbīr Aḥmad ʿUthmānī, *Fatḥ al-Mulhim*, 5:154.

[2] Ibid., 5:155.

In the conclusion of his research, ʿUthmānī mentioned both his viewpoint and the opinion of Kāshmīrī:

قَالَ فِي مَوْضِعٍ آخَرَ مِنْ رِسَالَتِهِ بَعْدَ سَرْدِ الْأَحَادِيْثِ: فَخَرَجَ مِنْ هَذِهِ الْأَحَادِيْثِ بِهَذَا الْوَجْهِ وَجْهٌ مِنْ كُفْرِهِمْ مِنْ أَهْلِ الْحَدِيْثِ، وَقَدْ نَسَبَهُ السِّنْدِيُّ عَلَى سُنَنِ النَّسَائِيِّ إِلَيْهِمْ، وَهُوَ قَوْلٌ فَحْلٌ، وَكَذَا نَسَبَهُ فِي فَتْحِ الْقَدِيْرِ إِلَيْهِمْ، وَخَرَجَ عَدَمُ الْفَرْقِ بَيْنَ الْجُحُودِ وَالتَّأْوِيْلِ فِي الْقَطْعِيَّاتِ. وَاللهُ سُبْحَانَهُ وَتَعَالَى أَعْلَمُ. وَخَرَجَ أَنَّ الْكُفْرَ قَدْ يَلْزَمُ مِنْ حَيْثُ لَا يَدْرِي، مَعَ مَا يَحْقِرُ أَحَدُكُمْ صَلَاتَهُ وَصِيَامَهُ مَعَ صَلَاتِهِمْ وَصِيَامِهِمْ، وَأَعْمَالَهُ مَعَ أَعْمَالِهِمْ، وَلَيْسَتْ قِرَاءَتُهُ إِلَى قِرَاءَتِهِمْ شَيْئًا، فَخُذْ هَذِهِ الْجُمَلَ النَّبَوِيَّةَ أَصْلًا فِي مَسْأَلَةِ التَّكْفِيْرِ، فَهِيَ كَأَحْرُفِ الْقُرْآنِ، كُلُّهَا شَافٍ كَافٍ.

After mentioning the hadith reports elsewhere, he [Kāshmīrī] said, 'Those of the traditionists who charged them [the Kharijites] with disbelief derived their view from these hadith reports. Al-Sindī—may God have mercy upon him—also charged them [with disbelief] in his commentary on al-Nasāʾī's *al-Sunan*, and this is a solid view. Similarly, the author of *Fatḥ al-Qadīr* [al-Munāwī] charged them [with disbelief] and mentioned that there is no distinction between denial and erroneous interpretation when it comes to [disbelief in] the unequivocal matters [*qaṭʿīyāt*]—and God Most High knows best. It is also derived [from these hadith reports] that disbelief may occur whilst one is unaware, in addition to the fact that 'one of you will see his prayers, fasting, deeds and recitation as insignificant in comparison to theirs'. Hence, you should take these prophetic words as a basis for the issue of charging [others] with disbelief, for they are like the letters of the Qurʾān: all of them heal and suffice.[1]

[1] Ibid.

Chapter 17

Today's Terrorists are Kharijites

ALTHOUGH WE HAVE DETAILED NUMEROUS HADITH REPORTS ABOUT the Kharijites here, there are scores more that we have not mentioned.[1] There is no denying the fact that every era has its share of people who possess the ideas, inclinations and proclivities of the Kharijites. The Prophet ﷺ made it clear that these groups would comprise immature youth who are sidetracked by propaganda and brainwashing and encouraged to commit wanton acts of violence.

It is also clear from the hadith reports that the Kharijites are not exclusive to any one given period and that they will continue to appear until the emergence of the Anti-Christ. The Prophet ﷺ said,

يَخْرُجُ قَوْمٌ مِنْ قِبَلِ الْمَشْرِقِ يَقْرَؤُونَ الْقُرْآنَ، لَا يُجَاوِزُ تَرَاقِيَهُمْ. كُلَّمَا قُطِعَ قَرْنٌ نَشَأَ قَرْنٌ، حَتَّى يَخْرُجَ فِي بَقِيَّتِهِمُ الدَّجَّالُ.

> 'There shall appear a group in the direction of the east who will recite the Qur'ān but it will not pass their throats. Every time a generation of them appears it will be cut down until the Anti-Christ appears from their last remnants'.[2]

We see from this hadith that the Prophet ﷺ informed that the Kharijites will continue to emerge and spread tumult until the appearance of the Anti-Christ, which is one of the major portents of the Final Hour. In the final days of his *Umma*, there shall emerge a group with the faces of humans but with the hearts of devils. Abū Hurayra ﷺ reported that the Prophet ﷺ said,

يَخْرُجُ فِي آخِرِ الزَّمَانِ رِجَالٌ يَخْتَلُّونَ الدُّنْيَا بِالدِّينِ. يَلْبَسُونَ لِلنَّاسِ جُلُودَ الضَّأْنِ

---

[1] For a more detailed listing of hadith reports about the Kharijites, see my other book, *al-Intibāh li al-khawārij wa al-ḥarūrā*.

[2] Narrated by Aḥmad b. Ḥanbal in *al-Musnad*, 2:209 §6952; al-Ṭabarānī in *al-Muʿjam al-awsaṭ*, 7:41 §6791; al-Ḥākim in *al-Mustadrak*, 4:556 §8558; al-Ṭayālisī in *al-Musnad*, p. 302 §2293; and Abū Nuʿaym in *Ḥilyat al-Awliyā'*, 6:54.

مِنَ اللِّيْنِ. أَلْسِنَتُهُمْ أَحْلَى مِنَ السُّكَّرِ، وَقُلُوبُهُمْ قُلُوبُ الذِّئَابِ. يَقُولُ اللهُ: أَبِي يَغْتَرُّونَ أَمْ عَلَيَّ يَجْتَرِءُونَ؟ فَبِي حَلَفْتُ لَأَبْعَثَنَّ عَلَى أُولَئِكَ مِنْهُمْ فِتْنَةً تَدَعُ الْحَلِيْمَ مِنْهُمْ حَيْرَانًا.

'In the final days there shall appear men who acquire the world by means of the religion. In front of people they will wear the garments of sheepskins, to exhibit their gentility, and their tongues will be sweeter than sugar, but their hearts will be those of wolves. God will say, "Do they delude in My name, or do they act haughtily before Me? I swear by My Being, I will surely send a tribulation against them that will leave the [seemingly] forbearing amongst them bewildered".'[1]

ʿAbd Allāh b. ʿAbbās ﵄ reported that the Messenger of God ﷺ said,

سَيَجِيءُ فِي آخِرِ الزَّمَانِ أَقْوَامٌ، يَكُونُ وُجُوهُهُمْ وُجُوهَ الْآدَمِيِّينَ، وَقُلُوبُهُمْ قُلُوبَ الشَّيَاطِينِ، أَمْثَالُ الذِّئَابِ الضَّوَارِيِّ، لَيْسَ فِي قُلُوبِهِمْ شَيْءٌ مِنَ الرَّحْمَةِ، سَفَّاكُونَ لِلدِّمَاءِ، لا يَرْعَوُونَ عَنْ قَبِيحٍ، إِنْ تَابَعْتَهُمْ وَارَبُوكَ، وَإِنْ تَوَارَيْتَ عَنْهُمُ اغْتَابُوكَ، وَإِنْ حَدَّثُوكَ كَذَبُوكَ، وَإِنِ ائْتَمَنْتَهُمْ خَانُوكَ. صَبِيُّهُمْ عَامِرٌ وَشَابُّهُمْ شَاطِرٌ وَشَيْخُهُمْ لَا يَأْمُرُ بِمَعْرُوفٍ وَلَا يَنْهَى عَنْ مُنْكَرٍ، الْاِعْتِزَازُ بِهِمْ ذُلٌّ، وَطَلَبُ مَا فِي أَيْدِيهِمْ فَقْرٌ، الْحَلِيمُ فِيهِمْ غَاوٍ، وَالْآمِرُ بِالْمَعْرُوفِ فِيهِمْ مُتَّهَمٌ، الْمُؤْمِنُ فِيهِمْ مُسْتَضْعَفٌ، وَالْفَاسِقُ فِيهِمْ مُشَرَّفٌ، اَلسُّنَّةُ فِيهِمْ بِدْعَةٌ، وَالْبِدْعَةُ فِيهِمْ سُنَّةٌ، فَعِنْدَ ذَلِكَ يُسَلَّطُ عَلَيْهِمْ شِرَارُهُمْ، وَيَدْعُو خِيَارُهُمْ فَلاَ يُسْتَجَابُ لَهُمْ.

'In the final days there shall appear groups of people with the faces of humans but with the hearts of devils, like that of raging wolves. There will not be found in their hearts even an iota of mercy. They will be given to shedding blood in abundance. They will not have any compunction

[1] Narrated by al-Tirmidhī in *al-Sunan*: *Kitāb al-zuhd* [The Book of Renunciation], 4:604 §2404.

> in committing odious acts. If you pledge your fealty to them they will betray you, and if you get away from them [for your safety] they will backbite you. When they speak to you they will lie, and if you trust them they will betray their trust. The children amongst them will run the household; the youth amongst them will be cunning; and their elder [leader] will not enjoin the good and forbid the evil. To feel honour through them is humiliation and to seek what is in their hands [i.e., their ideologies and arms] is poverty [it will destroy the economy]. The [seemingly] forbearing one amongst them will be an allurer; the one who enjoins the good and forbids the evil amongst them will be suspect; the believer amongst them will be weak; and the corrupt amongst them will be honoured. The Sunna will be seen as blameworthy innovation, and blameworthy innovation will be seen as Sunna. During that time, their evil ones will gain authority over them, and the best of them will supplicate [God] but they will not be answered'.[1]

These traditions vividly describe thc traits possessed by the modern-day terrorists. They have the faces of humans but the hearts of devils. They are devoid of mercy and full of contempt for others. They not only accuse Muslims of disbelief and polytheism, but they also target them in attacks, kill them and—to add insult to injury—film these gory scenes and disseminate them, thus bringing Islam and Muslims into disrepute.

Ibn Taymiyya said,

وَكَذَلِكَ الْخَوَارِجُ: لَمَّا كَانُوا أَهْلَ سَيْفٍ وَقِتَالٍ، ظَهَرَتْ مُخَالَفَتُهُمْ لِلْجَمَاعَةِ؛ حِيْنَ كَانُوا يُقَاتِلُونَ النَّاسَ. وَأَمَّا الْيَوْمَ فَلَا يَعْرِفُهُمْ أَكْثَرُ النَّاسِ.

> 'And likewise the Kharijites: since they were armed and inclined to fight, their opposition to the community [*jamā*ʿ*a*] manifested when they fought people. However,

[1] Narrated by al-Ṭabarānī in *al-Mu*ʿ*jam al-kabīr,* 11:99 §11169; and in *al-Mu*ʿ*jam al-ṣaghīr,* 2:111 §869.

> as for today, most people do not know of them [due to their religious disguise]'.[1]

This begs the question, if they were hidden before, how did they become known? Ibn Taymiyya answered that, saying:

> هَاتَانِ الْبِدْعَتَانِ ظَهَرَتَا لَمَّا قُتِلَ عُثْمَانُ ﵁ فِي الْفِتْنَةِ؛ فِي خِلَافَةِ أَمِيْرِ الْمُؤْمِنِيْنَ عَلِيِّ بْنِ أَبِي طَالِبٍ ﵁؛ وَظَهَرَتِ الْخَوَارِجُ بِمُفَارَقَةِ أَهْلِ الْجَمَاعَةِ، وَاسْتِحْلَالِ دِمَائِهِمْ وَأَمْوَالِهِمْ؛ حَتَّى قَاتَلَهُمْ أَمِيْرُ الْمُؤْمِنِيْنَ عَلِيُّ بْنُ أَبِي طَالِبٍ ﵁ مُتَّبِعًا فِي ذَلِكَ لِأَمْرِ النَّبِيِّ ﷺ. قَالَ الْإِمَامُ أَحْمَدُ بْنُ حَنْبَلٍ: صَحَّ الْحَدِيْثُ فِي الْخَوَارِجِ مِنْ عَشَرَةِ أَوْجُهٍ. وَهَذِهِ قَدْ رَوَاهَا صَاحِبُهُ مُسْلِمُ بْنُ الْحَجَّاجِ فِي صَحِيْحِهِ، وَرَوَى الْبُخَارِيُّ قِطْعَةً مِنْهَا. وَاتَّفَقَتِ الصَّحَابَةُ عَلَى قِتَالِ الْخَوَارِجِ حَتَّى أَنَّ ابْنَ عُمَرَ . . . قَالَ عِنْدَ الْمَوْتِ: مَا آسِي عَلَى شَيْءٍ إِلاَّ عَلَى أَنِّي لَمْ أُقَاتِلِ الطَّائِفَةَ الْبَاغِيَةَ مَعَ عَلِيٍّ، يُرِيْدُ بِذَلِكَ قِتَالَ الْخَوَارِجِ. . . . وَإِنَّمَا أَرَادَ الْمَارِقَةَ الَّتِي قَالَ فِيْهَا النَّبِيُّ ﷺ: تَمْرُقُ مَارِقَةٌ عَلَى حِيْنِ فُرْقَةٍ مِنَ النَّاسِ، يَقْتُلُهُمْ أَدْنَى الطَّائِفَتَيْنِ إِلَى الْحَقِّ. وَهَذَا حَدَّثَ بِهِ أَبُو سَعِيْدٍ. فَلَمَّا بَلَغَ ابْنَ عُمَرَ قَوْلُ النَّبِيِّ ﷺ فِي الْخَوَارِجِ، وَأَمْرُهُ بِقِتَالِهِمْ، تَحَسَّرَ عَلَى تَرْكِ قِتَالِهِمْ.
>
> The two innovations [declaring the Muslims disbelievers and considering their property lawful] appeared when ʿUthmān ﵁ was killed during the turmoil, and during the caliphate of the Commander of the Faithful, ʿAlī b. Abī Ṭālib ﵁. The Kharijites appeared by splitting off from the community and declaring their blood and wealth lawful, until the Commander of the Faithful, ʿAlī b. Abī Ṭālib ﵁ fought against them—following the command of the Prophet ﷺ. Imam Aḥmad b. Ḥanbal said, 'The hadith about them is authentic from ten different angles [chains of narration]'. These [hadith reports] were narrated by Muslim b. al-Ḥajjāj in his *Ṣaḥīḥ* collection, and al-Bukhārī narrated a portion of them. The Companions were in unanimous agreement that the Kharijites were to be fought; to the point that Ibn ʿUmar . . . said on

[1] Ibn Taymiyya, *al-Nubuwwāt*, p. 222.

> his deathbed, 'I regret nothing save that I did not fight with ᶜAlī against the rebellious faction'. By that he meant the Kharijites. . . . [H]e only meant the ones who 'passed through' [*māriqa*], about whom the Prophet ﷺ said, 'A group will pass through [*tamruq*] during a time in which people are disunited; the closest of the two groups to the truth will fight against them'. This is what Abū Saᶜīd narrated. Hence, when the statement of the Prophet ﷺ regarding the Kharijites reached Ibn ᶜUmar, he felt regret that he did not fight against them.[1]

From all of this we can gather that people generally mistake the Kharijites for righteous people due to their outward appearance and ostensible religiosity; however, they reveal their true colours when they take up arms and murder harmless people. The Kharijites are not identified by the name 'Kharijite' written on their foreheads; they are identified as Kharijites by their barbaric actions.

17.1 CONDEMNATION OF THOSE WHO SUPPORT THE KHARIJITE TERRORISTS

There are some people who have a soft spot in their hearts for the Kharijite terrorists. They do not consider them evil, and might even offer them physical, financial or moral support. Those who support the Kharijites are called *Qaᶜdiyya* [literally, 'the sitters']. Ibn Ḥajar al-ᶜAsqalānī said,

"الْقَعْدِيَّةُ" قَوْمٌ مِنَ الْخَوَارِجِ، كَانُوا يَقُولُونَ بِقَوْلِهِمْ، وَلَا يَرَوْنَ الْخُرُوجَ بَلْ يُزَيِّنُونَهُ.

> 'The *Qaᶜdiyya* are a folk from the Kharijites who held the beliefs of the latter but would only justify rebellion, without actually participating in it'.[2]

Elsewhere he wrote,

اَلْخَوَارِجُ الَّذِيْنَ أَنْكَرُوا عَلَى عَلِيٍّ ﵁ التَّحْكِيْمَ وَتبَرَّءُوا مِنْهُ وَمِنْ عُثْمَانَ ﵁ وَذُرِّيَّتِهِ

---

[1] Ibid., pp. 222–223.

[2] Ibn Ḥajar al-ᶜAsqalānī, *Fatḥ al-Bārī*, 1:432.

وَقَاتَلُوهُمْ، فَإِنْ أَطْلَقُوا تَكْفِيْرَهُمْ فَهُمُ الْغُلَاةُ مِنْهُمْ وَالْقَعْدِيَّةُ الَّذِيْنَ يُزَيِّنُونَ الْخُرُوجَ عَلَى الْأَئِمَّةِ وَلَا يُبَاشِرُونَ ذَلِكَ.

> 'The Kharijites are those who censured ʿAlī ﷺ because of the act of arbitration, and disavowed themselves from him and ʿUthmān ﷺ and his family and fought against them. If their charge of disbelief is general [to everyone except them], they are considered of the extreme [Kharijites]. The *Qaʿdiyya* justify rebelling against the Muslim governments but do not participate in it directly'.[1]

In *Tahdhīb al-tahdhīb*, he said,

"الْقَعْدُ" اَلْخَوَارِجُ كَانُوا لَا يَرَوْنَ بِالْحَرْبِ، بَلْ يُنْكِرُونَ عَلَى أُمَرَاءِ الْجَوْرِ حَسَبَ الطَّاقَةِ، وَيَدْعُونَ إِلَى رَأْيِهِمْ، وَيُزَيِّنُونَ مَعَ ذَلِكَ الْخُرُوجَ، وَيُحَسِّنُونَهُ.

> 'The *Qaʿdiyya* are Kharijites who do not believe in waging war; rather, they censure the unjust rulers according to their ability, invite others to their belief, and in addition to that, they beautify and justify rebellion [through religious garbs]'.[2]

In general, the *Qaʿdiyya* do not openly express their views. They work behind the scenes and support those who rebel. They sow the seeds of dissension, disruption and strife in the hearts of people, which is especially dangerous when conducted by one who is eloquent and who mixes his speech with references to the Sunna.

17.2 An Important Juristic Issue: Labelling the Terrorists as Kharijites is Based on the Qurʾān and Sunna, Not Independent Reasoning [*Ijtihād*]

Our judgement that the terrorists of today are Kharijites is not based on independent reasoning; rather, it is based on the Qurʾān

---

[1] Ibid., 1:459.

[2] Ibn Ḥajar al-ʿAsqalānī, *Tahdhīb al-tahdhīb*, 8:114.

and the Sunna. The Kharijites are not merely the sect of old that rebelled against our master, ʿAlī ﷺ. Certainly, they were their vanguard, but, as we have mentioned, the tribulation of the Kharijites has emerged time and time again, and will continue to emerge until the appearance of the Anti-Christ.

According to Sharīk b. Shihāb ﷺ, the Messenger of God ﷺ said about the Kharijites,

لَا يَزَالُونَ يَخْرُجُونَ حَتَّى يَخْرُجَ آخِرُهُمْ مَعَ الْمَسِيحِ الدَّجَّالِ، فَإِذَا لَقِيْتُمُوهُمْ فَاقْتُلُوهُمْ هُمْ شَرُّ الْخَلْقِ وَالْخَلِيْقَةِ.

'They shall continue to appear until the last of them appears with the Anti-Christ [al-Dajjāl]; so you should kill them when you encounter them [in the battlefield]. They are the most evil of the creation'.[1]

Similarly, Imam Aḥmad b. Ḥanbal and Imam Ibn Abī Shayba narrated,

لَا يَزَالُوْنَ يَخْرُجُوْنَ حَتَّى يَخْرُجَ آخِرُهُمْ، فَإِذَا رَأَيْتُمُوْهُمْ فَاقْتُلُوْهُمْ، قَالَهَا ثَلَاثًا. شَرُّ الْخَلْقِ وَالْخَلِيْقَةِ. قَالَهَا ثَلَاثًا.

'They will not cease to emerge, until the last group of them emerges [with the Anti-Christ]; so you should kill them when you encounter them [in the battlefield]. They are the most evil of creation'. He repeated these words three times.[2]

And Imam al-Ḥākim narrated a hadith report with these words,

لَا يَزَالُوْنَ يَخْرُجُوْنَ حَتَّى يَخْرُجَ آخِرُهُمْ، فَإِذَا رَأَيْتُمُوْهُمْ فَاقْتُلُوْهُمْ. قَالَهَا حَمَّادٌ ثَلَاثًا.

---

[1] Narrated by al-Nasāʾī in *al-Sunan*: *Kitāb taḥrīm al-dam* [The Book on the Prohibition of Bloodshed], chapter: 'Regarding the One Who Unsheathes His Sword and Wields it amongst People', 7:119 §4103; al-Nasāʾī in *al-Sunan al-kubrā*, 2:312 §3566; al-Bazzār in *al-Musnad*, 9:294 §3846; and al-Ṭayālisī in *al-Musnad*, 1:124 §923.

[2] Narrated by Aḥmad b. Ḥanbal in *al-Musnad*, 4:421 §19798; Ibn Abī Shayba in *al-Muṣannaf*, 7:559 §37917; and al-Ruyānī in *al-Musnad*, 2:26 §766.

هُمْ شَرُّ الْخَلْقِ وَالْخَلِيْقَةِ. قَالَهَا حَمَّادٌ ثَلَاثًا. وَقَالَ: قَالَ أَيْضًا: لَا يَرْجِعُوْنَ فِيْهِ.

> 'They will not cease to emerge, until the last group of them comes forth [with the Anti-Christ]; so you should kill them when you encounter them [in the battlefield]. [According to Ḥammād, a reporter of the tradition:] "The Messenger of God ﷺ repeated these words three times." [Ḥammād said:] The Messenger of God ﷺ added: "They will not turn from their doctrine and ideology".'[1]

In the preceding hadith reports, the Messenger of God ﷺ has clarified that the rebels will continuously form groups and emerge in Muslim states and societies. The word, *lā yazālūna yakhrujūna,* [they will not cease to emerge] indicate that all these groups will be Kharijites and will continue to appear until their last party rise with the Anti-Christ before the end of time.

17.3 Summary

This detailed discussion highlighting the signs, traits and features of the Kharijites proves beyond a shadow of a doubt that the modern-day terrorists are their contemporary embodiment. It is, therefore, our religious and national duty to expose them who they are and detail the threat they pose to peace and coexistence.

Although they mask themselves with the garb of religion, we should not be fooled, for their mischief and evil show us who they really are. They have no connection with Islam, no matter what religious trappings they take on. They are outside of the fold of Islam and have passed through it just as an arrow passes through a hunted game; their criminal acts cannot be associated with Islam or the Muslims.

Both the early and latter-day Islamic scholars have unanimously agreed that—in the light of the Qurʾānic verses and hadith reports—the Kharijite terrorists have nothing to do with Islam. Traditional Islamic teachings hold that such people are rebels

---

[1] Narrated by al-Ḥākim in *al-Mustadrak*, 2:160 §2647; and al-Haythamī in *Majmaʿ al-Zawāʾid*, 6:229.

and that it is the duty of the state to eliminate them. Having said that, a word of caution must be mentioned: the duty of removing the Kharijite cancer from society is the responsibility of the state alone. Vigilantism is not allowed in the Islamic Sacred Law. No individual or private band of citizens is allowed to take up arms against terrorists with the intention of eliminating them and restoring peace in society. Such a venture will inevitably lead to more harm than good and bring about drastic consequences.

The Messenger of God ﷺ foretold the perpetual emergence and rising of Kharijites in every era in the form of well-organized militant groups to put the Muslims on alert, and so that they might recognize them. The Muslims should not be mistaken by their guised faces and appearances, slogans and high claims on Shariah. Simultaneously, he declared that the state must come into action to eliminate them, in order to save the peaceful community from their terror, bloodshed and plunder. That is the reason why the Companions ﷺ joined our master ʿAlī ﷺ to uproot the terrorists, the Kharijites, at state level and founded a tradition for the coming generations.

Chapter 18

The Peaceful Method of Social and Political Struggle

18.1 The Peaceful Method of Struggle in the Muslim State

In this fatwa we have proven that it is impermissible to rebel against the Muslim state, even if its rulers are corrupt and oppressive. Certain questions naturally arise: What should Muslims do to counter the oppression and cruelty of the rulers? Should the rulers have free reign to do what they like? Should the followers of truth sit back idly as silent spectators? If not, then what are their responsibilities in those circumstances? If Islam disapproves of armed rebellion and, at the same time, condemns silence in the face of oppression, what options are available for the citizens of the Muslim state to bring about change?

18.2 The Qur'ānic Command to Enjoin the Good and Forbid the Evil

In Islamic terminology, the act of promoting good and preventing wrong is called 'enjoining the good and forbidding the evil' [*al-amr bi al-maʿrūf wa al-nahī ʿan al-munkar*]. This religiously mandated act is to be applied at the individual and governmental levels.

In the Qur'ān, God has commanded the believers to enjoin the good and forbid the evil. The importance of this command is reflected in the verse of the Qur'ān where it is listed amongst the qualities of 'the balanced *Umma*':

﴿كُنتُمْ خَيْرَ أُمَّةٍ أُخْرِجَتْ لِلنَّاسِ تَأْمُرُونَ بِٱلْمَعْرُوفِ وَتَنْهَوْنَ عَنِ ٱلْمُنكَرِ﴾

> '*You are the best nation raised up for mankind; you enjoin the good and forbid the evil*'.[1]

Elsewhere, God says,

﴿وَٱلْمُؤْمِنُونَ وَٱلْمُؤْمِنَٰتُ بَعْضُهُمْ أَوْلِيَآءُ بَعْضٍ يَأْمُرُونَ بِٱلْمَعْرُوفِ وَيَنْهَوْنَ عَنِ ٱلْمُنكَرِ﴾

[1] Qur'ān 3:110.

> *'And the believing men and women are allies to one another; they enjoin the good and forbid the evil'.*[1]

Although this responsibility falls on individuals in an Islamic society, we must bear in mind that isolated, individual efforts to change wrongs committed by the government are often without much effect. Efforts to bring change and reform in society should ideally be collective, which is why organized grassroot movements are justified in Islamic law.

18.3 The Collective Effort to Enjoin the Good and Forbid the Evil

The effort to enjoin the good and forbid the evil is both an individual and collective endeavour. God says in the Qur'ān,

﴿وَلْتَكُن مِّنكُمْ أُمَّةٌ يَدْعُونَ إِلَى ٱلْخَيْرِ وَيَأْمُرُونَ بِٱلْمَعْرُوفِ وَيَنْهَوْنَ عَنِ ٱلْمُنكَرِ وَأُوْلَٰئِكَ هُمُ ٱلْمُفْلِحُونَ﴾

> *'And let their arise amongst you a group that invites to good and enjoins what is right and forbids what is wrong. And it is they who are the successful'.*[2]

This verse informs us that enjoining the good and forbidding the evil on the collective level contributes to its effectiveness, productivity and benefit. This is in fulfilment of the Qur'ānic command:

﴿وَتَعَاوَنُوا۟ عَلَى ٱلْبِرِّ وَٱلتَّقْوَىٰ وَلَا تَعَاوَنُوا۟ عَلَى ٱلْإِثْمِ وَٱلْعُدْوَانِ﴾

> *'And help one another with piety and righteousness, and do not help one another with sin and transgression'.*[3]

---

[1] Ibid., 9:71.

[2] Ibid., 3:104.

[3] Ibid., 5:2.

18.4 HADITH REPORTS CONCERNING THE ACT OF ENJOINING THE GOOD AND FORBIDDING THE EVIL

The prophetic traditions speak of the importance of enjoining the good and forbidding the evil, and the dire consequences of neglecting them. Ḥudhayfa ﵁ reported that the Messenger of God ﷺ said,

فِتْنَةُ الرَّجُلِ فِي أَهْلِهِ وَمَالِهِ وَجَارِهِ تُكَفِّرُهَا الصَّلَاةُ وَالصَّدَقَةُ وَالْأَمْرُ بِالْمَعْرُوفِ وَالنَّهْيُ عَنِ الْمُنْكَرِ.

> 'The tribulations a man faces with regard to his family, wealth and neighbours are expiated by prayer, charity and the act of enjoining the good and forbidding the evil'.[1]

Ḥudhayfa ﵁ also reported that the Prophet ﷺ said,

وَالَّذِي نَفْسِي بِيَدِهِ، لَتَأْمُرُنَّ بِالْمَعْرُوفِ وَلَتَنْهَوُنَّ عَنِ الْمُنْكَرِ أَوْ لَيُوشِكَنَّ اللهُ أَنْ يَبْعَثَ عَلَيْكُمْ عِقَابًا مِنْهُ، ثُمَّ تَدْعُونَهُ فَلَا يُسْتَجَابُ لَكُمْ.

> 'By the One in whose Hand rests my soul, you must surely enjoin the good and forbid the evil, otherwise it is expected that God will send against you a punishment from Him, and then you will supplicate Him but will not be answered'.[2]

ʿAbd al-Raḥmān b. al-ʿAlāʾ al-Ḥaḍramī ﵁ said, 'Someone informed me that he heard the Messenger of God ﷺ say,

---

[1] Narrated by al-Bukhārī in *al-Ṣaḥīḥ*: *Kitāb al-manāqib* [The Book of Exemplary Virtues], chapter: 'The Signs of Prophethood in Islam', 3:1314 §3393; and Muslim in *al-Ṣaḥīḥ*: *Kitāb al-fitan wa ashrāṭ al-sāʿa* [The Book of Tribulations and the Portents of the Final Hour], chapter: 'Regarding the Tribulations That Will Descend Like a Crashing Wave', 4:2218 §2889.

[2] Narrated by al-Tirmidhī in *al-Sunan*: *Kitāb al-fitan* [The Book of Tribulations], chapter: 'What Has Come to Us Concerning the Act of Enjoining the Good and Forbidding the Evil', 4:468 §2169; Ibn Mājah in *al-Sunan*: *Kitāb al-fitan* [The Book of Tribulation], chapter: 'Enjoining the Good and Forbidding the Evil', 2:1327 §4004; and Aḥmad b. Ḥanbal in *al-Musnad*, 5:391 §23375.

إِنَّ مِنْ أُمَّتِي قَوْمًا يُعْطَوْنَ مِثْلَ أُجُورِ أَوَّلِهِمْ، فَيُنْكِرُونَ الْمُنْكَرَ.

"Indeed, from my *Umma* there are a folk who shall receive rewards equivalent to the rewards of the early ones [my Companions]—they forbid the evil".'[1]

Abū Hurayra ﷺ reported that the Messenger of God ﷺ said,

لَتَأْمُرُنَّ بِالْمَعْرُوفِ وَلَتَنْهَوُنَّ عَنِ الْمُنْكَرِ، أَوْ لَيُسَلِّطَنَّ اللهُ عَلَيْكُمْ شِرَارَكُمْ، ثُمَّ يَدْعُو خِيَارُكُمْ فَلَا يُسْتَجَابُ لَكُمْ.

'You must surely enjoin the good and forbid the evil, otherwise God will cause the evil ones in your midst to gain authority over you, and then the best of you will supplicate but you will not be answered'.[2]

Anas b. Mālik ﷺ said,

قُلْنَا: يَا رَسُولَ اللهِ، لَا نَأْمُرُ بِالْمَعْرُوفِ حَتَّى نَعْمَلَ بِهِ، وَلَا نَنْهَى عَنِ الْمُنْكَرِ حَتَّى نَجْتَنِبَهُ كُلَّهُ. فَقَالَ رَسُولُ اللهِ ﷺ: بَلْ مُرُوا بِالْمَعْرُوفِ وَإِنْ لَمْ تَعْمَلُوا بِهِ كُلِّهِ، وَانْهَوْا عَنِ الْمُنْكَرِ وَإِنْ لَم تَجْتَنِبُوهُ كُلَّهُ.

'We said, "O Messenger of God! We shall abstain from enjoining the good until we act on it ourselves, and we shall abstain from forbidding the evil until we also turn away from it". He replied, "No. Rather, you should enjoin the good, even if you do not act upon it entirely, and you should forbid the evil, even if you do not turn away from it entirely".'[3]

The aforementioned traditions inform us of the significance and importance of enjoining the good and forbidding the evil. This

[1] Narrated by Aḥmad b. Ḥanbal in *al-Musnad*, 4:62 §16643; and 5:375 §23299; and al-Haythamī in *Majmaʿ al-zawāʾid*, 7:261, 271.

[2] Narrated by al-Ṭabarānī in *al-Muʿjam al-awsaṭ*, 2:99 §1379; Ibn Abī Shayba in *al-Muṣannaf*, 7:460 §37221; al-Bazzār in *al-Musnad*, 1:292–293 §188; and Abū Yaʿlā in *al-Musnad*, 8:313 §6916.

[3] Narrated by al-Ṭabarānī in *al-Muʿjam al-awsaṭ*, 6:365 §6628; al-Bayhaqī in *Shuʿab al-Īmān*, 6:89 §7570; and al-Haythamī in *Majmaʿ al-zawāʾid*, 7:277.

praiseworthy act expiates sins, removes tribulations from our lives and serves as a shield against Divine wrath. If we take account of ourselves and our current predicament, we will see that we are suffering the consequences of our neglect of this righteous act. Our prayers go unanswered, natural disasters and calamities are increasing and lawlessness, murder, corruption and unemployment are on the rise. In short, there is not a single tribulation that has not engulfed us.

18.5 The Three Levels of Forbidding the Evil

The Prophet ﷺ has described to us three levels in the act of forbidding evil. Abū Saʿīd ؓ reported that the Prophet ﷺ said,

مَنْ رَأَى مِنْكُمْ مُنْكَرًا فَلْيُغَيِّرْهُ بِيَدِهِ، فَإِنْ لَمْ يَسْتَطِعْ فَبِلِسَانِهِ، فَإِنْ لَمْ يَسْتَطِعْ فَبِقَلْبِهِ وَذَلِكَ أَضْعَفُ الْإِيْمَانِ.

> 'Whoever amongst you witnesses an evil, let him reform it [practically] with his hand; if he is unable, then [let him denounce it] verbally; and if he is unable, then [let him abhor it] in his heart—and that is the weakest form of faith'.[1]

This hadith delineates three methods of condemning evil: through the hand, the tongue and the heart. This means that one should take practical steps to remove evil, speak out about it and detest it in his or her heart. Each of these three ways is a peaceful means of change. To forbid evil with one's hands is to struggle against it

---

[1] Narrated by Muslim in *al-Ṣaḥīḥ*: *Kitāb al-Īmān* [The Book of Faith], chapter: 'The Act of Forbidding Evil is a Part of Faith', 1:69 §49; al-Tirmidhī in *al-Sunan*: *Kitāb al-fitan* [The Book of Tribulation], chapter: 'What Has Come to Us Concerning the Interpretation of Forbidding Evil with the Hand, Tongue and Heart', 4:469 §2172; Abū Dāwūd in *al-Sunan: Kitāb al-malāḥim* [The Book of Tumultuous Battles], chapter: 'On Commanding and Forbidding', 4:123 §4340; al-Nasāʾī in *al-Sunan*: *Kitāb al-Īmān wa al-sharāʾiʿuhu* [The Book of Faith and its Revealed Laws], chapter: 'The Varying Ranks of the Faithful', 8:111 §5008; Ibn Mājah in *al-Sunan*: *Kitāb iqāmat al-ṣalāt wa al-Sunna fīhā* [The Book of Establishing the Prayer and the Sunna Therein], chapter: 'What Has Come to Us Concerning the Ritual prayer of Two Eids', 1:406 §1275.

in the physical realm; but it must be free of violence because good cannot be forced on others through oppression, as God says,

﴿لَآ إِكۡرَاهَ فِي ٱلدِّينِ﴾

'There is no compulsion in religion'.[1]

The command to physically forbid evil is communally obligatory upon those who are able; otherwise, the believers are ordered to denounce it verbally, and if that is not possible, they must at least detest it in their hearts. What is encompassed in the definition of evil? Here, people have restricted its usage to a more literal and limited sense. The fact remains that evil also includes domestic violence against women and deprivation of their rights, as well as every form of corruption, disruption, violence, violation of human rights, nepotism, and promotion of what is forbidden in the Islamic Sacred Law.

18.6 The Meaning of Forbidding Evil Physically

Imagine a society in which evil is widespread and the command to forbid it by hand is interpreted as the use of physical force. Every individual and group would have their own conception of good and begin imposing it on others. Such a situation would create unrest, lawlessness and violence. Furthermore, if 'forbidding the evil' is carried out by means of firearms and explosives, civil war will occur and more evil will spread.

How can the Islamic faith, which does not permit Muslims to take up arms and revolt against corrupt rulers for the sake of social justice and peace, allow the use of violence to prevent evil? Hence, for the common citizen, forbidding the evil is done through practical, non-violent means according to his or her ability.

If preventing evil means eradicating it by using physical force, then it becomes the responsibility of the government to undertake its execution. The government is the only entity vested with the authority to use force in the removal of evil—this, in fact, is what justifies its existence in the first place. God says,

---

[1] Qur'ān 2:256.

﴿ٱلَّذِينَ إِن مَّكَّنَّٰهُمْ فِى ٱلْأَرْضِ أَقَامُوا۟ ٱلصَّلَوٰةَ وَءَاتَوُا۟ ٱلزَّكَوٰةَ وَأَمَرُوا۟ بِٱلْمَعْرُوفِ وَنَهَوْا۟ عَنِ ٱلْمُنكَرِ وَلِلَّهِ عَٰقِبَةُ ٱلْأُمُورِ﴾

'[The believers are those] *who, if We establish their rule in the earth, establish the prayer, pay the Zakat, enjoin the good and forbid the evil. And to God belongs the final results of all things*'.[1]

18.7 Political and Democratic Struggle against Injustice and Oppression

Islam seeks to establish societies based on justice and equity: societies in which no one encroaches on the rights of others or seeks to wield his or her strength, authority, wealth or status unjustly. It is the responsibility of a Muslim to raise his or her voice and speak out against the oppression and excesses of individuals or governments. God has enjoined the believers to expose the cruelty of oppressors:

﴿لَّا يُحِبُّ ٱللَّهُ ٱلْجَهْرَ بِٱلسُّوٓءِ مِنَ ٱلْقَوْلِ إِلَّا مَن ظُلِمَ وَكَانَ ٱللَّهُ سَمِيعًا عَلِيمًا﴾

'*God does not like the public mention of evil except by the one who has been wronged. And God is All-Hearing, All-Knowing*'.[2]

As Muslims, we are urged to voice our protest against oppression and injustice. In fact, declaring a word of justice in the presence of an oppressive ruler is considered the highest form of jihad. Abū Saʿīd al-Khudrī ﷺ reported that the Messenger of God ﷺ said,

إِنَّ مِنْ أَعْظَمِ الْجِهَادِ كَلِمَةَ عَدْلٍ عِنْدَ سُلْطَانٍ جَائِرٍ.

'Indeed, from the greatest forms of jihad is a just word spoken before a tyrannical ruler'.[3]

---

[1] Ibid., 22:41.

[2] Ibid., 4:148.

[3] Narrated by al-Tirmidhī in *al-Sunan*: *Kitāb al-fitan* [The Book of Tribulations], chapter: 'What Has Come to Us Concerning the Fact That the Best Jihad is a

In a narration from Abū Dāwūd, the word 'tyrannical emir' is used in place of 'tyrannical ruler'.[1] The Prophet ﷺ forbade the believers from concealing the truth out of fear. Abū Saʿīd al-Khudrī ؓ reported that the Messenger of God ﷺ said,

لَا يَمْنَعَنَّ رَجُلًا هَيْبَةُ النَّاسِ أَنْ يَقُولَ بِحَقٍّ إِذَا عَلِمَهُ.

> 'Let not any man shrink from saying the truth out of fear of people if he knows it'.[2]

The Prophet ﷺ also warned people from abandoning the duty of forbidding the evil when they are capable,

مَا مِنْ قَوْمٍ يُعْمَلُ فِيْهِمْ بِالْمَعَاصِي، ثُمَّ يَقْدِرُونَ عَلَى أَنْ يُغَيِّرُوا، ثُمَّ لَا يُغَيِّرُوا إِلَّا يُوشِكُ أَنْ يَعُمَّهُمُ اللهُ مِنْهُ بِعِقَابٍ.

> 'There is no nation in which acts of disobedience are committed but they do not stop them, even though they are able, save that it is expected that God will cover them all with a punishment'.[3]

ʿAdī b. Ḥātim ؓ reported that the Messenger of God ﷺ said,

إِنَّ اللهَ ﷻ لَا يُعَذِّبُ الْعَامَّةَ بِعَمَلِ الْخَاصَّةِ حَتَّى يَرَوُا الْمُنْكَرَ بَيْنَ ظَهْرَانَيْهِمْ، وَهُمْ قَادِرُونَ عَلَى أَنْ يُنْكِرُوهُ فَلَا يُنْكِرُوهُ. فَإِذَا فَعَلُوا ذَلِكَ عَذَّبَ اللهُ الْخَاصَّةَ وَالْعَامَّةَ.

Just Word before a Tyrannical Ruler', 4:471 §2174.

[1] Narrated by Abū Dāwūd in *al-Sunan: Kitāb al-malāḥim* [The Book of Tumultuous Battles], chapter: 'Enjoining the Good and Forbidding the Evil', 4:124 §4344.

[2] Narrated by al-Tirmidhī in *al-Sunan*: *Kitāb al-fitan* [The Book of Tribulations], chapter: 'What Has Been Reported Regarding the Prophet ﷺ Informing His Companions of All That Would Occur until the Day of Resurrection', 4:483 §2191; Ibn Mājah in *al-Sunan*: *Kitāb al-fitan* [The Book of Tribulation], chapter: 'Enjoining the Good and Forbidding the Evil', 2:1328 §4007; and Aḥmad b. Ḥanbal in *al-Musnad*, 3:5 §11030.

[3] Narrated by Abū Dāwūd in *al-Sunan*: *Kitāb al-malāḥim* [The Book of Tumultuous Battles], chapter: 'Enjoining the Good and Forbidding the Evil', 4:122 §4338; Ibn Mājah in *al-Sunan*: *Kitāb al-fitan* [The Book of Tribulation], chapter: 'Enjoining the Good and Forbidding the Evil', 2:1329 §4009; and Aḥmad b. Ḥanbal in *al-Musnad*, 4:364 §19250.

'Indeed, God does not punish all for the actions of the few until the former witness evil in their midst and fail to stop it even though they are able. When that occurs, God shall punish them collectively: the few and the many'.[1]

Abū Bakr al-Ṣiddīq ﷺ said,

يَا أَيُّهَا النَّاسُ، إِنَّكُمْ تَقْرَءُونَ هَذِهِ الْآيَةَ: ﴿يَٰٓأَيُّهَا ٱلَّذِينَ ءَامَنُواْ عَلَيۡكُمۡ أَنفُسَكُمۡ لَا يَضُرُّكُم مَّن ضَلَّ إِذَا ٱهۡتَدَيۡتُمۡ﴾ وَإِنَّا سَمِعْنَا رَسُولَ اللهِ ﷺ يَقُولُ: إِنَّ النَّاسَ إِذَا رَأَوُا الْمُنْكَرَ فَلَمْ يُنْكِرُوهُ أَوْشَكَ أَنْ يَعُمَّهُمُ اللهُ بِعِقَابِهِ.

'O people! Surely, you all read the verse, "*O you who believe! Take care of your own selves. If you are guided, then no one who is astray can harm you*" [Qur'ān 5:105]. Indeed, we heard the Messenger of God ﷺ say, "It is to be expected that if a people witness evil but do not censure it, God will cover them all with His punishment".'[2]

Jarīr ﷺ reported that the Messenger of God ﷺ said,

مَا مِنْ رَجُلٍ يَكُونُ فِي قَوْمٍ يُعْمَلُ فِيهِمْ بِالْمَعَاصِي، يَقْدِرُونَ عَلَى أَنْ يُغَيِّرُوا عَلَيْهِ، فَلَا يُغَيِّرُوا إِلَّا أَصَابَهُمُ اللهُ بِعَذَابٍ مِنْ قَبْلِ أَنْ يَمُوتُوا.

'There are no people in the midst of whom a man does acts of disobedience, and they have the ability to stop him, but do not, except that God will afflict them with a punishment before they die'.[3]

---

[1] Narrated by Aḥmad b. Ḥanbal in *al-Musnad*, 4:192; Mālik in *al-Muwaṭṭā: Kitāb al-kalām* [The Book of Speech], chapter: 'What Has Come to Us Concerning the Punishment of All for the Acts of the Few', 2:991 §1799; and al-Ṭabarānī in *al-Muʿjam al-kabīr*, 17:139.

[2] Narrated by Aḥmad b. Ḥanbal in *al-Musnad*, 1:2 §1.

[3] Narrated by Abū Dāwūd in *al-Sunan: Kitāb al-malāḥim* [The Book of Tumultuous Battles], chapter: 'Enjoining the Good and Forbidding the Evil', 4:122 §4339; Ibn Mājah in *al-Sunan*: *Kitāb al-fitan* [The Book of Tribulation], chapter: 'Enjoining the Good and Forbidding the Evil', 2:1329 §4009; and Aḥmad b. Ḥanbal in *al-Musnad*, 4:364; Ibn Ḥibbān in *al-Ṣaḥīḥ*, 1:536 §300; and al-Ṭabarānī in *al-Muʿjam al-kabīr*, 2:332 §2382.

Abū ʿUbayda ﵁ reported that the Messenger of God ﷺ said,

إِنَّ بَنِي إِسْرَائِيْلَ لَمَّا وَقَعَ فِيْهِمُ النَّقْصُ كَانَ الرَّجُلُ يَرَى أَخَاهُ عَلَى الذَّنْبِ فَيَنْهَاهُ عَنْهُ. فَإِذَا كَانَ الْغَدُ لَمْ يَمْنَعْهُ مَا رَأَى مِنْهُ أَنْ يَكُونَ أَكِيْلَهُ وَشَرِيْبَهُ وَخَلِيْطَهُ. فَضَرَبَ اللهُ قُلُوبَ بَعْضِهِمْ بِبَعْضٍ، وَنَزَلَ فِيْهِمُ الْقُرْآنُ. فَقَالَ: ﴿لُعِنَ ٱلَّذِينَ كَفَرُواْ مِنۢ بَنِىٓ إِسْرَٰٓءِيلَ عَلَىٰ لِسَانِ دَاوُۥدَ وَعِيسَى ٱبْنِ مَرْيَمَ ذَٰلِكَ بِمَا عَصَواْ وَّكَانُواْ يَعْتَدُونَ﴾. فَقَرَأَ حَتَّى بَلَغَ: ﴿وَلَوْ كَانُواْ يُؤْمِنُونَ بِٱللَّهِ وَٱلنَّبِيِّ وَمَآ أُنْزِلَ إِلَيْهِ مَا ٱتَّخَذُوهُمْ أَوْلِيَآءَ وَلَٰكِنَّ كَثِيرًا مِّنْهُمْ فَٰسِقُونَ﴾. قَالَ: وَكَانَ نَبِيُّ اللهِ مُتَّكِئًا، فَجَلَسَ، فَقَالَ: لَا، حَتَّى تَأْخُذُوا عَلَى يَدِ الظَّالِمِ فَتَأْطَرُوهُ عَلَى الْحَقِّ أَطْرًا.

'When shortcomings befell the Children of Israel, a man would witness his brother committing a sin and forbid him from it, but the sin he saw from him would not prevent him from eating, drinking and mingling with him the next day. As a result, God afflicted them with hatred, and the Qurʾān revealed about them: "*Cursed were those who disbelieved amongst the Children of Israel by the tongue of David and Jesus the son of Mary. That was because they disobeyed and continually transgressed. . . . If only they had believed in God and the Prophet and what was revealed to him, they would not have taken them as protecting friends; but many of them are corrupt*".' Abū ʿUbayda added, 'The Messenger of God ﷺ was reclining, and then he sat up and said, "No [you cannot escape the same fate] until you hold the hand of the oppressor and prevent him and lead him to the truth!".'[1]

Al-Nuʿmān b. Bashīr ﵁ reported that the Prophet ﷺ said,

---

[1] Narrated by al-Tirmidhī in *al-Sunan*: *Kitāb tafsīr al-Qurʾān* [The Book of Qurʾānic Exegesis], chapter: 'From *Sūra al-Māʾida*', 5:252 §3048; Abū Dāwūd in *al-Sunan*: *Kitāb al-malāḥim* [The Book of Tumultuous Battles], chapter: 'Enjoining the Good and Forbidding the Evil', 4:121 §4336; Ibn Mājah in *al-Sunan*: *Kitāb al-fitan* [The Book of Tribulation], chapter: 'Enjoining the Good and Forbidding the Evil', 2:1327 §4006; and al-Ṭabarānī in *al-Muʿjam al-kabīr*, 10:146 §10268, and *al-Muʿjam al-awsaṭ*, 1:166 §519.

مَثَلُ الْمُدْهِنِ فِي حُدُودِ اللهِ وَالْوَاقِعِ فِيْهَا مَثَلُ قَوْمٍ اسْتَهَمُوا سَفِيْنَةً فَصَارَ بَعْضُهُمْ فِي أَسْفَلِهَا وَصَارَ بَعْضُهُمْ فِي أَعْلَاهَا. فَكَانَ الَّذِي فِي أَسْفَلِهَا يَمُرُّونَ بِالْمَاءِ عَلَى الَّذِيْنَ فِي أَعْلَاهَا فَتَأَذَّوْا بِهِ. فَأَخَذَ فَأْسًا فَجَعَلَ يَنْقُرُ أَسْفَلَ السَّفِيْنَةِ. فَأَتَوْهُ فَقَالُوا: مَا لَكَ؟ قَالَ: تَأَذَّيْتُمْ بِي وَلَا بُدَّ لِي مِنَ الْمَاءِ. فَإِنْ أَخَذُوا عَلَى يَدَيْهِ أَنْجَوْهُ وَنَجَّوْا أَنْفُسَهُمْ، وَإِنْ تَرَكُوهُ أَهْلَكُوهُ وَأَهْلَكُوا أَنْفُسَهُمْ.

> 'The likeness of the one who is lax in applying the prescribed limits of God and the one who transgresses against them is like that of a people who cast lots in boarding a ship. A group of them go to the lower deck and some of them stay on the upper deck. When those in the lower deck want water, one of them goes to the occupants of the upper deck until they are annoyed by him. He then starts to punch a hole in the lower deck [for water], and those of the upper deck go to him and ask, "What is wrong with you?" He replies, "I was annoying you, but I must have water!" If they take him by his hand and stop him they will save him and themselves, but if they leave him they will destroy him and themselves'.[1]

Since exposing the injustice and oppression of the rulers is an important responsibility on the Muslims, and since it must be peaceful and democratic, there are a number of ways in which it may be done in contemporary times:

- Using one's freedom of expression and denouncing oppression
- Speaking out against evil through books, literature and other forms of media
- Protesting against violations of human rights through peaceful demonstrations and rallies

---

[1] Narrated by al-Bukhārī in *al-Ṣaḥīḥ*: *Kitāb al-shahādāt* [The Book of Testimonies], chapter: 'On the Drawing of Lots for Resolving Problems', 2:954 §2540; al-Tirmidhī in *al-Sunan*: *Kitāb al-fitan* [The Book of Tribulations], chapter: 'What Has Come to Us Concerning the Act of Changing Wrongs with the Hand, Tongue or Heart', 4:470 §2173; Aḥmad b. Ḥanbal in *al-Musnad*, 4:270; and al-Bazzār in *al-Musnad*, 8:238 §3298.

- Organizing conferences and workshops that highlight political injustice
- Awakening the collective consciousness through speeches, writings and public consensus building
- Struggling at the political level to bring change to the government through constitutional and democratic means—sometimes these efforts become obligatory at the individual and organizational levels, and any failure to meet the challenge becomes an invitation to God's wrath
- Raising one's voice at the floor of parliament, calling for the rule of law and the granting of basic necessities and demanding the protection of human rights and the eradication of oppression and violence

18.8 Muslims Living in Non-Muslim Countries

Muslims who live in non-Muslim countries—whether as refugees, natural born citizens, permanent residents or students living there temporarily—are all duty-bound to obey the laws of the land (as long as the laws do not entail disobedience to God) and contribute positively to society at large. It is forbidden to violate the law, foment sedition or otherwise harm peaceful citizens.

We have the best example in the lives of the Prophet's Companions, who, at the Prophet's order ﷺ, immigrated to Christian Abyssinia (present-day Ethiopia) and enjoyed the support of its ruler, the Negus. God revealed in the Qur'ān,

﴿وَٱلَّذِينَ هَاجَرُواْ فِى ٱللَّهِ مِنۢ بَعْدِ مَا ظُلِمُواْ لَنُبَوِّئَنَّهُمْ فِى ٱلدُّنْيَا حَسَنَةً وَلَأَجْرُ ٱلْأَخِرَةِ أَكْبَرُ﴾

> '*And to those who migrated from their homes in the cause of God, after suffering oppression, We shall surely give a goodly home in this world; but the reward of the Hereafter will be even greater.*'[1]

Imam al-Qurṭubī commented on this verse in his exegesis: 'Qatāda said, "They are the Companions of Muhammad ﷺ. The pagans of

[1] Qur'ān 16:41.

Mecca wronged them and expelled them, until a group of them reached Abyssinia, then God Most High granted them an abode of migration and gave them helpers amongst the believers".'[1]

In another verse related to the Companions' immigration to Abyssinia, God said,

﴿يَٰعِبَادِيَ ٱلَّذِينَ ءَامَنُوٓاْ إِنَّ أَرۡضِي وَٰسِعَةٞ فَإِيَّٰيَ فَٱعۡبُدُونِ﴾

> *'O My servants who have believed! Indeed, My earth is vast so worship Me'.*[2]

Ibn Kathīr commented:

> This is a command from God Most High to His believing servants that they emigrate from the land in which they are unable to practise the religion to God's spacious earth, so they will be able to exercise the religion freely . . . so when the disenfranchised in Mecca found their stay there difficult, then immigrated to the land of Abyssinia so they could practise their religion in safety. And so, they found a most gracious host, the Negus, King of Ethiopia, may God Most High have mercy upon him.[3]

Umm Salama ﵂ said,

> 'When we arrived in Abyssinia, we were in the company of the best neighbour—the Negus! He granted us protection, allowing us to practise our religion, and we worshipped God Most High unharmed'.[4]

In a narration in Ibn Isḥāq's biography of the Prophet ﷺ, it is mentioned that Abyssinia was chosen as a place of immigration because it was a land of truthfulness, and its King oppressed

---

[1] Muhammad al-Qurṭubī, *al-Jāmiʿ li aḥkām al-Qurʾān*, 10:107.

[2] Qurʾān 29:56.

[3] Ibn Kathīr, *Tafsir al-Qurʾān al-Aẓīm*, 2:571.

[4] Ibn Hishām, *al-Sīra*, 1:413.

no one.[1] Ibn Hishām reported with a fully connected chain of narration from Zuhrī that Umm Salama ﷺ said,

> By God! We were upon that [peace and security] until a person from the Ethiopians challenged his kingdom. By God! I don't think we were ever as saddened as we were that day, fearing that this person might defeat the Negus and come to power, not acknowledging our rights as the Negus did. The Negus went out to meet him in battle whilst between them was the Nile. The Companions of the Messenger of God ﷺ said, 'Which man amongst us is willing to go out to witness the battle and then tell us the news?' Al-Zubayr b. al-ʿAwām said, 'I will', whereupon they said, 'Then it is you', and he was the youngest of them. They blew into a waterskin for him and he placed it on his chest. He then swam on it towards the place off of the Nile where the battle was taking place until he reached it. We then prayed to God Most High for the Negus, that he achieve victory over his enemy and gain authority in his land. By God! As we were expecting the outcome, suddenly, al-Zubayr raced towards us with [water] glistening off of his garments, saying, 'Shall I not give you all the good news? The Negus was victorious and God destroyed his enemy and gave him authority in his land!' By God! I don't think we were ever as delighted as we were on that day.[2]

This amazing narration teaches us many important lessons. We learn that Islam does not teach us a binary, black-or-white view of things, where others are either completely 'good' and 'Islamic' or completely 'bad' and 'un-Islamic'. At the time of the Companions' immigration to Abyssinia, the Negus was not a Muslim, yet the Companions had no problems describing him positively. We also learn the importance of living in an environment of peace and security for the proper practice of our religion—even if

---

[1] Ibid., 1:397.

[2] Ibid., 1:376.

that environment is not one hundred per cent 'Islamic' in every way. Most importantly, we learn from this story that it is from the etiquette of Islam to pray for the well-being and continued temporal authority of just rulers, whether they are Muslims or non-Muslims. In the contemporary context, this can include voting for a non-Muslim candidate that stands for justice or is, at least, better amongst others. Praying for the victory of a non-Muslim ruler is no different from voting him or her into office—both are permissible means, contrary to the claims of the Kharijites who claim that voting is polytheism that expels one from the religion.

18.9 Conclusion

I ask God Most High to make this fatwa a source of clarity and guidance for all of humanity. I pray that God, through the means of this fatwa, opens the eyes of the confused, establishes the proof against the corrupt and makes it a positive step in eliminating the scourge of terrorism that plagues our lands. And my final prayer is: All praise belongs to God, the Lord of the worlds, and may blessings and salutations be upon our master Muhammad, and upon his family, Companions and all who follow his excellent example until the Last Day. Amen.

Appendix

Scholars Cited in the Fatwa

ʿAbd al-Ḥaqq al-Dihlawī

ʿAbd al-Ḥaqq ‘Muḥaddith’ al-Dihlawī (d. 1052 AH), of Dehli, India. Al-Dihlawī settled in Mecca and studied hadith traditions and jurisprudence, and later settled in India, where he taught for over half a century and wrote over one hundred works.

ʿAbd al-Raḥmān al-Jazīrī

ʿAbd al-Raḥmān b. Muhammad ʿAwaḍ al-Jazīrī (d. 1941), born on the Egyptian island of Shandawīl in 1882 and educated at al-Azhar. He is the author of a contemporary and encyclopaedic work in comparative jurisprudence.

ʿAbd al-Raḥmān Mubārakpūrī

ʿAbd al-Raḥmān b. Ḥāfiẓ ʿAbd al-Raḥīm Mubārakpūrī, the famous *Ahl al-Ḥadīth* scholar of India (d. 1353 AH). He is the author of a commentary on the *Sunan* collection of Imam al-Tirmidhī, *Tuḥfat al-aḥwadhī.*

Ibn Ḥajar al-ʿAsqalānī

Shihāb al-Dīn Abū al-Faḍl Aḥmad b. Ḥajar al-ʿAsqalānī (d. 852 AH), known as ‘*al-Ḥāfiẓ*’ [the Hadith Master]. Ibn Ḥajar is a Shāfiʿī jurist, hadith scholar and author of the most famous and relied upon commentary of *Ṣaḥīḥ al-Bukhārī*, *Fatḥ al-Bārī*. He was given the title ‘the Leader of the Faithful in Hadith’.

Abū Bakr al-Ṣiddīq

Abū Bakr b. Abī Quḥāfa al-Taymī, better known as Abū Bakr al-Ṣiddīq [the Veracious] (d. 13 AH). A small trader of Mecca and the Prophet’s closest Companion, he accompanied the Prophet during his migration to Medina, and after his passing became the first of the four Rightly Guided Caliphs.

Abū Bakr Ibn al-ᶜArabī

Abū Bakr Ibn al-ᶜArabī (d. 543 AH), a Spanish scholar of hadith and Mālikī jurisprudence. Ibn al-ᶜArabī wrote an acclaimed commentary on the *Sunan* collection of Imam al-Tirmidhī.

Abū Dāwūd al-Sijistānī

Sulaymān b. al-Ashᶜab b. Isḥāq (d. 275 AH), the Shāfiᶜī scholar and hadith master. He is the compiler of *al-Sunan*, one of the famous canonical hadith collections, better known as *Sunan Abī Dāwūd*.

Abū Ḥāmid al-Ghazālī

Abū Ḥāmid al-Ghazālī al-Ṭūsī (d. 505 AH), the famous Persian polymath, and author of the highly acclaimed magnum opus, *The Revival of the Religious Sciences* (*Iḥyāʾ ᶜulūm al-dīn*). Al-Ghazālī was considered an authority in Shāfiᶜī jurisprudence, philosophy, theology and mysticism.

Abū Ḥanīfa

Nuᶜmān b. Thābit, known by his agnomen 'Abū Hanīfa' (d. 148 AH), was the founder of the Ḥanafī school of jurisprudence. The Ḥanafī school has the largest number of followers in the Muslim world, with its influence stretching from Egypt, Turkey, the Levant, Iraq, Transoxiana and the Indian Subcontinent.

Abū al-Ḥasan al-Māwardī

Aḥmad b. ᶜAlī b. Ḥabīb al-Māwardī (d. 450 AH), a scholar of the Shāfiᶜī school who served as a judge in several districts of Iraq. He is best known for his books *al-Aḥkām al-sulṭāniyya* on Islamic governance, and *Ādab al-dunyā wa al-dīn* on ethics.

Abū Hurayra ﵁

Abū Hurayra al-Dawsī al-Yamānī (d. 58 AH). One of the most copious and knowledgeable hadith narrators. It is reported that once Abū Hurayra complained to the Prophet ﷺ about his forgetfulness, whereupon the Prophet ﷺ placed his hand on his chest and supplicated, asking God to grant him a powerful memory.

Abū Isḥāq al-Shāṭibī

Ibrāhīm b. Mūsā b. Muhammad al-Shāṭibī (d. 790 AH), the famous Mālikī legal theorist. He is best known for his groundbreaking work on the 'objectives of the Shariah' (*Maqāṣid al-sharīʿa*), *al-Muwāfaqāt*.

Abū Jaʿfar al-Ṭaḥāwī

Aḥmad b. Muhammad, better known as Abū Jaʿfar (d. 321 AH). A nephew of the early Shāfiʿī jurist, al-Muzanī, al-Ṭaḥāwī later switched to the Ḥanafī school and was known for his mastery of hadith. His famous book of creed, *The Creed of Ṭaḥāwī*, represents one of the earliest formulations of Sunni doctrine, and is still studied to this day.

Aḥmad b. Ḥanbal

Aḥmad b. Ḥanbal al-Shaybānī (d. 241 AH), the famous hadith scholar after which the Ḥanbali school of jurisprudence is named. It is said that he committed over three hundred thousand hadith reports to memory, complete with their full chains of narration. The Ḥanbalī school, the smallest of the four Sunni schools of law, is mostly found in the Arabian Peninsula and parts of Syria and Iraq.

Aḥmad al-Qasṭalānī

Shihāb al-Dīn Aḥmad b. Muhammad al-Qasṭalānī (d. 923 AH), the Egyptian historian, hadith scholar and jurist. He is the author of a large commentary on *Ṣaḥīḥ al-Bukhārī*, *Irshād al-sārī* and a famous book on the biography of the Prophet Muhammad ﷺ, *al-Mawāhib al-laduniyya*.

ʿĀʾISHA B. ABĪ BAKR ﵂

ʿĀʾisha, the daughter of Abū Bakr (d. 58 AH), also know as Bint al-Ṣiddīq (the Daughter of the Veracious). She was the third and most beloved wife of the Prophet ﷺ. Due to her close relationship with the Prophet Muhammad ﷺ, she was privy to many of the details regarding his daily habits and sayings, and became one of the most knowledgeable jurists amongst the Companions.

ʿALĪ B. ABĪ ṬĀLIB ﵁

The fourth of the four Rightly Guided Caliphs, ʿAlī b. Abī Ṭālib (d. 40 AH) was the cousin and son-in-law of the Prophet ﷺ, having married his daughter Fāṭima ﵂. ʿAlī was the model of Muslim chivalry for the *Umma* and was renowned for his bravery, wisdom and clemency. After ʿUthmān b. ʿAffān ﵁ was assassinated, ʿAlī accepted the office of Caliph, which he held for about five years disturbed by rebellions. He was assassinated in Kufa by one of the Kharijites, who charged him with disbelief for having agreed to arbitration and negotiation with Muʿāwiya ﵁.

ʿĀLIM B. AL-ʿALĀʾ AL-ANDARĪTĪ

ʿAlim b. al-ʿAlāʾ al-Andarītī (d. 1398 AH), a famous Ḥanafi jurist of Central Asia and author of *al-Fatāwā al-tātārkhāniyya*, a collection of legal verdicts according to the Ḥanafī school.

BADR AL-DĪN AL-ʿAYNĪ

Badr al-Dīn al-ʿAynī (d. 855 AH), the Turkish Ḥanafī jurist and hadith scholar. Al-ʿAynī later settled in Egypt and wrote the acclaimed commentary on *Ṣaḥīḥ al-Bukhārī*, *ʿUmdat al-qārī*.

IBN ʿĀBIDĪN AL-SHĀMĪ

Sayyid Muhammad Amīn, better known as Ibn ʿĀbidīn al-Shamī (d. 1252 AH), the late Ottoman Ḥanafī jurist. Ibn ʿĀbidīn is the author of the most authoritative late work of Ḥanafī jurisprudence, *Radd al-Muḥtār*.

Ibn Bazzāz al-Kurdarī

Ibn Bazzāz al-Kurdarī (d. 827 AH), the famous Ḥanafī jurist. He was the author of *al-Fatāwā al-bazzaziyya*, a collection of legal verdicts according to the Ḥanafī school of jurisprudence.

Ibn Mufliḥ al-Ḥanbalī

Shams al-Dīn Ibn Mufliḥ (d. 763 AH), an influential Ḥanbalī jurist who studied under Ibn Taymiyya and included his juristic preferences in his book, *al-Furūʿ*.

Ibn Qudāma al-Maqdisī

Muwaffaq al-Dīn Ibn Qudāma al-Maqdisī (d. 620 AH), one of the famous Ḥanbalī jurists whose family emigrated from Nablus and settled in Damascus during the crusades. He is the author of the famous book *al-Mughnī*, a multi-volume commentary on Ḥanbalī jurisprudence.

Ibn Jarīr al-Ṭabarī

Muhammad b. Jarīr al-Ṭabarī (d. 310 AH), an early Qurʾānic exegete and historian. He is the author of the famous *Jāmiʿ al-bayān*, a large Qurʾānic exegesis that was heavily relied upon by other subsequent exegetes. He was also an independent scholar and founder of his own, no longer extant, school of jurisprudence.

Ibn Juzayy al-Kalbī

Muhammad b. Aḥmad Ibn Juzayy al-Kalbī al-Gharnāṭī, the esteemed Mālikī jurist, Qurʾānic exegete and master of the canonical readings of the Qurʾān. He is the author of *al-Qawānīn al-fiqhiyya*, an early work on comparative jurisprudence. He was killed as a martyr in the Battle of Ṭarīf in the year 741 AH.

IBN TAYMIYYA

Abū al-ʿAbbās Taqī al-Dīn Ibn Taymiyya al-Ḥarrānī (d. 728 AH), the controversial Ḥanbalī jurist and theologian. Ibn Taymiyya wrote a prolific number of works and was recognized for his scholarly output and keen memory.

IMAM AḤMAD RIḌĀ KHĀN

Aḥmad Riḍā Khān (d. 1921), the famous Indian Islamic scholar and reviver. Aḥmad Riḍā Khān was an Islamic authority and author of over one thousand books. Millions of Muslims in the Indian Subcontinent affiliate themselves with his scholarly legacy and positions.

IMAM AL-BUKHĀRĪ

Muhammad b. Ismāʿīl al-Bukharī (d. 256 AH), an orphan born in the city of Bukhara in present-day Uzbekistan. Al-Bukhārī is the author of *al-Jāmiʿ al-ṣaḥīḥ* (The Rigorously Authentic Compendium), better known as *Ṣaḥīḥ al-Bukhārī*, and considered the most authoritative and famous collection of hadith reports.

IMAM AL-ḤAṢKAFĪ

Muhammad ʿAlā al-Dīn al-Ḥaṣkafī (d. 1088 AH), the famous Turkish Ḥanafī scholar and grammarian. He is the author of *al-Durr al-Mukhtār* in Ḥanafī jurisprudence, which was subsequently explained in detail in the Ibn ʿĀbidīn's commentary, *Radd al-Muḥtār*.

IMAM AL-KĀSĀNĪ

Abū Bakr b. Masʿūd b. Aḥmad al-Kāsānī (d. 587 AH), an illustrious Ḥanafī jurist and student of Imam Abū Bakr al-Samarqandī. It is related that after he mastered his teacher's book of Ḥanafī jurisprudence, *al-Tuḥfa*, and wrote his extensive commentary on it, called *Badāʾiʿ al-ṣanāʾiʿ*, al-Samarqandī was so impressed that he married him to his daughter, stipulating his commentary as the dowry.

Imam Ibn Mājah

Muhammad b. Yazīd al-Rubʿī al-Qazwīnī (d. 273 AH), the Persian hadith master and Qurʾānic exegete. He is the author of *al-Sunan*, one of the canonical hadith collections.

Imam Mālik

Mālik b. Anas al-Aṣbaḥī (d. 179 AH), also known as the 'Imam of the Medinites', was the founder of the Mālikī school of jurisprudence. The Mālikī school flourishes in North Africa, sub-Saharan Africa, and parts of the Gulf region, such as the United Arab Emirates.

Imam al-Marghīnānī

Burhān al-Dīn al-Marghīnānī (d. 593 AH), known as 'Shaykh al-Islam' of the Ḥanafis. Al-Marghīnānī was the author of the highly influential jurisprudence manual *al-Hidāya*.

Imam Muslim

Muslim b. al-Ḥajjāj al-Nīshābūrī (d. 261 AH), the hadith master second only to his mentor, Imam al-Bukhārī, in authority in the hadith sciences. He is the author of the famous hadith collection, *Ṣaḥīḥ Muslim*, which together with al-Bukhārī's *Ṣaḥīḥ al-Bukhārī*, form the two most authoritative hadith collections.

Imam al-Nasāʾī

Aḥmad b. ʿAlī b. Shuʿayb al-Nasāʾī (d. 303 AH), the Shāfiʿī hadith scholar. He is the author of *al-Sunan*, one of the canonical hadith collections, and a compilation on the merits of ʿAlī b. Abī Ṭālib ﷺ. He was martyred in Damascus, having been beaten to death by Kharijites for his outspoken love for ʿAlī b. Abī Ṭālib.

Imam al-Nawawī

Muḥyī al-Dīn Yaḥyā b. Sharaf al-Nawawī (d. 676 AH), the late Shāfiʿī scholar of Damascus and author of a famous commentary on *Ṣaḥīḥ Muslim*. His positions on legal matters within the Shāfiʿī school of jurisprudence are considered authoritative, and his other works on hadith are some of the most highly read works in the Muslim world.

IMAM AL-SARAKHSĪ

Muhammad b. Aḥmad al-Sarkhasī (d. 490 AH) known as '*Shams al-Aʾimma*', or the 'Sun of the Imams'. Al-Sarakhsī is the author of *al-Mabsūṭ*, a famous commentary on Ḥanafī jurisprudence which spans thirty volumes.

IMAM AL-SHĀFIʿĪ

Muhammad b. Idrīs al-Shāfiʿī (d. 204 AH), a scion of the Qurashī line, was the founder of the Shāfiʿī school of jurisprudence. The Shāfiʿī school flourishes in Egypt, Syria, Yemen, East Africa and the Malay Archipelago.

IMAM AL-SHIRBĪNĪ

Muhammad Shirbīnī al-Khaṭīb (d. 977 AH), the Shāfiʿī jurist and 'teacher of teachers'. He is the author of *Mughnī al-muḥtāj*, a commentary on al-Nawawī's *Minhāj al-ṭālibīn*, noted for its clarity and reliability.

IMAM AL-TIRMIDHĪ

Muhammad b. ʿĪsā al-Tirmidhī (d. 279 AH), the hadith scholar and student of Imam al-Bukhārī. He is the author of *al-Sunan*, one of the canonical hadith collections, and the famous and celebrated *al-Shamāʾil al-Nabawiyya*, a collection of reports detailing the personal appearance, dress, habits and daily behaviour of the Prophet Muhammad ﷺ.

MUHAMMAD AL-QURṬUBĪ

Abū ʿAbd Allāh Muhammad b. Aḥmad b. Abī Bakr al-Qurṭubī (d. 671 AH), the famous Qurʾānic exegete and hadith scholar of Cordóva. He is the author of *al-Jāmiʿ li aḥkām al-Qurʾān*, a famous exegesis that focuses on the jurisprudential points extracted from the Qur'ān.

Mullā ʿAlī al-Qārī

Abū al-Ḥasan ʿAlī al-Qārī al-Makkī (d. 1014 AH), the famous latter-day Ḥanafī scholar who hailed from Herat, Afghanistan, and settled in Mecca. He was the author of several works in Ḥanafī jurisprudence, hadith commentary and biography.

Qāḍī ʿIyāḍ

Qāḍī ʿIyāḍ b. Mūsā al-Yaḥṣubī (d. 544 AH), a Mālikī jurist born in Gibraltar. Qāḍī ʿIyāḍ later settled in Grenada and served as a judge (hence the name 'Qāḍī'). He is the author of *al-Shifā bi taʿrīf ḥuqūq al-Muṣṭafā* ﷺ (*The Healing Through Acquainting One with the Rights of the Chosen One* ﷺ), which is perhaps the most famous book detailing the inner and outer characteristics and rights of the Prophet Muhammad ﷺ.

Shāh ʿAbd al-ʿAzīz al-Dihlawī

Ghulām Ḥalīm Shāh ʿAbd al-ʿAzīz 'Muḥaddith' al-Dihlawī (d. 1239 AH), the Indian polymath and son of polymath and reformer, Shāh Walī Allāh al-Dihlawī. Shāh ʿAbd al-ʿAzīz wrote an Urdu translation of the Qur'ān.

Sufyān al-Thawrī

Sufyān b. Saʿīd al-Thawrī (d. 161 AH), a well-known scholar and jurist of Kufa. Al-Thawrī was an early jurist whose legal views led to the development of the Thawrī legal school which is no longer extant. He was also known for his asceticism and withdrawal from governmental positions. Following a dispute with the caliph of his time, al-Thawrī spent his final year in hiding. His legal opinions and hadith transmissions have survived in the works of other jurists, and his opinions are authoritative.

TAQĪ AL-DĪN AL-SUBKĪ

ʿAlī b. ʿAbd al-Kāfī b. ʿAlī b. Tamām (d. 756 AH), the Egyptian Shāfiʿī scholar and hadith specialist. Al-Subkī later became a judge in Damascus and wrote the completion (*al-Takmila*) of Imam al-Nawawī's uncompleted work in Shāfiʿī jurisprudence, *Sharḥ al-muhadhhab*.

ʿUMAR B. ʿABD AL-ʿAZĪZ ﵁

ʿUmar b. ʿAbd al-ʿAzīz b. Marwān (d. 101 AH), sometimes called 'the fifth Rightly Guided Caliph'. He was known for his piety and asceticism, and strictly upheld the equal rights of converts.

ʿUMAR B. AL-KHAṬṬĀB ﵁

Also known as ʿUmar al-Fārūq [the Discerning], ʿUmar b. al-Khaṭṭāb (d. 23 AH). Initially one of the staunchest of the Prophet's opponents in Mecca, ʿUmar became one of its greatest defenders. As the second of the four Rightly Guided Caliphs, ʿUmar instituted numerous policies regarding non-Muslim citizens and administrative duties. He was assassinated by Persians in the Prophet's Mosque.

ʿUTHMĀN B. ʿAFFĀN ﵁

ʿUthmān b. ʿAffān b. Abī al-ʿĀṣ b. Umayya (d. 35 AH). A wealthy merchant in Mecca by migrating to Medina, ʿUthmān was also known as *Dhū al-Nūrayn*—the man of the two lights—because he married two of the Prophet's daughters: Ruqayya, and then, after her death, Umm Kulthūm ﵂. During the latter years of his caliphate, he was accused of nepotism, which resulted in his murder at the hands of a group of rebels who besieged his house and then stormed it, stabbing him to death as he was reading the Qurʾān.

Zakariyyā al-Anṣārī

Zakariyyā b. Muhammad b. Aḥmad b. Zakariyyā (d. 926 AH), the hadith master, Shāfiʿī jurist and judge of Egypt. He was the author of many indispensible works on legal theory, jurisprudence and Sufism.

Zayn al-Dīn b. al-Nujaym

Zayn al-Dīn b. al-Nujaym (d. 970 AH), the author of *al-Baḥr al-rāʾiq* in Ḥanafī jurisprudence and called 'the second Abū Ḥanīfa'.

Bibliography

ʿAbduh, Muhammad. *Al-Muslimūn wa al-Islām*. (No publisher information given)

Afrīqī, Ibn Manẓūr Jamāl al-Dīn Muhammad b. Mukrim al-. *Lisān al-ʿArab*. Beirut: Dār Ṣādir, n.d.

ʿAjlūnī, Ismāʿīl b. ʿUmar al-. *Kashf al-khafāʾ wa muzīl al-ilbās ʿamma ashtahara min al-aḥādīth ʿalā alsinat al-nās*. Beruit: Muʾassasa al-Risāla, 1985.

Ājurrī, Abū Bakr Muhammad b. Ḥusayn al-. *Al-Sharīʿa*. Riyadh: Dār al-Waṭan, 1999.

Albānī, Muhammad Nāṣir al-Dīn al-. *Silsila al-aḥādīth al-ṣaḥīḥa*. Beruit: al-Maktab al-Islāmī, 1985.

Anṣārī, ʿĀlim b. al-ʿAlāʾ al-. *Al-Fatāwā al-tātārkhāniyya fī al-fiqh al-Ḥanafī*. Beirut: Dar al-Kotob al-Ilmiyah, 2005.

Anṣārī, Zakariyyā b. Muhammad al-. *Manhaj al-ṭullāb*. Beirut: Dar al-Kotob al-Ilmiyah, 1418 AH.

Aṣfahānī, Abū Nuʿaym al-. *Musnad al-Imām Abī Ḥanīfa*. Riyadh: Maktaba al-Kawthar, 1415 AH.

——. *Kitāb al-arbaʿīn ʿalā madhhab al-mutaḥaqqiqīn min al-Ṣūfiyya*. Beruit: Dār Ibn Ḥazm, 1993.

——. *Ḥilyat al-Awliyāʾ wa ṭabaqāt al-aṣfiyāʾ*. Beirut: Dār al-Kitāb al-ʿArabī, 1985.

ʿAsqalānī, Ibn Ḥajar Aḥmad b. ʿAlī al-. *Al-Dirāya fī takhrīj aḥādīth al-Hidāya*. Beruit: Dār al-Maʿrifa, n.d.

——. *Hadyī al-sāri muqaddima Fatḥ al-Bārī*. Beruit: Dār al-Maʿrifa, n.d.

——. *Fatḥ al-Bārī sharḥ Ṣaḥīḥ al-Bukhārī*. Beruit: Dār al-Maʿrifa, 1379 AH.

——. *Tahdhīb al-tahdhīb*. Beirut: Dar al-Fikr, 1404 AH.

——. *Al-Iṣāba fī tamyīz al-Ṣaḥāba*. Beirut: Dār al-Jīl, 1412 AH.

ʿAynī, Badr al-Dīn al-. *ʿUmdat al-qārī sharḥ Ṣaḥīḥ al-Bukhārī*. Beruit: Dār Iḥyāʾ al-Turāth al-ʿArabī, n.d.

——. *Al-Bināya sharḥ al-Hidāya*. Beirut: Dar al-Kotob al-Ilmiyah, n.d.

Azdī, Maʿmar b. Rāshid al-. *Al-Jāmiʿ*. Beruit: al-Maktab al-Islāmī, 1403 AH.

Azharī, Muhammad b. Aḥmad al-. *Tahdhīb al-lugha*. Beirut: Dār Iḥyāʾ al-Turāth al-ʿArabi, 2001.

Baghawī, Abū Muhammad Ḥusayn b. Masʿūd b. Muhammad al-Farrāʾ al-. *Maʿālim al-Tanzīl*. Beruit: Dār al-Maʿrifa, 1987.

Baghdādī, Khaṭīb al-. *Tārīkh Baghdād*. Beirut: Dar al-Kotob al-Ilmiyah, n.d.

Baghdādī, ʿAbd al-Qādir al-. *Al-Farq bayn al-firaq*. Beirut: Dār al-Āfāq al-Jadīda, 1977.

Bahūtī, Manṣūr b. Yūnus al-. *Kashhāf al-qināʿ ʿan matn al-Iqnāʿ*. Beirut: Dar al-Fikr, 1402 AH.

Balādhurī, Aḥmad b. Yaḥyā al-. *Futūḥ al-buldān*. Beirut: Dar al-Kotob al-Ilmiyah, 1985.

Bayhaqī, Aḥmad b. al-Ḥusayn al-. *Al-Sunan al-kubrā*. Mecca: Maktaba Dār al-Bāz, 1994.

——. *Shuʿab al-Īmān*. Beruit: Dar al-Kotob al-Ilmiyah, 1990.

Bazzār, Aḥmad b. ʿAmr al-. *Al-Musnad (al-Baḥr al-zakhār)*. Beruit: Muʾassasa ʿUlūm al-Qurʾān, 1409 AH.

Bujayrimī, Sulaymān b. ʿUmar b. Muhammad al-. *Ḥāshiyat al-Bujayrimī ʿalā sharḥ minhāj al-ṭullāb*. Turkey: al-Maktaba al-Islāmiyya, n.d.

Bukhārī, Abū ʿAbd Allāh Muhammad b. Ismāʿīl b. Ibrāhīm b. Mughīra al-. *Al-Jāmiʿ al-ṣaḥīḥ*. Beruit: Dār Ibn Kathīr, 1987.

——. *Al-Tārīkh al-kabīr*. Beirut: Dar al-Kotob al-Ilmiyah, 2001.

——. *Al-Adab al-mufrad*.

Dihlawī, ʿAbd al-ʿAzīz al-. *Tuḥfat ithnā ʿashriyya*. Istanbul: Maktaba al-Ḥaqīqa, 1988.

Dihlawī, ʿAbd al-Ḥaqq al-. *Ashʿat al-lamaʿāt sharḥ mishkāt al-maṣābīḥ*. Sakhar: Maktaba Nūrīyya Riḍawīyya, 1962.

Dihlawī, Nadhīr Ḥusayn al-. *Fatāwā nadhīriyya*. Gujranwala: Maktaba al-Maʿārif al-Islāmiyya, 1988.

Dāraquṭnī, ʿAlī b. ʿUmar al-. *Al-Sunan*. Beruit: Dār al-Maʿrifa, 1966.

Dardīr, Aḥmad al-. *Al-Sharḥ al-kabīr*, Beirut: Dar al-Fikr, n.d.

Dārimī, ʿAbd Allāh al-. *Al-Sunan*. Beruit: Dār al-Kitāb al-ʿArabī, 1407.

Dasūqī, Muhammad b. Aḥmad b. ʿArafa al-. *Ḥāshiyat al-Dasūqī ʿalā al-sharḥ al-kabīr*. Beirut: Dar al-Fikr, n.d.

Daylamī, Abū Shujāʿ Shīrawayh al-. *Al-Firdaws bi maʾthūr al-khiṭāb*. Mecca: Dar al-Kotob al-Ilmiyah, 1986.

Dhahabī, Shams al-Dīn Muhammad b. Aḥmad al-. *Al-Kabāʾir*. Beruit: Dār al-Nadwa al-Jadīda, n.d.

——. *Siyar ʿalām al-nubalāʾ*. Beirut: Muʾassasa al-Risāla, 1413 AH.

Fawzān, Ṣāliḥ b. Fawzān al-. *Al-Jihād wa ḍawābiṭuhu al-sharʿiyya*.

Ḥākim, Muhammad b. ʿAbd Allāh al-. *Al-Mustadrak ʿalā al-ṣaḥīḥayn*. Beruit: Dar al-Kotob al-Ilmiyah, 1990.

Ḥanafī, Ibn Abī al-ʿIzz al-. *Sharḥ al-ʿaqīda al-ṭaḥāwiyya*. Beirut: al-Maktab al-Islāmī, 1988.

Ḥanbal, Aḥmad b. *Al-Musnad*. Beruit: Dar al-Kotob al-Ilmiyah, 1986.

——. *Faḍāʾil al-Ṣaḥaba*. Beruit: Muʾassasa al-Risāla, 1983.

Ḥanbalī, Ibn Rajab ʿAbd al-Raḥmān al-. *Jāmiʿ al-ʿulūm wa al-ḥikam*. Beruit: Dār al-Maʿrifa, 1408 AH.

Ḥaṣkafī, Muhammad ʿAlāʾ al-Dīn b. ʿAlī al-. *Al-Durr al-mukhtār fī sharḥ tanwīr al-abṣār*. Beirut: Dar al-Fikr, 1386 AH.

Haythamī, Nūr al-Dīn Abū al-Ḥasan ʿAlī al-. *Majmaʿ al-zawāʾid wa manbaʿ al-fawāʾid*. Cairo: Dār al-Rayān li al-Turāth, 1987.

Hindī, Ḥusām al-Dīn ʿAlāʾ al-Dīn ʿAlī al-Muttaqī al-. *Kanz al-ʿummāl*. Beruit: Muʾassasa al-Risāla, 1979.

Hitti, Philip K. *History of the Arabs*. Oxford: Macmillan Education Ltd., 1991.

Ḥuṣayn, Fahd al-. *Al-Fatāwā al-sharʿiyya fī al-qaḍāyā al-ʿaṣriyya*.

Ibn ʿAbd al-Barr, Yūsuf b. ʿAbd Allāh. *Al-Tamhīd li mā fī al-muwaṭṭa min al-maʿānī wa al-asānīd*. Marrakech: Ministry of Religious Affairs, 1387 AH.

——. *Al-Kāfī fī fiqh Ahl al-Madīna*. Beirut: Dar al-Kotob al-Ilmiyah, 1407 AH.

Ibn Abī al-Dunyā, ʿAbd Allāh b. Muhammad. *Al-Ahwāl*.

Ibn Abī ʿĀṣim, ʿAmr. *Al-Sunna*. Beruit: Al-Maktab al-Islāmī, 1400 AH.

——. *Al-Diyāt*. Karachi: Idāra al-Qur'ān wa al-ʿUlūm al-Islāmiyya, 1308 AH.

Ibn ʿĀbidīn, Muhammad. *Radd al-muḥtār ʿalā al-durr al-mukhtār ʿalā tanwīr al-abṣār*. Beirut: Dar al-Fikr, 1386 AH.

Ibn Abī Ḥātim, ʿAbd al-Raḥmān b. Muhammad Idrīs. *Tafsīr al-Qur'ān al-ʿAẓīm*. Sayda: al-Maktaba al-ʿAṣriyya, n.d.

Ibn Abī Shayba, ʿAbd Allāh b. Muhammad. *Al-Muṣannaf*. Riyadh: Maktaba al-Rushd, 1409 AH.

Ibn ʿĀdil, Abū Ḥafṣ Sirāj al-Dīn ʿUmar b. ʿAlī. *Al-Lubāb fī ʿulūm al-Kitāb*. Beruit: Dar al-Kotob al-Ilmiyah, 1998.

Ibn Aḥmad, ʿAbd Allāh. *Al-Sunna*. Damam: Dār Ibn al-Qayyim, 1406 AH.

Ibn Anas, Mālik. *Al-Muwaṭṭā*. Beruit: Dār Iḥyā' al-Turāth al-ʿArabī, 1985.

Ibn ʿAsākir, ʿAlī b. al-Ḥasan. *Tārīkh Dimashq al-kabīr*. Beirut: Dar al-Fikr, 1995.

Ibn al-Athīr, ʿAlī b. Muhammad. *Al-Kāmil fī al-tārīkh*. Beirut: Dār Ṣādir, 1979.

Ibn Baṭṭāl, ʿAlī b. Khalaf. *Sharḥ Ṣaḥīḥ al-Bukhārī*. Riyadh: Maktaba al-Rushd, 2003.

Ibn Bāz, ʿAbd al-ʿAzīz. *Khaṭa' man yaqūl anna ṭāʿat wullāt al-umūr wa munāṣaḥatahum 'fikran inhizāmiyan* [*sic*]'. www.binbaz.org.sa/mat/1934 (last accessed May 24, 2010).

Ibn Bazzāz, Muhammad b. Muhammad b. Shihāb. *Al-Fatāwā al-bazzāziyya ʿalā hāmish al-fatāwā al-ʿālamghirīyya*. Beirut: Dār al-Maʿrifa, 1973.

Ibn Fāris, Aḥmad. *Muʿjam maqāyīs al-lugha*. Damascus: Ittiḥād al-Kitāb al-ʿArab, 2002.

Ibn Ḥazm, ʿAlī Aḥmad b. Saʿīd. *Al-Muḥallā*. Beirut: Dār al-Āfāq al-Jadīda, n.d.

Ibn Ḥibbān, Abū Ḥātim Muhammad. *Al-Ṣaḥīḥ*. Beruit: Mu'assasa al-Risāla, 1993.

Ibn Hishām, Abū Muhammad ʿAbd al-Malik. *Al-Sīra*. Beruit: Mu'assasa al-Risāla, 1993.

Ibn Hubayra, ʿAwn al-Dīn Yaḥyā. *Al-Ifṣāḥ ʿan maʿānī al-ṣiḥāḥ fī al-fiqh ʿalā al-madhhab al-arbaʿa*. Riyadh: Dār al-Waṭan, 1417 AH.

Ibn Humām, Kamāl al-Dīn Muhammad b. ʿAbd al-Wāhid. *Fatḥ al-Qadīr sharḥ al-hidāya*. Quetta: Maktaba Rashīdiyya, n.d.

Ibn Ḥumayd, ʿAbd. *Al-Musnad*. Cairo: Maktaba al-Sunna, 1988.

Ibn Ibrāhīm, Abū Yūsuf Yaʿqūb. *Kitāb al-kharāj*. Beirut: Dār al-Maʿrifa, n.d.

Ibn Kathīr, Abū al-Fidāʾ Ismāʿīl b. ʿUmar. *Tafsīr al-Qurʾān al-ʿAẓīm*. Beruit: Dar al-Fikr, 1401 AH.

——. *Al-Bidāya wa al-nihāya*. Beirut: Maktaba al-Maʿārif, n.d.

Ibn Khuzayma, Muhammad b. Isḥāq. *Al-Ṣaḥīḥ*. Beruit: al-Maktab al-Islāmī, 1970.

Ibn Mandah, ʿAbd Allāh Muhammad b. Isḥāq. *Al-Īmān*. Beruit: Muʾassasa al-Risāla, 1406 AH.

Ibn Mufliḥ, Ibrāhīm b. Muhammad. *Al-Mubdiʿ fī sharḥ al-Muqniʿ*. Beirut: al-Maktab al-Islāmī, n.d.

Ibn Mufliḥ, Shams al-Dīn. *Al-Furūʿ*. Beirut: Dar al-Kotob al-Ilmiyah, 1418 AH.

Ibn Nujaym, Zayn al-Dīn. *Al-Baḥr al-rāʾiq sharḥ kanz al-daqāʾiq*. Beirut: Dār al-Maʿrifa, n.d.

Ibn Rushd, Muhammad b. Aḥmad. *Bidāyat al-mujtahid*. Beirut: Dar al-Fikr, n.d.

Ibn Saʿd, Muhammad. *Al-Ṭabaqāt al-kubrā*. Beirut: Dar Bayrūt, 1978.

Ibn Sallām, Abū ʿUbayd al-Qāsim. *Kitāb al-amwāl*. Beirut: Dar al-Fikr, 1308 AH.

Ibn Taymiyya, Aḥmad b. ʿAbd al-Ḥalīm. *Al-Nubuwwāt*. Beirut: Dār al-Kitāb al-ʿArabī, 1985.

——. *Majmūʿa al-fatāwā*. Maktaba Ibn Taymiyya, n.d.

Ibn Zanjawayh, Ḥamīd. *Kitāb al-amwāl*. Riyadh: Markaz al-Malik Fayṣal li al-Buḥūth wa al-Dirāsāt al-Islāmiyya, 1986.

Jaṣṣāṣ, Abū Bakr Aḥmad b. ʿAlī al-. *Aḥkām al-Qurʾān*. Beruit: Dār Iḥyāʾ al-Turāth al-ʿArabī, 1405 AH.

Jawziyya, Muhammad b. Abī Bakr Ayyūb Ibn Qayyim al-. *Aḥkām ahl al-dhimma*. Beirut: Dār Ibn Ḥazm, 1997.

Jazīrī, ʿAbd al-Raḥmān al-. *Al-Fiqh ʿalā al-madhāhib al-arbaʿa*. Beirut: Dār Iḥyāʾ al-Turāth al-ʿArabī, n.d.

Jazarī, Mubārak b. Muhammad al-. *Al-Nihāya fī gharīb al-āthār.* Beirut: al-Maktaba al-ʿIlmiyya, 1399 AH.

Kalbī, Muhammad b. Aḥmad b. Juzayy al-. *Al-Qawānīn al-fiqhiyya.* Beirut: Dar al-Fikr, n.d.

Karmī, Marʿī b. Yūsuf al-. *Ghāyat al-muntahā.* Beirut: al-Maktab al-Islāmī, n.d.

Kāsānī, ʿAlāʾ al-Dīn al-. *Badāʾiʿ al-sanāʾiʿ.* Beirut: Dār al-Kitāb al-ʿArabī, 1982.

Kawtharī, Muhammad Zāhid al-. *Majmūʿa al-ʿaqīda wa ʿilm al-kalām.* Beirut Dar al-Kotob al-Ilmiyah, 2004.

Khāzin, ʿAlī b. Muhammad b. Ibrāhīm al-. *Lubāb al-taʾwīl fī maʿānī al-Tanzīl.* Beruit: Dār al-Maʿrifa, n.d.

Khiraqī, ʿUmar b. Ḥusayn al-. *Mukhtaṣar al-Khiraqī min masāʾil al-Imām Aḥmad b. Ḥanbal.* Beirut: al-Maktab al-Islāmī, 1403 AH.

Maḥallī, Jalāl al-Dīn al- and Jalāl al-Dīn al-Suyūṭī. *Tafsīr al-Jalālayn.* Beruit: Dār Ibn Kathīr, 1998.

Maqdisī, Ibn Qudāma al-. *Al-Kāfī fī fiqh Ibn Ḥanbal.* Beirut: al-Maktab al-Islāmī, n.d.

——. *Al-Mughnī fī fiqh al-Imām Aḥmad b. Ḥanbal al-Shaybānī.* Beirut: Dar al-Fikr, 1405 AH.

Maqdisī, Muhammad b. ʿAbd al-Wāḥid al-. *Al-Aḥādīth al-mukhtāra.* Mecca: Maktaba al-Nahḍa al-Ḥaditha, 1990.

Mardāwī, ʿAlāʾ al-Dīn ʿAlī b. Sulaymān al-. *Al-Inṣāf fī maʿrifat al-rājiḥ min al-khilāf ʿalā madhhab al-Imām Aḥmad b. Ḥanbal.* Beirut: Dār Iḥyāʾ al-Turāth al-ʿArabī, n.d.

Marghīnānī, ʿAlī b. Abī Bakr b. ʿAbd al-Jalīl al-. *Al-Hidāya sharḥ al-bidāya.* Beirut: al-Maktaba al-Islāmiyya, n.d.

Marwadhī, Nuʿaym b. Ḥammād al-. *Al-Fitan.* Beruit: Muʾassasa al-Kutub al-Thaqāfiyya, 1408 AH.

Marwazī, Aḥmad b. ʿAlī al-. *Musnad Abī Bakr al-Ṣiddīq.* Beruit: al-Maktab al-Islamī, n.d.

Marwazī, Muhammad b. Naṣr al-. *Taʿẓīm qadr al-ṣalāt.* Medina: Maktaba al-Dār, 1302 AH.

Māturīdī, Abū Manṣūr Muhammad b. Muhammad b. Maḥmūd al-. *Taʾwīlāt Ahl al-Sunna.* Beirut: Muʾassasa al-Risāla, 2004.

Māwardī, ʿAlī b. Muhammad al-. *Al-Aḥkām al-sulṭāniyya*. Beirut: Dar al-Kotob al-Ilmiyah, 1978.

——. *Al-Iqnāʿ fī al-fiqh al-Shāfiʿī*. Beirut: Dar al-Kotob al-Ilmiyah, n.d.

Mubārakpūrī, Muhammad ʿAbd al-Raḥmān al-. *Tuḥfat al-aḥwadhī fī sharḥ Jāmiʿ al-Tirmidhī*. Beirut: Dar al-Kotob al-Ilmiyah, n.d.

Muhammad Mīqā, Ismāʿīl. *Mabādī al-Islām*.

Munāwī, ʿAbd al-Raʾūf b. Tāj al-Dīn al-. *Fayḍ al-Qadīr sharḥ al-Jāmiʿ al-ṣaghīr*. Egypt: Maktaba Tijāriyya al-Kubrā, 1356 AH.

Mundhirī, ʿAbd al-ʿAẓīm al-. *Al-Targhīb wa al-tarhīb*. Beruit: Dar al-Kotob al-Ilmiyah, 1417 AH.

Naḥās, Abū Jaʿfar Aḥmad b. Muhammad b. Ismāʿīl al-. *Maʿānī al-Qurʾān al-Karīm*. Mecca: Umm al-Qurā University Press, 1409 AH.

Nasāʾī, Aḥmad b. Shuʿayb al-. *Al-Sunan*. Beruit: Dar al-Kotob al-Ilmiyah, 1995.

Nawawī, Muḥyī al-Dīn Yaḥyā b. Sharaf al-. *Sharḥ al-Nawawī ʿalā Ṣaḥīḥ Muslim*. Beirut: Dār Iḥyāʾ al-Turāth, 1392 AH.

——. *Rawḍat al-ṭālibīn wa ʿumdat al-muftiyīn*. Beirut: al-Maktab al-Islāmī, 1405 AH.

Nīshābūrī, Abū ʿAwāna Yaʿqūb b. Isḥāq al-. *Al-Musnad*. Beruit: Dār al-Maʿrifa, 1998.

Nīshābūrī, Muslim b. al-Ḥajjāj al-. *Al-Jāmiʿ al-ṣaḥīḥ*. Beruit: Dār Iḥyāʾ al-Turāth al-ʿArabī, n.d.

——. *Al-Sunan al-kubrā*. Beruit: Dar al-Kotob al-Ilmiyah, 1991.

Pānipātī, Qāḍī Thanāʾ Allāh al-. *Al-Tafsīr al-maẓharī*. Quetta: Baluchistan Book Depot, n.d.

Qarāfī, Shihāb al-Dīn al-. *Al-Dhakhīra fī al-fiqh al-Mālikī*. Beirut: Dār al-Gharb, 1996.

——. *Al-Furūq* (*Anwār al-burūq fī anwāʿ al-furūq*). Beirut: Dar al-Kotob al-Ilmiyah, 1998.

Qārī, Mullā ʿAlī al-. *Mirqāt al-mafātīḥ sharḥ mishkāt al-maṣābīḥ*. Multan: Maktaba Imdādiyya, n.d.

Qasṭalānī, Aḥmad b. Muhammad al-. *Irshād al-sārī li sharḥ Ṣaḥīḥ al-Bukhārī*. Beruit: Dār al-Fikr, n.d.

Qazwīnī, Ibn Mājah al-. *Al-Sunan*. Beruit: Dār al-Fikr, n.d.

Qurashī, Yaḥyā b. Ādam al-. *Kitāb al-kharāj*. Lahore: al-Maktaba al-Islāmiyya, 1974.

Qurṭubī, Abū ʿAbd Allāh Muhammad b. Aḥmad al-. *Al-Jāmiʿ li aḥkām al-Qurʾān*. Cairo: Dār al-Shaʿb, 1372 AH.

——. *Al-Mufhim li ma ushkila min talkhīṣ kitāb Muslim*. Beruit: Dār Ibn Kathīr, 1999.

Rabīʿ, Ibn Ḥabīb al-. *al-Jāmiʿ al-ṣaḥīḥ/Musnad al-Imām al-Rabīʿ*. Beruit: Dār al-Ḥikma, 1415 AH.

Ruḥaybānī, Muṣṭafā b. Saʿd al-. *Maṭālib uwlī al-nuhā fī sharḥ ghāyat al-muntahā*. Damascus: al-Maktab al-Islāmī, 1961.

Rāzī, Fakhr al-Dīn Muhammad b. ʿUmar al-. *Mafātīḥ al-ghayb (al-tafsīr al-kabīr)*. Beruit: Dar al-Kotob al-Ilmiyah, 1421 AH.

Riḍā Khān, Aḥmad. *Al-ʿAṭāyā al-Nabawiyya fī al-fatāwā al-riḍ awiyya*. Lahore: Raza Foundation, Jāmiʿa Niẓāmiyya Riḍawiyya, 1991.

Ruʾyānī, Muhammad b. Ḥārūn al-. *Musnad al-Ṣaḥāba (Musnad al-Ruʾyānī)*. Cairo: Muʾassasa Qurṭuba, 1416 AH.

Samarqandī, Abū al-Layth Naṣr b. Muhammad b. Ibrāhīm, al-. *Baḥr al-ʿulūm*. Beirut: Dār al-Fikr, n.d.

Ṣanʿānī, ʿAbd al-Razzāq al-. *Al-Muṣannaf*. Riyadh: Al-Maktab al-Islāmī, 1403 AH.

Sarakhsī, Shams al-Dīn al-. *Al-Mabsūṭ*. Beirut: Dār al-Maʿrifa, 1978.

Shāfiʿī, Muhammad b. Idrīs. *Al-Musnad*. Beruit: Dar al-Kotob al-Ilmiyah, n.d.

——. *Al-Umm*. Beirut: Dār al-Maʿrifa, 1393.

Shāṭibī, Abū Isḥāq Ibrāhīm b. Mūsā al-. *Al-Iʿtiṣām*. Egypt: al-Maktaba al-Tijāriyya al-Kubrā, n.d.

Shahrastānī, Muhammad b. ʿAbd al-Karīm al-. *Al-Milal wa al-niḥal*. Beirut: Dār al-Maʿrifa, 2001.

Shawkānī, Muhammad b. ʿAlī al-. *Nayl al-awṭār sharḥ Muntaqā al-akhbār*. Beirut: Dār al-Jīl, 1973.

Shaybānī, Muhammad b. Ḥasan al-. *Al-Mabsūṭ*. Karachi: Idāra al-Qurʾān wa al-ʿUlūm al-Islāmiyya, n.d.

——. *Al-Ḥujja ʿalā Ahl al-Madīna*. Beirut: ʿĀlam al-Kutub, 1403 AH.

Shirbīnī, Muhammad Khaṭīb al-. *Al-Iqnāᶜ fī ḥill alfāẓ Abī Shujāᶜ*. Beirut: Dar al-Fikr, 1415 AH.

——. *Mughnī al-muḥtāj ilā maᶜrifat maᶜānī alfāẓ al-minhāj*. Beirut: Dār Iḥyāʾ al-Turāth al-ᶜArabī, 1982.

Sijistānī, Abū Dāwūd al-. *Al-Sunan*. Beruit: Dār al-Fikr, 1994.

Suyūṭī, Jalāl al-Dīn al-. *Al-Durr al-manthūr fī al-tafsīr bi al-maʾthūr*. Beruit: Dār al-Fikr, 1993.

Ṭabarānī, Sulaymān b. Aḥmad al-. *Al-Muᶜjam al-ṣaghīr*. Beruit: al-Maktab al-Islāmī, 1985.

——. *Al-Muᶜjam al-awsaṭ*. Cairo: Dār al-Ḥaramayn, 1415 AH.

——. *Al-Muᶜjam al-kabīr*. Mosul: Maktaba al-ᶜUlūm wa al-Ḥikam, 1983.

——. *Musnad al-Shāmiyyīn*. Beruit: Muʾassasa al-Risāla, 1985.

Ṭabarī, Abū Jaᶜfar Muhammad b. Jarīr al-. *Jāmiᶜ al-bayān fī tafsīr al-Qurʾān*. Beirut: Dār al-Fikr, 1405 AH.

——. *Ṭārīkh al-umam wa al-mulūk*. Beirut: Dar al-Kotob al-Ilmiyah, 1407 AH.

Ṭabarsī, Faḍl b. Ḥasan al-. *Al-Muʾtalif min al-mukhtalif bayn aʾimma al-salaf*. Qom: Maṭbaᶜa Sayyid al-Shahīd, 1410 AH.

Ṭaḥāwī, Abū Jāᶜfar Aḥmad b. Muhammad al-. *Sharḥ maᶜānī al-āthār*. Beirut: Dar al-Kotob al-Ilmiyah, 1399 AH.

——. *Al-ᶜAqīda al-ṭaḥāwiyya*. Beirut: Dar al-Kotob al-Ilmiyah, 1399 AH.

Tamīmī, Abū Yaᶜlā Aḥmad b. ᶜAlī al-. *Al-Musnad*. Damascus: Dār al-Maʾmūn li al-Turāth, 1984.

Tanūkhī, Saḥnūn b. Saᶜīd b. Ḥabīb al-. *Al-Mudawwana al-kubrā*. Beirut: Dār Ṣādir, n.d.

Ṭayālisī, Sulaymān b. Dāwūd Jārūd al-. *Al-Musnad*. Beruit: Dār al-Maᶜrifa, n.d.

Tirmidhī, Abū ᶜĪsā Muhammad b. ᶜĪsā al-. *Al-Sunan*. Beruit: Dār Iḥyāʾ al-Turāth al-ᶜArabī, n.d.

ᶜUthmānī, Shabbīr Aḥmad al-. *Fatḥ al-Mulhim bi sharḥ Ṣaḥīḥ al-Imām Muslim*. Damascus: Dār al-Qalam, 2006.

Watt, Montgomery. *Islamic Political Thought: The Basic Concepts*. Edinburgh: Edinburgh University Press, 1980.

Yaḥṣubī, Qāḍī ʿIyāḍ al-. *Ikmāl al-muʿlim bi fawāʾid Muslim.* Beruit: Dār al-Wafā, 1998.

——. *Al-Shifā bi taʿrīf ḥuqūq al-Muṣṭafā* ﷺ. Beirut: Dār al-Kitāb al-ʿArabī, n.d.

Zamakhsharī, Jār Allāh Abū al-Qāsim Maḥmūd b. ʿUmar al-. *Al-Kashshāf ʿan ḥaqāʾiq ghawāmiḍ al-Tanzīl.* Beruit: Dār Iḥyāʾ al-Turāth al-ʿArabī, n.d.

Indices

Index of Qur'ānic Verses

Index of Hadith Reports and Narrations

General Index